UNDERSTANDING SOVIET FOREIGN POLICY

READINGS AND DOCUMENTS

UNDERSTANDING SOVIET FOREIGN POLICY

READINGS AND DOCUMENTS

EDITED BY

Vladimir Wozniuk

Department of Government and Law
Lafayette College

McGRAW-HILL PUBLISHING COMPANY

New York St. Louis San Francisco Auckland Bogotá Caracas
Hamburg Lisbon London Madrid Mexico Milan Montreal New Delhi
Oklahoma City Paris San Juan São Paulo Singapore Sydney Tokyo Toronto

This book was set in Times Roman by the College Composition Unit
in cooperation with Monotype Composition Company.
The editors were Bert Lummus and Linda Richmond;
the production supervisor was Friederich W. Schulte.
The cover was designed by Rafael Hernandez.
R. R. Donnelly & Sons Company was printer and binder.

Permissions

page 63: Excerpt from chapter 4 of *Expansion and Coexistence: Soviet Foreign Policy 1917—1973*
by Adam B. Ulam, 2d ed. Copyright © 1974 by Holt, Rinehart and Winston. Reprinted by permission of the publisher.

page 99: Excerpt from ''Doubts'' in *Conversations with Stalin* by Milovan Djilas, translated by
Michael B. Petrovich, pp. 112-115. Copyright © 1962 by Harcourt Brace Jovanovich. Reprinted by
permission of the publisher.

UNDERSTANDING SOVIET FOREIGN POLICY
Readings and Documents

1 2 3 4 5 6 7 8 9 0   DOC   DOC   8 9 4 3 2 1 0 9

ISBN 0-07-071912-8

Library of Congress Cataloging in Publication Data

Understanding Soviet foreign policy: readings and documents/edited by Vladimir Wozniuk.
    p.   cm.

    Includes bibliographical references.
    ISBN 0-07-071912-8
    1. Soviet Union—Foreign relations—Sources.   2. Soviet Union—Foreign relations—(date).
I. Wozniuk, Vladimir.
DK 65.U53   1990
327.47—dc20   89-12766

ABOUT
THE AUTHOR

VLADIMIR WOZNIUK is Assistant Professor of Government and Law at Lafayette College in Easton, Pennsylvania. He is the author of a book, *From Crisis to Crisis: Soviet-Polish Relations in the 1970s* (1987), and a number of articles and reviews appearing in various scholarly journals, including *Comparative Strategy, Conflict, East European Quarterly, Journal of Church and State, Journal of Politics,* and *Soviet Studies*. He has also contributed op-ed pieces to newspapers such as *The Christian Science Monitor, The Chicago Tribune,* and *The Atlanta Journal-Constitution*.

This book is dedicated to my wife, Karen

CHRONOLOGICAL CONTENTS

Chapter Six: **Soviet Foreign Policy under Andropov and Chernenko—**
Generational Transition (1982–1985) **227**

Chapter Seven: **Soviet Foreign Policy under Gorbachev—A New Era?**
(1985–) **252**

TOPICAL CONTENTS

The Cold War

CPSU Evaluation of the International Situation

World Communism

Superpower Relations, Détente and Arms Control

The Developing World

LIST OF ACRONYMS

ABM	Antiballistic missile
AFP	Agence France-Presse (France Press Agency)
ALCM	Air-launched cruise missile
ASAT	Antisatellite weapon
BMD	Ballistic missile defense
CMEA	Council for Mutual Economic Assistance
Cominform	Communist Information Bureau
Comintern	Communist International (Third International)
CPC	Communist Party of China
CPCZ	Communist Party of Czechoslovakia
CPSU	Communist Party of the Soviet Union
CSCE	Conference on Security and Cooperation in Europe (Helsinki Talks)
CSR	Czechoslovak Socialist Republic
EEC	European Economic Community (Common Market)
FRG	Federal Republic of Germany (West Germany)
GDR	German Democratic Republic (East Germany)
ICBM	Intercontinental ballistic missile
INF	Intermediate-range nuclear forces
KGB	Committee for State Security
KMT	Kuomintang
LCY	League of Communists of Yugoslavia
MIRV	Multiple independently targeted reentry vehicle
MPA	Main Political Administration (of the armed forces)
MPLA	Popular Movement for the Liberation of Angola
NATO	North Atlantic Treaty Organization
NEP	New Economic Policy
NTBT	Nuclear Test Ban Treaty
NTMs	National Technical Means
PAP	Polish Press Agency
PDPA	People's Democratic Party of Afghanistan

PPR	Polish People's Republic
PRC	People's Republic of China
PUWP	Polish United Workers' Party
RSFSR	Russian Soviet Federated Socialist Republic
SALT	Strategic Arms Limitation Talks
SDI	Strategic Defense Initiative (Star Wars)
SFRY	Socialist Federated Republic of Yugoslavia
SLBM	Sea-launched ballistic missile
SLCM	Sea-launched cruise missile
SRV	Socialist Republic of Vietnam
START	Strategic Arms Reduction Talks
TASS	Telegraph Agency of the Soviet Union
TTBT	Threshold Test Ban Treaty
UAR	United Arab Republic
UNITA	National Union for the Total Independence of Angola
UNO	United Nations Organization
USSR	Union of Soviet Socialist Republics
WTO	Warsaw Treaty Organization

PREFACE

It has been said that necessity is the mother of invention. This book originated in the need for a collection of documents, speeches, and core readings for an undergraduate course in Soviet foreign policy. A part of this need had for over two decades been filled for many instructors by Alvin Z. Rubinstein's excellent *The Foreign Policy of the Soviet Union*, until that volume went out of print in 1984. As this instructor searched for a replacement to supplement other readings in the course, frustration set in. For although there was no dearth of excellent edited volumes of readings on the subject, none met the crucial triple criterion of covering the breadth of Soviet foreign policy since 1917, providing a documentary record of the most important foreign policy initiatives and achievements of the Soviet regime during its seven decades of existence, and illustrating both continuity and change in Soviet foreign policy from Lenin to Gorbachev. And so, this project was conceived.

Both instructor and student will find that this volume comprises more than 130 documents and readings which, it is hoped, will complement any of the primary texts or monographs that are usually utilized in college courses on Soviet foreign policy. The documents, the heart of the volume, span the period from 1917 to the present. Although this collection includes a number of classic pieces which have previously appeared in the Rubinstein volume and other texts (e.g., the Nazi-Soviet Pact, the Yalta Agreement, the Brezhnev Doctrine), it is distinguished by an abundance of documents that have never before appeared in any text (e.g., Yugoslavia's expulsion from the Cominform and the Treaty of Moscow) and that cover the period since 1972 (e.g., U.S.-Soviet summits since 1972, the INF Treaty, Afghan Accords, and Gorbachev's United Nations speech).

The organization of the volume is simple insofar as the logic of chronology is followed throughout. Early on in the editing and writing of this volume, the decision was made to follow the path of chronology rather than to organize the material on the basis of regions and issue areas. This was done in order to make the development of Soviet actions appear as organic as possible and thereby create a more accessible volume to the student-initiate of Soviet foreign policy. However, the reader will find that the chronological table of contents has been supplemented by a second table, more topical in nature, so that easy reference can be made to entire subject categories.

A basic presupposition underlying this book is that new leaders can make a difference in effecting policies[1]; therefore, *individuals* are key in the complex equation of determinants that shape and direct the foreign policy of a nation-state. In the Soviet case, the problem of grappling with the variables of individual and personality in foreign policy is at once more complex and easier to resolve than is the case with other nation-states. Easier because there have been only seven individuals since the inception of the Soviet experiment whose names have been attached to political regimes guiding the Soviet ship of state through the often turbulent waters of international politics. More complex because, despite the introduction of *glasnost* (openness) into Soviet society by Mr. Gorbachev, the workings of the Kremlin have remained shrouded in secrecy and shielded from the public eye, both within and outside the Soviet Union. We still know much less about Soviet leaders and Soviet politics than we would like to, and certainly much less than the Soviet student knows about similar subjects in the United States.

After an outline of the complex sources and determinants of Soviet foreign policy in Chapter 1, the remaining six chapters approach the subject from the aspect of political leadership—those few leaders who have emerged as either undisputed chiefs or *primis inter pares* in the Soviet political system: Vladimir I. Lenin, Joseph V. Stalin, Nikita S. Khrushchev, Leonid I. Brezhnev, Yuri V. Andropov, Konstantin U. Chernenko, and Mikhail S. Gorbachev. Of course, others in the highest echelons of the Soviet leadership have historically contributed to the shaping and molding of Soviet foreign policy as well.

The analytical and documentary materials in each chapter of this book, while focusing on the "top dogs" in the Soviet foreign policy decision-making hierarchy, also reflect the ongoing debate within the foreign policy establishment over the fundamental character and nature of Soviet foreign policy. Should Soviet foreign policy continue to promote revolutionary goals and keep faith with the Marxist-Leninist class analysis of society or should the Soviet Union compromise and follow a status quo path in international politics? Or to paraphrase Lenin, should the Soviet state advance or retreat? That debate has been resolved variously by subsequent generations of Soviet leaders since 1917; it is hoped that some of its flavor is passed on to the reader.

Each chapter of readings and documents is prefaced by an editorial introduction, which is then followed by analytical narratives that have been selected according to a number of evaluative criteria. First and foremost were consid-

---

[1]In this regard, see the discussion in Valerie Bunce, *Do New Leaders Make a Difference? Executive Succession and Public Policy under Capitalism and Socialism* (Princeton, Princeton University Press, 1981), pp. 3–7 and 167–178.

ered the expertise of the writers and the readability of the pieces. In this regard, the student will be exposed to some of the leading Western writers on Soviet affairs, including E. H. Carr, George Kennan, Merle Fainsod, Adam Ulam, Zbigniew Brzezinski, and Stephen Cohen. Second, the successful summation in a relatively short length of the complexities of a given problem or issue relevant to a particular leadership was deemed imperative for a manageable classroom text. Third, the contribution of the selection to the student's understanding of the reasons for differences among Soviet leaders on policy issues was weighed. Of course, not all classic writers on the subject could be accommodated in such limited space; some hard choices had to be made in the final editing of the volume. However, in selecting these authors, partiality for a single school or ideological predisposition was avoided. A variety of views is represented, ranging from conservative to moderate to liberal.

Each documentary entry is prefaced by editorial commentary that strives to place the given document in historical and policy perspectives. Again, an attempt has been made to keep most of these commentaries short and succinct, except where more extensive explanation is unavoidable. Because the purpose of these commentaries was seen to be primarily the exposition of context and relevance in as brief a space as possible, critical comments were avoided; these have been left for the most part to the analytical narratives found at the beginning of each chapter.

A word concerning sources. Some of the documents were translated by the editor; others were obtained already translated from U.S. and Soviet governmental (and some nongovernmental) sources. All translation sources have been labeled clearly. Whenever possible, texts not translated by the editor were checked against the original.

McGraw-Hill and I would like to thank the following reviewers for their many helpful comments and suggestions: Jonathan R. Adelman, University of Denver; Yaroslav Bilinsky, University of Delaware; Walter Clemens, Boston University; Linda Cook, Brown University; George V. Kacewicz, California State University—Long Beach; Andrzej Korbonski, University of California—Los Angeles; Vojtech Mastny, Boston University; Donald Pienkos, University of Wisconsin—Milwaukee; and Leonas Sabaliunas, Eastern Michigan University.

Vladimir Wozniuk

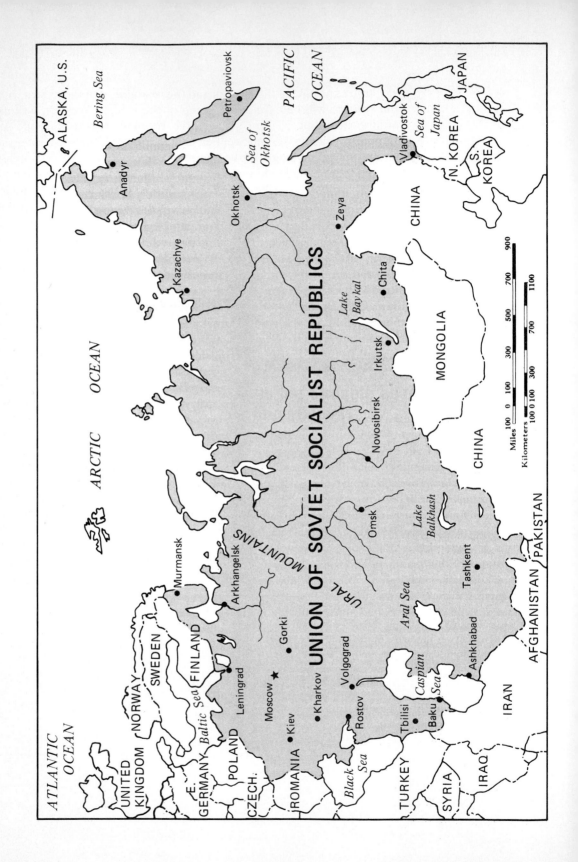

CHAPTER ONE

Sources and Determinants of Soviet Foreign Policy

What are the sources of Soviet foreign policy? Just as with any nation-state's foreign policy, the factors influencing the formulation of Soviet policy are diverse and complex, an admixture of internal and external variables.

Internal factors usually considered include the geography, history, ideology, and economic and political systems of Russian and Soviet society. To these can be added bureaucratic conflicts, which shape and mold policy, as well as the differences in personality among individual Soviet leaders from Lenin to Gorbachev. Analysis of these several factors goes a long way toward achieving a well-grounded understanding of the context of Soviet foreign policy and determining the extent of continuity between imperial Russian and Soviet foreign policies.

For nearly the entire period of the European Renaissance, the peoples of Russia remained on the periphery of both Asia and Europe, largely isolated from the West culturally and alternately subject to the depredations of Germanic conquerors and Asiatic nomads who made use of the vast Russian steppes to attack the ancient Russian lands.[1] Invasion after invasion from both West and East contributed to a siege mentality, one which has perhaps only recently shown signs of beginning to abate as the effects of the last invasion, by Nazi Germany in World War II, begin to fade in prominence among younger generations of Soviet citizens. According to a standard interpretation (Soviet as well as Western) of Russian history, the ramifications of this centuries-long situation

---

[1]See Nicholas Riasanovsky, *A History of Russia,* 4th ed. (New York: Oxford University Press, 1984), especially pp. 67–76.

were substantial. At a minimum, it contributed to the isolation of Russian civilization from its Western European neighbors and contributed to an increase in xenophobia among the Russians.[1]

Partly as a result of its slow adaptation to the industrial revolution of the nineteenth century, the Russian economy entered the twentieth century as among the most backward in Europe, a condition which the bolsheviks inherited in 1917.[2] Endemic economic problems have led to various Soviet initiatives toward the West in the attempt to lessen international pressure on the Soviet Union. Of particular note are recent initiatives by Mr. Gorbachev, who has explicitly made reference to the connection of the economy to "relaxation of tension" between East and West and the future character of Soviet foreign policy.[3]

The twin factors of the authoritarian heritage of Soviet political institutions and the official Soviet ideology of Marxism-Leninism must also be considered as central determinants in the formulation of Soviet foreign policy. One analyst has averred that "contemporary Soviet political culture is rooted in the historical experience of centuries of absolutism."[4] If so, is the Soviet communist system, as George Kennan suggested, merely "tsarism in overalls"?

The authoritarian tradition of Russian politics is a native factor, while the second, the Marxist tradition, is a Western import that was adapted to contemporary Russian conditions by Vladimir Ilyich Lenin, founder and theorist of the Soviet state. However, as Adam Ulam has observed, the resultant Marxist-Leninist ideology has been so blended with more traditional patriotic and nationalist ideas that "the ideology has become a servant of nationalism, but after sixty years of Soviet power this servant cannot be dismissed without gravely imperiling the position of the master. Furthermore, the only dimension in which the ideology remains relevant is that of foreign relations."[5]

Also important is the factor of differences in leadership personality, whose implications for the formulation of all aspects of state policy, foreign as well as domestic, have been observed for some time.[6] Joseph L. Nogee and Robert H. Donaldson have asserted that differences among the post-Stalin leaderships over foreign policy issues are among the most important internal variables that have acted to change Soviet foreign policy since World War II.[7]

Among the most important *external* variables that have been suggested as acting to change Soviet foreign policy since World War II are the growth of a multipolar international system, the appearance of polycentrism in the world communist movement, and the technological development of weapons of mass destruction.[8] As the two "camps" in the post–World War II world have given way to an increasingly broad array of independent actors in international politics, the implications of the new state of affairs have not been lost on Soviet leaders. Soviet doctrine and action have proven quite adaptive to a changing international environment. As successful as the Soviets have been in adapting, nowhere has the damage to Soviet international interests been so

---

[1]Ibid.

[2]The problem of relapsing into backwardness has been recognized. See, for example, Timothy Colton, *The Dilemma of Reform in the Soviet Union*, rev. ed. (New York: Council on Foreign Relations, 1986), pp. 37ff.

[3]See *Time Magazine*, September 1985, interview with Mr. Gorbachev.

[4]Stephen White, *Political Culture and Soviet Politics* (London: Macmillan, 1979), pp. 14 and 21.

[5]Adam Ulam, "Russian Nationalism," *The Domestic Context of Soviet Foreign Policy,* ed. Seweryn Bialer. (Boulder, CO: Westview, 1981), p. 14.

[6]See, for example, Harold Laswell, "Psychopathology and Politics," *The Political Writings of Harold Laswell* (New York: Free Press, 1951); Theodore W. Adorno, *The Authoritarian Personality* (New York: Harper & Row, 1950); and, more recently, James D. Barber, *The Presidential Character* (Englewood Cliffs, NJ: Prentice-Hall, 1977).

[7]Joseph L. Nogee and Robert H. Donaldson, *Soviet Foreign Policy Since World War II* (New York: Pergamon, 1987), pp. 5–7.

[8]Ibid.

extensive as in the emergence of polycentrism in international communism, beginning with the Yugoslav defection from the world communist movement in 1948. Finally, the development of means to destroy both socialist and capitalist society has led to the adoption of new tactics and strategies, such as "peaceful coexistence," to deal more effectively with the West.

In the two essays beginning this chapter, the debate over determinants is set before us by two prolific scholars of Soviet foreign policy, George F. Kennan and Thomas W. Wolfe. In explaining the historical and cultural determinants within the political system itself that he views as central, Kennan in his classic "containment" essay focuses on the basic continuity of Soviet policy as a function of systemic and historical factors. How relevant is Kennan's analysis today? Written as it was in 1947, many of the essay's concerns about rigidity in Soviet positions may be seen as somewhat dated, especially in light of Gorbachev's unquestionable compromises in recent years in arms control (INF) and regional problems (Afghanistan). But perhaps it is especially appropriate to review the piece once again in light of just these changes in Soviet policy: Has Kennan been vindicated after all in counseling the West to hold its ground until a mellowing of the Soviet system occurred?

It could be argued that what is most valuable about Kennan's argument and what gives the piece its longevity is the implicit reminder that Soviet-American relations have been best when the national interests of the two countries have coincided—and that has been seldom. Kennan explains the basic hostility of the Stalinist system to Western-style democracy. This basic incongruity of interests between East and West was easy to see during Stalin's reign, when the confrontational character of the Soviet system was unabashedly proclaimed and probes were launched to test Western will in both Europe (Berlin) and Asia (Korea) after the Grand Alliance (an alliance of convenience) had ended with

the defeat of Germany and Japan. Little wonder that the system was evaluated with near unanimity in the West as totalitarian in its basic character and compared with that of Nazi Germany.

Thomas Wolfe observes, however, that the degree of unanimity which once characterized Western opinion on the nature of the Soviet system has dwindled since the death of the great dictator Stalin. In part, this is because the unmitigated hostility that the Stalinist system embodied has gradually given way, and concurrently the style of Soviet foreign policy has undergone some important changes. These include a general reluctance to confront the West directly on issues considered to be vital security interests and a willingness to negotiate with the West over lowering the threshold of tension in the world. Whereas Kennan elucidates the factors of history and political culture impinging on the formation of Soviet interests, Wolfe explains the ways in which Western analysts have tried to understand the nature of decision making in Soviet foreign policy. He addresses the question of the totalitarian model's validity and outlines some alternative approaches to understanding contemporary Soviet foreign policy, including the "bureaucratic" paradigm.[1] He also briefly sketches the structural and institutional political framework in which Soviet foreign policy decisions are made and carried out.

It can be argued that the defining feature of Soviet foreign policy since 1917 has been its "dualism."[2] The tension between the revolutionary imperative in the Marxist-Leninist doctrine and the continuing need for compromise in order to preserve the Soviet state in a "hostile" capitalist world provides an indisputable strand of continuity in Soviet foreign policy from the bolshevik revolution to the present. Beginning with Lenin, alternating "left" and "right" pol-

---

[1] See Graham Allison, *The Essence of Decision: Explaining the Cuban Missile Crisis* (Boston: Little, Brown, 1971).
[2] See, for example, E. H. Carr, *The Bolshevik Revolution,* vol. 3 (London: Penguin, 1953), pp 79ff.

icies—more aggressive and assertive pursuit of revolutionary goals versus more accommodation toward, and interaction with, noncommunist forces—have characterized Soviet foreign policy.[1] The right phases began with Lenin's promotion of two interconnected doctrinal notions, in light of the superior power of the imperialist nations during the period of "capitalist encirclement" of the Soviet Union. These were peaceful coexistence and the support of "national lib-

eration movements" in the colonial world (what we now call the underdeveloped or third world). These doctrines helped outline a "transitional phase" from capitalism to socialism in the world revolutionary process, according to Lenin. The question today is whether or not a fundamental change is in the making regarding this dualistic approach of Soviet foreign policy.

Through the excerpts offered from speeches and writings of Soviet leaders spanning the breadth of Soviet history, we can see the right-left tension clearly. Moreover, we can see the peaks and valleys of relations between the Soviet Union and the capitalist world as the different elements of this dualism have been emphasized by Soviet leaders since Lenin.

---

[1]See, for example, Marshal Shulman, *Stalin's Foreign Policy Reappraised* (Cambridge, MA: Harvard University Press), pp. 1–7, and Francis Fukuyama, "Patterns of Soviet Third World Policy," *Problems of Communism,* 36/5, September–October 1987, pp. 3–4.

READING 1

The Sources of Soviet Conduct

X (George F. Kennan)

The political personality of Soviet power as we know it today is the product of ideology and circumstances: ideology inherited by the present Soviet leaders from the movement in which they had their political origin, and circumstances of the power which they now have exercised for nearly three decades in Russia. There can be few tasks of psychological analysis more difficult than to try to trace the interaction of these two forces and the relative role of each in the determination of official Soviet conduct. Yet the attempt must be made if that conduct is to be understood and effectively countered.

It is difficult to summarize the set of ideological concepts with which the Soviet leaders came into power. Marxian ideology, in its Russian-Communist projection, has always been in process of subtle evolution. The materials on which it bases itself are extensive and complex. But the outstanding features of Communist thought as it existed in 1916 may perhaps be summarized as follows: (a) that the central factor in the life of man, the factor which determines the character of public life and the "physiognomy of society," is the system by which material goods are produced and exchanged; (b) that the capitalist system of production is a nefarious one which inevitably leads to the exploitation of the working class by the capital-owning class and is incapable of developing adequately the economic resources of society or of distributing fairly the material goods produced by human labor; (c) that capitalism contains the seeds of its own destruction and must, in view of the inability of the capital-owning class to adjust itself to economic change, result eventually and inescapably in a revolutionary transfer of power to the working class; and (d) that imperialism, the final phase of capitalism, leads directly to war and revolution.

The rest may be outlined in Lenin's own words: "Unevenness of economic and political development is the inflexible law of capitalism. It follows from this that the victory of Socialism may come originally in a few capitalist countries or even in a single capitalist country. The victorious proletariat of that country, having expropriated the capitalists and having organized Socialist production at home, would rise against the remaining capitalist world, drawing to itself in the process the oppressed classes of other countries."[1] It must be noted that there was no assumption that capitalism would perish without proletarian revolution. A final push was needed from a revolutionary proletariat movement in order to tip over the tottering structure. But it was regarded as inevitable that sooner or later that push be given.

For 50 years prior to the outbreak of the Revolution, this pattern of thought had exercised great fascination for the members of the Russian revolutionary movement. Frustrated, discontented, hopeless of finding self-expression—or too impatient to seek it—in the confining limits of the Tsarist political system, yet lacking wide popular support for their choice of bloody revolution as a means of social betterment, these revolutionists found in Marxist theory a highly convenient rationalization for their own instinctive desires. It afforded pseudo-scientific justification for their impatience, for their categorical denial of all value in the Tsarist system, for their yearning for power and revenge and for their inclination to cut corners in the pursuit of it. It is therefore no wonder that they had come to believe implicitly in the truth and soundness of the Marxian-Leninist teachings, so congenial to

X, "The Sources of Soviet Conduct," *Foreign Affairs*, 25/4, July 1947, pp. 566–582, *excerpts*. Reprinted by permission of *Foreign Affairs*, July 1947.

[1]"Concerning the Slogans of the United States of Europe," August 1915. Official Soviet edition of Lenin's works.

their own impulses and emotions. Their sincerity need not be impugned....

Now it must be noted that through all the years of preparation for revolution, the attention of these men, as indeed of Marx himself, had been centered less on the future form which Socialism[1] would take than on the necessary overthrow of rival power which, in their view, had to precede the introduction of Socialism. Their views, therefore, on the positive program to be put into effect, once power was attained, were for the most part nebulous, visionary and impractical. Beyond the nationalization of industry and the expropriation of large private capital holdings there was no agreed program. The treatment of the peasantry, which according to the Marxist formulation was not of the proletariat, had always been a vague spot in the pattern of Communist thought; and it remained an object of controversy and vacillation for the first ten years of Communist power.

The circumstances of the immediate post-revolution period—the existence in Russia of civil war and foreign intervention, together with the obvious fact that the Communists represented only a tiny minority of the Russian people—made the establishment of dictatorial power a necessity. The experiment with "war Communism" and the abrupt attempt to eliminate private production and trade had unfortunate economic consequences and caused further bitterness against the new revolutionary regime. While the temporary relaxation of the effort to communize Russia, represented by the New Economic Policy, alleviated some of this economic distress and thereby served its purpose, it also made it evident that the "capitalistic sector of society" was still prepared to profit at once from any relaxation of governmental pressure, and would, if permitted to continue to exist, always constitute a powerful opposing element to the

Soviet regime and a serious rival for influence in the country. Somewhat the same situation prevailed with respect to the individual peasant who, in his own small way, was also a private producer.

Lenin, had he lived, might have proved a great enough man to reconcile these conflicting forces to the ultimate benefit of Russian society, though this is questionable. But be that as it may, Stalin, and those whom he led in the struggle for succession to Lenin's position of leadership, were not the men to tolerate rival political forces in the sphere of power which they coveted. Their sense of insecurity was too great. Their particular brand of fanaticism, unmodified by any of the Anglo-Saxon traditions of compromise, was too fierce and too jealous to envisage any permanent sharing of power. From the Russian-Asiatic world out of which they had emerged they carried with them a skepticism as to the possibilities of permanent and peaceful coexistence of rival forces. Easily persuaded of their own doctrinaire "rightness," they insisted on the submission or destruction of all competing power....

Now it lies in the nature of the mental world of the Soviet leaders, as well as in the character of their ideology, that no opposition to them can be officially recognized as having any merit or justification whatsoever. Such opposition can flow, in theory, only from the hostile and incorrigible forces of dying capitalism. As long as remnants of capitalism were officially recognized as existing in Russia, it was possible to place on them, as an internal element, part of the blame for the maintenance of a dictatorial form of society. But as these remnants were liquidated, little by little, this justification fell away; and when it was indicated officially that they had been finally destroyed, it disappeared altogether. And this fact created one of the most basic of the compulsions which came to act upon the Soviet regime: since capitalism no longer existed in Russia and since it could not be admitted that there could be serious or widespread opposition to the

---

[1]Here and elsewhere in this paper "Socialism" refers to Marxist or Leninist Communism, not to liberal Socialism of the Second International variety.

Kremlin springing spontaneously from the liberated masses under its authority, it became necessary to justify the retention of the dictatorship by stressing the menace of capitalism abroad.

This began at an early date. In 1924 Stalin specifically defended the retention of the "organs of suppression," meaning, among others, the army and the secret police, on the ground that "as long as there is a capitalist encirclement there will be danger of intervention with all the consequences that flow from that danger." In accordance with that theory, and from that time on, all internal opposition forces in Russia have consistently been portrayed as the agents of foreign forces of reaction antagonistic to Soviet power.

By the same token, tremendous emphasis has been placed on the original Communist thesis of a basic antagonism between the capitalist and Socialist worlds. It is clear, from many indications, that this emphasis is not founded in reality. The real facts concerning it have been confused by the existence abroad of a genuine resentment provoked by Soviet philosophy and tactics and occasionally by the existence of great centers of military power, notably the Nazi regime in Germany and the Japanese Government of the late 1930s, which did indeed have aggressive designs against the Soviet Union. But there is ample evidence that the stress laid in Moscow on the menace confronting Soviet society from the world outside its border is founded not in the realities of foreign antagonism but in the necessity of explaining away the maintenance of dictatorial authority at home.

Now the maintenance of this pattern of Soviet power, namely, the pursuit of unlimited authority domestically, accompanied by the cultivation of the semi-myth of implacable foreign hostility, has gone far to shape the actual machinery of Soviet power as we know it today. Internal organs of administration which did not serve this purpose withered on the vine. Organs which did serve this purpose became vastly swollen. The security of Soviet power came to rest on the iron discipline of the Party, on the severity and ubiquity of the secret police, and on the uncompromising economic monopolism of the state. The "organs of suppression," in which the Soviet leaders had sought security from rival forces, became in large measure the masters of those whom they were designed to serve....

II.

So much for the historical background. What does it spell in terms of the political personality of Soviet power as we know it today?

Of the original ideology, nothing has been officially junked. Belief is maintained in the basic badness of capitalism, in the inevitability of its destruction, in the obligation of the proletariat to assist in that destruction and to take power into its own hands. But stress has come to be laid primarily on those concepts which relate most specifically to the Soviet regime itself: to its position as the sole truly Socialist regime in a dark and misguided world, and to the relationships of power within it.

The first of these concepts is that of the innate antagonism between capitalism and Socialism. We have seen how deeply that concept has become imbedded in foundations of Soviet power. It has profound implications for Russia's conduct as a member of international society. It means that there can never be on Moscow's side any sincere assumption of a community of aims between the Soviet Union and powers which are regarded as capitalist. It must invariably be assumed in Moscow that the aims of the capitalist world are antagonistic to the Soviet regime, and therefore to the interests of the peoples it controls. If the Soviet government occasionally sets its signature to documents which would indicate the contrary, this is to be regarded as a tactical maneuver permissible in dealing with the enemy (who is without honor) and should be taken in the spirit of *caveat emptor*. Basically, the antagonism remains. It is postulated. And from it flow many of the phenomena which we find disturbing in the Kremlin's conduct of foreign policy: the secretiveness, the lack of frankness, the duplicity, the wary suspiciousness and the basic unfriendliness of purpose. These phenomena are there to stay, for the foreseeable future. There can be variations of degree and of emphasis. When there is something the Russians want from us, one or the other of these features of their policy may be thrust temporarily into the background; and when that happens there will always be Americans who will leap forward with gleeful announcements that "the Russians have changed," and some who will even try to take credit for having brought about such "changes." But we should not be misled by tactical maneuvers. These characteristics of Soviet policy, like the postulate from which they flow, are basic to the internal nature of Soviet power, and will be with us, whether in the foreground or the background, until the internal nature of Soviet power is changed.

This means that we are going to continue for a long time to find the Russians difficult to deal with. It does not mean that they should be considered as embarked upon a do-or-die program to overthrow our society by a given date. The theory of the inevitability of the eventual fall of capitalism has the fortunate connotation that there is no hurry about it. The forces of progress can take their time in preparing the final *coup de grace*. Meanwhile, what is vital is that the "Socialist fatherland"—that oasis of power which has been already won for Socialism in the person of the Soviet Union—should be cherished and defended by all good Communists at home and abroad, its fortunes promoted, its enemies badgered and confounded. The promotion of premature, "adventuristic" revolutionary projects abroad which might embarrass Soviet power in any way would be an inexcusable, even a counterrevolutionary act. The cause of Socialism is the support and promotion of Soviet power, as defined in Moscow.

This brings us to the second of the concepts important to contemporary Soviet outlook. That is the infallibility of the Kremlin. The Soviet concept of power, which permits no focal points of organization outside the Party itself, requires that the Party leadership remain in theory the sole repository of truth. For if truth were to be found elsewhere, there would be justification for its expression in organized activity. But it is precisely that which the Kremlin cannot and will not permit.

The leadership of the Communist Party is therefore always right, and has been always right ever since in 1929 Stalin formalized his personal power by announcing that the decisions of the Politburo were being taken unanimously.

On the principle of infallibility there rests the iron discipline of the Communist Party. In fact, the two concepts are mutually self-supporting. Perfect discipline requires recognition of infallibility. Infallibility requires the observance of discipline. And the two together go far to determine the behaviorism of the entire Soviet apparatus of power. But their effect cannot be understood unless a third factor be taken into account: namely, the fact that the leadership is at liberty to put forward for tactical purposes any particular thesis which it finds useful to the cause at any particular moment and to require the faithful and unquestioning acceptance of the thesis by the members of the movement as a whole. This means that truth is not a constant but is actually created, for all intents and purposes, by the Soviet leaders themselves. It may vary from week to week, month to month. It is nothing absolute and immutable—nothing which flows from objective reality. It is only the most recent manifestation of the wisdom of those in whom the ultimate wisdom is supposed to reside, because they represent the logic of history. The accumulative effect of these factors is to give to the whole subordinate apparatus of Soviet power an unshakable stubbornness and steadfastness in its orientation. This orientation can be changed at will by the Kremlin but by no other power. Once a given party line has been laid down on a given issue of current policy, the whole Soviet governmental machine, including the mechanism of diplomacy, moves inexorably along the prescribed path, like a persistent toy automobile wound up and headed in a given direction, stopping only when it meets with some unanswerable force. The individuals who are the components of this machine are unamenable to argument or reason which comes to them from outside sources. Their whole training has taught them to mistrust and discount the glib persuasiveness of the outside world. Like the white dog before the phonograph, they hear only the "master's voice." And if they are to be called off from the purposes last dictated to them, it is the master who must call them off. Thus the foreign representative cannot hope that his words will make any impression on them. The most that he can hope is that they will be transmitted to those at the top, who are capable of changing the party line. But even those are not likely to be swayed by any normal logic in the words of the bourgeois representative. Since there can be no appeal to common purposes, there can be no appeal to common mental approaches. For this reason, facts speak louder than words to the ears of the Kremlin; and words carry the greatest weight when they have the ring of reflecting, or being backed up by, facts of unchallengeable validity.

But we have seen that the Kremlin is under no ideological compulsion to accomplish its purposes in a hurry. Like the Church, it is dealing in ideological concepts which are of long-term validity, and it can afford to be patient. It has no right to risk the existing achievements of the revolution for the sake of vain baubles of the future. The very teachings of Lenin himself require great caution and flexibility in the pursuit of Communist purposes. Again, these precepts are fortified by the lessons of Russian history: of centuries of obscure battles between nomadic forces over the stretches of a vast unfortified plain. Here caution, circumspection, flexibility and deception are the valuable qualities; and their value finds natural appreciation in the Russian or the oriental mind. Thus the Kremlin has no compunction about retreating in the face of superior force. And being under the compulsion of no timetable, it does not get panicky under the necessity for such retreat. Its political action is a fluid stream which moves constantly, wherever it is permitted to move, toward a given goal. Its main concern is to make sure that it has filled every nook and cranny available to it in the basin of world power. But if it finds unassailable barriers in its path, it accepts these philosophically and accommodates itself to them. The main thing is that there should always be pressure, unceasing constant pressure, toward the desired goal. There is no trace of any feeling in Soviet psychology that that goal must be reached at any given time.

These considerations make Soviet diplomacy at once easier and more difficult to deal with than the diplomacy of individual aggressive leaders like Napoleon and Hitler. On the one hand it is more sensitive to contrary force, more ready to yield on individual sectors of the diplomatic front when that force is felt to be too strong, and thus more rational in the logic and rhetoric of power. On the other hand it cannot be easily defeated or discouraged by a single victory on the part of its opponents. And the patient persistence by which it is animated means that it can be effectively countered not by sporadic acts which represent the momentary whims of democratic opinion but only by intelligent long-range policies on the part of Russia's adversaries—policies no less steady in their purpose, and no less variegated and resourceful in their application, than those of the Soviet Union itself.

In these circumstances it is clear that the main element of any United States policy toward the Soviet Union must be that of a long-term patient but firm and vigilant containment of Russian expansive tendencies. It is important to note, however, that such a policy has nothing to do with outward histrionics: with threats or blustering or superfluous gestures of outward "toughness."

While the Kremlin is basically flexible in its reaction to political realities, it is by no means unamenable to considerations of prestige. Like almost any other government, it can be placed by tactless and threatening gestures in a position where it cannot afford to yield even though this might be dictated by its sense of realism. The Russian leaders are keen judges of human psychology, and as such they are highly conscious that loss of temper and of self-control is never a source of strength in political affairs. They are quick to exploit such evidences of weakness. For these reasons, it is a sine qua non of successful dealing with Russia that the foreign government in question should remain at all times cool and collected and that its demands on Russian policy should be put forward in such a manner as to leave the way open for a compliance not too detrimental to Russian prestige.

III.

In light of the above, it will be clearly seen that the Soviet pressure against the free institutions of the Western world is something that can be contained by the adroit and vigilant application of counterforce at a series of constantly shifting geographical and political points, corresponding to the shifts and maneuvers of Soviet policy, but which cannot be charmed or talked out of existence. The Russians look forward to a duel of infinite duration, and they see that already they have scored great successes. It must be borne in mind that there was a time when the Communist Party represented far more of a minority in the sphere of Russian national life than Soviet power today represents in the world community.... A great uncertainty hangs over the political life of the Soviet Union. That is the uncertainty involved in the transfer of power from one individual or group of individuals to others.

This is, of course, outstandingly the problem of the personal position of Stalin. We must remember that his succession to Lenin's pinnacle of preeminence in the Communist movement was the only such transfer of individual authority which the Soviet Union has experienced. That transfer took 12 years to consolidate. It cost the lives of millions of people and shook the state to its foundations. The attendant tremors were felt all through the international revolutionary movement, to the disadvantage of the Kremlin itself.

It is always possible that another transfer of preeminent power may take place quietly and inconspicuously, with no repercussions anywhere. But again, it is possible that the questions involved may unleash, to use some of Lenin's words, one of those "incredibly swift transitions" from "delicate deceit" to "wild violence" which characterize Russian history, and may shake Soviet power to its foundations....

Thus the future of Soviet power may not be by any means as secure as Russian capacity for self-delusion would make it appear to the men in the Kremlin. That they can keep power themselves, they have demonstrated. That they can quietly and easily turn it over to others remains to be proved. Meanwhile, the hardships of their rule and the vicissitudes of international life have taken a heavy toll of the strength and hopes of the great people on whom their power rests. It is curious to note that the ideological power of Soviet authority is strongest today in areas beyond the frontiers of Russia, beyond the reach of its police power.... And who can say with assurance that the strong light still cast by the Kremlin on the dissatisfied peoples of the western world is not the powerful afterglow of a constellation which is in actuality on the wane? This cannot be proved. And it cannot be disproved. But the possibility remains (and in the opinion of this writer it is a strong one) that Soviet power, like the capitalist world of its conception, bears within it the seeds of its own decay, and that the sprouting of these seeds is well advanced....

The Making of Soviet Foreign and Defense Policy

Thomas W. Wolfe

A. ASSUMPTIONS ABOUT THE SOVIET DECISIONMAKING PROCESS

Perhaps it would be useful first to say a few words about some of the basic assumptions and conceptual models which outside observers have tended to employ—either implicitly or explicitly—in analyzing the Soviet decisionmaking process. For our purposes, it may suffice to single out what appear to be the two most sharply contrasting conceptions or theoretical models of how decisions are made and policy priorities established and implemented in the Soviet system.

The first of these constructs has a lineage going back to the model of a self-perpetuating totalitarianism that was widely employed to depict the Soviet system under Stalin during its earlier stages of forced industrial growth and consolidation of communist authority and legitimacy. This model has undergone some revision in the course of time, in recognition of the fact that as the Soviet Union has evolved into a more mature and complex industrial society there has been a partial shift from the totalitarian "command system" of the Stalinist age to a system of rule in the Khrushchev and Brezhnev periods which appear somewhat more responsive to pluralistic pressures from below.

However, the basic political assumption underlying this model has remained essentially un-

changed during the transition from the harsh autocracy of the Stalinist period to the less rigid oligarchic rule of the present collective leadership, namely: A small leadership elite with highly centralized machinery of planning and control at its disposal is assumed to be in a position to make its own fully informed calculation of preferred policy alternatives and to dictate its decisions to all subordinate echelons of Party and government for implementation. In terms of contemporary decisionmaking theory, this model shares one of the central attributes of the so-called "rational choice" or "rational actor" paradigm, in which decisions are seen to be the result of carefully calculated choices by some unitary decisionmaking entity that selects optimum courses of action intended to maximize benefits and minimize losses in pursuit of its goals.[1]

When viewed through the conceptual lenses of this model, the Soviet policymaking process is seen as one in which the top political leadership is the master and never the captive of the overlapping bureaucracies over which it nominally presides, in which decisions come from the top down, and are the product of consensus among the ruling elite....

In recent years, however, this "totalitarian-rational choice" model has come to be challenged increasingly by Western scholars looking to the concepts of comparative systems analysis and the theory of complex organizations for other models better suited to reflect what were felt by many analysts to be processes of change, diversification and interest-group politics at work within the formal structure of Soviet institutions. One finds therefore that another paradigm or model has come into wide use, differing notably in some respects from its predecessor. This contrasting model combines elements of what the

Excerpted from Thomas W. Wolfe, *The Military Dimension in the Making of Soviet Foreign and Defense Policy* (P-6024), October 1977, The Rand Corporation, 1700 Main St., P.O. Box 2138, Santa Monica, CA 90406. This was originally prepared as a statement before the U.S. House of Representatives, Subcommittee on Europe and the Middle East, Committee on International Relations, 11 October 1977. Reprinted by permission.

[1]The "rational choice" model does not, of course, apply only to centralized systems of totalitarian stripe. In fact, it has a lot in common with the classical theory of the firm—operating on a mini-max calculus according to some recognized value or utility function.

literature of contemporary decisionmaking theory distinguishes as the "organizational process" and the "bureaucratic politics" models.[1]

The basic assumption upon which this alternative interpretive approach rests in any case is that no single centralized leadership entity—even in a totalitarian society—has the time or information at its disposal to make all the important decisions for the system. Since the top leadership cannot master all the details and complexities of the issues with which it deals, it must depend on inputs of information and technical judgment flowing upward from subordinate organizations. These organizations in turn tend to operate according to their own established rules and procedures. They have their own institutional momentum, vested interests to protect, axes to grind, constituencies to please, traditional claims on the budget, commitments to programs already laid down, and so on.

As seen by this model, the various bureaucracies—as centers of partial power in the system—have a claim to be heard; the way they marshal their arguments and the skill of their advocacy can help to structure the issues presented to the top leadership, so that in a sense the policy options open to it may already be somewhat circumscribed before they become a matter of decision. Further, while this model can allow for a dominant role by the Party apparatus in the Soviet decisionmaking process, it also accommodates the contention that other bureaucracies in the system have become more vocal and active in looking out for their special interests.

Although the Soviet government is not one of formal checks and balances, when viewed in terms of this model, the proliferation of power within a large and complex bureaucratic system like that in the Soviet Union may beget potential vetoes upon policy and therefore in some sense serve as a kind of random substitute for constitutional checks upon central authority. Another implication of this model is that the Soviet bureaucratic system, because of an inherent organizational tendency to depend on standard operating procedures, discourages innovatory action that breaks with established ways of doing things. The known difficulties of introducing new technology into the Soviet civilian economy and a seeming periodic need to import new technology from the West can be cited to buttress this point.[2]

Besides emphasizing the effect of bureaucratic phenomena upon Soviet policymaking, this model also views the top leadership itself as a far from homogeneous group prepared to speak with a single voice on the issues that come before it. Rather, the ruling oligarchy is presumed to have its own differing alignments of interest, and to engage in internal political maneuvering and to strike committee compromises that may

---

[1]Theoretically, the "organizational process" model holds that decisions in large organizations are less the product of rational or optimized pursuit of preferred outcomes than of largely routine procedures or SOPs for dealing with various classes of problems based on past experience, while the distinctive argument of the "bureaucratic politics" model is that decisions emerge primarily as the product of internal competition among bureaucratic actors and interest-groups, who tend to pursue values determined more by institutional or personal concerns than by some abstract calculus of national interest.

One of the first practical efforts by a Western analyst to bring out the differences between the "rational unitary actor" theory and the "organizational process" and "bureaucratic politics" models when applied to actual Soviet decisionmaking was Graham Allison's case study, *Essence of Decision: Explaining the Cuban Missile Crisis*, Little Brown, Boston, 1971.

For a useful review of Western decisionmaking theory and examination of its potential application to the study of Soviet foreign policy decisionmaking, see Arnold L. Horelick, A. Ross Johnson, and John D. Steinbruner, *The Study of Soviet Foreign Policy: A Review of Decision-Theory-Related Approaches*, R-1334, The Rand Corporation, Santa Monica, December 1973....

[2]For an argument that periodic transfusions of selected Western technologies have been a logical or rational choice as well as a necessity for the highly bureaucratized Soviet economic system, which in effect runs best on standard operating procedures in the intervals between doses of innovation from the outside, see Raymond Vernon, "Apparatchiks and Entrepreneurs: US-Soviet Economic Relations," *Foreign Affairs*, January 1974, pp. 253–255.

tend to water down its decisions and sometimes rob them of logical consistency.

In effect, then, unlike the older "totalitarian-rational choice" model, this newer one suggests that the policies which emerge from the Soviet decisionmaking process may represent something less than the product of optimum choice among a full array of alternatives. Even what appear to be unitary high-level decisions reached for the weightiest reasons of Soviet national interest may on occasion represent the cumulative result of many smaller and sometimes conflicting actions—as well as failures to act—at various levels of the bureaucratic system.

Needless to say, one ought to be wary of attempts to fit actual Soviet behavior into any given abstract model, or to explain Soviet priorities and decisions in terms of any single set of determinants—economic, strategic, ideological, historical, bureaucratic, or whatever. Neither of the illustrative models of the Soviet decisionmaking process sketched above may accurately convey the shape of Soviet reality, but it does seem to make some difference whether one's judgments are informed primarily by the first or the second of these conceptions. In the first case, the tendency may be to oversimplify the situation, to see the Soviet Union as a highly controlled society in which all decisions come down from the top and must therefore be directed toward some logically explicable purpose or intention in line with the professed philosophy of the top leadership. In the second instance, the tendency may be to read more into the interplay of elite politics and bureaucratic phenomena as a sign that the Soviet Union is well on the way to becoming a pluralist society than the situation actually warrants.[1]...

But...any good working model of the Soviet decisionmaking process must take account of the fact that latent bureaucratic pluralism in the Soviet Union is still strongly tempered by state controls and other pressures for conformity inherent in the Soviet system and Russian political tradition[2]...a "controlled-pluralism" model—one that provides room for some measure of institutional and functional pluralism and internal conflict, while also recognizing the limits imposed by conformist features of the Soviet setting[3]...may strike the right balance between the two theoretical examples we have been discussing here.

B. ANATOMY OF THE SOVIET DECISIONMAKING SYSTEM

With that, let me turn from theoretical constructs to a description of the structure or anatomy of the Soviet decisionmaking system as it can be observed from the outside, focusing especially on the places in the structure where military and foreign policy matters intersect with economic and other considerations....

(1) The Top Leadership Level

The Politburo In the Soviet Union the final power of decision on all matters of policy rests with the Party Politburo. Resolutions of the Central Committee, directives of the Council of Ministers, and decrees of the Supreme Soviet are all essentially decided in advance by the Politburo, among whose members...[the] Secretary General is clearly primus inter pares. The bylaws under which the Politburo operates are unknown, but it is the view of many observers...that most policy issues are settled by consensus.[4] If con-

[1]For a trenchant statement that argues this point, see William E. Odom, "A Dissenting View on the Group Approach to Soviet Politics," *World Politics*, July 1976, pp. 542–567.

[2]Kenneth A. Meyers and Dimitri Simes, *Soviet Decision Making, Strategic Policy, and SALT*, Georgetown University Center for Strategic and International Studies, Washington, December 1974, pp. 8–11.

[3]Ibid., p. 11....

[4]Brezhnev's comments on Politburo operations were made to a group of Western news correspondents in Mos-

sensus cannot be reached, formally equal power to vote on final decisions is apparently shared by the 14 full members of the Politburo. This prerogative is seldom exercised....A small subgroup or committee of Politburo members is usually charged with resolving a disputed issue.[1]

Central Committee Secretariat and Departments
...It is in the Central Committee departments, the heads of which operate under the supervision of members of the secretariat, that the bulk of the staff work immediately supporting the Politburo still appears to be accomplished. Only several of the departments whose work has varying degrees of relevance in foreign policy and national security matters need be mentioned here.

One of these, Defense Industry...is the principal staff element of the Central Committee apparatus concerned with the production aspects of weapons policy. Another is the International Department, which deals with foreign policy matters related to capitalist and third-world countries, and is said to wield more influence in the making of foreign policy than the Ministry of Foreign Affairs.[2]...The Department of Liaison with Ruling Communist and Workers Parties...is involved in foreign policy and security matters relating to countries under communist control. Another department, Administrative Organs,...has an area of responsibility which apparently includes matters of personnel selection and administration in the armed forces, as well as in the internal security and intelligence agencies.

A point of particular interest to this discussion is that there is no department in the Central Committee apparatus, nor any individual member of the supervisory secretariat, with responsibility for general military policy.[3] The Main Political Administration of the Armed Forces (MPA)...does serve simultaneously as a Central Committee department and as an overseer of the Party-political apparatus within the Ministry of Defense. However, its concerns are primarily with the ideological orientation and political instruction of military personnel, rather than with military policy formulation or management of military forces. At the same time, though the MPA does not directly supervise the operation-technical activities of the armed forces, it doubtless has some indirect influence in these areas, since many of the Soviet military writers who promulgate the Party's line on military affairs, including military doctrine, do so through journals controlled by the MPA, such as *Communist of the Armed Forces.*

Council of Ministers   ...Although the Council of Ministers is an important institution for executing Politburo decisions and for supervising the day-to-day running of the bureaucratic machinery of the Soviet state, it does not appear to function as a deliberative or decisionmaking body on new issues of policy. To be sure, as government executives in charge of the ministerial bureaucracies, the members of the Council of Ministers can certainly influence both the way in which policy issues reach the deliberative-decisionmaking level in the Politburo, and the way in which the policies adopted are carried out.

Where foreign and military affairs are concerned, however, such influence probably makes itself felt more at the ministry level than in the Council of Ministers itself. So far as one can tell, neither the full Council, numbering some 70 members, nor its presidium of 12 men, is directly

cow in June 1973, on the eve of his visit to the United States. See Theodore Shabad, "Brezhnev, Who Ought to Know, Explains Politburo," *New York Times*, June 15, 1973. For well–informed accounts of Politburo policymaking procedures, see: Vladimir Petrov, "Formation of Soviet Policy," *Orbis*, Fall 1973, pp. 827–831; Matthew P. Gallagher and Karl F. Spielmann, Jr., *Soviet Decision-Making for Defense*, Praeger Publishers, New York, 1972, pp. 28–33.
    [1]*New York Times*, June 15, 1973.
    [2]See Thomas Wolfe, *The SALT Experience: Its Impact on US and Soviet Strategic Policy and Decisionmaking*, R-1686-PR, The Rand Corporation, September 1975, p. 30.

    [3]Meyers and Simes, op. cit., p. 14.

engaged institutionally in the formulation of foreign and national security policy.

(2) High-Level Mediating Bodies

Just below the Politburo apex of the Soviet decisionmaking system and above the ministerial level are two somewhat enigmatic bodies that do not show up in the formally constituted organizational structure, but which play signficant roles in the formation of national security policy. Both operate at the interface between the top political leadership and the ministerial bureaucracies, and appear to perform mediating and coordinating functions that the formal Party-government machinery is not fitted to handle expeditiously.

The Defense Council One of these bodies, whose lineage can be traced back to the Council of Labor and Defense of Lenin's day and the Defense Commission which operated under Stalin in the 1930s, today goes by the name of Defense Council.[1]...The Defense Council apparently brings together selected members of the Politburo...with senior officers of the military high command and representatives of other Party and state agencies, depending on the subject matter.[2]

Little is known about the mandate of the Defense Council or the procedures under which it operates. In peacetime, it appears to provide a setting in which the political and military leaderships can interact on a broad variety of defense policy issues, rather than to concern itself with day-to-day managerial functions.[3] In wartime, the Defense Council presumably would be transformed into a body similar to the State Committee of Defense, or GKO, of World War II....

It would seem to be a reasonable conjecture that...the Defense Council also serves in turn as the body in which the military leadership finds its best opportunity to present a unified military position on important issues to the political leadership. What happens if a disputed issue goes unresolved here is an intriguing question which, given present knowledge of the inner politics of the Soviet elite, unfortunately cannot be answered.

Military-Industrial Commission ...The Military-Industrial Commission (its Russian acronym is VPK)...provides a forum for handling matters involving the various ministries that make up what is know as the defense-industry sector of the Soviet economy.[4] The VPK's membership has never been announced, but it is logical to suppose that the principal members are the heads of the eight major industrial ministries of the defense sector, together with participants from such agencies as the State Planning Committee (GOSPLAN), and the Ministry of Defense.

The functions of the VPK are thought to include the coordination of defense research and production activities that cut across individual ministerial lines. Some observers believe that this group...determines whether existing technologies are adequate to support a given program, and that it helps to distribute resources among programs as needed, but that its charter does not

---

[1]For references to the evolution of this institution, see, among others: Gallagher and Spielmann, op. cit., p. 18; John Erickson, *Soviet Military Power*, Royal United Services Institute for Defence Studies, London, 1971, p. 14; David Mark, in *The Military Budget and National Economic Priorities*, Part III, the Joint Economic Committee, 91st Congress, June 1969, p. 956....

[2]See Harriet Scott, "The Soviet High Command," *Air Force Magazine*, March 1977, p. 53.

[3]Gallagher and Spielmann, op. cit., p. 19. Some analysts have suggested, however, that the Defense Council may also

serve as the formal medium through which the Ministry of Defense receives its directives from the Politburo. See Malcom Mackintosh, "The Soviet Military Influence on Foreign Policy," *Problems of Communism*, September–October 1973, p. 4.

[4]See Andrew Sheren, "Structure and Organization of Defense-Related Industries," in *Economic Performance and the Military Burden in the Soviet Union*, Joint Economic Committee, Washington, 1973, p. 123; Karl F. Spielmann, "Defense Industrialists in the USSR," *Problems of Communism*, September–October 1976, pp. 58–61.

include establishing the relative priority of one major program versus another—a matter dealt with higher up at the Defense Council or Politburo level.[1] ...

(3) The Ministerial Bureaucracies

At this level, the two principal ministries involved in foreign affairs and defense policy matters are, of course, the Ministry of Foreign Affairs...and the Ministry of Defense....

Ministry of Foreign Affairs   ...Most observers agree that this ministry's role continues to lie primarily in the realm of implementing, rather than formulating, Soviet foreign policy. The MFA does have a division charged with foreign policy planning, as well as a Collegium of senior diplomatic officials which is prepared to furnish advice on foreign policy matters. However, recommendations from both of these bodies apparently are rarely sought at the level of the Politburo and Central Committee departments, which tend to task the Foreign Ministry with preparation of reports containing information and analyses, rather than policy recommendations.[2]

In the field of arms control, the Foreign Ministry has a disarmament section which deals with...disarmament activities. Staffed by arms control specialists, this section probably comes closer to approximating its American counterpart, ACDA [Arms Control and Disarmament Agency], than any other organization on the Soviet side, although it is a good deal smaller than ACDA....

The Ministry of Defense and the General Staff
Although there is no question about the Party's control over the military as an institution, and although the military aspects of Soviet policy are integrated with political, economic and other relevant considerations at the top leadership level and through the mediating bodies that have been described, the military establishment... does appear to enjoy a large measure of autonomy and authority in strategic and operational matters.[3] ...

Though formally an agency of the Ministry of Defense, the General Staff is institutionally powerful in its own right, and as the central organ of the military high command, it has direct controlling links with the main staffs of the various service branches, military districts, and operational forces. Through its Main Operations Directorate, one of its three major components,[4] the General Staff directs military operations, develops strategic concepts, targeting and war plans, and helps formulate general military policy.[5]

Traditionally, there has been a muted rivalry between the Ministry of Defense, which though not run by civilian appointees, represents the interface of the military establishment with political authority, and the General staff, which regards itself as the real seat of military professionalism and leadership in the USSR, and is a somewhat larger organization than the Ministry itself. Moreover, one of the enunciated tasks of the General Staff is to ensure "coordinated actions" by all defense entities, including "the main and central administrations of the Ministry of Defense,"[6] which would seem to suggest that the latter should march to the cadence set by the General Staff....

Both the Ministry of Defense and the General Staff have an interest in arms control, and have made organizational arrangements for dealing

---

[1]Meyers and Simes, op. cit., p. 20.
[2]Meyers and Simes, op. cit., p. 19.

---

[3]Meyers and Simes, op. cit., pp. 19–20.
[4]The other two main directorates deal with logistics and procurement, and technology and R&D. Other General Staff components are concerned with intelligence, communications and so on.
[5]Gallagher and Speilmann, op. cit., p. 39....
[6]Cited by Harriet Scott in *Air Force Magazine*, March 1977, p. 55. This General Staff responsibility for coordinated action extends also to Civil Defense USSR.

with it.[1] In the case of SALT, the bulk of the preparation of substantive Soviet positions at the ministry level apparently has been carried out within the military establishment.[2] There has also been strong military representation on the Soviet negotiating delegation from the beginning of SALT....

Other Ministries and State Agencies   [Other entities] that contribute in some measure to the making of Soviet foreign and defense policy include the eight military-industrial ministries that comprise the previously mentioned defense-industry sector of the Soviet economy,[3] as well as the Committee of State Security (KGB), the State Planning Committee (GOSPLAN), the State Committee on Science and Technology and the Academy of Sciences, along with some of its subordinate research institutes.

In the case of the military-industrial ministries, influence upon Soviet defense policy is exerted through a web of organizational, economic and political relationships too intricate to be traced without far more detailed attention than is possible here. But several points can be briefly made.

First, the defense industry bureaucracy is notable for its continuity, both organizationally and in terms of key personnel. Since the late 1930s when a separate cluster of defense industries and

their supporting R&D institutions was established, these industries have tended to keep their centralized or "vertical" organizational structure intact throughout various industrial shakeups, including the economic decentralization of the 1957–65 period. As a result, though growth and change have occurred in the defense sector, basic enterprise groupings and lines of ministerial authority have remained relatively more stable than in other economic sectors....

A second notable feature of the defense industry sector is its symbiotic realtionship with the military establishment. In the Soviet Union, not only production of military goods, but the bulk of military R&D is carried out in institutions under the jurisdiction of the defense-related industrial ministries.[4] At the upper levels of the military establishment and the defense industries, the close link between military requirements and their fulfillment by the R&D and production programs of the defense industry sector apparently has led to a mutual interest in preserving arrangements which have not only helped to maintain favorable budgetary shares for both parties, but which—despite problems in certain cases—have on the whole enabled the Soviet Union to compete successfully against the West in the field of military technology.

This community of interest has operated at sub-levels of the interlocking military-industrial bureaucracies also. A network of ties has emerged between weapons design-production groups in industry and their immediate customers in the military establishment. One result is the formation of what might be called informal

---

[1]An office identified as a "section" in the Ministry of Defense has arms control responsibilities, while in the General Staff the drafting of substantive positions is thought likely to take place within the Main Operations Directorate. See Marshall Shulman, "SALT and the Soviet Union," in Mason Willrich and John B. Rhinelander (eds.), *SALT: The Moscow Agreements and Beyond*, Free Press, New York, 1974, 110; Gallagher and Spielmann, op. cit., p. 39.

[2]Testimony to this effect occasionally has come from Soviet visitors to the US. For example, a department head from one of the academic research institutes of the USSR Academy of Sciences, when asked in 1973 whether his institute made direct contributions to SALT planning, replied: "We do not work on the development of a strategic arms limitation plan. That is Marshal Grechko's province." See Wolfe, *The SALT Experience*, p. 40.

[3]See above, p. 15....

---

[4]Scientific research institutes (NII), general design buros (OKB), and some plant facilities for experimental production comprise the R&D network within the defense industry sector, with cross ties at all levels with military representatives of the Ministry of Defense and the General Staff. See Sheren, loc. cit., pp. 30, 35; William T. Lee, "The 'Politico-Military-Industrial Complex' of the USSR," *Journal of International Affairs*, No. 1, 1972, pp. 74–76; David Holloway, "Technology and Political Decision in Soviet Armaments Policy," *Journal of Peace Research*, No. 4, 1974, p. 260.

subgroup "alliances" devoted to promoting particular weapons categories, for example, between working elements of the Ministry of General Machine Building, which is believed to be responsible for design and production of strategic ballistic missiles, and military representatives of the Strategic Rocket Forces....

The KGB...can be presumed to have some influence on the formulation of foreign and national security policy, although its role is understandably not spelled out in Soviet sources. One avenue of KGB influence is through the kinds of information it supplies. Together with the GRU, the intelligence organ of the General Staff, it gathers information abroad and processes it into finished intelligence, although which of the two agencies is charged with preparing final assessments for the top leadership is not clear. The KGB's responsibilities also extend to keeping tabs on the conduct of Soviet officials, and to maintaining secure communications lines with Soviet representatives all over the world, activities which probably give it at least indirect influence upon the shaping of policy decisions....

The State Planning Committee, or GOSPLAN, makes a substantial contribution to Soviet defense policymaking, especially as a prime source of advice for the top leadership...with regard both to resources required and those available to support civil and military production programs, respectively.

Integration of defense program planning with the overall five-year economic plan cycle in the Soviet Union is thought to be accomplished by preparing a parallel five-year defense plan, subject like the overall economic plan, to annual and mid-term modifications....

The State Committee on Science and Technology...has a broad charter covering the improvement of the national research effort. However, the extent to which it may have some institutionalized role in Soviet military policymaking is not clear.... The Central Committee's Department on Science and Educational Institutions...evidently has some oversight role with regard to scientific research institutions, but does not appear to steer R&D policy as such.

Finally...we come to the USSR Academy of Sciences and some of the research institutes that nominally operate under its wing. The Academy itself...apparently plays little direct role in policy matters, but a rather significant impact may be exerted by its members upon both military and foreign policy issues. One channel of influence is through personal contacts of senior scientists who have been invited periodically to high policy councils as consultants in their own fields of competence.[1] In the past, scientists given access to the top leadership generally were expected to provide individual professional advice, and not to represent the view of a "scientific lobby" or to voice political judgments; more recently, at least some members of the Soviet scientific community may have acquired a broader advisory role.[2] The practice of bringing in scientific experts as consultants or sometimes staff members in the Central Committee apparatus reportedly also has increased in recent years.[3]

Among the research institutes under the USSR Academy of Sciences which produce studies in the fields of foreign affairs, defense and arms control are the Institute of World Economy and International Relations [IMEMO], directed by N. N. Inozemtsev, and the newer Institute of the USA and Canada, directed by G. A. Arbatov. Since the late sixties both of these

---

[1] Khrushchev's frequent invitations to prominent scientists to discuss the military implications of their work were a case in point. See *Khrushchev Remembers: The Last Testament*, Little Brown & Co., New York, 1974, pp. 58–71.

[2] Cf. Shulman, in *SALT: The Moscow Agreements and Beyond*, p. 111.

[3] Most of the experts thus drawn into the Central Committee apparatus are said to be from the social and political sciences rather than the "hard" sciences. See Meyers and Simes, op. cit., p. 21.

institutions have established departments to deal with military-political aspects of international relations, headed in each instance by former General Staff officers with academic degrees.[1] A number of other retired or brevetted military officers also joined the staffs of the two institutes, and in most cases apparently have maintained their contacts with the General Staff and the Ministry of Defense....

The largely unknown factor is how much weight the work of these institutes may have in the actual framing of Soviet foreign and military policy. Since neither of the institutes ostensibly is authorized or asked to analyze Soviet strategic, economic and other problems, their inputs to policymaking presumably lie mainly in how they interpret developments abroad—which may differ somewhat from the interpetations provided by the regular Soviet intelligence organizations. Some outside observers feel that institute researchers probably have had a substantial impact on policymaking by providing an alternative transmission belt for information between the United States and the Soviet Union: others have the impression that the interaction between institute researchers and official policymakers has not been very close.[2] It is generally thought, on the other hand, that the directors of the two institutes may have considerably more influence than their reserach staffs by virtue of their Party standing.[3] ...

---

[1] The original chairman of the Division of Military-Political Problems of International Relations in [IMEMO] was Colonel V. M. Kulish, while the chairman of the Division of Military Aspects of Foreign Policy at Arbatov's institute was Colonel V. V. Larionov. Both men, well known by their writings outside the USSR, have since been replaced.

[2] Meyers and Simes, op. cit., pp. 34–38; Wolfe, *The SALT Experience*, pp. 48–49.

[3] Both Inozemtsev and Arbatov are candidate members of the Central Committee, which gives them positions of moderate but scarcely high prestige in terms of the Party hierarchy.

DOCUMENT 1

Imperialism, the Highest Stage of Capitalism

V. I. Lenin

1917

Editor's commentary: This excerpt is from one of Lenin's most influential works, written during his Swiss exile in 1916 as an explanation of the origins of World War I and the certain collapse of capitalism. In this work, Lenin revises the Marxist critique of capitalism and raises it to the level of international relations. The theory of the continual clash of capitalist-imperialist interests in the form of wars whose purpose is to "partition the world" has its origins here. The significance of the third world (the colonial holdings of the imperialist European powers) in Marxist-Leninist doctrine can be traced back to this important work.

IMPERIALISM AS A SPECIAL STAGE OF CAPITALISM

...Imperialism emerged as the development and direct continuation of the fundamental attributes of capitalism in general. But capitalism only became capitalist imperialism at a definite and very high stage of its development, when certain of its fundamental attributes began to be transformed into their opposites, when the features of the period of transition from capitalism to a higher social and economic system began to take shape and reveal themselves all along the line. The fundamental economic factor in this process is the substitution of capitalist monopolies for capitalist free competition. Free competition is

---

V. I. Lenin, *Imperialism, the Highest Stage of Capitalism* (New York: International Publishers, 1939), pp. 88–89 and 123–126, *excerpts*.

the fundamental attribute of capitalism and of commodity production generally. Monopoly is exactly the opposite of free competition; but we have seen the latter being transformed into monopoly before our very eyes, creating large-scale industry and eliminating small industry, replacing large-scale industry by still larger-scale industry, finally leading to such a concentration of production and capital that monopoly has been and is the result: cartels, syndicates and trusts, and merging with them, the capital of a dozen or so banks manipulating thousands of millions. At the same time monopoly, which has grown out of free competition, does not abolish the latter, but exists alongside it and hovers over it, as it were, and, as a result, gives rise to a number of very acute antagonisms, frictions and conflicts. Monopoly is the transition from capitalism to a higher system.

If it were necessary to give the briefest possible definition of imperialism we should have to say that imperialism is the monopoly stage of capitalism. Such a definition would include what is most important, for, on the one hand, finance capital is the bank capital of the few big monopolist banks, merged with the capital of the monopolist combines of manufacturers; and, on the other hand, the division of the world is the transition from a colonial policy which has extended without hindrance to territories unoccupied by any capitalist power, to a colonial policy of the monopolistic possession of the territories of the world which has been completely divided up....

THE PLACE OF IMPERIALISM IN HISTORY

We have seen that the economic quintessence of imperialism is monopoly capitalism. This very fact determines its place in history, for monopoly that grew up on the basis of free competition, and precisely out of free competition, is the transition from the capitalist system to a higher social economic order. We must take special note of the four principal forms of monopoly, or the four principal manifestations of monopoly capitalism, which are characteristic of the epoch under review.

Firstly, monopoly arose out of the concentration of production at a very advanced stage of development. This refers to the monopolist capitalist combines: cartels, syndicates, and trusts. We have seen the important role these play in modern economic life. At the beginning of the twentieth century, monopolies acquired complete supremacy in the advanced countries. And although the first steps towards the formation of the combines were first taken by countries enjoying the protection of high tariffs (Germany, America), Great Britain, with her system of free trade, was not far behind in revealing the same basic phenomenon, namely, the birth of monopoly out of the concentration of production.

Secondly, monopolies have accelerated the capture of the most important sources of raw materials, especially for the coal and iron industries, which are the basic and most highly cartelized industries in capitalist society. The monopoly of the most important sources of raw materials has enormously increased the power of big capital, and has sharpened the antagonism between cartelized and noncartelized industry.

Thirdly, monopoly has sprung from the banks. The banks have developed from most intermediary enterprises into the monopolists of finance capital. Some three or five of the biggest banks in each of the foremost capitalist countries have achieved the "personal union" of industrial and bank capital, and have concentrated in their hands the power to dispose of thousands upon thousands of millions which form the greater part of the capital and income of entire countries. A financial oligarchy, which throws a close net of relations of dependence over all the economic and political institutions of contemporary bourgeois society without exception—such is the most striking manifestation of this monopoly.

Fourthly, monopoly has grown out of colonial policy. To the numerous "old" motives of colonial policy, finance capital has added the struggle for the sources of raw materials, for the export of capital, for "spheres of influence," i.e., for spheres for profitable deals, concessions, monopolist profits, and so on; in fine, for economic territory in general. When the colonies of the European powers in Africa comprised only one-tenth of that territory (as was the case in 1876), colonial policy was able to develop by methods other than those of monopoly—by the "free grabbing" of territories, so to speak. But when nine-tenths of Africa had been seized (approximately by 1900), when the whole world had been divided up, there was inevitably ushered in a period of colonial monopoly and, consequently, a period of particularly intense struggle for the division and the redivision of the world.

The extent to which monopolist capital has intensified all the contradictions of capitalism is generally known. It is sufficient to mention the high cost of living and the oppression of the cartels. This intensification of contradictions constitutes the most powerful driving force of the transitional period of history, which began at the time of the definite victory of world finance capital.

Monopolies, oligarchy, the striving for domination instead of striving for liberty, the exploitation of an increasing number of small or weak nations by an extremely small group of the richest most powerful nations—all these have given birth to those distinctive characteristics of imperialism which compel us to define it as parasitic or decaying capitalism. More and more prominently there emerges, as one of the tendencies of imperialism, the creation of the "bond-holding" (*rentier*) state, the usurer state, in which the bourgeoisie lives on the proceeds of capital exports and by "clipping coupons." It would be a mistake to believe that this tendency to decay precludes the possibility of the rapid growth of capitalism. It does not. In the epoch of imperialism, certain branches of industry, certain strata of the bourgeoisie and certain countries betray to a more or less degree, one or other of these tendencies. On the whole capitalism is growing far more rapidly than before, but this growth is not only becoming more and more uneven in general; its unevenness also manifests itself, in particular, in the decay of the countries which are richest in capital (such as England).

. . . In its turn, this finance capital which has grown so rapidly is not unwilling (precisely because it has grown so quickly) to pass on to a more "tranquil" possession of colonies which have to be seized—and not only by peaceful methods—from richer nations. In the United States, economic development in the last decades has been even more rapid than in Germany, and *for this very reason* the parasitic character of modern American capitalism has stood out with particular prominence. On the other hand, a comparison of, say, the republican American bourgeoisie with the monarchist Japanese or German bourgeoisie shows that the most pronounced political distinctions diminish to an extreme degree in the epoch of imperialism—not because they are unimportant in general, but because in all these cases we are discussing a bourgeoisie which has definite features of parasitism.

The receipt of high monopoly profits by the capitalists in one of the numerous branches of industry, in one of numerous countries, etc., makes it economically possible for them to corrupt certain sections of the working class and for a time a fairly considerable minority, and win them to the side of the bourgeoisie of a given industry or nation against all the others. The intensification of antagonisms between imperialist nations for the division of the world increases this striving. And so there is created that bond between imperialism and opportunism, which revealed itself first and most clearly in England, owing to the fact that certain features of imperialist development were observable there much earlier than in other countries.

DOCUMENT 2

The Imperialist War of 1914–1918

Nikolai I. Bukharin

1920

Editor's commentary: By 1920 the civil war was winding down and the bolsheviks were consolidating their power at home. They thought that because of the Versailles treaty, with its harsh reparations demands on the losers, Germany and the rest of Europe would soon be overtaken by revolution. It was in this heady atmosphere that Nikolai I. Bukharin, a leading bolshevik whom Lenin called "the favorite of the whole party," penned (in collaboration with E. Preobrazhensky) the ABC of Communism. *This selection expands on the doctrinal themes that Lenin introduced in* Imperialism, the Highest Stage of Capitalism, *explaining who was really responsible for the war from the bolshevik perspective.*

The policy of Imperialism pursued by the "Great Powers" was bound, sooner or later, to lead to conflict. It is perfectly clear that the robber policy of all the "Great Powers" was the cause of the great war. Only a fool can still believe that the war broke out because the Serbians murdered the Austrian Crown Prince or because Germany attacked Belgium. At the beginning of the war there was much discussion as to who was to blame. The German capitalists asserted that Russia had attacked Germany, and the Russian capitalists declared with one voice that Russia had been attacked by Germany. In England, it was said that the war was being fought for the protection of the unfortunate Belgians. In France, likewise, it was written, said and sung that noble France entered the war on behalf of the heroic Belgian people. And at the same time it was stated throughout the length and breadth of Austria and Germany that they were protecting themselves from the onslaught of the Russian Cossacks, and were forced to wage a holy war of defense.

This was sheer nonsense from beginning to end, and was a betrayal of the working masses. The bourgeoisie made use of this betrayal in order to compel the soldiers to march off to the war. The bourgeoisie employed these means not for the first time. We have already seen how the lords of the syndicates introduced high tariffs in order, with the help of the robbery of their own countrymen, to carry on the struggle more effectively in foreign markets. The tariffs were for them a means of attack. The bourgeoisie, however, maintained that they wanted merely to defend home industries. It is the same in the case of war. The reason for the Imperialist war, which was intended to subject the world to the rule of finance capital, lay precisely in the fact that *all were aggressors*. That is perfectly clear now. The Czarist lackeys said that they were "defending" themselves. However, when the secret departments of the Ministries were burst open during the October revolution documentary evidence was found establishing the fact that Kerensky, as well as the Czar, in league with the English and French, had carried on the war from motives of plunder; that the Russians were to be allowed to take Constantinople, to plunder Turkey and Persia, and to seize the Austrian province of Galicia.

The German Imperialists were similarly unmasked. One has only to remember in this connection the peace of Brest-Litovsk, after which they carried out raids into Poland, Lithuania, Ukraine, and Finland. The German revolution disclosed several important facts. We now have documentary proof that Germany, actuated by a desire for loot, prepared for a sudden onslaught with the idea of seizing upon almost all foreign lands and colonies.

N. Bukharin and E. Preobrazhensky, *ABC of Communism* (Detroit, MI: The Marxian Educational Society, 1921), chapter 4, section 29, *excerpts*.

And what of the "noble" Allies? They also are now thoroughly exposed. Since they robbed Germany by the Peace of Versailles, and imposed an indemnity of 125 milliards [billions] upon her; since they took away her whole fleet, all her colonies, and almost all her locomotives, and drove off her milch cows, it is quite natural that no one should any longer believe in their generosity. They are plundering Russia in the same way, north and south. They also, therefore, carried on the war *for the sake of loot*.

The Bolsheviks said all this at the very beginning of the war. At that time few people believed it. Now, however, it is tolerably clear to every reasonable person. Finance capital is an avaricious, blood-soaked robber, no matter what the country of its origin—whether it be Russian, German, French, Japanese or American.

It is therefore absurd to say that in an *Imperialist* war one group of Imperialists is to blame and another not, or that one group attacks and another acts on the defensive. These excuses were thought out merely to deceive the workers. In reality, all the Imperialist groups attacked the small peoples in the first instance; they were all possessed of the idea of plundering the whole world, and of subjecting it to the rule of the finance capital of their own country.

The war was bound to be a world war. The whole world was parcelled out amongst the "Great Powers," and all the Powers were connected in the great world economy. Small wonder, therefore, that the war embraced almost all the divisions of the earth.

England, France, Italy, Belgium, Russia, Germany, Austria-Hungary, Serbia, Bulgaria, Roumania, Montenegro, Japan, the United States, China, and many other smaller States were drawn into the bloody struggle. The population of the world is approximately a milliard and a half, and all these people bore, directly or indirectly, the burden of the war which a handful of capitalist criminals has forced upon them. Such colossal armies as were placed in the field and such mighty weapons of destruction had never

previously been seen. Such power as capital possessed had never been known in the world. England and France compelled not only Englishmen and Frenchmen to subserve their financial interest, but hundreds of black and yellow-skinned slaves in subject territories as well. The civilized bandits did not shrink from employing cannibals in order to achieve their purpose. And all this was cloaked by professions of the noblest sentiments. . . .

The Tasks of the Communist University of the Toilers of the East in Relation to the Colonial and Dependent Countries of the East

Joseph V. Stalin

18 May 1925

Editor's commentary: Stalin adopted and developed many of the themes that Lenin himself put forward in revolutionary ideology and doctrine. The most important of these for subsequent Soviet foreign policy concerned revolutionary possibilities in the colonial empires. This speech stressed the importance for nascent revolutionaries in underdeveloped societies to maintain close contact with the successful proletarians of the developed world (i.e., the USSR) on the road to achieving true national liberation. The strategic imperative was the organization and formation of Communist parties out of existing progressive forces.

From a speech entitled "The Political Tasks of the University of the Peoples of the East," delivered at a meeting of students of the Communist University of the Toilers of the East, 18 May 1925, in J. V. Stalin, *Works* (Moscow: Foreign Languages Publishing House, 1953–1955). Originally appeared in *Pravda*, 22 May 1925.

Let us pass to...the question of the tasks of the Communist University of the Toilers of the East in relation to the colonial and dependent countries of the East.

What are the characteristic features of the life and development of these countries, which distinguish them from the Soviet republics of the East?

Firstly, these countries are living and developing under the oppression of imperialism.

Secondly, the existence of a double oppression, internal oppression (by the native bourgeoisie) and external oppression (by the foreign imperialist bourgeoisie), is intensifying and deepening the revolutionary crisis in these countries.

Thirdly, in some of these countries, India for example, capitalism is growing at a rapid rate, giving rise to and moulding a more or less numerous class of local proletarians.

Fourthly, with the growth of the revolutionary movement, the national bourgeoisie in such countries is splitting up into two parts, a revolutionary part (the petty bourgeoisie) and a compromising part (the big bourgeoisie), of which the first is continuing the revolutionary struggle, whereas the second is entering into a bloc with imperialism.

Fifthly, parallel with the imperialist bloc, another bloc is taking shape in such countries, a bloc between the workers and the revolutionary petty bourgeoisie, an anti-imperialist bloc, the aim of which is complete liberation from imperialism.

Sixthly, the question of the hegemony of the proletariat in such countries, and of freeing the masses of the people from the influence of the compromising national bourgeoisie, is becoming more and more urgent.

Seventhly, this circumstance makes it much easier to link the national-liberation movement in such countries with the proletarian movement in the advanced countries of the West.

From this at least three conclusions follow:

1. The liberation of the colonial and dependent countries from imperialism cannot be achieved without a victorious revolution: you will not get independence gratis.

2. The revolution cannot be advanced and the complete independence of the capitalistically developed colonies and dependent countries cannot be won unless the compromising national bourgeoisie is isolated, unless the petty-bourgeois revolutionary masses are freed from the influence of that bourgeoisie, unless the policy of the hegemony of the proletariat is put into effect, unless the advanced elements of the working class are organised in an independent Communist Party.
3. Lasting victory cannot be achieved in the colonial and dependent countries without a real link between the liberation movement in those countries and the proletarian movement in the advanced countries of the West.

The main task of the Communists in the colonial and dependent countries is to base their revolutionary activities upon these conclusions....

Hence, the immediate tasks of the revolutionary movement in the capitalistically developed colonies and dependent countries are:

1. To win the best elements of the working class to the side of communism and to create independent Communist Parties.
2. To form a national-revolutionary bloc of the workers, peasants and revolutionary intelligentsia against the bloc of the compromising national bourgeoisie and imperialism.
3. To ensure the hegemony of the proletariat in that bloc.
4. To fight to free the urban and rural petty bourgeoisie from the influence of the compromising national bourgeoisie.
5. To ensure that the liberation movement is linked with the proletarian movement in the advanced countries.

Such are the three groups of immediate tasks confronting the leading cadres in the colonial and dependent countries of the East....

What is the mission of the University of the Peoples of the East in relation to the colonial and dependent countries in view of all these circumstances? Its mission is to take into account all the specific features of the revolutionary development of these countries and to train the cadres coming from them in a way that will ensure the fulfillment of the various immediate tasks I have enumerated.

In the University of the Peoples of the East there are about ten different groups of students who have come here from colonial and dependent countries. We all know that these comrades are thirsting for light and knowledge. The task of the University of the Peoples of the East is to make them into real revolutionaries, armed with the theory of Leninism, equipped with the practical experience of Leninism, and capable of carrying out the immediate tasks of the liberation movement in the colonies and dependent countries with all their heart and soul....

Such, in general, are the political tasks of the University of the Peoples of the East in relation to the peoples of the Soviet East and of the colonial East.

Let us hope that the University of the Peoples of the East will succeed in carrying out these tasks with honour.

DOCUMENT 4

Those Who Fall Behind Get Beaten

Joseph V. Stalin

4 February 1931

Editor's commentary: This speech to Soviet "businessmen" is sometimes viewed as remarkably prescient in its call to make up in 10 years' time, at whatever cost necessary, the huge gap that

---

Excerpted from a speech entitled "The Tasks of Business Executives," given at the First All-Union Conference of Managers of Socialist Industry, 4 February 1931. J. V. Stalin, *Problems of Leninism*, 11th ed. (Moscow, 1953), pp. 448–458.

separated Soviet industry from that of the West. Ten years later, the Nazis attacked the USSR. It is bluntly stated that if Soviet industry does not catch up, the Soviet state—and by implication, communism—will be "crushed." Stalin characterizes the USSR as the loyal "shock brigade" of the international proletariat against capitalism and exhorts his audience with the Stakhanovite slogan "There are no fortresses which Bolsheviks cannot capture." In this speech the Marxist-Leninist progressive worldview is joined to the nationalist image of a helpless, traditional, and "backward" Mother Russia being beaten throughout history by hostile invaders.

...It is sometimes asked whether it is not possible to slow down the tempo somewhat, to put a check on the movement. No, comrades, it is not possible! The tempo must not be reduced! On the contrary, we must increase it as much as is within our powers and possibilities. This is dictated to us by our obligations to the workers and peasants of the USSR. This is dictated to us by our obligations to the working class of the whole world.

To slacken the tempo would mean falling behind. And those who fall behind get beaten. But we do not want to be beaten. No, we refuse to be beaten! One feature of the history of old Russia was the continual beatings she suffered because of her backwardness. She was beaten by the Mongol khans. She was beaten by the Turkish beys. She was beaten by the Swedish feudal lords. She was beaten by the Polish and Lithuanian gentry. She was beaten by the British and French capitalists. She was beaten by the Japanese barons. All beat her—because of her backwardness, military backwardness, cultural backwardness, political backwardness, industrial backwardness, agricultural backwardness. They beat her because to do so was profitable and could be done with impunity. Do you remember the words of the prerevolutionary poet: "You are poor and abundant, mighty and impotent, Mother Russia." Those gentlemen were quite familiar with the verses of the old poet. They beat her, saying: "You are abundant," so one can enrich oneself at your expense. They beat her saying: "You are poor and impotent," so you can be beaten and plundered with impunity. Such is the law of the exploiters—to beat the backward and the weak. It is the jungle law of capitalism. You are backward, you are weak—therefore you are wrong; hence, you can be beaten and enslaved. You are mighty—therefore you are right; hence we must be wary of you.

That is why we must no longer lag behind.

In the past we had no fatherland, nor could we have one. But now that we have overthrown capitalism and power is in our hands, in the hands of the people, we have a fatherland, and we will defend its independence. Do you want our socialist fatherland to be beaten and to lose its independence? If you do not want this, you must put an end to its backwardness in the shortest possible time and develop genuine Bolshevik tempo in building up a socialist system of economy. There is no other way. That is why Lenin said on the eve of the October Revolution, "Either perish, or overtake and outstrip the advanced capitalist countries."

We are fifty or a hundred years behind the advanced countries. We must make good this distance in ten years. Either we do it, or we shall be crushed. This is what our obligations to the workers and peasants of the USSR dictate to us.

But we have other, still more serious and more important obligations. They are our obligations to the world proletariat. They coincide with our obligations to the workers and peasants of the USSR. But we place them higher. The working class of the USSR is part of the world working class. We achieved victory not solely through the efforts of the working class of the USSR, but also thanks to the support of the working class of the world. Without this support we would have been torn to pieces long ago. It is said that our country is the shock brigade of the proletariat of all countries. This is a fitting definition. But this imposes very serious obligations upon us. Why does the international proletariat support us?

How did we merit this support? By the fact that we were the first to hurl ourselves into the battle against capitalism, we were the first to establish a working-class state, we were the first to start building socialism. By the fact that we are doing work which, if successful, will change the whole world and free the entire working class. But what is needed for success? The elimination of our backwardness, the development of a high Bolshevik tempo of construction. We must march forward in such a way that the working class of the whole world, looking at us, may say: This is my vanguard, this is my shock brigade, this is my working-class state, this is my fatherland; they are promoting their cause, which is *our* cause, and they are doing this well; let us support them against the capitalists and promote the cause of the world revolution. Must we not live up to the hopes of the world's working class, must we not fulfill our obligations to them? Yes, we must if we do not want utterly to disgrace ourselves.

Such are our obligations, internal and international. As you see, they dictate to us a Bolshevik tempo of development.

I will not say that we have accomplished nothing in regard to economic management during these years. In fact, we have accomplished a good deal. We have doubled our industrial output as compared with the prewar level. We have created the largest-scale agricultural production in the world. But we could have accomplished more had we tried hard during this period really to master production, the technique of production, the financial and economic side of it.

In ten years at most we must make good the distance which separates us from the advanced capitalist countries. We have all the "objective" possibilities for this. The only thing lacking is the ability to take proper advantage of these possibilities. And that depends on us. *Only* on us! It is time we learned to take advantage of these possibilities. It is time to put an end to the rotten policy of noninterference in production. It is time to adopt a new policy, a policy adapted to the present times—the policy of *intefering in every-*

thing. If you are a factory manager, then interfere in all the affairs of the factory, look into everything, let nothing escape you, learn and learn again. Bolsheviks must master technique. It is time Bolsheviks themselves became experts. In the period of reconstruction technique decides everything. And a business executive who does not want to study technique, who does not want to master technique, is a joke and not an executive.

It is said that it is hard to master technique. That is not true! There are no fortresses which Bolsheviks cannot capture. We have solved a number of most difficult problems. We have overthrown capitalism. We have assumed power. We have built up a huge socialist industry. We have swung the middle peasants to the path of socialism. We have already accomplished what is most important from the point of view of construction. What remains to be done is not so much: to study technique, to master science. And when we have done that we will develop a tempo of which we dare not even dream at present.

And we will do that if we really want to.

DOCUMENT 5

The International Situation

Andrei Zhdanov

September 1947

Editor's commentary: At the founding conference of the Communist Information Bureau in September

---

Speech by Andrei Zhdanov given at the founding conference of the Cominform in late September 1947. In U.S. Congress, House of Representatives, Committee on Foreign Affairs, *The Strategy and Tactics of World Communism*, 84th Congress, Second Session, House Document No. 619 (Washington, D.C.: U.S. Government Printing Office, 1948), pp. 211–230, *exerpts*.

1947, Andrei Zhdanov enunciated a foreign policy line that reiterated in ideological terms the realities of the East-West postwar confrontation, baptized by journalist Walter Lippmann as the "cold war." According to Stalin's chief lieutenant, two camps had congealed, the "anti-imperialist and democratic camp" of socialism and the "imperialist and anti-democratic camp" of capitalism. Although "peaceful coexistence" was proclaimed as a principle of relations, this speech, given as it was on the occasion of what was widely perceived in the West as the resurrection of the Communist International, signaled a deepening of the cold war and the more vigorous promotion of revolution abroad.

I. THE POST-WAR WORLD SITUATION

...The fundamental changes caused by the war on the international scene in the position of individual countries has entirely changed the political landscape of the world. A new alignment of political forces has arisen. The more the war recedes into the past, the more distinct become two major trends in post-war international policy, corresponding to the division of the political forces operating on the international arena into two major camps; the imperialist and anti-democratic camp, on the one hand, and the anti-imperialist and democratic camp, on the other. The principal driving force of the imperialist camp is the U.S.A....

The cardinal purpose of the imperialist camp is to strengthen imperialism, to hatch a new imperialist war, to combat Socialism and democracy, and to support reactionary and anti-democratic pro-fascist regimes and movements everywhere.

In the pursuit of these ends the imperialist camp is prepared to rely on reactionary and anti-democratic forces in all countries, and to support its former adversaries in the war against its wartime allies.

The anti-fascist forces comprise the second camp. This camp is based on the U.S.S.R. and the new democracies. It also includes countries that have broken with imperialism and have firmly set foot on the path of democratic development.... The purpose of this camp is to resist the threat of new wars and imperialist expansion, to strengthen democracy and to extirpate the vestiges of fascism.

The end of the Second World War confronted all the freedom-loving nations with the cardinal task of securing a lasting democratic peacesealing victory over fascism. In the accomplishment of this fundamental task of the post-war period the Soviet Union and its foreign policy are playing a leading role. This follows from the very nature of the Soviet Socialist state, to which motives of aggression and exploitation are utterly alien, and which is interested in creating the most favourable conditions for the building of a Communist society. One of these conditions is external peace. As the embodiment of a new and superior social system, the Soviet Union reflects in its foreign policy the aspirations of progressive mankind, which desires lasting peace and has nothing to gain from a new war hatched by capitalism.... The change in the general alignment of forces between the capitalist world and the Socialist world brought about by the war has still further enhanced the significance of the foreign policy of the Soviet state and enlarged the scope of its activity on the international arena....

Soviet foreign policy proceeds from the fact of the co-existence for a long period of the two systems—capitalism and socialism. From this it follows that co-operation between the U.S.S.R. and countries with other systems is possible, provided that the principle of reciprocity is observed and that obligations once assumed are honoured. Everyone knows that the U.S.S.R. has always honoured the obligations it has assumed. The Soviet Union has demonstrated its will and desire for co-operation.

Britain and America are pursuing the very opposite policy in the United Nations. They are doing everything they can to renounce their commitments and to secure a free hand for the prosecution of a new policy, a policy which envisages not co-operation among the nations, but the hounding of one against the other, violation of the rights and interests of democratic nations, and the isolation of the U.S.S.R.

Soviet policy follows the line of maintaining loyal, good-neighbor relations with all states that display the desire for co-operation. As to the countries that are its genuine friends and allies, the Soviet Union has always behaved, and will always behave, as their true friend and ally. Soviet foreign policy envisages a further extension of friendly aid by the Soviet Union to these countries....

DOCUMENT 6

Crisis of the World Capitalist System and Inevitability of Wars between Capitalist Countries

Joseph V. Stalin

1952

Editor's commentary: This excerpt is from one of Stalin's last important theoretical works, completed just prior to the convening of the 19th CPSU Congress (the first one since 1939). Although Stalin did not give the keynote address at the congress (this was left to Georgi Malenkov), this work became its centerpiece and was cited and paraphrased throughout. Expanding on themes first developed by Lenin in his Imperialism, the Highest Stage of Capitalism, *Stalin claims that wars will continue among capitalist powers increasingly desperate in their search for markets and resources; this is part of the general crisis of*

Excerpted from J. V. Stalin, *Problems of Socialism in the USSR* (Moscow: Foreign Languages Publishing House, 1952), pp. 31–41.

capitalism. Meanwhile, the socialist camp should not fear an attack by the capitalists because, he implies, they themselves are unsure of prevailing over socialism. Wars will continue among capitalist countries until imperialism itself is "abolished."

...Some comrades hold that, owing to the development of new international conditions since the Second World War, wars between capitalist countries have ceased to be inevitable. They consider that the contradictions between the socialist camp and the capitalist camp are more acute than the contradictions among the capitalist countries; that the U.S.A. has brought the other capitalist countries sufficiently under its sway to be able to prevent them going to war among themselves and weakening one another; that the foremost capitalist minds have been sufficiently taught by the two world wars and the severe damage they caused to the whole capitalist world not to venture to involve the capitalist countries in war with one another again—and that, because of all this, wars between capitalist countries are no longer inevitable.

These comrades are mistaken. They see the outward phenomena that come and go on the surface, but they do not see those profound forces which, although they are so far operating imperceptibly, will nevertheless determine the course of developments....

It is said that the contradictions between capitalism and socialism are stronger than the contradictions among the capitalist countries. Theoretically, of course, that is true. It is not only true now, today; it was true before the Second World War. And it was more or less realized by the leaders of the capitalist countries. Yet the Second World War began not as a war with the U.S.S.R., but as a war between capitalist countries. Why? Firstly, because war with the U.S.S.R., as a socialist land, is more dangerous to capitalism than war between capitalist countries, for whereas war between capitalist countries puts in question only the supremacy of certain capitalist countries over others, war with the U.S.S.R. must certainly put in question the existence of capitalism itself. Secondly, because the capitalists, although they clamour, for "propaganda" purposes, about the aggressiveness of the Soviet Union, do not themselves believe that it is aggressive, because they are aware of the Soviet Union's peaceful policy and know that it will not itself attack capitalist countries....

It is said that Lenin's thesis that imperialism inevitably generates war must now be regarded as obsolete, since powerful popular forces have come forward today in defense of peace and against another world war. That is not true.

The object of the present-day peace movement is to rouse the masses of the people to fight for the preservation of peace and for the prevention of another world war. Consequently, the aim of this movement is not to overthrow capitalism and establish socialism—it confines itself to the democratic aim of preserving peace. In this respect, the present-day peace movement differs from the movements of the time of the First World War for the conversion of the imperialist war into civil war, since the latter movements went further and pursued socialist aims.

It is possible that in a definite conjuncture of circumstances, the fight for peace will develop here or there into a fight for socialism. But then it will no longer be the present-day peace movement; it will be a movement for the overthrow of capitalism.

What is most likely, is that the present-day peace movement, as a movement for the preservation of peace, will, if it succeeds, result in preventing a *particular* war, in its temporary postponement, in the temporary preservation of a *particular* peace, in the resignation of a bellicose government and its supersession by another that is prepared temporarily to keep the peace. That, of course, will be good. Even very good. But, all the same, it will not be enough to eliminate the inevitability of wars between capitalist countries generally. It will not be enough, because for all the successes of the peace movement, imperialism will remain, continue in force—and consequently, the inevitability of wars will also continue in force.

To eliminate the inevitability of war, it is necessary to abolish imperialism.

On Peaceful Coexistence and Preventing War

N. S. Khrushchev

February 1956

Editor's commentary: In that part of his address to the Twentieth Party Congress which was made public, Khrushchev exhibited, for the most part, continuity with his predecessors. However, regarding the subject of the inevitability of war, he made an important change in elevating the Leninist tactic of peaceful coexistence to a strategy in light of a new circumstance: the existence of nuclear weapons. This new position became a contributing factor soon thereafter to the ideological dispute between the Soviet and Chinese Communists over the character of the struggle between socialism and capitalism.

THE INTERNATIONAL SITUATION OF THE SOVIET UNION

The emergence of socialism from within the bounds of a single country and its transformation into a world system is the main feature of our era. Capitalism has proved powerless to prevent this process of a world-historic significance.

Nikita S. Khrushchev, *Report of the Central Committee of the CPSU to the Twentieth Party Congress* (Moscow: Foreign Languages Publishing House, 1956), pp. 8–9 and 38–42, *excerpts.*

The simultaneous existence of two opposite world economic systems, the capitalist and the socialist, developing according to different laws and in opposite directions, has become an indisputable fact.

Socialist economy is developing towards the ever-increasing satisfaction of the material and cultural requirements of all members of society, the continuous expansion and improvement of production on the basis of higher techniques, and closer cooperation and mutual assistance between the socialist countries.

The trend of capitalist economy is that of the ever-increasing enrichment of the monopolies, the further intensification of exploitation and cuts in the living standards of millions of working people, particularly in the colonial and dependent countries, of increased militarization of the economy, the exacerbation of the competitive struggle among the capitalist countries, and the maturing of new economic crises and upheavals....

SOME FUNDAMENTAL QUESTIONS OF PRESENT-DAY INTERNATIONAL DEVELOPMENT

Comrades! I should like to dwell on some fundamental questions concerning present-day international developments....

These questions are the peaceful coexistence of the two systems, [and] the possibility of preventing wars in the present era....

Let us examine these questions in brief.

The Peaceful Coexistence of the Two Systems

The Leninist principle of peaceful coexistence of states with different social systems has always been and remains the general line of our country's foreign policy.

It has been alleged that the Soviet Union advances the principle of peaceful coexistence merely out of tactical considerations, considerations of expediency. Yet it is common knowledge that we have always, from the very first years of Soviet power, stood with equal firmness for peaceful coexistence. Hence, it is not a tactical move, but a fundamental principle of Soviet foreign policy.

This means that if there is indeed a threat to the peaceful coexistence of countries with differing social and political systems, it by no means comes from the Soviet Union or the rest of the socialist camp. Is there a single reason why a socialist state should want to unleash aggressive war? Do we have classes and groups that are interested in war as a means of enrichment? We do not. We abolished them long ago. Or, perhaps, we do not have enough territory or natural wealth, perhaps we lack sources of raw materials or markets for our goods? No, we have sufficient of all those and to spare. Why then should we want war? We do not want it, as a matter of principle we renounce any policy that might lead to millions of people being plunged into war for the sake of the selfish interests of a handful of multi-millionaires. Do those who shout about the "aggressive intentions" of the U.S.S.R. know all this? Of course they do. Why then do they keep up the old monotonous refrain about some imaginary "communist aggression"? Only to stir up mud, to conceal their plans for world domination, a "crusade" against peace, democracy, and socialism.

To this day the enemies of peace allege that the Soviet Union is out to overthrow capitalism in other countries by "exporting" revolution. It goes without saying that among us Communists there are no supporters of capitalism. But this does not mean that we have interfered or plan to interfere in the internal affairs of countries where capitalism still exists.... We often hear representatives of bourgeois countries reasoning thus: "The Soviet leaders claim that they are for peaceful coexistence between the two systems. At the same time they declare that they are fighting for communism, and say that communism is bound to win in all countries. Now if the Soviet Union is fighting for communism, how can there be any peaceful co-existence with it?" This view is the

result of bourgeois propaganda. The ideologists of the bourgeoisie distort the facts and deliberately confuse questions of ideological struggle with questions of relations between states in order to make the Communists of the Soviet Union look like advocates of aggression.

When we say that the socialist system will win in the competition between the two systems—the capitalist and the socialist—this by no means signifies that its victory will be achieved through armed interference by the socialist countries in the internal affairs of the capitalist countries. Our certainty of the victory of communism is based on the fact that the socialist mode of production possesses decisive advantages over the capitalist mode of production. Precisely because of this, the ideas of Marxism-Leninism are more and more capturing the minds of the broad masses of the working people in the capitalist countries, just as they have captured the minds of millions of men and women in our country and the People's Democracies. (*Prolonged applause*) We believe that all working men in the world, once they have become convinced of the advantages communism brings, will sooner or later take the road of struggle for the construction of socialist society. (*Prolonged applause*) Building communism in our country, we are resolutely against war. We always held and continue to hold that the establishemnt of a new socialist system in one or another country is the internal affair of the peoples of the countries concerned.... Indeed, there are only two ways: either peaceful coexistence or the most destructive war in history. There is no third way....

The Possibility of Preventing War in the Present Era

Millions of people all over the world are asking whether another war is really inevitable, whether mankind which has already experienced two devastating world wars must still go through a third one? Marxists must answer this question taking into consideration the epoch-making changes of the last decades.

There is, of course, a Marxist-Leninist precept that wars are inevitable as long as imperialism exists. This precept was evolved at a time when (1) imperialism was an all-embracing world system, and (2) the social and political forces which did not want war were weak, poorly organized, and hence unable to compel the imperialists to renounce war.

People usually take only one aspect of the question and examine only the economic basis of wars under imperialism. This is not enough. War is not only an economic phenomenon. Whether there is to be a war or not depends in large measure on the correlation of class, political forces, the degree of organization and the awareness and resolve of the people. Moreover, in certain conditions the struggle waged by progressive social and political forces may play a decisive role. Hitherto the state of affairs was such that the forces that did not want war and opposed it were poorly organized and lacked the means to check the schemes of the war-makers....

[But] now there is a world camp of socialism, which has become a mighty force. In this camp the peace forces find not only the moral, but also the material, means to prevent aggression. Moreover, there is a large group of other countries with a population running into many hundreds of millions which are actively working to avert war. The labor movement in the capitalist countries has today become a tremendous force. The movement of peace supporters has sprung up and developed into a powerful factor.

In these circumstances certainly the Leninist precept that so long as imperialism exists, the economic basis giving rise to wars will also be preserved remains in force. That is why we must display the greatest vigilance. As long as capitalism survives in the world, the reactionary forces representing the interests of the capitalist monopolies will continue their drive towards military gambles and aggression, and may try to un-leash war. But war is not fatalistically inevitable. Today there are mighty social and political forces possessing formidable means to prevent the imperialists from unleashing war, and if they actually try to start it, to give a smashing rebuff to the aggressors and frustrate their adventurist plans. To be able to do this all anti-war forces must be vigilant and prepared, they must act as a united front and never relax their efforts in the battle for peace. The more actively the peoples defend peace, the greater the guarantees that there will be no new war. (*Stormy, prolonged applause*)

DOCUMENT 8

On the Struggle against Imperialism

L. I. Brezhnev

March 1971

Editor's commentary: At the Twenty-fourth CPSU Congress, Brezhnev discussed the continuing crisis of capitalism and its eventual demise. He paid special tribute to the national liberation movements, the Soviet promotion of which had contributed in the struggle against imperialism across the globe during the 1960s. This investment was paying a handsome dividend particularly in Southeast Asia, where American "imperialism" was fighting a losing battle against Vietnamese "liberators." Brezhnev also attacked the Chinese and other "splitters" of the international communist movement, counseling the need for unity in the face of rejuvenated attacks of imperialism against the struggle for socialism.

L. I. Brezhnev, *Report of the Central Committee of the CPSU to the Twenty-fourth Party Congress* (Moscow: Novosti Press Agency, 1971), pp. 19–26, *excerpts.*

These remarks were made in the aftermath of the 1968 Soviet invasion of Czechoslovakia, an event which had further eroded communist unity.

Comrades, at its 23rd Congress and then in a number of its documents our Party has already given a comprehensive assessment of modern imperialism.... Allow me, therefore, in the light of the experience of the last few years to deal with some of the basic points which we must take account of in our policy.

The features of contemporary capitalism largely spring from the fact that it is trying to adapt itself to the new situation in the world. In the conditions of the confrontation with socialism, the ruling circles of the capitalist countries are afraid more than they have ever been of the class struggle developing into a massive revolutionary movement. Hence, the bourgeoisie's striving to use more camouflaged forms of exploitation and oppression of the working people, and its readiness now and again to agree to partial reforms in order to keep the masses under its ideological and political control as far as possible. The monopolies have been making extensive use of scientific and technical achievements to fortify their positions, to enhance the efficiency and accelerate the pace of production, and to intensify the exploitation and oppression of the working people.

However, adaptation to the new conditions does not mean that capitalism has been stabilised as a system. *The general crisis of capitalism has continued to deepen.*

Even the most developed capitalist states are not free from grave economic upheavals. The USA, for instance, has been floundering in one of its economic crises for almost two years now.... There are now almost eight million unemployed in the developed capitalist countries.

The contradictions between the imperialist states have not been eliminated either by the processes of integration or the imperialists' class concern for pooling their efforts in fighting against the socialist world. By the early 1970s, the main centres of imperialist rivalry have become clearly visible: these are the USA—Western Europe...—Japan. The economic and political competitive struggle between them has been growing ever more acute. The import bans imposed by official US agencies on an ever growing number of products from Europe and Japan and the European countries' efforts to limit their exploitation by US capital are only some of the signs of this struggle.

In the past five-year period, imperialist foreign policy has provided fresh evidence that imperialism has not ceased to be reactionary and aggressive.

In this context, one must deal above all with US imperialism, which in the last few years has reasserted its urge to act as a kind of guarantor and protector of the international system of exploitation and oppression. It seeks to dominate everywhere, interferes in the affairs of other peoples, high-handedly tramples on their legitimate rights and sovereignty....

And the continuing US aggression against the peoples of Vietnam, Cambodia and Laos is the main atrocity committed by the modern colonialists; it is the stamp of ignominy on the United States....

Comrades, we have no doubt at all that the attempts of imperialism to turn the tide of history, to make it flow in its favour, are bound to fail. However, we Communists are well aware that there is no room for passivity or self-complacency. The fighters against capitalist oppression are confronted by the last but the most powerful of the exploiting systems that have ever existed. That is why a long and hard struggle still lies ahead.

The *international working-class movement* continues to play, as it has played in the past, the role of time-tested and militant vanguard of the revolutionary forces. The events of the past five-year period in the capitalist world have fully borne out the importance of the working class as the chief and strongest opponent of the rule of the monopolies, and as a centre rallying all the anti-monopoly forces....

At the same time, comrades, imperialism is being subjected to ever greater pressure by the forces which have sprung from the national liberation struggle, above all by the young independent and anti-imperialist-minded states of Asia and Africa.

The main thing is that *the struggle for national liberation in many countries has in practical terms begun to grow into a struggle against exploitative relations, both feudal and capitalist....*

The great Lenin's prediction that the peoples of the colonies and dependent countries, starting with a struggle for national liberation, would go on to fight against the very foundations of the system of exploitation is coming true. And this, of course, is a heavy blow at the positions of capitalism as a whole, as a world social system.

Comrades, success in the struggle against imperialism largely depends on the cohesion of the anti-imperialist forces, above all of the *world communist movement*, their vanguard. In the last five years, our Party, together with the other fraternal Parties, has done much to strengthen this cohesion and the unity of the communist ranks.

It was a complex task. It was precisely in the period under review that the attempts on various sides to attack Marxism-Leninism as the ideological-theoretical basis for the activity of the communist movement have been most acute. The Chinese leadership went over to the establishment in a number of countries of splinter groupings under the signboard of the so-called "Marxist-Leninist parties," and has clearly tried to unite them in some way as a counterweight to the international communist movement. The trotskyites have now and again formed blocs with these groupings. Here and there tendencies towards nationalistic self-isolation have been stepped up, and both "Left" and Right-wing" opportunism have been revived.

The main aim has been to secure a turn towards the cohesion of the communist movement and consolidation of its ideological basis....

DOCUMENT 9

There Is No Alternative to Peaceful Coexistence

G. Trofimenko

July 1986

Editor's commentary: "Peaceful coexistence between different social systems" was, under Lenin and Stalin, a tactic which accepted the necessity to avoid direct confrontation with the imperialist enemy while socialism was weak. Khrushchev raised it to the level of a strategy, primarily because of the ever-present danger of nuclear war between East and West. However, competition short of direct confrontation was always accepted as a necessary tenet of Leninism. For Khrushchev and Brezhnev, this meant expansion of competition, including military support of national liberation movements in the third world. This article suggests that now, part of Gorbachev's "new thinking" includes a recasting of this notion of peaceful coexistence to mean "only and exclusively, peaceful competition," and an acceptance of the principle of "reasonable sufficiency" in the military balance. If implemented as a general principle, these suggested changes could substantially alter the superpower relationship.

Both in the Political Report of the CPSU Central Committee to the 27th Congress and in the new edition of the party's Programme, peaceful coexistence of states with different social systems is treated as a categorical imperative of today.

Naturally, we have existed side by side with the capitalist world for almost 70 years now and over half of that period has been marked by the presence of nuclear weapons in the arsenals of several states. Proceeding from that circumstance, some theorists and politicians in the

---

International Affairs (Moscow), July 1986, pp. 18–22, *excerpts.*

West, above all in the United States, have claimed that the Soviet Union allegedly lays it on too thick speaking of the extraordinary nature of the current international situation; they allege that everything goes normally in the world, that the military balance, which is acknowledged by Moscow as well, is more or less stable, and that the Soviet-US talks on limiting nuclear and space arms go on, and that, if so, why should one "work up" fears....

The destinies of humankind are directly contingent on present-day policies. And this crucial issue has been accorded topmost priority by the Soviet Communists who are aware of the complexity of dealing with the problem of securing a durable peace under conditions of confrontation and coexistence of the two different social systems, cohabitation that has not always been peaceful....

As is well known, the joint Soviet-American communique on the outcome of the Geneva summit does not contain an explicit mention of the term "peaceful coexistence." Yet, both the communique and the meeting itself have in fact implied the US side's recognition, if I am allowed to put it that way, of the inevitability of peaceful coexistence and the nonexistence of any other platform or any other prospect for relations between the two countries because, as has been stressed in the communique, "a nuclear war cannot be won and must never be fought."...

As to our country, it does not simply say "yes" to the process of cementing peaceful coexistence. The new peaceful initatives of the USSR, the new edition of the CPSU Programme and the fundamental provisions of the political Report of the CPSU Central Committee to the 27th Party congress—all consolidate the concept of peaceful coexistence as applied to the current crucial state of international relations by rendering it even more universal.

What new has the forum of the Soviet communists added in this regard? While not claiming to be all-embracing, I wish to highlight the following points. First and foremost, this is a concept of a nuclear-free world. What is involved here is that at present genuine security is guar-

anteed not by the highest possible but by the lowest possible level of strategic balance which should fully exclude nuclear arms and other types of weapons of mass destruction. Moreover, this is not merely a programme for complete elimination of mass-destruction weapons by the end of the century, accompanied by appropriate stabilizing reduction in conventional arms, but it is also a programme of restructuring the present-day system of international relations on the basis of the universal application of the principle of peaceful coexistence.

This is the principle that constitutes the centerpiece of the basis for a comprehensive system of international security as formulated by the 27th CPSU Congress, which can justly be termed a new code of peaceful coexistence of states in the modern age because it unites all aspects of interstate relations, be it military, political, economic or humanitarian, with a view to establishing a truly lasting peace on our planet.

Then, it is a fundamental provision regarding the need to approach security as an exclusively political problem. The character of present-day weapons leaves no country any hope of defending itself only with military and technical means, for instance, by creating defenses, no matter how formidable they were. Security can only be universal and should be ensured not through a global arms race but on the basis of international treaties and agreements aimed at not merely limiting the arms race but at attaining a verifiable reduction in the levels of the military potentials of states down to the limits of what is reasonably sufficient.

An indispensable part of the comprehensive security system should be a system of international economic security providing for protection against discrimination, sanctions and other methods of arm-twisting through non-military factors to the detriment of other states' partners in the world community.

This is also a question of harmonizing legitimate national interests through the aid of appropriate international procedures and institutions. The goal of this is to remove the most acute disagreements now existing among states and above all among major powers which, because of their economic and military potentials and their international prestige, are endowed with a particular responsibility for a course of world developments. As to the social faceoff between capitalism and socialism, it should take the form of, only and exclusively, peaceful competition.

Furthermore, under present-day conditions, peaceful coexistence urgently calls for creative cooperation on a world-wide scale in dealing with environmental and other global problems.

A good many other fundamental provisions promoting the concept of peaceful coexistence could also be mentioned. The main thing, however, is that the Soviet approach to restructuring international relations constitutes, in essence, an amalgam of the philosophy of moulding a safer world in the nuclear and space age with the platform of specific actions. Not only do the CPSU and the Soviet government call for doing away with the outdated stereotypes of thinking but with their actions and initiatives they provide a specific example of abandoning narrow, selfish interests and grasping the collective responsibility of all states, big and small, for the future of mankind at the threshold of the third millenium.

Suggested Readings

Adelman, Jonathan R. (ed.): *Communist Armies in Politics* (Boulder, CO: Westview, 1982).

Allison, Graham: *The Essence of Decision: Explaining the Cuban Missile Crisis* (Boston: Little, Brown, 1971).

Bialer, Seweryn (ed.): *The Domestic Context of Soviet Foreign Policy* (Boulder, CO: Westview, 1981).

Billington, James H.: *The Icon and the Axe* (New York: Random House, 1970).

Dmytryshyn, Basil: *USSR: A Concise History,* 4th ed. (New York: Scribner's, 1984).

Dunlop, John B.: *The Faces of Contemporary Russian Nationalism* (Princeton, NJ: Princeton University Press, 1983).

Hoffman, Erik P., and Frederick Fleron (eds.): *The Conduct of Soviet Foreign Policy* (New York: Aldine, 1980).

Hough, Jerry F., and Merle Fainsod: *How the Soviet Union Is Governed* (Cambridge, MA: Harvard University Press, 1979).

Hunt, R. N. Carew: *The Theory and Practice of Communism* (New York: Macmillan, 1957).

Korbonski, Andrzej: *The Soviet Union and the Third World: The Last Three Decades* (Ithaca, NY: Cornell University Press, 1987).

Meyer, Alfred G.: *Marxism: The Unity of Theory and Practice* (Ann Arbor, MI: University of Michigan Press, 1966).

Nogee, Joseph L., and Robert H. Donaldson: *Soviet Foreign Policy Since World War II,* 2d ed. (New York: Pergamon, 1984).

Petrov, Vladimir: "Formation of Soviet Foreign Policy," *Orbis* (Fall 1973), pp. 819–863.

Ponomarev, B., et al.: *History of Soviet Foreign Policy 1917–1945* (Moscow: Progress Publishers, 1969).

Riasanovsky, Nicholas: *A History of Russia,* 3d ed. (New York: Oxford University Press, 1977).

Rubinstein, Alvin Z.: *The Foreign Policy of the Soviet Union* (New York: Random House, 1972).

Schwartz, Morton: *The Foreign Policy of the USSR: Domestic Factors* (Encino, CA: Dickenson, 1975).

Simis, Konstantin M.: *USSR: The Corrupt Society* (New York: Simon & Schuster, 1982).

Skilling, H. Gordon, and Franklyn Griffiths (eds.): *Interest Groups in Soviet Politics* (Princeton, NJ: Princeton University Press, 1971).

Solzhenitsyn, Aleksander: *The Gulag Archipelago, 1918–1956,* 2 vols. (New York: Harper & Row, 1974).

Sonnenfeldt, Helmut, and William Hyland: "Soviet Perspectives on Security," *Adelphi Papers,* 150 (London: International Institute for Strategic Studies, Spring 1979).

Tokes, Rudolph L. (ed.): *Dissent in the USSR: Politics, Ideology and People* (Baltimore, MD: Johns Hopkins University Press, 1975).

Yanov, Alexander: *Detente after Brezhnev: The Domestic Roots of Soviet Policy* (Berkeley, CA: Institute of International Studies, University of California, 1977).

Zimmerman, William: *Soviet Perspectives on International Relations, 1956–1967* (Princeton, NJ: Princeton University Press, 1969).

CHAPTER TWO

Soviet Foreign Policy under Lenin—Beginnings (1917–1924)

Vladimir Ilyich Ulyanov studied law at the Universities of Kazan and Leningrad. Perhaps the most formative event in his early life was the execution of his brother in 1887 for an assassination attempt on Czar Alexander III. The remainder of his life was spent in single-minded pursuit of the goal of overthrowing the czarist political system in Russia and replacing it with a Marxist regime. In part to frustrate the czarist *okhrana* (secret police), he adopted the pseudonym Lenin which became attached to the political system that he first constructed in theory and then founded on the ruins of the collapsed czarist state in 1917.

Among the many theoretical works written by Lenin prior to October 1917 were two seminal pieces, *What Is To Be Done?* (1902) and *Imperialism, the Highest Stage of Capitalism* (1917). In the first, Lenin outlined the type of "vanguard" party that was needed in order for the revolution to succeed first in Russia, the "weakest link of capitalism," and then in other industrialized countries: conspiratorial and secretive, committed to violence, and nondemocratic in nature. The roots of Marxist-Leninist political thought can be traced to this classic work. In the second, Lenin explained the nature of the First World War; it was an imperialist war waged by capitalist robbers for new markets and colonies, and it reflected the last gasp of the capitalist system. Soon, it was hoped, all of Europe would be in the throes of an emancipating workers' revolution.

When the czar abdicated in February 1917 as a result of the deteriorating domestic situation and intense pressure to end an increasingly unpopular and costly war, Lenin returned to Russia from his Swiss exile in a sealed railway boxcar that the Germans provided him. His work in Russia, from his return until October, focused on first toppling the coalition of forces that were known collectively as the Provisional Government and then gaining exclusive power for the bolsheviks. These goals were achieved beginning on 6 November 1917.

As is the case for any opposition group in or outside of government, foreign policy had been only of theoretical and rhetorical concern to Lenin and the bolsheviks until the October Revolution. True, the peace issue had been instrumental in getting the bolsheviks the popular support they needed, especially in view of the fact that they were the only political organization to use it: Lenin promised an end to Russia's part in the "imperialist" war. But the bolsheviks quickly learned that theory and practice did not always jibe.

The German military leaders in particular were not interested in ambiguous and ideologically charged proclamations such as were reflected in the Soviet government's first formal foreign policy act, the Decree of Peace (Chapter 2, document 1), or in Leon Trotsky's "no war, no peace" formula (see Chapter 2, reading 1). They needed a peace treaty that would free up forces for the Western front. Only under intensified German military pressure, which threatened to destroy the fledgling Soviet Russian state, did the bolsheviks agree to conduct traditional diplomacy, resulting in the Brest-Litovsk peace treaty (Chapter 2, document 2). And it was Lenin who was directly responsible for this tactical retreat: two steps forward, one step back. The substantial losses formalized by Brest-Litovsk would be recovered in time. It was as a result of the Brest peace that Lenin emerged as undisputed leader of the bolsheviks—he alone foresaw what needed to be done.

For Lenin, survival was the paramount concern. The fledgling Soviet state's weakness stood in stark contrast to the strength of the Western Allies, who had emerged victorious over German militarism in World War I. Nevertheless, by 1920 Soviet achievements were substantial: the bolsheviks had gained the upper hand in the civil war against their enemies, primarily loyalist "white" forces, and had survived foreign pressure and incursion (in Arkhangelsk, Murmansk, and Vladivostok) after concluding their separate peace with Germany. Uncharacteristically, the heady feeling of success led to overconfidence, which carried Lenin away temporarily as the opportunity presented itself to export the revolution through Poland and into Germany in the summer of 1920, during the Second Congress of the Communist International (Chapter 2, document 3). The bolshevik defeat at Warsaw nearly turned into a disaster; this was the last adventure that bolshevism undertook in its early years. The world revolution was put on hold.

In this chapter's first selection, E. H. Carr traces the development of bolshevik foreign policy and Lenin's role in its formulation from the Great October Revolution of 1917 through the conclusion of the Rapallo treaty in 1922 by Germany and Soviet Russia, which broke the diplomatic isolation of both European pariahs. He explains the formulation and implementation of the bolsheviks' "dual policy" toward the West—exporting revolution through the Comintern while retaining good relations through traditional diplomatic channels—and recounts early successes and failures in the two main areas of Lenin's foreign policy orientation, Germany and China. The documents which follow mark the progress of early Soviet diplomacy from the naivete of revolutionary zeal to a sober, experience-based, security-minded orientation, which for the most part has governed the formulation and conduct of Soviet foreign policy since that time.

Early Soviet Diplomacy

E. H. Carr

FROM OCTOBER TO BREST-LITOVSK

The famous "decree on peace"—in reality, an appeal to the governments and peoples of the belligerent countries for the conclusion of a democratic peace—was the first act of foreign policy of the "provisional workers' and peasants' government," adopted by the second All-Russian Congress of Soviets on 26 October/8 November 1917, the day after the victorious revolution.... It was a proposal for the immediate conclusion of peace, addressed "to all the belligerent peoples and their governments" and broadcast throughout the world. It demanded not a socialist, but a "just, democratic" peace—a peace without annexations or indemnities, a peace based on the right of self-determination for all nations by "a free vote." It declared secret diplomacy abolished, and announced the intention of the government to publish the secret treaties of the past and conduct all future negotiations "completely openly before the whole people."...

Contempt for traditional foreign policy and an ingrained internationalism were a logical outcome of the view commonly taken at this time of the prospects of the regime. [Leon] Trotsky had expressed it emphatically on the morrow of the revolution:

> If the peoples of Europe do not arise and crush imperialism, we shall be crushed—that is beyond doubt. Either the Russian revolution will raise the whirlwind of struggle in the west, or the capitalists of all countries will stifle our struggle.[1]

Since European or world revolution was the acknowledged condition of the building of socialism in Russia and of the very survival of the regime, the fundamental aim of foreign policy must be to promote and further it. The methods of pursuing this aim were direct and simple. Among the early decrees of Sovnarkom [Council of People's Commissars] was one which appeared in *Pravda* of 13/26 December 1917, over the signatures of Lenin as president and Trotsky as People's Commissar for Foreign Affairs, resolving "to place at the disposal of the representatives abroad of the Commissariat of Foreign Affairs for the needs of the revolutionary movement two million rubles."[2] Within a few weeks of the revolution the People's Commissariat of Foreign Affairs (Narkomindel) had established a "section for international propaganda"...for circulation among German and Austrian prisoners of war and German troops on the eastern front.[3]...

The failure of the peace decree to evoke any response from the western allies and the pressing need, in spite of this failure, to end the war with Germany first forced on the Soviet leaders the conception of a policy directed to meet national interests and national requirements. From this point onwards, a certain duality appeared in Soviet foreign policy. It was always theoretically possible to ask whether, in any given issue of policy, priority should be given—or, in retrospect, whether it had been given—to Soviet national interest or to the international interest of world revolution; and this could, in the heat of the political controversy, be depicted as a choice between principle and expediency. But, since it

[1] *Vtoroi Vserosiiskii S''ezd Sovetov* (1928), pp. 86–87
[2] *Sobranie Uzakonenii, 1917–1918,* No. 8, art. 112; its appearance in Trotsky, *Sochineniya,* iii, ii, 151 indicates Trotsky's authorship.
[3] According to a report in *Vos'moi S''ezd RKP (B)* (1933), pp. 434–5, the section was staffed by German and Austro-Hungarian prisoners of war.

was difficult, at any period now in question, to diagnose any fundamental incompatibility between the two interests, the question remained largely unreal, or reduced itself to a question of tactics. Lenin had long ago contemplated the possibility that a proletarian revolution in a single country—even perhaps in backward Russia—would find itself temporarily isolated in a capitalist world, and was perhaps better prepared than most of his followers to take a realistic view of the resulting situation. After the triumph of the revolution, the illusion that foreign policy and diplomacy were no more than an evil legacy of capitalism, and that the headquarters of the proletarian dictatorship would be the general staff of a militant movement rather than the capital of an established state, was automatically and almost unconsciously dissipated. On the day after the revolution Sovnarkom assumed responsibility for the public affairs of a territory which, though lacking precise frontiers and even an official name, none the less formed a unit in a world divided into states. From the international standpoint the Soviet republic became a state in virtue of this fact and independently of any deliberate act of its new rulers. The instinct of self-preservation did the rest. The Bolsheviks had a sound motive to uphold and maintain the authority of the state against the encroachments of other states until such time as their dream of revolution in Europe should come true; and this meant, in the troubled conditions of the autumn of 1917, that they had, in spite of themselves, to have a foreign policy to bridge the interval. More specifically they had at all costs to take Russia out of the war; for the peasants who formed the rank and file of the army would only suppport a regime which gave them peace. But it took two to make peace as Lenin, unlike Trotsky, saw from the first; and this meant that, pending the coming of world revolution, it was necessary to win a respite from the warring capitalist countries. Thus a dual, and in some respects self-contradictory, foreign poicy was imposed on the Bolsheviks by the situation in which they found

themselves: to attempt to hasten the downfall of the capitalist governments and to attempt to negotiate with them....

Paradoxical as the claim appeared, the Bolsheviks were able to treat the Brest-Litovsk armistice as a victory. The occupation of Russian territory by the German armies was a *fait accompli*. Its recognition in the armistice agreement cost nothing; and all this would be undone by the impending German revolution. The non-transfer of German troops to the west was the proof of Bolshevik sincerity, freedom of propaganda the guarantee of Bolshevik victory. Both these had been secured: these, said Trotsky afterwards, were the two vital points on which the delegates had instructions not to yield.[1] Through the fraternization points Bolshevik ideas and Bolshevik literature seeped into the German army, spreading the seeds of disintegration through Germany's eastern front. The armistice was celebrated by a proclamation from Trotsky's pen addressed ''to the toiling peoples of Europe, oppressed and bled white.''

> We conceal from nobody [it read] that we do not consider the present capitalist governments capable of a democratic peace. Only the revolutionary struggle of the working masses against their governments can bring Europe near to such a peace. Its full realization will be assured only by a victorious proletarian revolution in all capitalist countries.

Trotsky admitted that ''we are compelled to undertake negotiations with those governments which still exist at the present moment,'' but claimed that ''in entering into negotiations with the present governments, saturated on both sides with imperialist tendencies, the Council of People's Commissars does not for a moment deviate from the path of social revolution.'' He went on to define the ''dual task'' of Soviet foreign policy:

---

[1]Trotsky, *Sochineniya*, iii, ii, 197.

In the peace negotiations the Soviet power sets itself a dual task: in the first place, to secure the quickest possible cessation of the shameful and criminal slaughter which is destroying Europe, secondly, to help the working class of all countries by every means available to us to overthrow the domination of capital and to seize state power in the interests of a democratic peace and of a socialist transformation of Europe and of all mankind.

And the manifesto ended with an exhortation to the proletarians of all countries to join in "a common struggle for the immediate cessation of the war on all fronts," and to close their ranks "under the banner of peace and social revolution."[1] The verbal contradiction in the concluding words aptly summed up the compromise inherent in the Soviet policy of the first weeks of the revolution....

The German government, like the allies, had rejected all proposals for a "just, democratic peace"; and the German soldiers, far from rising against their masters to consummate the proletarian revolution, were preparing to march obediently against revolutionary Russia. Lenin, following his usual practice, expounded his views in advance...[that] to make peace at whatever cost would in the long run be the best advertisement for world revolution:

> The example of a socialist Soviet republic in Russia will stand as a living model for the peoples of all countries, and the propagandist, revolutionary effect of this model will be immense. On one side, the bourgeois order and a naked out-and-out war of annexation between the two groups of robbers: on the other, peace and the socialist republic of Soviets.[2]...

Then on 3 March 1918,...the Brest-Litovsk treaty was signed. Under this treaty Russia renounced all rights over the city of Riga and its hinterland, the whole of Courland and Lithuania and a part of White Russia, the destiny of which was to be decided by Germany and Austria Hungary "in agreement with their population"; recognized the German occupation of Livonia and Estonia until "proper national institutions" had been established there; agreed to make peace with the Ukrainian Rada; and ceded Kars, Ardahan and Batum, whose populations would "reorganize" these districts in agreement with Turkey. Diplomatic intercourse between Soviet Russia and the central Powers was to be resumed on the ratification of the treaty. The financial clauses were less drastic, and there was a mutual waiver of indemnities and other claims....

In the last stages of the Brest-Litovsk discussions a new factor emerged which was destined to be of great importance in Soviet foreign policy. The dogmatic absolutism which assumed that the Soviet regime must maintain an attitude of equal and unqualified hostility to all capitalist governments (and they to it), and objected on this ground even to the conclusion of a separate peace, was not seriously tenable. According to any reasonable estimate, it was the split in the capitalist world which had enabled the Soviet Government to establish itself and was the best insurance of its survival. As [Karl] Radek wrote some years later, it was the "fundamental fact" which "stood at the cradle" of Soviet foreign policy.[3] Lenin cautiously recognized this in his *Theses on the Question of the Immediate Conclusion of a Separate and Annexationist Peace*:

> By concluding a separate peace, we are freeing ourselves in the largest measure *possible at the present moment* from both warring imperialist groups; by utilizing their mutual enmity we utilize the war,

[1]Klyuchnikov i Sabanin, *Mezhdunarodnaya Politika*, ii (1926), 100–2; Trotsky, *Sochineniya*, iii, ii, 206–9.

[2]Lenin, *Sochineniya*, xxii, 193–9; the theses were published for the first time in *Pravda* of 24 February 1918—the day after Lenin's view had been finally accepted by the party central committee—with a brief preface by Lenin explaining their origin (ibid., xxii, 289).

[3]K. Radek, *Die Auswärtige Politik Sowjet-Russlands* (Hamburg, 1921), pp. 80–1.

which makes a bargain between them against us difficult.[1]

From this recognition of the pragmatic value of the division in the enemy camp it was only a short step to the conscious exploitation of it as an asset of Soviet foreign policy, and to the abandonment of any doctrinal assumption of the uniform and unvarying hostility of the capitalist world....

The Brest-Litovsk crisis, wrote Lenin in *Pravda* in an article entitled "A Hard but Necessary Lesson," would "appear as one of the greatest historical turning-points in the history of the Russian—and international—revolution."[2] It was a significant eminence from which it was possible to look back on the past and forward to the future. The Brest-Litovsk crisis brought to a head the unresolved dilemma of the relations of Soviet Russia to the world, the dilemma of an authority which aspired to act at one and the same time as the driving-force of world revolution and as the sovereign power of a state in a world of states; and it was at this time that the durable foundations of Soviet foreign policy were laid....

That the survival of the revolution in Russia depended on its prompt extension to central and western Europe was so unquestioningly assumed that it was natural for the Bolsheviks to believe both that the revolution in Europe was imminent and that their primary task was to hasten and promote it. These beliefs, held with all the revolutionary enthusiasm of the October victory, would not be lightly abandoned. The acceptance of Brest-Litovsk seemed an assault on both these articles of faith. The existing positions in Europe, exclaimed [Nikolai] Bukharin at the seventh party congress, could only be described as "the collapse, the dissolution of the old capitalist relations" under the stress of war. He cited the strikes and the setting up of Soviets in Vienna and Budapest in January 1918, and the strikes in

Germany later in the same month, as proof that revolution in Europe was well on the way. This was the moment which Lenin chose to introduce a policy of peaceful cohabitation between Soviet Russia and the capitalist Powers....

Thus the final precipitate of the Brest-Litovsk crisis was a foreign policy which was designed equally to promote world revolution and the national security of the Soviet republic, and denied any inconsistency between these two essential aims. World revolution was the sole guarantee of national security; but national security was also a condition of the successful promotion of world revolution. Scarcely had the immediate pressure of German intervention been removed from the Soviet republic when the intervention of the opposing capitalist group began with the Japanese landing at Vladivostok on 4 April 1918. Thereafter, for two and a half years with one short intermission, Soviet Russia was in a state of undeclared war against the allied powers. In conditions of war no incompatibility could in any case occur between the two facets of Soviet foreign policy. Military weakness made revolutionary propaganda among the peoples of the hostile Powers the most effective defensive weapon in the Soviet armoury.

> The facts of world history [wrote Lenin in November 1918] have proved to those Russian patriots who will hear of nothing but the immediate interests of their country, conceived in the old style, that the transformation of our Russian revolution into a socialist revolution was not an adventure but a necessity since *there was no other choice*: Anglo-French and American imperialism will *inevitably* strangle the independence and freedom of Russia *unless* world-wide socialist revolution, world-wide Bolshevism triumphs.[3]

But the motive of national defence against the foreign invader and his agents could also be directly invoked, and invested Soviet policy, especially towards the end of this period, with an

---

[1] Lenin, *Sochineniya,* xxii, 198.
[2] Lenin, *Sochineniya,* xxii, 290.

[3] Lenin, *Sochineniya,* xxiii, 291.

aura of Russian patriotism. It was only when the civil war ended, and the establishment of peaceful relations with the capitalist Powers was once more placed on the agenda in the early months of 1921, that the controversies and embarrassments of the dual policy once more reared their head, as they had done in the more dramatic days of peace-making at Brest-Litovsk. In the meanwhile the two facets of Soviet foreign policy—the encouragement of world revolution and the pursuit of national security—were merely different instruments of a single consistent and integrated purpose.

THE DUAL POLICY

...An out-and-out revolutionary foreign policy thus continued to be practised side by side with a foreign policy which took account of "the state significance of the revolution." Brest-Litovsk was the first occasion on which the new regime had been compelled to conform to the customary usages of international relations and to assume obligations in its capacity as a territorial state. [Georgi] Chicherin's appointment [as foreign minister] no doubt ushered in the reign of a "passive" policy, when "the period for a revolutionary offensive policy was replaced by a period of retreats and manoeuvres."[1] But this change fitted in perfectly with the needs of a desperate situation; and it was noteworthy that, when Lenin, in a confidential memorandum written in May 1918 and not published in his lifetime, set out to define the policy of "retreats and manoeuvres" of which Brest-Litovsk was itself the prototype, he spoke in terms not of change but of continuity:

> The foreign policy of the Soviet power must not be changed in any respect. Our military preparation is still not completed, and therefore our general maxim remains as before—to tack, to retreat, to

wait while continuing this preparation with all our might....

In the Soviet attitude to the allies, the abortive movement towards accommodation in February and March faded away in face of the uncompromising character of allied hostility and the imminent threat of allied intervention. After the summer of 1918 no serious doubt could be entertained of allied determination to destroy the regime and to give assistance to any who sought to destroy it. The British landing at Murmansk at the end of June was followed by a British and French landing at Archangel at the beginning of August; during August American troops joined the British and French in north Russia and the Japanese in Vladivostok; in south Russia the "white" forces coalesced under the leadership of Denikin with allied encouragement, and, a little later, active allied support. The counter-revolutionary conspiracies of July and August in central Russia were organized and financed from abroad. On 31 August the offical British agent, Lockhart, was arrested on the charge of complicity in them, and two days later a detailed Soviet statement denounced "the conspiracy organized by Anglo-French diplomats."[2] The last bridge had been broken. No form of appeasement or conciliation was any longer open to the Soviet Government....

These catastrophic developments left a lasting mark on Soviet thought. The action of the allies confirmed and intensified the ideological aspect of Soviet foreign policy and made international revolution once more its principal plank, if only in the interest of national self-preservation. The vital question whether the coexistence of capitalist and socialist states was possible had at any rate been left open by the first pronouncements of the Soviet Government, and notably by the decree on peace; in some, at any rate, of the pronouncements of the spring and

---

[1]G. Chicherin, *Vneshnyaya Politika Sovetskoi Rossii za Dva Goda* (1920), p. 7.

[2]See Vol. 1, p. 175; the statement appeared in *Izvestiya* of 3 September 1918.

summer of 1918 it had been answered in the affirmative. Now it seemed irrefutably clear that this coexistence was impossible, at any rate with the countries of the Entente, and that revolutionary propaganda directed to the workers of these countries was the most effective, and indeed the only effective, weapon in the hands of a government whose military resources were still negligible. Soviet foreign policy from the autumn of 1918 to the end of 1920 was in all probability more specifically and exclusively coloured by international and revolutionary aims than at any other time. World revolution was in a certain sense the counterpart in Soviet foreign policy of war communism in economic policy. In form a logical, though extreme, development of communist doctrine, it was in fact imposed on the regime, not so much by doctrinal orthodoxy, as by the desperate plight of the civil war....

ISOLATION AND THE COMINTERN

The year 1919 was the year of Soviet Russia's most complete isolation from the outside world. It was also the year in which Soviet foreign policy took on its most outspokenly revolutionary complexion. The two circumstances were inter-connected, and it would be a mistake to attribute to premeditation the prominence assumed by the revolutionary aspect of Soviet policy at this time....

The fact of the foundation of a Third or Communist International, henceforth familiarly known as Comintern, was more important than anything done at its first congress. It adopted a "platform" and a manifesto "To the Proletarians of the Whole World," which reviewed the rise and fall of capitalism and the development of communism in the seventy-two (or more accurately seventy-one) years since Marx and Engels issued the *Communist Manifesto*, and was afterwards described by [Grigorii] Zinoviev as "a second *Communist Manifesto*."[1] The congress approved a set of the-

ses presented by Lenin in denunciation of bourgeois democracy and parliamentarianism and in defence of the dictatorship of the proletariat (this was the theme of Lenin's main speech at the congress)...and attacked the imperialism of the Entente Powers and the "white" terror. Finally, it issued an appeal "To the Workers of All Countries," whose urgent tone and topical content distinguished it from the other congress documents. This began by expressing the "gratitude and admiration" of the congress for "the Russian revolutionary proletariat and its directing party—the Communist Party of the Bolsheviks." The work of liberation and reform pursued by the Soviet power had, however, been interrupted by a civil war which was being waged with the aid of the Entente countries and would collapse at once without that aid. Hence it was the duty of the "working masses of all countries" to press upon their governments by all available means ("including, if necessary, revolutionary means") demands for the cessation of intervention, for the withdrawal of armies from Russia, for the recognition of the Soviet regime, for the establishment of diplomatic and commercial relations, and for the dispatch to Russia of "some hundreds or even thousands" of engineers, instructors and skilled workers to assist in the restoration and reorganization of transport.[2] The congress elected an "executive committee of the Communist International" (IKKI or, by its English initials, ECCI), containing representatives of the communist parties of Russia, Germany, Austria, Hungary, the Balkan federation, Scandinavia and Switzerland, to act, like the central committee of the party, in the name of the institution in the intervals between congresses; other parties joining Comintern before the next congress were to receive a seat on IKKI.[3]...

---

[1]*Vos'moi S''ezd RKP (B)* (1933), p. 138; it was drafted by Trotsky and appears in Trotsky, *Sochineniya*, xii, 38–49.

[2]The principal resolutions of the congress are in *Kommunisticheskii Internatsional v Dokumentakh* (1933), pp. 53–88.

[3]*Der I. Kongress der Kommunistischen Internationale* (Hamburg, 1921), pp. 200–1. The resolution laid down that, pending the arrival in Moscow of its other members, the functions of IKKI should be discharged by the Russian delegation.

The appeal "To the Workers of All Countries" to rally to the support of the Soviet regime in Russia was in some respects the most significant document of the first Congress of the Communist International. Beyond question the new organization had been conceived by its founders as in the fullest sense international—a successor of the defunct and discredited "Second International." Lenin, in one of his rare flights of rhetoric, described it at the moment of its foundation as "the forerunner of the international republic of Soviets."[1] But the conditions of its birth marked it out for a different destiny. The constant and ineradicable duality of purpose inherent in Lenin's outlook—the defence of the Soviet power in Russia and the furtherance of international revolution—coloured his view of the new instrument; and the partly unforeseen circumstances which put the effective control of it exclusively into Russian hands completed the organic link between Comintern and the Soviet regime. What had taken place in Moscow in March 1919 was not in fact the fusion of a number of national communist parties of approximately equal strength into an international organization, but the harnessing of a number of weak, in some cases embryonic and still unformed, groups to an organization whose main support and motive force was necessarily and inevitably the power of the Soviet state. It was Soviet power which created Comintern and gave it its influence and prestige; in return, it was natural to expect that international communist propaganda and action should help to defend that power at a moment when it was threatened by all the reactionary forces of the capitalist world. At this crucial moment of the civil war the supreme task naturally presented itself in Lenin's mind as "a struggle of the proletarian state surrounded by capitalist states."[2] National and international aims, the security of the Soviet regime and the interests of the proletarian revolution, were once more inextricably blended. In an article contributed by Lenin to the first number of *Kommunisticheskii Internatsional*, the journal of the new organization, the simple truth was stated with the emphasis of italics:

> The new third "International Workingmen's Association"[3] has *already begun to coincide* in a certain measure *with the Union of Soviet Socialist Republics*.[4]

The struggle was waged simultaneously on the two planes—the revolutionary plane and the plane of state action—without any sense of incompatibility between them. . . .

REVOLUTION OVER EUROPE

The outbreak of war with Poland in May 1920, bringing in its train a resumption of the civil war in the south against "white" forces led by Wrangel, reproduced on a smaller scale the situation of 1919. The Red Army was stronger, the military forces arrayed against it less imposing. But the country was exhausted, stocks were depleted and transport on the point of complete breakdown, so that the threat of 1920 seemed scarcely less grave than in the previous year. The incipient *rapprochement* with the west which had begun in the first months of 1920 was nipped in the bud, with the same result of replacing diplomatic contacts by revolutionary propaganda as the staple of Soviet foreign policy. But here one striking difference became apparent. In 1919 the propaganda of the Bolsheviks, though often effective locally, had been a hand-to-mouth affair, and not organized on an international scale. In 1920 Comintern was already a going concern capable of playing a conspicuous part on the international stage and forming an effective focus for revolutionary propaganda in many countries. . . . The

---

[1] Lenin, *Sochineniya*, xxiv, 26.
[2] Ibid., xxiv, 56.

[3] This was the official title of the First International founded in London in 1864.
[4] Lenin, *Sochineniya*, xxiv, 247.

revolutionary propaganda which now emanated from Moscow was more confident, more bombastic and more coherent than anything that had been attempted before, and gave a clearer impression of organized power behind it. The summer and autumn of 1920 proved to be the high-water mark of the prestige of Comintern and of its hopes of promoting revolution throughout the world....

Before the second congress of Comintern assembled in the [second] half of July 1920, a dramatic reversal had occurred in the fortunes of war. The Polish invader had been driven back far beyond the boundaries of the Ukraine; the Red Army was sweeping westward into Poland almost without opposition; and the fall of Warsaw—and the outbreak of the Polish revolution—seemed all but certain. Zinoviev, who presided at the congress, afterwards described the scene:

> In the congress hall hung a great map on which was marked every day the movement of our armies. And the delegates every morning stood with breathless interest before this map. It was a sort of symbol: the best representatives of the international proletariat with breathless interest, with palpitating heart, followed every advance of our armies, and all perfectly realized that, if the military aim set by our army was achieved, it would mean an immense acceleration of the international proletarian revolution.[1]...

When the second congress of Comintern ended on 7 August 1920, the Soviet advance on Warsaw was proceeding rapidly and almost unopposed, and optimism and enthusiasm were unbounded....On 16 August a powerful Polish counteroffenseive had been launched. Within a few days the Red Army was retreating as rapidly as it had advanced.

Many explanations were afterwards offered of the Soviet defeat. Later Soviet military experts, enjoying the advantages of hindsight, tended to condemn the whole campaign as a military miscalculation: the Red Army was inadequately equipped and prepared, in everything except enthusiasm, for so serious an enterprise as the invasion of Poland.[2]...Nobody, except in the brief intoxication of unexpectedly easy military triumphs, had really believed that the Red Army could conquer Poland. Lenin and those who had voted with him for the advance had all counted on the Red proletariat of Poland....When the Polish workers of Warsaw failed to rise, or even joined the national army to defend the capital, the enterprise was doomed. It was not the Red Army, but the cause of world revolution, which suffered defeat in front of Warsaw in August 1920....

The Soviet-Polish war of 1920 had far-reaching repercussions on more than one aspect of Soviet foreign policy. But these repercussions were not immediately felt in anything like their full force, nor were the broader lessons of the defeat digested at once. The military set-back was outweighed a few weeks later by the victory over Wrangel which finally ended the civil war with the rout of the last "white" invader; and the temporary sacrifice of territory to Poland was still compensated by the thought that the birth of a Soviet Poland in the near future would make frontiers unimportant. The enthusiasm generated at the second congress of Comintern and the drives set in motion by it were not immediately relaxed. Like the policies of war communism at home, the revolutionary offensive in Europe was continued throughout the winter of 1920–21. From its second congress Comintern had emerged as the central directing staff of the forces of world revolution with national parties in the principal countries grouped around it. The headquarters of Comintern, where, beneath all international trap-

---

[1] *Desyatyi S''ezd Rossiiskoi Kommunisticheskoi Partii* (1921), p. 271.

[2] An objective summary of the campaign, together with references to some of the military authorities, is in W. H. Chamberlin, *The Russian Revolution 1917–1921* (1935), ii, 311–14; Tukhachevsky's view, coinciding in the main with that of Trotsky, was expressed in lectures on the campaign delivered at the staff college in 1923, and reprinted *in extenso* in J. Pilsudski, *L'Annee 1920* (French transl. from Polish, 1929), pp. 203–55.

pings, the voice of the Russian party was ultimately decisive, dealt separately with parties which normally had no dealing with one another except through the intermediary of Comintern. This was the essence of the relations set up by the twenty-one conditions. The submission of these conditions to the Left parties in the principal European countries in the autumn and winter of 1920–21 was a turning point in the history of European socialism and of its attitude to Moscow....

REVOLUTION OVER ASIA

Marx gave little thought to colonial questions, since it did not occur to him that the colonial or backward regions of the world would be called on to play any part in the overthrow of capitalism. The First International ignored them. The Second International remained for a long time equally apathetic. At the Paris congress of 1901, under the influence of the South African War, Rosa Luxemburg, who was afterwards to give colonial exploitation a central place in her theory of the accumulation of capital, for the first time proposed a resolution deploring the twin evils of militarism and colonial policy. The Russian revolution of 1905 transferred the immediate centre of interest from Africa to Asia, where national revolutionary movements—the Persian revolution of 1906, the "young Turk" revolution of 1908, the Chinese revolution of 1912, and the beginnings of Indian nationalism—stirred in the wake of the Russian upheaval. In 1907 Kautsky wrote a pamphlet called *Socialism and Colonial Policy* in which he published for the first time a letter from Engels of 1881, prophesying a revolution in India and arguing that, once the proletariat had won its victory in Europe and North America, "this will give such a colossal impetus and such an example that the half-civilized countries will follow us of their own accord."[1] In 1908 an article by Lenin entitled

Explosive Material in World Politics found a new significance in the revolutionary movements in Persia, Turkey, India, and China: "The conscious European worker now has Asiatic comrades, and the number of these comrades will grow from hour to hour.[2]...

In the summer of 1920 Soviet policy still halted before the fateful choice between universal support of communist parties in foreign countries for the furtherance of world-wide revolution and cooperation with selected bourgeois governments, where national interests appeared to require it, even at the expense of the communist parties in the countries concerned. Optimism about the prospects of world revolution, which had seemed in partial eclipse during the winter of 1919–20, was once more general; and powerful circles in the Kremlin still shrank from military or diplomatic alliances with non-communist powers, and continued to believe in propaganda against all capitalist governments as the most effective, and indeed the only proper, instrument of Soviet foreign policy.

Such were the conditions when in July 1920 the second congress of Comintern set out to formulate a policy on what was known as "the national and colonial question." The task before the congress was to apply the principles of world revolution to the eastern peoples, to develop the doctrine of a common struggle in which all the workers of the world, west and east, had their part to play, and in particular, to strengthen the revolt under the leadership of the RSFSR against British imperialism....

The long discussion of the national and colonial question at the second congress was evidence of a new concentration of interest on eastern questions, which corresponded with the shift in Soviet policy at this time from west to east following the victories over Kolchak and Denikin in the civil war.[3] For the first time it became

---

[1]Marx i Engels, *Sochineniya*, xxvii, 238–9.

[2]Lenin, *Sochineniya*, xii, 306.
[3]See Vol. 1, pp. 330–4.

possible to interweave the national policy pursued by the RSFSR within its own borders with its foreign policy of support for national movements in revolt against imperialist Powers, and to contrast the autonomy or independence bestowed on national republics within the RSFSR with the fate of the Asiatic peoples directly or indirectly within the orbit of the western Powers.... The first step was to carry the eastern question into a setting more appropriate to it than a universal congress of Comintern in Moscow. The issue of the official journal of Comintern which appeared on the opening day of the second congress carried an invitation ''to the enslaved popular masses of Persia, Armenia, and Turkey'' to a congress which was to assemble at Baku on 15 August 1920.... As disappointment grew with the failing prospect of revolution in the west, ever stronger reliance was placed on the aid that would come from the east for the final overthrow of capitalist Powers. Lenin, in his last published article ''Better Less, But Better,'' noting the slowness with which the western countries were ''completing their development towards socialism,'' consoled himself with the consideration that ''the east has finally entered the revolutionary movement'' and reflected that ''Russia, India, China, etc. constitute a gigantic majority of the population of the world.''[1] The Baku congress may fairly be called the starting point of this process of calling in the east to redress the unfavourable balance of the west. Whether Soviet foreign policy was to follow revolutionary lines or to shape itself in a traditional mould of national interests, full recognition of the importance of the role of the east in determining its course may be said to date from the winter of 1920–21....

RAPALLO

For the Soviet Government, as for the German Government, the Rapallo treaty had the rare and refreshing character of an equal bargain; it was the first major diplomatic occasion on which either Soviet Russia or the Weimar republic had negotiated as an equal. The two outcasts of European society, overcoming the barrier of ideological differences, joined hands, and, in so doing, recovered their status and their self-esteem as independent members of the society. Confidence in the ability of the Soviet Government to play a successful role in the game of diplomacy as a European Power began with the treaty of Rapallo.

The long-range implications of the change in Soviet policy and outlook of which the Rapallo treaty was the expression were not yet fully recognized. It had been a commonplace among Soviet leaders that the RSFSR had been enabled to survive in its critical first two years by the divisions and jealousies within the capitalist world. Crude attempts had been made in 1918 to play off the Germans against the western allies and the western allies against the Germans. Lenin on one occasion said that the whole foreign policy of the regime during its first three years had been to ''utilize the division between the capitalist countries.''... But it was the Rapallo treaty which first made the balance of power a vital, though unavowed, principle of Soviet policy in Europe. The Genoa conference had confronted Soviet Russia with the danger, exaggerated by Soviet fears but not wholly lacking in substance, of a Europe united to exploit Russian resources and impose terms on Soviet Russia as an economically dependent ''backward'' country. This danger was conjured by wooing away one of the essential partners in such a project. The Rapallo treaty was not, strictly speaking, a treaty of alliance. It did not constitute on either side an exclusive association. Soviet Russia did not cease to be preoccupied with the improvement of her relations with the other European group, notably with Great Britain, or of her relations with the United States, still remote and still secure enough to adhere to neither European group. But Rapallo established the principle that the capi-

---

[1]Lenin, *Sochineniya*, xxvii, 415–17.

talist world must be prevented at all costs from uniting against the Soviet power and that this could be achieved by proffering the hand of friendship to one of the camps into which that world was divided; and since, throughout the Weimar period, Germany was the weaker of the two groups, this established a special relation between Soviet Russia and Germany....

The Genoa conference and the Rapallo treaty taken together gave Soviet Russia for the first time an assured status as a European Power. After the invitation to Genoa, the western Powers might quarrel with her, but could no longer ignore her. After Rapallo, she was the equal partner of another Great Power—another Power which had also been in temporary eclipse and also regarded the treaty as a way of escape from isolation and contempt. Broader opportunities of manoeuvre entered into Soviet diplomacy. Hitherto the main choice open to the Soviet Government had been whether to pursue a policy of temporary appeasement of capitalist governments through diplomatic procedures or whether to seek to undermine and overthrow them through revolutionary propaganda. What was new in 1922 was the ability within the limits of the first policy, to woo either one or the other of two capitalist groups which divided Europe between them—an option which the Soviet Government had tried in vain to exercise in the days of its extreme weakness. The second half of 1922 was, in domestic policy, the culmination of the first period of NEP. The famine of 1921 had been outlived; the harvest of 1922 was excellent; and the stimulus administered by NEP was making itself felt throughout the economy. In these conditions it was natural that the compromise with capitalism should find expression in foreign, as well as in domestic, affairs. It was a time of consolidation and no fresh adventures....

The retreat from the constant and active promotion of world revolution, which characterized Soviet foreign policy after March 1921, and had led by the end of 1922 to a marked consolidation of Soviet interests in Europe, was equally con-

spicuous in eastern affairs. The transition in eastern policy was in many respects less sharp and less difficult. While from 1920 onwards the emphasis on Soviet interest in Asia progressively increased, there was no non-European country where the prospects of proletarian revolution could be anything but remote, or where any native communist party was more than a slavish imitation of the Russian model or a direct emanation of Soviet influence. In these circumstances, the question which for so long embarrassed Soviet diplomacy in Europe—the question whether Moscow was more directly interested in stimulating the downfall of capitalist governments or in coming to terms with them—scarcely arose in Asia....

DOCUMENT 1

Decree of Peace

8 November 1917

Editor's commentary: The first act of the new government of Russia, one day after the successful revolution, was to declare peace unilaterally. The bolsheviks thought that their revolution was sui generis: *according to the progressive Marxist-Leninist worldview, a new era had dawned in world history and other proletarian revolutions would soon follow, changing relations among people and nations. The words of the peace decree reflect this idealism regarding matters of stubborn* realpolitik *in foreign relations, including minority and nationalities problems which had been among the causes of the war. Appointed People's Commissar*

"Decree of Peace," issued immediately after Petrograd workers, led by the bolsheviks, seized power. *Source:* U.S. Congress, House Committee on Un-American Activities, *The Communist Conspiracy: Strategy and Tactics of World Communism,* 84th Congress, 2nd session (1956), no. 2241, part 1, pp. 6–10, *excerpts.*

of Foreign Affairs, Leon Trotsky stated shortly after, "I will issue a few revolutionary proclamations and close up shop." Needless to say, the contempt which this view of formal diplomacy embodied survived only a short time as the bolsheviks were forced to deal with the outside world.

The Workers' and Peasants' Government, created by the revolution of October 24th and 25th [6 and 7 November] and based on the Soviet of Workers', Soldiers', and Peasants' Deputies, proposes to all warring peoples and their Governments to begin immediately negotiations for a just and democratic peace.

An overwhelming majority of the exhausted, wearied, and war-tortured workers and the laboring classes of all the warring countries are longing for a just and democratic peace.... Such a peace the Government considers to be an immediate peace without annexations (i.e., without seizure of foreign territory, without the forcible annexation of foreign nationalities) and without indemnities.

The Government of Russia proposes to all warring peoples immediately to conclude such a peace. It expresses its readiness to take at once without the slightest delay, all the decisive steps until the final confirmation of all terms of such a peace by the plenipotentiary conventions of the representatives of all countries and all nations....

The Government considers it to be the greatest crime against humanity to continue the war for the sake of dividing among the powerful and rich nations the weaker nationalities which were seized by them, and the Government solemnly states its readiness to sign immediately the terms of peace which will end this war...equally just for all nationalities without exceptions. At the same time the Government announces that it does not consider the above-stated conditions of peace as in the nature of an ultimatum, that is, it is ready to consider any other terms of peace, insisting, however, that such be proposed as soon as possible by any one of the warring countries and on condition of the most definite clarity and absolute exclusion of any ambiguousness, or any secrecy when proposing the terms of peace.

The Government abolishes secret diplomacy and on its part expresses the firm intention to carry on all negotiations absolutely openly before all the people, and immediately begins to publish in full the secret treaties concluded or confirmed by the government of landowners and capitalists from February up to November 7th, 1917. The Government abrogates absolutely and immediately all the provisions of these secret treaties in as much as they were intended in the majority of cases for the purpose of securing profits and privileges for Russian landowners and capitalists and retaining or increasing the annexations by the Great Russians.

While addressing the proposal to the Governments and peoples of all countries to start immediately open negotiations for the conclusion of peace, the Government expresses its readiness to carry on these negotiations by written communications, by telegraph, as well as by parleys of the representatives of various countries, or at a conference of such representatives. To facilitate such negotiations the Government appoints a plenipotentiary representative in neutral countries.

The Government proposes to all the Governments and peoples of all the warring countries to conclude an armistice immediately; at the same time, it considers desirable that this armistice should be conducted for a period of not less than three months—that is, a period during which it would be fully possible to terminate the negotiations for peace with the participation of the representatives of all peoples and nationalities drawn into the war or compelled to participate in it, as well as to call the plenipotentiary conventions of people's representatives of all countries for the final ratification of the terms of peace.

While addressing this proposal of peace to the Governments and peoples of all warring countries, the Provisional Workers' and Peasants'

Government of Russia appeals also in particular to the class-conscious workers of the three most forward nations of the world and the largest states participating in the present war—England, France, and Germany. The workers of these countries have been of the greatest service to the cause of progress and socialism.... The workers of the above-mentioned countries understand the duties which devolve upon them now in the cause of the liberation of humanity from the horrors of war and its consequences, a cause which these workers by their resolute and energetic activity will help us to bring to a successful end—the cause of peace, and, together with this, the cause of the liberation of the labouring and exploited.

DOCUMENT 2

The Peace Treaty of Brest-Litovsk

3 March 1918

Editor's commentary: Although the Treaty of Brest-Litovsk was enormously beneficial to the Germans in the short run, in the long run it allowed the fledgling Soviet Russian state to survive. The huge territorial concessions made to the Germans brought heavy criticism down on Lenin, who was seen to be compromising with the imperialist adversary. But within several months it became clear that Lenin had been right. After the November armistice, which ended the Great War, the bolsheviks regained all that had been given up at Brest-Litovsk.

Germany, Austria-Hungary, Bulgaria and Turkey for the one part, and Russia for the other

Leonard Shapiro, *Soviet Treaty Series,* vol. 1 (Washington, DC: Georgetown University Press, 1950), pp. 4–5. Reprinted by permission of Georgetown University Press.

part, being in accord to terminate the state of war and to enter into peace negotiations as speedily as possible, have appointed ...plenipotentiaries [who] have agreed upon the following stipulations:

I. Germany, Austria-Hungary, Bulgaria and Turkey for the one part, and Russia for the other part, declare that the state of war between them has ceased. They are resolved to live henceforth in peace and amity with one another.

II. The Contracting Parties will refrain from any agitation or propaganda against the Government or the public and military institutions of the other Party. In so far as this obligation devolves upon Russia, it holds good also for the territories occupied by the powers of the Quadruple Alliance.

III. The territories which formerly belonged to Russia, lying to the west of the line agreed upon by the Contracting Parties, will no longer be subject to Russian sovereignty; the line agreed upon is traced on the map submitted as an essential part of this Treaty of Peace.... The exact fixation of the line will be established by a Russo-German commission.

No obligations whatever toward Russia shall devolve upon the territories referred to, arising from the fact that they formerly belonged to Russia.

Russia refrains from all interference in the internal relations of these territories. Germany and Austria-Hungary propose to determine the future status of these territories in agreement with their population.

IV. As soon as a general peace is concluded and Russian demobilization is carried out completely, Germany will evacuate the territory lying to the east of the line designated in Paragraph I. of Article II, in so far as Article VI does not determine otherwise....

V. Russia will, without delay, carry out the full demobilization of her army inclusive of those units recently organized by the present Government.

Furthermore, Russia will either bring her warships into Russian ports and there detain them until the day of the conclusion of a general peace, or disarm them forthwith. Warships of the states which continue in the state of war with the powers of the Quadruple Alliance, in so far as they are within Russian sovereignty, will be treated as Russian warships....

VI. Russia obligates herself to conclude peace at once with the Ukrainian People's Republic and to recognize the Treaty of Peace between that state and the powers of the Quadruple Alliance. The Ukrainian territory will, without delay, be cleared of Russian troops and the Russian Red Guard. Russia is to put an end to all agitation or propaganda against the Government or the public institutions of the Ukrainian People's Republic.

Estonia and Livonia will likewise, without delay, be cleared of Russian troops and the Russian Red Guard....

Finland and the Asland Islands will immediately be cleared of Russian troops and the Russian Red Guard, and the Finnish ports of the Russian fleet and of the Russian naval forces....

VII. In view of the fact that Persia and Afghanistan are free and independent states, the Contracting Parties obligate themselves to respect the political and economic independence and territorial integrity of these states.

VIII. The prisoners of war of both Parties will be released to return to their homeland....

IX. The Contracting Parties mutually renounce compensation for their war expenses, i.e., of the public expenditures for the conduct of war, as well as compensation for war losses, i.e., such losses as were caused them and their nationals within the war zones by military measures, inclusive of all requisitions effected in enemy country.

X. Diplomatic and consular relations between the Contracting Parties will be resumed immediately upon the ratification of the Treaty of Peace....

DOCUMENT 3

The Foundation of the Communist International

March 1919

Editor's commentary: The Third, or Communist, International was created in Moscow in March 1919, during the Russian civil war. Its purpose was to promote revolution throughout Europe and the world. It was to supercede earlier international organizations of socialists, including the First International, founded by Karl Marx and lasting from 1864 to 1872, and the "bankrupt" Second, or Socialist, International which existed from 1889 to 1914. Lenin blamed the Second International's leaders for accepting "social patriotism" and the nationalist principles which fueled World War I instead of promoting "internationalism"—solidarity of the working class and all progressive forces across Europe against the war efforts of the imperialist powers. At its First and Second Congresses, the statutes and conditions for membership in the Communist International, or Comintern, secured Soviet control of the international communist movement and guaranteed that all parties within it would, in fact, emulate Lenin's bolshevik party.

STATUTES OF THE COMMUNIST INTERNATIONAL

...To all intents and purposes the Communist International should represent a single universal Communist party, of which the parties operating in every country form individual sections. The organized apparatus of the Communist International is to secure to the toilers of every country the possiblity at any given moment of

U.S. Congress, House Committee on Un-American Activities, *The Communist Conspiracy: Strategy and Tactics of World Communism*, part 1, 84th Congress, 2d session, House report no. 2242 (Washington, DC: U.S. Government Printing Office, 1956), pp. 24–28 and 39–44, *excerpts.*

obtaining the maximum of aid from the organized workers of the other countries.

For this purpose the Communist International confirms the following items of its statutes:

1. The new International Association of Workers is established for the purpose of organizing common activity of the workers of various countries who are striving towards a single aim: the overthrow of capitalism; the establishment of the dictatorship of the proletariat and of the International Soviet Republic; the complete abolition of classes and the realization of socialism—the first step of Communist Society.
2. The new International Association of Workers has been given the name of The Communist International.
3. All the parties and organizations comprising the Comintern bear the name of the communist party of the given country (section of the Comintern).
4. The World Congress of all parties and organizations which form part of the Comintern is the supreme organ of this International....
5. The World Congress elects an Executive Committee of the Communist International [ECCI] which serves as the leading organ of the Comintern....
6. The residence of the ECCI is every time decided at the World Congress of the Comintern.
7. A Special World Congress of the Comintern may be convened either by regulation of the ECCI or at the demand of one-half of the number of the parties....
8. The chief bulk of the work and greatest responsiblity in the ECCI lie with the party of that country where, in keeping with the regulations of the World Congress, the Executive Committee finds its residence at the time....
9. The Executive Committee is the leading organ of the Comintern between the conven-

tions....The Executive Committee makes the necessary appeals on behalf of the Comintern, and issues instructions obligatory on all the parties and organizations which form part of the Comintern. The ECCI enjoys the right to demand from the affiliated parties the exclusion of groups of members who are guilty of the infringement of international proletarian discipline, as well as the exclusion from the Comintern of parties guilty of the infringement of the regulations of the World Congress....

10. The ECCI enjoys the right to include in its ranks representatives of organizations and parties not accepted in the Comintern but which are sympathethic towards communism....
11. The organs of all the parties and organizations of the Comintern ...are obliged to publish all official regulations of the Comintern and of its Executive Committee.
12. The general state of things in the whole of Europe and of America makes necessary for the communists of the whole world an obligatory formation of illegal communist organizations along with those existing legally....
13. All the most important political relations between the individual parties forming part of the Comintern will generally be carried on through the medium of the ECCI....
14. The Trade Unions that have accepted the Communist platform and are united on an international scale under the control of the ECCI form Trade Union Sections of the Comintern....
15. The International League of Communist Youth is subordinate to the Comintern and its Executive Committee. One representative of the Executive Committee of the International League of Communist Youth with a decisive vote is delegated to the ECCI....
16. The ECCI confirms the International Secretary of the Communist Women's Move-

ment, and organizes a women's section of the Comintern.

17. In case a member of the Comintern goes to another country, he is to have the fraternal support of the local members of the Third International.

TWENTY-ONE CONDITIONS OF ADMISSION TO THE COMMUNIST INTERNATIONAL

The First Constituent Congress of the Comintern did not draw up precise conditions of admission to the Third International.... The Second Congress of the Comintern rules that the conditions for joining the Comintern shall be as follows:

1. The general propaganda and agitation should bear a really Communist character, and should correspond to the programme and decisions of the Third International. The entire party press should be edited by reliable Communists....

2. Every organization desiring to join the Comintern shall be bound systematically and regularly to remove from all the responsible posts in the labor movement...all reformists and followers of the "centre," and to have them replaced by Communists....

3. The class struggle in almost every country of Europe and America is entering the phase of civil war. Under such conditions the Communists can have no confidence in bourgeois laws. They should create everywhere a parallel illegal apparatus....

4. A persistent and systematic propaganda and agitation is necessary in the army, where communist groups should be formed in every military organization. Wherever, owing to repressive legislation, agitation becomes impossible, it is necessary to carry on such agitation illegally....

5. A systematic and regular propaganda is necessary in the rural districts....Communist work in the rural districts is acquiring a pre-

dominant importance during the present period....

6. Every party desirous of affiliating with the Third International should renounce not only avowed social patriotism, but also the falsehood and the hypocrisy of social pacifism....

7. Parties desirous of joining the Comintern must recognize the necessity of complete and absolute rupture with reformism....

8. In the colonial question and that of the oppressed nationalities there is necessary an especially distinct and clear line of conduct of the parties of countries where the bourgeoisie possesses such colonies or oppresses other nationalities. Every party desirous of belonging to the Third International should be bound to denounce without any reserve all the methods of "its own" imperialists in the colonies, supporting not only in words but practically a movement of liberation in the colonies....

9. Every party desirous of belonging to the Comintern should be bound to carry on systematic and persistent communist work in the labor unions, co-operatives and other labor organizations of the masses....

10. Any party belonging to the Comintern is bound to carry on a stubborn struggle against the Amsterdam "International" of yellow [Editor: socialist] labor unions....

11. Parties desirous of joining the Third International shall be bound to inspect the personnel of their parliamentary factions, to remove all unreliable elements therefrom....

12. All parties belonging to the Comintern should be formed on the basis of the principle of democratic centralization. At the present time of acute civil war the Communist Party will be able fully to do its duty only when it is organized in a sufficiently thorough way, when it possesses an iron discipline, and when its party centre enjoys the confidence of the members of the party, who are to en-

dow this centre with complete power, authority and ample rights.

13. The Communist parties of those countries where Communist activity is legal, should make a clearance of their members from time to time, as well as those of the party organizations, in order systematically to free the party from the petty bourgeois elements which penetrate into it.

14. Each party desirous of affiliating with the Comintern should be obliged to render every possible assistance to the Soviet Republics in their struggle against all counter-revolutionary forces [particularly the bolsheviks' opponents in the civil war]. The Communist parties should carry on a precise and definite propaganda to induce the workers to refuse to transport any kind of military equipment intended for fighting against the Soviet Republics, and should also by legal or illegal means carry on a propaganda amongst the troops sent against the workers' republics, etc.

15. All those parties which up to the present moment have stood upon the old social and democratic programmes should, within the shortest time possible, draw up a new Communist programme in conformity with the special conditions of their country and in accordance with the resolutions of the Comintern....

16. All the resolutions of the Congress of the Comintern, as well as the resolutions of the Executive Committee are binding for all parties joining the Communist International....

17. ...Each party desirous of joining the Comintern should bear the following name: Communist Party of such and such a country, section of the Third Communist International....

18. All the leading organs of the press of every party are bound to publish all the most important documents of the ECCI.

19. All those parties which have joined the Comintern, as well as those which have expressed a desire to do so, are obliged in as short a space of time as possible...to convene an Extraordinary Congress in order to discuss these conditions.

20. All those parties which at the present time are willing to join the Third International...should, prior to their joining the Third International, take care that not less than two-thirds of their committee members and of all their central institutions should be composed of comrades who have made an open and definite declaration prior to the convening of the Second Congress, as to their desire that the party should affiliate with the Third International....

21. Those party members who reject the conditions and the theses of the Third International are liable to be excluded from the party....

DOCUMENT 4

Speech to a Moscow Meeting of Communists

V. I. Lenin

November 1920

Editor's commentary: In this speech, Lenin discusses the need for a transition from the disastrous policies of war communism to a New Economic Policy (NEP): a "retreat" which would include trade concessions to the capitalist states, the avowed enemies of the bolsheviks. Lenin

U.S. Congress, House Committee on Un-American Activities, *The Communist Conspiracy: Strategy and Tactics of World Communism,* part 1, "Communism Outside the United States," section B, "The USSR," 84th Congress, 2d session, House report no. 2241 (Washington, DC: U.S. Government Printing Office, 1956), pp. 72–75, *excerpts.*

asserts that all political and economic concessions to the imperialist powers are merely a temporary retreat or respite in the ongoing war with imperialism; the war was not being terminated, but only entering a "new plane" or "different sphere." He also states that in the context of this different venue, contradictions among the capitalist imperialist powers themselves must be exploited in innovative ways. Several themes of classic Leninist theory and tactics emerge, including peaceful coexistence, "two steps forward, one step back," and capitalist encirclement.

Comrades, I have noticed with great pleasure, although, I must confess, with surprise, that the question of concessions is arousing enormous interest. Cries are heard on every hand, and chiefly among the rank and file. How is that, they ask: we have driven out our own exploiters, but are inviting foreign exploiters?...

The fundamental thing in the matter of concessions...from the standpoint of political considerations, is the rule which we have not only mastered theoretically but have also applied practically...namely, we must take advantage of the antagonisms and contradictions between two capitalisms, between two systems of capitalist states, inciting one against the other. As long as we have not conquered the whole world, as long as, from the economic and military standpoint, we are weaker than the capitalist world, we must adhere to the rule that we must know how to take advantage of the antagonisms and contradictions existing among the imperialists. Had we not adhered to this rule, every one of us would have long ago been hanging from an aspen tree, to the satisfaction of the capitalists. We gained our chief experience in this respect when we concluded the Brest Treaty. It must not be inferred that all treaties must be like the Brest Treaty or the Versailles Treaty. That is not so. There may be a third kind of treaty, one favourable for us.

Brest was notable for the fact that we were able for the first time, on an immense scale and amidst vast difficulties, to take advantage of the contradictions among the imperialists in such a way that in the long run socialism won. At the time of Brest there were two gigantically powerful groups of imperialist pirates: the German-Austrian group and the Anglo-Franco-American group. They were engaged in a furious struggle which was to decide the fate of the world for the immediate future. The fact that we were able to hold on, although from the military standpoint we were a nonentity, possessing nothing and steadily sinking into the depths of chaos economically,...was entirely due to the fact that we took proper advantage of the hostility between German and American imperialism. We made a tremendous concession to German imperialism, and by making a concession to one imperialism we at once safeguarded ourselves against the persecution of both imperialisms....

It was just this period which history accorded us as a breathing space that we took advantage of in order so to consolidate ourselves that it became impossible to defeat us by military force. We gained time, we gained a little time, and only sacrificed a great deal of space for it....At that time we did not sacrifice any fundamental interests: we sacrificed subsidiary interests and preserved the fundamental interests....

The example of the Brest Peace has taught us a lot. We are at present between two foes. If we are unable to defeat them both, we must know how to dispose our forces in such a way that they fall out among themselves; because, as is always the case, when thieves fall out, honest men come into their own. But as soon as we are strong enough to defeat capitalism as a whole, we shall immediately take it by the scruff of the neck. Our strength is growing, and very rapidly. While the Brest Peace was a lesson we shall never forget, one which, in respect to the inferences to be drawn from it, was richer than any propaganda or preaching, now, however, we have won, in the sense that we are standing on our own feet. We are surrounded by imperialist states, which detest the Bolsheviks with all their heart and soul, which are spending vast sums of money, ideological forces, the forces of the press, and so on, and which yet were unable in three years to defeat us in war, although we are, from the military and economic standpoint, infinitely weak....

But, of course, it would be a great mistake to think that concessions imply peace. Nothing of the kind. Concessions are nothing but a new form of war. Europe fought us, and now the war is moving into a new plane. Formerly, the war was conducted in the field in which the imperialists were infinitely stronger, the military field.... Nevertheless, we held our own in this field, and we undertake to continue the fight and are passing to an economic war.... We shall learn from them how to organise model enterprises by placing our own side by side with theirs. If we are incapable of doing that, it is not worth talking about anything. To procure the last word in technology in the matter of equipment at the present time is not an easy task, and we have to learn, learn it in practice....

Economically, we have a vast deal to gain from concessions. Of course, when settlements are created they will bring capitalist customs with them, they will demoralise the peasantry. But watch must be kept, we must put up our Communist influence in opposition at every step. This also is a kind of war, the military rivalry of two methods, of two formations, two kinds of economy—communist and capitalist. We shall prove that we are the stronger.... Of course, the task is a difficult one, but we said, and continue to say, that socialism has the power of example. Force is of avail in relations to those who want to restore their power. But that exhausts the value of force, and after that only influence and example are of avail. We must demonstrate the importance of communism practically, by example. We have no machines, the war has impoverished us, the war has deprived Russia of her economic resources; yet we do not fear this rivalry, because it will be useful to us in all respects.

This will also be a war in which not the slightest yielding is permissible.... As long as capitalism and socialism exist, we cannot live in peace: in the end, one or the other will triumph—a funeral dirge will be sung either over the Soviet Republic or over world capitalism. This is a respite in war. The capitalists will seek pretexts for fighting. If they accept the proposal and agree to concessions, it will be harder for them. On the one hand, we shall have the best conditions in the event of war; on the other hand, those who want to go to war will not agree to concessions. The existence of concessions is an economic and political argument against war. The states that might war on us will not war on us if they take concessions. For the point of view of the danger of a collision between capitalism and Bolshevism, it must be said that concessions are a continuation of the war, but in a different sphere. Every step of the enemy will have to be watched. Every means of administration, surveillance, influence and authority will be required. And this is war. We have fought a much bigger war, yet in this war we shall mobilise even larger numbers of the people than in that war. In this war literally everybody who toils will be mobilised; he will be told, and given to understand: "If capitalism does this or that, you workers and peasants who have overthrown the capitalists must do no less than they. Learn."

DOCUMENT 5

The Rapallo Treaty

16 April 1922

Editor's commentary: As E. H. Carr succinctly explained in the opening essay to this chapter, Rapallo ended the diplomatic isolation of the

Leonard Shapiro, *Soviet Treaty Series,* vol. 1 (Washington, DC: Georgetown University Press, 1950), pp. 168–169. Reprinted by permission of Georgetown University Press.

Soviet state. Secret clauses to the treaty, not included here, also provided for the testing of German armaments on Soviet soil, in contravention of the Versailles peace treaty ending World War I, and the sharing of technologies developed in this way with the Soviet state.

The German Government, represented by Reichsminister Dr. Walther Rathenau, and the Government of R.S.F.S.R., repesented by People's Commissar Chicherin, have agreed upon the following provisions:

I. The two Governments agree that all questions resulting from the state of war between Germany and Russia shall be settled in the following manner:

(a) Both Governments mutually renounce repayment for their war expenses and for damages arising out of the war, that is to say, damages caused to them and their nationals in the zone of war operations by military measures, including all requisitions effected in a hostile country. They renounce in the same way repayment of civil damages inflicted on civilians, that is to say, damages caused to the nationals of the two countries by exceptional war legislation or by violent measures taken by any authority of the state of either side.

(b) All legal relations concerning questions of public or private law resulting from the state of war, including the question of the treatment of merchant ships which fell into the hands of the one side or the other during the war, shall be settled on the basis of reciprocity.

(c) Germany and Russia mutually renounce repayment of expenses incurred for prisoners of war. The German Government also renounces repayment of expenses for soldiers of the Red Army interned in Germany. The Russian Government, for its part, renounces repayment of the sums Germany has derived from the sale of Russian Army material brought into Germany by these interned troops.

II. Germany renounces all claims resulting from the enforcement of the laws and measures of the Soviet Republic as it has affected German nationals or their private rights or the rights of the German state itself, as well as claims resulting from measures taken by the Soviet Republic or its authorities in any other way against subjects of the German state or their private rights, provided that the Soviet Republic shall not satisfy similar claims made by any third state.

III. Consular and diplomatic relations between Germany and the Federal Soviet Republic shall be resumed immediately. The admission of consuls to both countries shall be arranged by special agreement.

IV. Both Governments agree, further, that the rights of the nationals of either of the two Parties on the other's territory as well as the regulation of commercial relations shall be based on the most favored nation principle. This principle does not include rights and facilities granted by the Soviet Government to another Soviet state or to any state that formerly formed part of the Russian Empire.

V. The Two Governments undertake to give each other mutual assistance for the alleviation of their economic difficulties in the most benevolent spirit. In the event of a general settlement of this question on an international basis, they undertake to have a preliminary exchange of views. The German Government declares itself ready to facilitate, as far as possible, the conclusion and the execution of economic contracts between private enterprises in the two countries.

VI. Article I, Paragraph (b), and Article IV of this Agreement will come into force after the ratification of this document. The other Articles will come into force immediately.

Suggested Readings

Borkenau, Franz: *World Communism* (Ann Arbor, MI: University of Michigan Press, 1962).

Cohen, Stephen F.: *Rethinking the Soviet Experience: Politics and History Since 1917* (New York: Oxford University Press, 1985).

Davies, Norman: *White Eagle, Red Star: The Polish-Soviet War, 1919–1920* (New York: St. Martin's, 1972).

Degras, Jane: *The Communist International, 1919–1943: Documents,* 3 vols. (London: Oxford University Press, 1960).

Kennan, George: *Soviet Foreign Policy 1917–41* (New York: Van Nostrand, 1960).

————: *Russia and the West under Lenin and Stalin* (Boston: Little, Brown, 1960).

Lenin, V. I.: *Selected Works,* 12 vols. (New York: International Publishers, 1938).

Pipes, Richard: *The Formation of the Soviet Union: Communism and Nationalism, 1917–1923* (Cambridge, MA: Harvard University Press, 1964).

Seton-Watson, Hugh: *East Europe between the Wars, 1918–1941* (Cambridge: Cambridge University Press, 1945).

Shapiro, Leonard, and Peter Reddaway: *Lenin* (Boulder, CO: Westview, 1987).

Tucker, Robert C. (ed.): *The Lenin Anthology* (New York: W. W. North, 1975).

Ulam, Adam: *Expansion and Coexistence: The History of Soviet Foreign Policy, 1917–1973.* 2d ed. (New York: Praeger, 1974).

————: *The Bolsheviks* (New York: Macmillan/Collier, 1965).

CHAPTER THREE

Soviet Foreign Policy under Stalin—From Weakness to Strength (1925–1953)

After Lenin's death in January 1924, the intraparty struggle over the mantle of Lenin's leadership was gradually resolved in favor of Josef Vissarionovich Dzhugashvili, also known as Stalin, who successfully utilized his position as General Secretary of the Communist Party of the Soviet Union (CPSU) to install cadres loyal to him throughout the party and state apparatuses.[1] By the end of 1927, Stalin had skillfully outmaneuvered both the "left" and "right" opposition to him and emerged as the premier political figure in the Soviet Union. The former orthodox seminary student from the Georgian region of the Russian Empire[2] proved more than a match for popular and better-known party luminaries such as Trotsky, Zinoviev, and Bukharin. They instead were numbered among the millions who eventually were caught in the gears of the Stalinist machine of terror and repression, culminating in the bloody purges of 1936 to 1939.

Perhaps because Stalin's attentions were turned inward on the domestic political situation early on, his foreign policy views remained fairly conservative and mirrored Lenin's. Through the 1920s, the dual

---

[1] For a succinct explanation of the advantages to the General Secretary's position in the Soviet political system despite its only "nominal" powers, see Seweryn Bialer, "The Political System," *After Brezhnev: Sources of Soviet Conduct in the 1980s,* ed. Robert Byrnes (Bloomington, IN: Indiana University Press, 1983), pp. 17–20.

[2] For a provocative interpretation of the influence of Stalin's orthodox seminary background and Georgian heritage on his political behavior, see Isaac Deutscher, "Marxism and Primitive Magic," *The Stalinist Legacy: Its Impact on Twentieth Century World Politics,* ed. Tariq Ali (London: Penguin, 1985). Also see Donald D. Barry and Carol Barner-Barry, *Contemporary Soviet Politics: An Introduction,* 2d ed. (Englewood Cliffs, NJ: Prentice Hall, 1982), pp. 7–12, and especially note 19.

policy of the early bolsheviks continued to be promoted by Stalin, as did the regional emphases on Germany and China in Soviet policy. Stalin's faithful promotion of Lenin's perspective on the importance of the underdeveloped world in global Soviet revolutionary strategy (see Chapter 1, document 3) and support of peaceful coexistence with Western countries (Chapter 3, document 2) when it was profitable, are characteristic of this early orientation. Indeed, throughout his 25 years as virtual dictator of the bureaucratized system of terror that he constructed, little penchant for adventurism of any kind can be found in Soviet foreign policy.

But in the 1920s Soviet foreign policy under Stalin suffered several critical setbacks—which subsequently had a negative impact on the security of the Soviet state in the 1930s. First, the Comintern's support for a united front of the Chinese Communist party with the nationalist Kuomintang party led by Chiang Kai-shek resulted in the nearly complete destruction of the Chinese Communist party in Shanghai and other cities.[1] Second, Stalin's German plans backfired. The Comintern ordered German Communists not to collaborate with other leftists, but rather to seek the destruction of these more moderate elements, and thereby create a revolutionary situation in Germany. This had the effect of further polarizing German politics and contributed to the rise of the Nazis.[2]

The 1930s saw the Soviets in a desperate quest for security as nonaggression pacts were signed with neighboring countries and new diplomatic forays brought tangible, though somewhat belated benefits, including the establishment of relations with the United States (Chapter 3, document 4). This same quest for security led to the infamous Nazi-Soviet Pact of August 1939 (Chapter 3, document 7), which cleared the way for Hitler's attack on Poland and gave the Germans the necessary reassurance that the Soviet Union would stay out of any European war that Hitler might launch in the West.

The Soviet leaders believed that alliance with Hitler provided the best chance for security; it also allowed for Soviet territorial aggrandizement at the expense of Poland, Romania, and the Baltic states. Stalin's Machiavellian diplomacy with Hitler initiated the most recent round of Russo-Polish distrust, hostility, and animosity, and culminated in the total alienation of Poland from Soviet Russia after the Nazi discovery of a mass grave of several thousand Polish officers in the Katyn Forest near Smolensk in 1943 (Chapter 3, document 12), apparently a result of the Soviet occupation.[3]

Initially it seemed that Stalin had deftly succeeded in obtaining Soviet security at the expense of the West. For nearly two years, as war raged in east Central and Western Europe, the Soviet Union remained out of the fray. That Stalin believed Hitler would keep his part of the bargain reached in 1939 appears likely; this provides a logical explanation for the poor state of readiness of Soviet forces in the face of German legions gathering on the Soviet border and of many other indications that an attack was coming (Chapter 3, document 8). Stalin's faith in the pact is further substantiated by his behavior on 22 June 1941, when the Nazi attack finally came. The great dictator went into seclusion and emerged only on 3 July to call the nation to arms (Chapter 3, document 9). In his absence, it was left to Vyacheslav Molotov, the foreign minister who had negotiated the Nazi-Soviet Pact, to explain to the Soviet people that they were now at war with the formidable military machine of Nazi

---

[1]See Adam Ulam, *Expansion and Coexistence: Soviet Foreign Policy 1917–1973*, 2d ed. (New York: Praeger, 1974), pp. 178–179.

[2]See Alvin Z. Rubinstein, *Soviet Foreign Policy Since World War II: Imperial and Global*, 2d ed. (Boston: Little, Brown, 1985), p. 16.

[3]See J. K. Zawodny, *Death in the Forest: The Story of the Katyn Forest Massacre* (South Bend, IN: University of Notre Dame Press, 1962).

Germany, which had broken the nonaggression treaty between them.

Aid was immediately offered from the West, as Britain and the United States followed the old adage "the enemy of your enemy is your friend," and Stalin's past sins were forgiven in the common goal of defeating Hitler. This Grand Alliance was but a temporary marriage of convenience (Chapter 3, document 11) with little reason for continuing beyond the defeat of the mutual enemy. Indeed, as soon as the war was over, East and West began to contend over various aspects of the agreements they had reached at wartime meetings, including the Yalta conference (Chapter 3, document 16). By 1947, the character of the relationship between the former allies, Britain, the United States, and the Soviet Union, had changed into a cold war between two camps (Chapter 3, document 17–19) with different views of the future of world politics.[1]

The extension of Soviet power to Eastern Europe at the end of the war and within a few years the transplantation of the entire Stalinist political and economic system to that region appeared to indicate the relentless advance of Soviet power to the detriment of Western interests. In 1949, the victory of the Chinese Communist party over the Kuomintang, the establishment of the People's Republic of China (PRC), and the conclusion of an alliance between the USSR and the PRC (Chapter 3, document 22) seemed to fulfill Lenin's strategic goals; against all odds, communist systems had been successfully constructed in both Germany (East) and China. The fact that all was not well in the communist camp, evidenced by the excommunication of Tito's Yugoslavia from the Cominform (Chapter 3, document 20), had little effect on the general perception of communism's seemingly inexorable march across the Eurasian landmass.

By the time of Stalin's death in March 1953, the expansion of Soviet power had been temporarily stifled in Korea. The Korean war, instigated in June 1950 by the North Korean leader Kim Il Sung (Chapter 3, document 23), but presumably with Stalin's blessing, ended in a stalemate culminating in an armistice the summer after Stalin's death. The dictator's passing was mourned by millions and greeted with relief by still other millions, including the inner circle of his deputies, who had themselves lived in fear of another round of terror and purges that apparently was being planned.[2]

In this chapter's first reading, Adam Ulam discusses Stalin's early foreign policy. Expertly tracing the development of the Soviet strategy of expansion and tactics of coexistence during the 1920s and early 1930s, he explains Stalin's manipulation of the levers of power in the foreign affairs apparatus and the emerging idea of a distinctly "Soviet national interest." The successes and failures of Soviet foreign policy during that period are illustrated by Professor Ulam in his focus on Germany and China as the main targets of Soviet policy. In the second reading, Ghita Ionescu outlines the process of the building of the Stalinist empire and holds that this was already in Stalin's mind at the wartime conferences at Tehran and Yalta, where the die was cast against western interests in Eastern Europe. After analyzing Stalin's policy toward East and West, he suggests that Stalin's legacy, in both domestic and foreign policy, was a heavy burden for his successors to manage. The reader's attention is particularly directed to the treaties reproduced in this chapter, which reflect the changing directions and fortunes of Soviet foreign policy under Stalin.

---

[1]See George Kennan, "The Sources of Soviet Conduct," in Chapter 1 of this book.

[2]See Zbigniew Brzezinski, *The Soviet Bloc: Unity and Conflict* (New York: Praeger, 1961), pp. 146–150.

Stalin's Foreign Policy, 1924–1934

Adam B. Ulam

THE TRANSITION

...Stalin moved in foreign policy at first with his customary wariness and caution. He was not equipped for it by either background or experience. Other Communist leaders—Lenin himself, Zinoviev, Trotsky, Bukharin—had spent years abroad and were at home in French and German. Stalin knew no foreign languages (unless Russian, which he spoke to the end with an accent, be considered as such). He had spent his political life in underground revolutionary work, then in plodding behind-the-scenes administrative labors. He had none of the literary and theoretical polish then considered a prerequisite for a leader of international Communism.[1] For foreign diplomats and Communists alike, Trotsky and Zinoviev were household words, while Stalin was virtually unknown.

The pattern of foreign-policy–Comintern decision-making was thus barely disturbed by the emergence of the new dictator. Zinoviev remained at the head of the Comintern until 1926.

He was then replaced by Stalin's ally Bukharin. Chicherin continued at the head of the *Narkomindel* (the Foreign Commissariat). But before long the new pattern asserted itself, and the hand of the new master was felt.

Control and organization were the key elements in Stalin's philosophy of power. There was no place in the system for a freewheeling diplomat like Krasin or for a foreign Communist Party that was not tightly organized and controlled from Moscow. Soviet diplomats became more firmly controlled than before. The scruples and divisions among foreign Communists were no longer to be controlled by oratory or by the moral prestige of the Moscow leaders but by purges and tight organization. Trotsky's fall had already been followed by the purge of his followers in the diplomatic corps and the Comintern. In 1926–27 came the turn of the followers of Zinoviev and Kamenev, in 1930 those of Bukharin. In 1930, Litvinov was installed in the *Narkomindel,* and, for all the European renown that he was to acquire, he was simply a tool of Stalin's. (When he became inconvenient in view of the approaching Nazi-Soviet alliance he was cast aside in 1939. The legend of Litvinov's pro-Western attitudes made him useful again in 1941 as ambassador to Washington, and he retired in 1946 with the beginning of the cold war. The man who had been a Bolshevik and servant of the Soviet state for upward of forty years was not even given retirement pay, and he died in poverty and obscurity.) The Comintern in 1930 was entrusted to two of the most servile of Stalin's followers, Molotov and Manuilsky....No other agency of the Soviet government was to be purged as thoroughly and pitilessly as the Comintern.

Stalin did not like debates. Congresses both of the Comintern and of the Communist Party of the U.S.S.R.—annual affairs under Lenin—became less and less frequent, and when they did meet, the speeches were in fact recitations on themes proposed by the Secretary General and

---

Excerpt from chapter 4 of *Expansion and Coexistence: Soviet Foreign Policy 1917–1973,* 2d ed. Copyright © 1974 by Holt, Rinehart and Winston. Reprinted by permission of the publisher.

[1]Stalin's awareness of his limitations and his bitterness about them were poignantly expressed more than once. In 1925, he wrote that the "literary" type of Soviet leader was no longer in the front rank, and he gave as an example Anatol Lunacharsky, once a shining light of Bolshevism, now confined to the Commissariat of Education. In an interview with the German publicist Emil Ludwig, he contrasted his own career, that of a man who spent long years in revolutionary work and imprisonment in Russia, with those who had conducted their political work from the cafes of Vienna and Paris. It was a transparent and unfair reference to people like Zinoviev and Trotsky, who for all their years abroad had also suffered imprisonment in Tsarist Russia.

his closest servants. Several networks of control and espionage intertwined with the *Narkomindel* and the Comintern.[1]

The new dictator considered himself—and to a large extent he was—a pupil of Lenin's in foreign policy. But temperamentally he was averse to those elements of revolutionary romanticism and even adventurism that were not entirely absent in Lenin and were quite pronounced in, say, Zinoviev or Trotsky. Foreign Communism was now *consciously* thought of as an extension of the power of the Soviet Union, eventually as the extension of the power of the dictator. Lenin, at least in the beginning, was ready to make considerable sacrifices of Soviet state interest for the sake of a revolution in Germany. Stalin would have found such a policy inconceivable or, rather, incomprehensible. Lenin never reconciled his desires to have foreign parties be both mass parties and strictly disciplined. Under Stalin, strict discipline and mechanical obedience to the Soviet Union took priority over the number of members or votes cast in elections. It is unreasonable to think that Lenin would have been incapable of concluding a Nazi-Soviet pact, but Stalin's *Realpolitik* was unaccompanied by any lingering ideological compunctions. Lenin would not have raised his glass, as Stalin did, in a toast to the Führer, adding that he knew how much the German people loved him! For the father of Communism, the Germans at Brest-Litovsk were imperialist bandits with whom one had to to deal. To Stalin, Chiang Kai-shek and Hitler were, as long as they had power, perfectly plausible partners, and there was nothing shamefaced or requiring excuses in being their ally. Stalinism in foreign policy as in other respects was thus Leninism pushed to its logical conclusions, without those remnants of social democratic

and revolutionary scruples that Lenin never entirely discarded.

Stalin's frank avowal of the Soviet national interest and his exploitation of Russian nationalism belong properly to the years after 1933. Yet already in 1931 he rationalized the need for rapid and painful industrialization by the need for *Russia* to be strong. Old, backward Russia had been beaten, repeatedly—by the Poles, by the Japanese, by the West—because she had been poor and weak. He never took up Lenin's motif that the greatest strength of the Soviet Union was the love of millions of proletarians throughout the world. But we are anticipating our story. During the period under discussion, Soviet foreign policy evolved almost imperceptibly according to the pattern laid down in the years of great trials and hopes, 1918–21.

The actual story of Soviet foreign policy during the 1920's must of necessity be concentrated on two theaters, Germany and the Far East.... And here, as it was to be true forty years later, Germany and China were the key points. Even in the nature of the Soviet approach to those two countries we discern certain similarities, to be sure not exact, to our own day. Soviet relations with Germany and Soviet policy on Germany's role in Europe were then handled primarily from the viewpoint of formal Soviet diplomacy, rather than that of its Siamese twin, the Comintern, though the latter appeared intermittently on the scene. The Chinese problem appeared mainly as one for the world Communist movement and its tactics-ideology. In both cases, Soviet policy gravitated toward the weak spots in the world order. Germany was defeated, resentful, burdened with reparations, part of it under foreign occupation. China was in the throes of revolution and anarchy. The condition of both countries precluded the prospects of world stabilization and the re-establishment of a world Concert of Powers or, in Soviet parlance, of the unity of the capitalist world. Great Britain was eager for the reintegration of Germany into the European system; French policy was bent upon preserv-

---

[1]As early as 1926, Chicherin acknowledged to a Russian diplomat, a future defector, that his office was bugged.

ing Germany in subordinate status; and the clash of the two victorious powers on this issue appeared at times to the most optimistic Soviet observers to promise a new European war. In the Far East, Japanese ambitions in China were the underlying cause of the American-Japanese conflict, and here again, twenty years prematurely, the Soviets saw an early war between the two Pacific powers.

GERMANY AND EUROPE

...The Locarno agreement of 1925 was designed to accomplish...a stabilization of the European situation. In it, Germany pledged to observe her frontiers with France and Belgium—a reiteration of Versailles, but this time given without a *diktat*. Great Britain and Italy in turn guaranteed militarily the status quo in the West. Germany was to enter the League of Nations and take a seat on its council, thus signifying her return as a Great Power. When it came to Germany's eastern frontiers with Poland, they were not included in the Locarno guarantees but were left to the vague protection of Article 16 of the League Covenant, requiring joint action of members against an aggressor. But Article 16 was in turn watered down into virtual meaninglessness by the stipulation of all Locarno powers that reinterpreted action taken against aggression according "to an extent which is compatible with [a state's] military situation and takes its geographical location into account."[1] The exceptions and reinterpretations thus alleviated Russian fears that Germany, under her League of Nations obligations, might become a partner in a coalition against the U.S.S.R. or that Germany's claims on Poland were being abandoned....

The Treaty of Berlin of April 24, 1926, between the Soviet Union and Germany provided that both sides would stand by their former agree-

ment, which was to remain in force for five years. They pledged neutrality in the case of an attack upon either of them by a third party and abstention from any trade or financial boycott against one of the signatories.

For Russian diplomacy, Locarno—even if softened by the Treaty of Berlin and by the Germans' skill in qualifying their obligations under the League of Nations—represented an undoubted defeat. Germany was no longer a partner in the struggle against the European status quo; she now could and did play the Soviet Union against the West, and her partnership with Russia was no longer the main element but only one of many in her foreign policy. To be sure, economic and military collaboration went on, and in historical perspective their concrete results outweigh the Locarno and Berlin pacts, which in a few years would appear largely irrelevant in the new European setting. So would, for that matter, the Kellogg-Briand Pact on the renunciation of war and the disarmament negotiations, which were to drag on for years and occupy much of the Russian diplomats' time. Those heated diplomats' conferences, those struggles over a proviso, over the exact wording of this or that communique, over the timing of the Berlin Treaty as against the coming into effect of Locarno—all those petty dramas which occupied the attention of Europe in the 1920's and which generated so much dispute in the chanceries and parliaments appear to us now as ancient as the Congress of Vienna.

The activities of Soviet diplomacy during this period cannot, however, be downgraded. If we compare its achievement with what the Comintern or international communism managed to do for the extension of Soviet power and influence, we shall appreciate the importance of Chicherin's, Litvinov's and their colleagues' work. The Comintern sought in vain for a revolutionary opening in a Europe that had settled down....

The [Fifth Comintern] Congress [in 1925] ordered a more vigorous subordination of foreign Communist parties to Moscow than had been achieved through the Twenty-one Conditions. The Fifth Congress complemented the ideolog-

---

[1]Gerald Freund, *Unholy Alliance: Russian-German Relations from the Treaty of Brest Litovsk to the Treaty of Berlin* (London, 1957), pp. 234–35.

ical strait-jacket with an organizational one. The Executive Committee of the Comintern, resident in Moscow, was now empowered to issue directives binding all parties unconditionally, and to supervise their activities. The decisions of the central organs of the parties, even of their congresses, could now be annulled by the Executive Committee. The latter also received the right to expel foreign communists and even whole parties from the Comintern. Thus, foreign communist parties were now bound hand and foot by the hierarchy of the Comintern, which meant of course the ruling faction in Moscow, which in turn was very soon to mean Stalin. This pattern became known as the "bolshevization" of the International. But while "bolshevization" meant that from now on the Comintern was even more than before an obedient tool of Moscow, it meant also a recognition by its membership that the institution had lost vitality and significance.[1]

As against the negative achievement of world communism, the *Narkomindel,* through its skillful maneuvering, secured the recognition of Russia as once more a Great Power. The German gambit obtained valuable industrial and military advantages. Those seemingly endless and ineffective trade and financial negotiations resulted in a trickle of credits and concessions from the foreign capitalists, which, even if they did not meet the earlier and exorbitant expectations, speeded up the reconstruction of the Russian economy and provided for the importation of experts and technical skills. Of equal importance was the breach in the hostility of the external world, the implanting among governments and groups abroad of the idea that "one can do business with Russia." Without these foundations, Russia's extensive diplomatic activity in the 1930's crowned by the German-Soviet pact in 1939, would have been impossible. Had Russia scorned

diplomatic coexistence in the 1920's, had her policy in effect been what the Comintern declarations and speeches proclaimed, the real threats of the 1930's—German and Japanese militarism—could not have been deflected for a time or dealt with separately. Skillful diplomacy masked Soviet Russia's weakness during her most vulnerable period and accustomed Western diplomats to include her in their calculations and combinations....

CHINA AND THE FAR EAST

The story of Soviet policy in China, 1921–28, constitutes a companion piece to Russia's exertions, successes, and failures in Western Europe around the focal area of Germany. In both cases, the dates work better than they usually do for a historian, for 1928 is a definite landmark in both areas....

In the case of China, 1928 marks the end of the partnership of the Soviets with the Kuomintang, a catastrophe for the Chinese Communists, and their reversal to obscurity and apparent impotence. The two stories are instructive in their similarities and yet they are different. China, like Germany, was a theater on which were projected formal "Soviet" policy, Comintern policies, and the Soviet leaders' internal intrigues and quests for power. But while in the case of Germany the main plot concerned the relations of the two governments, in the case of China the main weight of activity was thrown into the fairly constant attempt to sway the country in a Communist direction.... In the Chinese drama, we are given several simultaneous action scenes: in one, Soviet diplomacy is courting some Chinese warlords; in another, action takes place in relation to the official Chinese government (if in fact China during the period can be asserted to have had a government) in Peking. But the main stage has the Chinese Communists collaborating with, infiltrating, and ultimately fighting the Kuomintang and its (from the Communist point of view) evil spirit Chiang Kai-shek....

With the government of the "Chinese Republic" in Peking (whose effective authority extended

---

[1]Stalin did not like discussions. Though the statute of the Comintern stated that its congresses were to be held "at least once in two years," after the Fifth Congress in 1924, four years were to elapse until the next one. The Seventh and the last Congress was held in 1935.

over some northern provinces of China *minus* Manchuria), the Soviets after several false starts finally signed a treaty on May 31, 1924. The treaty was a diplomatic triumph for Russia: though the Soviets promised to withdraw their troops from Outer Mongolia, the date was unspecified; and though Chinese sovereignty over that country was solemnly acknowledged, the treaty in effect recognized the Soviet protectorate over Mongolia. The Chinese Eastern Railway remained the property of the Soviet government, with some soothing concessions granted to spare Chinese pride....

But the most promising horse in the Chinese race was obviously the Kuomintang. This was the organization on which were centered the hopes of nationalistically and progressively minded Chinese everywhere, who dreamed of freeing their country from stultifying traditions, warlordism, and foreign imperialism; of bringing China into the twentieth century. Its founder and moving spirit, Dr. Sun Yat-sen, professed a philosophy not much different from that of other reformers of Asian societies who aspired to modernize and free their countries. It was a mixture of Western ideas, nationalism, and some very moderate doses of socialism, plus what was to become known much later as "one-party democracy." "His hope was to bring about the peaceful and benevolent transformation of Chinese society after first securing power for himself and his followers by purely military means."[1] But for all the popularity of his ideas among the younger generation of intellectuals, durable political power kept eluding him. His ephemerapolitical successes were scored as a result of a bargain with this or that warlord.

The Bolshevik Revolution was an eye-opener to the Kuomintang, as to many other similarly-oriented Asian political movements. What attracted their admiration and emulation was not the ideological content of Bolshevism, but the example of a small party which, through organizational discipline and superior propaganda techniques, managed to seize power in a backward society and to hold on to it despite the hostility of Western imperialists. It appeared as if the Communists were in possession of some magic political and organizational formulas that until then had eluded the Asian reformers....

Comintern emissaries...began in 1922 to press the Chinese Communists to enroll in the Kuomintang. In January 1923 came the famous Yoffe-Sun declaration. The Soviet diplomat reassured the Chinese nationalists that Soviet Russia had no desire to export Communism or Russians into China. Chinese Communists were to be admitted into the Kuomintang without giving up their separate party. Soviet help in arms and advisers was to be extended to the cause of Chinese nationalism....

Communist influence and advice transformed the Kuomintang from what it had been prior to the Yoffe-Sun agreement—a group of intellectuals seeking leverage within this or that warlord group—into a modern, well-organized mass party. Like its Bolshevik prototype, the Kuomintang developed extensive techniques for exploiting all the numerous social ills and grievances that afflicted the unhappy country—the peasants' exploitation by the landlord, the general land hunger, the Chinese workers' struggle to exact a minimum living wage from the foreign employers, the universal resentment against Western imperialism, which was blamed for keeping the country divided and backward. The price exacted for this achievement was the growing Communist power within the Kuomintang, which by 1926 made most of the foreign observers conclude prematurely that it was in fact a "front" for the Communist Party of China. It could not be questioned that much of its machinery, especially in the propaganda and organization departments, was run by the Communists, and that its military forces were being organized by Soviet advisers....

The course of events in 1927 in China is of a complexity surpassing that of the previous few

---

[1]Harold Isaacs, *The Tragedy of the Chinese Revolution* (Stanford, Calif., 1951), p. 57.

years and defying brief description. But it is clear what the Soviet scheme was. Chiang Kai-shek and the Right Kuomintang were to be helped up to the limit of their usefulness or, as Stalin said in a speech to Moscow Party workers in the spring of 1927, "They have to be utilized to the end, squeezed out like a lemon, and then thrown away."[1] Then, presumably, the same unenviable fate would be dealt to the Left Kuomintang. One thing that in the opinion of the ruling group in Moscow could disrupt this desirable sequence of events in China would be undue haste on the part of the Chinese Communists, who might arouse the suspicions of Chiang Kai-shek and the Left Kuomintang by any premature attempt to seize power on their own and by excessive agitation among the peasants and workers. Hence, the Chinese Communists were muzzled and once again told to hold in check their ambitions for power on their own....

The complicated structure of Soviet policies in China collapsed in 1927, as perhaps it was bound to in view of their oversubtle character and the personalities and issues involved. It was impossible for Chiang Kai-shek not to perceive the role assigned him by Moscow, and he hastened to strike at them before he could be "squeezed out like a lemon and then thrown away." Having captured Shanghai, largely with the help of the Communists, he proceeded on April 12 to massacre the local Communists and their supporters....

By 1928, Soviet policy in China was in a shambles. The Kuomintang appeared to be the wave of the future, conquering large parts of the country, coming to an accommodation with the most influential northern warlords, thus bidding fair to become the government of united China and recognized as such by most of the foreign powers. Its relations with the Soviet Union were now definitely severed. In vulgar terms, Chiang Kai-shek had beaten the Communists at their own game. This was recognized by the erstwhile Comintern vice-

roy in China, Borodin, on his departure for Russia and obscurity: "When the next Chinese general comes to Moscow and shouts 'Hail to the world revolution!' better send at once for the OGPU. All that any of them want is rifles."[2]

But if one views the Soviet policies in China from a historical perspective and apart from the emotion-laden Stalin-Trotsky debate, one is constrained to some different conclusions. The initial Soviet aim of weakening the grip of the imperial powers on China was certainly accomplished, through the agency of the Kuomintang. It was the latter's success and its threat to unite effectively all of China that prompted the Japanese military venture in Manchuria in 1931 and later on in the rest of China, tied the hands of Soviet Russia's most feared enemy in the Far East, and eventually brought about the American-Japanese war, an intra-imperialist conflict of which Soviet policymakers had dreamed since Lenin. This Kuomintang success would have been inconceivable without Soviet help between 1923 and 1926 and without Soviet advisers and military experts....

The lessons of China conclude the second great formative period of Soviet foreign policy, 1921–28. Between 1917 and 1921, Soviet Russia fought for and won the right to exist as a state. Between 1921 and 1928, she fought for and secured the right to exist as a *new type* of state—one which, while maintaining normal diplomatic and trade relations with the rest of the world, is at the same time the center and directing force of a world revolutionary movement. Furthermore, from a symmetry of those two aspects of Soviet foreign policy, expressed in its Comintern and *Narkomindel* branches, the activities of the Soviet Union abroad often took on an even more complex character. In China, as we noted, at one brief moment the Soviet regime followed four separate yet integrated lines of activity: it maintained diplomatic relations with the official government in Peking; it advised

---

[1]Robert C. North, *Moscow and the Chinese Communists* (Stanford, Calif., 1953), p. 96.

[2]Quoted in Conrad Brandt, *Stalin's Failure in China* (Cambridge, Mass., 1958), p. 153.

and helped the national movement (Chiang Kai-shek), which was conducting a military campaign that sought to overthrow that regime; it helped and abetted the coalition (Left Kuomintang) that sought to overthrow Chiang Kai-shek; finally, it controlled the Chinese Communists who sought to take over the Left Kuomintang! And, at least for a brief period, it obtained the acquiescence of all the parties concerned to its right to pursue that fourfold policy. The Chinese debacle did not affect the Soviet conviction that the interests of any given Communist movement must be sacrificed in favor of another ally if this policy promises to render greater dividends to the U.S.S.R. Thus, from the position of 1917–18—that Soviet Russia exists to promote the world revolution—the Communist view by 1928 had shifted to the position that the world revolutionary movement exists to defend and promote the interests of the U.S.S.R. Said Stalin, "He is a revolutionary who without reservation, unconditionally, openly... is ready to protect and defend the U.S.S.R.... He who thinks to defend the world revolutionary movement apart and against the U.S.S.R. is going against the revolution and will certainly slide into the camp of the enemies of the revolution."[1]

There is no question that the containment of Communism in Europe and Asia on the one hand, and the absence of a concrete threat of war on the other, contributed to the decision to embark upon the drastic plan of collectivization and industrialization that Stalin began to implement in 1928. None of the tantalizing possibilities of the early 1920's—a Franco-British war, a clash between the United States and England or between the United States and Japan—had come to pass. Communism both in China and in Germany was definitely stymied. While the decision to collectivize and industrialize was dictated by internal economic factors, its furious pace and the risks taken were undoubtedly related to foreign frustrations and the need to

channel a power drive that had been thwarted abroad to vast tasks at home. By the same token, while Stalin repeatedly invoked the threat of foreign intervention and war as the rationale for the First Five-Year Plan, there is little doubt that the regime would not have embarked on a campaign which debilitated Russia economically for several years and brought the peasantry to the verge of a revolt if it had seen a serious threat of imminent war. Implicit even in the very scheme of the First Five-Year Plan was a considerable importation of foreign machinery and influx of foreign technicians. How were those to be obtained, if the very countries from which they were to come were—if one believed the speeches of the Soviet leaders and the "revelations" of the show sabotage trials—about to pounce on the Soviet Union? Nor should one take too seriously the other aspect of Stalin's campaign oratory: his prediction of a vast economic crisis of capitalism, which, when it came with the depression of 1929 and the 1930's, was hailed as proof of the Communist leader's perspicacity. Predictions of shattering world crises were a perennial feature in Soviet oratory. When one did come, it was eagerly seized by proponents of Stalin's infallibility while the previous ones were forgotten. That is how prophets and economists make their reputation! Circumstantial evidence is very strong that in fact the Soviet leadership in 1928 expected economic stabilization in the capitalist world to continue for some years: the Five-Year Plan required great purchases in the main industrial countries, which in turn had to be financed largely by an increase in Soviet exports to them. A depression would, as it did in fact, make Germany, Britain, and the United States curtail their imports.[2]

The First Five-Year Plan and the onset of the depression mark very fundamental changes

---

[1]Jane Degras, *Soviet Documents on Foreign Policy, II: 1925–43,* (London and New York, 1952), p. 243.

[2]"The Plan no doubt tended towards a form of economic autarchy.... But the immediate result was to strengthen and not to weaken economic ties with the capitalist world." Max Beloff, *The Foreign Policy of Soviet Russia, 1929–1941* (London, 1947), I, 28.

in the world situation and in the tone of Soviet policies. With the latter, the change is, again, subtle and not so drastic as presented by some interpreters. Stalin does not "abandon" foreign Communism to concentrate exclusively on internal problems. But the relationship of the Soviet leaders to world Communism undergoes yet another shift. Moscow's analysis of the world situation changes drastically between 1928 and 1934. The invocation of the threat of war had been since 1921 part of the Communist ritual; the threat of capitalist intervention was at most half believed, though used unrestrainedly for propaganda purposes and as a weapon in the intra-Party struggle. By 1934, this threat was all too tangible and believable, and all the resources of Soviet diplomacy and of world Communism were thrown in to avoid Soviet entanglement or, if worse came to worst, Soviet isolation in a war.

The Building of the Empire

Ghita Ionescu

THE WATERSHED: TEHERAN AND AFTER

Like Lenin, and indeed like any genuine bolshevik, Stalin was a voluntarist, that is a revolutionary who, although he believes in some historically determined conditions for political and social changes, knows that they have to be effected by direct, or even violent action. While Lenin might have found some room in his assessment of a given situation for such impon-

derabilia as the people's needs, moods and claims, Stalin believed that these and other factors did not contribute essentially to the shaping of the situation, and in any case could be altered by the firm use of force. From this point of view his "socialism in one country" was a policy of bringing into shape new social and political realities exclusively and directly by the means in one's possession. Force was the lever and was also the yardstick. In every situation pressure should be brought to bear; but in no situation should one go farther than the limit of one's force, however promising and encouraging the reactions one could count on from friendly quarters.

In terms of strategy, political, diplomatic or military, this implied a preference for bases and jumping-off boards as near as possible to any potential trouble spot; for the sharpest and most effective tools for action; and for as overwhelming a superiority in forces, actual and potential, as could be built up before the action. Thus, as far as the instruments were concerned, Stalin preferred for his internal policies the secret police to the party and for external ones the Soviet army (and the external ramifications of the NKVD) to the foreign Communist parties or the Communist International. As far as the bases were concerned, territorial contiguity and defensive depth were what he aimed at. In 1940, he had obtained the Baltic states, the eastern part of Poland and Bessarabia. He surely thought of them as "marches" and "buffer-zones." But he assimilated them, territorially, politically and ideologically, into the USSR in an unmistakably imperialistic way. When in 1943 the war was drawing to an end, he was already considering, with an audacious sense of historical timing, his future relations with those countries, which, after the Reich's collapse, would be the neighbouring power "somewhere in Europe."

For those in search of the starting point of the Cold War, or indeed of European and Eastern European post-war history, the Teheran Conference of 27 November to 3 December 1943 is, in

Excerpt from *The Break-up of the Soviet Empire in Eastern Europe* (Baltimore and London: Penguin, 1967), pp. 11–12, 14–16, 18–19, 32–37, and 39–41. Reprinted by permission of Ghita Ionescu.

retrospect, the watershed....It already had its place in history as the first conference at which Churchill, Roosevelt and Stalin met together. Now it can be seen as the conference at which the fateful decision was taken, before the final attack on Europe, which was Hitler's fortress, to divide it into two exclusive zones of operation, with the Anglo-American forces in the West and the Soviet army in the East. In the minds of the Western Governments this was, of course, only a provisional military agreement; and not only did Stalin treat it again and again in his speeches as such but indeed the conference also issued declarations stressing the international harmony and justice upon which the future post-war collaboration of the Powers was to be based. But in Stalin's eyes this was the beginning of a new revolutionary advance by Russia. He came already prepared with the idea and had an easy game to play against the British and the Americans, who were unaware of his intentions and were not fully in agreement with each other on this particular issue of how to launch the offensive in Europe....

Much more ink has been spilt on the subject of the Yalta Conference of 4–11 February 1945, which is considered by many statesmen, historians and journalists as Stalin's greatest diplomatic *coup* against the naive British and Americans. Yet it can be seen in retrospect that there was an attempt at the Yalta Conference (at which some mistakes were undoubtedly made, as for instance the inclusion in the Soviet zone of influence of North Korea up to the 38th parallel) to redress some of the harm done in Teheran and before. Thus the Yalta Conference was the first, even if belated, occasion on which the United States showed a direct interest in Central and Eastern European affairs. Until then the American Chiefs of Staff had most categorically forbidden any commitments of American power in Europe beyond Germany (even Austria was at first included in the "Balkan zone" or in the Mediterranean).

The platonic agreements worked out at Yalta for some compromise on the Governments in Po-land and the other Eastern European countries could not of course change the *de facto* situation already created by the fact that the Soviet army was the sole master and arbiter of the region; but it put forward some principles which, vague though they were, nevertheless had to be trampled upon later by Stalin. From this particular point of view, Yalta was an attempt to improve, on paper at least, the situation already created by the fact that from 1944 the Soviet Union, because of the massive presence of Soviet troops, was able to play a direct and decisive part in the internal politics of every country in Eastern Europe.

The same is true also of the celebrated Stalin-Churchill agreement of October 1944, which many historians consider to be the decisive moment when Eastern Europe was lost to Russia. The agreement, one must admit, is far from being morally commendable. Churchill himself describes it in his *Second World War* in sober terms, when he speaks of the visit he and Eden paid to Moscow in October 1944:

> The moment was apt for business, so I said, "Let us settle about our affairs in the Balkans. Your armies are in Rumania and Bulgaria. We have interests, missions and agents there. Don't let us get at cross-purposes in small ways. So far as Britain and Russia are concerned, how would it do for you to have ninety per cent predominance in Rumania, for us to have ninety per cent of the say in Greece, and go fifty-fifty in Yugoslavia?" While this was being translated, I wrote out on a half-sheet of paper:
>
>> Rumania: Russian 90%, others 10%
>> Greece: Great Britain (in accord with USA) 90%, Russia 10%
>> Yugoslavia: 50-50%
>> Hungary: 50-50%
>> Bulgaria: Russia 75%, the others 25%
>
> I pushed this across to Stalin, who had by then heard the translation. There was a slight pause. Then he took his blue pencil and made a large tick upon it and passed it back to us. It was all settled in no more time than it takes to set it down.

Yet the fact remains that if there was going to be a bargain on such a basis, it was in Britain's favour—for while the Soviet armies were already in Rumania and in the other Eastern European countries, where they could with impunity do what they wished, they were not in Greece and could by this move be excluded from it. But, apart from the fact that for this and many other reasons Stalin decided not to press the matter of Greece, the deal did not materialize because, for one thing, Roosevelt's approval, required by Stalin, was conditional and partial. We can see now that it also failed because while Czechoslovakia and Poland were not even mentioned in the agreement their fate under Stalin did not differ from that of the other countries. And what was actually left of the Western share of fifty per cent in Hungary in 1956 when the Soviet tanks crushed the Hungarian revolution? And where was the difference in degree of domination between Rumania and Hungary and Bulgaria under the massive *Gleichschaltung* to which all the countries except Yugoslavia lying within the zone of exclusive operation of the Soviet army were subjected?

STALIN'S PLANS FOR EASTERN EUROPE

...Basically, Stalin believed that the doomed capitalist world would, after the Second World War, enter into a phase of rapid disintegration and dissolution amidst the collapse of the colonial empires, the rise of the working classes and the determining presence of Soviet Russia as the standard-bearer of world revolution. But there were many reasons for advancing only slowly. Stalin had to give his armies and his peoples a respite and proceed to partial disarmament. This would also lead to a speeding-up of disarmament and demobilization in the West and especially to a reduction of the American forces, which was so clamorously demanded by the American people.

American disarmament, with its corollary, the withdrawal of the American forces from Europe, presented only advantages for Stalin. With these prospects Stalin must have seen the wisdom of not precipitating "Communist revolutions" in the Eastern European countries. For this might have resulted in a total deterioration of relations with America and Britain, with whom economic collaboration still presented great advantages for Soviet reconstruction plans. It might also have frightened the peoples of other countries, especially in Europe, where there was a possibility that "coalition governments," similar to those apparently in power in Eastern Europe, might be established. In France and Italy, for instance, the establishment of such governments, in which key posts were held by the Communists, could lead to a gradual Communist take-over.

In 1945 Stalin's interest in Eastern Europe was still primarily strategic and economic. Ideological considerations were then of minor importance, and indeed Stalin's conflicts with Tito at this time sprang from his annoyance at Tito's "left-wing" determination to form an exclusively Communist Government and to proclaim Yugoslavia immediately as a Communist State. Both these actions lessened Yugoslavia's economic contribution to Russia, while increasing her political independence. Isaac Deutscher described Stalin's attitude in 1945 in these words:

> He was approaching the problems of the Russian zone of influence in a manner calculated to satisfy nationalist Russian demands and aspirations and to wreck the chances of communist Revolution in those territories. He prepared to exact and did in fact exact heavy reparations from Hungary, Bulgaria, Rumania, Finland and Eastern Germany.[1]

The Soviet army was to be given priority in Eastern Europe in order to establish once and for all its new positions and lines of communication. Economic "reparations" or "collaboration" were to be organized in such a way as to help reconstruction in Soviet Russia. "Mixed" Soviet companies were to be established in as many Eastern European countries as possible—Rumania, Bulgaria,

---

[1] Isaac Deutscher: *Russia After Stalin* (London, 1953), p. 79.

Hungary, Yugoslavia—which would syphon off the resources of the respective countries directly into the Soviet economy.

Massive trade agreements with "special" prices for the main commodities purchased by the Soviet Union, as for instance Polish coal, were to be signed under pressure. The entire region was to be put under the administrative supervision of the Soviet proconsular network: military, economic and police. Progressive denationalization and Russianization should be the aim. Finally, a type of quasi-Communist State, called a "people's democracy" and based on a coalition of forces, controlled by the Communist parties, was to be established in the countries of Eastern Europe.

If such a relationship with the West and with Eastern Europe could be reasonably established, Stalin would not need to use the more dramatic, violent and to him more congenial means of action to which he knew he could always resort if necessary....

Stalin's relations with the Chinese Communists had always been uneasy. As the leader of the CPSU and of the diplomacy of Soviet Russia, he had always looked on China as a strategic buffer against Japan. Twice in less than a quarter of a century he had advised the Chinese Communists to agree to collaborate with the Nationalist forces of the Kuomintang. The first time was in 1926 when the Chinese Communists were forced by the International and the CPSU to suspend their revolutionary action against the Kuomintang, with the result that Chiang Kai-shek, the leader of the Kuomintang, crushed the Communist organizations in the main towns. Mao Tse-Tung with a handful of friends took command of some hundred thousand peasants and marched for more than a year until half of them, but only half, reached Yennan and made contacts with the Russians. (This became known as "the long march" and was the birth of Mao's own party and army which was to lead him to supreme victory.) The second time was in 1945 when Stalin, for less obvious reasons, as Japan was already defeated, again advised Mao to reach an agreement with the Kuomintang. But this time Mao ignored Stalin's orders and with his own forces, like Tito in Yugoslavia and without any substantial Soviet help, began the return march, winning victory after victory.

As with Yugoslavia, Stalin knew that he had no hidden allies in the Chinese Communist Party or indeed in the Republic through whom he could direct their behavior and ideology. The Soviet army, his indispensable lever, was not on the spot, and his secret police had no functionaries camouflaged in the Chinese Politburo or Central Committee. It was reasonable to fear that sooner or later China would emerge as another Communist World Power and, like Yugoslavia in the West, challenge the political and ideological supremacy of the CPSU.

THE COERCIVE STATE

In light of these . . . considerations Stalin took the offensive during 1948–50 in three separate ways. First he decided to test by military means how prepared the West was to hold its main positions. This led him to the Berlin Blockade of 7 April 1948, which was defeated by the ingenious Western air-lift and by the moral resistance of the people of Berlin themselves. Afterwards Stalin ordered the Communist parties of France, Italy, West Germany and indeed all Western countries to launch a campaign of unrest against the economic stability of these countries and thereby to create pre-revolutionary situations in them. Concurrently he also denounced the Marshall Plan as an intolerable American intervention against which all European patriots should fight; and he not only refused it for Russia, but forced all the Eastern European countries, some of which had tentatively accepted it, to refuse it also.

As far as the purely political situation in Eastern Europe was concerned Stalin decided that the best way to stop the rot was to impose complete uniformity on the regimes. People's democracies, a junior variation of the Soviet State, were to be proclaimed everywhere . . . , and their constitutions so amended as to make it clear that they had been brought to life and remained in existence by virtue of Soviet Russia, to whom therefore they must be eternally indebted. (Even the Chinese constitution of 1948 included this formula.)...

The Eastern European people's democracies were...in some respects dictatorships of the proletariat, but their very existence as States and as political structures was based on the link with the Soviet Union. As dictatorships of the proletariat too their genuineness would be shown by their readiness to follow as closely as possible the mode of the Soviet State and of the Soviet constitutions. As *Bolshevik,* the theoretical organ of the CPSU, put in in 1959 (No. 17):

> The general laws of transition from capitalism to socialism discovered by Marx and Engels and experienced by Lenin and Stalin on the basis of the record of the Bolshevik Party and of the Soviet Union are binding upon all countries.

As such the basic features of these States were: the total leadership of the local communist party; massive and rapid industrialization; collectivization; and a coercive State.

There was no longer room in Stalin's refurbished empire for those people's democracies or Communist parties or leaders who would not accept either the commandments or the rule of allegiance and vow of gratitude to the Soviet Union. Thus, after a heated correspondence on 20 March 1948 between the Communist Party of the Soviet Union and Yugoslavia, the Cominform published on 28 June 1948 a communique which stated that "the Central Committee of the CP of Yugoslavia has placed itself and the Yugoslav party outside the family of the fraternal Communist Parties"—a clear excommunication. The main accusations against Yugoslavia were: the anti-Russian attitude shown by the Yugoslav Government and party towards the representatives of the Soviet army and State in Yugoslavia; the erroneous line taken by the Yugoslav party in the essential matter of agricultural policy, where they were now refusing to collectivize and were as such becoming a "kulak

party"; and the erroneous view that the People's Front was an organization superior to the party itself—an error equal to that of the Russian Social Democrats of Lenin's time.

Stalin expected that after this excommunication Tito would fall and a true Stalinist leadership would take the helm of the Yugoslav Communist Party. But Tito weathered the storm and the CPSU and Stalin were defeated. This constituted the first grave defeat of the supreme authority which Lenin and he had succeeded in imposing over the world Communist parties since the foundation of the Communist International on Russian soil and under Russian control in 1920.

Having thus so utterly failed in Yugoslavia, but in any case preferring to have the enemy outside rather than inside the empire, Stalin then proceeded ruthlessly with the purge of the "national Communists" from all the people's democracies....

By 1951 the echelons of power in Soviet-dominated Eastern Europe were manned by CPSU and the NKVD agents known to be entirely reliable. In addition, the infiltration of the administrative and party machines by Soviet agents was accelerated and intensified to unprecedented degrees. At all levels and in all channels, there was direct penetration and spying by Soviet personnel.[1] Brzezinski describes five main categories of Soviet control:

> The first link in the informal chain of imposed political control was direct consultation between the Soviet leadership and that of the countries concerned. The second was the permanent supervision of domestic events through reliance on the Soviet ambassadors. The third link was a close contact with various party organs, particularly those dealing with ideological matters, through frequent exchanges of experts and visits of Soviet "advisers." The fourth was the direct penetration of those governmental institutions particularly important as the instrument of power and force. And the fifth was

---

[1]Zbigniew K. Brzezinski: *The Soviet Bloc* (New York, 1961).

the isolation of the various communist states from the rest of the world and from one another. All this was buttressed by Soviet military might, both in the potential and the actual sense. These controls, unlike the autonomously operative ones, were subject to purposeful Moscow direction.

Stalin's third major political act during 1949 and 1950 was the establishment of an ideological hierarchy for the entire empire. The CPSU would stand supreme in all ideological matters over all parties both inside and outside the empire. In its turn the CPSU would have only one universal source of communist wisdom and inspiration: Stalin himself. This much was already familiar in the organization of Russia and of the International. But this time the rules were going to be applied to states and governments, creating a uniform coordinated statement of faith throughout the empire.

The first stage in the process was the founding on 22–23 September 1947 of the Communist Information Bureau, or Cominform. It contained the parties of the USSR, Yugoslavia, Poland, Czechoslovakia, Hungary, Rumania, Bulgaria, France and Italy (these last two as candidates for possible power in their respective countries) but not the Chinese Communist Party, which had even better prospects. In January 1949 there followed Cominform's economic counterpart: the Council for Mutual Economic Assistance (COMECON). Cominform published a journal and issued resolutions. It was through this paper and through these resolutions that the entire transformation from within of the doctrine of the "new road to socialism" was effected. This doctrine developed into one of abject submission to and imitation of the example of the Soviet Union and the CPSU. Cominform also had the right—which was obviously useful for the CPSU—to eliminate deviationist parties.... Cominform ensured that, in all these matters, the Eastern European communists as well as all Communists abroad believed not only that the CPSU knew the right and unique answers but that the CPSU itself was receiving them from one man alone: Stalin....

STALIN'S LEGACY

By 1951, the entire region of Eastern Europe in which Soviet troops were stationed was lying prostrate at Stalin's feet. Not only did no one oppose him and his rule, but all sang his praises and those of his country. In one way these were well deserved. For never before in history had Russia and a Russian ruler wielded such authority over so vast an expanse of territory. Both in the intensity with which it was exercised and in the geographical area over which it extended, Stalin's power was unsurpassed.

But how shallow was Stalin's victory in the last years of his rule! What was described as the building of Socialism was in reality forced labour, Soviet exploitation and the production of war materials. What should have been the "socialist transformation of agriculture" was instead the tenacious resistance of the Eastern European peasants to the expropriation of their land, accompanied by mass trials and deportations. "Proletarian internationalism" was in fact domination and exploitation by So-viet Russia and her apparatus of quasi-occupation. And what was described as bloc coordination or even integration was the overall control by the Soviet commercial and military organizations of economies which, having just emerged from the war and its aftermath, were expected from 1950 onwards to produce again for war.

For there was war, too, though far away. In a still insufficiently explained strategic move, Stalin had, in 1950, made the mistake of allowing the North Koreans, who were Russian rather than Chinese puppets, to attack South Korea in an effort to end the partition. This partition was, in obviously smaller dimensions, a replica in the Far East of the partition of Germany in Europe. The fact that Stalin gave permission to the North Koreans to attack is generally explained by the faulty information he received from his intelligence services to the effect that the United States, under President Truman, would not defend South Korea. Moreover, in an even more mystifying move, he instructed the Soviet delegation at the United Nations to absent itself from the meetings in which the Korean issue was discussed, thus giving to the United States and the West the enormous advantage of starting their defence of South Korea as a United Nations operation. Had Soviet Russia and her satellites been present at the meetings where this intervention was approved by the United Nations they could have easily vetoed it. Did Stalin hope to entangle the United States and Great Britain in a hopeless, slow war in Asia so as to give the Soviet forces an opportunity to stike a decisive and lightning blow in Germany and in Europe? Did he want to disperse the Western forces, exhaust their economies, unnerve their peoples and then launch the final attack? Did he take such risks because Russia, appreciably nearer the possibility of producing the atom bomb, no longer felt so inferior *vis-à-vis* the West? Or was it also a shrewder plan—more difficult to detect at the time—to allow China to become more deeply involved in a long contest with the United States and so diminish her potential demands on and rivalry with Soviet Russia?

Whatever the answer to these mysteries, the effects of the Korean war considerably aggravated the growing internal economic and even political difficulties of the Soviet bloc. It was especially in the satellites, the weakest link in the chain, that this was most noticeable. Increased demands on production led to industrial apathy, absenteeism and even strikes. The campaign for collectivization reached a painful stalemate, with the peasants entrenched in their villages. There was growing discontent and unrest among the urban populations because of the steady lowering of the standard of livng and because of the lack of the basic food and consumer goods. This led to increased activity by the secret police, to successive arrests, and to deportation and internment in the mushrooming labour camps. There was increasingly outspoken contempt and hatred of the Russians and growing signs of common determination among such vast and differing groups as workers, the students, and the intellectuals. The impact of Western propaganda increased. So did the appeal of Tito and the Yugoslavs, who were now so fully vindicated in everything they had said about Stalin's ultimate intentions and their consequences.

The signs of an impending shake-up were accumulating. Indeed, it had already begun in Czechoslovakia in 1952 with strikes and riots, which were dealt with by the local police. When the agitation spread to East Berlin and East Germany in 1953, however, Soviet tanks had to be used against the workers of this Communist State. Open revolt reappeared in 1956 in Poznan, whence it spread all over Poland and Hungary. By then, however, Stalin was dead. After a final convulsion of fear and suspicion which produced what was known as the "doctors' purge," he had died in March 1953, one of the most timely tyrants' deaths in history. His uncertain successors, left with an undeniably difficult legacy, immediately started to dissociate themselves and their country from the crisis which they proclaimed as Stalin's personal responsibility.

<hr>

DOCUMENT 1

Report of the Central Committee to the Fourteenth Congress of the CPSU

J. V. Stalin

18 December 1925

Editor's commentary: At the Fourteenth Party Congress, Stalin took center stage with his report to the Central Committee, in which he summarized

U.S. Congress, House Committee on Un-American Activities, *The Communist Conspiracy: Strategy and Tactics of World Communism*, part 1, "Communism Outside the United States," section B, "The USSR," 84th Congress, 2d session, House report no. 2241 (Washington, DC: U.S. Government Printing Office, 1956), pp. 105–109, *excerpts*.

the domestic and external conditions endangering the Soviet state. Two camps existed now that the chain of world capitalism had been broken by the bolshevik revolution. But the Soviet state was still weak and underdeveloped. A choice existed: to become an "appendage" of capitalism or to develop as a separate socialist entity. The hostile international situation of "capitalist encirclement" and the backward internal conditions within the Soviet Union gave rise to two themes that became characteristic of the 1920s and 1930s: the need for industrialization and building socialism in one country.

I. THE INTERNATIONAL SITUATION: THE CAPITALIST WORLD AND THE SOVIET UNION

I pass to the...series of contradictions...between the Soviet Union and the capitalist world.

The basic fact in this sphere is that an all-embracing world capitalism no longer exists. After the Land of Soviets came into being, after old Russia was transformed into the Soviet Union, all-embracing world capitalism ceased to exist. The world has split up into two camps: the camp of imperialism and the camp that is fighting imperialism. This is the first point that must be noted.

The second point that must be noted in this sphere is that two major countries are coming out at the head of the capitalist countries—England and America, as an Anglo-American alliance. Our country—the Soviet Union—is coming out at the head of the discontented who are engaged in mortal struggle against imperialism.

The third point is that the two major, but opposite, centres of attraction are being created and, in conformity with this, two lines of gravitation towards these centres all over the world: the Anglo-American—for the bourgeois governments, and the Soviet Union for the workers of the West and for the revolutionaries of the East. The power of attraction of the Anglo-American centre lies in its wealth; credits can be obtained there. The power of attraction of the Soviet Union lies in its revolutionary experience, its experience in the struggle for the emancipation of the workers from capitalism and of the oppressed nations from imperialism. I am speaking of the gravitation of the workers of Europe and of the revolutionaries of the East towards our country. You know what a visit to our country means to a European worker, or to a revolutionary from an oppressed country, how they make pilgrimages to our country, and what an attraction our country has for all that is honest and revolutionary all over the world.

Two camps, two centres of attraction.

The fourth point is that in the other camp, the camp of capitalism, there is no unity of interests and no solidarity; that a conflict of interests, disintegration, a struggle between victors and vanquished, a struggle among the victors themselves, a struggle among all the imperialist countries over colonies, over profits, reign there; and because of all this, stabilization in that camp cannot be durable. On the other hand, in our country a healthy stabilization is proceeding and gaining strenth, our economy is growing, our socialist construction is growing, and throughout the whole of our camp all the discontented elements and strata in the West and in the East are gradually and steadily rallying around the proletariat of our country, rallying around the Soviet Union.

In that camp, the camp of capitalism—there is strife and disintegration. In our camp, the camp of Socialism—there is solidarity and ever-increasing unity of interests against the common foe—against imperialism....

II. THE INTERNAL SITUATION IN THE SOVIET UNION

I pass to the second part of the Central Committee's report. This part deals with the internal situation in our state and with the Central Committee's policy on questions concerning the internal situation....We are working and building within a capitalist encirclement. This means that our economy and work of construction will develop in antagonism, in conflicts between our system of economy and the capitalist system of economy. This antagonism we cannot possibly avoid. It is the framework within which the struggle between the two systems, the socialist and the capitalist systems, must proceed. It means, furthermore, that our economy must be built up not only in opposition to the capitalist economy outside our country, but also in opposition to the different elements within it, the opposition of the socialist elements to the capitalist elements.

Hence the conclusion: we must build our economy in such a way as to prevent our country from becoming an appendage of the world capitalist system, to prevent it from being drawn into the general system of capitalist development as its subsidiary enterprise, so that our economy should develop not as a subsidiary enterprise of world capitalism but as an independent economic unit, based mainly on the home market, based on the link between our industry and peasant husbandry in our country.

There are two general lines: one proceeds from the assumption that our country must for a long time yet remain an agrarian country, must export agricultural produce and import equipment; that we must take this stand and develop along this line in the future. In essence, this line demands that we should pack up our industry.... To follow this line would mean that our country would never be able, or almost never be able, to become really industrialized; that instead of being an economically independent unit based on the home market, our country would, objectively, become an appendage of the general capitalist sytem. This line means the abandonment of our construction task.

That is not our line.

There is another general line, which proceeds from the assumption that we must exert all efforts to make our country an economically self-reliant, independent country based on the home market; a country that will serve as a centre of attraction for all those countries which gradually drop out of capitalism and enter the channel of socialist economy. This line demands the utmost expansion of our industry, in proportion and in conformity, however, with the resources at our command. It emphatically rejects the policy of converting our country into an appendage of the world capitalist sytem. It is our line of construction that the Party adheres to and will continue to adhere to in the future. This line is obligatory as long as the capitalist encirclement exists....

DOCUMENT 2

Report of the Central Committee to the Fifteenth Congress of the CPSU

J. V. Stalin

3 December 1927

Editor's commentary: At the Fifteenth Congress, Stalin continued to stress the themes he introduced two years earlier at the Fourteenth Congress. Although the prospects for expansion of the revolution were seen as improving, the line promoted by Stalin toward the "imperialist camp" is a cautious one, reflecting the sober realization that the Soviet Union was still an industrially backward state. Although world capitalism was now, by 1927, evidencing noticeable "contradictions and degeneration," it was still dangerous, and the necessity existed, according to Stalin (who quotes Lenin on this point), to continue good relations with the capitalists and promote "peaceful coexistence" at least until international conditions became more favorable for the system's ultimate collapse.

U.S. Congress, House Committee on Un-American Activities, *The Communist Conspiracy: Strategy and Tactics of World Communism,* part 1, "Communism Outside the United States," section B, "The USSR," 84th Congress, 2d session, House report no. 2241 (Washington, DC: U.S. Government Printing Office, 1956), pp. 132–135, *excerpts.*

I. THE GROWING CRISIS OF WORLD CAPITALISM AND THE EXTERNAL SITUATION OF THE U.S.S.R.

Our country, comrades, is living and developing in a capitalist encirclement. Its external situation is determined not only by its internal strength, but also by the state of this capitalist encirclement, by the situation in the capitalist countries which surround our country, by their strength and weakness, by the strength and weakness of the oppressed classes all over the world, by the strength and weakness of the revolutionary movement of these classes. Not to speak of the fact that our revolution is a part of the international revolutionary movement of the oppressed classes.

That is why I think that the Central Committee's report should start with a brief sketch of our country's international situation; with a brief sketch of the situation in the capitalist countries and of the state of the revolutionary movement in all countries....

THE CAPITALIST WORLD AND THE U.S.S.R.

(a)... Whereas the *temporary* postwar economic crisis of 1920–21, with its chaos within and breakdown of connections outside the capitalist countries, may be regarded as having been overcome, as a result of which the period of partial stabilization was ushered in, the *general* and *fundamental* crisis of capitalism observed as a result of the victory of the October Revolution and the dropping out of the U.S.S.R. from the world capitalist system, far from being overcome is, on the contrary, becoming more and more intense, and is shaking the very foundations of the existence of world capitalism....

The stabilization of capitalism is becoming increasingly decayed and unstable.

Whereas a year or two ago it was possible, and necesary, to speak of the ebb of the revolutionary tide in Europe, today, we have all grounds for asserting that *Europe is obviously entering the period of a new revolutionary upswing.* Not to mention the colonies and dependent countries, where the position of the imperialists is becoming more and more catastrophic.

(b) The hopes of the capitalists that the U.S.S.R. would be tamed, that it would undergo capitalistic degeneration, that its prestige among the workers of Europe and the masses of the working people in the colonies would decline, have collapsed. The U.S.S.R. is growing and developing precisely as a country in which Socialism is being built. Its influence among the workers and peasants all over the world is growing and gaining strength. The very existence of the U.S.S.R. as a country in which Socialism is being built is one of the greatest factors in the disintegration of world imperialism and in the undermining of its stability both in Europe and in the colonies.

...Hence the revival of interventionist tendencies among the imperialists, the policy of isolating the U.S.S.R., the policy of surrounding the U.S.S.R., the policy of preparing the conditions for war against the U.S.S.R.

The strengthening of interventionist tendencies in the camp of the imperialists and the danger of war (against the U.S.S.R.) is one of the fundamental factors in the present situation....

(c) The struggle between two tendencies in the relations between the capitalist world and the U.S.S.R., the tendency towards military aggression (primarily England) and the tendency to continue peaceful relations (a number of other capitalist countries), is, in view of this, the fundamental fact in our foreign relations at the present time....

Whereas a year or two ago it was possible, and necessary, to speak of a period of a certain equilibrium and "peaceful coexistence" between the U.S.S.R. and the capitalist countries, today, we have all grounds for asserting that *the period of "peaceful coexistence" is receding into the past,* making way for the period of imperialist raids and preparation for intervention against the U.S.S.R....

Hence the task of taking into account the antagonisms in the camp of the imperialists, of postponing war by "buying off" the capitalists, and of taking all measures to maintain peaceful relations.

We must not forget what Lenin said about very much in our work of construction depending upon whether we succeed in postponing war with the capitalist world, which is inevitable, but which can be postponed either until the moment when the proletarian revolution in Europe matures, or until the moment when the colonial revolutions have fully matured, or, lastly, until the moment when the capitalists fight among themselves over the division of the colonies.

Therefore, the maintenance of peaceful relations with the capitalist countries is an obligatory task for us.

Our relations with the capitalist countries are based on the assumption that the coexistence of two opposite systems is possible. Practice has fully confirmed this....

DOCUMENT 3

Report of the Central Committee to the Sixteenth Congress of the CPSU

J. V. Stalin

27 June 1930

Editor's commentary: By 1930, Stalin claimed the world revolutionary process was at a "turning point" because of the severe crisis in capitalism evidenced by the great depression in the West. He implied that as the economic situation improved in the Soviet Union and deteriorated in the capitalist world, a new political situation, one favoring the Soviet state, would materialize. Stalin took great satisfaction in pointing out that this state of affairs was foreseen by the CPSU several years earlier.

U.S. Congress, House Committee on Un-American Activities, *The Communist Conspiracy: Strategy and Tactics of World Communism,* part 1, "Communism Outside the United States," section B, "The USSR, House report no. 2241, 84th Congress, 2d session (Washington, DC: U.S. Government Printing Office, 1956), pp. 213–240, *excerpts.*

I. THE GROWING CRISIS OF WORLD CAPITALISM AND THE EXTERNAL SITUATION OF THE U.S.S.R.

Comrades! Since the Fifteenth Congress two and a half years have passed. Not a very long period one would think. Nevertheless, during this period most important changes have taken place in the life of peoples and states. To characterize the past period in two words it could be called the *turning point* period. It marked a turning point not only for us, for the U.S.S.R., but also for the capitalist countries all over the world. There is a fundamental difference between these two turning points, however. Whereas for the U.S.S.R. this turning point meant a turn in the direction of a new and bigger economic *upswing,* for the capitalist countries it meant a turn towards economic *decline.* Here, in the U.S.S.R., there is a *growing upswing* of socialist development both in industry and in agriculture. Among them, the capitalists, there is *growing* economic *crisis* both in industry and in agriculture.

Such is the picture of the present situation in a few words.

Recall the state of affairs in the capitalist countries two and a half years ago. Growth of industrial production and trade in nearly all the capitalist countries. Growth of production of raw materials and food in nearly all the agrarian countries. The halo around the United States as the land of the most full-blooded capitalism. Triumphant hymns of "prosperity." Grovelling to the dollar. Hymns in honour of the new technology, in honour of capitalist rationalization. Proclamation of an era of the "recovery" of capitalism and of the unshakable firmness of capitalist stabilization. "Universal" noise and clamour about the "inevitable doom" of the Land of Soviets, about the "inevitable collapse" of the U.S.S.R.

That was the state of affairs yesterday.

What is the picture today?

Today there is an economic crisis in nearly all the capitalist industrial countries. Today there is an agricultural crisis in all the agrarian countries. Instead of "prosperity" there is mass poverty and a colossal growth of unemployment. Instead of an upswing in agriculture there is the mass ruination of millions of peasants. The illusions about the omnipotence of capitalism in general and of North American capitalism in particular are collapsing. The triumphant hymns in honour of the dollar and of capitalist rationalization are sounding more and more faint. Pessimistic wailing about the "mistakes" of capitalism is growing louder and louder. And the "universal" clamour about the "inevitable doom" of the U.S.S.R. is giving way to "universal" venomous hissing about the necessity of punishing "that country" that dares to develop its economy when crisis is reigning all around.

Such is the picture today.

Things have turned out exactly as the Bolsheviks said they would two or three years ago....

DOCUMENT 4

Diplomatic Recognition by the United States

Exchange of Communications Between President Roosevelt and Mr. Litvinov

16 November 1933

Editor's commentary: In the face of the rise of Nazism and with the danger of war increasing in Europe, Stalin's desire to improve relations with capitalist nations was reciprocated. The correspondence here marks the official recognition of the

Establishment of Diplomatic Relations with the Union of Soviet Socialist Republics (Washington, DC: U.S. Government Printing Office, 1933), pp. 5–6 and 8–11, in U.S. House Committee on Un-American Activities, *The Communist Conspiracy: Strategy and Tactics of World Communism,* part 1, "Communism Outside the United States," section B, "The USSR," 84th Congress, 2d session (Washington, DC: U.S. Government Printing Office, 1956), pp. 257–259.

Soviet state by the United States. This was the first of several positive developments in the Soviet attempt to break out of isolation in the search for collective security against the threat of German revanchism. In this regard, the Soviet Union also joined, somewhat belatedly, the League of Nations on 18 September 1934. Accompanying the notes of diplomatic recognition were elaborate "guarantees" (demanded by the U.S. Congress) by the Soviet foreign minister that the Comintern would not act to subvert U.S. government and society.

The White House,
Washington, November 16, 1933

Mr. Maxim M. Litvinov,
People's Commissar for Foreign Affairs,
Union of Soviet Socialist Republics

My Dear Mr. Litvinov: I am very happy to inform you that as a result of our conversations the Government of the United States has decided to establish normal diplomatic relations with the Government of the Union of Soviet Socialist Republics and to exchange ambassadors.

I trust that the relations now established between our peoples may forever remain normal and friendly, and that our nations henceforth may cooperate for their mutual benefit and for the preservation of the peace of the world.

I am, my dear Mr. Litvinov,
Very sincerely yours,
Franklin D. Roosevelt

Washington, November 16, 1933

My Dear Mr. President: I am very happy to inform you that the Government of the Union of Soviet Socialist Republics is glad to establish normal diplomatic relations with the Government of the United States and to exchange ambassadors.

I too, share the hope that the relations now established between our peoples may forever remain normal and friendly, and that our nations henceforth may cooperate for their mutual benefit and for the preservation of the peace of the world.

I am, my dear Mr. President,
Very sincerely yours,
Maxim Litvinov,
People's Commissar for Foreign Affairs,
Union of Soviet Socialist Republics

Washington, November 16, 1933

My Dear Mr. President: I have the honor to inform you that coincident with the establishment of diplomatic relations between our two Governments it will be the fixed policy of the government of the Union of Soviet Socialist Republics:

1. To respect scrupulously the indisputable right of the United States to order its own life within its own jurisdiction in its own way and to refrain from interfering in any manner in the internal affairs of the United States, its territories or possessions.

2. To refrain, and to restrain all persons in government service and all organizations of the Government or under its direct or indirect control, including organizations in receipt of any financial assistance from it, from any act covert or overt liable in any way whatsoever to injure the tranquility, prosperity, order, or security of the whole or any part of the United States, its territories or possessions, and, in particular, from any act tending to incite or encourage armed intervention, or any agitation or propaganda having as an aim, the violation of the territorial integrity of the United States, its territories or possessions, or the bringing about by force of a change in the political or social order of the whole or any part of the United States, its territories or possessions.

3. Not to permit the formation or residence on its territory of any organization or group—and to prevent the activity on its territory of any organization or group, or of representatives or officials of any organization or group—which makes claim to be the government of, or makes attempt upon the territorial integrity of, the United States, its

territories or possessions; not to form, subsidize, support or permit on its territory military organizations or groups having the aim of armed struggle against the United States, its territories or possessions, and to prevent any recruiting on behalf of such organizations and groups.

4. Not to permit the formation or residence on its territory of any organization or group—and to prevent the activity on its territory of any organization or group, or of representatives or officials of any organization or group—which has as an aim the overthrow or the preparation for the overthrow of, or the bringing about by force of a change in, the political or social order in the whole or any part of the United States, its territories or possessions.

I am, my dear Mr. President,
Very sincerely yours,
Maxim Litvinov,
People's Commissar for Foreign Affairs,
Union of Soviet Socialist Republics

DOCUMENT 5

Report of the Central Committee to the Seventeenth Congress of the CPSU

J. V. Stalin

29 January 1934

Editor's commentary: By 1934, Stalin's confidence regarding the benefits accruing to the USSR as a result of the situation in the capitalist world had changed. The rise of fascism in Europe and

U.S. Congress, House Committee on Un-American Activities, *The Communist Conspiracy: Strategy and Tactics of World Communism,* part 1, "Communism Outside the United States," section B, "The USSR," House report no. 2241, 84th Congress, 2d session (Washington, DC: U.S. Government Printing Office, 1956) pp. 262–274, *excerpts.*

militarism in Asia boded ill for Soviet security. Consequently, Stalin moved to improve relations with France, Poland, and other capitalist states, including both the United States and Great Britain—who were four years previously among the major "imperialist" enemies of the USSR. A strong sense of concern is apparent in this address about war in both Europe and Asia possibly drawing in the Soviet Union.

I. THE CONTINUING CRISIS OF WORLD CAPITALISM AND THE POSITION OF THE SOVIET UNION IN INTERNATIONAL AFFAIRS

Comrades, more than three years have passed since the Sixteenth Congress. That is not a very long period. But it has been fuller in context than any other period. I do not think a single period in the last decade has been so rich in events as this one.

In the *economic* sphere these years have been years of continuing world economic crisis. The crisis has affected not only industry, but also agriculture as a whole. The crisis has raged not only in the sphere of production and trade; it has also invaded the sphere of credit and money circulation, and has completely upset the established credit and currency relations among countries. While formerly people here and there still debated as to whether there was a world economic crisis or not, now this is no longer a matter of debate; for the existence of the crisis and its devastating effects are only too obvious. Now the controversy centres around another question: Is there a way out of the crisis or not; and if there is, how is it to be effected?

In the *political* sphere these years have been years of growing tension in the relations among capitalist countries as well as within these countries. Japan's war on China and the occupation of Manchuria, which have strained relations in the Far East; the victory of fascism in Germany and the triumph of the idea of re-

venge, which have strained relations in Europe; the withdrawal of Japan and Germany from the League of Nations, which has given a new impetus to the growth of armaments and to the preparations for an imperialist war....

Amid the surging waves of economic perturbations and military-political catastrophes, the U.S.S.R. stands out alone, like a rock, continuing its work of socialist construction and its fight to preserve peace. While in the capitalist countries the economic crisis is still raging, the U.S.S.R. is advancing steadily both in the sphere of industry and in the sphere of agriculture. While in the capitalist countries feverish preparations are in progress for a new war, for a new redivision of the world and of spheres of influence, the U.S.S.R. is continuing its systematic and persistent struggle against the menace of war and for peace; and it cannot be said that the efforts of the U.S.S.R. in this sphere have been entirely unsuccessful.

Such is the general picture of the international situation at the present moment....

Of the many facts reflecting the successes of the peace policy of the U.S.S.R., two facts of indisputably material significance should be noted and singled out.

1. I have in mind, first, the change for the better that has taken place recently in the relations between the U.S.S.R. and Poland and between the U.S.S.R. and France....

In this connection some German politicians say that the U.S.S.R. has now taken an orientation towards France and Poland; that from an opponent of the Versailles Treaty it has become a supporter of that treaty. That is not true.... Our orientation in the past and our orientation at the present time is towards the U.S.S.R, and towards the U.S.S.R. alone. (*Loud applause.*)

2. Secondly, I have in mind the restoration of normal relations between the U.S.S.R. and the United States of America. There cannot be any doubt that this act is of great signifi-

cance for the whole system of international relations. It is not only that it improves the chances of preserving peace, and that it improves the relations between the two countries, strengthens commercial intercourse between them, and creates a base for their mutual collaboration....

Such are the two main facts which reflect the successes of the Soviet peace policy.

It would be wrong, however, to think that everything went smoothly in the period under review. No, not everything went smoothly, by a long way.

Recall, say, the pressure that was brought to bear upon us by England; the embargo on our exports, the attempt to interfere in our internal affairs....

Nor can we lose sight of the relations between the U.S.S.R. and Japan, which stand in need of very considerable improvement. Japan's refusal to conclude a pact of nonaggression, of which Japan stands in no less need than the U.S.S.R., once again emphasizes the fact that all is not well in the sphere of our relations....

Such is the situation as regards the foreign relations of the U.S.S.R.

Our foreign policy is clear. It is a policy of preserving peace and of strengthening commercial relations with all countries. The U.S.S.R. does not think of threatening anybody—let alone of attacking anybody. We stand for peace and champion the cause of peace. But we are not afraid of threats and are prepared to return the instigators of war blow for blow. (*Loud applause.*) Those who want peace and seek business relations with us will always have our support. But those who try to attack our country will receive a crushing repulse to teach them not to poke their pig snouts into our Soviet garden. (*Thunderous applause.*)

Such is our foreign policy. (*Thunderous applause.*)

The task is to continue this policy with unflagging perseverance and consistency.

DOCUMENT 6

Report of the Central Committee to the Eighteenth Congress of the CPSU

J. V. Stalin

10 March 1939

Editor's commentary: Soviet security had become more precarious by March 1939 than at any time since the period of foreign intervention and civil war. Stalin lists the efforts made by the Soviet Union to find greater security, including signing a number of bilateral nonaggression pacts with its neighbors, establishing diplomatic relations with the United States, and joining the League of Nations. Despite all Soviet efforts, impending war in Europe and raging war in Asia threatened to engulf the Soviet state on two fronts. In the meantime, the Great Purge (1936 to 1939) left the armed forces of the Soviet Union bereft of their most gifted leaders. This fact gives a strange twist to Stalin's blustering about the might of the Red Army and Navy.

I. THE SOVIET UNION AND INTERNATIONAL AFFAIRS

Comrades, five years have elapsed since the Seventeenth Party Congress. No small period, as you see. During this period the world has undergone considerable changes. States and countries, and their mutual relations, are now in many respects totally altered.

What changes exactly have taken place in this period in the international situation?...

For the capitalist countries this period was one of very profound perturbations in both the economic and political spheres. In the economic

"Report to the 18th Congress of the CPSU (B) on the Work of the Central Committee," 10 March, 1939, in J. V. Stalin, *Problems of Leninism* (Moscow: Foreign Languages Publishing House, 1953), pp. 746–759, *excerpts*.

sphere these were years of depression, followed, from the beginning of the latter half of 1937, by a period of new economic crisis.... In the political sphere they were years of serious political conflicts and perturbations. A new imperialist war is already in its second year, a war waged over a huge territory stretching from Shanghai to Gibraltar, and involving over five hundred million people. The map of Europe, Africa, and Asia is being forcibly redrawn. The entire postwar system, the so-called peace regime, has been shaken to its foundations.

For the Soviet Union, on the contrary, these were years of growth and prosperity, of further economic and cultural progress, of further growth of political and military might, of struggle for the preservation of peace throughout the world....

The Soviet Union and the Capitalist Countries

The war has created a new situation with regard to the relations between countries. It has enveloped them in an atmosphere of alarm and uncertainty. By undermining the postwar peace regime and overriding the elementary principles of international law, it has cast doubt on the value of international treaties and obligations. Pacifism and disarmament schemes are dead and buried. Feverish arming has taken their place. Everybody is arming, small states and big states, including primarily those which practise the policy of non-intervention. Nobody believes any longer in the unctuous speeches which claim that the Munich concessions to the aggressors and the Munich agreement opened a new era of "appeasement." They are disbelieved even by the signatories to the Munich agreement, Britain and France, who are increasing their armaments no less than other countries.

Naturally, the U.S.S.R. could not ignore these ominous developments. There is no doubt that any war, however small, started by the aggressors in any remote corner of the world constitutes a danger to the peaceable countries.... In view of this,

while our country is unswervingly pursuing a policy of maintaining peace, it is at the same time working very seriously to increase the preparedness of our Red Army and our Red Navy.

At the same time, in order to strengthen its international position, the Soviet Union decided to take certain other steps. At the end of 1934 our country joined the League of Nations, considering that despite its weakness the League might nevertheless serve as a place where aggressors can be exposed, and as a certain instrument of peace, however feeble, that might hinder the outbreak of war. The Soviet Union considers that in alarming times like these even so weak an international organization as the League of Nations should not be ignored. In May 1935 a treaty of mutual assistance against possible attack by aggressors was signed between France and the Soviet Union. A similar treaty was simultaneously concluded with Czechoslovakia. In March 1936 the Soviet Union concluded a treaty of mutual assistance with the Mongolian People's Republic. In August 1937 the Soviet Union concluded a pact of nonaggression with the Chinese Republic.

It was in such difficult international conditions that the Soviet Union pursued its foreign policy of upholding the cause of peace.

The foreign policy of the Soviet Union is clear and explicit.

1. We stand for peace and the strengthening of business relations with all countries. That is our position; and we shall adhere to this position as long as these countries maintain like relations with the Soviet Union, and as long as they make no attempt to trespass on the interests of our country.
2. We stand for peaceful, close and friendly relations with all the neighboring countries which have common frontiers with the U.S.S.R. That is our position; and we shall adhere to this position as long as these countries maintain like relations with the Soviet Union, and as long as they make no attempt to trespass, directly or indirectly, on the in-

tegrity and inviolability of the frontiers of the Soviet state.

3. We stand for the support of nations which are the victims of aggression and are fighting for the independence of their country.
4. We are not afraid of the threats of aggressors, and are ready to deal two blows for every blow delivered by instigators of war who attempt to violate the Soviet borders.

Such is the foreign policy of the Soviet Union. (*Loud and prolonged applause*.) . . .

The tasks of the Party in the sphere of foreign policy are:

1. To continue the policy of peace and of strengthening business relations with all countries;
2. To be cautious and not allow our country to be drawn into conflicts by warmongers who are accustomed to have others pull the chestnuts out of the fire for them;
3. To strengthen the might of our Red Army and Red Navy to the utmost;
4. To strengthen the international bonds of friendship with the working people of all countries, who are interested in peace and friendship among nations.

DOCUMENT 7

Treaty of Nonaggression between Germany and the Union of Soviet Socialist Republics, with Secret Additional Protocol

23 August 1939

Editor's commentary: Often discussed as an example of Machiavellian diplomacy in

---

U.S. Department of State, *Documents on German Foreign Policy, 1918–1945,* vol. 7 (Washington, DC: U.S. Government Printing Office, 1956), pp. 245–247.

international politics, the Molotov-Ribbentrop Pact of 1939 nevertheless bears Stalin's particular brand of realpolitik. In a single cynical move, Stalin gave Hitler a free hand to wage war secure in the knowledge that Stalin would not join the Western powers in a coalition and, at the same time, avenged the Red Army's defeat at the gates of Warsaw in 1920 by dismembering, with his new ally Hitler, the Polish state.

The Government of the German Reich and the Government of U.S.S.R., desirous of strengthening the cause of peace between Germany and U.S.S.R., and proceeding from the fundamental provisions of the Treaty of Neutrality, which was concluded between Germany and the U.S.S.R. in April 1926, have reached the following agreement:

Article I
The two Contracting Parties undertake to refrain from any act of violence, any aggressive action, and any attack on each other, either severally or jointly with other Powers.

Article II
Should one of the Contracting Parties become the object of belligerent action by a third Power, the other Contracting Party shall in no manner lend its support to this third Power.

Article III
The Governments of the two Contracting Parties will in the future maintain continual contact with one another for the purpose of consultation in order to exchange information on problems affecting their common interests.

Article IV
Neither of the two Contracting Parties will join any grouping of Powers whatsoever which is aimed directly or indirectly at the other Party.

Article V
Should disputes or conflicts arise between the Contracting Parties over questions of one kind or another, both Parties will settle these disputes

or conflicts exclusively by means of a friendly exchange of views or if necessary by the appointment of arbitration commissions.

Article VI
The present Treaty shall be concluded for a period of ten years, with the proviso that, in so far as one of the Contracting Parties does not denounce it one year before the expiry of this period, the validity of this Treaty shall be deemed to be automatically prolonged for another five years.

Article VII
The present treaty shall be ratified within the shortest possible time. The instruments of ratification will be exchanged in Berlin. The treaty shall enter into force immediately upon signature.

Done in duplicate in the German and Russian languages.

Moscow, August 23, 1939

For the Government of the German Reich: v. Ribbentrop

With full power of the Government of U.S.S.R.: V. Molotov

SECRET ADDITIONAL PROTOCOL

On the occasion of the signature of the Non-Aggression Treaty between the German Reich and Union of Soviet Socialist Republics, the undersigned plenipotentiaries of the two Parties discussed in strictly confidential conversations the question of the delimitation of their respective spheres of interest in Eastern Europe. These conversations led to the following result:

1. In the event of a territorial and political transformation in the territories belonging to the Baltic States (Finland, Estonia, Latvia, Lithuania), the northern frontier of Lithuania shall represent the frontier of the spheres of interest both of Germany and the U.S.S.R. In this connection the interest of Lithuania in the Vilna territory is recognized by both Parties.

2. In the event of a territorial and political transformation of the territories belonging to the Polish State, the spheres of interest of both Germany and the U.S.S.R. shall be bounded approximately by the line of the rivers Narev, Vistula and San.

The question of whether the interests of both Parties make the maintenance of an independent Polish State appear desirable and how the frontiers of this State should be drawn can be definitely determined only in the course of further political developments.

In any case both Governments will resolve this question by means of a friendly understanding.

3. With regard to South-Eastern Europe, the Soviet side emphasizes its interest in Bessarabia. The German side declares its complete political *desinteressement* in these areas.

4. This Protocol will be treated by both Parties as strictly secret.

Moscow, August 23, 1939

For the government of the German Reich: v. Ribbentrop

With full power of the government of the U.S.S.R.: V. Molotov

---

DOCUMENT 8

TASS Dispatch of 13 June 1941

Editor's commentary: This TASS statement was delivered to Ambassador Schulenburg of Germany in Moscow prior to its general release. In contrast to the realpolitik *which normally characterized Soviet foreign policy under Stalin, the text reflects*

U.S. Department of State, *Documents on German Foreign Policy, 1918–1945*, vol. 7 (Washington, DC: U.S. Government Printing Office, 1956), pp. 1027–1028, *excerpts.*

wishful thinking. Within eight days, the massive Nazi invasion of the Soviet Union began. Difficult as it is to explain the extent to which Stalin was prepared to go to mollify Hitler, historians are left with the speculation that Stalin trusted Hitler to keep his part of the bargain struck in the Nazi-Soviet Pact of 1939.

...There have been widespread rumors of "an impending war between the USSR and Germany" in the English and foreign press. These rumors allege:

1. That Germany supposedly has made various territorial and economic demands on the USSR and that at present negotiations are impending between Germany and the USSR for the conclusion of a new and closer agreement between them;
2. That the Soviet Union is supposed to have declined these demands and that as a result Germany has begun to concentrate her troops on the frontier of the Soviet Union in order to attack the Soviet Union;
3. That on her side the Soviet Union is supposed to have begun intensive preparations for war with Germany and to have concentrated her troops on the German border.

Despite the obvious absurdity of these rumors, responsible circles in Moscow have thought it necessary, in view of the persistent spread of these rumors, to authorize Tass to state that these rumors are a clumsy propaganda maneuver of the forces arrayed against the Soviet Union and Germany, which are interested in a spread and intensification of the war.

Tass declares that:

1. Germany has addressed no demands to the Soviet Union and has proposed no new closer agreement, and that therefore negotiations in this regard cannot be taking place;
2. According to the evidence in the possession of the Soviet Union, both Germany and the Soviet Union are fulfilling to the letter the terms of the Soviet-German Nonaggression Pact, so that in the opinion of Soviet circles the rumors of the intention of Germany to break the Pact and to launch an attack against the Soviet Union are completely without foundation, while the recent movements of German troops which have completed their operations in the Balkans, to the eastern and northern parts of Germany, must be explained by other motives which have no connection with Soviet-German relations;
3. The Soviet Union, in accordance with her peace policy, has fulfilled and intends to fulfill the terms of the Soviet-German Nonaggression Pact; as a result, all the rumors according to which the Soviet Union is preparing for a war with Germany are false and provocative;
4. The summer calling-up of the reserves of the Red Army which is now taking place and the impending maneuvers mean nothing but a training of the reservists and a check on the operation of the railway system, which as is known takes place every year; consequently, it appears at least nonsensical to interpret these measures of the Red Army as an action hostile to Germany.

DOCUMENT 9

Radio Address to the Soviet People after the Nazi Attack

J. V. Stalin

3 July 1941

Editor's commentary: Those who heard Stalin's first address to the Soviet people after his mysterious

Soviet War Documents, USSR Information Bulletin, Special Supplement (Washington, DC: USSR Embassy, December 1943), pp. 3–7, *excerpts.*

absence from the public eye on the heels of the German invasion remember it as a somber but inspiring occasion. The gist of the speech was not the promotion of the ideals or the system of communism, but simply an appeal to national survival instincts. There is irony in Stalin's pleas to ethnic minorities of the Soviet state, some of which collaborated with the enemy for what they thought would be liberation of their homeland from communist oppression.

Comrades! Citizens! Brothers, and Sisters! Men of our Army and Navy! I am addressing you, my dear friends!

The perfidious military attack on our motherland begun on June 22 by Hitler's Germany is continuing. In spite of the heroic resistance of the Red Army, and although the enemy's finest divisions and finest air-force units have already been smashed and have met their doom on the field of battle, the enemy continues to push forward, hurling fresh forces into the attack. Hitler's troops have succeeded in capturing Lithuania, a considerable part of Latvia, the western part of Byelorussia, and part of the Western Ukraine. The fascist air force is extending the range of operations of its bombers, and is bombing Murmansk, Orsha, Mogilev, Smolensk, Kiev, Odessa and Sevastopol. A grave danger hangs over our country.

How could it have happened that our glorious Red Army surrendered a number of our cities and districts to the fascist armies? Is it really true that the German-fascist troops are invincible, as is ceaselessly trumpeted by boastful fascist propagandists? Of course not! History shows that there are no invincible armies and never have been. Napoleon's army was considered invincible but it was beaten successively by Russian, English, and German armies. Kaiser Wilhelm's German army in the period of the first imperialist war was also considered invincible, but it was beaten several times by Russian and Anglo-French forces and was finally smashed by the Anglo-French

forces. The same must be said of Hitler's German-fascist army today. This army has not yet met with serious resistance on the continent of Europe. Only on our territory has it met serious resistance. And if as a result of this resistance the finest divisions of Hitler's German-fascist army have been defeated by our Red Army, it means that this army too can be smashed and will be smashed, as were the armies of Napoleon and Wilhelm.

As to part of our territory having nevertheless been seized by German-fascist troops, this is chiefly due to the fact that the war of fascist Germany on the USSR began under conditions favorable for the German forces and unfavorable for the Soviet forces. The fact of the matter is that the troops of Germany, as a country at war, were already fully mobilized, and the 170 divisions hurled by Germany against the USSR and brought up to the Soviet frontiers were in a state of complete readiness, only awaiting the signal to move into action, whereas the Soviet troops had still to effect mobilization and to move up to the frontiers.

Of no little importance in this respect is the fact that fascist Germany suddenly and treacherously violated the non-aggression pact she concluded in 1939 with the USSR, disregarding the fact that she would be regarded as the aggressor by the whole world. Naturally, our peace-loving country, not wishing to take the initiative in breaking the pact, could not have resorted to perfidy. It may be asked: how could the Soviet Government have consented to conclude a non-aggression pact with such treacherous fiends as Hitler and Ribbentrop? Was this not an error on the part of the Soviet Government? Of course not! Nonaggression pacts are pacts of peace between two states. It was such a pact that Germany proposed to us in 1939. Could the Soviet government have declined such a proposal? I think that not a single peace-loving state could decline a peace treaty with a neighboring state, even though the latter was headed by such fiends and cannibals as Hitler and Ribbentrop. But that, of course, only on the one indispensable condition, namely, that this peace treaty did not infringe, either directly or indirectly, on the territorial integrity, independence and honor of the peace-loving state. As is well known, the non-aggression pact between Germany and the USSR was precisely such a pact.

What did we gain by concluding the nonaggression pact with Germany? We secured our country peace for a year and a half and the opportunity of preparing its forces to repulse fascist Germany should she risk an attack on our country despite the pact. This was a definite advantage for us and a disadvantage for fascist Germany.

What has fascist Germany gained and what has she lost by treacherously tearing up the pact and attacking the USSR? She has gained certain advantageous positions for her troops for a short period, but she has lost politically by exposing herself in the eyes of the entire world as a bloodthirsty aggressor. There can be no doubt that this shortlived military gain for Germany is only an episode, while the tremendous political gain of the USSR is a serious and lasting factor that is bound to form the basis for the development of decisive military successes of the Red Army in the war with fascist Germany....

What is required to put an end to the danger hovering over our country, and what measures must be taken to smash the enemy?

Above all, it is essential that our people, the Soviet people, should understand the full immensity of the danger that threatens our country and abandon all complacency, all heedlessness.... The enemy is cruel and implacable. He is out to seize our land watered with our sweat, to seize our grain and oil secured by our labor. He is out to restore the rule of the landlords, to restore Tsarism, to destroy the national culture and the national state existence of the Russians, Ukrainians, Byelorussians, Lithuanians, Letts, Estonians, Tatars, Uzbeks, Moldavians, Georgians, Armenians, Azerbaijanians and the other free peoples of the Soviet Union, to Germanize them, to convert them into slaves of the German princes and barons. Thus the issue is one of life or death for the Soviet State, of life or death for the peoples of the USSR; the issue is whether the peoples of the Soviet Union shall remain free or fall into slavery....

This war with fascist Germany cannot be considered an ordinary war. It is not only a war between two armies; it is also a great war of the entire Soviet people against the German-fascist forces. The aim of this national war in defense of our country against the fascist oppressors is not only elimination of the danger hanging over our country, but also aid to all European peoples groaning under the yoke of German fascism. In this war of liberation we shall not be alone. In this great war we shall have loyal allies in the peoples of Europe and America, including the German people who are enslaved by the Hitlerite despots. Our war for the freedom of our country will merge with the struggle of the peoples of Europe and America for their independence, for democratic liberties. It will be a united front of peoples standing for freedom and against enslavement and threats of enslavement by Hitler's fascist armies.

In this connection, the historic utterance of the British Prime Minister, Mr. Churchill, regarding aid to the Soviet Union, and the declaration of the United States Government signifying its readiness to render aid to our country, which can only evoke a feeling of gratitude in the hearts of the peoples of the Soviet Union, are fully comprehensible.... Comrades! Our forces are numberless. The overweening enemy will soon learn this to his cost.... All our forces—for the support of our heroic Red Army and our glorious Red Navy! All forces of the people—for the demolition of the enemy! Forward, to our victory!

Soviet-Polish Agreements

London, 30 July, and Moscow, 20 August 1941

Editor's commentary: The Soviet leaders were quick to try to mend fences with their new allies after the Nazi attack. Poland, which had ceased to exist as a result of the Nazi-Soviet Pact of 1939, now reappeared on Soviet maps, and the Polish government-in-exile in London was officially recognized by Moscow, as the Soviet Union, in order to placate the Allies, renounced the territorial gains it had made at Polish expense in 1939.

DIPLOMATIC RECOGNITION

The Soviet Information Bureau reports the signing at London on July 30, 1941 of an agreement between the Government of the USSR and the Polish Government.

The agreement was signed for the USSR by Ivan Maisky, Ambassador Extraordinary and Plenipotentiary of the USSR in Great Britain, and for the Polish Government by Premier Wladyslaw Sikorski. The text follows:

1. The Government of the USSR recognizes the Soviet-German treaties of 1939 as to territorial changes in Poland as having lost their validity. The Polish Government declares Poland is not bound by any agreement with any third power which is directed against the USSR.
2. Diplomatic relations will be restored between the two Governments upon the signing of this agreement, and an immediate exchange of Ambassadors will be arranged.

USSR Information Bulletin, vol. 1, no. 16, 1 August 1941, pp. 2–3, and no. 33, 21 August 1941, pp. 2–3.

3. The two Governments mutually agree to render one to another aid and support of all kinds in the present war against Hitlerite Germany.
4. The Government of the USSR expresses its consent to the formation on territory of the USSR of a Polish Army under a commander appointed by the Polish Government in agreement with the Soviet Government, the Polish Army on territory of the USSR being subordinated in an operational sense to the Supreme Command of the USSR, in which the Polish Army will be represented. All details as to command, organization and employment of this force will be settled in a subsequent agreement.
5. This agreement will come into force immediately upon signature and without ratification. The present agreement is drawn up in two copies in the Russian and Polish languages. Both texts have equal force.

To this agreement the following protocol was appended:

The Soviet Government grants amnesty to all Polish citizens now detained on Soviet territory either as prisoners of war or on other sufficient grounds, as from the resumption of diplomatic relations.

MILITARY AGREEMENT

The Soviet Information Bureau yesterday announced:

In conformity with the Soviet-Polish agreement of July 30, 1941, a military agreement was concluded in Moscow on August 14 of this year between the Supreme Command of the USSR and the Supreme Command of Poland.

The Agreement was signed for the USSR by the representative of the Supreme Command of the USSR, Major General Vasilevski, and for Poland by the representative of the Supreme Council of Poland, Major General Sziszko-Bogusz.

The Commander-in-Chief of the Polish Armed Forces General Sikorski has appointed General Anders to command the Polish Army on territory of the USSR. General Anders has begun the formation of a Polish Army.

DOCUMENT 11

On the Grand Alliance and the Need for a Second Front

J. V. Stalin

3 October 1942

Editor's commentary: Western media had created, in line with the necessities of Allied solidarity, a romantic image of the heroic Soviet resistance, intentionally disregarding the record of Stalin's cynical diplomacy. A popular image had also been created of the large-scale American assistance keeping the Soviets going in their war effort. In this short response to an Associated Press correspondent's questions, a slightly different picture emerges. The assistance in which Stalin is interested is a second front in Europe; he reduces the significance of U.S. lend-lease aid.

Soviet War Documents: USSR Information Bulletin Special Supplement (Washington, DC: Embassy of the USSR, December 1943), p. 32.

Henry C. Cassidy, Moscow correspondent of the United States Associated Press, addressed the Chairman of the Council of People's Commissars of the USSR Joseph Stalin with a request to reply orally or in writing to three questions which interest the American public. Stalin replied with the following letter:

Dear Mr. Cassidy:

Owing to pressure of work and the consequent inability to grant you an interview, I shall confine myself to a brief written answer to your questions.

1. *Question:* What place does the possibility of a second front occupy in Soviet estimates of the current situation?

Answer: A very important place, one might say, a place of first-rate importance.

2. *Question:* To what extent is Allied aid to the Soviet Union proving effective and what could be done to amplify and improve this aid?

Answer: As compared with the aid which the Soviet Union is giving to the Allies by drawing upon itself the main forces of the German-fascist armies, the aid of the Allies to the Soviet Union has so far been little effective. In order to amplify and improve this aid, only one thing is required: that the Allies fulfill their obligations fully and on time.

3. *Question:* What remains the Soviet capacity for resistance?

Answer: I think that the Soviet capacity of resisting the German brigands is in strength not less, if not greater, than the capacity of fascist Germany or of any other aggressive power to secure for itself world domination.

With respect,

(Signed) J. Stalin

The Katyn Forest Massacre

1943

Editor's commentary: In 1943, the German occupation forces in the USSR unearthed mass graves of several thousand bodies, victims of mass executions who were identified as Polish officers and intellectuals. Soviet authorities adamantly denied any part and blamed the Nazis. Evidence pointed to the Soviets, who had occupied western Poland from September 1939 until spring 1941, the mass executions likely having taken place sometime in 1940. International outrage at this discovery was quickly subordinated to the Allies' need for unity to defeat Hitler. As a gesture to the Allies, Stalin "dissolved" the Comintern. However, by the early 1950s, the entire episode was brought up again as the cold war grew hot in Korea, and old cases, including Katyn, were reopened by the U.S. government.

THE SOVIET VERSION OF KATYN

The Hitlerite fiends have again been nailed to the pillory. A complete picture has been reconstructed of the monstrous atrocities perpetrated by the German-fascist bandits in Katyn. Today we publish the findings of a special commission for the investigation of the circumstances of the shooting of Polish officers, prisoners of war, by the German-fascist invaders in the forest of Katyn.

The "Katyn affair" is typical of the vile and fraudulent methods so widely resorted to by the

"On the Shooting of Polish War Prisoners by the Germans at Katyn," *Pravda*, 26 January 1944, as reprinted in *USSR Information Bulletin*, vol. 4, no. 12, 29 January 1944, pp. 5–6, *excerpts*; "House Select Committee to Conduct an Investigation and Study of the Facts, Evidence, and Circumstances of the Katyn Forest Massacre," 2 July 1952, reprinted in U.S. Congress, House Committee on Un-American Activities, *The Communist Conspiracy: Strategy and Tactics of World Communism*, part 1, "Communism Outside the United States," section B, "The USSR," 84th Congress, 2d session (Washington, DC: U.S. Government Printing Office, 1956), pp. 428–430, *excerpts*.

Hitlerite bandits in the furtherance of their criminal aims. Prior to the attack of the German-fascist bandits on the Soviet Union there was a camp in the Smolensk Region for Polish war prisoners who were engaged in road building.

During the Red Army's retreat the situation was such that it was impossible to evacuate the Polish war prisoners and they all fell into the hands of the Hitlerite butchers. The German-fascist bandits, continuing the bloody policy which they had practiced in Poland of the complete extermination of the Poles, in the autumn of 1941 shot the war prisoners in the Smolensk Region. In order to cover up this atrocious crime and to further their vile political ends the Hitlerite bandits resorted to a monstrous fraud.

In the spring of 1943 they published a statement in which they attempted to fasten the guilt for the crime committed in the Katyn forest on Soviet authorities and declared that the massacre was committed in the spring of 1940. It was not for nothing that this iniquitous frameup was conceived in the spring of 1943. The winter of 1942–1943, during which the Red Army administered serious defeats to Hitler's army, was marked by the sharp deterioration of the military and political situation of fascist Germany, and by the further strengthening of the unity of the Allied Powers. Fearing retribution, and at the same time seeking to set the Russians and Poles at loggerheads, the Germans—faithful to Hitler's precept of not shrinking from the most repulsive and vilest atrocities—attempted to calumniate Soviet organs of government by ascribing their own villainies to them.

This attempt failed. Another abominable fraud of the German-fascist butchers was exposed to the eyes of the world. The Hitlerites' preposterous fabrication and vile slander was immediately exposed by a communique of the Soviet Information Bureau and by our press. The freedom-loving peoples of all countries repudiated with contempt the base calumniation of the Soviet people who were displaying miracles of heroism, courage and nobility.

And only the emigrant Polish government fell an easy prey to the bait of the Hitlerite intriguers and stepped forward in the role of Hitler's lieutenants. The Polish government took an active part in the malicious anti-Soviet campaign of slander launched by the German invaders in connection with the "Katyn massacre." At a time when the peoples of the USSR were shedding their blood in an arduous struggle against Hitler's Germany and mustering all their effort for the defeat of the common enemy of the Russian and Polish peoples and all democratic countries, the Polish government, to gratify the Hitlerites, dealt the Soviet Union a treacherous stab in the back.

By the fault of the Polish government, owing to its active participation in the Germans' malicious anti-Soviet slander campaign, diplomatic relations were broken off between the Soviet Government and the Polish government.

Now in the light of the evidence in possession of the special commission—the testimony of over 100 interrogated witnesses, the findings of medical experts, documents and other material dug up from the graves in the Katyn forest—the whole disgusting chain of German-fascist intrigue, murder and fraud which together comprise the "Katyn affair" has been brought to light. Documents published today prove incontrovertibly that the Polish war prisoners were in the camps west of Smolensk up to and including September, 1941, and that in the autumn of 1941 the German occupation authorities organized the wholesale shooting of the Polish war prisoners in the Katyn forest. . . .

The findings of the special commission expose the methods by which the German-fascist butchers fabricated the "Katyn affair." They tried by means of intrigue, coaxing, bribery, threats and brutal torture to find "witnesses" and to extort false evidence from them. More, they not only shot the war prisoners in the Katyn camp but brought there the corpses of prisoners shot in other places. The report of the special commission states that "in preparation for this malicious fraud the German occupation authorities employed in the work of uncovering the graves and removing documents and other material, the evidence of which might incriminate them, about 500 Russian war prisoners, who when this work was completed, were shot by the Germans."

The sadistic ill-treatment by the Hitlerites of their victims, the wholesale massacres and the methods of these massacres, are in the same category with the monstrous crimes which the Hitlerite murderers perpetrated on Soviet soil and which were exposed at the Krasnodar and Kharkov trials.

The investigations of the special commission furnish documentary proof that the massacres in the Katyn forest were committed on direct orders from Berlin in pursuance of the policy of physically exterminating the Slav peoples. . . .

U.S. GOVERNMENT FINDINGS

This committee unanimously finds, beyond any question of reasonable doubt, that the Soviet NKVD (People's Commissariat of Internal Affairs) committed the mass murders of the Polish officers and intellectual leaders in the Katyn Forest near Smolensk, Russia.

The evidence, testimony, records and exhibits recorded by this committee through the investigations and hearings during the last 9 months overwhelmingly will show the people of the world that Russia is directly responsible for the Katyn massacre. Throughout our entire proceedings, there has not been a scintilla of proof or even any remote circumstantial evidence presented that could indict any other nation in this international crime.

It is an established fact that approximately 15,000 Polish prisoners were interned in three Soviet camps: Kozielsk, Starobielsk, and Ostashkov in the winter of 1939–40. With the exception of 400 prisoners, these men have not been heard from, seen, or found since the spring of 1940. Following the discovery of the graves in 1943, when the Germans occupied this territory, they claimed there were 11,000 Poles buried in Katyn. The Russians recovered the territory from the Germans in September 1943 and likewise they stated that 11,000 Poles were buried in those mass graves.

Evidence heard by this committee repeatedly points to the certainty that only those prisoners interned at Kozielsk were massacred in the Katyn Forest. Testimony of the Polish Red Cross officials definitely established that 4,143 bodies were actually exhumed from the 7 mass graves. On the basis of further evidence, we are equally certain that the rest of the 15,000 Polish officers—those interned at Starobielsk and Ostashkov—were executed in a similar brutal manner. Those from Starobielsk were disposed of near Kharkov, and several witnesses stated that the Ostashkov prisoners were placed on barges and drowned in the White Sea. Thus the committee believes that there are at least two other ''Katyns'' in Russia.

No one could entertain any doubt of Russian guilt for the Katyn massacre when the following evidence is considered:

1. The Russians refused to allow the International Committee of the Red Cross to make a neutral investigation of the German charges in 1943.
2. The Russians failed to invite any neutral observers to participate in their own investigation in 1944, except a group of newspaper correspondents taken to Katyn who agreed ''the whole show was staged'' by the Soviets.
3. The Russians failed to produce sufficient evidence at Nuremberg—even though they were in charge of the prosecution—to obtain a ruling on the German guilt for Katyn by the International Military Tribunal.
4. This committee issued formal and public invitations to the Government of the U.S.S.R. to present any evidence pertaining to the Katyn Massacre. The Soviets refused to participate in any phase of this committee's investigation.
5. The overwhelming testimony of prisoners formerly interned at the three camps, of medical experts who performed autopsies on the massacred bodies, and of observers taken to the scene of the crime conclusively confirms this committee's findings.
6. Polish Government leaders and military men who conferred with Stalin, Molotov, and NKVD chief Beria for a year and a half attempted without success to locate the Polish prisoners before the Germans discovered Katyn. This renders further proof that the Soviets purposely misled the Poles in denying any knowledge of the whereabouts of their officers when, in fact, the Poles already were buried in the mass graves at Katyn.
7. The Soviets have demonstrated through their highly organized propaganda machinery that they fear to have the people behind the iron curtain know the truth about Katyn. This is proven by their reaction to our committee's efforts and the amount of newspaper space and radio time devoted to denouncing the work of our committee. They also republished in all newspapers behind the iron curtain the allegedly ''neutral'' Russian report of 1944. The worldwide campaign of slander by the Soviets against our committee is also construed as another effort to block this investigation....

DOCUMENT 13

The Dissolution of the Communist International

22 May 1943

Editor's commentary: Below is the text of a resolution passed by the Presidium of the Executive Committee of the Communist International, announcing the dissolution of the

Pravda, 22 May 1943. *Source:* U.S. Congress, House Committee on Un-American Activities, *The Communist Conspiracy: Strategy and Tactics of World Communism,* part 1, ''Communism Outside the United States,'' section B, ''The USSR,'' 84th Congress, 2d session, House report no. 2243 (U.S. Government Printing Office, 1956), pp. 85–88, *excerpts.*

Communist International as the directing center of the international working class movement, in part to soothe Western public opinion after the discovery by the Nazis of the Soviet-perpetrated Katyn Forest massacre. It is interesting to note that in this statement the role of the "vanguard of the workers" in the anticipated liberation of Europe from Nazi occupation is not diminished.

The historic role of the Communist International, which was founded in 1919 as a result of the political union of the great majority of old, prewar working-class parties, consisted in upholding the principles of Marxism...in helping to promote the consolidation in a number of countries of the vanguard of the foremost workers in real working-class parties, and in helping them to mobilise the workers for the defence of their economic and political interests and for the struggle against Fascism and the war the latter was preparing and for support of the Soviet Union as the chief bulwark against Fascism....

But long before the war it became more and more clear that, with the increasing complications in the internal and international relations of the various countries, any sort of international centre would encounter insuperable obstacles in solving the problems facing the movement in each separate country. The deep differences of the historic paths of development of various countries, the differences in their character and even contradictions in their social orders, the differences in the level and tempo of their economic and political development, the differences, finally, in the degree of consciousness and organisation of the workers, conditioned the different problems facing the working class of the various countries.

The whole development of events in the last quarter of a century, and the experience accumulated by the Communist International convincingly showed that the organisational form of uniting the workers chosen by the first congress of the Communist International answered the conditions of the first stages of the working-class movement but has been outgrown by the growth of this movement and by the complications of its problems in separate countries, and has even become a drag on the further strengthening of the national working-class parties....

THE FUNDAMENTAL TASK

In the countries of the Hitlerite *bloc* the fundamental task of the working class...consists in giving all help for the defeat of this *bloc,* by sabotage of the Hitlerite military machine from within, and by helping to overthrow the Governments who are guilty of the war. In the countries of the anti-Hitlerite coalition, the sacred duty of the widest masses of the people, and in the first place of the foremost workers consists in aiding by every means the military efforts of the governments of these countries aimed at the speediest defeat of the Hitlerite *bloc* and the assurance of the friendship of nations based on their equality.

...At the same time, the war of liberation of the freedom-loving peoples against the Hitlerite tyranny, which has brought into movement the masses of the people, uniting them without difference of party or religion in the ranks of a powerful anti-Hitlerite coalition, has demonstrated with still greater clearness that the general national upsurge and mobilisation of the people for the speediest victory over the enemy can be best of all and most fruitfully carried out by the vanguard of the working-class movement of each separate country....

THE PROPOSAL

...The Presidium of the Executive Committee of the Communist International, in the circumstances of the World War not being able to convene a congress of the Communist International, puts forward the following proposal for ratification by the sections of the Communist International:

The Communist International, as the directing centre of the International Working-Class

Movement, is to be dissolved, thus freeing the section of the Communist International from their obligations arising from the statutes and resolutions of the Congresses of the Communist International.

The Presidium of the Executive Committee of the Communist International calls on all supporters of the Communist International to concentrate their energies on whole-hearted support of and active participation in the war of liberation of the peoples and States of the anti-Hitlerite coalition for the speediest defeat of the deadly enemy of the working class and toilers—German-Fascism and its associates and vassals.

The Presidium of the Executive Committee of the Communist International

(Signed): G. Dimitrov, E. Ercoli, W. Florin, K. Gottwald, V. Kolarov, J. Koplenig, O. Kuusinen, D. Manuilsky, A. Marty, W. Pieck, M. Thorez, A. Zhdanov.

The following representatives of Communist Parties also append their signatures to the present resolution: Bianco (Italy), Dolores Ibarruri (Spain), Lekhtinin (Finland), Anna Pauker (Rumania), Matthias Rakosi (Hungary).

Moscow, May 15, 1943

DOCUMENT 14

Soviet Government Statements on Soviet-Polish Relations

January 1944

Editor's commentary: As the German front receded from the Soviet Union and into Eastern Europe, changes became apparent in the Soviet attitude toward the Polish government-in-exile in London. Most important was a revision of earlier Soviet statements regarding the restoration of Poland to its prewar borders. The Treaty of Riga of 1921, which had established these borders, was denounced as "imposed" on the Soviet state. The Soviet Union was now intent on retaining territory it had acquired as a result of the Nazi-Soviet pact. As "compensation" the Soviet statement suggests that "ancient Polish lands" should be reclaimed from Germany. These territorial revisions and the Polish problem as a whole remained major issues of conflict among the Allies into the postwar period.

DECLARATION OF THE SOVIET GOVERNMENT ON SOVIET-POLISH RELATIONS

TASS, 11 January 1944

On January 5 in London was published a declaration of the emigre Polish Government on Soviet-Polish relations which contains a number of incorrect assertions, including an incorrect assertion about the Soviet-Polish frontier.

As is well known, the Soviet constitution established the Soviet-Polish frontier in conformity with the will of the population of Western Ukraine and Western Byelorussia, as expressed through a plebiscite conducted on a broad democratic basis in 1939. Then the territories of the Western Ukraine in which Ukrainians form the overwhelming majority of the population were incorporated with the Soviet Ukraine, and the territories of Western Byelorussia in which Byelorussians form an overwhelming majority of the population were incorporated with Soviet Byelorussia. The injustice committed by the Riga Treaty of 1921, which was imposed upon the Soviet Union, in regard to the Ukrainians inhabiting the Western Ukraine and the Byelorussians inhabiting Western Byelorussia, was thus rectified.

The incorporation of Western Ukraine and Western Byelorussia with the Soviet Union not only did not violate the interests of Poland, but

USSR Information Bulletin, vol. 4, no. 5 (13 January 1944), p. 1, and vol. 4, no. 8, (20 January 1944), p. 1.

on the contrary created a reliable foundation for stable and permanent friendship between the Polish people and its neighbors—the Ukrainian and Byelorussian and Russian peoples.

The Soviet Government has repeatedly stated that it stands for the reestablishment of a strong and independent Poland and for friendship between the Soviet Union and Poland. The Soviet Government declares again that it seeks to establish friendship between the USSR and Poland on the basis of stable, good neighborly relations and mutual respect and, if the Polish people will so desire—on the basis of an alliance for mutual assistance against the Germans as the chief enemies of the Soviet Union and Poland....

At present the possibility is opening for the rebirth of Poland as a strong and independent state. However, Poland must be reborn not through the seizure of Ukrainian and Byelorussian lands, but through the restoration to Poland of lands which belonged to Poland from time immemorial and were wrested by the Germans from her. Only in this way trust and friendship could be established between the Polish, Ukrainian, Byelorussian and Russian peoples.

The eastern frontiers of Poland can be established by agreement with the Soviet Union. The Soviet Government does not regard the frontiers of 1939 as unalterable. These frontiers can be modified in Poland's favor so that the areas in which the Polish population forms a majority be turned over to Poland. In this case the Soviet Polish frontier could pass approximately along the so-called Curzon line, which was adopted in 1919 by the Supreme Council of the Allied Powers, and which provides for inclusion of the Western Ukraine and Western Byelorussia into the Soviet Union.

The western frontiers of Poland must be extended through incorporation with Poland of ancient Polish lands previously wrested by Germany, without which it is impossible to unite the whole Polish people in its state, which thereby will receive a needed outlet to the Baltic Sea.

The just aspiration of the Polish people for its full reunion in a strong and independent state must receive recognition and support.

The emigre Polish government, isolated from its people, proved incapable of establishment of friendly relations with the Soviet Union. It also proved incapable of organizing active struggle against the German invaders within Poland herself. Furthermore, by its incorrect policy it not infrequently plays into the hands of the German occupationists.

However, the interests of Poland and the Soviet Union consist in that stable, friendly relations be established between our countries and that the people of Poland and the Soviet Union unite in struggle against the common external enemy, as demanded by the common cause of all the Allies.

TASS STATEMENT

17 January 1944

In connection with the declaration of the Polish government in London of January 15, TASS has been authorized to state the following:

1. The declaration of the Polish government, in which the main question of the recognition of the Curzon line as the Soviet-Polish frontier is completely evaded and ignored, cannot be regarded otherwise than as a rejection of the Curzon line.

2. As to the proposal of the Polish government on the opening of official negotiations between it and the Soviet Government, the Soviet Government believes that this proposal is intended to mislead public opinion, since it is not difficult to understand that the Soviet Government cannot enter into official negotiations with a government with which diplomatic relations have been interrupted. Soviet circles remind that diplomatic relations with the Polish government were interrupted through the fault of that government because

of its active participation in the hostile anti-Soviet slanderous campaign of the German occupationists in connection with the alleged Katyn murders.

3. In the opinion of Soviet circles, the above circumstances demonstrate once more that the present Polish government does not wish to establish good-neighborly relations with the Soviet Union.

Conversations with Stalin

Milovan Djilas

1944

Editor's commentary: Milovan Djilas was Josip Broz Tito's second-in-command in Yugoslavia during and after the Second World War. By the early 1950s, Djilas began to have second thoughts about aspects of communism, resulting in his classic critique of the communist system, The New Class. *In* Conversations with Stalin, *Djilas recalls wartime and early postwar meetings with Stalin in the Kremlin. These excerpts are from 1944 and presage both the establishment of Soviet control over Eastern Europe and the eventual conflict between Stalin and Tito in 1948. They also suggest Stalin's affinity for military affairs and power politics in the mold of his predecessors, the Russian czars.*

...Stalin teased Tito with obvious deliberateness—in a manner that had in it as much malice as jest. He did it by speaking unfavorably of the Yugoslav Army while flattering the Bulgarian

---

Excerpt from "Doubts" in *Conversations with Stalin,* Michael B. Petrovich (trans.), pp. 112–115. Copyright © 1962 by Harcourt Brace Jovanovich. Reprinted by permission of the publisher.

Army. That previous winter Yugoslav units including many draftees who were engaged for the first time in very serious frontal attacks had suffered defeats, and Stalin, who was apparently well informed, took the opportunity to point out, "The Bulgarian Army is better than the Yugoslav. The Bulgars had their weaknesses and enemies in their ranks. But they executed a few score—and now everything is in order. The Bulgarian Army is very good—drilled and disciplined. And yours, the Yugoslav—they are still Partisans, unfit for serious front-line fighting. Last winter one German regiment broke up a whole division of yours. A regiment beat a division!"

A bit later Stalin proposed a toast to the Yugoslav Army, but he did not forget to add to it, "But which will yet fight well on level ground!"

Tito had kept from reacting to Stalin's comments. Whenever Stalin made some witty remark at our expense, Tito looked at me silently with a strained smile, and I returned his look with solidarity and sympathy. But when Stalin said that the Bulgarian Army was better than the Yugoslav, Tito could not stand it, and shouted that the Yugoslav Army would quickly rid itself of its weaknesses.

One could detect in the relations between Stalin and Tito something special, tacit—as though these two had a grudge against one [an]other, but each was holding back for his own reasons. Stalin took care not to offend Tito personally in any way, but at the same time he kept taking sideswiping jabs at conditions in Yugoslavia. On the other hand, Tito treated Stalin with respect, as one would one's senior, but resentment could also be detected, especially at Stalin's remarks on Yugoslav conditions.

At one point Tito brought out that there were new phenomena in socialism and that socialism was now being achieved in ways different from those of the past, which gave Stalin an opportunity to say, "Today socialism is possible even under the English monarchy. Revolution is no longer necessary everywhere. Just recently a delegation of British Labourites was here, and we talked about this in particular. Yes, there is much that is new. Yes, socialism is possible even under an English king.''

As is known, Stalin never upheld such a view publicly. The British Labourites soon gained a majority at the elections and nationalized over twenty per cent of the industrial production. Nevertheless, Stalin never recognized these measures as being socialistic nor the Labourites as being socialists. I maintain that he did not do so primarily because of differences and clashes with the Labour Government in foreign policy.

In the course of the conversation about this, I interjected that in Yugoslavia there existed in essence a Soviet type of government; the Communist Party held all the key positions and there was no serious opposition party. But Stalin did not agree with this. ''No, your government is not Soviet—you have something in between De Gaulle's France and the Soviet Union.''

Tito remarked that in Yugoslavia something new was taking shape. But this discussion remained unfinished. Within myself I could not agree with Stalin's view; neither did I think that I differed with Tito.

Stalin presented his views on the distinctive nature of the war that was being waged: ''This war is not as in the past; whoever occupies a territory also imposes on it his own social system. Everyone imposes his own system as far as his army can reach. It cannot be otherwise.''

He also pointed out, without going into long explanations, the meaning of his Panslavic policy. ''If the Slavs keep united and maintain solidarity, no one in the future will be able to move a finger. Not even a finger!'' he repeated, emphasizing his thought by cleaving the air with his forefinger.

Someone expressed doubt that the Germans would be able to recuperate within fifty years. But Stalin was of a different opinion. ''No, they will recover, and very quickly. That is a highly developed industrial country with an extremely qualified and numerous working class and technical intelligentsia. Give them twelve to fifteen years and they'll be on their feet again. And this is why the unity of the Slavs is important. But even apart from this, if the unity of the Slavs exists, no one will dare move a finger.''

At one point he got up, hitched up his pants as though he was about to wrestle or to box, and cried out almost in a transport, ''The war shall soon be over. We shall recover in fifteen or twenty years, and then we'll have another go at it.''

There was something terrible in his words: a horrible war was still going on. Yet there was something impressive, too, about his cognizance of the paths he had to take, the inevitability that faced the world in which he lived and the movement that he headed.

The rest of what was said that evening was hardly worth remembering. . . .

<hr>

DOCUMENT 16

The Yalta Agreement

12 February 1945

Editor's commentary: The key agreement reached at Yalta between Stalin, Churchill, and Roosevelt outlined the basic mechanics of political administration of postwar Germany and the political character of Eastern European governments. A separate secret agreement (not reproduced here) also provided for Soviet entry into the war against Japan as soon as Germany was defeated. It is not difficult to see the sources of subsequent friction and disagreement among the Allies over interpretation, particularly over the issue of Polish independence and free elections. Yalta has been seen as a sellout of Eastern Europe by an enfeebled Roosevelt to Stalin. However, it is important to note, as Ghita Ionescu explains at the

Department of State Bulletin, vol. 12, no. 295, 18 February 1945, pp. 213–216, *excerpts.*

beginning of this chapter, that others bear a good deal of the responsibility. Also, liberation of nearly all of Eastern Europe by the Red Army played the decisive role in the political order that was eventually established in that region.

...The following statement is made by the Prime Minister of Great Britain, the President of the United States of America, and the Chairman of the Council of People's Commissars of the Union of Soviet Socialist Republics on the results of the Crimean Conference:

THE DEFEAT OF GERMANY

We have considered and determined the military plans of the three allied powers for the final defeat of the common enemy.... The fullest information has been interchanged. The timing, scope and coordination of new and even more powerful blows to be launched by our armies and air forces into the heart of Germany from the East, West, North, and South have been fully agreed and planned in detail.

Our combined military plans will be made known only as we execute them, but we believe that the very close working partnership among the three staffs attained at this Conference will result in shortening the War. Meetings of the three staffs will be continued in the future whenever the need arises.

Nazi Germany is doomed. The German people will only make the cost of their defeat heavier to themselves by attempting to continue a hopeless resistance.

THE OCCUPATION AND CONTROL OF GERMANY

We have agreed on common policies and plans for enforcing the unconditional surrender terms which we shall impose together on Nazi Germany after German armed resistance has been finally crushed. These terms will not be made known until the final defeat of Germany has been accomplished. Under the agreed plan, the forces of the three powers will each occupy a separate zone of Germany. Coordinated administration and control has been provided for under the plan through a central control commission consisting of the Supreme Commanders of the three powers with headquarters in Berlin. It has been agreed that France should be invited by the three powers, if she should so desire, to take over a zone of occupation, and to participate as a fourth member of the control commission. The limits of the French zone will be agreed by the four governments concerned through their representatives on the European Advisory Commission.

It is our inflexible purpose to destroy German militarism and Nazism and to ensure that Germany will never again be able to disturb the peace of the world. We are determined to disarm and disband all German armed forces; break up for all time the German General Staff that has repeatedly contrived the resurgence of German militarism; remove or destroy all German military equipment; eliminate or control all German industry that could be used for military production; bring all war criminals to just and swift punishment and exact reparation in kind for the destruction wrought by the Germans; wipe out the Nazi Party, Nazi laws, organizations and institutions, remove all Nazi and militarist influences from public office and from the cultural and economic life of the German people; and take in harmony such other measures in Germany as may be necessary to the future peace and safety of the world. It is not our purpose to destroy the people of Germany, but only when Nazism and militarism have been extirpated will there be hope for a decent life for Germans, and a place for them in the comity of nations.

REPARATION BY GERMANY

We have considered the question of the damage caused by Germany to the allied nations in this war and recognized it as just that Germany be obliged to make compensation for this damage in kind to the greatest extent possible. A commission for the compensation of damage will be established. The commission will be instructed to consider the question of the extent and methods for compensating damage caused by Germany to the allied countries. The commission will work in Moscow.

UNITED NATIONS CONFERENCE

We are resolved upon the earliest possible establishment with our Allies of a general international organization to maintain peace and security. We believe that this is essential, both to prevent aggression and to remove the political, economic and social causes of war through the close and continuing collaboration of all peace-loving peoples....

DECLARATION ON LIBERATED EUROPE

...The establishment of order in Europe and the rebuilding of national economic life must be achieved by processes which will enable the liberated people to destroy the last vestiges of Nazism and Fascism and to create democratic institutions of their own choice. This a principle of the Atlantic Charter....

To foster the conditions in which the liberated peoples may exercise these rights, the three governments will jointly assist the people in any European liberated state or former Axis satellite state in Europe where in their judgment conditions require (a) to establish conditions of internal peace; (b) to carry out emergency measures for the relief of distressed people; (c) to form interim governmental authorities broadly representative of all democratic elements in the population and pledged to the earliest possible establishment through free elections of governments responsive to the will of the people; and (d) to facilitate where necessary the holding of such elections.

The three governments will consult the other United Nations and provisional authorities or other governments in Europe when matters of direct interest to them are under consideration....

POLAND

A new situation has been created in Poland as a result of her complete liberation by the Red Army. This calls for the establishment of a Polish Provisional Government which can be more broadly based than was possible before the recent liberation of Western Poland. The Provisional Government which is now functioning in Poland should therefore be reorganized on a broader democratic basis with the inclusion of democratic leaders from Poland itself and from Poles abroad. This new government shall be called the Polish Provisional Government of National Unity.... This Polish Provisional Government of National Unity shall be pledged to the holding of free and unfettered elections as soon as possible on the basis of universal suffrage and secret ballot. In these elections all democratic and anti-Nazi parties shall have the right to take part and to put forward candidates....

The three heads of government consider that the eastern frontier of Poland should follow the Curzon line with digressions from it in some regions of five to eight kilometres in favor of Poland. They recognize that Poland must receive substantial accessions of territory in the north and west. They feel that the opinion of the new Polish Provisional Government of National Unity should be sought in due course on the extent of these accessions and that the final delimitation of the western frontier of Poland should thereafter await the Peace Conference.

YUGOSLAVIA

We have agreed to recommend to Marshal Tito and Dr. Subasic that the agreement between them should be put into effect immediately, and that a new government should be formed on the basis of that agreement....

UNITY FOR PEACE AS FOR WAR

Our meeting here in the Crimea has reaffirmed our common determination to maintain and strengthen in the peace to come that unity of purpose and of action which has made victory possible and certain for the United Nations in this war. We believe that this is a sacred obligation which our Governments owe to our peoples and to all the peoples of the world....

Victory in this war and establishment of the proposed international organization will provide the greatest opportunity in all history to create in the years to come the essential conditions of such a peace.

Signed: Winston S. Churchill,
Franklin D. Roosevelt, J. Stalin

DOCUMENT 17

Speech of 9 February 1946

J. V. Stalin

Editor's commentary: In one of Stalin's earliest postwar speeches to the Supreme Soviet, he reemphasized the Marxist-Leninist perspective that the war which had just concluded was the fault of capitalism, thereby questioning implicitly continuation of the alliance with the Western Allies. While Stalin also suggested that some attention will be paid to improving living conditions of the Soviet people after all the hardships they endured during the war, major Soviet sacrifices were seen as necessary to restore and surpass Soviet prewar industrial might (defense industry) and technical-scientific knowledge (atomic power).

U.S. Congress, House Committee on Foreign Affairs, *The Strategy and Tactics of World Communism*, 80th Congress, 2d session, House document no. 619 (Washington, DC: U.S. Government Printing Office, 1948), pp. 168–178, *excerpts.*

Comrades! Eight years have elapsed since the last election to the Supreme Soviet. This was a period abounding in events of decisive moment. The first four years passed in intensive effort on the part of Soviet men and women to fulfill the third Five-Year Plan. The second four years embrace the events of the war against the German and Japanese aggressors, the events of the Second World War. Undoubtedly, the war was the principal event in the past period.

It would be wrong to think that the Second World War was a casual occurrence or the result of mistakes of any particular statesmen, though mistakes undoubtedly were made. Actually, the war was the inevitable result of the development of world economic and political forces on the basis of modern monopoly capitalism. Marxists have declared more than once that the capitalist system of world economy harbors elements of general crises and armed conflicts and that, hence, the development of world capitalism in our time proceeds not in the form of smooth and even progress but through crises and military catastrophes.

The fact is, that the unevenness of development of the capitalist countries usually leads in time to violent disturbance of equilibrium in the world system of capitalism, that one group of capitalism considers itself worse provided than others with raw materials and markets usually making attempts to alter the situation and repartition the "spheres of influence" in its favor by armed force. The result is a splitting of the capitalist world into two hostile camps and war between them.

Perhaps military catastrophes might be avoided if it were possible for raw materials and markets to be periodically redistributed among the various countries in accordance with their economic importance, by agreement and peaceable settlement. But that is impossible to do under present capitalist conditions of the development of world economy.

Thus the First World War was the result of the first crisis of the capitalist system of world economy, and the Second World War was the result of a second crisis....

PLANS FOR FUTURE

Now a few words about the Communist Party's plans of work for the immediate future. As is known these plans are set forth in the new Five-Year Plan which is shortly to be endorsed. The principal aims of the new Five-Year Plan are to rehabilitate the ravaged areas of the country, to restore the prewar level in industry and agriculture, and then to surpass this level in more or less substantial measure. To say nothing of the fact that the rationing system will shortly be abolished (*stormy, prolonged applause*), special attention will be devoted to extending the production of consumer goods, to raising the living standard of the working people by steadily lowering the prices of all goods (*stormy, prolonged applause*), and to the widespread construction of all manner of scientific research institutions (*applause*) that can give science the opportunity to develop its potentialities. (*Stormy applause.*)

I have no doubt that if we give our scientists proper assistance they will be able in the near future not only to overtake but to surpass the achievements of science beyond the boundaries of our country. (*Prolonged applause.*)

As regards the plans for a longer period ahead, the Party means to organize a new mighty upsurge in the national economy, which would allow us to increase our industrial production, for example three times over as compared with the prewar period. We must achieve a situation where our industry can produce annually up to 50 million tons of pig iron (*prolonged applause*), up to 500 million tons of coal (*prolonged applause*), and up to 60 million tons of oil (*prolonged applause*). Only under such conditions can we consider that our homeland will be guaranteed against all possible accidents. (*Stormy applause.*) That will take three more Five-Year Plans, I should think, if not more. But it can be done and we must do it. (*Stormy applause.*)...

DOCUMENT 18

The American Plan for the Enthrallment of Europe

Andrei Zhdanov

September 1947

Editor's commentary: At the founding conference of the Communist Information Bureau, Andrei Zhdanov delivered the Marxist-Leninist critique of both the Marshall Plan and the Truman Doctrine as aggressive imperialist schemes to "enslave" the Western Europeans and acquire military bases from which a new war could be launched against the Soviet Union and its allies. Zhdanov exhorted European Communists to struggle against these plans.

The aggressive and frankly expansionist course to which American imperialism has committed itself since the end of World War II finds expression in both the foreign and home policy of the United States.... Although the U.S.A. suffered comparatively little from the war, the vast majority of the Americans do not want another war, with its accompanying sacrifices and lim-

U.S. Congress, House Committee on Foreign Affairs, *The Strategy and Tactics of World Communism*, 80th Congress, 2d session, House document no. 619 (Washington, DC: U.S. Government Printing Office, 1948), pp. 211–230.

itations. This has induced monopoly capital and its servitors among the ruling circles in the United States to resort to extraordinary means in order to crush the opposition at home to the aggressive expansionist course and to secure a free hand for the further prosecution of this dangerous policy.

...The expansionist foreign policy inspired and conducted by the American reactionaries envisages simultaneous action along all lines: (1) strategical military measures, (2) economic expansion, and (3) ideological struggle....

At this present juncture the expansionist ambitions of the United States find concrete expression in the Truman doctrine and the Marshall Plan. Although they differ in form of presentation, both are an expression of a single policy, they are both an embodiment of the American design to enslave Europe.

The main features of the Truman doctrine as applied to Europe are as follows:

1. Creation of American bases in the Eastern Mediterranean with the purpose of establishing American supremacy in that area.
2. Demonstrative support of the reactionary regimes in Greece and Turkey as bastions of American imperialism against the new democracies in the Balkans....
3. Unremitting pressure on the countries of the new democracy, as expressed, in false accusations of totalitarianism and expansionist ambitions....

The unfavorable reception which the Truman doctrine was met with accounts for the necessity of the appearance of the Marshall Plan which is a more carefully veiled attempt to carry through the same expansionist policy....

The assessment given by the countries of the anti-imperialist camp of the "Marshall Plan" has been completely confirmed by the whole course of developments. In relation to the "Marshall Plan," the camp of democratic countries have proved that they are a mighty force standing guard over the independence and sovereignty of all European nations, that they refuse to yield to browbeating and intimidation, just as they refuse to be deceived by the hypocritical manoeuvres of dollar diplomacy....

The exposure of the American plan for the economic enslavement of the European countries is an indisputable service rendered by the foreign policy of the USSR and the new democracies....

The chief danger to the working class at this present juncture lies in underrating its own strength and overrating the strength of the enemy....The Communist Parties must therefore head the resistance to the plans of imperialist expansion and aggression along every line—state, economical and ideological; they must rally their ranks and unite their efforts on the basis of a common anti-imperialist and democratic platform, and gather around them all the democratic and patriotic forces of the people.

A special task devolves on the fraternal Communist Parties of France, Italy, Great Britain and other countries. They must take up the standard in defence of the national independence and sovereignty of their countries....If, in their struggle against the attempts to economically and politically enthrall their countries, they are able to take the lead of all the forces prepared to uphold the national honour and independence, no plans for the enthrallment of Europe can possibly succeed.

Establishment of the Communist Information Bureau

September 1947

Editor's commentary: The birth of the Cominform was seen by the West as a thinly veiled attempt to resurrect the disbanded Comintern. Stalin no doubt saw the need for some formal organizational structures to facilitate the presentation of communist unity in an Eastern Europe occupied by Soviet forces. The Cominform was likely meant to fill that need. Its base was to be Belgrade, not Moscow. However, it soon ran into trouble as the Yugoslav Communist leader Tito refused to accept Stalin's dictates for Yugoslavia.

TEXT OF RESOLUTION

The text of a resolution adopted by the conference follows:

The conference states that the absence of connections between Communist parties who have taken part in this conference is in the present situation a serious shortcoming. Experience has shown that such division between Communist parties is incorrect and harmful. The requirement for an exchange of experience and voluntary coordination of actions of the separate parties has become particularly necessary now in conditions of the complicated post-war international situation and when the disunity of Communist parties may lead to damage for the working class.

Because of this, members of the conference agreed on the following:

First, to set up an Information Bureau of representatives of the Communist party of Yugoslavia, the Bulgarian Workers party (of Communists) of Rumania, the Hungarian Communist party, the Polish Workers party, the All-Union Communist party (bolshevik), the Communist party of France, the Communist party of Czechoslovakia, the Communist party of Italy.

Second, the task given to the Information Bureau is to organize and exchange experience and, in case of necessity, coordinate the activity of communist parties on foundation of mutual agreement.

Third, the Information Bureau will have in it representatives of the Central Committee—two from each Central Committee. Delegations of the Central Committee must be appointed and replaced by the Central Committees.

Fourth, the Information Bureau is to have printed an organ—fortnightly and, later on, weekly. The organ is to be published in French and Russian and, if possible, in other languages.

Fifth, the Information Bureau is to be in Belgrade.

From a communiqué of 5 October 1947. *Source:* U.S. Congress, House Committee on Foreign Affairs, *Strategy and Tactics of World Communism*, 80th Congress, 2d session, House document no. 619 (Washington, DC: U.S. Government Printing Office, 1948), pp. 207–211, *excerpts*.

Expulsion of Yugoslavia from the Cominform

28 June 1948

Editor's commentary: Attempts by Stalin to subvert Yugoslav sovereignty were resisted by Tito and many loyal to him in the Yugoslav Party. Soviet criticism about the process of building socialism in Yugoslavia and complaints about how Soviet diplomats and military advisers in Yugoslavia were

For a Lasting Peace, for a People's Democracy! [the Cominform's newspaper], 1 July 1948, p. 1, *excerpts*.

being treated became the vehicle by which Stalin indicted the Yugoslavs for "betraying" communism. The exchange of a series of letters from March to June 1948 culminated in the expulsion of Yugoslavia from the nine-member Cominform. The Cominform note indicting Tito also encouraged Yugoslavs to "replace" their leaders. The Soviet-Yugoslav break destroyed the unity of what had been until that time monolithic international communism. This unity would never again be fully restored even after Stalin's death and Khrushchev's move to reintegrate Yugoslavia into the movement. With the split, independent "national communism" became a viable alternative model to a Soviet-sponsored and dominated system. Stalin's fabled threat that "I will bend my little finger and Tito will be no more" proved to be impossible to effect.

RESOLUTION OF THE INFORMATION BUREAU CONCERNING THE SITUATION IN THE COMMUNIST PARTY OF YUGOSLAVIA

The Information Bureau…upon discussing the situation in the Communist Party of Yugoslavia and announcing that the representatives of the Communist Party of Yugoslavia had refused to attend the meeting of the Information Bureau, unaminously reached the following conclusions:

1. The Information Bureau notes that recently the leadership of the Communist Party of Yugoslavia has pursued an incorrect line on the main question of home and foreign policy, a line which represents a departure from Marxism-Leninism….

2. The Information Bureau declares that the leadership of the Yugoslav Communist Party is pursuing an unfriendly policy toward the Soviet Union and the CPSU (B). An undignified policy of defaming Soviet military experts and discrediting the Soviet Union, has been carried out in Yugoslavia. A special regime was instituted for Soviet civilian experts in Yugoslavia, whereby they were under surveillance of Yugoslav state security organs and were continually followed….

All these and similar facts show that the leaders of the Communist Party of Yugoslavia have taken a stand unworthy of Communists, and have begun to identify the foreign policy of the Soviet Union with the foreign policy of the imperialist powers, behaving toward the Soviet Union in the same manner as they behave to the bourgeois states. Precisely because of this anti-Soviet stand, slanderous propaganda about the "degeneration" of the CPSU and the "degeneration" of the USSR, and so on, borrowed from the arsenal of counter-revolutionary Trotskyism, is current within the Central Committee of the Communist Party of Yugoslavia.

The Information Bureau denounces this anti-Soviet attitude of the leaders of the Communist Party of Yugoslavia, as being incompatible with Marxism-Leninism and only appropriate to nationalists.

3. In home policy, the leaders of the Communist Party of Yugoslavia are departing from the positions of the working class and are breaking with the Marxist theory of classes and class struggle. They deny that there is a growth of capitalist elements in their country, and consequently, a sharpening of the class struggle in the countryside….

4. The Information Bureau considers that the leadership of the Communist Party of Yugoslavia is revising the Marxist-Leninist teachings about the Party….

5. The Information Bureau considers that the bureaucratic regime created inside the Party by its leaders is disastrous for the life and development of the Yugoslav Communist Party. There is no inner Party democracy, no elections, and no criticism and self-criticism in the Party. Despite the unfounded assurances of Comrades Tito and Kardelj, the majority of the Central Committee of the Communist Party of Yugoslavia is composed of co-opted,

and not of elected members. The Communist Party is actually in a state of semi-legality....

6. The Information Bureau considers that the criticism made by the Central Commitee of the Communist Party of the Soviet Union (B) and Central Committees of the other Communist parties of the mistakes of the Central Committee of the Communist Party of Yugoslavia, and who in this way rendered fraternal assistance to the Yugoslav Communist Party, provides the Communist Party of Yugoslavia with all the conditions necessary to speedily correct the mistakes committed....

7. Taking into account the situation in the Communist Party of Yugoslavia, and seeking to show the leaders of the Party the way out of this situation, the Central Committee of the Communist Party of the Soviet Union (B) and the Central Committees of other fraternal parties, suggested that the matter of the Yugoslav Communist Party should be discussed at a meeting of the Information Bureau, on the same, normal party footing as that on which the activities of other Communist Parties were discussed at the first meeting of the Information Bureau.

   However, the Yugoslav leaders rejected the repeated suggestions of the fraternal Communist Parties to discuss the situation in the Yugoslav Party at a meeting of the Information Bureau....

   The refusal of the Yugoslav Party to report to the Information Bureau on its actions and to listen to criticism by other Communist Parties means, in practice, a violation of the equality of the Communist Parties and is, in fact, tantamount to a demand for a privileged position for the Communist Party of Yugoslavia in the Information Bureau..

8. ...The Information Bureau unanimously concludes that by their anti-Party and anti-Soviet views, incompatible with Marxism-Leninism, by their whole attitude and their refusal to attend the meeting of the Information Bureau, the leaders of the Communist Party of Yu-

goslavia have placed themselves in opposition to the Communist Parties affiliated to the Information Bureau, have taken the path of seceding from the united socialist front against imperialism, have taken the path of betraying the cause of international solidarity of working people, and have taken up a position of nationalism.

The Information Bureau condemns this anti-Party policy and attitude of the Central Committee of the Communist Party of Yugoslavia.

The Information Bureau considers that, in view of all this, the Central Committee of the Communist Party of Yugoslavia has placed itself and the Yugoslav Party outside the family of the fraternal Communist Parties, outside the united Communist front and consequently outside the ranks of the Information Bureau.

The Information Bureau considers that the basis of these mistakes made by the leadership of the Communist Party of Yugoslavia lies in the undoubted fact that nationalist elements, which previously existed in a disguised form, managed in the course of the past five or six months to reach a dominant position in the leadership of the Communist Party of Yugoslavia, and that consequently the leadership of the Yugoslav Communist Party has broken with the international traditions of the Communist Party of Yugoslavia and has taken the road of nationalism....

The Information Bureau does not doubt that inside the Communist Party of Yugoslavia there are sufficient healthy elements, loyal to Marxism-Leninism, to the international traditions of the Yugoslav Communist Party and to the united socialist front.

Their task is to compel their present leaders to recognize their mistakes openly and honestly and to rectify them; to break with nationalism, return to internationalism; and in every way to consolidate the united socialist front against imperialism.

Should the present leaders of the Yugoslav Communist Party prove incapable of doing this, their job is to replace them and to advance a new internationalist leadership of their Party.

The Information Bureau does not doubt that the Communist Party of Yugoslavia will be able to fulfill this honourable task.

DOCUMENT 21

Soviet Views on NATO

1 April 1949

Editor's commentary: The following TASS statement concerning the formation of the North Atlantic Treaty Organization (NATO) is void of rhetoric and instead criticizes the treaty in light of UN agreements concluded during and after World War II. The statement maintains that the creation of NATO also abrogated previous bilateral agreements reached between the former allies. Summarizing, the Soviet argument against NATO was twofold: first, the Soviets were not threatening anyone, and second, the treaty upset previous agreements that the Soviet Union had with NATO members.

"On 31 March the Government of the Soviet Union forwarded through its ambassadors to the Governments of the United States of America, Great Britain, France, Belgium, Holland, Luxembourg, and Canada the following memorandum concerning the North Atlantic Treaty:

On 18 March the State Department of the United States published the text of the North Atlantic Treaty which the governments of the United States of America, Great Britain, France,

Belgium, the Netherlands, Luxembourg, and Canada intend to sign within the next few days.

The text of the North Atlantic Treaty fully supports what was said in the announcement of the USSR Ministry of Foreign Affairs of 29 January of this year, which is attached hereto, both as regards the aggressive aims of this treaty and the fact that the North Atlantic Treaty finds itself contradicting the principles and aims of the United Nations Organization and the commitments of the governments of the United States of America, Great Britain, and France, which were assumed by them under other treaties and agreements. The declarations contained in the North Atlantic Treaty, concerning its designation for defense and its recognition of the United Nations Organization's principles, serve aims which have nothing in common either with the tasks of self-defense of the parties to the treaty or with real recognition of the aims and principles of the United Nations Organization.

The parties to the North Atlantic Treaty are such great powers as the United States, Great Britain, and France. Therefore the treaty is directed neither against the United States of America, nor Great Britain, nor France. Of the great powers only the Soviet Union is excluded from among the parties to this treaty, which can be explained only by the fact that this treaty is directed against the Soviet Union. That the North Atlantic Treaty is directed against the USSR, as well as against the countries of people's democracy, was definitely pointed out also by official representatives of the United States of America, Great Britain, and France.

To justify the conclusion of the North Atlantic Treaty, references are being made to the fact that the Soviet Union has defensive treaties with the countries of people's democracy. These references, however, are utterly untenable.

All the treaties of the Soviet Union of friendship and mutual assistance with the countries of people's democracy possess a bilateral character and are directed only against the possibility of a repetition of German aggression, the danger

Pravda, 1 April 1949, p. 2, *excerpts*. Editor's translation.

of which not a single peace-loving state can forget. And so, the possibility of interpreting them as treaties which are to any degree at all aimed against the allies of the USSR in the last war, against the United States or Great Britain or France, is absolutely precluded.

Moreover, the USSR has the same kind of treaties against a repetition of German aggression not only with the countries of people's democracy, but also with Great Britain and France.

In contradistinction to this, the North Atlantic Treaty is not a bilateral, but a multilateral, treaty, which creates a closed grouping of states and, what is especially important, completely ignores the possibility of a repetition of German aggression; as a result, it does not have as its goal the prevention of a new German aggression. And, inasmuch as of the great powers which constituted the anti-Hitlerite coalition only the USSR is not a party to this treaty, the North Atlantic Treaty must be regarded as a treaty directed against one of the chief allies of the United States, Great Britain, and France in the last war—against the USSR....

The North Atlantic pact is designed to intimidate the states which do not agree to bow to the dictate of the Anglo-American grouping of powers which have laid claim to world domination, although the Second World War confirmed anew the bankruptcy of all such claims: it ended in the debacle of fascist Germany, which also had claims to world domination.

Among the participants in the North Atlantic Treaty are also countries whose governments expect to benefit at the expense of richer parties to the treaty and make various plans regarding the procurement of new credits and other material advantages.

At the same time, one cannot help but see the baselessness of the anti-Soviet motives of the North Atlantic Treaty, inasmuch as it is known to all that the Soviet Union does not intend to attack anyone and in no way threatens the United States of America, Great Britain, France, or the other parties to the treaty.

The conclusion of the North Atlantic Treaty and the creation of a new grouping of powers is motivated by the weakness of the United Nations Organization. It is completely apparent, however, that the North Atlantic Treaty does not serve the cause of strengthening the United Nations Organization, but on the contrary leads to the undermining of the very foundations of this international organization, because the establishment of the above grouping of powers not only does not correspond to the aims and principles of the United Nations Organization, but also runs counter to the charter of this organization.

The parties to the North Atlantic Treaty refer to the fact that this treaty is allegedly a regional agreement envisaged by article 52 of the United Nations Charter. But such references are utterly baseless and untenable. There can be no question whatsover of any regional character of this Treaty, inasmuch as the union of states envisaged by this Treaty embraces states situated in both hemispheres of the globe and does not have as its goal the settlement of any regional problems. This is also confirmed by the fact that, as has already been announced, states which are not members of the United Nations Organization (Italy, Portugal) are being drawn into participation in the North Atlantic Treaty, even though article 52 of the United Nations Charter has in view the conclusion of regional agreements only among members of the United Nations Organization.

Neither can the creation of the North Atlantic grouping of states be in any way justified by the right of each member of the UNO to individual or collective self-defense in conformity with article 51 of the charter. Suffice it to say that such a right under the charter of the UNO can arise only in the case of armed attack against a member of the organization, whereas, as is known to all, neither the United States of America, Britain, France, nor the other parties to the pact are threatened by any armed attack.

It is clear that references to articles 51 and 52 of the UNO Charter are untenable and made only in order to disguise the aggressive aims of this military grouping of states which is being created with the conclusion of the North Atlantic Treaty....

On the basis of all of the above, the Soviet government arrives at the following conclusions:

1. The North Atlantic Treaty has nothing in common with the aims of the self-defense of the states who are parties to the treaty, whom no one threatens, and whom no one is preparing to attack. On the contrary, this treaty has an obviously aggressive character and is aimed against the USSR, which even official representatives of the states who are parties to the treaty do not conceal in their public pronouncements.

2. The North Atlantic Treaty not only does not contribute to the strengthening of peace and international security, which is the duty of all members of the United Nations Organization, but it is in direct contradiction to the principles and aims of the UNO Charter and leads to the undermining of the United Nations Organization.

3. The North Atlantic Treaty is counter to the treaty between Great Britain and the Soviet Union concluded in 1942, according to which both states assumed the obligation to cooperate in the maintenance of peace and international security and 'not to conclude any alliances and not to participate in any coalitions directed against the other High Contracting Party.'

4. The North Atlantic Treaty is counter to the treaty between France and the Soviet Union concluded in 1944, according to which both states assumed the obligation to cooperate in the maintenance of peace and international security and 'not to conclude any alliance and not to take part in any coalition directed against one of the High Contracting Parties.'

5. The North Atlantic Treaty is counter to the agreements between the Soviet Union, the United States of America, and Great Britain concluded at the Yalta and Potsdam conferences, as well as at other conferences of the representatives of these powers held both during and after the Second World War, consonant with which the United States of America and Great Britain, just as the Soviet Union, assumed the obligations to cooperate in the consolidation of general peace and international security and to contribute to the strengthening of the United Nations Organization.''

DOCUMENT 22

The Sino-Soviet Alliance

14 February 1950

Editor's commentary: With the establishment of the People's Republic of China (PRC) in October 1949, the international prestige accruing to the communist model of organization of society grew appreciably. The 30-year treaty of alliance and cooperation between the USSR and the PRC created great apprehensions in the West. It formed what seemed to be a solid bloc of like-minded communist governments hostile to the West which now spanned from the Baltic to the Pacific and threatened further expansion. The details of the general points outlined in the treaty of friendship were specified in two separate, modest agreements accompanying it: one provided for the return of the Chinese Changchun Railway and Port Arthur and Port Dalny to China, and the other provided for $300 million worth of credits at 1 percent interest for Chinese development.

U.S. Senate, Committee on Armed Services and Committee on Foreign Relations, *The Military Situation in the Far East,* part 5 (Washington, DC: U.S. Government Printing Office, 1951), pp. 3171–3173.

Negotiations were recently held in Moscow between J. V. Stalin, Chairman of the Council of Ministers of the USSR, and A. Y. Vyshinsky, Minister of Foreign Affairs of the USSR, on the one hand, and Mr. Mao Tse-tung, chairman of the Central People's Government of the People's Republic of China and Mr. Chou En-lai, Prime-Minister of the State Administrative Council and Minister of Foreign Affairs, on the other, during which important political and economic questions on relations between the Soviet Union and the People's Republic of China were considered.

These negotiations, which proceeded in an atmosphere of cordiality and friendly mutual understanding, confirmed the desire of both parties to strengthen and develop in every way relations of friendship and cooperation between them, as well as their desire to cooperate for the purpose of insuring universal peace and the security of the nations.

The negotiations ended with the signing in the Kremlin on February 14 of:

1. A Treaty of Friendship, Alliance, and Mutual Assistance between the Soviet Union and the People's Republic of China;
2. An agreement on the Chinese Changchun Railway, Port Arthur, and Dalny, in accordance with which, after the signing of a peace treaty with Japan, the Chinese Changchun Railway is to be handed over to the complete ownership of the People's Republic of China, and Soviet troops are to be withdrawn from Port Arthur;
3. An agreement on the granting by the Government of the Soviet Union to the Government of the People's Republic of China of long-term economic credits for paying for deliveries of industrial and railway equipment from the USSR.

The aforementioned Treaty and agreement were signed on behalf of the USSR by A. Y. Vyshinky, and on behalf of the People's Republic of China by Mr. Chou En-lai.

In connection with the signing of the Treaty of Friendship, Alliance, and Mutual Assistance and the Agreement on the Chinese Changchun Railway, Port Arthur and Dalny, Mr. Chou En-lai and A. Y. Vyshinksy exchanged notes to the effect that the respective Treaty and agreements concluded on August 14, 1945, between [nationalist] China and the Soviet Union have become invalid, and also that both Governments affirm a full guarantee of the independent position of the Mongolian People's Republic as a result of the referendum of 1945 and of the establishment with it of diplomatic relations by the People's Republic of China.

Simultaneously, Mr. Chou En-lai and A. Y. Vyshinksy also exchanged notes on the decision of the Soviet Government to hand over gratis to the Government of the People's Republic of China property acquired by Soviet economic organizations from Japanese owners in Manchuria, and also on the decision of the Soviet Government to hand over gratis to the Government of the People's Republic of China all buildings of the former military cantonment in Peking. . . .

TREATY OF FRIENDSHIP, ALLIANCE, AND MUTUAL ASSISTANCE BETWEEN THE UNION OF SOVIET SOCIALIST REPUBLICS AND THE PEOPLE'S REPUBLIC OF CHINA

The Presidium of the Supreme Soviet of the Union of Soviet Socialist Republics and the Central People's Government of the People's Republic of China;

Filled with determination jointly to prevent, by the consolidation of friendship and cooperation between the Union of Soviet Socialist Republics and the People's Republic of China, the rebirth of Japanese imperialism and a repetition of aggression on the part of Japan or any other state which should unite in any form with Japan in acts of aggression;

Imbued with the desire to consolidate lasting peace and universal security in the Far East and throughout the world in comformity with the aims and principles of the United Nations organization;

Profoundly convinced that the consolidation of good neighborly relations and friendship between the Union of Soviet Socialist Republics and the People's Republic of China meets the fundamental interests of the people of the Soviet Union and China;

Resolved for this purpose to conclude the present Treaty and appointed as their plenipotentiary and representatives:

The Presidium of the Supreme Soviet of the Union of Soviet Socialist Republics—Andrei Yanuaryevich Vyshinsky, Minister of Foreign Affairs of the Union of Soviet Socialist Republics;

The Central People's Government of the People's Republic of China—Chou En-Lai, Prime minister of the State Administrative Council and Minister of foreign affairs of China;

Who after exchange of their credentials, found in due form and good order, agreed upon the following:

Article I

Both High Contracting Parties undertake jointly to take all the necessary measures at their disposal for the purpose of preventing a repetition of aggression and violation of peace on the part of Japan or any other state which should unite with Japan, directly or indirectly, in acts of aggression. In the event of one of the High Contracting Parties being attacked by Japan or states allied with it, and thus being involved in a state of war, the other High Contracting Party will immediately render military and other assistance with all the means at its disposal.

The High Contracting Parties also declare their readiness in the spirit of sincere cooperation, to participate in all international actions aimed at ensuring peace and security throughout the world, and will do all in their power to achieve the speediest implementation of these tasks.

Article II

Both the High Contracting Parties undertake by means of mutual agreement to strive for the ear-liest conclusion of a peace treaty with Japan, jointly with the other Powers which were allies during the Second World War.

Article III

Both High Contracting Parties undertake not to conclude any alliance directed against the other High Contracting Party, and not to take part in any coalition or in actions or measures directed against the other High Contracting Party.

Article IV

Both High Contracting Parties will consult each other in regard to all important international problems affecting the common interests of the Soviet Union and China, being guided by the interests of the consolidation of peace and universal security.

Article V

Both the High Contracting Parties undertake, in the spirit of friendship and cooperation and in conformity with the principles of equality, mutual interests, and also mutual respect for the state sovereignty and territorial integrity and noninterference in internal affairs of the other High Contracting Party—to develop and consolidate economic and cultural ties between the Soviet Union and China, to render each other every possible economic assistance, and to carry out the necessary economic cooperation.

Article VI

The present Treaty comes into force immediately upon its ratification; the exchange of instruments of ratification will take place in Peking.

The present Treaty will be valid for 30 years. If neither of the High Contracting Parties gives notice one year before the expiration of this term of its desire to denounce the Treaty, it shall remain in force for another five years and will be extended in compliance with this rule.

Done in Moscow on February 14, 1950, in two copies, each in the Russian and Chinese languages, both texts having equal force.

Signed: By Authorization of the Presidium of the Supreme Soviet of the Union of Soviet Socialist Republics—A. Y. Vyshinsky.

By Authorization of the Central People's Government of the People's Republic of China—Chou En-lai.

DOCUMENT 23

Soviet Statement on the Korean War

June 1950

Editor's commentary: On 25 June 1950, North Korean troops crossed the 38th parallel, which had been designated by agreement among the Allies the official boundary between North and South Korea at the end of World War II. The United States convened an emergency session of the UN Security Council, which was able to agree on action against the aggressors without the Soviet representative vetoing the resolution: the Soviet representative had walked out of the UN earlier that year in protest of the decision not to seat its ally, the People's Republic of China, as the official representative of the Chinese people. Deputy Foreign Minister Gromyko maintained the "illegality" of the UN decision to send troops to Korea.

Department of State Bulletin, vol. 23, no. 575, 10 July 1950, p. 48.

In connection with the statement of the Government of the United States of America transmitted by you on June 27, the Soviet Government has instructed me to state the following:

1. In accordance with facts verified by the Soviet Government, the events taking place in Korea were provoked by an attack by forces of the South Korean authorities on border regions of North Korea. Therefore the responsibility for these events rests upon the South Korean authorities and upon those who stand behind their back.

2. As is known, the Soviet Government withdrew its troops from Korea earlier than the Government of the United States and thereby confirmed its traditional principle of noninterference in the internal affairs of other states. And now as well the Soviet Government adheres to the principle of the impermissibility of interference by foreign powers in the internal affairs of Korea.

3. It is not true that the Soviet Government refused to participate in meetings of the Security Council. In spite of its full willingness, the Soviet Government has not been able to take part in the meetings of the Security Council in as much as, because of the position of the Government of the United States, China, a permanent member of the Security Council, has not been admitted to the Council which has made it impossible for the Security Council to take decisions having legal force.

Suggested Readings

Bialer, Seweryn (ed.): *Stalin and His Generals: Soviet Military Memoirs of World War II* (New York: Pegasus, 1969).

Clemens, Diane S.: *Yalta* (London: Oxford University Press, 1970).

Davis, Lynn E.: *The Cold War Begins: Soviet-American Conflict Over Eastern Europe* (Princeton, NJ: Princeton University Press, 1974).

Deutscher, Isaac: *Stalin* (New York: Oxford University Press, 1970).

Djilas, Milovan: *Conversations with Stalin* (New York: Harcourt, Brace & World, 1962).

Fainsod, Merle: *Smolensk Under Soviet Rule* (New York: Vintage, 1963).

Hammond, Thomas T. (ed.): *The Anatomy of Communist Takeovers* (New Haven, CT: Yale University Press, 1975).

Kacewicz, George: *Great Britain, the Soviet Union and the Polish Government in Exile (1939–1945)* (The Hague: Nijhoff, 1979).

Kennan, George F.: *Memoirs: 1925–1950* (Boston: Little Brown, 1957).

Leonhard, Wolfgang: *Child of the Revolution* (Chicago: Regnery, 1958).

Mastny, Vojtech: *Russia's Road to the Cold War: Diplomacy, Warfare, and the Politics of Communism, 1941–45* (New York: Columbia University Press, 1979).

Medvedev, Roy A.: *Let History Judge: The Origins and Consequences of Stalinism* (New York: Knopf, 1971).

———: *On Stalin and Stalinism* (Oxford: Oxford University Press, 1979).

Paterson, Thomas G.: *Soviet-American Confrontation: Postwar Reconstruction and the Origins of the Cold War* (Baltimore, MD: Johns Hopkins University Press, 1973).

Sabaliunas, Leonas: *Lithuania in Crisis: Nationalism to Communism, 1939–40* (Bloomington, IN: Indiana University Press, 1972).

Shulman, Marshall D.: *Stalin's Foreign Policy Reappraised* (Cambridge, MA: Harvard University Press, 1963).

Stalin, Joseph V.: *On the Great Patriotic War of the Soviet Union* (Moscow: Foreign Languages Publishing House, 1945).

Taubman, William: *Stalin's American Policy: From Entente to Detente to Cold War* (New York: W. W. Norton, 1982).

Thornton, Richard C.: *The Comintern and the Chinese Communists, 1928–1931* (Seattle, WA: University of Washington Press, 1969).

Tucker, Robert C. "The Emergence of Stalin's Foreign Policy," *Slavic Review,* vol. 36, no. 4 (December 1977).

Ulam, Adam: *Stalin: The Man and His Era* (Boston: Beacon Press, 1987).

———: *Tito and the Cominform* (Cambridge, MA: Harvard University Press, 1952).

Zawodny, J. K.: *Death in the Forest: The Story of the Katyn Forest Massacre* (South Bend, IN: University of Notre Dame Press, 1962).

CHAPTER FOUR

Soviet Foreign Policy under Khrushchev— The Emergence of a Superpower (1953–1964)

Nikita Sergeevich Khrushchev holds the distinction of being the only top Soviet leader and First Secretary of the CPSU to date to have been ousted from his position instead of dying in office. Perhaps there are lessons for Gorbachev in Khrushchev's fate. Khrushchev attempted, like Gorbachev today, to reform the Soviet bureaucracy; these initiatives were perceived by the party bureaucracy as threatening its power. Although the reasons for both Khrushchev's rise to power and his subsequent ouster have more to do with domestic politics than foreign affairs,[1] the erratic foreign policy which was characteristic of Khrushchev's years in power was undoubtedly a contributing factor in his ultimate demise.

From the time of Stalin's death in 1953, the highest circles of the Soviet leadership were engaged in an intense struggle for political primacy in the Kremlin, culminating in Khrushchev's political disgrace of his opponents, Georgii Malenkov and Vyacheslav Molotov, in 1957. The First Secretary, Khrushchev, finally emerged victorious, but, as it turned out, with an incomplete victory. Issues of foreign policy became increasingly important for Khrushchev after the revelations about Stalin at the Twentieth Party Congress in February 1956. The "troika" of Khrushchev, Prime Minister Malenkov, and Soviet President Nikolai Bulganin jointly conducted Soviet foreign policy from Stalin's death until Khrushchev's emergence as the number one man in the Kremlin. A reorientation of Soviet foreign policy toward

---

[1] See Carl Linden, *Khrushchev and the Soviet Leadership, 1957–1964* (Baltimore, MD: The Johns Hopkins University Press, 1966).

a more compromising and less confrontational posture could be seen in various forums and initiatives, including the Geneva summit of 1955, the raising of the doctrine of peaceful coexistence to the level of strategy (see Chapter 1, document 7), and the move by Soviet leaders to mend fences within international communism by welcoming Tito of Yugoslavia back into the fold of the international communist movement (Chapter 4, document 4).

The Khrushchev years were marked by tremendous advances and equally tremendous failures in foreign policy. It was under Khrushchev that the Soviet Union emerged as a superpower strategically capable of delivering nuclear weapons to American soil and increasingly able and willing to challenge the position of global supremacy that the United States had held since the end of World War II. Also during this time, two international organizations were established by the Soviet Union in the "socialist commonwealth": the Warsaw Treaty Organization (Chapter 4, document 2) and the Council for Mutual Economic Assistance, or Comecon.[1] It was also under Khrushchev that the Third World achieved priority status in Soviet competition with the "imperialist camp": peaceful coexistence did not mean relinquishing class struggle, but rather shifting its venue. Last but not least, impressive technological advances with important foreign policy implications included the launching of the first artificial earth satellite and the first successful testing of an intercontinental ballistic missile (Chapter 4, documents 7 and 8).

Significant setbacks for Soviet foreign policy during the Khrushchev years included the Hungarian revolution of 1956 (Chapter 4, document 5), the Sino-Soviet split (Chapter 4, document 19), the Cuban missile crisis (Chapter 4, document 15), and the Berlin crises of the late 1950s and early 1960s (Chapter 4, document 12). It is probably true that among the "hare-brained schemes" that were responsible for Khrushchev's ouster, the Cuban missile crisis loomed especially large.[2] The inability to bluff the West out of Berlin by "rocket rattling" and making other threats did not become a severe liability for Khrushchev. However, the rupture that occurred in the Sino-Soviet relationship, though not Khrushchev's sole responsibility, became the most portentous foreign policy legacy of his tenure. Efforts to repair the fabric of the world communist movement after Tito's defection in 1948 had come to naught as the schism between Beijing and Moscow widened and soon dwarfed any previous interparty dispute. Khrushchev was able to remain in power until October 1964, when he ostensibly asked to be retired "for reasons of health" from the CPSU Presidium.

This chapter's first selection is by Zbigniew Brzezinski, writing while Khrushchev was still in power. He outlines how a "new course" was taken after Stalin's passing and how Khrushchev positioned himself on international issues important to the international communist movement in his quest for the number one position in the Kremlin. He discusses the importance of the Twentieth Party Congress and the "secret speech" that debunked Stalin's personality cult. These actions had implications subsequently for the events of the Polish and Hungarian revolutions some twenty months later. Merle Fainsod gives us a picture of Khrushchev the man and his mixed record of achievements and failures. This excerpt is, in its own way, a eulogy of a complex figure in Soviet politics, a devoted Communist who only under Gorbachev began to be rehabilitated in the Soviet Union, as the quest for reform expanded to include more critical analysis of previous attempts at changing the Soviet system.

---

[1]Actually, Comecon was created by Stalin in 1949. It was not until 1959, however, that it began to function as a viable institution.

[2]Linden, op. cit., p. 155. Indirect criticism of Khrushchev's "subjectivism" and "hare-brained scheming" appeared in *Pravda,* 17 October 1964.

The New Course: Stalinism Dissipated

Zbigniew Brzezinski

Stalin's death did not lead to the immediate disintegration of the Stalinist system. It did deprive it of the crucial psychological ingredient of personal fear—a fear shared by the subdued populations of East Europe, to whom Stalin was symbol of the Soviet might, and by their Communists leaders trained in the stiff Stalinist school of the Comintern and promoted through the rigorous competitions of the great purges. For the time being, however, the institutions of power remained, particularly the links between the Soviet secret policy and the satellite networks, and the Stalinist conception of the relations between the USSR and the Communist bloc as well. The new Soviet leadership groped carefully in the initial stages, seeking to maintain continuity with the past while attempting to develop its own solutions to a variety of domestic and external problems left by the Stalinist legacy. The surgical solutions which Stalin might have been contemplating in the closing days of his life now had to give way to a prolonged cure.

Soon both the institutions of Soviet power in the communist-ruled states as well as the theoretical framework governing their relations to the USSR were subjected to the pressures of changed conditions and new requirements. As the ingredient of power, so dependent on the personal impact of Stalin, gradually, almost imperceptibly, shrank, the Stalinist monopoly of ideology and power in Soviet-satellite relations slowly gave way to a greater reliance on ideology. The dilemma was that Stalinism as an ideology was so dependent on power that by itself it could not cope with the post-Stalin situation in the Communist camp. Under the circumstances, the ideological framework linking the communist states had to be made more elastic to permit greater variation in domestic policies within the context of overall unity. By 1956 and 1957 the search for new solutions was taking the form of a widespread dialogue between various Communist parties, leaders, newspapers, and intellectuals.[1] In effect, the Stalinist unity of ideology and power was dissipated within less than four years of his death....

PROBLEMS OF SOVIET SUCCESSION

Stalin was not merely the Soviet dictator but also the leader of international Communism. Yet, in view of the central position of the USSR, it was only fitting that the succession be resolved, initially at least, within the framework of Soviet domestic considerations. The competition for power produced immediate and broad disagreements on policy, even if only as a function of the succession crisis. In addition, Stalin's death brought to the surface certain dilemmas which had long been obscured by the single-minded purposefulness of Stalinism as long as the dictator

Excerpted from *The Soviet Bloc: Unity and Conflict* (Cambridge, MA: Harvard University Press) pp. 153–157 and 164–181. Copyright © 1960, 1967 by the President and Fellows of Harvard college. Reprinted by permission of the publishers.

[1] Admittedly, it is difficult to distinguish between ideological conflict which is politically motivated and that which primarily involves pure doctrine, especially when doctrinal positions form a basis for eventual political action. Nonetheless, one can point to certain ideological disputes in which problems of power are so involved that it is not unreasonable to suspect that the dialogue on theory is a mere sham for a brutal power struggle. The least one can say is that ideology and power have become inseparable at such a juncture. This would appear to have been the case with many of the disputes which developed after Stalin's death among various communist leaders and parties in East Europe, including the USSR, and also in the case of the positions taken by the Chinese and French communist parties. There is also, however, the more genuine conflict of ideas in which power plays only a secondary role. This seems to have been the situation with much of the ideological disputes which went on inside Poland, conducted by intellectuals not tied to specific posts of authority.

was at the helm. Dormant political and economic issues now demanded immediate attention and resolution. Unavoidably, such Soviet domestic preoccupations tended to leave the Communist leaderships in the neighboring states somewhat to their own resources.

Among the most imporant items on the agenda of the new "collective" leadership were the creation of some stable leadership arrangement which would safeguard the dominant interests of the upper levels of the political elite and prevent a violent and disruptive conflict; a reorganization of the party and administrative structure which had grown too large and unwieldy under Stalin; a diminution in world tensions which were imposing a heavy strain on Soviet and Communist development; and finally, a review of the Stalinist economic formula which favored heavy capital development at the expense of consumption and agriculture....

The first year and a half following Stalin's death was dominated, within the limits of an uneasy "collective" leadership, by Georgi Malenkov. The initial succession problem which the new regime faced was that of the secret police which had grown powerful under Stalin and which now seemed to be reaching out for total power.[1] The echoes of the July 1953 announcement of Lavrenti Beria's arrest and the Christmas Eve 1953 execution of the former secret police chief and six of his top associates had particular significance for the East European Communist parties smarting for the preceding years under police surveillance. The subsequent stress on "socialist legality," though still largely verbal, in itself represented a factor potentially limiting the formerly unchecked interference of the police in party matters.... The measure of duality of party and state administration which had developed under Stalin remained largely unchanged, and,

indeed, the effort to avoid a concentration of power in one man's hands resulted in the appointment of different individuals to head the party and the administration....

In foreign policy, the Malenkov period coincided with a reduction in world tensions, the most outstanding feature of which was the Korean armistice of July 27, 1953. In his August speech Malenkov took credit for a "normalization" in relations with Turkey, Iran, and Afghanistan, and for an exchange of envoys with Yugoslavia. As far as East Europe was concerned, Malenkov stood fast on the position that the People's Democracies were firmly tied to the USSR; much like Stalin earlier, he did not feel compelled to devote more than a passing phrase to them. One might well speculate, on rereading Stalin's "Economic Problems of Socialism in the USSR" that had the old dictator remained alive, Soviet foreign policy would not have been very much different. The Malenkov policy, too, seemed to take the permanence of the Soviet bloc much for granted and to count on growing tensions within the capitalist bloc to undermine the cohesion which had developed in the face of the earlier Soviet threat. In broad terms, the Malenkov policy may be characterized as a general continuation of Stalinism politically, possibly from sheer momentum, balanced by an attempt to reduce the harshness of the Stalinist economic policies. It was an attempt, in brief, to pursue a new course in economics without basically altering the framework of essentially Stalinist politics....

KHRUSHCHEV'S CONCEPTION OF THE COMMUNIST CAMP

During 1954, the Soviet political scene was dominated by the rapid growth in the stature of the first secretary of the party and by the increasingly peremptory tone of his pronouncements. As one authoritative observer has noted, "the step-by-step ascent of Khrushchev to a position of undisputed leadership represents a striking re-

---

[1]At the time many observers were inclined to feel that the secret police was the actual ruler of the USSR. See the remarks by G. Kennan and H. Arendt in C. J. Friedrich, ed., *Totalitarianism* (Cambridge, 1954), pp. 76–77, 82–83.

capitulation of the Stalinist experience,''[1] and it was accomplished primarily in terms of domestic issues and through the manipulation of domestic forces. By skillfully seizing the initiative in pressing for new and dynamic schemes of internal reconstruction, Khrushchev assumed the role of the Leninist revolutionary struggling against the vested interests of the bureaucrats, and he succeeded in mobilizing the party around him. His insistence, in February 1954, on a new agricultural policy, his shuffles of the party *apparat*, as well as his active interest in the parties of the People's Democracies (demonstrated through personal visits to Poland, Czechoslovakia, and China), made him appear as the dynamic innovator so necessary to keeping a totalitarian system from stagnating. Naturally, this produced resentment from those sections of society interested in stability, but in late 1954 and early 1955, Khrushchev succeeded in gaining the support of the Central Committee of the party on the critical issue of the methods of industrialization and of the rate of development of heavy industry.[2]

In retrospect, it appears that the Soviet leadership was at the time divided into three groups: some Soviet leaders favored relatively ''softer'' methods on the international front and some domestic economic concessions; others, accepting the proposition that Soviet interests would be best served by a foreign policy somewhat less Stalinist in form though not in content, differed fundamentally on the domestic economic line and insisted on heavy industrial development; still others supported domestic and external policies essentially Stalinist both in form and content. To the degree that it is possible to generalize about

as complex an issue as the policy outlook of specific Soviet leaders, it would appear that the first attitude was held by Malenkov, the second by Khrushchev,[3] and the third by Molotov. It was a combination of the last two that united to remove Malenkov on the issue of domestic policy, although Molotov was apparently unable to carry the day on the international issue. Thus, in international politics, the new Khrushchev-Bulganin team continued the efforts to present the USSR as genuinely striving to settle all international issues, reflecting the assessments made late in 1952. The Geneva Conference held in the summer of 1955 between the heads of governments of the United States, the United Kingdom, France, and the USSR (and with the First Secretary of the CPSU participating) was the culmination of this policy. It is likely that the Soviet leaders hoped that a measure of relaxation would allow the contradictions in the capitalist camp to mature while permitting the USSR and the People's Democracies to press their domestic industrialization unhindered by threats of war. Furthermore, the Soviet and other Communist leaders might have reasoned that such diminution of international tensions, symbolized by the Geneva handshakes with the leaders of the West, implicitly meant the West's acceptance of the status quo in East Central Europe.

In some respects it could be argued that the Communist calculations were well founded. However, the 1955 spell of international good will had a further and unexpected consequence. While possibly extinguishing any lingering hopes of Western ''liberation'' of East Europe, it also reduced the fears of the communist ruling elites and undermined the feeling that they must ''sink or swim'' with the USSR. The internal Soviet ambivalence in policy and the reduction in in-

---

[1]M. Fainsod, ''The CPSU Since Stalin,'' *Problems of Communism,* January–February 1958, p. 8. For a detailed analysis of Khrushchev's rise, see Fainsod's ''What Happened to 'Collective Leadership'?'' *Problems of Communism,* July–August 1959; also M. Rush, *The Rise of Khrushchev* (Washington, 1958).

[2]See *Pravda,* December 21, 1954 (article by V. Kruzhkov) and January 24, 1955 (article by D. Shepilow) for good statements of the Khrushchev position.

---

[3]Khrushchev, however, already in mid-1954 dissociated himself from Malenkov's willingness to concede that an all-out nuclear war would spell the end of humanity and firmly contended that such a conflict would mean the final destruction of capitalism.

ternational tensions produced the belief that the People's Democracies could now afford to frame their policies to fit their domestic requirements. The Stalinist "dilemma of the one alternative" was upset with the fading of the external enemy, while the Soviet return to heavy industrial development imediately put to the test the willingness of the parties—as well as their ability—to emulate the USSR under these new circumstances, even when such imitation imposed domestic strains. The situation was now quite different from the Malenkov New Course period.

That Khrushchev expected the People's Democracies to follow the new Soviet economic policy seems clear. Admitting that some "disproportions" had existed in the past, the Soviet leadership adopted the position that such errors had now been corrected and that correction of errors is not a substitute for policy....

The Khrushchev formula for the USSR and for the Soviet bloc involved no basic change in the foreign policy approach of the preceding two years, but domestically it stressed a return to an economic policy of maintaining heavy capital development while at the same time striving to improve agricultural productivity and to revitalize the economy. A by-product was to be an improvement in the standard of living, but without loss in heavy industrial development.... Khrushchev had to face the political problem squarely. The formula which he apparently developed in the course of the following year involved increasing emphasis on common economic practices while tolerating an undefined and limited measure of political autonomy, unthinkable during Stalinism.... These efforts to develop some indigenous support for the various communist regimes were to be matched by close, formal institutional ties which would fill the vacuum left by the disappearance of the personal Stalinist ingredient, and by greater emphasis on common ideological bonds which would result from similar economic undertakings....

Observing Sino-Soviet relations and bearing in mind the great dependence of the East European regimes on the USSR, Khrushchev could feel justified in altering the Stalinist formula in the direction of greater reliance on a community of economic patterns and emphasis on ideological uniformity. Such a framework could effectively contain the inherent pressures for diversity, but without the need for continuous Soviet involvement which Stalinism had demanded. In the words of Khrushchev's *Pravda*: "The historical experience of the Soviet Union and of the People's Democracies shows that, given unity in the chief fundamental matter of ensuring the victory of socialism, various ways and means may be used in different countries to solve the specific problems of socialist construction, depending on historical and national features."[1] In keeping with this, the return of the various states to a policy of rapid industrialization was a qualified one. Everywhere lip-service was paid to the pre-eminence of heavy industry. Nowhere did a full return to the Stalinist rate of industrialization take place.

With Stalin gone, and the post-Stalin circumstances producing greater diversity, the Stalinist method of informal political ties had to be buttressed through formalization. Khrushchev, even though somewhat of a "vulgar Marxist" in his notions concerning the source of cohesion between socialist states, was still sufficiently steeped in Leninism-Stalinism to recognize the importance of political bonds. This awareness was no doubt sharpened by certain international factors (such as the inclusion of West Germany into NATO), which made a more formal arrangement desirable. During Stalin's lifetime the independent state forms of the communist-ruled nations had been emptied of most of their political content, but now there was the danger that such forms could become impediments to real international Soviet unity as the local regimes gradually began to emphasize a more domestic point of view. Since the formal abolition of

---

[1]*Pravda*, July 16, 1955.

these states as independent entities was no longer feasible—and, on the contrary, in some cases it was even desirable to increase their number, as was done with East Germany—it was necessary to adopt a solution based on their continued existence and probability of growing importance. The answer to this and to NATO was the creation of the Warsaw Pact and the invigoration of the dormant Council of Economic Mutual Assistance (CEMA).

The creation of the Warsaw Pact was presaged by a conference held in Moscow in November 1954 between the Soviet government, represented by Molotov, and the heads of the Communist governments. The conference took a firm stand against the Western policy of West German remilitarization and warned that the Communist states would be forced to act jointly if this should come about.[1] The Warsaw Pact was, accordingly, partially an answer to the German development. The pact, entitled "On Friendship, Cooperation, and Mutual Aid," was signed in Warsaw on May 14, 1955, by all the European Communist states and the USSR. It contained a general political agreement and a military convention.[2] The states reaffirmed their unity of purpose and, in the vaguely phrased fifth clause of the agreement, allowed for the disposition of troops under a joint command as deemed appropriate by them and the command for purposes of mutual defense. No further agreements for the stationing of foreign troops on the soil of any one of the signatories was made (a matter regularized only after the Hungarian and Polish events in 1956), but the pact itself represented a formal "legalizing" of the stationing of Soviet troops, especially since the military convention assigned the joint command to a Soviet officer

and stipulated that troop disposition would be made according to mutual arrangements of the governments concerned (that is, between the USSR and the country concerned). The official Chinese observer, Pen Teh-huai, the former Korean War commander, associated himself with the pact and promised Chinese support in the case of foreign aggression.

The preponderance of Soviet power in East Europe should not obscure the political significance of the Warsaw Pact. It represented the single most important formal commitment binding the states to the USSR, officially limiting their scope of independent action, and legalizing the presence (and hence the political influence) of the Soviet troops stationed in some of them. The gradual return of "content" to the forms of state independence was in this fashion balanced by a treaty structure which provided for joint consultation on all major issues and Soviet command of all troops, and which did not provide any procedures for withdrawal from such treaty arrangement or for the removal of the Soviet forces.[3] Finally, since the sharp point of the the pact was directed against Germany, which some of the treaty members deeply feared, an element of mutual self-interest was also present.

These formal political ties were to be further buttressed by an increased reliance on the CEMA. After several years of relative inactivity, during which it occupied itself primarily with channeling trade between the Communist states, the CEMA became more vigorous after 1954. Meetings of the Council were held at least annually,...the council's organization was de-

---

[1]*Moskovskoe soveshchanie* (Moscow, 1954), for the official speeches and communique.

[2]For texts and speeches, see *Varshavskoe Soveshchanie Evropeiskikh Gosudarstv* (Moscow, 1955); for a semiofficial Communist evaluation, L. Gelberg, *Uklad Warszawski* (Warsaw, 1957).

[3]The Political Consultative Committee created by the Warsaw Pact met in Prague in January 1956 and decided to meet regularly not less than twice a year and to create a standing commission for foreign-policy coordination and standing secretariat. In a sense this meant the abandonment of the Stalinist technique of bilateralism (*Zasedaniia Politicheskovo Konsultativnovo Komiteta,* Moscow 1956, p. 53). The international military command, however, was not set up; the satellites did not appoint liaison officers to it; and control remained in Soviet hands. This underscored the primary political purpose of the treaty.

veloped and its objectives defined. Its basic goal was to facilitate mutual exchange of experience and techniques; to promote a division of labor and specialization in industrial production; to co-ordinate investment and the subsequent five-year plans.[1] The division of labor was a departure from the Stalinist notions of an essentially au-tarkic construction of socialist industrialization,[2] while the political significance of the economic cooperation was openly stated. "Intensification of the coordination of the national economic plans of the USSR and the People's Democra-cies is needed to strengthen socialism," *Pravda* observed, commenting on the activities of the council.[3]...

In this fashion the slightly greater measure of political flexibility in the bloc would be balanced by common economic interests and ideological commitment. Indeed, Khrushchev might well have hoped that the last two would more than compensate for any retreat from the rigid Stalin-ist insistence on political subordination which, in some cases, impeded the development of even "objective" ties. It is symptomatic that, unlike Malenkov's, the burden of Khrushchev's infor-mal criticisms of Stalinist policies in East Eu-rope involved political aberrations rather than economic ones (which in some measure had helped to produce the political).[4] Paralleling So-viet domestic re-emphasis of the party, the ex-cessive Stalinist reliance on controls was giving way in the hope that close Party relations would also revitalize the common ideological bonds.[5] While Soviet power remained a crucial back-ground factor, ideology based on economy was to replace power masked by ideology.

THE ISSUE OF YUGOSLAVIA

Within this revised framework the conflict with Yugoslavia lost most of its meaning and, indeed, could only impede the implementation of Khrush-chev's vision. On *this* score, Khrushchev might have been supported by some members of the displaced Malenkov group. In any case, given the changes in East Europe and recalling Tito's loyalty to the USSR prior to 1948, a portion of the Soviet leadership apparently concluded late in 1954 that the Soviet-Yugoslav rift was ideo-logically barren and largely a product of the late dictator's pathological hatreds and phobias. Not-ing that, domestically, Tito had been a forceful Communist, the Soviet leadership appears to have assumed that an arrangement stressing com-mon party bonds while accepting Tito's domes-tic autonomy would establish a pattern for sim-ilarly firm Communist regimes elsewhere. They would be bound together through the rigorous party dictatorships run on similar doctrinal as-sumptions, reinforced by integrated economic processes. Khrushchev realized he could not wipe out Tito's national Communism, but he hoped to harness it.

The decision to improve relations was made sometime in the fall of 1954, but the limits of the projected improvement were left undefined and, in the summer of 1955, caused a sharp exchange of views within the Soviet leadership, particu-

---

[1]Cf. V. Siroky, "Economic Cooperation on the Level of the Growing Tasks of the Socialist States," *Pravda,* April 6, 1956; R. Fidelski, *Wspolpraca Gospodarcza Polski z Kra-jami Socjalistycznymi* (Warsaw, 1959).

[2]Under the plan, East Germany was to specialize in the production of precision instruments and electrical equipment; Poland: rolling stock, ships, mining equipment, chemicals; Czechoslovakia: machine building, automobiles, engines; Hungary: diesel engines, motor trains, buses; Rumania: oil pipes, drilling equipment. Standing comittees, functional in nature and distributed among the various capitals, were also set up. Reflecting the importance of these committees was the fact that the various members states were normally rep-resented by the respective ministers or vice-ministers. R. Fidelski, ibid., pp. 81–83.

[3]*Pravda,* July 27, 1956.

[4]For instance, I. Nagy, *On Communism* (New York, 1957), p. 143.

[5]Characteristically, high CPSU officials were appointed as ambassadors to the various communist states: for instance, in Poland, the appointment in May 1955 of P. K. Ponomar-enko, former first secretary in Kazakhstan, and in October 1957 of P. A. Abrasimov, former party secretary of Belorus-sia.

larly between Khrushchev and Mikoyan on one side and Molotov on the other. Initially, however, even Molotov might have approved a "normalization" in relations, for during 1954 the Soviet peace campaign directed against the Western European Defense Community (EDC) went into high gear and the Yugoslav position of "positive neutrality" also involved a rejection of the Western scheme. In the fall of 1954, Soviet newspapers carried several articles citing the Yugoslav views[1] but without the usual derogatory references to Tito, and even quoting verbatim lengthy passages of Tito's criticisms of the EDC and the Atlantic Pact.[2] Following a series of friendly gestures...it was announced that direct talks between the Yugoslav and Soviet leaderships would be held in May 1955. The Soviet press emphasized that the Belgrade talks would end a situation which "had been only to the advantage of the enemies of peace."[3]

Khrushchev strove from the very outset of the talks, which began on May 27, to stress common ideological party issues and to put them on a Communist-to-Communist plane. Even in his apologetic airport speech Khrushchev adhered to this intention, while also revealing the basic assumptions of his thinking:

> The strongest ties are established between the peoples of both countries which have as their guiding force Parties that base all their activities on the teaching of Marxism-Leninism. The Parties that take the Marxist-Leninist teaching as their guide achieve complete mutual understanding because they have a common aim—struggle for the interests of the working class and the working peasants, for the interest of the working people.[4]

The agreement, however, that was signed on June 2 was purely a joint declaration of the two states and did not cover party or ideological matters as Khrushchev had wished.[5] Nonetheless, it explicitly acknowledged that Yugoslavia was a state building socialism and it did contain some implicit ideological concessions to the Yugoslavs. Reference was made to "mutual respect for...different forms of Socialist development" and, at the end of the eight-point agreement involving state matters (to which the Yugoslavs wished to restrict the conference), provision was made for "the exchange of Socialist experience."[6]

The Yugoslav reserve was understandable. Having gradually emerged with an ideological position and certain institutional arrangements which they considered as their own creative contribution to Marxism-Leninism, they feared the new Soviet policy of minimizing ideological and party differences before a clear-cut, un-Stalinist principle of diversity was acknowledged. They might well have been disturbed also by the equivocation of the Soviet leaders on the subject of the 1948 resolution which had expelled Yugoslavia from the Cominform. Even though the Yugoslavs were formally acting as if it had been renounced, the Soviet leaders pointedly rejected only the November 1949 Cominform resolution which had so violently condemned the Yugoslavs as Gestapo spies and such; little was said about the 1948 declaration which had charged them with a variety of ideological sins.[7] To Khrush-

---

[1]For instance, *Pravda, Izvestia,* September 17, 1954, citing *Borba.*

[2]Ibid., September 22, 1954. For Tito's views on the EDC, see R.B. Farrell, *Jugoslavia and the Soviet Union, 1948–1956* (The Shoe String Press, 1956), p. 163; also *Pravda,* April 22, 1955.

[3]*Pravda,* May 18, 1955.

[4]*For a Lasting Peace, For a People's Democracy!,* May 27, 1955.

[5]A Yugoslav ambassador stated to this writer that the agreement was based on a Yugoslav draft.

[6]*New York Times,* June 2, 1955; *Pravda* explicitly mentioned the points quoted above in its commentary on the agreement.

[7]In 1958, both the organ of the SED [Socialist Unity Party, of East Germany] and Khrushchev himself asserted, with no direct Yugoslav rebuttals, that the Yugoslav leadership had been told that it was the 1949 resolution only which was being denounced. See *Pravda,* July 12, 1958; *Einheit,* no. 5, 1958. The November 1949 declaration, entitled "The Communist Party of Yugoslavia in the Hands of Murderers and Spies," in effect urged Tito's liquidation.

chev, however, allowing the Yugoslavs to place a somewhat wider interpretation on the revision of the past, and even having to acknowledge indirectly a tolerance of diversity implied by the agreement, represented a small price to be paid for drawing Yugoslavia back into the fold. Such a step would minimize ideological differences and strengthen the bonds between the Soviet Union and the other People's Democracies in this post-Stalin period. Past Yugoslav experience could even serve to reinforce the argument for the imitation of Soviet experience....

Khrushchev, while admitting that the 1948 resolution had been fundamentally correct in its evaluation, claimed that unless the Soviet Union adopted a policy of drawing Yugoslavia back into the political and ideological fold, the other Communist states in the post-Stalin phase might be tempted to emulate the Yugoslav example, thereby causing the USSR unnecessary difficulties.... The last few months of 1955 were accordingly marked by the gradual falling into line of the other Communist states on the Yugoslav question, although with markedly less enthusiasm. Khrushchev continued to apply pressure on the neighbors of Yugoslavia, and one by one they withdrew from their anti-Titoist positions.

THE TWENTIETH PARTY CONGRESS

Domestically, Khrushchev was busy consolidating his position. The CPSU's Twentieth Party Congress had been scheduled for February 1956, at which time the official party program was to be expounded and top party posts filled. Domestic issues accordingly occupied the Soviet leadership a good deal. The earlier July session had also discussed current problems of industrialization; in September an amnesty for certain political offenders had been decreed, a press campaign for more effective struggle against illegality developed, and the Stalinist architectural style repudiated. In consolidating his position, Khrushchev was raising the Leninist banner, calling for more revolutionary zeal, and appealing to the anti-bureaucratic prejudices of the masses. It was not the heavy capital development which was denying them the fruits of Soviet industrialization but the priviledged and inefficient bureaucrats who were to blame, he argued, subtly linking his opponents with the bureaucrats. However, his domestic preoccupation did not lead him to neglect foreign policy. The agreement with Tito was followed by the Geneva Conference and, later in the fall, by the triumphant tour of Asia by Khrushchev and Bulganin. The new leadership, by word and deed, was demonstrating to its adherents its determination to cope in an imaginative way with the legacy of Stalinism.

In ideological matters, continued stress was laid on the significance of doctrine in the relations among Communist states. A curious episode, probably linked with the July plenum, gave the party's theoretical journal, *Kommunist,* an opportunity to expound on this subject more fully. In September, Molotov, in a published letter, retracted a statement made by him earlier in the year to the effect that the foundations of a socialist society had already been built in the USSR. The statement could have implied that a complete socialist society had not yet been constructed in the USSR. In withdrawing the statement as "theoretically erroneous and politically harmful," Molotov did not see fit to repudiate a further part of his original sentence, in which he had asserted that the People's Democracies "have made only the first, though highly important, steps in the direction of socialism."[1] A major disproportion in levels between the USSR and the other states was thus implicitly asserted. *Kommunist*'s editorial, commenting on the issue, stated that Molotov's original formulation was harmful because it underestimated the ideological and socio-economic importance of the Soviet system, particularly in view of the "present-day struggle for Communism." The editorial

---

[1]*Kommunist,* No. 14 (1955), p. 127.

went on to stress the vital need of the party to struggle against the "cult of the personality" which is part "of the struggle of the new with the old," and to stress pointedly the party's intolerance "of the complacency and conceit of certain leaders and cases of isolation from the masses."[1]

Having used the ideological issue as a point of departure for an attack on the domestic conservatives, *Kommunist* shifted to the international problem. Restating once again the thesis that the crisis within capitalism was deepening, the editorial charged that those responsible for foreign policy had been neglectful of the Marxist-Leninist orientation. It then noted that domestic construction of socialism in the USSR is inherently linked with the general problem of the socialist camp, or "commonwealth," as the editorial called it, "headed by the Soviet Union," since it involves a continuous search for theoretical formulations to guide the patterns of development, to decide what is general and what is particular, and to bind the socialist states in true proletarian internationalism. Soviet primacy is derived from its advanced historical stage and is accordingly justified ideologically. The Khrushchev formulation of the relations between Communist states was then explicitly stated:

A new, socialist type of international relations arose with the formation of the commonwealth of socialist states. These are relations of fully equal rights, genuine friendship, fraternal cooperation in the sphere of politics, economics and culture, and mutual assistance in the construction of a new life. These relations are determined by the nature of the socio-economic system of the countries of the socialist camp; by the unity of their fundamental interests and ultimate great aim, the building of communism; and by the single Marxist-Leninist world view of the Communist and Workers' parties....[2]

Khrushchev's notion hence did not abandon Soviet primacy, but attempted to place it on a new and, as he hoped, firmer basis. He thus found himself agreeing with Tito that Stalinism—more as a form of consciousness which lags behind the new reality than as an actual force—was becoming an impediment to the achievement of Soviet domestic and external objectives.

In this light, Khrushchev's performance at the Twentieth Party Congress becomes even more meaningful. His speech on Stalin, a stunning surprise in the vigor if its condemnation, was designed to shake the Stalinist orientation prevailing among many party members at home and abroad. Khrushchev may have been carried away in his delivery, but there is little doubt that the speech was designed to destroy the myth of Stalin's infallibility, which would in turn permit Khrushchev to be more selective in deciding which portions of the legacy could be retained and which portions already represented a moribund past.... The shattering effect of the speech on the delegates, despite the fact that they had been prepared by an earlier, also violently anti-Stalin speech by Mikoyan, is a matter of historical record. But a proper perspective on the speech should take into consideraton that its primary design—to shake the rigid Stalinist attitudes which were impeding the task of adapting the Stalinist legacy—was meant to apply to the entire bloc.

More positive conceptions emerged from Khrushchev's formal public address[3] and were echoed by some of the other leaders. However, with the exception of the admission that under certain favorable circumstances socialism may be established by nonviolent parliamentary devices and the assertion that war was no longer inevitable due to the power of the communist bloc, no startling changes in the existing trends were foreseen. Rather, these trends were given

---

[1]Ibid.
[2]Ibid.

[3]Text in *Current Digest of the Soviet Press*, VIII, no. 4, 1956.

a formal, explicit, and coherent form. The disintegration of the "imperialist colonial system" was analyzed and the development of "the zone of peace" noted as contributing to the decline of aggressive imperialism. With respect to relations with Communist states, Khrushchev now verbalized what he had been tacitly conceding since the summer of 1955: (1) ways to socialism may indeed differ and may in the future become "more and more varied" although socialism will presumably be the same; (2) "alongside the Soviet form of reorganizing society on socialist foundations, we have the form of People's Democracy," Khrushchev stated. Hence the two do differ (although his references to substantive differences were limited to the Chinese handling of private industry and trade and to the Yugoslav "unique specific forms of economic management"). There was still a paucity of detail in Khrushchev's speech on what is tolerable and what is not in the construction of socialism. But he did concede that, unlike the USSR, the construction may proceed by peaceful change if the working class shows sufficient strength and with the further stipulation that "in all the forms of transition to socialism an absolute and decisive requirement is political leadership of the working class, headed by its vanguard. The transition to socialism is impossible without this."...

A restoration of uniformity would have required Soviet resources for the subordination and maintenance of Communist regimes, but this was made almost permanently unpopular because of the domestic rigidities it imposed. Such a policy would also have conflicted with the broad international stance adopted by the USSR after Stalin's death and, indeed, with some of the domestic reforms. Limited diversity opened a vista for the emergence of self-supporting Communist regimes but at the price of cohesion of the bloc. Khrushchev's somewhat ambiguous formula attempted to straddle this dilemma by superimposing ideological party unity on an acceptance of some domestic institutional diversity, which in turn he hoped would be balanced by growing economic ties. But this involved a rejection of Stalin the man and Stalinism the dogma, and these had been part of the power element which had buttressed and long since merged with ideology. Dissipating it, Khrushchev placed a tremendous burden on the ideology. At the same time the ideology had to cope with the domestic problems left behind by Stalnism and with the pressures emanating from the independent, but now legitimately Communist, Yugoslav position as well as from developing domestic events in Hungary and Poland. Their effect on relations among Communist states was to prove of critical importance and the Khrushchev formula was yet to face its test.

READING 2

Khrushchevism in Retrospect

Merle Fainsod

To understand Khrushchevism, one must begin with Khrushchev the man, with what he was like in his days of power. Shrewd, earthy, endowed with boundless energy, a bouncing confidence, and a quick, if coarse, wit, he was the very epitome of the self-made man in any society. Like most self-made men, he believed profoundly that the social order which nurtured him and conferred its highest honors on him was a society whose virtues could not be impugned....

In the course of his lifetime, Khrushchev saw Russia transformed from a relatively backward country into one of the world's leading industrial and military powers, and he was understandably proud of this rapid progress and his own

Reprinted from *Marxism in the Modern World*, ed. Milorad M. Drackhovitch, with the permission of the publishers, Stanford University Press. Copyright © 1965 by the Board of Trustees of the Leland Stanford Junior University.

role in it. He gave every evidence of believing that the Soviet Union not only embodies the most progressive and just social structure that mankind has attained, but that it is also blazing a trail into the future that people everywhere will enthusiastically follow. "I am convinced more than ever," he told reporters toward the end of his American trip, "that the holiest of holies, the best that man can create, is socialist society, the Communist system."[1]

Nor can such remarks be dismissed as mere propaganda—the public pronouncements which a Soviet leader is duty-bound to make, and which do not necessarily mirror his fundamental outlook. Difficult as it is to be certain that one has ever penetrated the inner recesses of a man's character, the self-portrait that emerges from Khrushchev's countless impromptu remarks is fairly clear: he saw himself as a man of faith, believing that communism provides a key to the world's problems. He was a propagandist in every fiber of his being, but propaganda in his case was inseparable from his deepest convictions. In a characteristic speech to the Fifth World Congress of Trade Unions in 1961, he observed: "It may be said that Khrushchev is again handing out propaganda. If you think so, you are not mistaken. Yes, I was, am, and always shall be a propagandist. As long as the heart continues beating in my breast, I shall propagate the ideas of Marxism-Leninism, the ideas of Communist construction!"[2] . . .

CHOICES AND IMPERATIVES

To understand Khrushchevism as it took shape after Stalin's death, one must begin with the man; but one must also understand the situation in which he found himself and the necessities to

which he was compelled to adapt. Stalin's legacy to his successors was replete with problems. His impressive achievements in forcing the pace of Soviet industrialization, in building military power, and in expanding his domain into Eastern and Central Europe, were all purchased at a heavy price. Soviet agriculture remained backward and stagnant, and the food available to Soviet consumers was monotonous, scarce, and high-priced. Stalin's obsession with the development of heavy industry meant that light industry was ignored and underdeveloped, and shortages of consumer goods and housing were acute and widespread. The system of terror on which Stalin relied to protect his own security and to enforce his regime of deprivation and sacrifice had its debilitating effects. It bred a cowed and submissive populace for whom the regime was "they" and not "we." Frightened bureaucrats shrank from exercising initiative; there was a frozen and congealed quality about Soviet life that tended to rob it of all dynamism and revolutionary appeal. The East European satellites formed an extension of the Soviet prisonhouse. Yugoslavia, to be sure, had broken away amid the curses of the Cominform; and in the East, Communist China presented a special case with its own independent power base. For the rest, the Communist bloc was managed by puppets utterly dependent on Stalin. The Soviet empire was, in effect, sealed off from the West, and as a result of the Korean War the Soviet Union and the United States were involved in a spiraling arms race that threatened the world with a nuclear holocaust.

This was the situation that confronted Stalin's successors. As communists, the choices open to them were not infinite. They could not be expected to preside over the liquidation of Stalin's empire. As party leaders, they might seek other means than Stalin's to promote Communist objectives; but they shared with him not merely a common experience but also a common commitment. What they now also shared with one an-

---

[1] *Let Us Live in Peace and Friendship—The Visit of N. S. Khrushchev to the USA*, Moscow, Foreign Languages Publishing House, 1959, p. 338.

[2] N. S. Khrushchev, *Communism—Peace and Happiness for the Peoples*, Moscow, Foreign Languages Publishing House, 1963, Vol. II, p. 365.

other was a responsibility they could not escape: they had to make their own decisions.

The tone set by the new leadership in the months after Stalin's death was one of relaxion of tension at home and abroad. Amnesties, price cuts, and promises of more consumer goods and housing augured a new disposition to seek popular support. The ending of the Korean War contributed toward an easing of relations with the West. So far as we know, Khrushchev participated in and approved of these actions, as he no doubt also ratified the decision to suppress the East German rising in June 1953 and joined in the purge of Beria [Lavrentii Beria, chief of Stalin's secret police] soon afterward....

As his power and prestige mounted, the range of his interest broadened, and he began to place his own personal stamp on foreign as well as domestic policy. The Khrushchevian style was characterized by boldness as well as opportunism; above all, it was marked by a willingness to experiment and to strike out in new directions without necessarily calculating or anticipating costs and consequences. Khrushchev's most dramatic initiatives during this period were reserved for the field of foreign affairs. Of these, perhaps the most impressive were his efforts to woo Tito back into the Soviet bloc and to strengthen Soviet influence among the new nations of Asia and Africa.

THE WATERSHED

While the new dynamism thus introduced into Soviet foreign policy reflected the Khrushchevian touch, it remained for the 20th Party Congress, held in February 1956, to define the content of what has since come to be described as Khrushchevism. The high spot of the Congress was the "secret speech" in which Khrushchev combined a wide-ranging condemnation of Stalin's methods of rule with sensational disclosures of his terrorist crimes. What inspired Khrushchev to open this Pandora's box is still open to debate and may long remain so. Khrushchev himself defended the speech as a necessary surgical operation to restore the health of the party. In repudiating Stalin's terrorist practices, he in effect offered his personal guaranty that he would not repeat them. More positively, he held out a vision of a Soviet society in which citizens could breathe more freely, officialdom could exercise initiative without fearing the consequences, the bond between party and people would be strengthened, and the authority of the regime would be built on the rational foundations of regularized procedures, concern with popular welfare, and confidence rather than fear.

The destalinization campaign, the restatement of the theory of peaceful coexistence, and other innovations launched by Khrushchev at the 20th Party Congress were intended both to broaden the appeal of the Communist movement and to strengthen Khrushchev's own position within it. In the end, they came close to destroying Khrushchev, and they released divisive forces within the Communist world that have not yet run their full course. Within the Soviet Union, the ferment stirred up by Khrushchev's "secret speech" infected wide circles of the intelligentsia and student youth, inspiring a protest literature that went beyond denunciations of Stalin to criticism of the Soviet system itself. Within the bloc, the disarray assumed proportions serious enough to threaten the Soviet hold over Eastern Europe.

The gathering unrest came to a climax in October 1956. The bloody repression of the revolt in Hungary and the reimposition of cultural curbs within the Soviet Union in reaction to the revolt served to tarnish the image of Khrushchev as the great liberalizer. In the aftermath of Hungary, Khrushchev's prestige declined sharply. His handling of Hungarian events contributed to an exacerbation of relations with Tito. The Chinese party leadership gave him public support, but as subsequent disclosures have made clear, they were privately highly critical of his destalinization campaign, of his ideological initiatives, and above all of his failure to consult with them. Within the Soviet party itself, his Presidium opponents began to organize a cabal to unseat him, and by dint of the additional support they gathered in opposition to his industrial reorganization plans, they were able, by May 1957, to mobilize a seven-to-four majority against him and to confront him with a demand for his resignation.

It is a measure both of the power concentrated in the office of the First Secretary and of Khrushchev's capacity to turn adverse developments to his own advantage that he was able to triumph even in these circumstances. By transferring the arena of the struggle to the Central Committee, where his followers were strongly installed, he turned the tables on his opponents and emerged from the encounter stronger than ever. In October of the same year he further consolidated his position by ousting his erstwhile supporter, Marshal Zhukov, from the Presidium and moving quickly to bring the armed forces under firm party control.

At this stage of Khrushchev's career, fortune seemed to be smiling on him. He had rid himself of his Presidium opponents, and his position as party leader appeared to be unassailable. He had surmounted the crisis in Eastern Europe, and while restiveness was still evident, there were no threats of armed uprisings. The ferment among Soviet youth and intellectuals gave every outward appearance of having subsided; in any case, it presented no organized challenge to the regime's power.

Most important of all, the world was now treated to a startling demonstration of Soviet accomplishments in rocketry. In the excitement that attended the launching of Sputnik I on October 4, 1957, the simultaneous dismissal of Marshal Zhukov was all but forgotten. The Soviet space exploits had obvious military implications, and Khrushchev was not slow to point out that they marked a significant shift in the balance of power. He quickly initiated a major drive to translate Soviet rocket superiority into diplomatic gains. In a militant speech to a Polish-Soviet Friendship Meeting in Moscow on November 10, 1958, he ignited the Berlin crisis with a demand for the liquidation of the occupation regime in West Berlin. This time, Khrushchev overreached himself. The decision of the Western powers to stand firm exposed the emptiness of his ultimatums, bluster, and threats.

NEW ALTERNATIVES

It is worth pausing at this point to sketch out the problems and choices that Khrushchev faced. Despite undoubted industrial progress and dramatic space achievements, there were limits to the pressure that Moscow could apply on the West. The United States was still a formidable thermonuclear power with larger resources than the Soviet Union, and any confrontation that imperiled vital American interests raised the danger of a thermonuclear holocaust, with potentially disastrous consequences for both sides. As long as relations between the United States and the Soviet Union remained tense and difficult, the stage was set for the continuation of an expensive arms race that diverted resources from domestic development and spelled persisting hardships for the Soviet people. An easing of relations with the United States, by contrast, opened up tempting perspectives of more rapid improvement in the Soviet standard of living and accelerated economic development.

A real detente with the West, however, could only be achieved at the price of accepting the status quo in world affairs and foregoing opportunities for revolutionary advance, at least for a defined period. However expedient such a course of action might appear from the Soviet point of view, it held out dangers for Soviet relations with its allies in the world Communist movement. It subordinated their interest to those of the Soviet Union. It implied, for example, that Communist China would not be able to count on Soviet assistance in pressing its campaign to regain Taiwan, and that Chinese expansionist ambitions elsewhere would have to be curbed to serve Soviet national needs. It meant that Khrushchev might be forced to impose brakes on the revolutionary enthusiasm of Communist parties anxious to come to power, and might thus be maneuvered into a position where he could be accused of betraying the revolutionary cause.

It is unlikely that these sharply defined alternatives were either recognized or accepted by Khrushchev. Like leaders elsewhere who face multiple pressures and impulses, he sought to escape hard choices and found himself responding to events and pursuing policies with contradictory implications. Thus, Khrushchev's professed, and probably real, desire to achieve a relaxation of tension with the United States which would enable him to concentrate greater resources on internal development was periodically negated by actions that placed a strain on the Soviet-American relationship. The Berlin ultimatums and the building of the wall between East and West Berlin, the Congo adventure, and the Cuban missile crisis were symptomatic of the unresolved dilemma in an area where doctrinal commitments and considerations of *Realpolitik* clashed.

Equally difficult problems and choices confronted Khrushchev in working out his relations with his main ally in the Communist bloc. The alternative of responding to Chinese demands for increased militancy opened up serious risks. In the underdeveloped areas, it meant breaking the links that Soviet foreign policy had so carefully forged with the neutralist leaders of the new nations. In relations with the West, it meant risking a sharp increase in the danger of thermonuclear war and intensifying the arms race. In domestic terms, it meant slowing down the Soviet rate of economic growth and negating Khrushchev's vision of a welfare communism which would magnify the Soviet appeal both at home and abroad.

Faced with these alternatives, Khrushchev chose to stand firm on the policy lines to which he was committed. Indeed, as the bitterness and virulence of the Sino-Soviet dispute mounted and prospects of reconciliation faded, the positions of both sides hardened. In the wake of the Cuban missile crisis of 1962, with its sobering reminder of how close the world had come to thermonuclear extinction, Khrushchev demonstrated a renewed eagerness to improve his relations with the United States and the West. He turned his back on Communist China to sign a nuclear test-ban treaty with the United States and Britain, joined in establishing the so-called "hot line" between Washington and Moscow, undertook in cooperation with the United States to ban missiles in orbit and to cut back the production of fissionable material, negotiated a consular convention with the United States as well as a number of agreements on cultural exchanges, pressed restraint on Castro, and relaxed tension over Berlin. All these efforts to "normalize" relations with the West were greeted by Peking as additional confirmation of Khrushchev's apostasy from true Marxism-Leninism. They served to deepen a split that was rapidly becoming unbridgeable.

Khrushchev's decision to seize the "peace issue" even at the cost of further alienating Peking was not without its positive advantages. To the extent that Khrushchev could make good his indictment of the Chinese leaders as "madmen" and "adventurers" who were prepared to risk world destruction in order to realize their ambitions, he could count on widespread support not only in the Soviet Union but among all people, Communist as well as non-Communist, who feared nuclear war....

LESSONS IN FAILURE

Khrushchev's record was least impressive in the foreign policy field. Whereas Stalin could point to a vast expansion of the Communist empire in Europe and Asia, achieved in a period when the Soviet Union was in a much weaker position vis-a-vis the United States, Khrushchev, with much greater power at his command, was unable to register any large-scale gains. The accessions of North Vietnam and Cuba to the Communist camp were not insignificant victories, but taken together they hardly began to match Stalin's triumphs. In Europe Khrushchev was unable to break out of the stalemate inherited from Stalin; his unsuccessful efforts to dislodge the Western powers from West Berlin by threats and ultimatums that had to be withdrawn represented a major loss of face. The rebuff he received during the Cuban missile crisis further tarnished the myth of Soviet invincibility and revealed Khrushchev as an adventurer whose bluff could be called by a willingness to stand firm.

Fortunately for the world, Khrushchev's determination to test the resolution of his antagonists was combined with a vivid appreciation of the dangers of thermonuclear warfare. In contrast to Stalin Khrushchev operated under a compelling necessity to adjust the strategy and tactics of Soviet foreign policy to the realities of the thermonuclear age. These realities not only brought to the fore the common interest that he shared with Western leaders in avoiding mutual destruction; they also impelled him to seek ways of advancing the Communist cause that would minimize the risks of igniting a thermonuclear holocaust. Khrushchevian policies in the underdeveloped world fitted into this pattern. Trade, military and economic aid, technical assistance, and cultural penetration were the prime levers by which the Soviet Union sought to heighten its influence in these areas. In the interest of cementing relations with the nationalist leaders of these states, Khrushchev discouraged premature revolutionary bids for power by local Communists. From the point of view of the latter, anxious to strike out for power, Khrushchevism was all brakes and no forward charge. However valid Khrushchev's long-term prognosis for the underdeveloped world may turn out to be, it was ill-suited to a mood of revolutionary impatience, and it only provided fuel for the Chinese charge that Khrushchevism represented a betrayal of the cause of world revolution.

Whatever Khrushchev's claims to greatness, his contributions to the unity of world communism are not likely to be listed among them. In the eyes of his Chinese antagonists and their allies in the international Communist movement, Khrushchevism became a term of contempt, the symbol of a peculiarly degenerate form of revisionism that sacrifices the revolutionary elan of Leninism to serve the bourgeoisified interests of the chauvinist great power masquerading as a Communist state. His most poignant legacies to his successors may well be the recognition that a common ideological heritage provides no guaranty of political unity among communist powers, and that imperial conflict is no monopoly of the capitalist world. It should, perhaps, come as no great surprise that so powerful a force as nationalism should reappear in a Communist guise, but for those who have taken professions of brotherhood among Communist nations at face value, it has nevertheless come as a profound shock.

That Khrushchev should have contributed to the disintegration of the Communist world empire is a phenomenon that invites explanation. But it would be superficial to attribute the development solely to Khrushchev's personal idiosyncrasies. However much clashes of personality may have served to exacerbate relations between Khrushchev and Mao, the causes of their differences were more deep-seated, with roots in the very different array of domestic and foreign problems to which they felt impelled to respond. When a Communist regime sinks its roots in national soil, its perception of its needs cannot avoid being colored by the environment in which it functions and by the pressures under which it operates.

END OF AN ERA?

Insofar as Khrushchevism was something more than Khrushchev, it must be seen as an ideological expression of the stage of development in which the Soviet Union found itself. After decades of deprivation and sacrifice under Stalin, the regime came under strong pressure to raise the living standards of its own people and was understandably reluctant to make further sacrifices to lift the level of poorer Communist countries up to its own. A relatively advanced industrial power with a vested interest in preserving its hard-won gains, the Soviet Union was not prepared to support a reckless and adventurous revolutionary strategy that would pose unacceptable risks of thermonuclear extinction. As the historic leader and most powerful nation in the Communist camp, it was anything but eager to build up rivals who would challenge its mandate to direct Communist tactics everywhere. As a residuary legatee of Russian national interests, it tended to see China as a threat, in national as well as in Communist terms. In all these senses, Khrushchevism served to articulate the conservative interests of a mature Communist power with a relatively high stake in the preservation of the status quo.

If Khrushchevism bred its polar opposite in Maoism, both unwittingly conspired to create a situation in which even such a previously abject Soviet satellite as Rumania was emboldened to proclaim its economic independence and every communist regime or party is now tempted to place its own interests in the forefront whenever and wherever it can. The confrontation of Khrushchevism and Maoism became more than a contest for world Communist leadership; it set the stage for the emergence of Communist forces that sought to escape the discipline of both. The ultimate irony of Khrushchevism was the belated discovery that a Communist world empire could not be built on Soviet interests alone.

Reply to U.S. Embassy in Moscow Concerning Food Riots and Demonstrations in East Germany

V. M. Molotov

June 1953

Editor's commentary: After the death of Stalin, tensions rose across Soviet-occupied Eastern Europe. In the third week of June 1953, the accumulated misery and dissatisfaction over Stalinist deprivation of the German population resulted in food riots and demonstrations, which were suppressed by Soviet tanks in the eastern zones of occupation. This letter by the Soviet foreign minister denies any crisis in East Germany that was not of the making of Western provocateurs.

Dear Mr. Chargé d'Affaires: In your letter of July 10, it is said that the President of the U.S.A. is allegedly concerned over the food situation in the eastern part of Germany and that the Government of the U.S.A. has assigned $15 million for sending and distributing certain food products among the population of this part of Germany.

In connection with this, I consider it necessary to call the attention of the Government of the U.S.A. to the following:

From your communication, it is clear that the Government of the U.S.A. has been incorrectly informed regarding the situation in the eastern part of Germany. In this it is impossible to see anything unexpected inasmuch as you state that information regarding Eastern Germany has been received from such sources as the American High Commissioner in Germany and Bonn Chancellor Adenauer, who bear the chief responsibility for the infractions of the socialist order in the eastern part of Berlin which you mention. If on June 17 there had not been organized on their part the dispatch from the American sector of Berlin of whole groups of hirelings and criminal elements for setting fire to food and other stores, for attacking officials, state institutions of the German Democratic Republic, etc., then in general there would have taken place no infractions of order in Berlin.

From your letter it is also evident that the Government of the U.S.A. took the decision to send $15 million worth of food products even without having asked the opinion of the Government of the German Democratic Republic in this connec-

Department of State Bulletin, vol.29, no. 734, 20 July 1953, p. 68.

tion. Such manners at the present time would insult even the population of a colony, to say nothing of the German people and its legal democratic government.

From all this it follows that in the given case, the U.S.A. Government has not shown any sort of solicitude as to the food supply for the German people, but has decided to resort to a propaganda maneuver having nothing in common with concern for the real interests of the German population.

By the present letter, I request you to transmit to the Government of the U.S.A. that on the strength of stable, friendly relations established between the Soviet Union and the German Democratic Republic, the Soviet Government has even earlier given food assistance to the German population. The Soviet Government is also ready in the future, when there shall be need of it, to grant the population of the German Democratic Republic all necessary food and other assistance in correspondence with the existing agreement between the Governments of the U.S.S.R. and the G.D.R.

Molotov

DOCUMENT 2

The Warsaw Treaty

14 May 1955

Editor's commentary: Not coincidentally, the Warsaw Treaty was signed on 14 May 1955, one day before the conclusion of the Austrian State

---

"Treaty of Friendship, Cooperation, and Mutual Assistance Between the People's Republic of Albania, the People's Republic of Bulgaria, the Hungarian People's Republic, the German Democratic Republic, the Polish People's Republic, the Romanian People's Republic, the Union of Soviet Socialist Republics, and the Czechoslovak Republic," *United Nations Treaty Series,* vol. 219, no. 2962 (1955), pp. 24–33.

Treaty allowing for the withdrawal of Soviet occupation forces, which were there as a result of agreement made by the Allies of World War II. Although the inclusion of West Germany in NATO on 9 May 1955 was given as the main reason for the treaty, its initial purpose was to legitimize the presence of Soviet forces in other Central and Eastern European states after this withdrawal. This sent a strong message to the member states that the Austrian withdrawal was not a precedent for further such actions. The treaty became a mechanism by which Soviet political and military control could be more effectively maintained in Eastern and Central Europe. The Warsaw Treaty Organization remains today as one of two international organizations of the Soviet bloc—the other being the Council for Mutual Economic Assistance, or Comecon.

The Contracting Parties,

Reaffirming their desire to create a system of collective security in Europe based on the participation of all European States, irrespective of their social and political structure, whereby the said States may be enabled to combine their efforts in the interests of ensuring peace in Europe;

Taking into consideration, at the same time, the situation that has come about in Europe as a result of the ratification of the Paris Agreements, which provide for the constitution of a new military group in the form of a "West European Union," with the participation of a remilitarized West Germany and its inclusion in the North Atlantic bloc, thereby increasing the danger of a new war and creating a threat to the national security of peace-loving States;

Being convinced that in these circumstances the peace-loving States of Europe must take the necessary steps to safeguard their security and to promote the maintenance of peace in Europe;

Being guided by the purposes and principles of the charter of the United Nations;

In the interests of the further strengthening and development of friendship, cooperation, and mutual assistance in accordance with the principles of respect for the independence and sovereignty of States and of nonintervention in their domestic affairs;

Have resolved to conclude the present Treaty of Friendship, Cooperation, and Mutual Assistance and...have agreed as follows:

Article 1

The Contracting Parties undertake, in accordance with the Charter of the United Nations, to refrain in their international relations from the threat or use of force and to settle their international disputes by peaceful means in such a manner that international peace and security are not endangered.

Article 2

The Contracting Parties declare that they are prepared to participate, in a spirit of sincere cooperation, in all international action for ensuring international peace and security and will devote their full efforts to the realization of these aims.

In this connection, the Contracting Parties shall endeavor to secure, in agreement with other States desiring to cooperate in this manner, the adoption of effective measures for the general reduction of armaments and the prohibition of atomic, hydrogen, and other weapons of mass destruction.

Article 3

The Contracting Parties shall consult together on all important international questions involving their common interest, with a view to strengthening international peace and security.

Whenever any one of the contracting Parties considers that a threat of armed attack on one or more of the States parties to the Treaty has arisen, they shall consult together immediately with a view to providing for their joint defense and maintaining peace and security.

Article 4

In the event of an armed attack in Europe on one or more of the States Parties to the Treaty by any State or group of States, each State Party to the Treaty shall, in the exercise of the right of individual or collective self-defense, in accordance with Article 51 of the United Nations Charter, afford the State or States so attacked immediate assistance, individually and in agreement with the other States Parties to the Treaty, by all the means it considers necessary, including the use of armed force. The States Parties to the Treaty shall consult together immediately concerning the joint measures necessary to restore and maintain international peace and security.

Measures taken under this article shall be reported to the Security Council in accordance with the provisions of the United Nations Charter. These measures shall be discontinued as soon as the Security Council takes the necessary action to restore and maintain international peace and security.

Article 5

The Contracting Parties have agreed to establish a Unified Command, to which certain elements of their armed forces shall be allocated by agreement between the Parties, and which shall act in accordance with jointly established principles. The Parties shall likewise take such other concerted action as may be necessary to reinforce their defensive strength, in order to defend the peaceful labor of their peoples, guarantee the inviolability of their frontiers and territories, and afford protection against possible aggression.

Article 6

For the purpose of carrying out the consultations provided for in the present Treaty between the States Parties thereto, and for the consideration of matters arising in connection with the application of the present Treaty, a Political Consultative Committee shall be established, in which each State Party to the Treaty shall be represented by a member of the Government or by some other specially appointed representative.

The Committee may establish such auxiliary organs as may prove to be necessary.

Article 7

The Contracting Parties undertake not to participate in any coalitions or alliances, and not to conclude any agreements, the purposes of which are incompatible with the purposes of the present Treaty.

The Contracting Parties declare that their obligations under international treaties at present in force are not incompatible with the provisions of the present Treaty.

Article 8

The Contracting Parties declare that they will act in a spirit of friendship and cooperation to promote the further development and strengthening of the economic and cultural ties among them, in accordance with the principles of respect for each other's independence and sovereignty and of nonintervention in each other's domestic affairs.

Article 9

The present Treaty shall be open for accession by other States, irrespective of their social and political structure, which express their readiness, by participating in the present Treaty, to help in combining the efforts of the peace-loving States to ensure the peace and security of the peoples. Such accessions shall come into effect with the consent of the States Parties to the Treaty after the instruments of accession have been deposited with the Government of the Polish People's Republic.

Article 10

The present Treaty shall be subject to ratification, and the instruments of ratification shall be deposited with the Government of the Polish People's Republic.

The Treaty shall come in force on the date of deposit of the last instrument of ratification. The Government of the Polish People's Republic shall inform the other States Parties to the Treaty of the deposit of each instrument of ratification.

Article 11

The present Treaty shall remain in force for twenty years. For Contracting Parties which do not, one year before the expiration of that term, give notice of termination of the Treaty to the Government of the Polish People's Republic, the treaty shall remain in force for a further ten years.

In the event of the establishment of a system of collective security in Europe and the conclusion for that purpose of a General European Treaty concerning collective security, a goal which the contracting Parties shall steadfastly strive to achieve, the present Treaty shall cease to have effect as from the date on which the General European Treaty comes into force.

Done at Warsaw, this fourteenth day of May, nineteen hundred fifty-five, in one copy, in the Russian, Polish, Czech, and German languages, all the texts being equallly authentic. Certified copies of the present Treaty shall be transmitted by the Government of the Polish People's Republic to all the other Parties to the Treaty.

IN FAITH WHEREOF the Plenipotentiaries have signed the present Treaty and have thereto affixed their seals.

By authorization of the Presidium of the National Assembly of the People's Republic of Albania: (Signed) M. Shehu.

By authorization of the Presidium of the National Assembly of the People's Republic of Bulgaria: (Signed) V. Chervenkov

By authorization of the Presidium of the Hungarian People's Republic: (Signed) A. Hegedus

By authorization of the President of the German Democratic Republic: (Signed) O. Grotewohl

By authorization of the Council of State of the Polish People's Republic: (Signed) J. Cyrankiewicz

By authorization of the Presidium of the Grand National Assembly of the Romanian People's Republic: (Signed) G. Gheorghiu Dej

By authorization of the Presidium of the Supreme Soviet of the Union of Soviet Socialist Republics: (Signed) N. Bulganin

By authorization of the President of the Czechoslovak Republic: (Signed) V. Siroky

DOCUMENT 3

Austrian State Treaty

15 May 1955

Editor's commentary: This treaty's significance for Soviet foreign policy lies in the fact that its conclusion produced the first withdrawal in the postwar period of Soviet troops from occupied territory. The conditions under which such an event could take place are outlined in the excerpts below. It was the agreement of Austria to observe neutrality in European and world politics, similar to the position of Switzerland, that allowed for such an historic event. Interestingly, the signing of the Austrian State Treaty took place one day after the conclusion of the Warsaw Pact, 14 May 1955 (see Chapter 4, document 2).

Article 1—Reestablishment of Austria as a Free and Independent State
The Allied and associated Powers recognize that Austria is reestablished as a sovereign, independent and democratic State.

Article 2—Maintenance of Austria's Independence
The Allied and Associated Powers declare that they will respect the independence and territorial integrity of Austria as established under the present Treaty.

Article 3—Recognition by Germany of Austrian Independence
The Allied and Associated Powers will incorporate in the German Peace Treaty provisions for securing from Germany the recognition of Austria's sovereignty and independence and the renunciation by Germany of all territorial and political claims in respect of Austria and Austrian territory.

Article 4—Prohibition of Anschluss
1. The Allied and Associated Powers declare that political or economic union between Austria and Germany is prohibited. Austria fully recognizes its responsibilities in this matter and shall not enter into political or economic union with Germany in any form whatsoever.

2. In order to prevent such union Austria shall not conclude any agreement with Germany, nor do any act, nor take any measures likely, directly or indirectly, to promote political or economic union with Germany, or to impair its territorial integrity or political or economic independence....

Article 5
The frontiers of Austria shall be those existing on 1st January 1938.
[Articles 6 and 7 guarantee basic human rights and the protection of ethnic minorities.]

Article 8—Democratic Institutions
Austria shall have a democratic government based on elections by secret ballot and shall guarantee to all citizens free, equal and universal suffrage as well as the right to be elected to public office....

Article 9—Dissolution of Nazi Organizations
1. Austria shall complete the measures, already begun...to destroy the National Socialist Party and its affiliated and supervised organizations....

Article 10—Special Clauses on Legislation
1. Austria undertakes to maintain and continue to implement the principles contained in the laws and legal measures adopted by the Austrian Government and Parliament since 1st May 1945, and

---

"State Treaty for the Re-establishment of an Independent and Democratic Austria," *Department of State Bulletin*, vol. 32, no. 832, July 6, 1955, pp. 916–932, *excerpts*.

approved by the Allied Commission for Austria, aimed at liquidation of the remnants of the Nazi regime and at the re-establishment of the democratic system....

Article 11—Recognition of Peace Treaties
Austria undertakes to recognize the full force of the Treaties of Peace with Italy, Roumania, Bulgaria, Hungary and Finland and other agreements or arrangements which have been or will be reached by the Allied and Associated Powers in respect of Germany and Japan for the restoration of peace.
[Articles 12–19 circumscribe the character of future military affairs within the Austrian state.]

Article 20—Withdrawal of Allied Forces
1. The agreement on the Machinery of Control in Austria of 28th June, 1946 shall terminate on the coming into force of the present Treaty.
2. On the coming into force of the present Treaty, the Inter-Allied Command established under paragraph 4 of the Agreement on Zones of Occupation in Austria and the Administration of the City of Vienna of 9th July 1945, shall cease to exercise any functions with respect to the City of Vienna. The Agreement on Zones of Occupation of Austria shall terminate upon completion of withdrawal from Austria of the forces of the Allied and Associated Powers in accordance with paragraph 3 of the present Article.
3. The forces of the Allied and Associated Powers and members of the Allied Commission for Austria shall be withdrawn from Austria within ninety days from the coming into force of the present Treaty....
4. The Government of Austria shall accord to the forces of the Allied and Associated Powers and the members of the Allied commission for Austria pending their withdrawal from Austria the same rights, immunities and facilities as they enjoyed immediately before the coming into force of the present Treaty.
5. The Allied and Associated Powers undertake to return to the Government of Austria...
(a) all currency which was made avaliable

free of cost to the Allied and Associated Powers...
(b) All Austrian property requisitioned by Allied forces or the Allied Commission and which is still in their possession.
[The remainder of the treaty concerns economic matters.]

DOCUMENT 4

The Crimes of Stalin—Yugoslavia and the Camp of Socialism

N. S. Khrushchev

February 1956

Editor's commentary: Khrushchev's "secret speech" at the Twentieth Party Congress blamed much of what went wrong in Soviet domestic and foreign policy on Stalin's arbitrary dictatorial rule. In attempting to restore the unity of the world communist movement, damaged by the expulsion of Yugoslavia from the Cominform in 1948, Khrushchev denounced Stalin's treatment of Yugoslavia and, by implication, international communism. The restoration of good relations with Yugoslavia is seen to be "in the interest of the whole camp of socialism."

The willfulness of Stalin showed itself not only in decisions concerning the international life of the country but also in the international relations of the Soviet Union.

"The Crimes of the Stalin Era: Special Report to the 20th Congress of the Communist Party of the Soviet Union" (closed session, 24–25 February 1956), *The New Leader*, p. 48. Reprinted with permission of *The New Leader*. Copyright 1962 by *The New Leader*.

The July [1955] plenum of the Central Committee studied in detail the reasons for the development of conflict with Yugoslavia. It was a shameful role which Stalin played here. The "Yugoslav affair" contained no problems which could not have been solved through party discussions among comrades. There was no significant basis for the development of this "affair"; it was completely possible to have prevented the rupture of relations with that country. This does not mean, however, that the Yugoslav leaders did not make mistakes or did not have shortcomings. But these mistakes and shortcomings were magnified in a monstrous manner by Stalin, which resulted in a break of relations with a friendly country.

I recall the first days when the conflict between the Soviet Union and Yugoslavia began artificially to be blown up. Once, when I came from Kiev to Moscow, I was invited to visit Stalin, who, pointing to the copy of a letter lately sent to Tito, asked me, "Have you read this?"

Not waiting for my reply, he answered, "I will shake my little finger—and there will be no more Tito. He will fall."...

But this did not happen to Tito. No matter how much or how little Stalin shook not only his little finger but everything else that he could shake, Tito did not fall. Why? The reason was that, in this case of disagreement with the Yugoslav comrades, Tito had behind him a state and a people who had gone through a severe school of fighting for liberty and independence, a people which gave support to its leaders.

You see to what Stalin's mania for greatness led. He had completely lost consciousness of reality; he demonstrated his suspicion and haughtiness not only in relation to individuals in the USSR, but in relations to whole parties and nations.

We have carefully examined the case of Yugoslavia and have found a proper solution which is approved by the peoples of the Soviet Union and of Yugoslavia as well as by the working masses of all the people's democracies and by all progressive humanity. The liquidation of the abnormal relationship with Yugoslavia was done in the interest of the whole camp of socialism, in the interest of strengthening peace in the whole world....

DOCUMENT 5

Soviet Statement on Hungary

30 October 1956

Editor's commentary: Khrushchev's "secret speech" to the Twentieth CPSU Congress in February 1956 had unintended effects. The summer and autumn of that year witnessed unrest in Poland and Hungary. While the turmoil in Poland was resolved in October without Soviet military intervention, the situation in Hungary became incendiary. On 23 October a "counterrevolution" began in the city of Budapest. The Soviets responded in force to assist their Hungarian clients. However, on 30 October conditions seemed to relax somewhat, as the Soviet government statement included here suggests. But the withdrawal of Soviet tanks from Budapest promised by the Soviets was only a temporary exigency; on 4 November the tanks returned to crush the Hungarian revolution. International outrage was muted as the world's attention was turned to another hot spot, the Middle East, where the Suez crisis was raging at the same time.

The principles of peaceful coexistence, friendship, and cooperation among all states have always been and still form the unshakable foun-

---

Moscow Radio, 30 October 1956, as transcribed in *Department of State Bulletin*, vol. 35, no. 907, 12 November 1956, pp. 745–746, *excerpts*.

dation of the foreign relations of the USSR. This policy finds its most profound and consistent expression in the relationship with socialist countries. United by the common ideal of building a socialist society and the principles of proletarian internationalism, the countries of the great commonwealth of socialist nations can build their relations only on the principle of full equality, respect of territorial integrity, state independence and sovereignty, and noninterference in one another's domestic affairs....

In the process of the establishment of the new regime and the deep revolutionary transformation in social relations there were not a few difficulties, unsolved problems, and out-and-out mistakes, including some in the relations between the socialist states—violations and mistakes which infringed the principles of equality in relations between socialist states.

The 20th Congress of the Communist Party of the Soviet Union resolutely condemned these mistakes and violations and demanded that the Soviet Union apply Lenin's principles of the equality of nations in its relations with other socialist states. This statement took complete cognizance of the historical past and the peculiarities of each country which has taken the road of building a new life....

As recent events have shown, the need has arisen for an appropriate declaration to be made on the position of the Soviet Union in the mutual relations between the USSR and other socialist countries, primarily in the economic and military spheres. The Soviet Government is ready to discuss with the governments of other socialist states measures insuring the further development and strengthening of economic ties between socialist countries, in order to remove any possibilities of violating the principle of national sovereignty, mutual advantage, and equality in economic relations.

This principle should extend also to advisers. It is common knowledge that during the first period of the formation of the new social-ist order, at the request of the governments of the people's democracies, the Soviet Union sent to these countries a certain number of specialists—engineers, agronomists, scientific workers, and military advisers. During the latter period the Soviet Government on many occasions asked the socialist states about the recall of its advisers.

In view of the fact that by now the people's democracies have formed their own qualified national cadres in all spheres of economic and military construction, the Soviet Government considers it as urgent to examine, together with other socialist states, the question whether a further stay of USSR advisers in these countries is expedient....

With a view to insuring the mutual security of the socialist countries, the Soviet government is ready to examine with other socialist countries that are parties to the Warsaw Teraty the question of Soviet troops stationed on the territory of these countries. In this the Soviet Government proceeds from the general principle that the stationing of troops of one state that is a party to the Warsaw Treaty on the territory of another state that is a party to the Warsaw Treaty should take place on the basis of an agreement among all its participants and not only with the agreement of the state on whose territory these troops are stationed or are planned to be stationed at its request....

The Soviet government regards it as indispensable to make a statement in connection with the events in Hungary.

The course of the events has shown that the working people of Hungary, who have achieved great progress on the basis of their people's democratic order, correctly raise the question of the necessity of eliminating serious shortcomings in the field of economic building, the further raising of the material well-being of the population, and the struggle against bureaucratic excesses in the state apparatus.

However, this just and progressive movement of the working people was soon joined by forces of black reaction and counterrevolution, which are trying to take advantage of the discontent of part of the working people to undermine the foundations of the people's democratic order in Hungary and to restore the old landlord and capitalist order.

The Soviet government and all the Soviet people deeply regret that the development of events in Hungary has led to bloodshed. On the request of the Hungarian People's Government the Soviet Government consented to the entry into Budapest of the Soviet Army units to assist the Hungarian People's Army and the Hungarian authorities to establish order in the town. Believing that the further presence of Soviet Army units in Hungary can serve as a cause for even greater deterioration of the situation, the Soviet Government has given instructions to its military command to withdraw the Soviet army units from Budapest as soon as this is recognized as necessary by the Hungarian Government.

At the same time, the Soviet government is ready to enter in relevant negotiations with the Government of the Hungarian People's Republic and other participants of the Warsaw Treaty on the question of the presence of Soviet troops on the territory of Hungary.

The defense of socialist achievements by the people's democracy of Hungary is at the present moment the chief and sacred duty of workers, peasants, and intelligentsia, and of all the Hungarian working people.

The Soviet Government expresses confidence that the peoples of the socialist countries will not permit foreign and internal reactionary forces to undermine the basis of the people's democratic regimes, won and consolidated by the heroic struggle and toil of the workers, peasants, and intelligentsia of each country.

They will make all efforts to remove all obstacles that lie in the path of further strengthening the democratic basis of the independence and sovereignty of their countries, to develop further the socialist basis of each country, its economy and culture, for the sake of the constant growth of the material welfare and the cultural level of all the peoples. They will consolidate the fraternal unity and mutual assistance of the socialist countries for the strengthening of the great cause of peace and socialism.

DOCUMENT 6

Letter to President Eisenhower Concerning Suez Crisis

N. A. Bulganin

5 November 1956

Editor's commentary: This letter from Soviet Premier Bulganin was in response to a protest written the previous day by President Eisenhower concerning the Soviet intervention in Hungary. Bulganin ignored the pleas of Eisenhower concerning Hungary and instead shrewdly and cynically turned the tables on the President by inviting the United States to participate in a Middle East expedition to return control of the Suez Canal to the Egyptians, led by Gamel Abdel Nasser, from whom a British-French-Israeli force had wrested it several days earlier.

Since 1955, the Soviets had shared a good relationship with the Egyptians, and took advantage of this event to continue to cultivate for themselves the image of champion of Arab rights in the Middle East. The Soviets were also, in effect, scolding the Americans: they knew full well that although the United States had condemned this act of aggression in the Middle East, it had failed to control the actions of its own allies and would not move against them. The Middle East situation was fortuitous for the USSR at this time, overshadowing as it did the Soviet intervention in

Department of State Bulletin, vol. 35, no. 908, 19 November 1956, pp. 796–797.

Hungary, where Soviet tanks crushed the Hungarian "counterrevolution."

Esteemed Mr. President: In this troubled and responsible moment for the cause of universal peace, I approach you on behalf of the Soviet Government. One week has passed already since the armed forces of Britain, France, and—obedient to the will of external forces—Israel, without any reason attacked Egypt, bringing in their wake death and destruction. Inhuman bombardment by the British and French Air Force against Egyptian airfields, ports, installations, towns, and inhabited localities is taking place. Anglo-French troops have landed on Egyptian territory. From the invaders' fire tremendous values created by the hands of the Egyptian people are perishing and the toll of human life is mounting every day.

An aggressive war against Egypt, against the Arab peoples whose whole fault is that they upheld their freedom and independence, is unfolding before the eyes of the entire world. The situation in Egypt calls for immediate and most resolute action on the part of the UN Organization. In the event such action is not undertaken, the UN Organization will lose its prestige in the eyes of mankind and will fall apart.

The Soviet Union and the United States are permanent members of the Security Council and the two great powers which possess all modern types of arms, including atomic and hydrogen weapons. We bear particular responsibility for stopping war and reestablishing peace and calm in the area of the Near and Middle East. We are convinced that if the Governments of the USSR and the United States will firmly declare their will to insure peace and oppose aggression, the aggression will be put down and there will be no war.

Mr. President, at this threatening hour, when the loftiest moral principles and the foundations and aims of the United Nations are being put to the test, the Soviet Government approaches the Government of the United States with a proposal of close cooperation in order to put an end to aggression and to top any further bloodshed.

The United States has a strong navy in the zone of the Mediterranean. The Soviet Union also has a strong navy and a powerful air force. The joint and immediate use of these means by the United States and the Soviet Union according to a decision of the United Nations would be a sure guaranty of ending the aggression against the Egyptian people, against the people of the Arab East.

The Soviet Government turns to the US Government with an appeal to join their forces in the United Nations for the adoption of decisive measures to put an end to the aggression. The Soviet Government has already turned to the Security Council and the special extraordinary session of the General Assembly with suitable proposals. Such joint steps of the United States and the Soviet Union do not threaten the interests of Britain and France. The popular masses of Britain and France do not want war. They, like our people, desire the maintenance of peace. Many other states also, together with Britain and France, are interested in the immediate pacification and resumption of the normal functioning of the Suez Canal, interrupted by the military operations.

The aggression against Egypt has not been committed for the sake of free navigation along the Suez Canal, which was safeguarded. The piratical war was launched with the aim of restoring colonial order in the East, an order which had been overthrown by the people. If this war is not stopped it carries the danger of turning into a third world war.

If the Soviet Union and the United States will support the victim of the aggression, then other states, members of the United Nations, will join us in these efforts. By this the authority of the United Nations will be considerably enhanced and peace will be restored and strengthened.

The Soviet Government is ready to enter into immediate negotiations with the government of the United States on the practical realization of the above-mentioned proposals, so that effective action in the interests of peace might be undertaken within the next hours.

At this tense moment of history, when the fate of the entire Arab East is being decided, and at the same time the fate of the world, I await your favorable reply.

With sincere respect,
Bulganin

DOCUMENT 7

TASS Announcement of Successful Soviet ICBM Test

27 August 1957

Editor's commentary: The successful test of an intercontinental ballistic missile (ICBM) by the Soviet Union served warning on the United States that the age of relative U.S. strategic invulnerability was fast approaching its end. Coupled with the successful launch of Sputnik *several weeks later, the USSR became the clear leader in rocket technology, the strategic implications of which for the United States were myriad.*

In accordance with the plan of scientific research work in the Soviet Union, successful tests of an intercontinental ballistic rocket as well as detonations of nuclear and thermonuclear weapons have been carried out.

I. Recently, the launch of a long-distance, intercontinental, multi-stage ballistic rocket was accomplished.

Tests of the rocket were successful and completely bore out the correctness of calculations and the chosen design. The flight of the rocket occurred at a very great, as yet unachieved, al-

---

Pravda, 27 August 1957, p. 2. Editor's translation.

titude. Traversing a huge distance in a short time, the rocket landed in a specified region.

The obtained results show that there is the possibility of rocket launches to any region of the globe. The solution of the problem of creating intercontinental ballistic rockets allows the attainment of distant regions while not resorting to strategic aviation, which at the present time is vulnerable to contemporary means of anti-aircraft defense.

Bearing in mind the huge contribution to the development of science and the great significance of this scientific-technical achievement for the strengthening of the defensive capabilities of the Soviet state, the Soviet government expressed its thanks to the large collective of workers who took part in the development and manufacture of the intercontinental rocket and the complex of facilities assuring its launch.

II. In recent days in the Soviet Union there has been conducted a series of nuclear and thermonuclear (hydrogen) weapons detonations. In the interest of assuring the safety of the population, the detonations were carried out at a high altitude. The tests were successful.

In connection with the aforementioned tests TASS is authorized to announce:

For many years in the United Nations Organization the problem of disarmament has been discussed without results, including the question of the banning of atomic and hydrogen weapons and the question of stopping their testing.

The Soviet government, steadfastly conducting a policy of peace, more than once has introduced concrete proposals concerning the vital need of reduction of armed forces and armed states, of the cessation of tests of this type of weapon and of other measures connected with the question of disarmament. However, from the side of the Western powers up to this time no real steps have been made in the area of disarmament. On the contrary, from their side all sorts of obstacles are found as excuses on the road to the achievement of agreements regarding this most important problem of our age.

As is well known, the United States and its partners not only reject the banning of atomic and nuclear weapons, but also in fact do not wish to enter into an agreement on the unconditional and urgent cessation of the testing of nuclear weapons, conducting at the same time a large series of tests of these weapons.

Running into such a clearly negative attitude on the part of the Western powers, and first of all the U.S.A., to the positive resolution of the question of disarmament, the Soviet government finds it necessary to take all essential measures in the interests of insuring the security of the Soviet state.

At the same time, the Soviet government will continue persistently to seek agreements on the cessation of tests and the banning of atomic weapons, and the entire question of disarmament, in positive solutions in which all the peoples of the world are interested.

DOCUMENT 8

TASS Announcement of Sputnik Launch

5 October 1957

Editor's commentary: On 4 October 1957, the Soviet Union took the lead in the space race by accomplishing the first successful launch of an earth orbit satellite. The strategic significance of this achievement, coupled with the successful test of an ICBM in August of the same year, was not lost on American leaders. Note the evident pride in references to both Russian scientific history and the socialist model of development as factors contributing to the Soviet achievement of space flight.

Pravda, 5 October 1957, p. 1. Editor's translation.

For a number of years in the Soviet Union scientific research and experimental design work have been conducted toward the creation of an artificial earth satellite.

As has already been announced in the press, the first satellite launches in the USSR were planned for implementation in accordance with the program of scientific research of the International Geophysical Year.

As a result of this great intensive labor of scientific research institutes and design offices the first artificial satellite in the world was created. On 5 October 1957, in the USSR, a successful launch of the first satellite was carried out. According to preliminary data, the rocket imparted to the satellite the necessary orbital speed of nearly 8,000 meters per second. At the present time, the satellite is making an elliptical trajectory around the earth, and its flight can be observed in the rays of the rising and setting sun with the help of the simplest optical instruments (binoculars, telescopes, etc.).

The satellite has the form of a globe of 58 cm. diameter and weighs 83.6 kg. In it have been placed two radio transmitters, continually emitting radio signals at frequencies of 20.005 and 40.002 megaherz.... Powerful transmitters insure good reception of radio signals to a wide circle of ham operators. The signals appear as telegraph messages with the length of almost 0.3 seconds, with a pause of the same length. The broadcast at one frequency occurs at the time of the pause of the signal at the other frequency.

Scientific stations, located in different parts of the Soviet Union, are conducting observations of the satellite and are plotting its trajectory. Inasmuch as the density of the rarefied upper layers of the atmosphere is sufficiently unknown, at the present time there are no data for the precise determination of the life of the satellite and the place of its entry into the dense layers of the atmosphere. Calculations have shown that as a result of the great speed of the satellite at the end of its existence it will burn up upon reaching the upper layers of the atmosphere at an altitude of several dozen kilometers.

In Russia at the end of the nineteenth century it was by the work of the prominent scientist K. E. Tsiolkovsky that the scientifically based possibility of achieving cosmic flight with the assistance of rockets was first established.

The successful launch of the first man-made earth satellite brings about a most important contribution to the storehouse of world science and culture. A scientific experiment accomplished at such a great altitude has enormous meaning for the understanding of properties of the cosmic expanses and the study of the earth as a planet of our solar system.

During the International Geophysical Year, the Soviet Union intends to accomplish the launch of several more artificial earth satellites. These subsequent satellites will have an increased size and weight and through them will be conducted a wide program of scientific research.

Artificial satellites of the earth pave the way to interplanetary travel, and apparently our contemporaries are fated to be witnesses to the fact that liberated and politically conscious labor of the people of the new socialist society makes reality of the most daring dreams of mankind.

DOCUMENT 9

The Rapacki Plan

October 1957

Editor's commentary: This plan for a central European nuclear-free zone was initially introduced by Polish Foreign Minister Adam Rapacki in October 1957. The memorandum below was handed by Rapacki to U.S. Ambassador to Poland

Department of State Bulletin, vol. 38, no. 986, 19 May 1958, pp. 822–823, *excerpts.*

Jacob D. Beam on 14 February 1958, in hopes that further negotiations would produce the desired result. Although the proposal was construed by the United States as a propaganda effort on the part of the USSR and its allies, in retrospect, it could possibly have prevented many of the costly arms-related problems of subsequent years, thereby adding to the security of both sides. However, during the Eisenhower administration the U.S. defense of Europe became heavily reliant upon nuclear weapons, which were more cost-effective than standing armies—giving "more bang for the buck." This made denuclearization of Europe a difficult proposition.

MEMORANDUM

On October 2, 1957, the Government of the Polish People's Republic presented to the General Assembly of the United Nations a proposal concerning the establishment of a denuclearized zone in Central Europe. The governments of Czechoslovakia and of the German Democratic Republic declared their readiness to accede to that zone.

The Government of the Polish People's Republic proceeded with the conviction that the establishment of the proposed denuclearized zone could lead to an improvement in the international atmosphere and facilitate broader discussions on disarmament as well as the solution of other controversial internal issues, while the continuation of nuclear armaments and making them universal could only lead to a further solidifying of the division of Europe into opposing blocks and to a further replication of this situation, especially in Central Europe.

In December 1957 the Government of the Polish People's Republic renewed the proposal through diplomatic channels.

Considering the wide repercussion which the Polish initiative has evoked and taking into account the propositions emerging from the discussion which has developed on this proposal, the Government of the PPR hereby presents a more detailed elaboration of its proposal, which may facilitate the opening of negotiations and reaching of an agreement on this subject.

I. The proposed zones should include the territory of: Poland, Czechoslovakia, German Democratic Republic and German Federal Republic. In this territory nuclear weapons would neither be manufactured nor stockpiled, the equipment and installations designed for their servicing would not be located there; the use of nuclear weapons against the territory of this zone would be prohibited.

II. The contents of the obligations arising from the establishment of the denuclearized zone would be based upon the following premises:

1. The states included in this zone would undertake the obligation not to manufacture, maintain nor import for their own use and not to permit the location on their territories of nuclear weapons of any type, as well as not to install nor to admit to their territories of installations and equipment designed for servicing nuclear weapons, including missiles' launching equipment.

2. The four powers (France, United States, Great Britain, and USSR) would undertake the following obligations;

(a) Not to maintain nuclear weapons in the armaments of their forces stationed on the territories of states included in this zone; neither to maintain nor to install on the territories of these states any installations or equipment designed for servicing nuclear weapons, including missiles' launching equipment.

(b) Not to transfer in any manner and under any reasons whatsoever, nuclear weapons nor installations and equipment designed for servicing nuclear weapons—to governments or other organs in this area.

3. The powers which have at their disposal nuclear weapons should undertake the obligation not to use these weapons against the territory of the zone or against any targets situated in this zone....

4. Other states, whose forces are stationed on the territory of any state included in the zone, would also undertake the obligation not to maintain nuclear weapons in the armaments of these forces and not to transfer such weapons to governments or to other organs in this area....

On the basis of the above proposals the government of the Polish People's Republic suggests to initiate negotiations for the purpose of a further detailed elaboration of the plan for the establishment of the denuclearized zone, of the documents and guarantees related to it as well as of the means of implementation of the undertaken obligations.

The government of the PPR has reasons to state that acceptance of the proposal concerning the establishment of a denuclearized zone in Central Europe will facilitate the reaching of an agreement relating to the adequate reduction of conventional armaments and of foreign armed forces stationed on the territory of the states included in the zone.

DOCUMENT 10

Speech to the Twenty-first CPSU Congress

N. S. Khrushchev

5 February 1959

Editor's commentary: Khrushchev's optimistic closing address to the Twenty-first Congress emphasized the great opportunities which the Soviet Union perceived before it: decolonization was producing new independent states at a rapid pace, and these states were now on the side of the socialist camp in the struggle with imperialism.

Documents of the 21st Congress of the Communist Party of the Soviet Union (Ottawa, Canada: USSR Embassy Public Affairs, 1959), pp. 12–19, *excerpts.*

The policy of peaceful coexistence would assure that while the process of building socialism in the developing world took root, war would not break out with the West. Included here are also some excerpts which reveal the sensitivity of the Soviets to their own strategic inferiority at the time, a condition that would eventually lead to Khrushchev's attempt to install medium-range missiles in Cuba in 1962.

...The problem of peace and peaceful coexistence is the question of questions, because the people of any country, whatever the social system there, are making it their concern to have a good life, to work in peace, and to create better conditions for life.

We maintain that the peoples must live in peace, regardless of the social pattern of the states, and that disputes arising between states must be solved peacefully, not by war.

Great changes have taken place in the world today. We have countries making up the world socialist system. On the other hand, we have countries making up the world imperialist system. But we also have countries which, though not socialist, cannot be classed as countries of the imperialist system either. These countries, which have won national independence as a result of their movements for liberation, want to take their own road. They want to skip the capitalist stage of development so as, once having finished with colonial oppression, to embark upon the building of society along new lines.

Many leaders in these countries say they want to build socialism. True, they say "communism" with difficulty and it is not always clear what they mean by socialism. But one thing is unquestionable. These leaders look upon the socialist countries with goodwill. They do not regard the socialist countries as antagonists, as being against their aspirations to build a new life without the imperialist and colonial oppression. That is why the socialist countries have good friendly relations with these states, and normal economic relations are developing between them. We are jointly acting for peace and the security of the peoples, for a ban on atomic and hydrogen weapons, and against the colonialist policy of the imperialists.

So, if we take the countries making up the world socialist system and the countries valiantly fighting against imperialism and colonialism for freedom and national independence, we shall see that now the scales have already tipped in favour of these peace-loving countries, not of the imperialist states. Further, in territory, population, and material wealth, the peace-loving countries are superior to the imperialist states.

A cardinal conclusion to be deduced from an analysis of the present alignment of forces in the world is that most of the colonies, which but recently were imperialism's reserve and rear, have stopped being so. In the long struggle of the peoples, these countries have become active forces for peace. They are fighting against imperialism and colonialism, for freedom and national independence, and they are for the peaceful coexistence of states with different social orders....

American military figures and statesmen often declare that the United States has more favourable conditions than the Soviet Union from the military point of view, since the former possess a network of military bases on the territory of European and Asian countries which may be used to strike a blow at our country, while the Soviet Union has few intercontinental rockets so far, according to them....

If one state believes that at the present moment the enemy has no weapon capable of striking a blow at its own territory, it may be tempted to use this convenient opportunity for unleashing war. If certain American statesmen believe that at present their territory is invulnerable, they can jump at the conclusion that this is a convenient moment to unleash war....

Comrades, an improvement in the relations between the United States and the Soviet Union is a specially important factor in relaxing international tension. Not so long ago the government of the Soviet Union and the Government of the

United States of America exchanged rather sharp messages. This is due to the fact that they concerned very acute international problems. Some actions of the United States alarmed the peace-loving peoples and we could not but express our attitude to those actions.

Today these events are a thing of the past. It is necessary to look ahead. The Soviet Government on its part is doing everything possible for a relaxation of international tension and improvement of relations with all countries. We believe that the President and the other leaders of the United States, if they really want peace, as they stated in the conversation with A. I. Mikoyan, will recognize the necessity for the peaceful co-existence of states and, on this basis, they will build their relations with the Soviet Union and the other socialist countries....

DOCUMENT 11

Soviet Government Statement on the U-2 Incident

May 1960

Editor's commentary: The U-2 spy plane incident squelched the idea of a summit between Eisenhower and Khrushchev. Perhaps more important, it displayed the increasing effectiveness of Soviet technology to deal with what had been for so long vastly superior American capabilities. This incident was a propaganda coup for the Soviet Union and continued to pay dividends to Soviet public diplomacy as Francis Gary Powers, the pilot of the aircraft, was put on trial in Moscow as a spy.

Department of State Bulletin, vol. 42, no. 1092, 30 May 1960, pp. 852–854, *excerpts*. This note was delivered by the Soviet Ministry of Foreign Affairs to the American Embassy in Moscow on 10 May.

The Government of the Union of Soviet Socialist Republics considers it necessary to state the following to the Government of the United States of America:

On May 1 of this year at 5 hours 36 minutes, Moscow time, a military aircraft violated the boundary of the Union of Soviet Socialist Republics and intruded across the borders of the Soviet Union for a distance of more than 2,000 kilometers. The government of the Union of Soviet Socialist Republics naturally could not leave unpunished such a flagrant violation of Soviet state boundaries. When the intentions of the violating aircraft became apparent, it was shot down by Soviet rocket troops in the area of Sverdlovsk.

Upon examination by experts of all data at the disposal of the Soviet side, it was incontrovertibly established that the intruder aircraft belonged to the United States of America, was permanently based in Turkey and was sent through Pakistan into the Soviet Union with hostile purposes.

As Chairman of the USSR Council of Ministers N. S. Khrushchev made public on May 7 at the final session of the USSR Supreme Soviet, exact data from the investigation leave no doubts with respect to the purpose of the flight of the American aircraft which violated the USSR border on May 1. This aircraft was specially equipped for reconnaissance and diversionary flight over the territory of the Soviet Union. It had on board apparatus for aerial photography for detecting the Soviet radar network and other special radio-technical equipment which form part of USSR anti-aircraft defenses. At the disposal of the Soviet expert commission which carried out the investigation, there is indisputable proof of the espionage-reconnaisance mission of the American aircraft: films of Soviet defense and industrial establishments, and tape recording of signals of Soviet radar stations and other data.

Pilot Powers, about whose fate the Embassy of the United States of America inquired in its note of May 6, is alive and, as indicated in the aforementioned speech of Chairman of the USSR Council of Ministers N. S. Khrushchev, will be brought to account under the laws of the Soviet state. The pilot has indicated that he did everything in full accordance with the assignment given him....

This and other information revealed in speeches of the head of the Soviet Government completely refuted the US State Department's concocted and hurriedly fabricated version, released May 5 in the official announcement for the press, to the effect that the aircraft was allegedly carrying out meteorological observations in the upper strata of the atmosphere along the Turkish-Soviet border.

After the complete absurdity of the aforementioned version had been shown and it had been incontrovertibly proven that the American aircraft intruded across the borders of the Soviet Union for aggressive reconnaissance purposes, a new announcement was made by the US State Department on May 7 which contained the forced admission that the aircraft was sent into the Soviet Union for military reconnaissance purposes and, by that very fact, it was admitted that the flight was pursuing aggressive purposes....

The Government of the Union of Soviet Socialist Republics cannot avoid pointing out that the State Department's statement, which is unprecedented in its cynicism, not only justifies provocative flights of aircraft of the armed forces of the United States of America but also acknowledges that such actions are "a normal phenomenon" and thus in fact states that in the future the United States intends to continue provocative invasions into the confines of the airspace of the Soviet Union for the purpose of intelligence....

The Soviet Government would sincerely like to hope that the Government of the United States of America recognizes in the final analysis that the interests of preserving and strengthening peace among peoples including the interests of the American people itself, whose striving for peace was well demonstrated during the visit of

the head of the Soviet Government, N. S. Khrushchev, to the United States of America, would be served by cessation of the aforementioned dangerous provocative activities with regard to the Union of Soviet Socialist Republics, by cessation of the "cold war," and by a search through joint efforts with the Soviet Union and with other interested states for solution of unsettled international problems, on a mutually acceptable basis which is awaited by all peoples.

DOCUMENT 12

The Soviet Stand on Germany

N. S. Khrushchev

1961

Editor's commentary: The German problem played a central role in Soviet foreign policy from 1917 until 1970, when the Treaty of Moscow marked the resolution of postwar issues, including borders and recognition of sovereignty. Also, attendant to the occupation of West Berlin by the Western allies were all the problems implied by an enclave within hostile territory. Stalin's attempt to blockade Berlin in 1948 and 1949 and test the resolve of the West to remain there met with failure. But the problem of the enclave did not disappear. Most significantly, it continued to plague the viability of the East German state, as tens of thousands, especially those well educated, "voted with their feet" and fled the communist system of the East through West Berlin.

In this memorandum, Khrushchev assesses the situation of Berlin as abnormal and threatens to "turn the keys" of West Berlin over to the East

---

"Soviet Aide Memoire of June 4," handed to President Kennedy by Premier Khrushchev during their meeting in Vienna, *Department of State Bulletin*, vol. 45 no. 1154, 7 August 1961, pp. 231–233, *excerpts*.

Germans if the status of Germany is not resolved to Soviet satisfaction, a resolution contrary to the postwar Four Power Agreement. Berlin began to fade in significance as a point where Soviet pressure could be applied to Western interests after the building of the Berlin Wall in the summer of 1961.

1. The years-long delay in arriving at a peace settlement with Germany has largely predetermined the dangerous course of events in the postwar period. The major decisions of the Allies on the eradication of militarism in Germany, which once were considered by the Governments of the United States and the USSR as the guarantee of stable peace, have been implemented only partially and now are actually not observed in the greater part of the German territory. Of the governments of the two German states that were formed after the war it is only the Government of the German Democratic Republic [GDR] that recognizes and adheres to those agreements. The Government of the Federal Republic of Germany [FRG] openly proclaims its negative attitude to those agreements, cultivates sabre-rattling militarism, and advocates the review of the German frontiers and the results of World War II. It tries to establish a powerful military base for its aggressive plans, to kindle a dangerous hotbed of conflicts on German soil and to set the former Allies in the anti-Hitler coalition against each other....

2. The Soviet Government is earnestly striving toward removing the sources of tension between the United States and the USSR and to proceed to constructive, friendly cooperation. The conclusion of a German peace treaty would allow the two countries to come much closer to the attainment of this goal....

3. Proceeding from a realistic evaluation of the situation, the Soviet Government stands for the immediate conclusion of a peace treaty with Germany. The question of a peace treaty is one that concerns the national security of the USSR and of many other states. The time has already passed for allowing the situation in Germany to remain unchanged. All the conditions for the conclusion of a peace treaty matured a long time ago and this treaty must be concluded....

4. The Soviet Government is not pursuing the goal of harming the interests of the United States or other powers in Europe. It does not propose to change anything either in Germany or in West Berlin in favor of any one state or group of states. The USSR deems it necessary in the interests of consolidating peace formally to recognize the situation which has developed in Europe after the war, to legalize and to consolidate the inviolability of the existing German borders, to normalize the situation in West Berlin on the basis of reasonable consideration for the interests of all the parties concerned.

In the interests of achieving agreement on a peace treaty the Soviet Union does not insist on the immediate withdrawal of the FRG from NATO. Both German states could for a certain period, even after the conclusion of a peace treaty, remain in the military alliances to which they now belong.

The Soviet proposal does not tie the conclusion of a peace treaty to the recognition of the GDR or the FRG by all the parties to this treaty. It is up to each Government to decide whether or not to recognize this or that State.

If the US is not prepared to sign a joint peace treaty with the two German states, a peaceful settlement could be achieved on the basis of two treaties. In that case the states that participated in the anti-Hitlerite coalition would sign a peace treaty with two German states or with one German state, at their own discretion. These treaties need not be completely identical in wording but they must contain the same kind of provisions on the most important points of a peaceful settlement.

5. The conclusion of a German peace Treaty would also solve the problem of normalizing the situation in West Berlin. Deprived of a stable international status, West Berlin is a place where the Bonn revanchist circles constantly maintain

extreme tension and organize all kinds of provocations very dangerous to the cause of peace. We are duty-bound to prevent a development where intensification of West German militarism could lead to irreparable consequences due to the unsettled situation in West Berlin.

At present the Soviet Government does not see a better way to solve the West Berlin problem than by transforming it into a demilitarized free city. The implementation of the proposal to turn West Berlin into a free city, with the interests of all parties duly taken into consideration, would normalize the situation in West Berlin. The occupation regime now being maintained has long already outlived itself and has lost all connection with the purposes for which it was established, as well as with the Allied agreements concerning Germany that established the basis for its existence.

The occupation rights will naturally be terminated upon the conclusion of a German peace treaty, whether it is signed with both German states or only with the GDR, within whose territory West Berlin is located.... In short, West Berlin, as the Soviet Government sees it, should be strictly neutral. Of course, the use of Berlin as a base for provocative activities, hostile to the USSR, the GDR or any other State, cannot be permitted in the future, nor can Berlin be allowed to remain a dangerous hotbed of tension and international conflicts.

The USSR proposes that the most reliable guarantees be established against interference in the affairs of the free city by any State. Token troop contingents of the US, the UK, France and the USSR could be stationed in West Berlin as guarantors of the free city. The USSR would have no objection either to the stationing in West Berlin, for the same purpose, of military contingents from neutral States under the aegis of the UN. The status of the free city could be duly registered by the United Nations and consolidated by the authority of that international organization. The Soviet side is prepared to discuss any other measures that would guarantee the freedom and independence of West Berlin as a free, demilitarized city....

6. The Soviet government proposes that a peace conference be called immediately, without delay, that a German peace treaty be concluded, and that the problem of West Berlin as a free city be solved in this way. If for any motives the Governments of the United States or other Western Powers are not ready for this at the present time, an interim solution could be adopted for a specified period of time....

7. The Soviet Government is prepared to consider any constructive proposals of the United States Government on a German peace treaty and on normalizing the situation in West Berlin. The Soviet Government will show a maximum of good will in order that the question of a German peace treaty may be settled by mutual agreement between the USSR, the US and other States concerned. The signing of a German peace treaty by all the members of the anti-Hitlerite coalition and the settlement of the question of a neutral status for West Berlin on this basis would create better conditions for trust among States and for the the solution of such important international problems as disarmament and others. But, if the United States does not show that it realizes the necessity of concluding a peace treaty, we shall deplore it because we shall be obliged to sign a peace treaty, which it would be impossible and dangerous to delay, not with all the states but only with those that wish to sign it.

The peace treaty would specifically define the status of West Berlin as a free city and the Soviet Union, just as the other parties to the treaty, would of course observe it strictly; measures would also be taken to ensure that this status be respected by other countries as well. At the same time this would also mean putting an end to the occupation regime in West Berlin with all its implications. In particular, questions of using the means of communication by land, water, or air within the territory of the GDR would have to be settled solely by appropriate agreements with the GDR. That is but natural, since control over such means of communication is an inalienable right of every sovereign State.

8. The conclusion of a German treaty would be an important step towards the final post-war settlement in Europe for which the Soviet Union is persistently striving.

Soviet Statements on the Bay of Pigs Incident

April 1961

Editor's commentary: Nikita Khrushchev turned to maximum Soviet advantage the Bay of Pigs fiasco, the first real foreign policy test of the new Kennedy administration, which had inherited from the Eisenhower administration the plan to use Cuban emigrés to liberate Cuba from communist control. The relish with which this foreign policy blunder was greeted in the Kremlin is apparent in the two documents included here, a letter from Khrushchev to Kennedy and an official Soviet government pronouncement.

KHRUSHCHEV'S LETTER TO JFK, 18 APRIL 1961

Dear Mr. President: I address this message to you at an alarming hour which is fraught with danger against universal peace. An armed aggression has been started against Cuba. It is an open secret that the armed bands which have invaded that country have been prepared, equipped, and armed in the United States. The planes which bomb Cuban towns belong to the United States

Department of State Bulletin, vol. 44, no. 1141, 8 May 1961, pp. 661–667, *excerpts.*

of America, the bombs which they drop have been put at their disposal by the American government.

All this arouses in the Soviet Union, the Soviet Government, and the Soviet people an understandable feeling of indignation. Only recently, exchanging views through our representatives, we talked with you about the mutual wish of the parties to exert joint efforts directed toward the improvement of relations between our countries and the prevention of a danger of war. Your statement a few days ago to the effect that the United States of America would not participate in military actions against Cuba created an impression that the leading authorities of the United States are aware of the consequences which aggression against Cuba could have for the whole world and the United States of America itself.

How are we to understand what is really being done by the United States now that the attack on Cuba has become a fact?

It is yet not too late to prevent the irreparable. The Government of the U.S. can still prevent the flames of war kindled by the interventionists on Cuba from spreading into a conflagration which it will be impossible to cope with. I earnestly appeal to you, Mr. President, to call a halt to the aggression against the Republic of Cuba. The military techniques and the world political situation now are such that any so-called "small war" can produce a chain reaction in all parts of the world.

As for the U.S.S.R., there must be no mistake about our position. We will extend to the Cuban people and the Government all the necessary aid for the repulse of the armed attack on Cuba. We are sincerely interested in the relaxation of international tension, but if others go in for its aggravation, then we will answer them in full measure. In general it is impossible to carry on affairs in such a way that in one area the situation is settled and the fire is put out, and in another area a new fire is lit.

I hope that the U.S. Government will take into consideration these reasons, dictated only by concern that steps should not be permitted which might lead the world to a catastrophe of war.

SOVIET GOVERNMENT STATEMENT, 18 APRIL 1961

The Government of the Republic of Cuba has announced that in the morning of 15 April airplanes of the U.S. B-26 bomber type subjected separate districts of the capital of Cuba—Havana—and a number of other inhabited localities to barbarous bombing. There were many killed and injured among the inhabitants of the capital.

Following the bombing, early in the morning of 17 April armed forces of the interventionists landed at various places on the Cuban coast. The landing took place under the cover of U.S. aircraft and warships.

Cuban Government troops and the People's militia are engaged in fighting the invading gangs.

In connection with the invasion of Cuba the Government of the Soviet Union states:

The attack on Cuba is an open challenge to all freedom-loving peoples, a dangerous provocation against peace in the area of the Caribbean Sea, against universal peace. There can be no justification of this criminal invasion. The organizers of the aggression against Cuba are encroaching on the inalienable right of the Cuban people to live freely and independently. They are trampling underfoot the elementary norms of international relations, the principle of peaceful coexistence of states.

...What territory served as a starting point for the piratical attack on Cuba?

It was the territory of the United States and that of the neighboring countries which are under its control. Whose are the arms with which the counterrevolutionary gangs are equipped? They are U.S. arms. With whose funds have they been supported and are they being maintained? With funds appropriated by the United States....

The Government of the U.S.S.R. appeals to the governments of all member states of the United Nations to take all necessary measures for the immediate cessation of aggressive actions against Cuba, the continuation of which may give rise to the most serious consequences for universal peace. In this hour, when the sovereignty and independence of Cuba, a sovereign member of the United Nations, are in danger, the duty of all country members of the United Nations is to render it all necessary aid and support.

The Soviet government reserves the right, if armed intervention in the affairs of the Cuban people is not stopped, to take all measures with other countries to render the necessary assistance to the Republic of Cuba.

DOCUMENT 14

Report of the Central Committee to the Twenty-second CPSU Congress

N. S. Khrushchev

17 October 1961

Editor's commentary: The sections of Khrushchev's report to the Twenty-second CPSU Congress on the international situation are characterized by almost unqualified optimism about socialism and its progress since 1959. Khrushchev kept returning in the speech to peaceful coexistence as the most important factor in Soviet foreign policy. He highlighted the growth of third world influence in world politics as an important development in the struggle against imperialism, which, although collapsing as a system, continued to be dangerous.

Pravda, 18 October 1961, pp. 2–4, *excerpts*. Editor's translation.

I. THE CONTEMPORARY WORLD SITUATION AND THE INTERNATIONAL POSITION OF THE SOVIET UNION

Comrades, the main content of the period following the Twentieth CPSU Congress is the competition between the two world social systems—the socialist and capitalist. It has become the core, the main characteristic of world development of the present historical stage. In social development, two lines, two historical tendencies, are becoming more and more distinct. One is the line of social progress, of peace and creativity. The other is the line of reaction, oppression and war....

In the course of the peaceful competition of the two systems capitalism has suffered a profound moral defeat in the eyes of all the peoples. Ordinary people are becoming convinced daily that capitalism is incapable of solving any of the imminent problems confronting humanity. More and more it is apparent that only on the path of socialism can a solution to these problems be found. Trust in the capitalist system and the capitalist path of development is ever dwindling....

Events show that our party's course, worked out by the Twentieth Congress, was the right one: the congress noted that the primary characteristic of the epoch has been the appearance of socialism beyond the bounds of one country and its conversion into a world system. In the period since the Twentieth Congress a new important shift has occurred: the world socialist system is becoming a decisive factor in the development of society.

The party drew a conclusion about the inevitability of the collapse of colonialism. Under the powerful blows of the national liberation movement the colonial system has actually just about collapsed.

The party advanced the important thesis that in the present epoch wars between states are not inevitable, that they can be prevented. The events of past years serve to confirm this conclusion also. They have shown that the mighty forces that stand watch over peace have earnest means today by which to prevent the imperialists from unleashing a world war. What has become even more apparent is the superiority of the forces of peace and socialism over the forces of imperialism and war.

Briefly, comrades, this six year period has been good for us on a global scale!...

Comrades, the Twentieth Congress of the party, having analyzed the situation in the countries of capitalism, drew the conclusion that they were moving unswervingly toward new economic and social upheavals. Has this conclusion been borne out? Yes, it has. In recent years there has been further aggravation of contradictions both within the capitalist countries and among them. Colonial empires have been collapsing, and the struggle of the working class and the national liberation movement of the peoples have widened in scope.

The general tendency of the further decay of capitalism has continued to act inexorably. The economy of the capitalist countries, although experiencing some growth of production, has become even more unstable and recalls a man sick with fever—so often are its temporary recoveries overtaken by depressions and crises. The main capitalist country, the U.S.A., has experienced two critical recessions in five years. In the postwar period there have been, all told, four such recessions....The social gains that the working class achieved in the past are dwindling. On the whole, the condition of working people, especially in the economically underdeveloped countries, is deteriorating....

Comrades, on the world stage during the period under review, important chages have come about in the distribution of forces. The world socialist system has become a reliable shield protecting not only the peoples of the countries that are friendly to us, but also the whole of humanity against military adventures of imperialism. And the fact that the preponderance of strength is on the side of the socialist community of nations is of the greatest fortune for all humanity.

Moreover, peaceloving forces have grown all over the world.

Just a few years ago there were two opposing camps in international relations—socialism and imperialism. Now an active part in international affairs is being taken by those countries of Asia, Africa, and Latin America which have freed (and are freeing) themselves from foreign oppression. Those countries are frequently called neutralist, although they can be considered neutral only in the sense that they do not belong to any of the existing military-political alliances. However, the majority of these countries are by no means neutral regarding the root problem of our day—the problem of war and peace. As a rule, they are for peace and against war. The countries which have won their liberty from colonialism are becoming a significant factor of peace, and in the struggle with colonialism and imperialism. It is no longer possible to settle the fundamental issues of world politics without due regard for their interest.

In the capitalist countries themselves the masses of peoples are more and more vigorously active against war. The working class and all working people are fighting against the arms race and ruinous policy of the warmongers.

And so, growing forces now oppose the aggressive policy of the imperialist powers. *The struggle of the countries of socialism and all peaceloving forces against preparation of new aggression and war is the main content of world politics today....*

The principles of peaceful coexistence, worked out by Lenin and developed in the documents of our party, remain permanently as the general course of Soviet foreign policy. The foreign policy of the Soviet government gives convincing evidence of the fidelity of the party and the whole Soviet people to Lenin's peaceloving course....the peaceful coexistence of countries with different social systems can be maintained and insured only through the self-sacrificing struggle of all peoples against the aggressive aspirations of the imperialists. The greater the might of the socialist camp and the more vigorously the struggle for peace is waged within the capitalist countries themselves, the more difficult it is for the imperialists to realize their aggressive designs.

Peace and peaceful coexistence—these are not quite the same thing. Peaceful coexistence is not simply the absence of war; it is not a temporary, unstable truce between wars. It is the coexistence of two opposed social systems, based on mutual renunciation of resort to war as a means of resolving interstate disputes.

The experience of history teaches that you cannot placate an aggressor with concessions. Concessions to the imperialists on vitally important matters do not result in a policy of peaceful coexistence, but rather capitulation in the face of aggressive forces. We will never allow this. (*Applause.*) The imperialists should understand by now that it is no longer they who are the arbiters of the destiny of humanity, and that, whether they want it or not, socialism will exist, develop, and gain strength. (*Thunderous applause.*) But for the present, it does not seem that the imperialist gentlemen have grasped the plain truth. We can expect of them adventuristic actions that would mean disaster for hundreds of millions of people. That is why we must not aid and abet the aggressors, but rein them in. (*Prolonged applause.*)...

DOCUMENT 15

The Cuban Missile Crisis

October 1962

Editor's commentary: The Cuban missile crisis, spanning two weeks in October 1962, was the closest that the two superpowers have come to

---

Department of State Bulletin, vol. 47, no. 1220, pp. 741–749, *excerpts.*

direct conflict and nuclear war in the post–World War II period. The attempt by the USSR to deploy medium-range ballistic missiles with nuclear warheads in Cuba, and in so doing redress the strategic imbalance which then favored the United States, was met with categorical opposition by President Kennedy and his advisers, who chose to blockade Cuba in response. The following letters are part of the correspondence related to the resolution of the crisis. It has been speculated that Khrushchev's letter of October 27, the first item below, was not written by Khrushchev, but by others in the Soviet Presidium. It requested a quid pro quo that the Kennedy administration found unacceptable—to exchange the missile sites in Cuba for U.S. missiles in Turkey, thereby saving face for the Soviets. In his "first" letter of 26 October, Khrushchev had agreed to remove the missiles with only the guarantee that the United States would never invade Cuba. Kennedy shrewdly responded to the "first" letter, ignoring the letter of 27 October. The Kremlin finally agreed on 28 October to remove the missiles and end the crisis. One of Kennedy's advisers said, "We were eyeball to eyeball, and the other guy blinked." A crash program in ICBMs was initiated soon thereafter by the Soviet Union to achieve strategic parity and assure that such a result would never again occur.

CHAIRMAN KHRUSHCHEV'S MESSAGE OF OCTOBER 27, 1962

Dear Mr. President: It is with great satisfaction that I studied your reply to Mr. U Thant on the adoption of measures in order to avoid contact by our ships and thus avoid irreparable fatal consequences. This reasonable step on your part persuades me that you are showing solicitude for the preservation of peace, and I note this with satisfaction....

I understand your concern for the security of the United States, Mr. President, because this is the first duty of the president. However, these questions are also uppermost in our minds. The same duties rest with me as Chairman of the USSR Council of Ministers. You have been worried over our assisting Cuba with arms designed to strengthen its defensive potential—precisely defensive potential—because Cuba, no matter what weapons it had, could not compare with you since these are different dimensions, the more so given up-to-date measures of extermination.

Our purpose has been and is to help Cuba, and no one can challenge the humanity of our motives aimed at allowing Cuba to live peacefully and develop as its people desire. You want to relieve your country from danger and this is understandable. However, Cuba also wants this. All countries want to relieve themselves from danger. But how can we, the Soviet Union and our government, assess your actions which, in effect, mean that you have surrounded the Soviet Union with military bases, surrounded our allies with military bases, set up military bases literally around our country, and stationed your rocket weapons at them? This is no secret. High-placed American officials demonstratively declare this. Your rockets are stationed in Britain and in Italy and pointed at us. Your rockets are stationed in Turkey.

You are worried over Cuba. You say that it worries you because it lies at a distance of 90 miles across the sea from the shores of the United States. However, Turkey lies next to us. Our sentinels are pacing up and down and watching each other. Do you believe that you have the right to demand security for your country and the removal of such weapons that you qualify as offensive, while not recognizing this right for us?....

I think that one could rapidly eliminate the conflict and normalize the situation. Then people would heave a sigh of relief, considering that the statesmen who bear the responsiblity have sober minds, an awareness of their responsibility, and an ability to solve complicated problems and not allow matters to slide to the disaster of war.

This is why I make this proposal: We agree to remove those weapons from Cuba which you regard as offensive weapons. We agree to do this and to state this commitment in the United Nations. Your representatives will make a statement to the effect that the United States, on its part, bearing in mind the anxiety and concern of the Soviet state, will evacuate its analogous weapons from Turkey. Let us reach an understanding on what time you and we need to put this into effect....

We, having assumed this commitment in order to give satisfaction and hope to the peoples of Cuba and Turkey and to increase their confidence in their security, will make a statement in the Security Council to the effect that the Soviet Government gives a solemn pledge to respect the integrity of the frontiers and the sovereignty of Turkey, not to intervene in its domestic affairs, not to invade Turkey, not to make available its territory as a place d'armes for such invasion, and also will restrain those who would think of launching an aggression against Turkey either from Soviet territory or from the territory of other states bordering on Turkey.

The US Government will make the same statement in the Security Council with regard to Cuba. It will declare that the United States will respect the integrity of the frontiers of Cuba, its sovereignty, undertakes not to intervene in its domestic affairs, not to invade and not to make its territory available as place d'armes for the invasion of Cuba, and also will restrain those who would think of launching an aggression against Cuba either from US territory or from the territory of other states bordering on Cuba....

Nikita Khrushchev

PRESIDENT KENNEDY'S MESSAGE OF OCTOBER 27

Dear Mr. Chairman: I have read your letter of October 26th with great care and welcomed the statement of your desire to seek a prompt solution to the problem. The first thing that needs to be done, however, is for work to cease on offensive missile bases in Cuba and for all weapons systems in Cuba capable of offensive use the rendered inoperable, under effective United Nations arrangements.

Assuming this is done promptly, I have given

my representatives in New York instruction that will permit them to work out this weekend—in cooperation with the Acting Secretary General and your representative—an arrangement for a permanent solution to the Cuban problem along the lines suggested in your letter of October 26th. As I read your letter, the key elements of your proposals—which seem generally acceptable as I understand them—are as follows:

(1) You would agree to remove these weapons systems from Cuba under appropriate United Nations observation and supervision; and undertake, with suitable safeguards, to halt the further introduction of such weapons systems into Cuba.

(2) We, on our part, would agree—upon the establishment of adequate arrangements through the United Nations to ensure the carrying out and continuation of these commitments—(a) to remove promptly the quarantine measure now in effect and (b) to give assurances against an invasion of Cuba. I am confident that other nations of the Western Hemisphere would be prepared to do likewise.

If you will give your representative similar instructions, there is no reason why we should not be able to complete these arrangements and announce them to the world within a couple of days. The effect of such a settlement on easing world tensions would enable us to work toward a more general arrangement regarding "other armaments," as proposed in your second letter which you made public....

But the first ingredient, let me emphasize, is the cessation of work on missile sites in Cuba and measures to render such weapons inoperable, under effective international guarantees. The continuation of this threat, or a prolonging of this discussion concerning Cuba by linking these problems to the broader questions of European and world security, would surely lead to an intensification of the Cuban crisis and a grave risk to the peace of the world. For this reason I hope we can quickly agree along the lines outlined in this letter and in your letter of October 26th.

John F. Kennedy

CHAIRMAN KHRUSHCHEV'S MESSAGE OF OCTOBER 28

Dear Mr. President: I have received your message of 27 October. I express my satisfaction and thank you for the sense of proportion that you have displayed and for realization of the responsibility which now devolves on you for the preservation of the peace of the world.

I regard with great understanding your concern and the concern of the United States people in connection with the fact that the weapons you describe as offensive are formidable weapons indeed. Both you and we understand what kind of weapons these are.

In order to eliminate as rapidly as possible the conflict which endangers the cause of peace, to give an assurance to all people who crave peace, and to reassure the American people, who, I am certain, also want peace, as do the people of the Soviet Union, the Soviet Government, in addition to earlier instruction on the discontinuation of further work on weapons construction sites, has given a new order to dismantle the arms which you described as offensive, and to crate and return them to the Soviet Union....

Nikita Khrushchev

DOCUMENT 16

The "Hot Line" Agreement

20 June 1963

Editor's commentary: The "hot-line" agreement sought to improve communication between the leaders of the superpowers by providing speedier and more direct contact, especially critical in times of crisis. The Cuban missile crisis of the previous year inspired the two countries to take this significant step.

For use in time of emergency the Government of the United States of America and the Government of the Union of Soviet Socialist Republics have agreed to establish as soon as technically feasible a direct communications link between the two Governments.

Each Government shall be responsible for the arrangements for the link on its own territory. Each Government shall take the necessary steps to ensure continuous functioning of the link and prompt delivery to its head of government of any communications received by means of the link from the head of government of the other party.

Arrangements for establishing and operating the link are set forth in the Annex which is attached hereto and forms an integral part hereof.

DONE in duplicate in the English and Russian languages at Geneva, Switzerland, this 20th day of June, 1963.

DOCUMENT 17

Open Letter from the Central Committee of the CPSU to All Communists

14 July 1963

Editor's commentary: The veiled polemics between the CPSU and the Communist Party of China (CPC) were over a wide range of issues relevant to the international communist movement and the struggle between the two camps. These polemics surfaced in public after 1962. This open

Document 16: "Memorandum of Understanding Between the USA and USSR Regarding the Establishment of a Direct Communications Link," *Arms Control and Disarmament Agreements* (Washington, DC: Arms Control and Disarmament Agency/U.S. Government Printing Office, 1980), p. 31.

Document 17: *Pravda*, 14 July 1963, pp. 1–4, as translated in *Current Soviet Documents*, vol. 1 no. 20, 5 August 1963, pp. 3–16, *excerpts*.

letter from the CPSU criticizes the anti-peaceful coexistence stance of the Chinese and the denunciations of Soviet socialism emanating from Beijing. The now-famous line that "the atomic bomb adheres to no class principle" originated in this response to the bellicose attitude of the Chinese, who were apparently not concerned about the effects of a nuclear attack against Soviet territory.

Dear Comrades! The CPSU Central Committee deems it necessary to address an open letter to you in order to set out its position on fundamental questions of the international communist movement in connection with the letter of the Central Committee of the Communist Party of China of June 14, 1963....

It turns out that the Chinese comrades do not believe in the ability of the peoples of the socialist countries, of the international working class and of all democratic and peaceloving forces, to frustrate the plans of the warmongers and achieve peace for our and future generations. What lies behind the fine revolutionary phrases of the Chinese comrades? Disbelief in the forces of the working class and its revolutionary capabilities, disbelief both in the possibility of peaceful coexistence and in the victory of the proletariat in the class struggle. All peaceloving forces unite in the struggle to avert war. In their class composition and in their class interests they differ, but they can be united by the struggle for peace, for averting war, because the atomic bomb adheres to no class principle—it destroys everybody within the range of its devastating action....

The Chinese comrades obviously underestimate all of the danger of a thermonuclear war. "The atomic bomb is a paper tiger," it "is not terrible at all," they contend. The main thing, they say, is to put an end to imperialism as quickly as possible, but how and with what losses this will be achieved seems to be a secondary question. For whom, it may be asked, is it a secondary question? Is it for the hundreds of millions of people who are doomed to

death in the event a thermonuclear war is unleashed? Is it for the states that will be razed from the face of the earth in the very first hours of such a war?

No one, not even the big states, has the right to play with the destinies of millions of people. Those who do not want to exert efforts so as to exclude world war from the life of the peoples, to avert the mass annihilation of people and the destruction of the values of human civilization, deserve condemnation.

The June 14 letter of the CPC Central Committee says a good deal about "inevitable sacrifices" allegedly in the name of the revolution. Some responsible Chinese leaders have also declared that it is possible to sacrifice hundreds of millions of people in war. "The victorious peoples," it is asserted in *Long Live Leninism!*, the book approved by the CPC Central Committee, "will create with tremendous speed on the ruins of destroyed imperialism a civilization one thousand times higher than under the capitalist system, and will build their truly bright future.

Is it permissible to ask the Chinese comrades: do they realize what sort of "ruins" a global nuclear rocket war would leave behind?...

We stand fully for the destruction of imperialism and capitalism. We not only believe in the inevitable destruction of capitalism, but are doing everything possible for this to be accomplished by class struggle, and as soon as possible. Who should decide this historic question? First of all, the working class, guided by its vanguard—the Marxist-Leninist Party, the working people of each country.

The Chinese comrades propose another thing. They openly say: "On the ruins of destroyed imperialism"—in other words, as the result of the unleashing of war—"a bright future will be built." If one is to agree with this, then indeed there is no need for the principle of peaceful coexistence, for the struggle to strengthen peace. We cannot agree to such an adventurist path; it contradicts the essence of Marxism-Leninism....

DOCUMENT 18

Limited Test Ban Treaty

5 August 1963

Editor's commentary: The Limited Test Ban Treaty was one of the first significant moves by the superpowers toward effective arms control. Modest in its intent, it created an environment conducive to the realization of other arms control agreements.

The Governments of the United States of America, the United Kingdom of Great Britain and Northern Ireland, and the Union of Soviet Socialist Republics, hereinafter referred to as the "Original Parties,"

Proclaiming as their principal aim the speediest possible achievement of an agreement on general complete disarmament under strict international control in accordance with the objectives of the United Nations which would put an end to the armaments race and eliminate the incentive to the production and testing of all kinds of weapons, including nuclear weapons,

Seeking to achieve the discontinuance of all test explosions of nuclear weapons for all time, determined to continue negotiations to this end, and desiring to put an end to the contamination of man's environment by radioactive substances,

Have agreed as follows:

Article I

1. Each of the Parties to this Treaty undertakes to prohibit, to prevent, and not to carry out any nuclear weapon test explosion, or any other nuclear explosion, at any place under its jurisdiction or control:

"Treaty Banning Nuclear Weapon Tests in the Atmosphere, in Outer Space and Under Water," in *Arms Control and Disarmament Agreements* (Washington, DC: Arms Control and Disarmament Agency/U.S. Government Printing Office, 1980), pp. 41–42.

(a) in the atmosphere; beyond its limits, including outer space; or under water, including territorial waters or high seas; or

(b) in any other environment if such explosion causes radioactive debris to be present outside the territorial limits of the State under whose jurisdiction or control such explosion is conducted....

2. Each of the parties to this Treaty undertakes furthermore to refrain from causing, encouraging, or in any way participating in, the carrying out of any nuclear weapon test explosion, or any other nuclear explosion, anywhere which would take place in any of the environments described or have the effect referred to, in paragraph 1 of this Article.

Article II

1. Any party may propose amendments to this Treaty. The text of any proposed amendment shall be submitted to the Depositary Governments which shall circulate it to all Parties to this Treaty. Thereafter, if requested to do so by one-third or more of the Parties, the Depositary Governments shall convene a conference, to which they shall invite all the Parties, to consider such amendment.

2. Any amendment to this Treaty must be approved by a majority of the votes of all the Parties to this Treaty, including the votes of all of the Original Parties....

Article III

1. This Treaty shall be open to all States for signature. Any State which does not sign this Treaty before its entry into force in accordance with paragraph 3 of this Article may accede to it at any time.

2. This Treaty shall be subject to ratification by signatory States....

3. This Treaty shall enter into force after its ratification by all the Original Parties and the deposit of their instruments of ratification.

Article IV

This Treaty shall be of unlimited duration.

Each party shall in exercising its national sovereignty have the right to withdraw from the Treaty if it decides that extraordinary events...have jeopardized the supreme interests of its country. It shall give notice of such withdrawal to all other Parties to the Treaty three months in advance.

Article V

This Treaty, of which the English and Russian texts are equally authentic, shall be deposited in the archives of the Depositary Governments. Duly certified copies...shall be transmitted by the Depositary Governments to the Governments of the signatory and acceding States.

IN WITNESS WHEREOF the undersigned, duly authorized, have signed this Treaty.

DONE in triplicate at the city of Moscow the fifth day of August, one thousand nine hundred and sixty-three.

On Khrushchev's Phoney Communism

17 July 1964

Editor's commentary: This scathing polemic evaluated Khrushchev's doctrinal innovations as a "betrayal" of socialism and summarized Mao Zedong's ideological differences with Soviet communism. The attack is on both peaceful coexistence elevated to a strategy and the "restoration" of capitalism by the Soviet Union. The publication of this piece signified, perhaps more than any other single document, the point of no return in the dispute between the two communist powers; it brought into question the validity of Soviet leadership in the world

"On Khrushchev's Phoney Communism and Its Historical Lessons for the World," *Peking Review,* no. 29, 17 July 1964, pp. 7–28, *excerpts.*

communist movement. After this, there was progressively less chance that the Sino-Soviet dispute could be patched over while Mao was alive to claim the mantle of leadership of the movement, based on his understanding of "uninterrupted revolution."

The theories of the proletarian revolution and the dictatorship of the proletariat are the quintessence of Marxism-Leninism. The questions of whether revolution should be upheld or opposed and whether the dictatorship of the proletariat should be upheld or opposed have always been the focus of struggle between Marxism-Leninism and all brands of revisionism, and they are now the focus of struggle between Marxist-Leninists the world over and the revisionist Khrushchev clique.

At the Twenty-second congress of the CPSU, the revisionist Khrushchev clique developed their revisionism into a complete system not only by rounding off their antirevolutionary theories of "peaceful coexistence," "peaceful competition," and "peaceful transition" but also by declaring that the dictatorship of the proletariat is no longer necessary in the Soviet Union, and advancing the absurd theories of the "state of the whole people" and the "party of the entire people."...

Under the signboard of "peaceful coexistence," Khrushchev has been colluding with US imperialism, wrecking the socialist camp and the international communist movement, opposing the revolutionary struggles of the oppressed peoples and nations, practicing great power chauvinism and national egoism, and betraying proletarian internationalism. All this is being done for the protection of the vested interests of a handful of people which he places above the fundamental interests of the people of the Soviet Union, the socialist camp and the whole world....

As a result of Khrushchev's revisionism, the first socialist country in the world built by the great Soviet people with their blood and sweat is now facing an unprecedented danger of capitalist restoration....

Khrushchev's ''communism'' takes the United States for its model. Imitation of the methods of management of US capitalism and the bourgeois way of life has been raised by Khrushchev to the level of state policy....

Thus it can be seen that Khrushchev's ''communism'' is indeed ''goulash communism,'' the ''communism of the American way of life'' and ''communism seeking credits from the devil.'' No wonder he often tells representatives of Western monopoly capital that once such ''communism'' is realized in the Soviet Union, ''you will go forward to communism without any call from me.''

There is nothing new about such ''communism.'' It is simply another name for capitalism. It is only a bourgeois label, sign, or advertisement....

The Soviet people, the people of all socialist countries and the revolutionary people the world over will certainly learn lessons from the Khrushchev clique's betrayal. In the struggle against Khrushchev's revisionism, the international communist movement has grown and will continue to grow mightier than before.

Marxist-Leninists have always had an attitude of revolutionary optimism towards the future of proletarian revolution. We are profoundly convinced that the brilliant light of the dictatorship of the people, of socialism and of Marxism-Leninism, will shine forth over the Soviet land. The Proletariat is sure to win the whole world and communism is sure to achieve complete and final victory on earth.

Suggested Readings

Adomeit, Hannes: *Soviet Risk-Taking and Crisis Behavior* (London: Allen & Unwin, 1982).

Allison, Graham: *Essence of Decision: Explaining the Cuban Missile Crisis* (Boston: Little, Brown, 1971).

Bloomfield, Lincoln, Walter Clemens, and Franklyn Griffiths: *Khrushchev and the Arms Race: Soviet Interests in Arms control and Disarmament, 1954–1964* (Cambridge, MA: MIT Press, 1966).

Brzezinski, Zbigniew: *The Soviet Bloc: Unity and Conflict* (Cambridge, MA: Harvard University Press, 1967).

Crankshaw, Edward: *The New Cold War: Moscow and Peking* (Baltimore: Penguin, 1963).

Dallin, Alexander, Jonathan Harris, and Grey Hodnett (eds.): *Diversity in International Communism: A Documentary Record, 1961–1963* (New York: Columbia University Press, 1963).

Fejto, François: *A History of the People's Democracies: Eastern Europe Since Stalin* (New York: Praeger, 1971).

Garthoff, Raymond: *Soviet Strategy in the Nuclear Age* (New York: Praeger, 1958).

Griffith, William E.: *The Sino-Soviet Rift* (Cambridge, MA: MIT Press, 1964).

Khrushchev, Nikita S.: *The Soviet Stand on Germany* (New York: Crosscurrents, 1961).

———: *Khrushchev Remembers*, 2 vols., trans. and ed. Strobe Talbott (Boston: Little, Brown, 1974).

Laqueur, Walter Z.: *The Soviet Union and the Middle East* (New York: Praeger, 1959).

Linden, Carl: *Khrushchev and the Soviet Leadership, 1957–1964* (Baltimore: Johns Hopkins University Press, 1966).

Lowenthal, Richard: *World Communism: the Disintegration of a Secular Faith* (New York: Oxford University Press, 1966).

Rubinstein, Alvin Z.: *The Soviets in International Organizations: Changing Policy toward Developing Countries, 1953–1963* (Princeton: Princeton University Press, 1964).

Smolansky, Oles: *The Soviet Union and the Arab East under Khrushchev* (Bucknell, PA: Bucknell University Press, 1974).

Wolfe, Thomas W.: *Soviet Strategy at the Crossroads* (Cambridge, MA: Harvard University Press, 1964).

Zagoria, Donald: *The Sino-Soviet Conflict, 1956–1961* (Princeton: Princeton University Press, 1962).

CHAPTER FIVE

Soviet Foreign Policy under Brezhnev—The Attainment of Parity (1964–1982)

Leonid Ilyich Brezhnev was able to supplant his former patron, Nikita S. Khrushchev, as First Secretary[1] only with the help of a majority of Presidium members in 1964. Key among them were Nikolai V. Podgorny, chairman of the Presidium of the Supreme Soviet (president),[2] and Alexei N. Kosygin, chairman of the USSR Council of Ministers (prime minister). This troika was to preside over "a period of consolidation" in Soviet politics.[3] The collective leadership apparently agreed to refrain from any experimentation in either the domestic or foreign arenas, especially after Khrushchev's disasters in both.[4] They did not, however, jettison their predecessor's doctrinal innovations regarding peaceful coexistence and the necessity of avoiding nuclear war in the contemporary era. The implications of these points of continuity for subsequent developments in East-West relations were not insignificant.

Brezhnev's eighteen years of CPSU leadership[5] comprises the better part of a generation and stands second only to Stalin's length of tenure as chief of the Politburo. Although periodization carries with it the risk of oversimplification, the Brezhnev era as it relates to Soviet foreign

---

[1] "Brezhnev soon emerged as *primus inter pares*—at the latest, by March 1966, when he resumed the old title of General Secretary of the CPSU at the XXIIIrd Congress." Robin Edmonds, *Soviet Foreign Policy: The Brezhnev Years* (New York: Oxford University Press, 1983), p. 39.

[2] Podgorny actually became president in December 1965.

[3] See Edmonds, op. cit. p. 39.

[4] See Carl Linden, *Khrushchev and the Soviet Leadership, 1957–1964* (Baltimore, MD: The Johns Hopkins University Press, 1966).

[5] After Podgorny's forced retirement in 1977, Brezhnev also took upon himself the largely ceremonial title of president.

policy can be divided, for ease of analysis, into two periods: 1964 to 1975, a time of unparalleled expansion of Soviet power and interests; and 1976 to 1982, a period of steady decline in Soviet fortunes internationally. This periodization can be seen as roughly parallel, with a slight lag, to a decline in the rate of expansion of the Soviet domestic economy, which became by the mid-1970s of significant concern to Soviet planners.[1]

Period 1: 1964–1975 Brezhnev's first eleven years in power were characterized by an unprecedented growth in Soviet international power and prestige. In relations between East and West, this period saw the realization of important and historic Soviet military and diplomatic goals, including the achievement of strategic parity with the United States, followed by the watershed SALT I treaty (Chapter 5, document 11), the resolution of the German problem (Chapter 5, document 8), and the birth of detente (Chapter 5, documents 12 and 13).

In relations with the third world, successes were just as impressive. The Indo-Soviet relationship continued throughout this first period of Brezhnev's reign to improve and represented a model for other third world nations to emulate (Chapter 5, document 2). Soviet inroads were made in the Middle East after the Arab-Israeli (June) war of 1967: Soviet-Egyptian relations initially promised to surpass the Soviet-Indian relationship as a paradigm for third world emulation (Chapter 5, document 10). In 1971, the Aswan Dam, a great Soviet engineering feat, was put into service. Soviet interest in Southeast Asia paralleled the expansion of American involvement after 1964 (Chapter 5, document 1), and the scales continued to tip steadily in favor of the Soviets' Vietnamese allies until the American defeat in 1974. New opportunities were discovered in postcolonial Africa as Angola began

a long civil war after its emancipation from Portugal, which itself had nearly experienced a Communist victory at the ballot box in the same year. Indeed, by 1974 the "correlation of forces" between capitalism and socialism were seen to be shifting in general in favor of the socialist camp led by the Soviet Union.[2]

This is not to say that there were no problems facing the Soviet leaders during this time. This period was marred by serious disruptions in the socialist world. The "Prague Spring" of 1968 in Czechoslovakia caused great anxiety among the Soviet leaders and resulted in both the August invasion of that country by Warsaw Pact troops and the enunciation of a doctrine of "limited sovereignty of socialist states," referred to thereafter as the Brezhnev Doctrine (Chapter 5, document 6). In relations with China, the end of the 1960s saw an increase in tension on the Sino-Soviet frontier (Chapter 5, document 7), even leading in some places to large-scale military engagements which threatened to widen still further. Clearly, the socialist camp had seen better days of unity and cohesion.

There were also signs toward the end of this first period that detente was not going to be allowed to result in a zero-sum game in favor of the USSR. Questions began to be raised in the West about the intentions of Soviet leaders as the Soviet military continued to deploy new and impressive strategic hardware and Soviet power seemed to grow unchecked. Human rights concerns also were raised in the West, even after the Final Act of the Conference on Security and Cooperation in Europe was signed by the representatives of thirty-six nations in Helsinki, Finland, in July 1975. Helsinki was a two-sided coin. Although it was seen by some as a Western sell-out of Eastern Europe because it legitimated the territorial status quo, its human rights clauses also gave ammunition to Eastern European dis-

---

[1]See Timothy J. Colton, *The Dilemma of Reform in the Soviet Union,* rev. ed. (New York: Council on Foreign Relations, 1986), pp. 34–36.

[2]See Sh. Sanakoyev, "The World Today: The Problem of the Correlation of Forces," *International Affairs* (Moscow), November 1974, pp. 40–50.

sidents and thereby contributed to growing instability across Eastern Europe after 1975. This was especially true in Poland, where the domestic political situation began to deteriorate precipitously after 1975.

Period 2: 1976–1982 Numerous problems facing Soviet foreign policy were recognized in Brezhnev's address to the Twenty-fifth CPSU Congress in 1976 (Chapter 5, document 16), especially regarding the socialist camp and China. The high-water mark of detente had passed with the election of Jimmy Carter to the U.S. presidency in 1976. By 1978, the Soviets were being squeezed out of the Middle East as a key player in that region. Egypt, now turned to a compromise solution sponsored by the United States at Camp David (Chapter 5, document 17). During 1979, the SALT II treaty (Chapter 5, document 18) encountered significant problems in the U.S. Senate; then, over the Christmas holidays the Soviets intervened in Afghanistan to assist a failing client regime there (Chapter 5, document 19). This intervention doomed the SALT II treaty (Chapter 5, document 18).

Problems were compounded yet again for Soviet leaders shortly thereafter as the Solidarity trade union challenged Soviet-sponsored communism in Poland from the summer of 1980 until December 1981, when General Wojciech Jaruzelski declared martial law (Chapter 5, documents 23 to 25). Trade sanctions against the Soviet Union were announced by a number of countries, including the United States (Chapter 5, document 26). During the last two years of Brezhnev's rule, positive developments in foreign affairs were limited to relatively minor successes, such as the development of a closer working relationship with the revolutionary Sandinista government of Nicaragua (Chapter 5, document 28). Both Soviet domestic and foreign policies were characterized during this time by lethargy and inertia—the regime had particularly overextended its foreign policy resources. These facts continued to burden the Soviet leadership after Brezhnev passed away at the end of 1982. His successors inherited a troubled legacy.

In this chapter's opening reading, R. P. Barston gives a concise synopsis of the legacy of the Brezhnev years. He sees four sets of considerations shaping Soviet foreign policy during this time: (1) the need to stabilize the arms race; (2) the resolution of the German problem and European security issues; (3) the need to continue the "ideological struggle" in the third world; and (4) the continued strained relationship with the People's Republic of China. His analysis of the Brezhnev period follows these four categories. The rest of the chapter serves as both a documentary history of the rise and fall of detente and a detailing of the formidable problems of nationalism with which the Soviets have had to grapple continuously in key countries of the Warsaw Pact.

READING 1

Soviet Foreign Policy in the Brezhnev Years

R. P. Barston

Soviet foreign policy has undergone a number of important modifications since the overthrow of Nikita Khrushchev in 1964. With the death of Leonid Brezhnev in November 1982, it is once more under a major review if not revision in the short term.... It is the aim of this article to examine the major assumptions underlying foreign policy in the Brezhnev period and to discuss the boundaries and limits of detente.

CENTRAL FOREIGN POLICY ASSUMPTIONS

Since Brezhnev's consolidation of political power by 1968, Soviet foreign policy has been shaped by at least four sets of considerations. The first of these was an acceptance of the need to stabilize the arms race without undermining those areas in which the Soviet Union had an advantage in strategic delivery systems by extending arms control beyond the early forms of agreements of the 1960s—the Partial Test Ban Treaty (1963), Non-Proliferation Treaty (1968) and Outer Space Treaty (1969)—to central strategic systems and anti-ballistic missile (ABM) systems. Secondly, Soviet decision-makers placed importance on resolving the German problem and other related European questions, on terms which would formalize the status of East Germany (GDR) and the frontiers of central Europe. In the third place, at a formal and operational level foreign policy has been influenced by the requirement of continuing the political and ideological struggle in areas of opportunity outside Europe. Fourth, Soviet diplomacy has operated on the basis of the continued hostility of the People's Republic of China, for which the triangular relationship with Washington, Tokyo and the PRC has been of central importance, as well as the need to establish a diplomatic and military *cordon sanitaire* around the PRC. The fall of South Vietnam in 1975 provided a further set of possibilities not only vis-à-vis the reunified Vietnam but also the Indochina client states.

The first and second of these foreign policy assumptions formed the core of the Soviet conception of detente. The concept became formalized in the peace programme of the 24th Party Congress in March 1971. It substantially differed from the main line of peaceful co-existence articulated by Khrushchev at the 20th Party Congress, especially in the extent to which it envisaged increased co-operation with the United States in the control of strategic weapons, and, by implication, a reduction in the tactics of overt confrontation, which might damage agreement on central nuclear issues. The concept was above all based upon what Soviet decision-makers regarded as a favourable alteration in the balance of forces in part brought about by the development of Soviet-American strategic parity. Writing on what might be called the "classical" period of Soviet-American detente from 1971–5, Nikolai Lebedev, Rector of the Moscow State Institute for International Relations, refers to it as a "new stage in international relations." Detente was thus the central feature of Brezhnev's foreign policy—the crucial component was military detente, which was seen as separate from political detente. The concept of detente, whilst not replacing peaceful co-existence,[1] nevertheless altered the balance of co-operative and conflictual elements in Soviet foreign policy. This changed emphasis, which reflected the mutually

"Soviet Foreign Policy in the Brezhnev Years," *The World Today*, vol. 39, no. 3, March 1983, pp. 81–90, published by the Royal Institute of International Affairs, London. Reprinted by permission.

---

[1] *Report of the Central Committee of the CPSU*, 24th Congress (Moscow, 1971), p. 24.

perceived need for the control of the arms race, reducing the possibility of accidental war breaking out and the establishment of mechanisms for promoting trade and scientific cooperation, found expression in the "Basic Principles of Relations" with the United States, attached to the SALT I agreement in 1972.[1] But the ambiguity of detente proved to be the major drawback in the development of Soviet-American relations in the 1970s. Although the "Basic Principles of Relations" set out general guidelines, both superpowers had different conceptions of the contents of detente and what was both acceptable and permissible within that framework. The boundaries and limits of detente subsequently remained ill-defined in two crucial areas: the implications of intervention in third party disputes and domestic jurisdiction.

SOVIET EUROPEAN POLICY

The German question has dominated much of post-war Soviet foreign policy. By 1969 Soviet policy on Germany had been modified to take into account the growing economic and commercial contacts and diplomatic ties opening up between Eastern Europe and West Germany (FRG) in the post-Adenauer era, as well as with other Western countries. Prior to this, the building of the Berlin Wall served to reinforce the existence of two separate Germanies, although the issue of reunification was not closed for the Soviet Union. In addition, periodic East-West political crises over Berlin in the 1960s and 1970s merely served to underline the more fundamental aspects of the German problem and the sensitive state of FRG-GDR relations. Soviet policy on Germany, however, was modified by 1969 as part of the Soviet approach to European political detente, which aimed to reduce confrontation by promoting Soviet–West German bilateral relations, and, relations between East Germany and the Federal Republic. The latter was also seen as assisting the Soviet aim of gradually detaching the FRG from close ties with the United States, something which had proved impossible during the Adenauer period.[2] One consideration, however, remained unchanged: the need to prevent the FRG from ever becoming a significant military threat to the Soviet Union. Yet, as we shall note below, it is precisely the difficulties in achieving this aim, which have contributed to the growing Soviet concern over the state of detente.

Following the revision of Soviet policy towards Germany, the visit of Chancellor Brandt to Moscow paved the way for rapid progress in Soviet relations from 1970–4. In 1970, the Soviet Union concluded the Renunciation of Force Treaty with West Germany. It was not, however until the resignation of [East German leader Walter] Ulbricht in May 1971 and his replacement by [Erich] Honecker, that the pace of the Four-Power negotiations on Berlin and intra-German negotiations increased, culminating in the signature of the Four-Power Berlin agreement and the Basic Treaty (*Grundvertrag*) in 1972.[3] The visit of President Brezhnev to Bonn in 1973 proved to be the high point of Soviet-FRG relations. The Soviet Union's *Westpolitik* had, along with the treaties signed by the FRG with Poland and Czechoslovakia, created a series of bilateral frameworks which have never been fully developed. The Basic Treaty did serve the Soviet aim of confirming the "inviolability" of the post-war frontiers of Europe. The Soviet Union, too, was able through the bilateral relationship developed with the FRG to counter United States attempts to pursue a policy of "linkage," which

---

[1]For Henry Kissinger's assessment of the significance of the "Basic Principles of Relations," see Henry Kissinger, *The White House Years* (London: Weidenfeld and Nicolson, 1979), pp. 1253–4. . . .

[2]See Terence Pritte, *Adenauer: A Study in Fortitude* (London: Tom Stacey Ltd, 1972).

[3]For background, see Hilary Black, "The East-West German Treaty," *The World Today*, December 1972.

tried to tie together progress on the German question and the Helsinki and Vienna mutual balanced force reduction talks (MBFR). The transference of discussion on confidence-building measures and disarmament to the Helsinki framework from MBFR was also part of the Soviet preference for a pan-European approach to arms control and security. Yet, despite the short-term benefits, the Helsinki process, as continued through the Belgrade and Madrid review conference, has proved costly to the Soviet Union because of the critical attention given to human rights. In bilateral terms, the Soviet Union's relations with West Germany gradually declined after 1974 in the wake of the Guillaume espionage affair and Brandt's subsequent replacement by Helmut Schmidt. Although Brezhnev visited Bonn in 1978, little was achieved.

In the field of arms control, the conclusion of the SALT I Agreement in 1972 was a major feature of Soviet-American military detente, which complemented Soviet European policy. In addition to the ABM Treaty and counter-force ceilings, the accompanying scientific and economic agreements included provisions for a joint Soviet-American Trade Council. The Trade Council was set up the following year and met until the US withdrew after the Soviet intervention in Afghanistan in December 1979. Although the SALT I process itself was continued through the Vladivostok Accords signed between President Ford and Leonid Brezhnev in 1974, the effect of the intrusion of Watergate on East-West relations underlined two further key aspects of the "classical" period of detente: the importance of personality and the need for frequent high-level personal diplomacy. In another sense, the concept for strategic forces of "equal aggregates with freedom to mix" agreed at Vladivostok highlighted the problems of verification and interpretation of arms control agreements. These questions were to play a crucial part in the debate within the United States on the effectiveness of the SALT agreements and the subsequent shelv-

ing of the SALT II agreement.[1] In addition, the growing criticism of the Vladivostok agreement was linked to questions of United States trade with the Soviet Union. The Jackson and Stevenson amendments of the Trade Act in 1974–5 in effect made the development of credits for US-Soviet trade conditional on increased Jewish emigration, which the Soviet Union rejected in January 1975. As William G. Hyland notes: "for the first time, a sociological-political change within the USSR became an official object of US foreign policy, a complete turnover of the containment/evolution theory."[2]

SOVIET FOREIGN POLICY OUTSIDE EUROPE

Soviet foreign policy outside Europe has been modified in a number of important ways since the mid-1960s which have affected the evolution of detente. In the Khrushchev period, the Soviet Union's approach to the Middle East, Africa and Asia was in part shaped by strategic considerations, for example, vis-à-vis Egypt from the mid-1950s, but also by the perceived need to establish political relations with newly independent states emerging in a period of rapid decolonization. Attention in particular focused on states such as Guinea, Ghana, Ethiopia, Mali, Somalia, Nigeria, Sierra Leone and Indonesia through credit aid programmes, arms supplies and "show" projects. However, the limited success of these political initiatives, largely brought about because of the political volatility and nationalist sensitivities of these regimes, forced a reappraisal of Soviet policy by the end of the Khrushchev period. Subsequently, Soviet pol-

---

[1]See Howard Margolis and Jack Ruina, "SALT II: notes on shadow and substance," *Technology Review* (MIT), October 1979, pp. 30–6. Also Richard Burt, "SALT after Vladivostok," *The World Today,* February 1975, and Lawrence Freedman, "SALT II and the strategic balance," *ibid,* August 1979.

[2]William G. Hyland, "Soviet-American Relations: A New Cold War?" RAND R-2763-FF/RC, May 1981, p. 31.

icy has been influenced more by economic and strategic considerations as well as the need to build up more stable relations with selected Third World countries. In South Asia, for example, relations with India, developed since the mid-1950s, were upgraded, against the context of deterioration in Sino-Soviet relations especially from 1969, through the conclusion in August 1971 of the 20-year Soviet-Indian Treaty of Friendship and Co-operation. India was careful to insist, however, through Article 4, that the agreement did not signal an end to India's non-alignment. The expulsion of Soviet advisers by Egypt in 1972 proved a major setback to the Soviet Union's attempts to establish long-term influence in the Middle East. The break in Soviet-Egyptian relations had a profound impact on both the subsequent evolution of Soviet policy towards the region and relations with the United States. Earlier, Soviet-American relations were severely tested during the so-called "autumn of crises," involving super-power conflict over Jordan, Cienfuegos, Chile and also over the US mining of North Vietnamese ports. In the October 1973 Arab-Israeli conflict, the Soviet Union again showed restraint; although a massive airlift of supplies to Egypt was mounted through Yugoslavia and Syria, the Soviet Union ultimately conceded to American pressure triggered by the Stage-three nuclear alert. The "autumn of crises" and events in the Middle East, including the Arab-Israeli war, suggested that, whilst the Soviet Union would go to considerable lengths to protect its clients, it was not prepared at that point to jeopardize fundamentally the development of the embryonic detente with the United States.

Following the 1973 Arab-Israeli War, the Soviet Union was forced to seek alternative naval and military bases as well as other compensating political relationships as a result of the Egyptian decision first to limit access to port facilities at Alexandria and later in 1976 to abrogate the Soviet-Egyptian Treaty. In an attempt to redress this, Soviet attention turned increasingly to the Horn of Africa, first through a treaty of friendship with Somalia in 1974 and, to compensate for the loss of port facilities at Berbera in 1976–7, to Ethiopia, with whom a similar treaty was signed in 1978. In addition, Syria and Iraq were regarded as important potential members of an anti-Egyptian-American front the Soviet Union attempted to construct after 1975. Yet, the long-standing conflict between the two major factions of the Ba'ath parties in Syria and Iraq underlined the extent to which inter- and intra-Arab differences severely limited Soviet influence in the Middle East. For its part, too, Iraq opposed Soviet discussions with the United States in October 1977 aimed at resuming the Geneva conference on the Arab-Israeli dispute.[1] Whilst the Egyptian-US-Israeli Camp David summit served to unify briefly a disparate set of Arab interests in opposition to Egypt, the Camp David agreement itself isolated the Soviet Union further from the central political process connected with resolution of the Arab-Israeli dispute. The Soviet condemnation of the Camp David Agreement in September 1978, along with calls for a return to the multilateral Geneva framework as preferable to unilateral United States initiatives, confirmed the growing deterioration in super-power relations which developed after 1975.

The decline in Soviet-American relations was influenced to a considerable extent by the marked shift in methods of Soviet foreign policy outside Europe between 1975 and 1979. The period is marked by a series of opportunistic interventions using surrogate forces either from Cuba or Eastern Europe, which reflected the growing militarization of Soviet foreign policy and increasing influence of the military in decision-making. The first of these—the Angolan civil war (1975–6)—provided an opportunity, at a time of considerable disarray in American

---

[1] For a discussion of Iraqi policy, see Robert O. Freedman, "Soviet Policy Towards Ba'athist Iraq," in Robert H. Donaldson (ed.), *The Soviet Union and the Third World* (Boulder, CO: Westview Press, 1981), pp. 161–91.

foreign policy after Watergate, both to compensate for losses in Egypt and, more importantly, to reaffirm Soviet ideological aspirations and credentials under peaceful co-existence. The Angolan civil war also offered long-range but at that stage ill-defined options in Southern Africa as a whole. It is extremely doubtful that Soviet involvement in the civil war on the side of the MPLA [Movement for the Liberation of Angola] was intended to counter Chinese support for UNITA [National Union for the Total Independence of Angola] or FMLA forces.[1] In the two other major cases—the Somali-Ethiopian conflict (1977–8) and Yemen—Soviet involvement would seem to have been influenced by the need to obtain facilities in the Horn of Africa to support the "long-reach" naval policy initiated by Admiral Gorshkov in the mid-1960s. In South East Asia, Soviet policy again responded decisively to developments in Indochina, especially the deterioration in Sino-Vietnamese relations after the fall of South Vietnam. The Soviet decision to conclude a "special relationship" with Vietnam, which joined CMEA in June 1978, through the Treaty of Friendship on 3 November 1978, seems to have taken account the likely adverse implications of this for relations with the Association of South East Asian Nations (ASEAN), given Vietnam's regional ambitions. The agreement was thus regarded by the Soviet Union as a means of limiting Chinese influence in the Indochina region. The Soviet Union accordingly supported Vietnam's invasion of Kampuchea in December 1978 and provided intelligence and military supplies to the Vietnamese after the PRC launched a limited invasion of Vietnam in February 1979. Whilst the cutting of aid and business links by ASEAN with Vietnam initially was an acceptable cost of the agreement with Viet-

nam, as a result of the invasion, there has been growing Soviet frustration at the financial burden caused by the intractability of the Kampuchean conflict between the Heng Samrin regime and loose anti-Vietnamese coalition forces. Indeed, Soviet policy has recently shifted to favour dealing directly with Kampuchea, and cultivating links with Vientane.[2]

In pursuing an interventionist policy outside traditional areas of influence, Soviet decision-makers appear to have considered that these actions were not or should not be construed as being contrary to detente.[3] That is to say, Soviet involvement in national liberation struggles or in areas in which there is not direct United States presence are regarded as entirely legitimate and without prejudice to Soviet-American politico-military detente. In contrast, the United States saw Soviet actions as undermining the basic principles of detente—the assumption of moderation and restraint in conflict. Reviewing the reasons for the decline in Soviet-American relations after 1975, President Carter stated:

> The Soviet Union can choose either confrontation or co-operation. The United States is adequately prepared to meet either choice. We would prefer co-operation through a detente that increasingly involves similar restraint by both sides, similar readiness to resolve disputes by negotiation and not violence, similar willingness to compete peacefully and not militarily. Anything less than that is likely to undermine detente...[4]

THE SECOND AUTUMN OF CRISES

The autumn of 1979 proved to be a fundamental turning point in Soviet relations with the United States. In the second autumn of crises, three issues—the NATO decision about theater nuclear

---

[1]For a discussion of the evolution of the Angolan civil war, see T. Hodges, "The struggle for Angola," *Round Table,* April 1976, pp. 173–84. Also Stephen Larrabee, "Moscow, Angola and the dialectics of detente," *The World Today,* May 1976.

[2]See *Pravda,* 7 January 1982, for details of Kampuchean economic development and Soviet aid.
[3]See N. I. Lebedev, *A New Stage in International Relations* (Oxford: Pergamon Press, 1978).
[4]President Carter's speech, 7 June 1978, to US Naval Academy at Annapolis, Maryland.

forces (TNF), the SALT ratification debate and the Soviet intervention in Afghanistan—brought a marked decline in Soviet-US relations, to the point that detente, as a framework for Soviet-American relations, had by the following year been virtually abandoned.

The NATO modernization plan involving the deployment of ground and sea-launched cruise missiles and Pershing II intermediate range ballistic missiles (IRBMs: range 1,800 miles) brought together for the Soviet Union two of the major preoccupations in its foreign policy: arms control and European security. The NATO plan was regarded as a major threat not only to the Soviet Union itself but to stability within Europe. Western Europe was no longer the "hostage" of the past, but a Europe into which new elements of strategic uncertainty had been introduced. In response to the NATO proposals, Brezhnev outlined in October 1979, a counter-plan[1] which involved the withdrawal of 20,000 troops, 1,000 tanks, a nuclear "freeze" in Europe and confidence-building measures, on condition that NATO did not go ahead with plans to develop and deploy cruise and Pershing II missiles. The Soviet proposals met with little positive response from the West. The degree of Soviet concern can also be seen in the unusual visit of the Soviet Foreign Minister, Andrei Gromyko, to Bonn prior to the December NATO Council meeting, in which an attempt was made to persuade the FRG to reverse its decision on the NATO modernization plan. The Soviet intervention in Afghanistan in December 1979 led directly to President Carter's decision to shelve the SALT II agreement. For the Soviet Union, the protracted debate after the Vienna summit and Senate attempts to modify the agreement were an unnecessary intrusion. More importantly, the political effect of the decision not to continue the ratification process on the Soviet Union was to call into question at least two of the central assumptions in Brezhnev's foreign policy: that military detente through arms control brought strategic and economic advantages to the Soviet Union. In the United States, the conservative critique of SALT II, focusing not only on the SALT Protocol, but also on the Backfire bomber issue, the 3000 heavy ICBM concession and SS-20 deployment, paved the way for defence budgetary changes made by the Reagan Administration, based on the view that strategic parity had ceased to exist and that the Soviet Union in fact had moved to a position of overall strategic superiority.[2]

FOREIGN POLICY IN TRANSITION

By 1980 the politico-strategic calculus of the Soviet Union had become far more complex and filled with uncertainties and dilemmas. Between 1980 and 1982 Soviet-American relations continued to decline for the most part quite rapidly.[3] The sombre character of Brezhnev's address to the 26th Party Congress reflected Soviet unease at the increasing range of problems and instability in East-West relations. Although detente remained formally within the Soviet political vocabulary, relations with the United States were seen far more in terms of seeking at best a limited modus operandi. Three issues in particular—the Polish problem, Afghanistan and technology transfer—contributed, however, to the continuing decline in Soviet-American relations and highlighted a number of dilemmas for Soviet foreign policy. In the first place, growing involvement in Afghanistan and an inability to extricate Soviet forces worked against any significant improvement in relations with the United States, and for that matter, prevented a rapprochement with China. In the Polish case, the Soviet dilemma revolved around how to control events in Poland without incurring penalties from the

---

[1]See *Pravda*, 7 October 1979.

[2]See Paul Nitze, "SALT II and American strategic considerations," *Comparative Strategy*, Vol. 2, no. 1, 1980, pp. 9–24.

[3]See *Pravda*, 2 February 1981.

West, given the dependence of the Polish economy on West European financial credits. Although considerable military pressure was put on Poland in December 1980 and in March 1981, the Soviet Union refrained from direct military intervention. Nevertheless, the imposition of martial law by the Polish authorities, with Soviet assistance, resulted in further sanctions by Western Europe and the United States. Third, the Soviet Union placed consistent importance under Brezhnev on the acquisition of high technology, either formally through the development of bilateral relations, for example with the FRG, or through economic intelligence.[1] United States restrictions on export licenses for equipment of the Urengoi-West European pipe-line, and general tightening of legislation of the transfer of high technology following the Nunn report, particularly soured Soviet-United States relations.

A distinct hardening of attitudes to the United States was reflected in President Brezhnev's speech to the Soviet armed forces on 27 October and at the 65th anniversary of the Bolshevik revolution of 7 November 1982. At the Moscow military parade, the Soviet Defence Minister, Dimitri Ustinov, underlined the shift in Soviet policy when he accused the United States and its allies of mounting "a political, ideological and economic offensive against socialism."[2] The other important change in Soviet policy in the final phase of the Brezhnev period, corresponding with the deterioration in relations with the United States, was in terms of commencing a cautious revision of Sino-Soviet relations. The change of Soviet policy was foreshadowed, formally at least, in Brezhnev's speech at Tashkent in March 1982, and seems undoubtedly to have been influenced by the increasing uncertainties vis-à-vis European security and the difficulties in Soviet-American relations....

SOME CONCLUDING OBSERVATIONS

The end of the Brezhnev era has brought to a close a distinctive phase of post-war Soviet foreign policy....That period is perhaps above all distinguished by the breakdown of the "classical" period of detente and the emergence of a far more complex and less predictable range of issues on the Soviet foreign-policy agenda with regard to the United States, Europe and the Middle East. At the centre of the agenda for the Andropov collective leadership is the uncertainty surrounding the new adversarial relationship with the United States as reflected in the lack of progress in the Geneva strategic arms reduction talks, the "launch on warning" posture, taken in the context of the debate on Pershing missiles and further revised proposals on European theatre nuclear weapons. In other areas, only minor foreign-policy adjustments have been made, for example, vis-à-vis Finland and Albania. The major exception, of course, is in Sino-Soviet relations. The process of revision, begun during the final phase of Brezhnev's period of office, has been further continued at the diplomatic level and through the new November 1982 Soviet frontier act.[3] According to the Politburo member Konstantin Chernenko, the Soviet Union was now ready to make its frontier with China a "border of friendship." The future development of Sino-Soviet relations depends on the extent to which the USSR is prepared to revise policy on Soviet troop deployment on the Sino-Soviet border, Afghanistan and vis-à-vis Vietnam. It seems likely that changes of policy in some of these areas may occur. Whether they will remove the dilemmas in Soviet foreign policy or create new uncertainties remains to be seen.

---

[1]See *The Guardian*, 30 September 1982, for details of the Nunn Report and the Racal case, and *ibid,* 16 November 1982, on technology transfer. Also Vladimir Sobeslavsky, "East-West detente and technology transfer," *The World Today,* October 1980.

[2]*The Guardian*, 8 November 1982.

[3]See *Pravda*, 26 November 1982, for the text of the Law on State Borders.

Soviet Government Statement in Support of the Democratic Republic of Vietnam

9 February 1965

Editor's commentary: As the United States was drawn further into the rice paddies of South Vietnam in the cause of containing communism, the Soviet Union and other communist countries drew closer to the North Vietnamese and began to supply them with the materiel necessary to wage war against a superpower. This statement of 9 February 1965 appeared as major demonstrations occurred in Moscow and a mob attacked the U.S. Embassy there, ostensibly in response to the U.S. bombings of North Vietnamese cities on 7 February. Several weeks later, on 26 March, the Soviet Union concluded a military assistance pact with North Vietnam against U.S. "imperialism."

Reports of new serious provocations by the United States armed forces against the Democratic Republic of Vietnam [DRV] have come in during the past two days. On February 7, a large number of jet planes, based on aircraft carriers of the American Seventh Fleet, bombed the town of Dong-Hoi and a number of other populated localities in the DRV. The raid of U.S. planes on Dong-Hoi was repeated on February 8. The American planes bombed and strafed many houses and even a hospital. There was loss of human life.

The piratical raids by planes of the American air force on the populated localities of the DRV evoke the wrath and resolute condemnation of the Soviet people and of all the peoples who oppose imperialist arbitrariness and aggression.

In an attempt to create at least a semblance of a pretext for these new acts of armed aggression against the DRV, U.S. official circles refer to the fact that in the course of the liberation struggle the South Vietnamese patriots are dealing blows at military installations on the territory of U.S.-occupied South Vietnam. But who gave the US the right to retaliate against the actions of guerillas in South Vietnam, against the defeats that the occupationists and their henchmen are suffering there, by bombing the territory of a third country—the DRV? It is clear to every thinking person that there is not a single grain of truth in these explanations. They are nothing but a dodge to try to camouflage the predatory policy of the United States in the area of Indochina.

The people of South Vietnam are waging a hard and just struggle against the foreign intervention. They want only one thing—to settle their domestic affairs alone, without any foreign interference. They are fighting for national freedom and will win it. . . .

The Soviet government cautioned the ruling circles in the United States against attempts to encroach on the sovereignty of a fraternal socialist country—the DRV—and it hoped that the people in Washington would display a realistic attitude in their approach to the situation taking shape on the Indochinese peninsula. But, to all appearances, any sense of realism has been betrayed by those who are resorting to aggression against the peace-loving state—the DRV.

It seems that Washington simply cannot give up the illusion that aggression against the DRV can be carried out with impunity. Indeed, compared with the United States, the DRV is a small state and is less armed, but the people of the DRV are defending a just cause, defending their national independence, their freedom, and they have reliable and strong friends.

The Soviet Union has invariably supported the establishment of normal and improved relations with the United States. But the development of relations requires mutuality; and there must be no misunderstanding about this. This process is

---

Pravda, 9 February 1965, as translated in *Soviet Documents*, vol. 3, no. 9, 1 March 1965, pp. 3–5.

incompatible with aggressive political manifestations, which are likely to reduce to naught the various steps undertaken in the interest of improving Soviet-American relations.

The Soviet Government resolutely supports the statements made by the government of the DRV in protest against the military actions conducted by the United States against the DRV, against the build-up of United States armed forces and weapons in South Vietnam. It fully subscribes to the demand of the DRV Government to stop these actions, to ensure strict observance of the 1954 Geneva agreements on Vietnam, to defend peace in Indochina and Southeast Asia.

In the face of the above-mentioned actions of the United States, the Soviet Union will be forced, along with its allies and friends, to take further measures to safeguard the security and strengthen the defense capability of the DRV. No one should doubt that the Soviet Union will do this, that the Soviet peoples will fulfill their international duty in relation to the fraternal socialist country.

DOCUMENT 2

The Tashkent Declaration

10 January 1966

Editor's commentary: The leaders of India and Pakistan met in Soviet Uzbekistan to negotiate an end to the fighting which had broken out between their two countries in 1965. They both expressed their appreciation to Soviet arbitrators, including Alexei Kosygin, "for their constructive, friendly, and noble role" in sponsoring and hosting the meeting. The world public opinion value of this

Pravda, 11 January 1966, p. 1. Editor's translation.

Soviet action was substantial, especially in the third world. The declaration follows in full.

The prime minister of India and the president of Pakistan...state their firm determination to restore normal and peaceful relations between their countries and to promote mutual understanding and friendly relations between their peoples. They regard the achievement of these goals as vitally important for the prosperity of the 600 million people of India and Pakistan.

I. The prime minister of India and the president of Pakistan agree that the two sides should apply all efforts for the creation of good-neighborly relations between India and Pakistan in conformity with the charter of the United Nations. They affirm their commitment in accordance with the charter not to resort to force and to resolve their disputes by peaceful means. They agreed that the continuation of tensions between the two sides does not correspond to the interests of peace in their region.... In this regard, Jammu and Kashmir were discussed and each of the sides set forth its respective position.

II. The prime minister of India and the president of Pakistan agreed that all the armed personnel of both countries will withdraw not later than 25 February 1966 to the positions which they occupied before 5 August 1965, and both sides will observe the conditions of cease-fire on the line of cease-fire.

III. The prime minister of India and the president of Pakistan agreed that relations between India and Pakistan will be constructed on the basis of the principle of nonintervention in the internal affairs of one another.

IV. The prime minister of India and the president of Pakistan agreed that both sides will not encourage any propaganda directed against the other side....

V. The prime minister of India and the president of Pakistan agreed that the high commissioner of India in Pakistan and the high commissioner of Pakistan in India return to their posts and normal activity of the diplomatic missions of both countries be resumed.

VI. The prime minister of India and the president of Pakistan agreed to examine measures for the resumption of economic and trade relations, communications, cultural exchanges, and also to take steps for the fulfillment of existing agreements between India and Pakistan.

VII. The prime minister of India and the president of Pakistan agreed...to carry out the repatriation of prisoners.

VIII. The prime minister of India and the president of Pakistan agreed that the sides will continue the discussion of questions connected with the problem of refugees and illegal immigration....They further agreed to discuss the question of the return of property and assets in the possession of both sides as a result of the conflict.

IX. The prime minister of India and the president of Pakistan agreed that meetings will be continued between the sides both on the very highest and on other levels regarding questions which directly concern both countries. Both sides recognize the necessity to create joint Indo-Pakistani organs, which will present reports to their governments on making decisions regarding what further steps should be undertaken.

The prime minster of India and the president of Pakistan declare their feelings of deep gratitude and thanks to the leaders of the Soviet Union, the Soviet government and personally to the chairman of the Council of Ministers of the USSR for their constructive, friendly, and noble role in the organization of this meeting, which led to the mutually satisfactory results. They express also to the government and friendly people of Uzbekistan their sincere thanks for their kindly reception and their generous hospitality.

They invite the chairman of the Council of Ministers of the USSR to witness this declaration.

(Signed) Prime Minister of India, Dal Bahadur SHASTRI

President of Pakistan, Mohammed AIYUB KHAN

TASHKENT, 10 January 1966

The Sino-Soviet Dispute: CPSU Central Committee Letter of January 1966

Editor's commentary: The removal of Khrushchev from the apex of the Soviet leadership did little to assuage the Sino-Soviet dispute. The polemics over ideology which had gone on for more than three years between the Soviet Union and the People's Republic of China did not abate, but rather continued to increase and encompass more and more areas of Sino-Soviet relations. The Chinese were just entering the disastrous period of the Great Proletarian Cultural Revolution, the great upheaval of Chinese society promoted by Chairman Mao, when a summary letter of all the spurned attempts of the CPSU to better relations was forwarded to the CPC.

...In its concern to create a favorable political atmosphere, the Central Committee of the CPSU has put a unilateral end to open polemics. In so doing, we have yielded to the wishes of the Chinese leaders and we have invited to Moscow for the observances of the October Revolution's forty-seventh anniversary a delegation of the Chinese party and the government headed by comrade Chou En-lai, president of the Central Committee of the CPC and prime minister of the PRC.

This version of the text, thought to be authentic, was published in *Le Monde,* 23 March 1966, *excerpts.* Editor's translation.

At the beginning of February 1965, the Soviet delegation led by comrade Kosygin, member of the Presidium of the CC of the CPSU and president of the Council of Ministers of the USSR, made use of his stay in Beijing in order to make new contacts with the leaders before moving on to the Democratic Republic of Vietnam and the Democratic Republic of Korea. We have entered into these negotiations in all sincerity, in the hope of conducting them from the outset on an objective basis and in a spirit which will lead to concrete results. In the course of these conversations, conducted with the delegation of the Chinese party and the state led by Chou En-lai, the First Secretary of the CC of the CPC, comrade Brezhnev, made the following statement:

> We estimate that, after the October plenum of the CC of the CPSU, new favorable opportunities have appeared for the progressive elimination of the difficulties existing between our two parties. These will allow us to render normal the situation in the international communist movement and to realize an understanding on fundamental principles of Marxist-Leninism, of the 1957 and 1960 declarations. We intend to continue further on this path and express our sincere hope to see the Central Committee of the CP of China adopt the same conclusions.

We made known a detailed program dedicated to the normalization of Sino-Soviet relations, between the parties as well as the states. This program contains some proposals for the beginning of meetings of mixed delegations from the Soviet Union and China at the highest levels concerning the termination of polemics on both sides, concrete suggestions on the extension of commerce, scientific, technical and cultural cooperation, and the coordination of the foreign affairs of China and the USSR.

Nevertheless, our efforts have met with no understanding and have foundered on the opposition of the Chinese leaders. The Central Committee of the CPC has totally ignored the proposal of convening "at the summit." The leaders of the Chinese CP have not accepted the extension of economic, technical, and cultural cooperation, and have moreover undertaken new steps to restrict it. In April 1965, the government of the People's Republic of China officially renounced cooperation with the Soviet Union in the construction of a series of industrial projects as specified by the treaty of 1961. At the beginning of July, the People's Republic of China withdrew from the joint institute for nuclear research. The Chinese government has rejected the Soviet proposal for working together with other socialist states in the exploration and utilization of space.

All of this demonstrates that the leaders of the Chinese CP want to see the bad relations between the People's Republic of China and the USSR aggravated further. The Chinese leaders are frequently declaring that the Communist Party of China is conducting a political struggle against the Soviet Union. Against all good sense, they present it as "the struggle of the proletariat state against the bourgeois state."

The anti-Soviet line thus becomes an integral element of the entire ideological corpus of the Chinese CP inside as well as outside the country.

It is suggested to the Chinese people that the Soviet Union is one of their principal enemies. In Chinese enterprises and offices meetings are organized and each of the participants is forced to make criticisms of the Soviet Union. The organization of anti-Soviet demonstrations has been built into the system. On 6 March 1965 such a demonstration was even organized in front of the embassy of the USSR.

The Chinese leaders ceaselessly and actively undermine the order of Soviet state and society. Radio Beijing emits in the direction of the USSR declarations and statements whose aim is to provoke a conflict between the different social groups of Soviet people, to obstruct the friendship which unites the people of the Soviet Union and to destroy the trust accorded to the party and its organizations. This operation directly calls them to such political actions against the

Central Committee of the CP of the USSR and the Soviet government....

Report of the Central Committee to the Twenty-third Congress of the CPSU

L. I. Brezhnev

29 March 1966

Editor's commentary: Addressing a CPSU Congress as General Secretary for the first time since occupying that post in 1964, L. I. Brezhnev did not differ substantially from his predecessor (Khrushchev) in his evaluation of the international situation. Socialism was "making steady progress" in the world, the "crisis of capitalism" continued to foreshadow capitalism's ultimate demise, and the struggle for national liberation in the third world was, with the support of the CPSU, continuously bearing new fruit.

THE WORLD SYSTEM OF SOCIALISM...

It is a pleasure to note that the socialist system is being steadily consolidated in the fraternal countries, that the new social relations are being perfected, that the standard of living is rising and that the international prestige of the socialist states is increasing.

The world socialist system is making steady progress....

Comrades, cooperation and solidarity are the main sources of the strength of the socialist sys-

23rd Congress of the Communist Party of the Soviet Union (Moscow: Novosti Press Agency, 1966), pp. 11–41, *excerpts.*

tem. The development and deepening of this co-operation is in accordance with the vital interests of each individual country and of the socialist system as a whole; it promotes the cohesion of our ranks in the struggle against imperialism.

Such cohesion is particularly necessary in the present situation, when the American imperialists, broadening their aggression against the Vietnamese people, have launched an unprovoked attack against the Democratic Republic of Vietnam, a socialist country. The CPSU is working consistently for united action by all socialist countries in assisting fighting Vietnam....

While speaking of the consolidation of the world socialist system, comrades, we must at the same time note that our relations with the parties of two socialist countries, with the Communist Party of China and the Albanian Party of Labor, unfortunately remain unsatisfactory.

Our party and the Soviet people would sincerely like friendship with People's China and its Communist Party. We are prepared to do everything possible to improve our relations with people's Albania, and with the Albanian Party of Labor....

EXACERBATION OF THE CONTRADICTIONS OF THE CAPITALIST SYSTEM...

...The capitalist system as a whole is gripped by a general crisis. Its internal contradictions are growing more acute. In their efforts to surmount these contradictions and hold their ground in the struggle against socialism, the bosses of the bourgeois world pinned strong hopes on state regulation of the economy, scientific and technical progress and on greater military production. However, this has not nor could it have cured capitalism of its basic ailments. Although economic growth in the main capitalist countries has been more rapid since the war than between the two world wars, it is obvious that capitalist economy has remained unstable. Periods of relative rises in production are succeeded by recessions. Such rises and drops have occurred in many capitalist countries, particularly in the United States.

When to this is added the mounting inflation, the tremendous growth of the national debt and the indebtedness of the population, it becomes clear that the hidden destructive forces inherent in the capitalist economy are still operating; it will not escape new upheavals.

The law of the uneven economic and political development of capitalist countries is operating implacably; the contradictions between the capitalist states are growing more acute. For a number of years economic growth in the West-European countries and Japan was more rapid than in the United States, but in the last few years the tables have turned. Economic growth in the USA has been accelerated, while in Western Europe and Japan rates of growth have sharply fallen....

DEVELOPMENT OF THE NATIONAL LIBERATION MOVEMENT...

...In the past few years the cause of national liberation has made considerable progress. The world has witnessed the emergence of another 17 independent states, including the Algerian People's Democratic Republic, Kenya, Uganda, Tanzania, Zambia and others. Almost the whole of Asia and Africa have now shaken off the yoke of colonial slavery. This is a great gain in the peoples' liberation struggle against imperialism....

Wherever they can, the imperialists try to utilise the internal contradictions in the newly-free countries. They provoke clashes between various social, national and tribal groups and strive to set various politicians against each other; they try to move to power those belonging to the most reactionary and corrupt elements, who enrich themselves through ties and collaboration with foreign capital. In some countries they succeed in setting up anti-popular regimes, whose rep-resentatives are not averse to being the direct accomplices of imperialism in the international arena as well....

Our party and the Soviet state will continue to:

render the utmost support to the peoples who are fighting for their liberation and work for the immediate granting of independence to all colonial countries and peoples;

promote all-sided cooperation with countries that have won national independence and help them to develop their economy, train national cadres and oppose neocolonialism;

strengthen the fraternal links of the CPSU with the Communist Parties and revolutionary democratic organisations in Asian, African and Latin American countries.

The successes of the national liberation movement are inseparably bound up with the successes of world socialism and the international working class. The firm and unbreakable alliance of these great revolutionary forces is the guarantee of the final triumph of the cause of national and social liberation.

DOCUMENT 5

Check the Israeli Aggressor

July 1967

Editor's commentary: In the June 1967 Middle East war Israel was vastly outnumbered, yet emerged victorious over the coalition of Arab armies that had tried to destroy it. Taking advantage of this situation, the USSR claimed solidarity with the

---

International Affairs (Moscow), July 1967, pp. 3–5, *excerpts.*

Arab states' "just" cause, and along with most of the socialist camp, broke relations with Israel. In explaining the Soviet stance, this polemical editorial from the Soviet journal International Affairs *refers to the conflict "in the immediate vicinity of its frontiers," thereby implying the legitimacy of Soviet interests by virtue of the USSR's being a* regional *Middle East actor.*

...The Israeli Government, by unleashing its aggression against the Arab peoples, has shown once again that it is playing irresponsibly and criminally with the future of its own people. It has sown such hatred among the peoples of the Arab East and the whole world that this must have an effect on the future of Israel. Israeli leaders insist that "they have been waging this struggle for Israel's survival as a state." But, if anything could undermine the very basis of its existence, the Soviet Government declared in its statement, "it is the road of reckless adventurism in politics that the governing circles of Israel have chosen."

The Arabs are peace-loving people. No matter how much US and Israeli propaganda shout about their aggressiveness, they stand for peace and are prepared to safeguard this cause of peace with other nations. The Arab peoples need peace, the more so because many of them have started to tackle most difficult tasks in securing economic independence and implementing deep-going social and eocnmic reforms. The flames of war, kindled by the Tel Aviv militarists, have inflicted heavy material damage on the economy of the Arab countries, and that was also one of the aims of the aggression....

Today, when the Arab countries have become the objective of an Israeli attack carefully prepared by the imperialists, the Soviet Union has shown by the resolute acts that it wants to hold the aggressor and its patrons in check. The Soviet state could not remain indifferent to the fact that a hotbed of war had arisen in the immediate vicinity of its frontiers, and that aggression had been committed against friendly Arab states. The USSR has given the Arabs the broadest political, diplomatic and material help in their just struggle. This country has repeatedly issued serious warnings to the reckless Israeli militarists concerning their responsibility before the world and the grave consequences of their aggressive line. But when it became clear that Tel Aviv was turning a deaf ear to the demands of the Soviet Union and all peace-loving mankind to stop intervention, the Soviet Government broke off diplomatic relations with Israel, in view of Israel's cynical disregard of international law and gross violations of the UN Security Council's decision; other socialist states have also broken off diplomatic relations with the aggressor....

The statement issued by the Central Committees of the Communist and Workers' Parties and Governments of Bulgaria, Hungary, the GDR, Poland, the Soviet Union, Czechoslovakia and Yugoslavia made it quite clear that "unless the Government of Israel stops its aggression and withdraws its troops behind the armistice line, the Socialist states who have signed this statement will do everything necessary to help the peoples of the Arab countries give a decisive rebuff to the aggressor, safeguard their legitimate rights, put out the flames of war in the Middle East and restore peace in the area."

Israel has been warned and it must be clear about the stand of the peace-loving Socialist states. The aggressors should not forget that they will not evade responsibility for the violation of peace and encroachment on the sovereign rights of the peoples. The Socialist countries will not allow the imperialist forces to have their own way....

Those who hope that their crimes will go unpunished are mistaken, international law is not a mere abstraction, and the peoples will not allow themselves to be addressed in terms of force. The Israeli aggressors and their patrons will have to answer for their crimes against the Arab countries and the whole of mankind.

The Prague Spring and the Brezhnev Doctrine

1968

Editor's commentary: The excerpts from the two documents which follow outline the basic issues in the dispute between the Prague Spring reformers led by Alexander Dubček in 1968 and those promoting the orthodox Marxist-Leninist line in Czechoslovakia. The first is in the form of a warning given to the Czechoslovak reformers after the appearance of their "Two Thousand Words Manifesto," calling for political reforms in Czechoslovakia, including an end to censorship. The second is the ex post facto *justification of the invasion, as given in a* Pravda *editorial, which became known as the Brezhnev Doctrine of limited sovereignty of socialist states, emphasizing the primacy of defending "socialist gains" over the bourgeois notion of national sovereignty.*

(A) THE WARSAW LETTER, 18 JULY 1968

The development of events in your country evokes deep anxiety in us. It is our deep conviction that the offensive of the reactionary forces, backed by imperialism, against your party and the foundations of the socialist system in the Czechoslovak Socialist Republic threatens to push your country off the road of socialism and thus jeopardizes the interests of the entire socialist system.... We cannot agree to have hostile forces push your country from the road of socialism and create a threat of severing Czech-

oslovakia from the socialist community. This is something more than your cause. It is the common cause of our countries, which have joined in the Warsaw Treaty....

You are aware of the understanding with which the fraternal parties treated the decisions of the January plenary meeting of the Central Committee of the Communist Party of Czechoslovakia, as they believed that your party, firmly controlling the levers of power, would direct the entire process in the interest of socialism and not let anti-Communist reaction exploit it to grind its own ax. We shared the conviction that you would protect and cherish the Leninist principle of democratic centralism....

Unfortunately, events have taken another course.

Capitalizing on the weakening of party leadership in the country and demagogically abusing the slogan of "democratization," the forces of reaction triggered off a campaign against the Communist Party of Czechoslovakia and its honest and devoted cadres, clearly seeking to abolish the party's leading role, subvert the socialist system, and place Czechoslovakia in opposition to the other socialist countries....

Anti-socialist and revisionist forces have laid hands on the press, radio and television, making them a rostrum for attacking the Communist Party, disorienting the working class and all working folk, spewing forth uncurbed anti-socialist demagogy, and undermining friendly relations between the Czechoslovak Socialist Republic and the other socialist countries....

This is precisely why the reaction has been able publicly to address the entire country and to print in political platform under the title of "The 2,000 Words," which contains an outright call for struggle against the Communist Party and constitutional authority, for strikes and disorders. This call represents a serious danger to the party, the national front, and the socialist state, and is an attempt to introduce anarchy.... Far from being repudiated, this platform, being so extensively circulated at a responsible movement

---

Excerpts from *(a)* TASS release, 18 July 1968, and *(b)* Sergei Kovalev, "International Obligations of Socialist Countries," *Pravda,* 26 September 1968, p. 4, as translated in Richard Lowenthal, "The Sparrow in the Cage," *Problems of Communism,* vol. 17, no. 6 (November–December) 1968, pp. 2–28, *excerpts.*

on the eve of the extraordinary Congress of the Communist Party of Czechoslovakia, has, on the contrary, found obvious advocates in the party rank and file and its leadership, who second the anti-socialist calls.... A situation has thus arisen which is absolutely unacceptable for a socialist country....

Matters have gone so far that the joint staff exercises of our troops, with the participation of several units of the Soviet Army..., are being used for groundless accusations of violations of the sovereignty of the CSSR....

Czechoslovakia can retain her independence and sovereignty only as a socialist country, as a member of the socialist community.... It is our conviction that a situation has arisen in which the threat to the foundations of socialism in Czechoslovakia jeopardizes the common vital interests of other socialist countries....

That is why we believe that a decisive rebuff to the forces of anti-communism and decisive efforts to preserve the socialist system in Czechoslovakia are not only your task but ours, too.

The cause of defending the power of the working class and of all working people, as well as Czechoslovakia's socialist gains, demands that a bold and decisive offensive should be launched against right-wing and anti-socialist forces; that all the defensive means set up by the socialist state should be mobilized; that a stop should be put to the activity of all political organizations that come out against socialism; that the party should take control of the mass-information media—press, radio, and television—and use them in the interests of the working class, of all working people, and of socialism; that the ranks of the party itself should be closed on the principled basis of Marxism-Leninism; that the principle of democratic centralism should be undeviatingly observed; and that a struggle should be undertaken against those whose activity helps the enemy....

We express the conviction that the Communist Party of Czechoslovakia, conscious of its responsibility, will take the necessary steps to block the path of reaction. In this struggle, you can count on the solidarity and all-around assistance of the fraternal socialist countries.

(B) THE BREZHNEV DOCTRINE, 26 SEPTEMBER 1968

In connection with the events in Czechoslovakia, the question of the relationship and interconnection between the socialist countries' national interests and their internationalist obligations has assumed particular urgency and sharpness. The measures taken jointly by the Soviet Union and other socialist countries to defend the socialist gains of the Czechoslovak people are of enormous significance for strengthening the socialist commonwealth, which is the main achievement of the international working class.

At the same time it is impossible to ignore the allegations being heard in some places that the actions of the five socialist countries contradict the Marxist-Leninist principle of sovereignty and the right of the nations to self-determination.

Such arguments are untenable primarily because they are based on an abstract, non-class approach to the question of sovereignty and the right of nations to self-determination.

There is no doubt that the peoples of the socialist countries and the Communist parties have and must have freedom to determine their country's path of development. However, any decision of theirs must damage neither socialism in their own country, nor the fundamental interests of the other socialist countries, nor the worldwide workers' movement, which is waging a struggle for socialism. This means that every Communist party is responsible not only to its own people but also to all the socialist countries and to the entire Communist movement. Whoever forgets this is placing sole emphasis on the autonomy and independence of communist parties, lapsing into one-sidedness, and shirking his internationalist obligations....

Each Communist party is free to apply the principles of Marxism-Leninism and socialism in its own country, but it cannot deviate from these principles (if, of course, it remains a Communist party). In concrete terms this means primarily that no Communist party can fail to take into account in its activities such a decisive fact of our time as the struggle between the two antithetical social systems—capitalism and socialism. This struggle is an objective fact that does not depend on the will of people and is conditioned by the division of the world into the two antithetical social systems....

It should be stressed that even if a socialist country seeks to take an "extrabloc" position, it in fact retains its national independence thanks precisely to the power of the socialist commonwealth—and primarily to its chief force, the Soviet Union, and the might of its armed forces. The weakening of any link in the world socialist system has a direct effect on all the socialist countries, which cannot be indifferent. Thus, the anti-socialist forces in Czechoslovakia were in essence using talk about the right to self-determination to cover up demands for so-called neutrality and the CSSR's withdrawal from the socialist commonwealth. But implementation of such "self-determination," i.e., Czechoslovakia's separation from the socialist commonwealth, would run counter to Czechoslovakia's fundamental interests and would harm the other socialist countries. Such "self-determination," as a result of which NATO troops might approach Soviet borders and the commonwealth of European socialist countries could be dismembered, in fact infringes on the vital interest of these countries' peoples, and fundamentally contradicts the right of these peoples to socialist self-determination. The Soviet Union and other socialist states, in fulfilling their internationalist duty to the fraternal peoples of Czechoslovakia and defending their own socialist gains, had to act and did act in resolute opposition to the anti-socialist forces in Czechoslovakia....

The assistance given to the working people of the CSSR by the other socialist countries, which prevented the export of counterrevolution from the outside, is in fact a struggle for the Czechoslovak Socialist Republic's sovereignty against those who would like to deprive it of this sovereignty by delivering the country to the imperialists.

Over a long period of time and with utmost restraint and patience, the fraternal Communist parties of the socialist countries took political measures to help the Czechoslovak people to halt the anti-socialist forces' offensive in Czechoslovakia. And only after exhausting all such measures did they undertake to bring in armed forces.

The allied socialist countries' soldiers who are in Czechoslovakia are proving in deeds that they have no task other than to defend the socialist gains in that country. They are not interfering in the country's internal affairs, and they are waging a struggle not in words but in deeds for the principles of self-determination of Czechoslovakia's peoples, for their inalienable right to decide their destiny themselves after profound and careful consideration, without intimidation by counterrevolutionaries, without revisionist and nationalist demagoguery.

Those who speak of the "illegality" of the allied socialist countries' actions in Czechoslovakia forget that in a class society there is and can be no such thing as non-class law. Laws and the norms of law are subordinated to the laws of the class struggle and the laws of socialist development. These laws are clearly formulated in the documents jointly adopted by the Communist and Workers' parties.

The class approach to the matter cannot be discarded in the name of legalistic considerations. Whoever does so forfeits the only correct, class-oriented criterion for evaluating legal norms and begins to measure events with the yardsticks of bourgeois law....

There is no doubt that the actions taken in Czechoslovakia by the five allied socialist countries, actions aimed at defending the fundamental interests of the socialist commonwealth and primarily at defending Czechoslovakia's independence and sovereignty as a socialist state, will be increasingly supported by all who really value the interests of the present-day revolutionary movement, the peace and security of peoples, democracy and socialism.

DOCUMENT 7

Diplomatic Note from USSR Government to the Government of the PRC

2 March 1969

Editor's commentary: Doctrinal polemics and theoretical argument gave way in 1969 to more tangible forms of conflict between the Soviet Union and China on the rivers Ussuri and Amur, which form a common frontier between them. Disputed ownership of island territories was at the heart of the matter, as fighting broke out between Chinese regular forces and Soviet "border guards." The conflict threatened to widen in the weeks that followed, as neither side seemed willing to compromise. Not until the death of Mao Zedong did the slow process of improvement in relations between the two communist giants begin.

The Soviet government is informing the government of the People's Republic of China of the following.

On 2 March at 4:10 Moscow time Chinese authorities organized an armed provocation on the Sino-Soviet border in the region of the border

point Nizhe-Mikhailovka (the island of Damansk) on the Ussuri River. A Chinese detachment crossed the Soviet state border and made for Damansk island. According to Soviet border personnel guarding this region, the Chinese side suddenly opened fire with light machine guns. . . . The actions of the Chinese violators of the border were supported by an ambush from the Chinese shores of the Ussuri River. In this provocative attack on Soviet border guards more than 200 Chinese soldiers took part. As a result of this bandit raid there are dead and wounded Soviet border guards.

The impudent armed intrusion across the boundaries of Soviet territory appears as an organized provocation of Chinese authorities and pursues the goal of aggravating the situation on the Soviet-Chinese border.

The Soviet government is lodging a resolute protest with the government of the People's Republic of China regarding the dangerous provocative actions of Chinese authorities on the Soviet-Chinese border.

The Soviet government demands an immediate investigation and the strictest punishment of the individuals responsible for the organization of this provocation. It insists on the adoption of urgent measures which would exclude any violation of the Soviet-Chinese border.

The Soviet government reserves the right to take resolute measures for the termination of the provocations on the Soviet-Chinese border and warns the government of the People's Republic of China that all responsibility for the possible consequences of adventuristic politics, directed toward the aggravation of the situation on the borders between China and the Soviet Union, lies with the government of the People's Republic of China.

The Soviet government in relations with the Chinese people is guided by feelings of friendship, and it intends to carry on with this policy. But unthinking provocative actions of the Chinese authorities will be met from our side with a rebuff and will be nipped in the bud.

Pravda, 4 March 1969, p. 2. Editor's translation.

Treaty between the USSR and the FRG

12 August 1970

Editor's commentary: The Treaty of Moscow between the Soviet Union and West Germany led the way to other agreements, including one between Poland and the FRG and another concerning the status of Berlin; taken together, these agreements ushered in the era of European detente. The Soviets were especially happy to conclude this treaty and begin a more profitable trading relationship with the countries of Western Europe, and especially West Germany. The most important points of the treaty included the recognition of the territorial and political status quo in Eastern Europe by the FRG. In effect, this new approach toward Moscow, part of West German ostpolitik, *buried the Hallstein Doctrine, which refused to recognize the legitimacy of an East German government or the territory ceded to Poland as part of the postwar Soviet-sponsored rearrangement of borders.*

Article 1

The Union of Soviet Socialist Republics and the Federal Republic of Germany consider the maintenance of international peace and the achievement of relaxation of tensions among the important goals of their policy.

They express the aspiration to cooperate for the normalization of the situation in Europe and the development of peaceful relations between all European states, proceeding in this regard from the actual situation existing in that region.

Article 2

The Union of Soviet Socialist Republics and the Federal Republic of Germany will conduct themselves in their mutual relations and also in ques-

---

Pravda, 13 August 1970, p. 1, *excerpts.* Editor's translation.

tions of European and international security in comformity with the goals and principles set forth in the charter of the United Nations. Accordingly, they will resolve their differences exclusively by peaceful means. In conformity with article 2 of the charter of the United Nations they take upon themselves the responsibility to abstain from threat or use of force, as in their mutual relations, so in questions affecting European and international security.

Article 3

In accordance with the goals of the principles set forth above, the Union of Soviet Socialist Republics and the Federal Republic of Germany are united in the recognition of the fact that peace in Europe can be preserved only in the event that nobody encroaches on present borders. They take upon themselves the responsibility to observe strictly the territorial integrity of all states in Europe with their current borders;

they state that they have no territorial ambitions whatsoever against anyone and will not advance such ambitions in the future;

they consider as inviolable now and in the future the borders of all states in Europe, as they are on the day of the present treaty's signing, and among them the Oder-Neisse line, which is the Western border of the Polish People's Republic and the border between the Federal Republic of Germany and the German Democratic Republic.

Article 4

The present treaty between the Union of Soviet Socialist Republics and the Federal Republic of Germany does not affect other earlier bilateral and multilateral treaties and agreements concluded by them.

Article 5

The present treaty is subject to ratification and will come into force on the day of the exchange of the ratification instruments, which will be effected in Bonn.

DONE in Moscow, 12 August 1970, in two copies, each in the Russian and the German languages, both texts being equally valid.

For the USSR: A. Kosygin, A. Gromyko
For the FRG: W. Brandt, W. Schell.

Report of the Central Committee to the Twenty-fourth Congress of the CPSU

L. I. Brezhnev

30 March 1971

Editor's commentary: After the Twenty-third CPSU Congress, the international situation of socialism had undergone substantial changes. Most notably, certain "difficulties and complications" in world socialism had emerged as a result of the Prague Spring reform movement in Czechoslovakia in 1968. The necessity for greater unity and cohesion in the communist movement was stressed by Brezhnev because of the fissures that had developed in the world communist movement in the wake of the Warsaw Pact intervention, which terminated the Czech experiment of "socialism with a human face," and continued tension with China.

FOR THE FURTHER DEVELOPMENT OF THE FRIENDSHIP AND COOPERATION OF THE SOCIALIST COUNTRIES

The Central Committee's attention has been constantly centered on questions of further cohesion and development of the world socialist system, and on relations with the fraternal socialist countries and their Communist Parties.

The world socialist system has a quarter-century behind it. From the standpoint of the development of revolutionary theory and practice, these have been exceptionally fruitful years. The socialist world has given the communist and working-class movement experience which is of tremendous and truly historic importance....

At the same time, it is known that some difficulties and complications have continued to appear in the socialist world, and this has also had an effect on the development of relations between individual states and the Soviet Union. However, this has not changed the dominant tendency of strengthening the friendship and solidarity of the socialist countries. On the whole, our cooperation with the fraternal countries has been developing successfully and strengthening in every sphere....

We resolutely reject the slanderous inventions concerning the policy of our Party and our state that are being disseminated from Peking and instilled in the minds of the Chinese people. It is all the more absurd and harmful to sow dissent between China and the USSR considering that this is taking place in a situation in which the imperialists have been stepping up their aggressive action against the freedom-loving peoples. More than ever before the situation demands cohesion and joint action by all antiimperialist, revolutionary forces, instead of fanning hostility between two such states as the USSR and China.

We shall never foresake the national interests of the Soviet state. The CPSU will continue to work tirelessly for the cohesion of the socialist countries and the world Communist movement on a Marxist-Leninist basis. At the same time, our Party and the Soviet Government are deeply convinced that an improvement of relations between the Soviet Union and the People's Republic of China would be in line with the fundamental, long-term interests of both countries, the interests of socialism, the freedom of the peoples and stronger peace. That is why we are prepared in every way to help not only to normalize relations but also to restore good-neighborliness and friendship between the Soviet Union and the People's Republic of China, and we express the confidence that this will eventually be achieved....

Pravda, 30 March 1971, pp. 2–10, as translated in *Reprints from the Soviet Press*, vol. 12, nos. 9–10, 14 May 1971, pp. 7–27, *excerpts*.

Comrades, the political crisis in Czechoslovakia has been fairly prominent in the international events of recent years. There seems to be no need to have to set out the factual side of the matter, which is well known. Let us deal only with some of the conclusions drawn from what has taken place, which we believe to be the most essential.

The Czechoslovak events were a fresh reminder that in countries which have taken the path of socialist construction the various remaining internal antisocialist forces may, in certain conditions, become active and even mount direct counterrevolutionary action, in the hope of getting support from outside, from imperialism, which, for the most part, is always prepared to form blocs with such forces.

The danger of Right-wing revisionism, which on the pretext of "improving" socialism, seeks to destroy the revolutionary essence of Marxism-Leninism and paves the way for the penetration of bourgeois ideology, has been fully brought out in this connection.

The Czechoslovak events showed very clearly how important it is constantly to strengthen the Party's leading role in socialist society, steadily to improve the forms and methods of Party leadership, and to display a creative Marxist-Leninist approach to the solution of pressing problems of socialist development. . . .

DOCUMENT 10

Treaty of Friendship and Cooperation between the USSR and UAR (Egypt)

28 May 1971

Editor's commentary: The Soviet Union had expectations that the relationships it was building with third world countries would pay off in strategic terms. High on the list was the

relationship with Egypt (part of the United Arab Republics at this time). A visit to the Soviet Union in July 1970 by the most famous Arab nationalist, Nasser of Egypt, augured well for future Soviet-Egyptian relations, which had been steadily improving since the 1967 Arab-Israeli war. On 28 May 1971 a treaty of friendship was signed by Anwar Sadat and N. Podgorny. By concluding this treaty, the USSR was serving notice about its intentions to be a permanent actor in Middle East affairs. The Soviet Union began to supply the Arabs with sophisticated weapons and presented a united front with them against "Israeli aggression." But the close relationship between Egypt and the Soviet Union fell apart soon after the signing of the treaty. Sadat was interested in pressing the advantage he thought he had acquired as a result of Soviet armaments. Apparently unhappy with Soviet advice for restraint and with other aspects of his ties to the USSR, Sadat evicted some 10,000 Soviet advisers in 1972. He then pressed what he considered to be an Egyptian military advantage. The attack on Israel during Yom Kippur 1973 failed to achieve Egyptian aims. This failure eventually led Sadat to take another tack: a diplomatic solution brokered by the United States, which led to a severe setback for Soviet Middle East policy.

The Union of Soviet Socialist Republics and the United Arab Republic . . . agree on the following:

Article 1

The High Contracting Parties solemnly declare that unbreakable friendship will always exist between the two countries and their peoples. They will continue to develop and strengthen the existing relations of friendship and all-around cooperation between them in the political, economic, scientific, technological, cultural and other fields, on the basis of principles of respect for the sovereignty, territorial integrity, noninterference in each other's internal affairs, equality, and mutual benefit.

Pravda, 28 May 1971, as translated in *Reprints from the Soviet Press,* vol. 12, no. 13, 25 June 1971, pp. 25–29.

Article 2

The USSR, as a socialist state, and the UAR, which has set itself the aim of reconstructing society along socialist lines, will cooperate closely, and in all fields, in ensuring conditions for preserving and further developing the social and economic gains of their peoples.

Article 3

Being guided by a desire to contribute in every way toward maintaining international peace and the security of the peoples, the USSR and the UAR will continue with all determination to make efforts toward achieving and ensuring a fair and lasting peace in the Middle East in accordance with the aims and principles of the United Nations Charter.

In pursuing a peace-loving foreign policy, the High Contracting Parties will come out for peace, relaxation of international tensions, the achievement of general and complete disarmament, and prohibition of nuclear and other types of weapons of mass destruction.

Article 4

Being guided by the ideals of freedom and equality of all peoples, the High Contracting Parties condemn imperialism and colonialism in all their forms and manifestations. They will continue to come out against imperialism, and for the full and final elimination of colonialism, in pursuance of the UN Declaration of Granting Independence to All Colonial Countries and Peoples, and unswervingly wage struggle against racism and apartheid.

Article 5

The High Contracting Parties will continue to expand and deepen all-around cooperation and exchanges of experience in the economic and scientific-technological fields....

The two sides will expand trade and sea shipping between the two states on the basis of the principles of mutual benefit and most favored nation treatment.

Article 6

The High Contracting Parties will further promote cooperation between them in the fields of science, art, literature, education, health services, the press, radio, television, the cinema, tourism, physical culture and other fields.

The two sides will promote broader cooperation and direct ties between political and public organizations....

Article 7

Being deeply interested in ensuring peace and the security of the peoples, and attaching great importance to the concertedness of their actions in the international arena in the struggle for peace, the High Contracting Parties will, for this purpose, regularly consult each other at different levels on all important questions affecting the interests of both states.

In the event of the development of situations creating, in the opinion of both sides, a danger to peace or a violation of peace, they will contact each other without delay in order to concert their positions with a view to removing the threat that has arisen or reestablishing peace.

Article 8

In the interests of strengthening the defense capacity of the UAR, the High Contracting Parties will continue to develop cooperation in the military field on the basis of appropriate agreements between them. Such cooperation will provide specifically for assistance in training UAR military personnel, in mastering the armaments and equipment supplied to the UAR with a view to strengthening its capacity to eliminate the consequences of aggression as well as increasing its ability to stand up to aggression in general.

Article 9

Proceeding from the aims and principles of this Treaty, each of the High Contracting Parties states that it will not enter into alliances and will not take part in any groupings of states, in actions or measures directed against the other High Contracting Party.

Article 10

Each of the High Contracting Parties declares that its commitments under the existing international treaties are not in contradiction to the provisions of the present Treaty and it undertakes not to enter into any international agreements incompatible with it.

Article 11

The present Treaty will be operative for 15 years since the day it enters into force.

If neither of the High Contracting Parties declares one year before the expiration of this term its desire to terminate the Treaty, it will remain in force for the next five years, and so henceforth, until one of the High Contracting Parties, one year before the expiration of the current five-year period, gives written warning of its intention to terminate it.

Article 12

The present Treaty is subject to ratification and shall come into force on the day of exchange of ratification instruments, which will take place in Moscow in the near future.

The present Treaty is executed in two copies, each in Russian and Arabic, with both texts being equally authentic.

Executed in the City of Cairo on May 27, 1971, which corresponds to 3 Rabia as-sani 1391, Hidjra.

For the USSR, N. Podgorny

For the UAR, Anwar Sadat.

DOCUMENT 11

Anti-Ballistic Missile Treaty and SALT I Agreement

26 May 1972

Editor's commentary: The ABM Treaty and SALT I, signed by Richard Nixon and Leonid Brezhnev, were two heads of the same coin, limiting defensive systems in the first case and offensive weapons in the second. Together, they constitute the first major milestone toward control of the superpower arms race.

During the Reagan administration, the ABM Treaty became a bone of contention between the superpowers. A wide-ranging debate raged during this time over "narrow" versus "broad" interpretations of key articles regarding missiles, radars, and related technologies covered by the treaty (articles 1–5). This was in large measure the product of the U.S. decision to develop the Strategic Defense Initiative (SDI). Although somewhat muted since the last of the four Reagan-Gorbachev summits (May 1988), this ongoing debate has continued to focus on the relationship of the treaty to SDI. Soviet spokesmen continue to stress the "narrow" interpretation of the treaty, disallowing certain kinds of testing and deployment of space weapons and exotic technologies. What follow are the texts of the basic agreements, not including the several protocols and understandings which were separately concluded.

(A) TREATY BETWEEN THE UNITED STATES OF AMERICA AND THE UNION OF SOVIET SOCIALIST REPUBLICS ON THE LIMITATION OF ANTI-BALLISTIC MISSILE SYSTEMS

The United States of America and the Union of Soviet Socialist Republics, hereinafter referred to as the Parties...

Have agreed as follows:

Article I

1. Each Party undertakes to limit anti-ballistic missile (ABM) systems and to adopt other measures in accordance with the provisions of this Treaty.

2. Each Party undertakes not to deploy ABM systems for a defense of the territory of its country and not to provide a base for such a defense, and not to deploy ABM systems for defense of an individual region except as provided for in Article III of this Treaty.

Department of State Bulletin, vol. 66, no. 1722, 26 June 1972, pp. 918–920, *excerpts.*

Article II

1. For the purposes of this Treaty an ABM system is a system to counter strategic ballistic missiles or their elements in flight trajectory, currently consisting of:

(a) ABM interceptor missiles, which are interceptor missiles constructed and deployed for an ABM role, or of a type tested in an ABM mode;

(b) ABM launchers, which are launchers constructed and deployed for launching ABM interceptor missiles; and

(c) ABM radars, which are radars constructed and deployed for an ABM role, or of a type tested in an ABM mode.

2. The ABM system components listed in paragraph 1 of this Article include those which are:

(a) operational; (b) under construction; (c) undergoing testing; (d) undergoing overhaul, repair or conversion; or (e) mothballed.

Article III

Each Party undertakes not to deploy ABM systems or their components except that:

(a) within one ABM system deployment area having a radius of one hundred and fifty kilometers and centered on the Party's national capital, a Party may deploy: (1) no more than one hundred ABM launchers and no more than one hundred ABM interceptor missiles at launch sites, and (2) ABM radars within no more than six ABM radar complexes, the area of each complex being circular and having a diameter of no more than three kilometers; and

(b) within one ABM system deployment area having a radius of one hundred and fifty kilometers and containing ICBM silo launchers, a Party may deploy: (1) no more than one hundred ABM launchers and no more than one hundred ABM interceptor missiles at launch sites, (2) two large phased-array ABM radars comparable in potential to corresponding ABM radars operational or under construction on the date of signature of the Treaty in an ABM system deployment area containing ICBM silo launchers, and

(3) no more than eighteen ABM radars each having a potential less than the potential of the smaller of the above-mentioned two large phased array ABM radars.

Article IV

The limitations provided for in Article II shall not apply to ABM systems or their components used for development or testing, and located within current or additionally agreed test ranges. Each Party may have no more than a total of fifteen ABM launchers at test ranges.

Article V

1. Each Party undertakes not to develop, test, or deploy ABM systems or components which are sea-based, air-based, space-based, or mobile land-based.

2. Each Party undertakes not to develop, test, or deploy ABM launchers for launching more than one ABM interceptor missile at a time from each launcher, not to modify deployed launchers to provide them with such a capability, not to develop, test or deploy automatic or semiautomatic or other similar systems for rapid reload of ABM launchers.

Article VI

To enhance assurance of the effectivenenss of the limitations on ABM systems and their components provided by the Treaty, each Party undertakes:

(a) not to give missiles, launchers, or radars, other than ABM interceptor missiles, ABM launchers, or ABM radars, capabilities to counter strategic ballistic missiles or their elements in flight trajectory, and not to test them in an ABM mode, and

(b) not to deploy in the future radars for early warning of strategic ballistic missile attack except at locations along the periphery of its national territory and oriented outward.

Article VII

Subject to the provisions of this Treaty, modernization and replacement of ABM systems or their components may be carried out.

Article VIII
ABM systems or their components in excess of the numbers or outside the areas specified in this Treaty, as well as ABM systems or their components prohibited by this Treaty, shall be destroyed or dismantled under agreed procedures within the shortest possible agreed period of time.

Article IX
To assure the viability and effectiveness of this Treaty, each Party undertakes not to transfer to other States, and not to deploy outside its national territory, ABM systems or their components limited by this Treaty.

Article X
Each Party undertakes not to assume any international obligations which would conflict with this Treaty.

Article XI
The Parties undertake to continue active negotiations for limitations on strategic offensive arms.

Article XII
1. For the purpose of providing assurance of compliance with the provisions of this Treaty, each Party shall use national technical means of verification at its disposal in a manner consistent with generally recognized principles of international law.
2. Each Party undertakes not to interfere with the national technical means of verification of the other Party operating in accordance with paragraph 1 of this Article.
3. Each Party undertakes not to use deliberate concealment measures which impede verification by national technical means of compliance with the provisions of this Treaty. This obligation shall not require changes in current construction, assembly, conversion, or overhaul practices.

Article XIII
1. To promote the objectives and implementation of the provisions of this Treaty, the Parties shall establish promptly a Standing Consultative Commission, within the framework of which they will:
(a) consider questions concerning compliance with the obligations assumed and related situations which may be considered ambiguous;
(b) provide on a voluntary basis such information as either Party considers necessary to assure confidence in compliance with the obligations assumed;
(c) consider questions involving unintended interference with national technical means of verification;
(d) consider possible changes in the strategic situation which have a bearing on the provisions of this Treaty;
(e) agree upon procedures and dates for destruction or dismantling of ABM systems or their components in cases provided for by the provisions of this Treaty;
(f) consider, as appropriate, possible proposals for further increasing the viability of this Treaty; including proposals for amendments in accordance with the provisions of this Treaty;
(g) consider, as appropriate, proposals for further measures aimed at limiting strategic arms.
2. The Parties through consultation shall establish, and may amend as appropriate, Regulations for the Standing Consultative Commission governing procedures, composition and other relevant matters.

Article XIV
1. Each Party may propose amendments to this Treaty. Agreed amendments shall enter into force in accordance with the procedures governing the entry into force of this Treaty.
2. Five years after entry into force of this Treaty, and at five-year intervals thereafter, the Parties shall together conduct a review of this Treaty.

Article XV
1. This Treaty shall be of unlimited duration.

2. Each Party shall, in exercising its national sovereignty, have the right to withdraw from this Treaty if it decides that extraordinary events related to the subject matter of this Treaty have jeopardized its supreme interest. It shall give notice of its decision to the other Party six months prior to withdrawal from the Treaty. Such notice shall include a statement of the extraordinary events the notifying Party regards as having jeopardized its supreme interest.

Article XVI

1. This Treaty shall be subject to ratification in accordance with the constitutional procedures of each Party. The Treaty shall enter into force on the day of the exchange of instruments of ratification.

2. This Treaty shall be registered pursuant to Article 102 of the Charter of the United Nations.

DONE at Moscow on May 26, 1972, in two copies, each in the English and Russian languages, both texts being equally authentic.

For the USA: Richard Nixon, President of the USA

For the USSR: Leonid I. Brezhnev, General Secretary of the CPSU

(B) INTERIM AGREEMENT ON LIMITATION OF STRATEGIC OFFENSIVE ARMS (SALT I)

Article I

The Parties undertake not to start construction of additional fixed land-based intercontinental ballistic missile (ICBM) launchers after July 1, 1972.

Article II

The Parties undertake not to convert land-based launchers for light ICBMs, or for ICBMs of older types deployed prior to 1964, into land-based launchers for heavy ICBMs of types deployed after that time.

Article III

The Parties undertake to limit submarine-launched ballistic missile (SLBM) launchers and modern ballistic missile submarines to the numbers operational and under construction on the date of signature of this Interim Agreement, and in addition to launchers and submarines constructed under procedures established by the Parties as replacements for an equal number of ICBM launchers of older types deployed prior to 1964 or for launchers on older submarines.

Article IV

Subject to the provisions of this Interim Agreement, modernization and replacement of strategic offensive ballistic missiles and launchers covered by this Interim Agreement may be undertaken.

Article V

1. For the purpose of providing assurance of compliance with the provisions of this Interim Agreement, each Party shall use national technical means of verification at its disposal in a manner consistent with generally recognized principles of international law.

2. Each Party undertakes not to interfere with the national technical means of verification of the other Party operating in accordance with paragraph 1 of this Article.

3. Each Party undertakes not to use deliberate concealment measures which impede verification by national technical means of compliance with the provisions of this Interim Agreement. This obligation shall not require changes in current construction, assembly, conversion, or overhaul practices.

Article VI

To promote the objectives and implementation of the provisions of this Interim Agreement, the Parties shall use the Standing Consultative Commission established under Article XIII of the Treaty on the Limitation of Anti-Ballistic Missile Systems in accordance with the provisions of that Article.

Article VII

The Parties undertake to continue active negotiations for limitations on strategic offensive arms. The obligations provided for in this Interim Agreement shall not prejudice the scope or terms of the limitations on strategic offensive arms which may be worked out in the course of further negotiations.

Article VIII

1. This Interim Agreement shall enter into force upon exchange of written notices of acceptance by each Party, which exchange shall take place simultaneously with the exchange of instruments of ratification of the Treaty on the Limitation of Anti-Ballistic Missile Systems.

2. This Interim Agreement shall remain in force for a period of five years unless replaced earlier by an agreement on more complete measures limiting strategic offensive arms. It is the objective of the Parties to conduct active follow-on negotiations with the aim of concluding such an agreement as soon as possible.

3. Each Party shall, in exercising its national sovereignty, have the right to withdraw from this Interim Agreement if it decides that extraordinary events related to the subject matter of the Interim Agreement have jeopardized its supreme interests. It shall give notice of its decision to the other Party six months prior to withdrawal from this Interim Agreement. Such notice shall include a statement of the extraordinary events the notifying Party regards as having jeopardized its supreme interests.

DONE at Moscow on May 26, 1972, in two copies, each in the English and Russian languages, both texts being equally authentic.

For the USA: Richard Nixon, President of the USA

For the USSR: Leonid I. Brezhnev, General Secretary of the CC of the CPSU

DOCUMENT 12

Basic Principles of Relations between the United States of America and the Union of Soviet Socialist Republics

29 May 1972

Editor's commentary: The several points contained in this document constitute the "basic principles of detente" between the superpowers, signed in Moscow by Richard Nixon and Leonid Brezhnev. Problems in the document became apparent within several years as the interpretation of just what constituted "peaceful coexistence" (a loaded phrase for Leninists) between the two powers varied considerably. "Linkage" became a popular word in the American political lexicon, emphasizing the interconnectedness of regional issues, human rights, and strategic interests on the part of the United States. The Soviet interpretation of detente did not reflect the same concept of linkage.

The United States of America and the Union of Soviet Socialist Republics,

Guided by their obligations under the charter of the United Nations and by a desire to strengthen peaceful relations with each other and to place these relations on the firmest possible basis,

Aware of the need to make every effort to remove the threat of war and to create conditions which promote the reduction of tensions in the world and the strengthening of universal security and international cooperation,

Believing that the improvement of US-Soviet relations and their mutually advantageous development in such areas as economics, science and culture, will meet these objectives and contrib-

Department of State Bulletin, vol. 46, no. 1722, 26 June 1972, pp. 898–899.

ute to better mutual understanding and business like cooperation, without in any way prejudicing the interests of third countries,

Conscious that these objectives reflect the interests of the peoples of both countries,

Have agreed as follows:

First

They will proceed from the common determination that in the nuclear age there is no alternative to conducting their mutual relations on the basis of peaceful coexistence. Differences in ideology and in the social systems of the USA and the USSR are not obstacles to the bilateral development of normal relations based on the principles of sovereignty, equality, non-interference in internal affairs and mutual advantage.

Second

The USA and the USSR attach major importance to preventing the development of situations capable of causing a dangerous exacerbation of their relations. Therefore, they will do their utmost to avoid military confrontations and to prevent the outbreak of nuclear war. They will always exercise restraint in their mutual relations, and will be prepared to negotiate and settle differences by peaceful means. Discussions and negotiations on outstanding issues will be conducted in a spirit of reciprocity, mutual accommodation and mutual benefit.

Both sides recognize that efforts to obtain unilateral advantage at the expense of the other, directly or indirectly, are inconsistent with these objectives. The prerequisites for maintaining and strengthening peaceful relations between the USA and the USSR are the recognition of the security interests of the Parties based on the principle of equality and the renunciation of the use or threat of force.

Third

The USA and the USSR have a special responsibility, as do other countries which are permanent members of the United Nations Security Council, to do everything in their power so that conflicts or situations will not arise which would serve to increase international tensions. Accordingly, they will seek to promote conditions in which all countries will live in peace and security and will not be subject to outside interference in their internal affairs.

Fourth

The USA and the USSR intend to widen the juridical basis of their mutual relations and to exert the necessary efforts so that bilateral agreements which they have concluded and multilateral treaties and agreements to which they are jointly parties are faithfully implemented.

Fifth

The USA and the USSR reaffirm their readiness to continue the practice of exchanging views on problems of mutual interest and, when necessary, to conduct such exchanges at the highest level, including meetings between leaders of the two countries.

The two governments welcome and will facilitate an increase in productive contacts between representatives of the legislative bodies of the two countries.

Sixth

The Parties will continue their efforts to limit armaments on a bilateral as well as on a multilateral basis. They will continue to make special efforts to limit strategic armaments. Whenever possible, they will conclude concrete agreements aimed at achieving these purposes.

The USA and the USSR regard as the ultimate objective of their efforts the achievement of general and complete disarmament and the establishment of an effective system of international security in accordance with the purposes and principles of the United Nations.

Seventh

The USA and the USSR regard commercial and economic ties as an important and necessary element in the strengthening of their bilateral relations and thus will actively promote the growth of such ties. They will facilitate cooperation between the relevant organizations and enterprises of the two countries and the conclusion of appropriate agreements and contracts, including long-term ones.

The two countries will contribute to the improvement of maritime and air communications between them.

Eighth

The two sides consider it timely and useful to develop mutual contacts and cooperation in the fields of science and technology. Where suitable, the USA and the USSR will conclude appropriate agreements dealing with concrete cooperation in these fields.

Ninth

The two sides reaffirm their intention to deepen cultural ties with one another and to encourage fuller familiarization with each other's cultural values. They will promote improved conditions for cultural exchanges and tourism.

Tenth

The USA and the USSR will seek to ensure that their ties and cooperation in all the above-mentioned fields and in any others in their mutual interest are built on a firm and long-term basis. To give a permanent character to these efforts, they will establish in all fields where this is feasible joint commissions or other joint bodies.

Eleventh

The USA and the USSR make no claim for themselves and would not recognize the claims of anyone else to any special rights or advantages in world affairs. They recognize the sovereign equality of all states.

The development of US-Soviet relations is not directed against third countries and their interests.

Twelfth

The basic principles set forth in this document do not affect any obligations with respect to other countries earlier assumed by the USA and the USSR.

Moscow, May 29, 1972

For the United States of America: Richard Nixon, President of the USA

For the Union of Soviet Socialist Republics: Leonid I. Brezhnev, General Secretary of the CC CPSU

DOCUMENT 13

Agreement between the Governments of the United States of America and the Union of Soviet Socialist Republics Regarding Trade

18 October 1972

Editor's commentary: The U.S.-Soviet trade agreement, in abridged form below, was another of the fruits of the Nixon-Brezhnev era of detente, providing for mutual most favored nation status. It was part of a series of accords regarding economic concerns, including an agreement settling in full the World War II lend-lease dispute between the United States and the USSR. The trade agreement outlined here encountered significant problems in the Senate as Senator Henry Jackson (D-Washington) sought to link trade benefits accruing to the USSR in this arrangement with Jewish emigration. This, in turn, helped to create a rocky road for detente in the 1970s and contributed to its ultimate demise.

The Government of the United States of America and the Government of the Union of Soviet Socialist Republics...

Have agreed as follows:

Article 1

1. Each Government shall accord unconditionally to products originating in or exported to the

---

Department of State Bulletin, vol. 67, no. 1743, 20 November 1972, pp. 595–598, *excerpts.*

other country treatment no less favorable than that accorded to like products originating in or exported to any third country in all matters relating to:

(a) customs duties and charges of any kind imposed on or in connection with importation or exportation including the method of levying such duties and charges;

(b) international taxation, sale, distribution, storage and use;

(c) charges imposed upon the international transfer of payments for importation or exportation; and

(d) rules and formalities in connection with importation or exportation.

2. In the event either Government applies quantitative restrictions to products originating in or exported to third countries, it shall afford to like products originating in or exported to the other country equitable treatment vis-à-vis that applied in respect of such third countries. . . .

Article 2

1. Both Governments will take appropriate measures, in accordance with the laws and regulations then current in each country, to encourage and facilitate the exchange of goods and services between the two countries on the basis of mutual advantage and in accordance with the provisions of this Agreement. In expectation of such joint efforts, both Governments envision that total bilateral trade in comparison with the period 1969–1971 will at least triple over the three-year period contemplated by this Agreement. . . .

Article 3

Each Government may take such measures as it deems appropriate to ensure that the importation of products originating in the other country does not take place in such quantities or under such conditions as to cause, threaten or contribute to disruption of its domestic market. . . .

Article 4

All currency payments between natural and legal persons of the USA and foreign trade and other appropriate organizations of the USSR

shall be made in United States dollars or any other freely convertible currency mutually agreed upon by such persons and organizations.

Article 5

1. The Government of the USA may establish in Moscow a Commercial Office of the USA and the Government of the USSR may establish in Washington a Trade Representation of the USSR. The Commercial Office and the Trade Representation shall be opened simultaneously on a date and at locations to be agreed upon. . . .

Article 6

1. In accordance with the laws and regulations then current in each country, natural and legal persons of the USA and foreign trade organizations of the USSR may open their representations in the USSR and the USA, respectively. Information concerning the opening of such representations and provision of facilities in connection therewith shall be provided by each Government upon the request of the other Government. . . .

Article 7

1. Both Governments encourage the adoption of arbitration for the settlement of disputes arising out of international commercial transactions concluded between natural and legal persons of the USA and foreign trade organizations of the USSR, such arbitration to be provided for by agreements in contracts between such persons and organizations. . . .

Article 8

The provisions of this Agreement shall not limit the right of either Government to take any action for the protection of its security interests.

Article 9

1. This agreement shall enter into force upon the exchange of written notices of acceptance. This Agreement shall remain in force for three years, unless extended by mutual agreement.

2. Both Governments will work through the Joint US-USSR Commercial Commission established in accordance with the Communique issued in Moscow on May 26, 1972, in overseeing

and facilitating the implementation of this Agreement in accordance with the terms of reference and rules of procedure of the commission.

3. Prior to the expiration of this Agreement, the Joint US-USSR Commercial Commission shall begin consultations regarding extension of this Agreement or preparaton of a new agreement to replace this Agreement.

IN WITNESS WHEREOF, the undersigned, duly authorized, have signed this Agreement on behalf of their respective Governments.

DONE at Washington in duplicate this 18th day of October 1972, in the English and Russian languages, each being equally authentic.

For the Government of the USA: Peter G. Peterson

For the Government of the USSR: N. Patolichev

DOCUMENT 14

Threshold Test Ban Treaty

3 July 1974

Editor's commentary: This treaty, concluded during Nixon's last trip to Moscow before his resignation from the U.S. Presidency in 1974, was the only palpable fruit of the Moscow summit of that year. It limited the size of underground nuclear weapons tests to 150 kilotons. However, along with the Treaty on Underground Nuclear Tests for Peaceful Purposes, it remained dormant as the Senate delayed action into the late 1980s. When President Reagan went to Moscow in May 1988 to sign the INF accords, problems of verification plaguing these treaties were still being debated. Soviet

―――――――――

"Treaty between the USA and the USSR on the Limitation of Underground Nuclear Weapons Tests," *Arms Control and Disarmament Agreements* (Washington, DC: Arms Control and Disarmament Agency/U.S. Government Printing Office, 1980), pp. 167–168.

spokesmen have frequently used these unratified accords as evidence of lack of U.S. interest in broad-based arms control efforts.

The United States of America and the Union of Soviet Socialist Republics, hereinafter referred to as the Parties....

Have agreed as follows:

Article I

1. Each Party undertakes to prohibit, to prevent, and not to carry out any underground nuclear weapon test having a yield exceeding 150 kilotons at any place under its jurisdiction or control, beginning March 31, 1976.

2. Each Party shall limit the number of the underground nuclear weapon tests to a minimum.

3. The Parties shall continue their negotiations with a view toward achieving a solution to the problem of the cessation of all underground nuclear weapon tests.

Article II

1. For the purpose of providing assurance of compliance with the provisions of this Treaty, each Party shall use national technical means of verification at its disposal in a manner consistent with the generally recognized principles of international law.

2. Each Party undertakes not to interfere with the national technical means of verification of the other Party operating in accordance with paragraph 1 of this Article.

3. To promote the objectives and implementation of the provisions of this Treaty the Parties shall, as necessary, consult with each other, make inquiries and furnish information in response to such inquiries.

Article III

The provisions of this Treaty do not extend to underground nuclear explosions carried out by the Parties for peaceful purposes. Underground nuclear explosions for peaceful purposes shall be governed by an agreement which is to be negotiated and concluded by the Parties at the earliest possible time.

Article IV

This Treaty shall be subject to ratification in accordance with the constitutional procedures of each Party. This Treaty shall enter into force on the day of the exchange of instruments of ratification.

Article V

1. This Treaty shall remain in force for a period of five years. Unless replaced earlier by an agreement in implementation of the objectives specified in paragraph 3 of Article 1 of this Treaty, it shall be extended for successive five-year periods unless either Party notifies the other of its termination no later than six months prior to the expiration of the Treaty....

2. Each Party shall, in exercising its national sovereignty, have the right to withdraw from this Treaty if it decides that extraordinary events related to the subject matter of this Treaty have jeopardized its supreme interests. It shall give notice of its decision to the other Party six months prior to withdrawal from this Treaty. Such notice shall include a statement of the extraordinary events the notifying Party regards as having jeopardized its supreme interests.

3. This Treaty shall be registered pursuant to Article 102 of the Charter of the United Nations.

DONE at Moscow on July 3, 1974, in duplicate, in the English and Russian languages, both texts being equally authentic.

DOCUMENT 15

Brezhnev-Ford Summit at Vladivostok

24 November 1974

Editor's commentary: Anxious to continue the work that Nixon had begun in stabilizing U.S.-Soviet relations, the new President, Gerald Ford, met with Brezhnev at the summit in Vladivostok, where

the principles of SALT were reaffirmed on the road to a second SALT agreement.

(A) JOINT STATEMENT ON STRATEGIC ARMS

During their working meeting in the area of Vladivostok on November 23–24, 1974, the President of the USA Gerald R. Ford and General Secretary of the Central Committee of the CPSU L. I. Brezhnev discussed in detail the question of further limitations of strategic offensive arms.

They reaffirmed the great significance that both the United States and the USSR attach to the limitation of strategic offensive arms. They are convinced that a long-term agreement on this question would be a significant contribution to improving relations between the US and the USSR, to reducing the danger of war and to enhancing world peace. Having noted the value of previous agreements on this question, including the Interim Agreement of May 26, 1972, they reaffirm the intention to conclude a new agreement on the limitation of strategic offensive arms, to last through 1985.

As a result of the exchange of views on the substance of such a new agreement, the President of the USA and the General Secretary of the Central Committee of the CPSU concluded that favorable prospects exist for completing the work on this agreement in 1975.

Agreement was reached that further negotiations will be based on the following provisions.

1. The new agreement will incorporate the relevant provisions of the Interim Agreement of May 26, 1972, which will remain in force until October 1977.

2. The new agreement will cover the period from October 1977 through December 31, 1985.

3. Based on the principles of equality and

Department of State Bulletin, vol. 71, no. 1852, 23 December 1974, pp. 879–880, *excerpts*.

equal security, the new agreement will include the following limitations:

a. Both sides will be entitled to have a certain agreed aggregate number of strategic delivery vehicles;

b. Both sides will be entitled to have a certain agreed aggregate number of ICBMs and SLBMs [sea-launched ballistic missiles] equipped with multiple independently targetable warheads (MIRVs).

4. The new agreement will include a provision for further negotiations beginning no later than 1980–1981 on the question of further limitations and possible reductions of strategic arms in the period after 1985.

5. Negotiations between the delegations of the US and USSR to work out the new agreement incorporating the foregoing points will resume in Geneva in January 1975.

(B) JOINT US-SOVIET COMMUNIQUÉ SIGNED AT VLADIVOSTOK

24 November 1974

In accordance with the previously announced agreement, a working meeting between the President of the United States of America Gerald R. Ford and the General Secretary of the Central Committee of the Communist Party of the Soviet Union L. I. Brezhnev took place in the area of Vladivostok on November 23 and 24, 1974. . . .

I. The United States of America and the Soviet Union reaffirmed their determination to develop further their relations in the direction defined by the fundamental joint decisions and basic treaties and agreements concluded between the two States in recent years.

They are convinced that the course of American-Soviet relations, directed towards strengthening world peace, deepening the relaxation of international tensions and expanding mutually beneficial cooperation of states with different social systems meets the vital interests of the peoples of both States and other peoples.

Both sides consider that based on the agreements reached between them important results have been achieved in fundamentally reshaping American-Soviet relations on the basis of peaceful coexistence and equal security. These results are a solid foundation for progress in reshaping Soviet-American relations.

Accordingly, they intend to continue, without a loss in momentum, to expand the scale and intensity of their cooperative efforts in all spheres as set forth in the agreements they have signed so that the process of improving relations between the US and the USSR will continue without interruption and will become irreversible.

Mutual determination was expressed to carry out strictly and fully the mutual obligations undertaken by the US and the USSR in accordance with the treaties and agreements concluded between them.

II. Special consideration was given in the course of the talks to a pivotal aspect of Soviet-American relations: measures to eliminate the threat of war and to halt the arms race.

Both sides reaffirm that the Agreements reached between the US and the USSR on the prevention of nuclear war and the limitation of strategic arms are a good beginning in the process of creating guarantees against the outbreak of nuclear conflict and war in general. They expressed their deep belief in the necessity of promoting this process and expressed their hope that other states would contribute to it as well. For their part the US and the USSR will continue to exert vigorous efforts to achieve this historic task.

A joint statement on the question of limiting strategic offensive arms is being released separately.

Both sides stressed once again the importance and necessity of a serious effort aimed at preventing the dangers connected with the spread of nuclear weapons in the world. In this connection they stressed the importance of increasing the effectiveness of the Treaty on the Non-Proliferation of Nuclear Weapons.

It was noted that, in accordance with previous agreements, initial contacts were established between representatives of the US and of the USSR on questions related to underground nuclear explosions for peaceful purposes, to measures to overcome the dangers of the use of environmental modification techniques for military purposes, as well as measures dealing with the most dangerous lethal means of chemical warfare. It was agreed to continue an active search for mutually acceptable solutions of these questions.

III. In the course of the meeting an exchange of views was held on a number of international issues: special attention was given to negotiations already in progress in which the two Sides are participants and which are designed to remove existing sources of tension and to bring about the strengthening of international security and world peace.

Having reviewed the situation at the Conference on Security and Cooperation in Europe, both Sides concluded that there is a possibility for its early successful conclusion. They proceed from the assumption that the results achieved in the course of the conference will permit its conclusion at the highest level and thus be commensurate with its importance in ensuring the peaceful future of Europe.

The USA and the USSR also attach high importance to the negotiations on mutual reduction of forces and armaments and associated measures in Central Europe....

In the course of the exchange of views on the Middle East both Sides expressed their concern with regard to the dangerous situation in that region. They reaffirmed their intention to make every effort to promote a solution of the key issues of a just and lasting peace in that area on the basis of the United Nations resolution 338, taking into account the legitimate interests of all the peoples of the area, including the Palestinian people, and respect for the right to independent existence of all States in the area....

IV. The state of relations was reviewed in the field of commerical, economic, scientific and technical ties between the USA and the USSR. Both Sides confirmed the great importance which further progress in these fields would have for Soviet-American relations, and expressed their firm intention to continue the broadening and deepening of mutually advantageous cooperation.

The two Sides emphasized the special importance accorded by them to the development of a long term basis of commercial and economic cooperation, including mutually beneficial large-scale projects. They believe that such commercial and economic cooperation wil serve the cause of increasing the stability of Soviet-American relations....

President Ford affirmed the invitation to L. I. Brezhnev to pay an official visit to the United States in 1975. The exact date of the visit will be agreed upon later.

> For the USA: Gerald R. Ford, President of the USA
>
> For the USSR: L. I. Brezhnev, General Secretary of the CC CPSU

DOCUMENT 16

Report of the Central Committee to the Twenty-fifth Congress of the CPSU

L. I. Brezhnev

25 February 1976

Editor's commentary: At the Twenty-fifth CPSU congress, great successes were acclaimed in Soviet foreign policy since 1971 and the last party

"Report of the Central Committee to the 25th CPSU Congress," *Foreign Broadcast Information Service*, Soviet Union, special supplement (Washington, DC: *n.p.*, 25 February 1976, pp. 1–27, *excerpts*.

congress—Helsinki and detente with the US; successful third world socialist revolutions, as in Angola; arms control agreements; and generally rising Soviet prestige, as U.S. power seemed to be receding after the defeat in Vietnam. Detente was successful, according to Brezhnev, because of the changing "correlation of forces" in favor of the USSR. Soviet policy was now truly global, with "no spot on earth" being unimportant in Soviet eyes. But the first half of the decade had been the high-water mark for Soviet prestige. A fractured international commmunist movement, domestic unrest in Eastern Europe, and increasing economic problems at home all belied Soviet optimism after 1975. Interestingly, in this speech Brezhnev refers to the desire of the USSR to establish good relations with China on the basis of "peaceful coexistence" thereby rejecting the notion of the similar characters of the Soviet and Chinese systems.

THE WORLD SITUATION AND THE INTERNATIONAL ACTIVITY OF THE CPSU

[On Friendship and Cooperation with Socialist Countries]

... First of all, one must speak about the victory the Vietnamese people have gained. Imperialism's greatest postwar attempt by force of arms to deal with a socialist state and crush a national liberation revolution has ended in failure. The heroism and self-sacrifice of the Vietnamese people, combined with the resolute support for it by the countries of socialism and the progressive public of the whole world, have proved stronger than the armies of interventionists and their accomplices. The cause of freedom and independence have triumphed....

Of course, the question of relations with China is of special significance and it stands apart. The policy of its present leadership is openly directed against the majority of socialist states. Furthermore, it directly merges with the positions of the most extreme reactionaries in the world, starting with militarists and enemies of detente in

Western countries, and ending with racists in South Africa and the fascist rulers in Chile. This policy is not only entirely alien to socialist principles and ideals, but has in fact become an important reserve of imperialism in its struggle against socialism....

In relations with China, our Party firmly sticks to the course defined by the 24th Congress. The correctness of this course has been proved by life itself. We shall continue to wage a struggle against Maoism—a principled and uncompromising struggle.

At the same time, I would like to stress once more that in relations with China, as in relations with other countries, we observe the principles of equality, respect of sovereignty and territorial integrity, non-interference in domestic affairs of each other, and nonuse of force. In a word, we are ready to normalize relations with China on the principles of peaceful coexistence.

Furthermore, one can say with confidence that if in Peking they return to a policy which is really based on Marxism-Leninism and abandon their course, which is hostile to the socialist countries and embark on a course of cooperation and solidarity in the world of socialism, then this will meet with the appropriate response from us and will open up the possibility of development of good relations between the USSR and the PRC, corresponding to the principles of socialist internationalism. The ball is in the Chinese court.

[On Greater Cooperation with the Third World]

Comrades, in the period under review the ties between the Soviet Union and the countries which have liberated themselves from colonial dependence, or developing countries, have expanded and become more lasting....

The class struggle is intensifying. This is manifested in various ways. New progressive advances have taken place in the economic and political life in the Arab, African and Asian countries which have a socialist orientation. There are also countries where the development has gone further along the capitalist path....

The Soviet Union's attitude toward the complex processes in the developing countries is clearcut and definite: The Soviet Union does not meddle in the domestic affairs of other countries and peoples. Respect for the sacred right of each people and each country to select their own road of development is a firm principle of Leninist foreign policy. However, we do not hide our views. In the developing countries, as everywhere, we are on the side of the forces of progress, democracy and national independence, and we treat them as friends and comrades-in-arms....

[Development of Relations with the Capitalist States]

The struggle to assert the principles of peaceful coexistence, for lasting peace and detente and, in the long term, to prevent the risk of a new world war, has been and still is the main element in our relations with capitalist states. It can be said that in the past 5-year period considerable progress was made in this direction. The switch-over from cold war, from an explosively dangerous confrontation between the two blocs to detente, was related, above all to the changes in the balance [correlation] of forces in the international arena....

The results of the Conference [on Security and Cooperation in Europe] are largely linked with the future. The prospects for peaceful coexistence have been mapped out in a large number of fields.... Now it is important to put all the principles and agreements made at Helsinki into practice. The Soviet Union acts and will continue to act in this way. Recently we put forward certain proposals for the development of European cooperation in a number of important fields. We will continue to make efforts in this direction. We expect a similar approach from all the other participants in the European conference. Thus, there are achievements in establishing peaceful relations in Europe, and they are not small achievements, comrades....

As a result of the talks with US President Nixon in Moscow and Washington, and then the meetings with President Ford in Vladivostok and Helsinki, important principled mutual understanding was reached between the leaders of the Soviet Union and the United States on the need to develop peaceful, equitable relations between both countries. This was reflected in all the Soviet-American agreements, accords and other documents.... What is the main significance of these documents?

Altogether, they form a solid political and legal basis for the development of mutually-advantageous cooperation between the USSR and the United States on the principles of peaceful coexistence. To a certain extent they reduce the danger of an outbreak of a nuclear war. This is what we see as the main outcome of the development of Soviet-American relations in the past 5 years.

There are also good prospects for our future relations with the United States, as long as they continue to be developed on this jointly created realistic basis when, with the obvious differences in the class structure of both states and their ideologies, there are firm intentions to settle differences and disputes not by force, not by threats or brandishing weapons, but by peaceful political means....

DOCUMENT 17

A Dead-End Middle East Settlement

Yevgeny Primakov

February 1979

Editor's commentary: This analysis of Camp David's results is by a member of the USSR Academy of Sciences and one of the key Soviet

International Affairs (Moscow), February 1979, pp. 38–46, *excerpts.*

experts on the Middle East. The tone of the piece reveals residual bitterness over the failed Egyptian-Soviet relationship and the subsequent turn to the West by Anwar Sadat. The Camp David process, sponsored by President Jimmy Carter to bring peace between Egypt and Israel and then to the rest of the Middle East, was rejected by most of the Arab world. Labeled a "separate deal" by the Soviets, the Camp David accord is opposed and criticized in every detail. In its place, an international conference with a role for all regional powers and both superpowers is called for.

The first point that should be noted is that the Egyptian-Israeli treaty has not only been worked out with US assistance and participation but is a direct outgrowth of American Middle East policy. What is more, it is not the result of "intensive, multi-level search for a peace formula," as the American press has been trying to make out, but the product of a sustained effort to secure the imperialist interests of the US and its ally—Israel....

In broad outline, the Egyptian-Israeli deal can be defined as an act besuited to the interests of Israel's expansionist policy. It is nothing short of a gift to Israel, which has committed many acts of aggression against Arab countries and wants to keep what she has gained.

First, the Egyptian-Israeli treaty provides for Israeli troops to be withdrawn only from the Sinai Peninsula and, in point of fact, sanctions the continued Israeli occupation of the West Bank and the Gaza strip as well as the Golan Heights. The agreement between Sadat and Begin on "self-government" for Palestinians inhabiting the West Bank and the Gaza strip, as written into the "Framework for Peace in the Middle East" means nothing in the sense of ending Israeli occupation; in fact, it envisages the continued presence of the Israeli army in the territories and what is more, at strategically important regions, under the pretext of "ensuring the security" of Israel....

Second, the Egyptian-Israeli treaty does immense damage to the just cause of the Arab people of Palestine, who have been struggling for over 30 years to assert their legitimate right of self-determination, including the creation of a national state.

The separate deal makes no mention of this right....

Third, the Egyptian-Israeli treaty falls far short of nullifying the results of Israeli aggression, even for Egypt alone. Under this treaty Egypt's sovereignty over Sinai will be considerably limited after the territory is returned to it. There is an obvious premeditated discrimination against Egypt in the width of the demilitarized zones on either side of the border. Israel, with US aid, is setting up two air bases in the Negev Desert close to that border—thereby retaining, in fact, her military-strategic control over Sinai....

Fourth, the separate Egyptian-Israeli treaty worsens conditions for the *continued* struggle to nullify the effects of the 1967 Israeli aggression. It puts the strongest Arab protagonist of this struggle—Egypt—out of action. In the opinion of the overwhelming majority of Arab observers, the separate deal is a plot to widen the rift in the Arab world and erode the very idea of joint anti-imperialist and anti-Zionist action by Arab countries. Under the treaty, Sadat assumed certain commitments which imply Egypt's total abstention from aiding the other Arab countries and forces in their resistance to Israel's expansionism....

Finally, and this is the *fifth* point, the very character and implications of the separate deal will be increasingly instrumental in turning Egypt into a tool to further US interests and, notably, to help oppose the progressive regimes in the Arab world. The press in a number of Arab countries has stressed that, freed from confrontation with Israel, Sadat will be more "tempted" to use "redundant" armed forces against neighbouring Libya, whose relations with Egypt remain extremely strained....

Thus, the Egyptian-Israeli treaty creates but a semblance of a settlement and is basically directed against the safeguarding of a just and, hence, stable peace in the Middle East.

Will the US and Israel pull off their separate deal with Egypt? Whatever the real answer to this question, the strategic miscalculations of its sponsors are indisputable. The best evidence to this effect was, of course, provided by the successful Arab summit in Baghdad early last November. It brought together the leaders of all Arab states, except Egypt, and they unanimously recorded their oppositon to the separate Egyptian-Israeli treaty. Egypt has found herself completely isolated in the Arab world. An adverse view of the Egyptian-Israeli compact has also been taken by Saudi Arabia, which many in the USA regarded—and not without reason in some cases—as the mainstay of American policy in the region....

In contrast to US Middle East policy, which is based on piecemeal separatist agreements, the Soviet Union stands for a fundamental and comprehensive Middle East settlement. This means resolving all the problems rather than picking issues out of context and opposing some aspects of settlement to others. Far from bringing a Middle East settlement any nearer, separate negotiations and agreements which bypass the interests of other Arab countries concerned impede agreement and lead to a deadend. Nor do the separate talks and agreements promise stable peace for Israel itself. By letting it reap the fruit of its aggressive policy, they maintain an explosive situation in the Middle East, pregnant with further armed conflicts.

Therefore, as the Soviet leaders have emphasized more than once, the only right and sure way of securing a fundamental solution to all aspects of the Middle East problem in its entirety is through negotiations within the framework of the specially convened Geneva Middle East Peace Conference, with the attendance of all the parties involved in the conflict. Only this tried and tested approach will defuse the explosive situation in the Middle East and assure peace and security for all the people of that region. There is no other way.

SALT II Treaty, Strategic Weapons Data Base, and Joint Statement of Principles and Basic Guidelines for Subsequent Negotiations on the Limitation of Strategic Arms

18 June 1979

Editor's commentary: The conclusion of the SALT II talks in Vienna between Jimmy Carter and Leonid Brezhnev seemed to suggest that despite problems with detente, the SALT process would proceed unimpeded into the 1980s. However, events soon overwhelmed arms control and detente itself. Within seven months, the Soviet Union intervened in Afghanistan and by doing so, killed the chance of Senate ratification of the SALT II treaty and the continuation of "business as usual" in arms control, as the word "linkage" echoed in the halls of Congress. The three documents which follow constitute the SALT II accords.

(A) TREATY BETWEEN THE USA AND THE USSR ON THE LIMITATION OF STRATEGIC OFFENSIVE ARMS

Article I
Each Party undertakes, in accordance with the provisions of this Treaty, to limit strategic offensive arms quantitatively and qualitatively, to exercise restraint in the development of new types of strategic offensive arms, and to adopt other measures provided for in this Treaty.

"Treaty Between the USA and the USSR on the Limitation of Strategic Offensive Arms," "Memorandum of Understanding Between the USA and the USSR Regarding the Establishment of a Data Base on the Numbers of Strategic Offensive Arms," and "Joint Statement...," *Arms Control and Disarmament Agreements* (Washington, DC: Arms Control and Disarmament Agency/U.S. Government Printing Office, 1980), pp. 207–237, *excerpts*.

Article II

For the purposes of this Treaty:

1. Intercontinental ballistic missile (ICBM) launchers are land-based launchers of ballistic missiles capable of a range in excess of the shortest distance between the northeastern border of the continental part of the territory of the USA and the northwestern border of the continental part of the territory of the USSR, that is, a range in excess of 5,500 kilometers.

2. Submarine-launched ballistic missile (SLBM) launchers are launchers of ballistic missiles installed...on any submarine, regardless of its type.

3. Heavy bombers are considered to be:

(a) currently, for the USA, bombers of the B-52 and B-1 types, and for the USSR, bombers of the Tupolev-95 and Myasishchev types; (b) in the future, types of bombers which can carry out the mission of a heavy bomber in a manner similar or superior to that of bombers listed in subparagraph (a) above; (c) types of bombers equipped for cruise missiles capable of a range in excess of 600 kilometers; and (d) types of bombers equipped for ASBMs.

4. Air-to-surface ballistic missiles (ASBMs) are any such missiles capable of a range in excess of 600 kilometers and installed in an aircraft or on its external mountings.

5. Launchers of ICBMs and SLBMs equipped with multiple independently targetable reentry vehicles (MIRVs) are launchers of the types developed and tested for launching ICBMs or SLBMs equipped with MIRVs.

6. ASBMs equipped with MIRVs are ASBMs of the types which have been flight-tested with MIRVs.

7. Heavy ICBMs are ICBMs which have a launch-weight greater or a throw-weight greater than that of the heaviest, in terms of either launch-weight or throw-weight, respectively, of the light ICBMs deployed by either Party as of the date of signature of this Treaty.

8. Cruise missiles are unmanned, self-propelled, guided, weapon-delivery vehicles which sustain flight through the use of aerodynamic lift over most of their flight path and which are flight-tested from or deployed on aircraft, that is, air-launched cruise missiles, or such vehicles which are referred to as cruise missiles in subparagraph 1(b) of Article IX.

Article III

1. Upon entry into force of this Treaty, each Party undertakes to limit ICBM launchers, SLBM launchers, heavy bombers, and ASBMs to an aggregate number not to exceed 2,400.

2. Each Party undertakes to limit, from January 1, 1981, strategic offensive arms referred to in paragraph 1 of this Article to an aggregate number not to exceed 2,250, and to initiate reductions of those arms which as of that date would be in excess of this aggregate number.

3. Within the aggregate numbers provided for in paragraphs 1 and 2 of this Article and subject to the provisions of this Treaty, each Party has the right to determine the composition of these aggregates....

Article IV

1–3. Each Party undertakes not to start construction of additional fixed ICBM launchers...not to relocate fixed ICBM launchers...not to convert launchers of light ICBMs, or of ICBMs of older types deployed prior to 1964, into launchers of heavy ICBMs of types deployed after that time.

4. Each Party undertakes in the process of modernization and replacement of ICBM silo launchers not to increase the original internal volume of an ICBM silo launcher by more than thirty-two percent....

5. Each Party undertakes:

(a) not to suppply ICBM launcher deployment areas with ICBMs in excess of a number consistent with normal deployment, maintenance, training, and replacement requirements.

(b) not to provide storage facilities for or to store ICBMS in excess of normal deployment requirements at launch sites of ICBM launchers.

(c) not to develop, test, or deploy systems for rapid reload of ICBM launchers.

6. Subject to the provisions of this Treaty, each Party undertakes not to have under construction at any time strategic offensive arms referred to in paragraph 1 of Article III in excess of numbers consistent with a normal construction schedule.

7. Each Party undertakes not to develop, test, or deploy ICBMs [heavier than]...heavy ICBMs, deployed by either Party as of the date of signature of this Treaty.

8. Each Party undertakes not to convert land-based launchers of ballistic missiles which are not ICBMs into launchers for launching ICBMs, and not to test them for this purpose.

9. Each Party undertakes not to flight-test or deploy new types of ICBMs....

12. Each party undertakes not to flight-test or deploy SLBMs with a number of reentry vehicles greater than [14]....

13. Each Party undertakes not to flight-test or deploy ASBMs with a number of reentry vehicles greater than [10]....

14. Each Party undertakes not to deploy at any one time on heavy bombers equipped for cruise missiles capable of a range in excess of 600 km. a number of such cruise missiles which exceeds the product of 28 and the number of such heavy bombers.

Article V

1. Within the aggregate numbers provided for in paragraphs 1 and 2 of Article III, each Party undertakes to limit launchers of ICBMs and SLBMs equipped with MIRVs, ASBMs equipped with MIRVs, and heavy bombers equipped for cruise missiles capable of a range in excess of 600 kilometers to an aggregate number not to exceed 1,320....

5. Within the aggregate numbers provided for in paragraphs 1, 2, and 3 of this Article and subject to the provisions of this Treaty, each Party has the right to determine the composition of these aggregates.

Article VI

1. The limitations provided for in this Treaty shall apply to those arms which are:

(a) operational; (b) in the final stage of construction; (c) in reserve, in storage, or mothballed; (d) undergoing overhaul, repair, modernization, or conversion.

2. Those arms in the final state of construction are:

(a) SLBM launchers on submarines which have begun sea trials; (b) ASBMs after a bomber of a type equipped for such missiles has been brought out of the shop, plant...; (c) other strategic offensive arms which are finally assembled in a shop, plant or other facility....

3. ICBM and SLBM launchers of a type not subject to the limitation provided for in Article V, which undergo conversion into launchers of a type subject to that limitation, shall become subject to that limitation as follows:

(a) fixed ICBM launchers when work on their conversion reaches the stage which first definitely indicates that they are beng so converted; (b) SLBM launchers on a submarine when that submarine first goes to sea after their conversion has been performed.

4. ASBMs on a bomber which undergoes conversion from a bomber of a type equipped for ASBMS which are not subject to the limitation provided for in Article V into a bomber of a type equipped for ASBMS which are subject to that limitation shall become subject to that limitation when the bomber is brought out of the shop, plant, or other facility where such conversion has been performed.

5. A heavy bomber of a type not subject to the limitation provided for in paragraph 1 of Article V shall become subject to that limitation when it is brought out of the shop, plant, or other facility where it has been converted into a heavy bomber of a type equipped for cruise missiles capable of a range in excess of 600 kilometers....

6. The arms subject to the limitation provided for in this Treaty shall continue to be subject to these limitations until they are dismantled, are

destroyed, or otherwise cease to be subject to these limitations under procedures to be agreed upon.

7. In accordance with the provisions of Article XVII, the Parties will agree in the Standing Consultative Commission upon procedures to implement the provisions of this Article.

Article VII

1. The limitations provided for in Article III shall not apply to ICBM and SLBM test and training launchers or to space vehicle launchers for exploration and use of outer space....

2. The Parties agree that:

(a) there shall be no significant increase in the number of ICBM or SLBM test and training launchers or in the number of such launchers of heavy ICBMs;

(b) construction or conversion of ICBM launchers at test ranges shall be undertaken only for purposes of testing and training;

(c) there shall be no conversion of ICBM test and training launchers or of space vehicle launchers into ICBM launchers subject to the limitations provided for in Artricle III.

Article VIII

1. Each Party undertakes not to flight-test cruise missiles capable of a range in excess of 600 kilometers or ASBMs from aircraft other than bombers or to convert such aircraft into aircraft equipped for such missiles.

2. Each Party undertakes not to convert aircraft other than bombers into aircraft which can carry out the mission of a heavy bomber as referred to in subparagraph 3(b) of Article II.

Article IX

1. Each Party undertakes not to develop, test, or deploy:

(a) ballistic missiles capable of a range in excess of 600 kilometers for installation on waterborne vehicles other than submarines, or launchers of such missiles;

(b) fixed ballistic or cruise missile launchers for emplacement [in any watery environment]....

(c) systems for placing into Earth orbit nuclear weapons or any other kind of weapons of mass destruction, including fractional orbital missiles;

(d) mobile launchers of heavy ICBMs;

(e) SLBMs which have a launch weight greater or a throw-weight greater than that of the heavies...;

(f) ASBMs which have a launch-weight or greater or a throw-weight greater than that of the heavies...

2. Each Party undertakes not to flight-test from aircraft cruise missiles capable of a range in excess of 600 kilometers which are equipped with multiple independently targetable warheads and not to deploy such cruise missiles on aircraft.

Article X

Subject to the provisions of this Treaty, modernization and replacement of strategic offensive arms may be carried out.

Article XI

1. Strategic offensive arms which would be in excess of the aggregate numbers provided for in this Treaty as well as strategic offensive arms prohibited by this Treaty shall be dismantled or destroyed....

2. Dismantling or destruction...shall begin on the date of the entry into force of this Treaty and shall be complete within the following period from that date: four months for ICBM launchers; six months for SLBM launchers; and three months for heavy bombers....

4. Dismantling or destruction of strategic offensive arms prohibited by this Treaty shall be complete within the shortest possible agreed period of time, but not later than six months after the entry into force of this Treaty.

Article XII

1. In order to ensure the viability and effectiveness of this Treaty, each Party undertakes not to circumvent the provisions of this Treaty, through any other state or states, or in any other manner.

Article XIII

1. Each Party undertakes not to assume any international obligations which would conflict with this Treaty.

Article XIV

The Parties undertake to begin, promptly after the entry into force of this Treaty, active negotiations with the objective of achieving, as soon as possible, agreement on further measures for the limitation and reduction of strategic arms. It is also the objective of the Parties to conclude well in advance of 1985 an agreement limiting strategic offensive arms to replace this Treaty upon its expiration.

Article XV

1. For the purpose of providing assurance of compliance with the provisions of this Treaty, each Party shall use national technical means of verification at its disposal in a manner consistent with generally recognized principles of international law.

2. Each party undertakes not to interfere with the national technical means of verification of the other Party's operation in accordance with paragraph 1 of this Article.

3. Each Party undertakes not to use deliberate concealment measures which impede verification....

Article XVI

1. Each Party undertakes, before conducting each planned ICBM launch, to notify the other Party well in advance ... except for single ICBM launches from test ranges or from ICBM launcher deployment areas, which are not planned to extend beyond its national territory....

Article XVII

1. To promote the objective and implementation of the provisions of this Treaty, the Parties shall use the Standing Consultative Commission established by the Memorandum of Understanding Between the Government of the USA and the Government of the USSR Regarding the Establishment of a Standing Consultative Commission of December 21, 1972.

2. Within the framework of the Standing Consultative Commission, with respect to this Treaty, the Parties will:

(a) consider questions concerning compliance with the obligation assumed and related situations which may be considered ambiguous;

(b) provide on a voluntary basis such information as either Party considers necessary to assure confidence in compliance with the obligations assumed;

(c) consider questions involving unintended interference with national technical means of verification, and questions involving unintended impeding of verification by national technical means of compliance with the provisions of this Treaty;

(d) consider possible changes in the strategic situation which have a bearing on the provisions of this Treaty;

(e) agree upon procedures for replacement, conversion, and dismantling or destruction, of strategic offensive arms in cases provided for in the provisions of this Treaty...;

(f) consider, as appropriate, possible proposals for further increasing the viability of this Treaty....

Article XVIII

Each Party may propose amendments to this Treaty. Agreed amendments shall enter into force in accordance with the procedures governing the entry into force of this Treaty.

Article XIX

1. This Treaty shall be subject to ratification in accordance with constitutional procedures of each Party. This Treaty shall enter into force on the day of the exchange of instruments of ratification and shall remain in force through December 31, 1985, unless replaced earlier by an agreement further limiting strategic offensive arms.

2. This Treaty shall be registered pursuant to Article 102 of the Charter of the United Nations.

3. Each Party shall, in exercising its national sovereignty, have the right to withdraw from this Treaty if it decides that extraordinary events related to the subject matter of this Treaty have jeopardized its supreme interests. It shall give notice of its decision to the other Party six months prior to withdrawal from the Treaty. Such notice shall include a statement of the extraordinary events the notifying Party regards as having jeopardized its supreme interest.

DONE at Vienna on June 18, 1979, in two copies, each in the English and Russian languages, both texts being equally authentic.

(B) STRATEGIC WEAPONS DATA BASE FOR SALT II

For the Purposes of the Treaty Between the United States of America and the Union of Soviet Socialist Republics on the Limitation of Strategic Offensive Arms, the Parties have considered data on numbers of strategic offensive arms and agree that as of November 1, 1978 there existed the following numbers of stategic offensive arms subject to the limitation provided for in the Treaty which is being signed today.

	U.S.A.	U.S.S.R.
Launchers of ICBMs	1,054	1,398
Fixed Launchers of ICBMs	1,054	1,398
Launchers of ICBMs equipped with MIRVs	550	576
Launchers of SLBMs	656	950
Launchers of SLBMs equipped with MIRVs	496	128
Heavy bombers	574	156
Heavy bombers equipped for cruise missiles capable of a range in excess of 600	0	0
Heavy bombers equipped only for ASBMs	0	0
ASBMs	0	0
ASBMs equipped with MIRVs	0	0

At the time of entry into force of the Treaty the Parties will update the above agreed data in the categories listed in this Memorandum.

DONE at Vienna on June 18, 1979, in two copies, each in the English and Russian languages, both texts being equally authentic.

(C) JOINT STATEMENT OF PRINCIPLES AND BASIC GUIDELINES FOR SUBSEQUENT NEGOTIATIONS ON THE LIMITATIONS OF STRATEGIC ARMS

The United States of America and the Union of Soviet Socialist Republics . . . Have agreed as follows:

First
The Parties will continue to pursue negotiations, in accordance with the principle of equality and equal security, on measures for the further limitation and reduction in the numbers of strategic arms, as well as for their further qualitative limitation,

In furtherance of existing agreements between the Parties on the limitation and reduction of strategic arms, the Parties will continue, for the purposes of reducing and averting the risk of outbreak of nuclear war, to seek measures to strengthen strategic stability by, among other things, limitations on strategic offensive arms most destabilizing to the strategic balance and by measures to reduce and to avert the risk of surprise attack.

Second
Further limitations and reductions of strategic arms must be subject to adequate verification by national technical means, using additionally, as appropriate, cooperative measures contributing to the effectiveness of verification by national technical means. . . .

Third
The Parties shall pursue in the course of these negotiations, taking into consideration factors that determine the strategic situation, the following objectives:

(1) significant and substantial reductions in the numbers of strategic offensive arms;

(2) qualitative limitations on strategic offensive arms, including restrictions on the development, testing, and deployment of new types of strategic offensive arms and on the modernization of existing strategic offensive arms....

Fourth
The Parties will consider other steps to ensure and enhance strategic stability, to ensure the equality and equal security of the Parties, and to implement the above principles and objectives. Each Party will be free to raise any issue relative to the further limitation of strategic arms. The Parties will also consider further joint measures, as appropriate, to strengthen international peace and security and to reduce the risk of outbreak of nuclear war.

Vienna, June 18, 1979

For the United States of America: Jimmy Carter, President of the United States of America

For the Union of Soviet Socialist Republics: L. Brezhnev, General Secretary of the CPSU, Chairman of the Presidium of the Supreme Soviet of the U.S.S.R.

DOCUMENT 19

The Soviet View of the Afghan Revolution

28 and 30 December 1979

Editor's commentary: The 1979 "Christmas" invasion of Afghanistan was launched by the Kremlin to guarantee the survival of a crumbling Marxist-Leninist regime in the turbulent political environment of Kabul. In April 1978 a "treaty of friendship" was concluded between the USSR and Afghanistan after the old regime had been ousted by "progressive" forces. A period of intense factional struggle ensued. Finally, in December 1979 the leader of the People's Democratic Party of Afghanistan, H. Amin, who had taken power by executing his predecessor, N. Taraki, was himself executed by a new Soviet-installed regime led by B. Karmal, who was flown in directly from the Soviet Union to replace him. The three selections that follow include an appeal for "friendly assistance," a Soviet announcement of unequivocal support of the Afghan revolution, and the official Soviet interpretation of events. In coming to the defense of the "revolutionary gains" of the revolution, Soviet leaders created for themselves a difficult doctrinal situation, one which dogged them even after the Soviet military withdrawal in 1989.

THE AFGHAN GOVERNMENT'S APPEAL [28 DECEMBER 1979]

Kabul Radio today broadcast a statement by the government of the Democratic Republic of Afghanistan. It says:

The government of Afghanistan, taking into consideration the continuing and widening interference and provocation of the country's external enemies and in order to defend the gains of the April revolution, territorial integrity and national independence, and to maintain peace and security, and basing itself on the Treaty of Friendship, Good-Neighborliness and Cooperation of 5 December 1978, has appealed to the USSR with an urgent request to provide immediate political, moral and economic aid, including military aid.

The government of the Soviet Union has met the request of Afghanistan.

TASS, 28 and 30 December 1979, and Moscow Radio, 28 December 1979, as translated and transcribed in *Foreign Broadcast Information Service,* Soviet Union (Washington, DC: *n.p.,* 28 and 31 December 1979, pp. D3, D5 & D7, D11.

BREZHNEV'S CONGRATULATIONS [28 DECEMBER 1979]

To Comrade Babrak Karmal, General Secretary of the Central Committee of the People's Democratic Party of Afghanistan, Chairman of the Revolutionary Council and Prime Minister of the Democratic Republic of Afghanistan.

I heartily congratulate you on being elected as general secretary of the Central Committee of the People's Democratic Party of Afghanistan and to the senior state posts of the Democratic Republic of Afghanistan.

On behalf of the Soviet leadership and myself personally, I wish you great successes in all your diverse activity for the good of the friendly Afghan people. I am sure that in the present conditions the Afghan people will succeed in defending the gains of the April revolution and the sovereignty, independence and national dignity of the new Afghanistan.

[signed] L. Brezhnev

"ON EVENTS IN AFGHANISTAN" [30 DECEMBER 1979]

...The uncalled-for interference of imperialist forces in the internal affairs of Afghanistan [and] constant armed intrusions from the outside created a great danger for the country. In 1978–1979, the Afghan government turned many times to the Soviet Union with requests of support, specifically with...requests of military aid in response to armed interference by imperialist forces.

The Soviet Union believed that imperialist forces,...convinced of [the] irreversibility of the changes that have taken place in Afghanistan, would not go beyond a certain limit, would show consideration for realities. At the same time, our country made no secret that it will not allow Afghanistan being turned into a bridgehead for preparation of imperialist aggression against the Soviet Union.

But enemies of People's Afghanistan did not stop armed struggle against it. Imperialist interference started assuming forms and proportions still broader and more dangerous for the Afghan people.

External imperialist reaction has been making continuous efforts also for...disorganizing the ranks of the People's Democratic Party of Afghanistan.

Reaction found a helper for implementation of its anti-popular designs among the very leadership of Democratic Afghanistan. H. Amin turned out to be that helper. By deception and intrigues he got hold of the main levers of management of the state and then overthrew the lawful president N. Taraki and killed him. By his criminal actions, gross violation of law and order, by cruelty and abuse of power, Amin was undermining the ideals of the April Revolution. On his hands is the blood of many representatives of the industrious Afghan people, party leaders, honored military men, Moslem dignitaries [and] other honest citizens. Amin in actual fact teamed with the enemies of the April Revolution.

In conditions when interference from outside and terror unleashed by Amin within the country created a real threat to the democratic system, there were patriotic forces in Afghanistan which rose not only against foreign aggression but also against the usurper. Relying on the support of the people, they removed Amin. Revolutionary law and order was restored in the country. The People's Democratic Party and the state are directing their efforts to protect the gains of the April revolution, sovereignty, independence and national dignity of Afghanistan.

...The Afghan Government has made again an insistent request that the Soviet Union should give immediate aid and support in the struggle against external aggression.

The Soviet Union decided to grant this request and to send to Afghanistan a limited Soviet military contingent that will be used exclusively for assistance in rebuffing the armed interference from the outside. The Soviet contingent will be completely pulled out of Afghanistan when the reason that necessitated such an action exists no longer.

Making this decision, the Soviet Union proceeded from the community of the interests of Afghanistan and our country in the questions of security recorded in the 1978 Treaty of Friendship, Good-neighborliness and Cooperation, out of the interest of preserving peace in the region.

Article Four of the Soviet-Afghan treaty says:

"Acting in the spirit of the traditions of friendship and good-neighborliness, as well as the United Nations Charter, the parties to the treaty will be consulting each other and with mutual consent will be taking appropriate measures to ensure security, independence and territorial integrity of both countries. In the interest of reinforcing defence potential of the parties to the treaty, they will continue developing cooperation in the military sphere."

The request of the Afghan leadership and the positive response of the Soviet Union to this request also stem from the provisions of Article 51 of the United Nations Charter that envisages the inalienable right of states to collective and individual self-defence to rebuff an aggression and restore peace....

DOCUMENT 20

Soviet Commentary on SALT II Treaty's Demise

9 March 1980

Editor's commentary: This Pravda *criticism of President Carter's decision to withdraw the SALT II treaty from the floor of the Senate makes no mention of the primary reason for this move—the*

Soviet intervention in Afghanistan, which put the final nail in the coffin of detente and the SALT process. The Soviets knew that SALT was in trouble even before the Afghan invasion. Clearly, a decision was made that Soviet interests in Afghanistan were more important than the already troubled SALT II treaty. Further, they continued to bank on European public opinion's pressure on the alliance, which was undergoing considerable stress due to the decision to deploy medium-range missiles in response to the Soviet SS-20 buildup of the mid-1970s. Subsequently, all these Soviet moves ended in failure.

President J. Carter sent Congress a message in connection with the presentation to that legislative body of the annual report on the activity of the Arms Control and Disarmament Agency. In the message, there are contained assertions that strategic arms limitation "has held a central place in the measures carried out by the United States" and that the U.S. "as before, gives sincere support to the process of mutual arms limitation."

As some observers note, similar statements can be explained to a considerable extent by the short-term election campaign considerations of the administration, which cannot not take into account the fact that the overwhelming majority of Americans, as public opinion polls show, definitely favors the limitation of the strategic arms race and the achievement of real progress on the road to disarmament.

Proceeding from this fact, Carter says that he intends "to ask the Senate, after more urgent problems have been resolved, to again take up" the discussion of the Soviet-American SALT II treaty, the ratification of which has been frozen by the current master of the White House. As is known, the postponement of a decision on the question of the treaty's ratification has called forth a negative reaction from Washington's allies, who believe that ratification responds to the interests not only of the security of the USSR and the U.S.A. but also of the cause of the re-

---

"Concerning J. Carter's Message to Congress," *Pravda,* 9 March 1980, p. 5. Editor's translation.

laxation of tension and strengthening peace in the entire world.

The position taken by the present head of the Washington administration, who signed the SALT II treaty and thereby assumed certain commitments, is distinguished by its evident ambiguity. On the one hand, he states his "support for efforts in the field of arms limitation," while on the other hand he postpones ratification of the treaty, referring to the presence of some allegedly "unsuitable" military and political conditions. Moreover, the administration and the "hawks" in Congress have used the very process of the discussion of SALT II in Senate committees to impose decisions to speed up the nuclear arms race.

Thus, the administration has claimed that the adoption of decisions on MX strategic missile production and on the Western European deployment of new American medium-range nuclear missiles would help to accelerate the process of ratifying the SALT II treaty. MX missile production has already begun, preparations for deployment are under way, and a decision on the deployment of medium-range missiles has been imposed on Washington's NATO allies. However, the process of ratification of the SALT II treaty not only has not moved an inch but, on the contrary, has been artificially frozen. Isn't this just another example of the inconsistency and unpredictability of the present Washington administration's policy?

Now assertions resound from Washington that the U.S., in spite of everything, intends to "fulfill the conditions" of the treaty as if it had already been ratified. However, it may be asked: Who needs gestures of this sort, and who will believe in the sincerity of Washington, which assumed certain treaty commitments but is refusing to consolidate them according to established legal order? And who can rely on Washington's verbal assurances just when it so easily disavows the signatures it has put to dozens of international agreements? It should be perfectly clear that the SALT II treaty will enter into force only after it

is ratified by the legislative bodies of the parties that signed it.

DOCUMENT 21

Soviet Evaluation of Polish Solidarity Crisis

1 September 1980

Editor's commentary: The first official Soviet commentary on the crisis in Poland came one day after the Gdansk Accords were signed by the Polish government and representatives of the Interfactory Committee (Solidarity), the first such agreements ever in the East bloc. Note, however, that no mention was made of the historic accords between the government and the opposition, while Poland's security role in the Warsaw Pact is stressed. The initial Soviet denunciation was against "antisocialist elements," who were planning a "counterrevolution" in Poland. Similar charges had been leveled twelve years earlier during the Czechoslovak Prague Spring.

The Polish press is at present devoting attention to the fact that the antisocialist elements are not letting up their attempts to use the complex situation which has been created in the country in order to aggravate both political and economic difficulties.

Trybuna Ludu, the organ of the [Polish United Workers' Party (PUWP)] Central Committee, says: "Antisocialist elements in a number of places are striving for a continuation of the

---

A. Petrov, "The Intrigues of Socialist Poland's Enemies," *Pravda*, 1 September 1980, p. 5, as translated in *Foreign Broadcast Information Service*, Soviet Union (Washington, DC: *n.p.*, 2 September 1980), pp. F1–F2.

strikes, presenting for this purpose new demands, including political ones, and whipping up tension. They ignore the fact that this poisons the political atmosphere in the country and threatens the emergence of anarchy in public life, and they ignore the possible consequences for the state and the people." It is obvious from press reports that antisocialist elements succeeded in penetrating a number of enterprises on the Polish coast, primarily in Gdansk, in abusing the trust of part of the working class, and in using the economic difficulties for their counter-revolutionary aims.

Government commissions have [taken into] practical consideration the demands put forward by the workers' representatives. The viewpoint of the government commissions in Gdansk and Szczecin and the results of their negotiations were expounded at the [PUWP] Central Committee Plenum held on 30 August.

However, antisocialist elements are continuing to put to the foreground political demands, which reveal their real intention, which are remote from the economic and social interests of the Polish working class. The tactics of such elements, who are operating at a series of enterprises on the coast, are in fact directed toward a continuation of the work stoppages and disorganization of the life of the country.

They are inflicting direct damage to real socialism in the Polish land. They want to destroy the link between the party and working class, the chief source of strength of the [PUWP] and the Polish state. It is precisely for this reason that the antisocialist elements find support among Poland's enemies operating from outside. It is precisely for this reason that the mass information media in the West are building up a slanderous and provocatory campaign against the Polish People's Republic.

These actions are aimed at hindering in every possible way the restoration of a normal rhythm of work and public life in Poland, at inflicting the maximum possible damage to its economic and social development and to the socialist gains of the Polish people. Is this not demonstrated by the fact that, while the Polish people and their economy need supplies of foodstuffs and raw materials essential to Polish agriculture, industry and factories, the reactionary trade unions in the United States refuse to load ships going to Poland. And all this is done under the guise of "solidarity" with Polish workers.

The rightwing press of the FRG continues to publish material of an inflammatory and revanchist nature. The newspaper *Deutsche Wochenzeitung* proposes, for instance, that the "former German territories" be demanded from the Government of the Polish People's Republic as a guarantee for the granting of credit. A provocative demonstration of CDU [Christian Democratic Union] supporters was held in Bonn under the slogan of a revised "political structure" for socialist Poland.

The antisocialist elements in Poland are trying to coordinate their actions with the reactionary Polish emigres and subversion centers operating in the West. It is becoming clearer with each passing day that the inflammatory activity from abroad is dictated not at all by the concern for the well-being of the Polish working people. The aim of these circles is to inflict damage on the socialist gains of the Polish people, to attempt to turn Poland from the path it embarked on by the wish of the people after the liberation from the German fascist aggressors.

Trybuna Ludu notes that Poland occupies an important place on the European Continent and in European politics, and that it is a member of the defense alliance of the Warsaw Pact member states and is a member of CEMA. Poland plays an important role in the center of Europe as an element of peace and stability on the European Continent.

Trybuna Ludu justly emphasizes that "everyone who is fully aware of his responsibility should have a clear idea of the line which separates just demands from those demands which threaten the interests of the state."

DOCUMENT 22

Report of the Central Committee to the Twenty-sixth Congress of the CPSU

L. I. Brezhnev

23 February 1981

Editor's commentary: By 1981, Soviet foreign policy had run into several intractable problems, the foremost of which were Poland and Afghanistan. The Solidarity crisis in Poland was still in process as Brezhnev addressed this congress, and the Afghanistan intervention now appeared to be a long-term commitment as guerrilla resistance stiffened. Setbacks in the third world and a revitalized American commitment, voiced by the new American President, Ronald Reagan, to outspend the Soviet Union militarily and thereby contain Soviet expansionism, implied tough times ahead for Soviet foreign policy. Indeed, the tone of Brezhnev's keynote address is the least optimistic of any given during his administration.

DEVELOPMENT OF THE WORLD SOCIALIST SYSTEM

It should be noted...that lately our countries have been having to deal with their constructive tasks under more complicated conditions. The deterioration of the world economy and spiraling prices are making themselves felt. The slowing of the process of detente and the arms race imposed by the imperialist powers are no small burden for us as well.

Another point is the visible sharpening of the ideological struggle. For the West, this struggle is not confined to the battle of ideas—it includes

---

Report of the Central Committee of the CPSU to the 26th Congress of the CPSU (Washington, DC: USSR Embassy Information Department), *excerpts.*

a whole system of methods designed to subvert or soften up the socialist world.

The imperialists and their accomplices are systematically conducting a hostile campaign against the socialist countries. They malign and distort everything that goes on within the socialist world. For them, all that matters is to turn people against socialism.

Recent events have shown again and again that our class opponents are learning from their defeats. Their actions against the socialist countries are increasingly refined and treacherous.

And wherever imperialist subversive activity is compounded with mistakes and miscalculations in domestic policy, there arise conditions that stimulate elements hostile to socialism. This is what has happened in fraternal Poland, where opponents of socialism, supported by outside forces, are, by stirring up anarchy, seeking to channel events onto a counterrevolutionary course. As was noted at the latest plenary meeting of the Central Committee of the Polish United Workers' Party, the very foundations of the socialist state in Poland are in jeopardy.

At present, the Polish comrades are engaged in redressing the critical situation. They are striving to heighten the Party's action capacity and to tighten links with the working class and the other working people, and are working on a concrete program to restore the health of the Polish economy.

Last December's meeting of leaders of the Warsaw Treaty countries in Moscow rendered Poland important political support. It showed clearly that the Polish Communists, the Polish working class, and the working people of that country can firmly rely on their friends and allies. We will not abandon fraternal socialist Poland in its hour of need—rather, we will firmly back it.

For the events in Poland show once again how important it is for the Party, for the strengthening of its leading role, to pay close heed to the voice of the masses, resolutely to combat all signs of bureaucratic routine and voluntarism, actively to develop socialist democracy, and to conduct a considered and realistic policy in foreign economic relations.

The history of world socialism has seen all sorts of trials. There have been difficult times, and critical situations. But Communists have always courageously faced the attacks of the adversary, and have invariably won. This is how it has been in the past and this is how it is going to be in the future. And let no one doubt our common determination to secure our interests and to defend the socialist gains of the peoples....

DEVELOPMENT OF RELATIONS WITH THE NEWLY FREE COUNTRIES

...Imperialism launched a real, undeclared war against the Afghan revolution. This also created a direct threat to the security of our own southern frontier. In the circumstances, we were compelled to render the military aid asked for by that friendly country.

The plans of Afghanistan's enemies have collapsed. The considered policy of the People's Democratic Party and the Government of Afghanistan headed by Comrade Babrak Karmal, faithful to the national interests, has strengthened the people's power.

As for the Soviet military contingent, we will be prepared to withdraw it with the agreement of the Afghan Government. But before this is done, the infiltration of counterrevolutionary gangs into Afghanistan must be completely stopped—which must be secured in accords between Afghanistan and its neighbors. Dependable guarantees are required for there being no new intervention. Such is the fundamental position of the Soviet Union, and we keep to it firmly.

The revolution in Iran, which was a major event on the international scene in recent years, is of a specific nature. However complex and contradictory, it is essentially an anti-imperialist revolution, though reaction both within the country and abroad is seeking to change this aspect of it.

The people of Iran are looking for their own road to freedom and prosperity. We sincerely wish them success, and are prepared to develop good relations with that country on the principles of equality and, of course, reciprocity....

Comrades, an important place in the Soviet Union's relations with the newly free countries is, of course, accorded to our cooperation with India. We welcome the increasing role played by that large country in international affairs. Our ties with it continue to expand. In both our countries, Soviet-Indian friendship has become a deep-rooted popular tradition.

As a result of the recent negotiations in Delhi with Prime Minister Indira Gandhi and other Indian leaders, the entire range of Soviet-Indian relations has been taken substantially further.

Joint action with peaceful and independent India will continue to be one of the important areas of Soviet foreign relations....

RELATIONS WITH CAPITALIST STATES...

Comrades, in the period under review the USSR continued to follow Lenin's policy of peaceful coexistence and mutually beneficial cooperation with capitalist states, while firmly repulsing the aggressive designs of imperialism.

A further aggravation of the general crisis of capitalism was witnessed during these years. To be sure, capitalism has not stopped developing. But it is immersed in what is already the third economic recession of the past ten years....

The difficulties experienced by capitalism also affect its policy, including foreign policy. The struggle over the basic issues of the capitalist countries' foreign policy course has grown more bitter. Visibly more active of late are the opponents of detente, of limiting armaments, and of improving relations with the Soviet Union and other socialist countries....

It is universally recognized that in many ways the international situation depends on the policy of the USSR and the USA. As we see it, the state of relations between them at present, and the acuteness of the international problems requiring a solution, necessitate a dialogue, and an active dialogue at that, at all levels. We are prepared to hold such a dialogue.

Experience shows that the crucial link here is meetings at summit level. This was true yesterday and is still true today.

The USSR wants normal relations with the USA. There is simply no other sensible approach, from the point of view of the interests of both our nations and of humanity as a whole....

DOCUMENT 23

CPSU Letter to the Polish United Workers' Party Central Committee

12 June 1981

Editor's commentary: In June 1981, the CPSU Central Committee forwarded to the Polish United Workers' Party (PUWP) Central Committee an open letter that constituted a not-so-veiled threat: if the Polish house were not put in order soon and Solidarity activism in Polish society not halted, the consequences to Poland would be catastrophic. Although this was not the first warning that the Soviet Union gave to Poland, it was the most ominous. It focused on all the past errors of the PUWP that contributed to the rise of such a grassroots phenomenon as Solidarity and implied that any further retreat in the face of the "enemy" could lead to Warsaw Pact intervention.

Dear comrades! The Central Committee of the CPSU addresses this letter to you . . . deeply wor-

---

"To the Central Committee of the Polish United Workers' Party," *TASS,* 12 June 1981, as reported in *Foreign Broadcast Information Service,* Soviet Union (Washington, DC: *n.p.,* 12 June 1981), pp. F1–F4, *excerpts.*

ried about the destinies of socialism in Poland, about Poland as a free independent state.

Our letter is motivated by our comradely interest in the affairs of the party of Polish communists, the entire fraternal Polish people [and] socialist Poland. . . . Soviet and Polish communists stood shoulder to shoulder in the battle against Nazism, were together throughout all the post-war years. Our party [and the] Soviet people helped their Polish comrades build a new life, and we cannot be but alarmed that a mortal danger is threatening today the revolutionary gains of the Polish people.

We will say it frankly: Some trends in the development of the Polish People's Republic, especially in the field of ideological and economic policy of its former leadership, were a source of our concern for . . . a number of years. In full conformity with the spirit of the relations which have taken shape between the CPSU and PUWP, the Polish leaders were told about this in the course of talks at summit level and other meetings. Regrettably, these friendly warnings, just as the sharply critical pronouncements within the PUWP itself, were not taken into consideration and were even ignored. As a result a deep crisis has broken out in Poland, which has encompassed the entire political and economic life of the country.

We met with full understanding the change in the leadership of the PUWP, the striving to rectify the crude mistakes connected with the violation of the laws of building socialism [and] to restore the confidence of the masses . . . in the party and to strengthen socialist democracy. From the very first days of the crisis we considered it important that the party should resolutely repulse the attempts by the enemies of socialism, to take advantage of the difficulties, which have arisen in their far-reaching aims.

But this was not done. Endless concessions to the anti-socialist forces and their solicitations have brought about a situation in which the PUWP was retreating step by step under the onslaught of the internal counter-revolution, which relies on the support of imperialist subversive centers from abroad.

Today the situation is not just dangerous. It has brought the country to the critical point. It is impossible to assess it otherwise. The enemies of socialist Poland are not making any particular effort to conceal their intentions. They are engaged in a struggle for power, and are already capturing it. They are gaining control of one position after another. The counter-revolution uses as its strike force the extremist wing of Solidarity, drawing by deception the workers who joined that trade union association into a criminal conspiracy against the people's power. The wave of anti-communism and anti-Sovietism is mounting. The imperialist forces are making ever more brazen attempts to interfere in Polish affairs.

The extremely serious danger which is hanging over socialism in Poland is a threat also to the very existence of the independent Polish state. If the worst were to happen and the enemies of socialism seized power, were Poland deprived of defence by the socialist community, the greedy hands of the imperialists would immediately reach out to it, and who could then guarantee the independence, sovereignty and borders of Poland as a state? Nobody....

We would like to make special mention of the fact that in recent months counter-revolutionary forces have been actively spreading all sorts of anti-Soviet fabrications aimed at eliminating the fruit of the work done by our parties, at reviving nationalistic, anti-Soviet sentiments among various sections of... Polish society. These slanderers and liars stop at nothing. They are even trying to assure that the Soviet Union "plunders" Poland. And this is being said notwithstanding the fact that the Soviet Union gave and continues giving enormous additional material aid to Poland at this difficult time.... This is being said about a country, which by its supplies of oil, gas, ore and cotton at prices from 30 to 50 percent lower than world [market] prices, actually nourishes the main branches of Polish industry.

Esteemed comrades! In addressing this letter to you, we proceed not only from our concern about the situation in fraternal Poland, about the conditions and prospects for further Soviet-Polish cooperation. We are no less concerned, in common with the other fraternal parties, about the fact that the offensive by the hostile anti-socialist forces in the Polish People's Republic threatens the interests of the whole of our community, its cohesion, integrity and security of borders. Yes, our common security. The imperialist reaction, which supports and encourages the Polish counter-revolutionaries, does not conceal its hopes to sharply change... the balance of forces in Europe and in the world in their favour.

The crisis in Poland is actively used by imperialism to slander the socialist system, the ideals and principles of socialism, and is used for fresh attacks against the international communist movement.

So, a historical responsibility rests on the PUWP not only for the destiny of its homeland, its independence and progress, [and] for the cause of socialism in Poland. You, comrades, shoulder enormous responsibility also for the common interests of the socialist community.

We hold that there is still the possibility to prevent the worst, to prevent a national catastrophe. There are many honest and staunch communists in the PUWP who are ready to struggle for the ideals of Marxism-Leninism, for [an] independent Poland. There are many people in Poland, who are dedicated to the cause of socialism. The working class... even those who were drawn by deception into the machinations of the enemy, will in the long run follow the party.

The point is to mobilize all the healthy forces of society to repulse the class enemy, to struggle against the counter-revolution. And this requires in the first place revolutionary determination of the party itself, its activists and leadership. Yes, leadership. Time is not waiting. The party can and must find the strength in itself to change the course of events and... before the 9th Congress of the PUWP direct them into the necessary channel.

We would like to be confident that the Central Committee of the party of communists of fraternal Poland will prove to be equal to its historical responsibility.

We want to assure you, dear comrades, that in these difficult days, as was always the case in the past, the Central Committee of the CPSU, all Soviet communists and the entire Soviet people [sympathize] with your struggle. Our stand was clearly expressed by the statement by Comrade L. I. Brezhnev at the 26th Congress of the CPSU: "We will not abandon fraternal, socialist Poland in its hour of need, we will stand by it!"

DOCUMENT 24

Solidarity's Message to the Workers of Eastern Europe and the Soviet Response

September 1981

Editor's commentary: The crisis in Poland had dragged on for more than a year when the Soviets responded to Solidarity's First National Congress, where calls were made for strikes to be staged in Eastern Europe and the Soviet Union. Within three months, martial law was imposed by General Wojciech Jaruzelski, who presented himself as the "savior" of Polish sovereignty at a critical moment in Polish history.

Warsaw Radio, 9 September 1981, as translated and transcribed in *Foreign Broadcast Information Service*, Eastern Europe (Washington, DC: *n.p.*, 10 September 1981), p. G1; and Warsaw Radio, 18 September 1981, as translated and transcribed in *Foreign Broadcast Information Service*, Soviet Union (Washington, DC: 18 September 1981), pp. F1–F2.

MESSAGE TO THE WORKING PEOPLE OF EASTERN EUROPE

Delegates assembled in Gdansk at the first...Solidarity congress send workers of Albania, Bulgaria, Czechoslovakia, GDR, Romania, Hungary and all nations of the Soviet Union greetings and expressions of support. As the first independent trade union in our postwar history, we are profoundly aware of the fact that we share the same fate. We assure you that despite lies disseminated in your countries, we are an authentic representative organ of workers with 10 million members, an organ that was created as a result of workers' strikes.

Our goal is to struggle to improve the lives of all working people. We support those of you who have decided to embark on the difficult path of struggle for a free union movement. We believe that it will not be long now before our representatives will be able to meet your representatives in order to exchange their experiences as unionists.

THE SOVIET RESPONSE

Stanislaw Kania, first secretary of the [PUWP] Central Committee and Wojciech Jaruzelski, chairman of the Council of Ministers, received Soviet Ambassador Boris Aristov, who on behalf of the highest party and state leadership of the USSR said that the CPSU Central Committee and the Soviet Government are forced to draw the attention of the [PUWP] Central Committee and the Government of the Polish People's Republic to the growth of anti-Sovietism in Poland, which has increased to such an extent that it has reached dangerous limits.

The facts testify that an acute and unbridled campaign against the Soviet Union and its foreign and domestic policy is...being extensively waged in the country and that it is going unpunished. These are not isolated, irresponsible attacks but the coordinated action of enemies of socialism with a precisely determined political thrust. Their main goal is to smear and slander the first socialist state in the world and the very idea of socialism, to arouse enmity and hatred among the Poles toward the Soviet Union and Soviet people, to break the bonds of fraternal friendship linking our peoples and as a result to tear Poland from the socialist community and to liquidate socialism in Poland.

The anti-Soviet campaign is penetrating increasingly deeply into different spheres of the country's social life, including ideology, culture, and the system of education.... The history of relations between our countries is being sharply distorted. Fierce propaganda against the Soviet Union is to be discerned on the pages of various publications, on cinema screens and on theatrical stages.... It is to be heard openly in public speeches to mass audiences by the ringleaders of KSS-KOR [Social Self-Defense Committee], the Confederation for an Independent Poland and Solidarity.

The first round of the [Solidarity] trade union congress in essence became a platform from which slanders and insults were directed at our state. An outrageous provocation was the so-called message to the working people of Eastern Europe, adopted in Gdansk. Anti-Soviet forces continue to sully the memory of Soviet soldiers who in the hundreds of thousands gave their lives for the freedom and independence of the Polish nation. These forces are defiling their graves. Threats are appearing against soldiers of Soviet Army units, which are standing guard over the western boundaries of the socialist community, of which the Polish People's Republic is also a part.

The antisocialist forces are...evoking an atmosphere of extreme nationalism in Poland, giving it a distinctly anti-Soviet character, while the scale of intensity and degree of hostility of the current anti-Soviet campaign in Poland is taking on anti-Soviet characteristics which are kindled in some imperialist states.

This cannot but give rise to this question in our country: Why, on the part of official author-ities in Poland, have no decisive steps been taken up to now to put an end to the hostile campaign against the USSR, with which People's Poland is linked by friendly relations and alliance obligations? This stand even contradicts the Constitution of the Polish People's Republic, where the principle of strengthening friendship and cooperation with the Soviet Union is written.

We do not know of one single case of instigators of anti-Soviet provocations meeting with a sharp reaction from the authorities and being punished.

What is more, they are being given access to hold meetings...; the mass media are being made available; and technical means are allocated, although it is known in advance for what purposes they will be used. More than once we drew the attention of the leadership of the [PUWP] and the Government of the Polish People's Republic to the rising tide of anti-Sovietism in Poland. We spoke about this during the meeting in Moscow in March, and in April in Warsaw. We wrote about this with complete openness in the letter of the CPSU Central Committee on 5 June. We also talked about it during the meeting in the Crimea in August of this year....

The Soviet people, who made enormous sacrifices in the name of the liberation of Poland from fascist bondage and who unselfishly helped and are helping your country, have a full moral right to demand that an end be put to the anti-Soviet impudence in the Polish People's Republic.

The CPSU Central Committee and the Soviet Government consider that further tolerance of any...anti-Sovietism causes tremendous damage to Polish-Soviet relations and is in direct contradiction with the [allied] commitments...taken on by Poland, and to the vital interests of the Polish people. We expect that the leadership of the [PUWP] and the Government of the Polish People's Republic will without delay take resolute and radical steps in order to stop the malicious anti-Soviet propaganda and acts which are hostile to the Soviet Union.

DOCUMENT 25

Jaruzelski Announcement of Martial Law in Poland and TASS Reaction

13 and 14 December 1981

Editor's commentary: On 13 December 1981, after nearly a year and a half of the Solidarity crisis, which had precipitated an incendiary situation in Poland, General Wojciech Jaruzelski, head of the Polish government and Communist party, declared a state of emergency which lasted nineteen months and caused the internment of hundreds of Solidarity activists. The announcement came after a new series of strikes and demonstrations were called for by Solidarity, a situation which would have further paralyzed a Polish economy already seriously damaged.

The greater part of the exhausted Polish population greeted the announcement of martial law with equanimity, as another harsh winter approached and depleted stocks of food and fuel promised no happy holiday season. To no one's surprise, the Soviets, who had been manipulating the situation in Poland for many months and implicitly threatening intervention, greeted the announcement warmly and emphasized especially Jaruzelski's guarantees to maintain a close Soviet-Polish alliance and to fulfill all Polish obligations to the Warsaw Pact.

JARUZELSKI SPEECH (13 DECEMBER)

Citizens of the Polish People's Republic. I turn to you today as a soldier and as the head of the Polish Government. I turn to you in matters of supreme importance. Our country has found itself at the edge of an abyss. The achievements of many generations, the house erected from Pol-

---

Warsaw Radio, 13 December 1981; and TASS, 14 December 1981, as transcribed in *Foreign Broadcast Information Service*, Soviet Union (Washington, DC: *n.p.*, 14 December 1981), pp. F2–F9, *excerpts.*

ish ashes, is being ruined. The structures of the state are ceasing to function. New blows are being struck every day at the dying economy. Our living conditions are imposing on people an increasingly greater burden. Lines of painful division are running through every work enterprise and through many Polish homes. The atmosphere of endless conflicts, of misunderstandings and of hatred is sowing psychological devastation and injuring the traditions of tolerance. Strikes, strike readiness and protest actions have become the norm. Even school children are being dragged into it.

Yesterday evening many public buildings were occupied. Exhortations for a physical settling of accounts with the "Reds," with people who hold different views, are being made. Acts of terrorism, of threats, of mob trials and also of direct coercion abound. The wave of impudent crimes, of assaults and break-ins is sweeping the country. Fortunes amounting to millions are being accrued by economic underground sharks and are growing. Chaos and demoralization have assumed the proportions of a disaster.

The nation has come to the end of its psychological endurance. Many people are beginning to despair. Now it is not days but hours that separate us from a national catastrophe. Honesty compels one to ask the question: Did things have to come to this?

In assuming the office of chairman of the Council of Ministers, I believed that we could lift ourselves up. Have we thus done everything to stop the spiral of the crisis? History will assess our activities. There have been errors, and we are drawing conclusions from them. Above all, however, the past months have been a busy time for the government, a time of wrestling with enormous difficulties.

Unfortunately, however, the national economy has been turned into an arena for political struggle. A deliberate torpedoing of government activities has brought about a situation in which results are not commensurate with the work put in with our efforts. We cannot be said to lack good will, moderation and patience. Sometimes there has been, perhaps, even too much of it....

The self-preservation instinct of the nation must be heard. Adventurists must have their hands tied before they push the homeland into the abyss of fratricide.

Citizens. Great is the burden of responsibility that falls on me at this dramatic moment in Polish history. It is my duty to take this responsibility. Poland's future is at stake—the future for which my generation fought and for which it gave the best years of its life.

I announce that today a Military Council of National Salvation has been established. Today at midnight, the Council of State, in accordance with the Constitution, introduced martial law throughout the country. I want everyone to understand the motives and the aims of our action. We are not striving for a military coup, for a military dictatorship. The nation has enough strength, enough wisdom to develop an efficient democratic system of socialist rule. In such a system the Armed Forces will be able to remain where they belong—in the barracks. No Polish problem can, in the long run, be solved through force. The Military Council for National Salvation is not replacing constitutional organs of power. Its sole task is the protection of legal order in the country and the creation of executive guarantees that will make it possible to restore order and discipline. This is the last path we can take to initiate the extrication of the country from the crisis, to save the country from disintegration....

In this difficult moment I address myself to our socialist allies and friends. We greatly value their trust and constant aid. The Polish-Soviet alliance is, and will remain, the cornerstone of the Polish raison d'etat, the guarantee of the inviolability of our borders.

Poland is, and will remain, a lasting link in the Warsaw Pact, an unfailing member of the socialist community of nations....

TASS RESPONSE (14 DECEMBER)

Events of great importance have taken place in the Polish People's Republic. In accordance with the provisions of the Constitution the Council of State of the Polish People's Republic has introduced martial law throughout the country and a Martial Council for National Redemption has been established with W. Jaruzelski at the head.

The head of the Martial Council for National Redemption stated that the measures taken are designed to create conditions for taking Poland out of a crisis situation, to protect legality and to restore public order.

All these steps taken in Poland, are of course, its internal affair. A different interpretation of these events, made by certain circles in the West, can only be regarded as an attempt to interfere in affairs which lie within the competence of the Poles only.

It is no secret to anyone that the enemies of socialism in Poland, aiming to overthrow the existing social system and deliberately deepening the crisis in the country and disorganizing its economy, have jeopardized the independence of the Polish People's Republic.

These forces strove by all means to undermine the fraternal friendship between the Polish and Soviet peoples, friendship which shaped up in the joint struggle against fascism and which received all-round development in the course of the subsequent decades. By putting forward an anti-socialist, counter-revolutionary programme they created by their actions a direct threat to the fulfillment by Poland of its allied commitments under the Warsaw Treaty, which directly affected the interests of security of all states, parties to this treaty. It is no accident that the enemies of independent socialist Poland inside the country have the support of certain external circles in the West.

TASS is authorized to state that the Soviet leadership, all the Soviet people closely follow the events in Poland and around it. They have received with a feeling of satisfaction W. Jaruzelski's statement that the Polish-Soviet alliance has been and remains the cornerstone of Polish state interest, a guarantee of the inviolability of the Polish frontiers and that Poland has been and remains an unbreakable part of the Warsaw Treaty, a member of the socialist community of states.

The Soviet people wish the fraternal Polish people success in solving the difficult problems before their country, problems of historical importance for the destinies of the Polish state, to reliably ensure the further development of the Polish People's Republic along the path of socialism and peace.

DOCUMENT 26

TASS on U.S. Sanctions

30 December 1981

Editor's commentary: In response to the declaration of martial law in Poland on 13 December 1981, which formally ended the Solidarity era, the United States imposed trade sanctions on both Poland and the Soviet Union. The Soviet response to these sanctions is particularly angry and filled with counteraccusations. While it is difficult to tell how these sanctions affected the USSR, it is clear that the move affected negatively the Polish economy, accelerating the precipitous decline that had begun in the mid-1970s and continued through to the end of the 1980s.

The U.S. administration has undertaken a provocative act with the aim of still further poisoning the international climate, increasing tension,

---

TASS, 30 December 1981, as transcribed in *Foreign Broadcast Information Service*, Soviet Union (Washington, DC: *n.p.*, 30 December 1981), pp. F1–F2, *excerpts.*

making confrontation harsher and pursuing a harder militarist line in foreign policy.

Enraged by the collapse of their plans for the restoration of capitalism in Poland by the hands of their agents from among the counterrevolutionary rabble of KSS-KOR [Social Self-Defense Committee], Confederation for an Independent Poland and Solidarity, the Washington rulers are hastening to whip up to the maximum a campaign of hatred toward the countries of socialism, primarily toward the USSR, to undermine the foundations of Soviet-American relations, which have been worked out by tremendous efforts, and to reduce these relations to a minimum.

President Reagan has published a statement in which he announced the introduction of a whole range of unilateral discriminatory measures against the Soviet Union—from stopping Aeroflot flights to the United States to reviewing bilateral Soviet-American relations in the field of trade and scientific-technical cooperation, agreements which have been signed by the U.S. Government.

In order to justify this unprecedented crude diktat—absolutely impermissible in generally accepted international practice with regard to a sovereign state—the leader of the U.S. administration resorted to direct forgery and lies by asserting that the Soviet Union allegedly "interfered" in Polish affairs and bears "direct responsibility" for the situation which has come about in Poland.

The White House boss clearly needed these unsubstantiated accusations in order to distort generally known facts which bear witness to the fact that the trials which have fallen to the lot of the Polish people are primarily the result of direct interference in Poland's affairs by American imperialism. It is American imperialism which has carried out subversive activity against the Polish People's Republic through the CIA. It is precisely the United States which reared the Polish counterrevolution, incited it to unleash a fratricidal war that would plunge Poland into an abyss of chaos and lead it to national catastrophe.

None other than Washington rendered financial and other aid to the KSS-KOR members, the "Confederates" and Solidarity extremists, infiltrated CIA agents into these organizations, and through the Free Europe and Voice of America radio stations daily directed the provocative activity of counterrevolutionary antisocialist forces in undermining the people's power.

The measures taken in the Polish People's Republic with the aim of creating conditions for coming out of the state of crisis, in defense of legality and the restoration of public order are its own internal affair. The blind rage of the Washington administration about these legitimate actions of sovereign Poland show only that Washington has lost every vestige of common sense. It has reached the point at which Reagan, having without foundation at the beginning of his statement accused the Soviet Union of "interference" in Polish affairs, which is pure fiction, at the end of his statement demands that the USSR...should intervene in Poland with the aim of canceling the measures taken by the Polish People's Republic Government to stabilize and normalize the situation in that country. At the same time, Reagan threatened further acts of blackmail and pressure....

The White House's latest attempt to embark again on the long since bankrupt path of threats and blackmail can therefore be regarded as nothing other than a deliberate attempt by top U.S. ruling circles to worsen even more the international situation, to throw the world back to the gloomy times of the "cold war" and to untie the hands of U.S. imperialism so that it can pursue a militarist policy aimed at achieving world domination.

The White House stubbornly refused to come to terms with the indisputable fact that times have changed and that no one can turn back the tides of history. The Reagan administration's adventurist, reckless course is doomed to shameful failure.

DOCUMENT 27

Brezhnev on Sino-Soviet Relations

24 March 1982

Editor's commentary: During a speech in Tashkent, L. I. Brezhnev discussed Soviet plans to improve relations with Asian countries, including India, Japan, and China. It is the Chinese emphasis in this speech that drew the attention of international political analysts. Brezhnev was, in effect, holding out an olive branch to the Chinese Communist party. However, obstacles to normalization of Sino-Soviet relations from the Chinese perspective continued to include Afghanistan, Cambodia (Kampuchea), and Soviet troop levels on the Sino-Soviet frontier, only the last of which the Soviets were willing to discuss at that time and for several years following.

...First, despite the fact that we openly criticized and continue to criticize many aspects of the policy, especially the foreign policy, of the Chinese leadership as being at variance with socialist principles and standards, we have never tried to interfere in the internal life of the People's Republic of China. We did not deny and do not deny now the existence of a socialist social system in China, although Beijing's joining with the policy of imperialists in the world arena contradicts, of course, the interests of socialism.

Second, we have never supported and we do not now support in any form the so-called concept of two Chinas and have fully recognized and continue to recognize the PRC's sovereignty over Taiwan island.

Moscow Television, 24 March 1982, as translated and transcribed in *Foreign Broadcast Information Service*, Soviet Union (Washington, DC: *n.p.*, 25 March 1982), pp. R1–R7, *excerpts.*

Third, there has not been and there is no threat to the People's Republic of China from the Soviet Union. We have not had and do not have any territorial claims to the PRC and we are ready to continue talks on existing border questions for the purpose of reaching mutually acceptable decisions at any moment. We are also ready to discuss the question of possible measures to strengthen mutual trust in the area of the Soviet-Chinese frontiers.

Fourth, we remember well the time when the Soviet Union and People's China were united by bonds of friendship and comradely cooperation. We have never considered the state of hostility and estrangement between our countries normal. We are prepared to come to terms on measures acceptable to both sides to improve Soviet-Chinese relations on the basis of mutual respect for each other's interests, noninterference in each other's affairs and mutual benefit—certainly, not to the detriment of third countries—without any preliminary conditions. This refers to economic, scientific, and cultural, as well as political, relations, as the two sides become ready for these or other concrete steps in any of these spheres....

DOCUMENT 28

Joint Soviet-Nicaraguan Communiqué

9 May 1982

Editor's commentary: Moscow's policy of supporting national liberation movements continued to hold a central place in Soviet foreign policy throughout Brezhnev's reign. In the late 1970s Central

---

TASS, 9 May 1982, as transcribed in *Foreign Broadcast Information Service,* Soviet Union (Washington, DC: 10 May 1982), pp. K2–K4, *excerpts.*

America for the first time presented unprecedented opportunities for the extension of Soviet influence with the successful anti-Somoza revolution in Nicaragua and civil war in El Salvador. The joint Soviet-Nicaraguan communiqué issued at the end of a visit by Sandinista leader Daniel Ortega to Moscow included an agreement for the Soviets to provide important economic and technical assistance to the Sandinista regime, which continued to fight a counterinsurgency supported by the United States.

A state delegation of the Republic of Nicaragua, led by Commandante of the Revolution Daniel Ortega Saavedra, member of the national leadership of the Sandinista Front of National Liberation (FSLN), coordinator of the guiding council of the Government of National Reconstruction, stayed in the Soviet Union on an official friendly visit from May 4–9, 1982, at the invitation of the CPSU Central Committee, the Presidium of the USSR Supreme Soviet and the Soviet Government....

The sides emphasized the importance of contacts between the CPSU and the FSLN, and expressed satisfaction with the level of cooperation between the two parties, and a wish to continue to broaden and deepen these relations.

The successful development of trade-economic, scientific-technical and cultural contacts between the Soviet Union and the Republic of Nicaragua was noted, and the striving of the two countries to further develop the mutually beneficial cooperation was emphasized.

An inter-governmental agreement on further development of economic and technical cooperation as well as protocols envisaging the deliveries of machinery and equipment from the USSR to Nicaragua and rendering of assistance in the development of hydropower and mining industries, agriculture, communications, and other branches of the Nicaraguan economy were signed during the visit....

The Soviet side expressed resolute solidarity with the efforts by the heroic Nicaraguan people to attain their goals, understanding of the difficult tasks facing Nicaragua, and wishes of successes in their solution. It stressed the inalienable right of the Nicaraguan people to decide the fate of their country on their own in an atmosphere free from outside pressure and threats.

Daniel Ortega thanked the Soviet peoples for this solidarity and support.

An exchange of opinions on international issues revealed the community of the sides' views on major problems of the present-day international situation. It was characterized as complicated and causing serious concern. The cause of that is the growth of the aggressiveness of the forces of imperialism and reaction led by the United States of America, their attempts to undermine the process of detente, spiral the arms race and kindle enmity and mistrust among the peoples.

Of particular danger are the US large-scale military preparations, including the deployment of military contingents specially intended for interference in the internal affairs of countries which Washington includes at will into the sphere of its "vital interests."

In the Western Hemisphere, like in other regions, imperialism and its accomplices in a bid to suppress the peoples' legitimate striving for independence and independent development deliberately whip up tension, resort to provocations and subversive actions.

The sides strongly demanded that the United States discontinue threats against Nicaragua, Cuba and other nations in Central America and the Caribbean. They denounced the American interference in El Salvador, the U.S. support for the anti-people regime in that country, favoured a political solution of the problem through ne-

gotiations, and voiced their solidarity with the patriotic, democratic and revolutionary forces in Latin America.

The Nicaraguan side informed the Soviet side about its foreign policy initiatives within the framework of the policy of non-alignment, and declared that it is applying constant efforts in the struggle for peace, detente and international security....

The sides denounced the imperialist policy of economic sanctions, trade and economic blockades and other discriminatory measures which disrupt normal ties and cooperation between states.

The Soviet Union and the Republic of Nicaragua reaffirmed their determination to work actively for the lessening of international tension, and settlement of conflict situations and disputes in various parts of the world through negotiations on a fair basis.

Both sides expressed profound satisfaction with the talks held in an atmosphere of cordiality and complete mutual understanding, and pointed out that the results of the visit by the Nicaraguan state delegation are a new important contribution to strengthening and developing relations of friendship and cooperation between the Soviet Union and the Republic of Nicaragua.

Daniel Ortega, on behalf of the national leadership of the Sandinista National Liberation Front and the guiding council of the National Reconstruction Government of the Republic of Nicaragua, invited General Secretary of the CPSU Central Committee, President of the Presidium of the USSR Supreme Soviet Leonid Brezhnev to pay an official friendly visit to Nicaragua. The invitation was accepted with gratitude.

Suggested Readings

Amalrik, Andrei: *Will the Soviet Union Survive Until 1984?* (New York: Harper & Row, 1970).

Anderson, Richard D.: "Soviet Decisionmaking and Poland," *Problems of Communism* (March–April 1982), pp. 22–36.

Arbatov, Georgii, and William Oltmans: *The Soviet Viewpoint* (New York: Dodd, Mead, 1981).

Blasier, Cole: *The Giant's Rival: The USSR and Latin America* (Pittsburgh, PA: University of Pittsburgh Press, 1983).

Breslauer, George W.: *Khrushchev and Brezhnev as Leaders: Building Authority in Soviet Politics* (Winchester, MA: Allen & Unwin, 1982).

Caldwell, Lawrence T., and William Diebold: *Soviet-*

American Relations in the 1980s: Superpower Politics and East-West Trade (New York: McGraw-Hill, 1981).

Conquest, Robert: "The Limits of Detente," *Foreign Affairs* (Summer 1968), pp. 733–742.

Dawisha, Karen: *The Kremlin and the Prague Spring* (Berkeley, CA: University of California Press, 1984).

Donaldson, Robert H. (ed.): *The Soviet Union in the Third World: Successes and Failures* (Boulder, CO: Westview, 1981).

Edmonds, Robin: *Soviet Foreign Policy: The Brezhnev Years* (New York: Oxford University Press, 1983).

Ellison, Herbert J. (ed.). *The Sino-Soviet Conflict: A Global Perspective* (Seattle, WA: University of Washington Press, 1982).

Gati, Charles: *Hungary and the Soviet Bloc* (Durham, NC: Duke University Press, 1986).

Gelman, Harry: *The Brezhnev Politburo and the Decline of Detente* (Ithaca, NY: Cornell University Press, 1984).

Golan, Galia: *Yom Kippur and After: The Soviet Union and the Middle East Crisis* (New York: Cambridge University Press, 1977).

Hammond, Thomas T.: *Red Flag Over Afghanistan: The Communist Coup, the Soviet Invasion, and the Consequences* (Boulder, CO: Westview Press, 1984).

Hyland, William G.: "US-Soviet Relations: the Long Road Back," *Foreign Affairs* (America and the World, 1981), pp. 525–550.

Menon, Rajan.: *Soviet Power and the Third World* (New Haven, CT: Yale University Prtess, 1986).

Ploss, Sidney: *Moscow and the Polish Crisis* (Boulder, CO: Westview, 1986).

Porter, Bruce D.: *The USSR in Third World Conflicts* (New York: Cambridge University Press, 1984).

Remington, Robin A.: *The Warsaw Pact* (Cambridge, MA: MIT Press, 1972).

Rubinstein, Alvin Z.: *Soviet Policy toward Turkey, Iran, and Afghanistan: The Dynamics of Influence* (New York: Praeger, 1982).

Simes, Dimitri K.: *Detente and Conflict: Soviet Foreign Policy, 1972–1977* (Beverly Hills, CA: Sage, 1977).

Ulam, Adam: *Dangerous Relations: The Soviet Union in World Politics 1970–1982* (New York: Oxford University Press, 1983).

Valenta, Jiri: *Soviet Intervention in Czechoslovakia: Anatomy of a Decision* (Baltimore, MD: Johns Hopkins University Press, 1979).

Wolfe, Thomas: *Soviet Power and Europe, 1945–1970* (Baltimore, MD: Johns Hopkins University Press, 1970).

Wozniuk, Vladimir: *From Crisis to Crisis: Soviet-Polish Relations in the 1970s* (Ames, IA: Iowa State University Press, 1987).

Zagoria, Donald S. (ed.): *Soviet Policy in East Asia* (New Haven, CT: Yale University Press, 1982).

CHAPTER SIX

Soviet Foreign Policy under Andropov and Chernenko—Generational Transition (1982–1985)

For several prominent reasons, the legacy of Leonid Brezhnev's eighteen-year rule was to be a great burden for whomever would succeed him as top Soviet leader.

First, Soviet economic growth had perceptibly slowed by the late 1970s and continued to do so through the end of the 1980s. Whereas the growth rate between 1966 and 1970 was a robust 4.9 percent, the following two Five-Year Plans evidenced declines to 3.1 and 2.3 percent respectively.[1] The results of this slowdown included an erosion of living standards, the quality of which had been increasing steadily since the death of Stalin.

Second, the Soviet Union had intervened in a neighboring Muslim country, Afghanistan, to help "defend the gains of socialism" there, a situation that, by November 1982, had become a costly and bloody occupation with no clear victory in sight.

Third, direct Soviet pressure amounting to an indirect intervention in the affairs of Poland during 1980 and 1981 assisted the rollback of gains made by the independent Polish trade union, Solidarity, the first such union in the history of the Soviet bloc. During this time Solidarity led a challenge to "business as usual" by a corrupt and faction-ridden regime which had mismanaged the Polish economy. While Soviet pressure assisted in securing the Soviet position of dominance in Poland in the short term, it also resulted in a long and costly Soviet subsidy of the Polish economy.

---

[1] See Timothy J. Colton, *The Dilemma of Reform in the Soviet Union*, rev. ed. (New York: Council on Foreign Relations, 1986), pp. 34–35.

Fourth, the result of both the Afghan and Polish situations was to provide the new American administration, led by Ronald Reagan, who was sworn into office in January 1981, with the political ammunition to embark on an unprecedented arms buildup that threatened to eclipse the great Soviet military achievements of the 1970s, during which time the USSR had acquired strategic parity in certain areas and superiority in others. The Soviet gains which had been made during the heyday of *detente* now seemed fragile and in jeopardy.

It was in this difficult and precarious situation that an ailing Yuri V. Andropov took the reins of party leadership in November 1982, only to be replaced a short 14 months later by another aging member of the Politburo, Konstantin U. Chernenko, who had spent his career as a close associate of Brezhnev.

Andropov seemed to be the right man for the difficult dual task of getting the Soviet system moving again and forcing the West to recognize and accept the achievements of Soviet power. Early in the 1950s, and during the Hungarian "counterrevolution" of November 1956, he had been Soviet ambassador to Hungary. Therefore, it can be presumed that he played an important role in the restoration of the Soviet-sponsored system in Hungary after Soviet tanks crushed the uprising. He was appointed a CPSU secretary in 1962 and then head of the Committee for State Security (KGB) in 1967, where he continued to serve until his appointment to the General Secretaryship, having also been brought into the Politburo along the way in 1973.[1]

Chernenko, on the other hand, apparently owed his entire career to the political patronage of Brezhnev. His record was rather unremarkable, and until Brezhnev's death, he had been known more for lighting his patron's cigarettes than for anything substantive in terms of policy or administration.[2] While the choice of Andropov over Chernenko surprised some Western observers, it indicated clearly that the Soviet oligarchy required a strong-willed and discipline-oriented leader to assist in getting a stagnating system going once again during what was widely perceived as a difficult leadership succession phase in Soviet politics. The subsequent selection of Chernenko to lead the party upon Andropov's death in February 1984, as Stephen Cohen suggests (in this chapter's opening reading), was likely a compromise with old-line party bureaucrats: a last hurrah for the septuagenarian Brezhnevite remnants in positions of party authority. In any case, Chernenko's reign did not even surpass Andropov's brief tenure—he passed away in March 1985.

Apart from the brevity of the Andropov-Chernenko interregnum, the salient characteristic of this transition period was its continuity, in general terms, with the Brezhnev era. This is not to say that there were no innovations. It was Andropov who laid considerable stress on greater social discipline at home in the attempt to address the serious shortcomings of the Soviet economy. He also intensified a large-scale propaganda offensive of Soviet foreign policy toward Western Europe in the attempt to forestall deployment of Western intermediate-range nuclear forces (INF) to counter the large buildup of Soviet INF which had taken place in the 1970s.[3] It was also during the Andropov administration that proposals were first floated for serious negotiations on the INF issue (Chapter 6, document 1), eventually culminating in the resolution of the issue by Gorbachev in 1987.

However, it was also during this period preceding the generational transition that U.S.-Soviet relations reached their lowest point since the 1960s. Perhaps no two events more suc-

---

[1]For Andropov's official biography, see *Pravda*, 13 November 1982, p. 1.

[2]For Chernenko's official biography, see *Pravda*, 14 February 1984, p. 1.

[3]On Andropov's innovations, see Zhores A. Medvedev, *Andropov* (New York: Penguin, 1984), pp. 173–194.

cinctly expressed the quality of these relations from 1982 to 1985 than the shooting down of Korean Airlines passenger flight 007 by Soviet forces and Ronald Reagan's characterization of the Soviet Union as an "evil empire" (Chapter 6, document 2 and 3). In retrospect, it seems that toward the end of the Chernenko period, the Soviet leadership was considering the formulation of a game plan to move forward positively in the resolution of many international problems plaguing the Soviet leadership and to begin to repair the damage which many years of neglect and corruption under Brezhnev had done to the domestic economy. It was with eager anticipation of the new possibilities which a younger generation of Soviet leaders might offer that both American and Soviet observers greeted the news of the ancien regime's passing when Chernenko died in March 1985.

Why There Was No Andropov Era

Stephen F. Cohen

Within a year after Yuri Andropov succeeded Leonid Brezhnev as Soviet leader, and well before his death, it was already clear that the "Andropov Era" so widely heralded in the Western press would not unfold.

Most Western commentators predicted that after the growing problems and weak leadership of Brezhnev's last years, Andropov would become a "strongman," perhaps even ruling through the K.G.B., which he headed for fifteen years, and would change Soviet domestic and foreign policy in significant ways. Some initial developments under Andropov seemed to support that expectation: new high-level appointments; more energetic diplomatic overtures toward China and the United States, and toward a resolution of the war in Afghanistan; a surge of reformist rhetoric in the central press; and highly publicized campaigns to fight official corruption, restore "labor discipline" and increase the authority of plant managers.

But after a year, little had changed, certainly far less than during the first year of Khrushchev's or Brezhnev's leadership. Andropov's three domestic campaigns seemed to be petering out, while the Soviet press lapsed into its more self-satisfied tone. Meanwhile, the Soviet Union remained mired militarily in Afghanistan, deadlocked in negotiations with the Chinese and embroiled in a worsening confrontation with the United States.

Nor did Andropov become a strongman, even though in June 1983 he finally attained the ceremonial office of President. Despite several vacancies, only one new voting member was appointed to the Politburo. It was still composed largely of Brezhnev's people, not Andropov's. The same was true of the hundreds of top bosses who actually run the Soviet system, from Moscow ministers to regional party secretaries. The overwhelming majority remained Brezhnev men, aged symbols of unsolved problems and complacent leadership.

Moreover, Andropov, who sought to contrast himself to the long-enfeebled Brezhnev by being a visibly active leader, virtually disappeared from public life after the Korean airliner catastrophe on September 12, 1983. He did not even appear on the anniversary of the Revolution, on November 5. Unless Andropov was already completely incapacitated, poor health is no explanation. Confronted with foreign policy disasters of the magnitude of the airliner incident, ailing leaders of great states manage at least token appearances to reaffirm their authority. As a result, there was again widespread gossip in Moscow about a forthcoming succession—this time, to Andropov himself.

Thus, whereas we can speak meaningfully of a characteristic Russia of Lenin, Stalin, Khrushchev or even Brezhnev, there was no Andropov's Russia, only persistent signs that there would be none. The reasons involve three little-understood features of Soviet politics today.

First, the office of General Secretary of the Communist Party, the top leadership position, is not so inherently powerful that its occupant automatically becomes a dictator. It took Andropov's predecessors as General Secretary—Stalin, Khrushchev and Brezhnev—five years or more to achieve supremacy. Moreover, each General Secretary after Stalin had exercised less personal power than his predecessor.

The post was particularly weakened under Brezhnev. Still unnerved by their memories of Stalin's capricious terror and Khrushchev's incessant reorganizations, party, state and military bosses opposed the emergence of another strong leader. Brezhnev acquiesced to that sentiment and based his eighteen-year reign on conserva-

Sovieticus: American Perceptions and Soviet Realities (New York: W. W. Norton, 1986), pp. 60–64. Reprinted by permission of W.W. Norton.

tive policies that guaranteed the tenure of those officials, thus enhancing their institutional power. Andropov, therefore, was constrained not simply by the swollen power of the Soviet military, as Washington Sovietologists speculated, but by a more general diffusion of power throughout the system, at the expense of the General Secretary. As the oldest and least healthy man ever to assume the post, Andropov had no chance to revitalize it. Indeed, it is possible he was chosen for that reason.

The second constraint on the leader's power is longstanding policy division in the Soviet political elite. Despite the country's economic problems, for example, Soviet officials are deeply divided among those who believe in muddling through, those who want to restore draconian Stalinist measures and those who urge decentralization. The result has been decades of policy immobilism. Nor is there consensus on international affairs. On the central question of Soviet-American relations, Soviet officials are bitterly split between advocates of cold war with the West as Russia's historical destiny, and proponents of the necessity of detente. Here the result has been decades of erratic policy.

Finally, Andropov's first year was one of relentless confrontations and crises abroad—Poland and Afghanistan, Reagan's anti-Soviet crusade, Lebanon, Central America and the Caribbean. None of them were of Andropov's making, but their result was to redouble every Soviet obstacle to internal change, as international tensions always do. Thus, while American hard-liners insist that cold war is necessary because the Soviet system will never change, their policies make such change almost impossible.

Everything we know about Andropov suggests that he was both reform-minded and politically cautious. Had he lived longer, he might have put his imprint on the Soviet system. Instead, he will be remembered as a transitional figure who opened the door more widely to a younger generation of leaders. Indeed, perhaps the most significant development during Andropov's tenure was the emergence of a new inner circle in charge of government and economic affairs. Composed of Mikhail Gorbachev, Grigory Romanov, Geidar Aliev, Nikolai Ryzhkov and Vladimir Dolgikh, the average age of its members was about 58, a full political generation younger than Brezhnev and Andropov.

Many Western analysts argue that the succession of a new generation of officials throughout the Soviet system will make a major difference in policy. But that generation is also deeply divided between friends and foes of change. And it too will inherit a Soviet Union that increasingly resembles the lumbering bureaucratic Russia of weak czars rather than the dynamic leader-dominated "totalitarianism" of Stalin or of Orwell's *1984*.

(November 19, 1983)

DOCUMENT 1

Arms Reduction Plan

Yuri Andropov

21 December 1982

Editor's commentary: On the occasion of the sixtieth anniversary of the USSR, Yuri Andropov spoke to an audience in the Kremlin concerning the status of Soviet communism and proposed at the same time a four-point arms reduction plan: (1) each side would cut 25 percent of its strategic arsenals, (2) a freeze on levels of nuclear weapons would be instituted, (3) Soviet medium-range missiles would be reduced to the level of French and British

TASS, 21 December 1982, as transcribed in *Foreign Broadcast Information Service*, Soviet Union (Washington, DC: *n.p.*, 21 December 1982), pp. P1–P11, *excerpts*.

medium-range forces, and (4) all tactical and theater nuclear weapons would be eliminated from Europe. The first of these proposals became the kernel from which Gorbachev's 50 percent strategic arms reduction idea grew, leading to the resurrection of serious negotiations regarding the Strategic Arms Reduction Talks (START). It is also interesting to note Andropov's unequivocal rejection of the "zero option" on the INF issue—the eventual solution accepted by both sides in 1987.

...[One] of the main avenues leading to a real scaling down of the threat of nuclear war is that of reaching a Soviet-American agreement on limitation and reduction of strategic nuclear armaments. We approach negotiations of the matter with the utmost responsibility, and seek an honest agreement that will do no damage to either side and will, at the same time, lead to a reduction of the nuclear arsenals.

So far, unfortunately, we see a different approach by the American side. While calling for "radical reductions" in words, what it really has in mind is essentially a reduction of the Soviet strategic potential. For itself, the United States would like to leave a free hand in building up strategic armaments. It is absurd even to think that we can agree to this. It would, of course, suit the Pentagon, but can on no account be acceptable to the Soviet Union and, for that matter, to all those who have a stake in preserving and consolidating peace.

Compare to this the proposals of the USSR. They are based on the principle of preserving parity. We are prepared to reduce our strategic arms by more than 25 per cent. U.S. arms, too, must be reduced accordingly, so that the two states have the same number of strategic delivery vehicles. We also proposed that the number of nuclear warheads should be substantially lowered and that improvement of nuclear weapons should be maximally restricted....

And while the negotiations are under way, we offer what is suggested by common sense: to freeze the strategic arsenals of the two sides. The U.S. government does not want this, and now everyone can understand why: It has embarked on a new, considerable build-up of nuclear armaments.

Washington's attempts to justify this build-up are obviously irrelevant. The allegation of a "lag" behind the USSR which the Americans must close is a deliberate untruth. This has been said more than once. And the talk that new weapons systems, such as the MX missile, are meant "to facilitate disarmament negotiations" is altogether absurd.

No programmes of a further arms build-up will ever force the Soviet Union to make unilateral concessions. We will be compelled to counter the challenge of the American side by deploying corresponding weapons systems of our own—an analogous missile to counter the MX missile, and our own long-range cruise missile, which we are already testing, to counter the U.S. long-range cruise missile.

Those are not threats at all. We are wholly averse to any such course of events, and are doing everything to avoid it. But it is essential that those who shape U.S. policy, as well as the public at large, should be perfectly clear on the real state of affairs. Hence, if the people in Washington really believe that new weapons systems will be a "trump" for the Americans at negotiations, we want them to know that these "trumps" are false. Any policy directed to securing military superiority over the Soviet Union has no future and can only heighten the threat of war....

We consider this important for all regions of the world, and especially for Europe, where a flare-up of any kind may trigger a worldwide explosion.

At present, that continent is beset by a new danger—the prospect of several hundred U.S. missiles being deployed in Western Europe. I have got to say bluntly: This would make peace still more fragile.

As we see it, the peril threatening the European nations, and, for that matter, the nations of the whole world, can be averted. It is definitely possible to save and strengthen peace in Europe—and this without damage to anyone's security. It is, indeed, for this purpose that we have been negotiating with the United States in Geneva for already more than a year on how to limit and reduce nuclear weapons in the European zone.

The Soviet Union is prepared to go very far. As everybody knows, we have suggested an agreement renouncing all types of nuclear weapons—both of medium range and tactical—designed to strike targets in Europe. But this proposal has come up against a solid wall of silence. Evidently, they do not want to accept it, but are afraid to reject it openly. I want to reaffirm again that we have not withdrawn this proposal.

We have also suggested another variant: that the USSR and the NATO countries reduce their medium-range weaponry by more than two-thirds. So far, the United States will not have it. For its part, it has submitted a proposal which, as if in mockery, is called a "zero option." It envisages elimination of all Soviet medium-range missiles not only in the European, but also in the Asiatic part of the Soviet Union, while NATO's nuclear missile arsenal in Europe is to remain intact and may even be increased. Does anyone really think that the Soviet Union can agree to this? It appears that Washington is out to block an agreement and, referring to collapse of the talks, to station its missiles on European soil in any case.

The future will show if this is so. We, for our part, will continue to work for an agreement on a basis that is fair to both sides. We are prepared, among other things to agree that the Soviet Union should retain in Europe only as many missiles as are kept there by Britain and France—and not a single one more. This means that the Soviet Union would reduce hundreds of missiles, including dozens of the latest missiles known in the West as SS-20. In the case of the USSR and the USA this would be really an honest "zero" option as regards medium-range missiles. And if, later, the number of British and French missiles were scaled down, the number of Soviet ones would be additionally reduced by as many.

Along with this there must also be an accord on reducing to equal levels on both sides the number of medium-range nuclear-delivery aircraft stationed in this region by the USSR and the NATO countries.

We call on the other side to accept these clear and fair terms, to take this opportunity while it still exists. But let no one delude himself: We will never let our security or the security of our allies be jeopardized. It would also be a good thing if thought were given to the grave consequences that the stationing of new U.S. medium-range weapons in Europe would entail for all further efforts to limit nuclear armaments in general. In short, the ball is now in the court of the USA....

DOCUMENT 2

TASS Response to President Reagan's "Evil Empire" Speech

9 March 1983

Editor's commentary: The Soviet understanding of the reasons behind Ronald Reagan's now-famous "evil empire" speech given to a national gathering of evangelicals in Florida was not wildly off the mark. TASS saw this as part of an orchestrated program to justify the large increases in military spending, which in fact the Reagan administration had requested from Congress. It also attributed the speech, in part, to Reagan's own virulent anticommunism, which TASS referred to as "lunatic." Such exchanges during the Andropov and Chernenko years marked the lowest point in U.S.-Soviet relations under Reagan.

TASS, 9 March 1983, as transcribed in *Foreign Broadcast Information Service,* Soviet Union (Washington, DC: n.p., 10 March 1983), pp. A1–A2, *excerpts.*

President Reagan made another of his provocative speeches reaffirming once again that the present Washington administration can only think in terms of confrontation and bellicose, lunatic anticommunism.

Addressing the 41st annual convention of the National Evangelical Association in the city of Orlando (the state of Florida), he said he considers communism the source of evil in the modern world. In addition, the White House boss, who in the whole of his lifetime has never opened a book by the classics of Marxism-Leninism, has the cheek to assert that the founders and followers of the great doctrine reject every morality beyond the framework of the class concepts.

Reagan's pathological hatred for socialism and communism caught the attention of the UPI news agency, which noted that his utterances are a revival of the worst rhetoric of the times of the cold war.

At the same time, Reagan's statement came as an expression of the extreme militarism of the present Washington administration and of its reluctance to seek mutually acceptable agreements with the USSR to curb the lethal danger of the arms race for mankind. Admitting that the peoples of the world live in a "perilous age," the White House boss at the same time underscored his determination to "build up America's military might" by spending fresh hundreds of billions of dollars to achieve these ends.

The President admitted that the existence of radical ideological contradictions between socialism and capitalism did not mean that the US [and USSR] had to isolate [themselves] from each other and to give up the search for understanding with the Soviet Union and other socialist countries. He even asserted that he was going to do everything possible "to convince" the Soviet Union of the "peaceful intentions" of the United States. But here, however, Reagan reiterated the so-called "initiatives" of his administration at the strategic arms limitation and reductions talks and those on nuclear arms limitations in Europe, designed to break the existing rough parity of forces in the world, to force the USSR into unilateral disarmament and to achieve a decisive military edge over it....

It is for this reason that Reagan saw fit to "show the path of truth" to the convention's participants and to deliver to them a "lecture" demanding "not to hinder" the administration in its pursuit of the policy of stepping up the arms race. To add insult to injury, Reagan is invoking "religious morality" to try to justify the arms race, pronouncing the buildup of the US military might to be "a good thing."

The White House boss said that the religious workers must oppose those failing to support the administration's efforts designed to make America strong and free. In the process, without taking the trouble of adducing any proof, the President ascribed to the Soviet Union some mythical "aggressive aspirations." The US president's speech came as fresh testimony that the present Washington administration is stubbornly seeking a way out of the changes unfavourable to US imperialism in the modern world, through foreign policy adventures and the arms race....

DOCUMENT 3

Official Statement by Yuri Andropov on KAL 007

September 1983

Editor's commentary: This official statement by the CPSU General Secretary released by TASS on 28 September 1983 was in response to President Reagan's 26 September United Nations address. The hostile tone of this admittedly indignant statement is explained as a result of the ostensibly unfair characterization of the Soviet Union by the Reagan administration after Korean airliner 007

International Affairs (Moscow), November 1983, pp. 1–6, *excerpts.*

was shot down over Soviet airspace. The Soviets maintained consistently that the plane was on a spy mission for U.S. intelligence. The second part of the statement is particularly targeted at Western European public opinion on the INF issue: would the Europeans reject the NATO deployments, thereby vindicating Soviet strategy? In the first week of November, Great Britain began to receive the missiles. On 22 November the first ones arrived in Germany; the Soviet delegation walked out of the Geneva talks on 23 November.

The Soviet leadership deems it necessary to make known to Soviet people and other peoples and all those who are responsible for shaping the policy of states its assessment of the course pursued in international affairs by the present US Administration.

Briefly speaking, it is a militarist course which poses a grave threat to peace. Its essence is to try and assure for the United States dominant positions in the world without reckoning with the interests of other states and peoples.

Precisely these aims are served by the unprecedented build-up of the US military potential, the large-scale programmes of manufacturing weapons of all types—nuclear, chemical and conventional. Now it is planned to project the unrestricted arms race into outer space as well....

If anyone had any illusions about a possible evolution for the better in the policy of the present American administration, such illusions have been completely dispelled by the latest developments. For the sake of its imperial ambitions, that Administration goes to such lengths that one begins to doubt whether Washington has any brakes at all to prevent it from crossing the line before which any sober-minded person must stop.

The insidious provocation involving a South Korean plane engineered by US special services is also an example of extreme adventurism in politics. We have elucidated thoroughly and authentically the factual aspect of this act. The guilt of its organizers, however they might prevaricate and whatever false versions they might put forward, has been proved.

The Soviet leadership has expressed regret over the loss of human lives due to that unprecedented, criminal subversion. These lives are on the conscience of those who would like to arrogate to themselves the right not to reckon with the sovereignty of states and the inviolability of their borders, who masterminded and carried out the provocation, who literally on the following day hastily pushed through Congress colossal military appropriations and are now rubbing their hands in glee.

Thus, the "humanism" of the statesmen who are seeking to blame others for the death of the people aboard the plane is materialized in new mountains of weapons of mass destruction—from MX missiles to containers with nerve gas....

In the six and a half decades of its existence the Soviet state has successfully withstood many trials, including severe ones. Those who attempted to encroach on the integrity of our state, its independence and our system found themselves on the garbage heap of history....

Of course, the malicious attacks on the Soviet Union produce here a natural feeling of indignation, but we have strong nerves, and we do not base our policy on emotions. Our policy rests on common sense, realism, a sense of profound responsibility for the destiny of the world....

The Soviet-American talks on the burning problem—reduction of nuclear armaments in Europe—have been going on for two years now. The position of the Soviet side is directed at finding mutually acceptable solutions on a fair, just basis, solutions which do not infringe anyone's legitimate interest. At the same time, those two years have made it clear that our partners in the talks at Geneva are by no means there to reach an accord. Their task is different—to play for time and then start the deployment in Western Europe of ballistic Pershing 2 and long-range cruise missiles. And they do not particularly try to conceal this....

The operation of stationing these American nuclear missiles in Europe is seen from the Washington control tower as perfectly simple and maximally advantageous for the United States—advantageous at the expense of Europe. The European allies of the US are regarded as hostages. This is a frank, but cynical policy. What is really unclear is this: have those political leaders who—disregarding the interest of their peoples, the interests of peace—are helping to implement the ambitious militaristic policy of the US Administration given thought to this?

Here nothing should be left unsaid. If, contrary to the will of the majority of people in West European countries, American nuclear missiles appear on the European continent, this will be [a] major move fundamentally inimical to peace on the part of the US leaders and the leaders of other NATO countries who act at one with them....

All who raise today their voice against the senseless arms race and in defence of peace can be sure that the policy of the Soviet Union, of other socialist countries, is directed at attaining precisely these aims. The USSR wants to live in peace with all countries, including the United States. It does not nurture aggressive plans, does not impose the arms race on anyone, does not impose its social order on anyone.

Our aspirations and strivings are implemented in concrete proposals directed at effecting a decisive turn for the better in the world situation. The Soviet Union will continue to do everything possible to uphold peace on earth.

DOCUMENT 4

Soviet Response to Beginning of U.S. INF Deployments

Yuri Andropov

25 November 1983

Editor's commentary: The diplomatic part of the "two-track" approach taken by NATO during the latter 1970s in response to Soviet intermediate-range missile deployments failed. A tireless peace campaign against counterdeployments in Western Europe continued throughout the late 1970s and early 1980s. Soviet leaders no doubt hoped that the peace movement would assist in derailing NATO policy. However, in late 1983, the decision was taken by Western European governments to deploy U.S. Pershing and cruise missiles. Yuri Andropov's official statement on this decision included both an announcement that Soviet participation in the Geneva arms talks would now cease, and several threats, overt and veiled, regarding Soviet countermeasures. This statement reflects the tension and bitterness of the early 1980s, a period that has been referred to as a second cold war.

The leadership of the Soviet Union has already apprised Soviet people and other peoples of its assessment of the present US Administration's militarist course and warned the US Government and the Western countries which are at one with it about the dangerous consequences of that course.

However, Washington, Bonn, London, and Rome have failed to heed the voice of reason—the siting of the American medium-range missiles is starting on the territory of the FRG, Britain, and Italy. Thus the appearance of the American Pershings and cruise missiles on the European continent is becoming an accomplished fact.

For almost 40 years—longer than ever in modern history—Europe has been living under conditions of peace. This has been possible thanks to the consistently peace-loving policy of the socialist community countries, to the efforts of the continent's peace-loving forces, and also to the realistic position of sober-minded politicians in the West. The approximate equilibrium of military forces, including nuclear forces, which has

Pravda, 25 November 1983, p. 1, as translated in *Foreign Broadcast Information Service*, Soviet Union (Washington, DC: *n.p.*, 25 November 1983), pp. AA1–AA3, excerpts.

taken shape in Europe between the North Atlantic alliance states and the Warsaw Pact states has objectively served the cause of European security and stability.

Now the United States and NATO as a whole are taking a step aimed at tilting the scales their way. The nuclear missiles being deployed close to the borders of the Soviet Union and its allies are by no means intended for the defense of Western Europe——no one is threatening it. The siting of the American missiles on European soil increases not Europe's security but the real danger that the United States will bring disaster on the peoples of Europe....

We have also stated clearly that the appearance of the New American missiles in West Europe will render impossible the continuation of the negotiations on nuclear arms in Europe which have been taking place in Geneva.

The decisions adopted in recent days by the FRG, British, and Italian Governments unequivocally testify that, despite the will of their own peoples, despite their countries' security interests, and despite the interest of European and world peace, these governments have given the "green light" to the installation of the US missiles. Thereby they, together with the US government, have assumed all the responsibility for the consequences of a shortsighted policy about which the Soviet Union gave advance warning.

Having carefully weighed all the aspects of the situation which has been created, the Soviet leadership has adopted the following decisions.

First: Since the United States by its action has wrecked the possibility of achieving a mutually acceptable accord at the talks on questions of limiting nuclear arms in Europe and since their continuation in these conditions would only be a cover for actions by the United States and a number of other NATO countries aimed at undermining European and international security, the Soviet Union considers it impossible to participate further in these talks.

Second: The commitments unilaterally adopted by the Soviet Union with the objective of creating more favorable conditions for achieving success at the talks are abrogated. The moratorium on the deployment of Soviet medium-range nuclear systems in the European part of the USSR is thereby abrogated.

Third: By agreement with the governments of the GDR and the CSSR the preparatory work begun some time ago, as was announced, for the siting of enhanced-range operational-tactical missiles on the territory of these countries will be accelerated.

Fourth: Since by siting its missiles in Europe the United States is increasing the nuclear threat to the Soviet Union, corresponding Soviet means will be deployed in ocean regions and seas taking this circumstance into account. In terms of their characteristics these means of ours will be equal to the threat created for us and our allies by the US missiles being sited in Europe.

Of course, other measures aimed at safeguarding the security of the USSR and the other socialist community countries will also be taken.

In embarking on the implementation of the decisions we have taken, we state that the countermeasures from the Soviet side will be restricted strictly to the limits which will be dictated by the NATO countries' actions. The Soviet Union—and we stress this once again—does not seek military superiority, and we will do only what is absolutely necessary to ensure that the military balance is not disrupted.

If the United States and the other NATO countries display a readiness to return to the situation which existed prior to the commencement of the siting of US medium-range missiles in Europe, the Soviet Union too will be ready to do likewise. And then the proposals which we submitted earlier regarding questions of limiting and reducing nuclear arms in Europe would come into force again. In this event, that is, provided the previous situation is reestablished, the USSR's unilateral pledges in this sphere would also come back into force.

The Soviet Union declares most definitely and firmly that it continues to adhere to a principled course toward ending the arms race, and above all the nuclear arms race, and toward reducing and ultimately totally eliminating the threat of nuclear war. It will continue to make every effort to achieve these noble aims....

DOCUMENT 5

An Act of Banditry against Grenada

February 1984

Editor's commentary: The invasion of Grenada by U.S. troops in 1984 provided grist for the Soviet propaganda mill in the third world. This quasi-academic article reviews the history of U.S. "imperialism" in Central America and the Caribbean; it is a representative example of the kind of attack that was leveled at the "terrorism" of the Reagan administration after the Grenada invasion.

Washington's terroristic act against Grenada in defiance of all norms of international law has again exposed the predatory nature of the hegemonistic policy pursued by the most reactionary US imperialists. The American invaders of Grenada occupied other people's land and turned it into a torture-chamber for an entire nation. Washington never hesitates to resort to repressions and psychological terror in a bid to extirpate the ideas of anti-imperialist revolution in the Caribbean and Central American countries.

The US powers that be have always attached special importance to that region in their policy,

---

International Affairs (Moscow), February 1984, pp. 63–70, *excerpts.*

and beginning in the mid-19th century they worked hard to obtain the "key to two Oceans"—the future Panama Canal. In the first third of the 20th century, after building the canal and bringing to power regimes toeing Washington's line in those countries by occupying Nicaragua, the Dominican Republic and Haiti, and also by imposing fettering treaties upon Cuba and Panama, the USA turned the Caribbean into an "American lake" surrounded by a network of its military bases.

The area, first and foremost Mexico and Venezuela, as well as other countries, has vast deposits of oil, iron, chromium, nickel, bauxites and other strategic commodities. Key shipping lanes pass through the Panama Canal and the Caribbean. At the same time, following the victory of the people's revolution in Cuba, the region gradually became a most explosive center of national liberation struggle. About ten young independent nations emerged from the ruins of the British Empire in the 1960s and the 1970s. In El Salvador and Guatemala the people launched an armed struggle against the pro-American regimes, and people's revolutions triumphed in Nicaragua, Grenada and Surinam in the late 1970s and the early 1980s. The dominion of Yankee imperialism was shaken and jeopardized in the longer term.

THE SHADOW OF THE CIA OVER THE REVOLUTIONARY ISLAND

The USA retaliated by mounting a perfidious aggression against tiny Grenada, a state whose population can be housed in three or four New York skyscrapers and whose territory is about one-third of that of New York. The imperialist superpower's attack on that country caused anxiety and indignation throughout the world. In Latin America, to quote Peruvian TV, it had the effect of an electric shock....

Washington could not reconcile itself to changes on Grenada and was particularly against the development of close contacts between

Grenada and Cuba. We, Maurice Bishop said, do not recognize the right of the US to tell us with whom we can develop relations and with whom we cannot....

In the years of the people's government in Grenada the CIA organized there a number of counterrevolutionary plots and attempts on Bishop's life.... One of them, for instance, was made during a meeting in St. George's when a powerful explosion took place under a stand where Maurice Bishop and other members of the government were standing. By sheer chance they remained unhurt but three other people died and more than 20 were wounded....

The propaganda war became especially intense in the summer of 1983 when the American Administration started urging the Caribbean countries to "isolate" Grenada and to study the question of military action against it. The discord in the Grenadan leadership and the assassination of Maurice Bishop were among the pretexts for it. However, the events within a country cannot serve as a pretext for justifying the American aggression. Fidel Castro justly posed the questions: "Since when has the government of the United States become the arbiter of international conflicts... in any country?" This is tantamount to any power proclaiming the "right" to invade the United States after the assassination of John Kennedy....

INTERNATIONAL TERRORISM AS STATE POLICY

The unprovoked armed attack of US imperialism on the young state... evoked anger and condemnation among the broad sections of the world public. It was perceived as a flagrant violation of the fundamental principles of international law formalized in the UN Charter....

The world community unambiguously denounced the imperial ambitions of the USA and its attempts to impose its will upon other nations with the help of arms. This, however, did not embarrass the current chief of the White House at all. One hundred countries at the UN, he declared, "do not agree with us on almost every question brought to their consideration every time we are involved. This nevertheless does not make me lose my appetite."...

Latin American countries, especially those in the Caribbean, perceived the aggression against Grenada as a direct threat to their security; they have had a good idea of their northern neighbour's "big stick" ever since the beginning of this century. "The invasion of Grenada," *Le Monde* wrote, "is a demonstration... intended primarily, if you will, for regional consumption. It is addressed to Cuba, Nicaragua and Salvadoran guerrillas." *Financial Times* of London expressed a similar opinion: "Militarism is most striking in US policy in Central America. The countries immediately surrounding the region, such as Mexico and Venezuela, have the strongest incentives for understanding the problems of El Salvador and Nicaragua."

Washington's support for the Somoza bands making incursions into Nicaragua; the presence of 6,000 American servicemen in neighbouring Honduras under the pretext of manoeuvres, and the plans to bring their number to 11,000; the consent extorted from Costa Rica to accept 1,000 American soldiers to "build roads" in the region neighboring with Nicaragua; the more than 20,000 servicemen on ships of the US Navy constantly running along Central American shores and, finally, the formation by the "Green Berets" of a 25,000-strong army of Honduran, Guatemalan and Salvadoran punitive troops in Honduras all prompt Western observers to surmise that the operation in Grenada could be a dress rehearsal of a direct American aggression against Nicaragua. All the more so since Howard Baker, Republican majority leader in the US Senate, publicly declared that he deemed it possible to carry out the "Grenada action" vis-à-vis Nicaragua and upheld the "right' of the USA to send the Marines to other countries.

No state in the region can now feel safe....

DOCUMENT 6

Soviet Protest of the Mining of Nicaraguan Harbors

21 March 1984

Editor's commentary: Politburo member and vice-chairman of the USSR's Council of Ministers Andrei Gromyko personally handed to the U.S. chargé d'affaires this official Soviet protest of the mining of Nicaraguan harbors after a Soviet vessel was damaged by an exploding mine off the coast of Nicaragua.

The government of the Union of Soviet Socialist Republics states to the government of the United States of America the following:

On 20 March 1984, while approaching the Nicaraguan port of Sandino, the Soviet tanker *Lugansk* struck a mine and was damaged. Among the members of the ship's crew there were some injured.

The Soviet government holds the U.S. government responsible for that grave crime—an act of banditry and piracy.

It is common knowledge—and the U.S. Administration itself makes no secret of it—that the United States is directly interfering in the affairs of sovereign states of Central America and waging an undeclared war against Nicaragua. Official agencies of the U.S. finance, train, and equip bands of mercenaries and terrorists that invade Nicaraguan territory, commit robbery and violence, and kill peaceful civilians. It is also known that included in these groups are representatives of American special services. In such a manner, the United States is carrying out in practice a policy of state terrorism. . . .

A new and extremely dangerous manifestation of this policy has become actions aimed against foreign ships that are making commercial trips to Nicaragua or are near its coasts. Mines are being laid in vast areas of the ocean adjacent to Nicaragua, in its territorial waters, and even in its ports, and other explosive devices are being used. Already several foreign ships have struck them. Attacks are being made on commercial vessels proceeding to Nicaraguan ports.

The Soviet Union in the most categorical terms condemns the United States policy of terrorism, arbitrariness, and interference in the affairs of sovereign, independent states as incompatible with generally accepted norms of laws and morality and creating a threat to peace and international security, and insists that it be ended.

The government of the USSR files a resolute protest to the government of the U.S.A. in connection with the criminal act against the Soviet ship *Lugansk* and warns that the United States will bear total responsibility for the consequences with which the continuation of actions of this kind is fraught.

The government of the USSR reserves the right to demand compensation for the Soviet citizens who suffered and reimbursement of the material damage done to property of the USSR.

Pravda, 22 March 1984, 1. Editor's translation.

DOCUMENT 7

The Iran-Iraq War

April 1984

Editor's commentary: As the Iran-Iraq war dragged on into its fourth year, Soviet commentators began to side publicly with Iraq's cause. In part, this was

---

Krasnaya zvezda, 21 April 1984, p. 6, as translated in *Foreign Broadcast Information Service,* Soviet Union (Washington, DC: *n.p.,* 1 May 1984), pp. H5–H6, *excerpts.*

because it seemed that Iran might press its manpower advantage to a military victory and thereby threaten even greater instability in the Persian Gulf region, a situation which could affect Soviet security directly. Although this commentary from the Soviet military paper Krasnaya zvezda *indicts the Western arms trade for fueling the war, nothing is said about the military supplies Moscow contributed, particularly early on in the war, to its client state Iraq.*

. . . The Iranian ruling circles are using a number of measures in an attempt to boost the morale of the soldiers who are being sent to their deaths: They are whipping up religious fanaticism and militarist frenzy at the battlefront and on the home front and crudely slandering the country's democratic forces and terrorizing them.

The Paris paper *Le Matin* made a point of drawing attention to the link between the Iranian command's stepping up of combat actions at the front and the execution of democratic patriots. The latter, incidentally, was greeted with ill-concealed glee by many bourgeois news media in the West.

The chauvinistic propaganda, which has assumed unprecedented dimensions, sometimes makes it known that Baghdad's capitulation, demanded by Tehran, is just a step on the path toward the implementation of much more far-reaching designs. For example, what about the inscription on the building of the Iranian Ministry of Islamic Guidance: "We will spread our revolution to the entire world, because it is an Islamic revolution. Until the rallying cry 'There is no God but Allah' is heard all over the earth, the struggle will continue." Commentary would be superfluous in this case.

What, one wonders, are the Iranian leaders actually relying on in the long drawn-out war with Iraq, in a war that has already led to severe shortages of food in the country as well as [of] other essential goods and even medicines for the wounded, and to a flourishing black market and increasing crime. What they have to rely on is

considerably greater manpower and economic resources than Iraq possesses, a more advantageous geographical location in terms of military strategy, and, finally, religious fanaticism.

The Iranian population of approximately 40 million (Iraq has a population of 14 million) enabled them, according to the figures of Western diplomats in Tehran, to mobilize and mass between 750,000 and 1 million people along a front extending for 1200 km. This massive army includes 250,000 regular soldiers and about 300,000 "Islamic revolutionary guards," the rest being volunteers intoxicated by religious propaganda. According to Iranian officials, 1 million militiamen have undergone elementary combat training. They have to spend a few weeks and even months at the front.

For both Iran and Iraq the main item of state revenue that finances purchases of weapons and ammunition continues to be oil exports. Soon after the start of the war they fell sharply. But here too Iran has a clear advantage in that it has much broader access to the Persian Gulf and Arabian Sea, where the main oil routes are. According to preliminary data, Iran will make $30 billion from oil sales this year. The annual income from Iraqi oil, exported mainly through the only operating pipeline, which crosses Turkish territory, has already fallen to $8 billion.

According to Western military analysts, Iraq offsets the aforementioned Iranian advantages with a numerical and qualitative superiority in terms of air power, tanks, and artillery. Other factors are the heightened morale of Iraqi servicemen, who are fighting on their own territory, and the moral support they are receiving from the population. Iran's considerably large currency reserves are offset to some extent by the financial aid the Arab countries of the Persian Gulf are giving to Iraq.

Tehran is spending billions of dollars not only on rebuilding what has been destroyed by the war—work in which Japanese, Italian and other foreign firms are involved. Very large amounts of money are being spent on weapons, combat equipment, and ammunition on the extensive Western military market. And it is this that exposes the perfidious, hypocritical role of the US Administration, which goes on and on about its phony commitment to halting the Iran-Iraq conflict. In fact, it is doing all it can to ensure continuing Iranian and Iraqi bloodshed, which weakens two countries that have declared a struggle against the imperialist threat and Israeli aggression, splits the Arab and the even-wider Muslim world, and creates an albeit false pretext for further increasing the US military presence in the Persian Gulf zone and for preparations for an armed invasion of the region's countries....

DOCUMENT 8

Pravda on President Reagan's "Bombing" Joke

15 August 1984

Editor's commentary: The Soviet response to the bizarre "start bombing" radio incident, during which Ronald Reagan reportedly thought the microphones were turned off, was to make the greatest possible political capital from the affair. It is interesting to note, however, that the Soviets apparently anticipated that this blunder would hurt Reagan in his bid for a second term. Of course, it did not.

The world public is disturbed by an incident which took place last Saturday, 11 August, at the U.S. President's ranch in California, when a recording of his regular radio address to the coun-

---

Pravda, 15 August 1984, p. 4, as translated in *Foreign Broadcast Information Service,* Soviet Union (Washington, DC: *n.p.,* 15 August 1984), pp. A1–A4, *excerpts.*

try was being prepared. Mr. Reagan decided to limber up during the so-called "sound test" and suddenly, "having weakened," blurted out what is constantly on his mind but what on the threshold of the election campaign he has recently been forced to keep quiet about.

"Dear Americans," he said, suddenly coming up to the microphone, "I am glad to inform you that I have just signed legislation outlawing Russia forever. The bombing will start in 5 minutes."

Technicians recording the President's address to the country froze in horror. But the President just smiled, and they realized that Reagan was merely "testing his voice" before beginning to read the routine, previously prepared text devoted to everyday economic problems.

White House staffers immediately made immense efforts to prevent the words spoken carelessly by their boss from becoming public knowledge. But, as they say, a word is like a sparrow: If it flies out, you won't catch it....

Journalists rushed to the President's residence for an explanation. A perplexed White House spokesman refused to confirm or deny the report of what had happened. He declared that "any words spoken by the President before the recording of a radio address starts are not intended for the press."

A large-scale political scandal has blown up. Although members of Reagan's entourage, trying to play down the significance of his words, assured everybody that the President had simply been "joking," this escapade was regarded as a provocation not only in U.S. political circles but also abroad.

AFP [French Press Agency] reported from Los Angeles on 13 August that "by his dubious joke about the possibility of war with the Soviet Union, Reagan has clearly placed himself in a delicate position on the eve of the elections.... Senior White House officials, who are accompanying the US President in California and who tried at first to prevent further spread of the leak of information, were obviously not quite them-

selves at the thought that Reagan's pronouncement could affect his chances at the elections."

The agency declared that "the President's
blunder," which White House staff are trying to
represent as a witty joke, would further
strengthen "the image of a champion of war,
ready to press the button and start a nuclear
conflict."

As soon as the news of Reagan's insolent action became generally known, a wave of condemnation arose everywhere in the United States
and in the countries allied with it. "Reagan's utterance," the American agency ASSOCIATED
PRESS notes, "will hardly be forgotten soon,
for it appears at a time when the bad relations
between Moscow and Washington have become one of the issues of the presidential election campaign. Reagan's past sharp utterances
addressed to the Soviet Union, including his
words regarding the 'empire of evil,' have resulted in the President being accused of pursuing an unconcealed policy of confrontation
vis-à-vis the USSR." . . .

While R. Reagan stays at his ranch, the Pentagon continues the arms race at full speed. Congress is discussing the biggest draft military budget in US history. From time to time senators
and members of the House of Representatives
cut down this or that item in the budget, but these
reductions do no damage to the numerous arms
programs advocated by the Pentagon and the
President. . . .

President Reagan's attempts in the last 6
months to turn the facts inside out and to present
the matter as if it is not the United States, but
the Soviet Union, which opposes a halt to the
arms race and the establishment of peaceful international economic cooperation can only deceive those who want to be deceived.

People are not blind. They can see who is in
favor of peace, and who dreams of military solutions. And R. Reagan's escapade at the American radio microphone of 11 August is new evidence of what dangerous plans the American
Administration is hatching.

Striving to weaken the vigilance of peace-
loving forces, the US leaders often issue statements to the effect that the United States allegedly does not intend to use the mountains of
weapons it is accumulating, but to use their presence only in order to "deter" the Soviet Union
and other socialist countries. But these gentlemen should finally realize that the Soviet Union
and its allies are not countries that can be in-
timidated.

The Soviet Union and its allies have everything necessary to defend their security and to
rebuff any aggression. The response that the
United States received, having deployed their
first-strike nuclear missiles in West Europe,
shows sufficiently convincingly that no one at
any time will succeed in bringing to their knees
the people who have won their freedom at a high
cost and are fully determined to defend themselves and to defend the cause of peace.

The incident at the President's ranch on Saturday, 11 August, serves as yet another confirmation of the need to observe the greatest vigilance in the face of the aggressive plans of the
United States and NATO.

DOCUMENT 9

Interview with Konstantin Chernenko

16 October 1984

*Editor's commentary: One mark of continuity
between Andropov's and Chernenko's foreign
policies can be found in attempts to reconstruct a
mutually beneficial U.S.-Soviet arms control*

Interview conducted by Dusko Doder, *The Washington
Post*, 17 October 1984, p. A26. Copyright *The Washington
Post*. Reprinted by permission.

relationship. Although a good deal of the polemical character of Soviet public diplomacy remained, embryonic signs of changed emphases in Soviet policy and the willingness to entertain serious negotiations over the entire range of questions involved in INF and START appeared in this Washington Post interview with Chernenko. Note that during the oral part of the interview, the Soviet leader at times seemed somewhat confused and at one point actually needed assistance in answering the question posed to him. In less than 5 months, Chernenko passed away, and the reins of leadership were picked up by a new and energetic Soviet leadership, which developed these themes more fully.

Following are the written questions put to President Konstantin Chernenko and his answers, in unofficial translation.

Q: **President Reagan has said that the United States is prepared to resume a dialogue with the Soviet Union on a broad range of questions including arms control. What is the attitude of the Soviet Union toward President Reagan's expression of readiness for talks?**

A: In the past, we have already heard words about the U.S. administration's readiness for talks. But they have never been supported by real deeds..., particularly in the field of arms limitation and a reduction of the war danger.

Every time we put forward concrete proposals, they would run into a blind wall. Let me give some examples.

Such was the case last March when we identified a whole set of problems. Reaching agreement on them—or at least on some of them—would mean a real shift both in Soviet-U.S. relations and in the international situation as a whole. But what they did was simply to shirk responding to our proposals.

Such was the case in June when we proposed reaching agreement on preventing the militarization of outer space. This time we were answered, but with what? An attempt was made to substitute the very subject of negotiations. It was proposed to discuss issues related to nuclear weapons, i.e., issues which had previously been discussed at the talks in Geneva that were wrecked by the United States itself.

At the same time, the United States not only refused to remove the obstacles created by the deployment of the new U.S. missiles in Western Europe but is going ahead with their deployment.

And what about outer space? Instead of preventing an arms race in space, we were invited to proceed to working out some rules for such a race, and in fact to legalize it. Obviously, we cannot agree to that. Our objective is genuinely peaceful outer space and we shall persistently strive for this objective.

These are the facts.

Turning now to President Reagan's statement which you have referred to. If what the president has said about readiness to negotiate is not merely a tactical move, I wish to state that the Soviet Union will not be found wanting. We have always been prepared for serious and business-like negotiations and have repeatedly said so.

We are ready to proceed to negotiations with a view to working out and concluding an agreement to prevent the militarization of outer space, including complete renunciation of antisatellite systems, with a mutual moratorium—to be established from the date of the beginning of the talks—on testing and deployment of space weapons....

The Soviet proposal that the nuclear powers freeze quantitatively and qualitatively all nuclear weapons at their disposal also remains valid....

There is a real opportunity to finalize the agreement on the complete and general prohibition of nuclear weapon tests. Should there be no such tests, these weapons will not be improved, which will put the brakes on the nuclear arms race.

Here too, the United States could prove in deeds the sincerity of its declarations in favor of nuclear arms limitation. The United States can also prove it by ratifying the Soviet-American treaties on underground nuclear explosions.

These treaties were signed as far back as 1974 and 1976....

The Soviet Union has repeatedly called upon Washington to follow our example in assuming an obligation not to be the first to use nuclear weapons. Every time the answer was "no."

Imagine the reverse situation: the United States assumes an obligation not to be the first to use nuclear weapons, and calls upon us to reciprocate while we say "no," this does not suit us and we reserve the right to a first nuclear strike. What would people in the United States think of our intentions in that case? There can be no two views on that score....

Q: A view is widely spread that recently a shift has become discernible which could lead to better Soviet-U.S. relations. What do you think about this and what is your view of the prospects for these relations in the time to come?

A: Indeed, sentiments in favor of a shift for the better in Soviet-U.S. relations are widely spread in the world. This, in our view, reflects the growing understanding of the importance of these relations, particularly in the current international situation.

Unfortunately, so far there has been no ground to speak of such a shift in Soviet-U.S. relations as a fact of life. Is it possible? The resolution of the problems to which I referred earlier would help to bring it about.

I am convinced there is no sound alternative at all to a constructive development of Soviet-U.S. relations. At the same time, we do not overlook the fact that we have different social systems and world outlooks....

I have already said in the past and I wish to stress it once again: we stand for good relations with the U.S.A. and experience shows that they can be such. This requires a mutual desire to build relations as equals, to mutual benefit and for the good of peace.

Following is an abridged text of the oral interview with Chernenko.

Q: I want to use this opportunity to hear your opinion as to what specific steps the Soviet leadership would like to see after the American elections to get out of the current impasse in Soviet-American relations.

A: First of all, of course, the elections should take place in order to answer what will happen after the elections. The elections are in the future and therefore to determine now, in advance, what, when and where we are going to discuss is obviously too early....

Whoever is the president in America, our policy—a policy of peace which we are carrying out persistently and systematically—is going, I think, to remain the same. The same. That is why peace is the main question for us, and I think that any president who comes to the White House after the election will, I think, be thinking about the same question.

As a matter of fact, two great countries can, as we became convinced in the past and are being convinced each day, can do a great deal, in fact they can do everything, in order that flames of another world war do not flare up. This is our objective, this is our direction, our general direction, and we think that any sober-minded person can understand us correctly.

We are doing this not because we...like it, but because we experience in reality what such a war means, war without a hydrogen bomb, without such bombs. And what about a war with atomic bombs? We are now convinced that this is a very terrible weapon and naturally we would like to see in the face of [the] American president a partner in this sacred human task—for peace....

Q: Are you optimistic about the present development of Soviet-American relations?

A: Well there are considerable possibilities in Soviet-American relations, very considerable possibilities. We have been making attempts, and you know if we enumerate the numbers of our proposals, which we have advanced and which I mentioned in my answer, you can easily see that...

Chernenko's foreign policy adviser Andrei Alexandrov-Agentov: So far, there is no...

Chernenko: No, so far there is no serious shift, businesslike shifts, such moves which could convince people and which could be convincing in themselves. In principle, I am an optimist, an optimist, but that does not mean an endless optimism, since there are limits to everything. I think nevertheless that things are going to get normalized if the American side indeed takes some practical steps in the direction of the struggle for peace. Practical steps.

Q: And should not both sides take some small steps?

A: You see, you will find the answer there [in the written responses]. And not small steps but big steps that we have made in the direction of peace. But the White House is silent on this question. They are silent and they do not answer...or they do not even simply notice them. Or they consciously do not respond. One thing is clear: there has been no practical shift in the direction of peace by the White House. You can see that yourself.

It is necessary of course to translate those talks, all our agreements, questions and answers onto practical tracks. Here is the essence of the issue. It is not that we lack peace proposals, there are very many of them, but there are no practical solutions, no practical approaches for their resolution.

This is the most important point. And small steps, yes, yes, they only cloud people's eyes. That's it. But I believe that my answers to your questions are also one of our steps, our practical steps, on this important road.

DOCUMENT 10

For Outer Space without Weapons

28 December 1984

Editor's commentary: The Soviet campaign to achieve a ban on space weapons gained momentum in the first months after the

announcement of the Strategic Defense Initiative by the Reagan administration and continued to pick up steam into the Gorbachev era. This editorial is typical of the Soviet public response to the prospects of another arms race, with all its attendant strategic and economic implications.

...A system of antimissile defense with elements of space basing is being developed in the United States. The Pentagon strategists hope to use it as a cover for working out the possibility of delivering nuclear strikes against the other side and escaping retribution. Though the plans for gaining military supremacy and impunity of aggression can bear no scrutiny, the very planning of "star wars" is extremely dangerous to the cause of universal peace. This is recognized by many experts and politicians in the United States and other NATO countries, and not only outside that alliance.

Unless a reliable barrier is raised in the way of militarization of outer space, such militarization will cancel out everything that has been achieved so far in the sphere of arms limitations, it will give a boost to the arms race in other fields, and will dramatically increase the nuclear war threat. It is urgently necessary to prevent such a dangerous process and to do this without delay, before it becomes irreversible.

For many years now the USSR has been working vigorously to prevent the militarization of space. As early as in 1958, soon after the first Earth satellites had been put in orbit, our country raised the question of banning the use of outer space for military purposes—raised it formally in the United Nations General Assembly. Subsequently the Soviet Union was the initiator of a number of major international agreements which set the stage for further efforts to resolve this problem. Today the question of preventing

---

Pravda, 28 December 1984, as translated in *Reprints from the Soviet Press,* vol. 40, no. 1, 15 January 1985.

the militarization of space figures prominently on the agenda of international affairs.

The Soviet Government is calling for a permanent ban on the use of force in space and from space with respect to the Earth, and also from Earth with respect to targets in space. It suggests banning and scrapping a whole class of space attack weapons, including spaced-based antisatellite and anti-missile systems, as well as all the land-, air- and sea-based systems designed to attack targets in space.

The USSR backs its concrete proposals with practical moves. Our country has announced a unilateral moratorium on launching antisatellite weapons into space for as long as the USA and other countries do likewise.

These constructive Soviet initiatives are meeting with widespread support among the peace-loving states and peoples. The 39th session of the UN General Assembly has almost unanimously adopted a resolution calling for the exclusion of space from the sphere of the arms race (150 countries have voted for this resolution with only the USA abstaining). The resolution reflects the essence of the Soviet proposal, submitted for consideration by the Assembly, "On the Use of Outer Space Exclusively for Peaceful Purposes, for the Benefit of Mankind." The voting in the UN has confirmed that the international community sees the prevention of the militarization of near-Earth space as a most pressing task requiring the earliest possible solution.

Fully determined to secure meaningful progress in reducing the war danger, the USSR is preparing for new Soviet-American talks it has itself proposed in order to achieve mutually acceptable accords on the whole range of the inter-related issues dealing with nuclear and space weapons.

The Soviet Union is ready to consider the most radical solutions, solutions which would help the world advance along the track leading to the end of the arms race. It is particularly important to prevent escalation of the race into outer space.

Weapons of death must be banned from Earth and from space. Such is the will of the Soviet people and of all peace-loving nations.

DOCUMENT 11

Thirty Years of Soviet-Indian Cooperation

M. Sergeichik

1 February 1985

Editor's commentary: This commemoration of the thirtieth anniversary of Soviet-Indian cooperation by the chairman of the USSR State Committee for Foreign Economic Relations accentuated the importance that India holds in the entire framework of Soviet third world policy. In many ways, India has remained the success story of Soviet relations with the nonaligned world. In contrast to setbacks in the Middle East, Africa, and Asia, India has continued to be the model that the USSR would like other nonaligned nations to emulate, in both the economic and the political contexts. Soviet-Indian relations have remained stable irrespective of individual leaders and other political developments, and Soviet investments in India have paid off handsomely in terms of the competition between East and West in the third world.

The peoples of the Soviet Union and India have long been united by bonds of friendship and cooperation. As was stated at the 26th Congress of the CPSU, "Joint action with peaceful and independent India will continue to be one of the important areas of Soviet foreign policy."

India occupies a very special place in the overall spectrum of the Soviet Union's relations with developing countries. It has been making tangible contributions toward maintaining peace and strengthening international security, ending the arms race and doing away with the threat of nu-

Pravda, 1 February 1985, as translated in *Reprints from the Soviet Press*, vol. 40, no. 4, 28 February 1985. *Excerpts*.

clear war, toward promoting understanding and friendship among nations. The Treaty of Peace, Friendship and Cooperation concluded in August 1971 has been a factor of great importance in the consolidation of Soviet-Indian relations, having proved effective both as an instrument of broadening Soviet-Indian cooperation and as a means of ensuring political stability in Asia and the rest of the world.

"The Soviet Union and India are linked together by close ties of economic, scientific, technological and cultural cooperation. There is perhaps no area of our social life in which close contacts have not been established between our countries," Konstantin Chernenko, General Secretary of the CPSU Central Committee and President of the Presidium of the Supreme Soviet of the USSR, said at the time he presented national awards to Soviet and Indian spacemen.

Trade, economic, scientific and technological cooperation with our country, based on the principles of equality, mutual benefit and nonintervention in one another's internal affairs, have played an important part in promoting and strengthening India's economic independence and advancing a number of leading sectors of its national economy.

Soviet-Indian economic cooperation is 30 years old to the day. It was started with the signing of an intergovernmental agreement on assistance to India in the construction of the Bhilai Steel Plant....

The obelisk in tribute to Soviet-Indian friendship in Bhilai carries Jawaharlal Nehru's words: A dream is coming true—Bhilai is one of the places impressed on the nation's mind as a meaningful symbol of a new epoch in its life.

It is worth recalling that when India gained its independence in 1947, it had to face a wide range of tricky problems, what with overcoming the onerous heritage of its colonial past and creating its new, independent economy. The Soviet Union gave it every aid. Our cooperation was from the very outset a cog in the policy framed by the Nehru Government to strengthen eco-

nomic independence through accelerated industrialization and the establishment and full-scale promotion of a public sector. Its large scale, stability and reliability have always been some of its distinguishing features. It covers practically all of the basic sectors of the Indian economy. Fifty-eight industrial and other projects have been built in India with Soviet assistance during the last three decades, and some thirty more are either in the designing stage or under construction....

The projects of Soviet-Indian cooperation constitute the industrial backbone of the Indian public sector. In addition to their purely economic importance they are also of great social significance. Many of them have been built in remote, formerly backward areas which now have turned into large industrial centers with modern cities and townships completely equipped with social and cultural establishments. Numerous auxiliary enterprises have sprung up around the newly built plants. These enterprises provide jobs for large numbers of people....

The Long-Term Program of Economic, Trade, Scientific and Technical Cooperation between the USSR and India, signed in March 1979, plays a prominent role in promoting economic and commercial relations between the two countries. The Program spells out the trends and forms the further development of Soviet-Indian cooperation for the next 10 to 15 years....

In summing up the 30-year history of Soviet-Indian economic cooperation, one can certainly say that it is an important aspect of the diversified relations between the Soviet Union and India, and that it will be further developed and improved.

As Prime Minister Rajiv Gandhi of India said in his address over the All-India radio and television, India has always highly valued its diversified and time-tested relationship with the Soviet Union, relations based on cooperation, friendship and vital support when it was needed most.... India may rest assured that the Soviet Union is ready to extend assistance in further consolidating its economy and in enhancing its international prestige.

An Important Document in the History of Soviet-Chinese Relations

I. Alexeyev

13 February 1985

Editor's commentary: Late in Chernenko's tenure the thirtieth anniversary of the Sino-Soviet Treaty of Friendship was marked in the Soviet government's newspaper, Izvestia. This article presented itself as a review of Sino-Soviet relations since 1950. Rejecting Chinese demands for preconditions (Afghanistan, Cambodia, territorial issues) before normalization of relations, the tone of the article is nonetheless hopeful. The positive overtures begun in Brezhnev's last year in power finally resulted in better relations under Gorbachev.

Just a little over thirty-five years ago, on February 14, 1950, a Treaty of Friendship, Alliance and Mutual Assistance between the Soviet Union and the People's Republic of China was signed in Moscow. What made the treaty a document of the greatest historical significance was that it was concluded at a time when China faced a political, military and economic blockade organized by US imperialism. Hence, a treaty of alliance with the USSR was of major importance to the PRC in that strained situation.

Izvestiia, 13 February 1985, as translated in *Reprints from the Soviet Press,* vol. 40, nos. 5–6, 15–31 March 1985, pp. 57–62. *Excerpts.*

The event was welcomed both in China and the Soviet Union. China found the Soviet Union to be a reliable friend and ally in the drive to overcome its economic backwardness, strengthen its international positions, and build a socialist society....

The Soviet-Chinese Treaty embodied the highest principles of international friendship and cooperation. It was an example of a new type of international relations, typical of the fraternal socialist nations. There was close contact and a systematic exchange of opinions and experience between the CPSU and the CPC, and between the Governments and various departments of the two countries. Sino-Soviet cooperation in international affairs covered a wide range of issues relating to the confrontation of the two world social systems, socialism and imperialism, and to the struggle of the socialist community for peace and international security. Economic, scientific, technological and cultural relations between the Soviet Union and China developed on a broad scale....

In their message to the Soviet leaders on the 5th anniversary of the Soviet-Chinese Treaty, Mao Zedong, Liu Shaoqi and Zhou Enlai, commending the Soviet Union's cooperation and assistance, wrote that they [the USSR] "have shown to the whole world the great vital force of such international relations of a new type.... The Treaty of Friendship, Alliance and Mutual Assistance between China and the Soviet Union is a great, peaceful treaty, a symbol of the deep friendship between China and the Soviet Union."

The 8th Congress of the Communist Party of China, held in 1956, reaffirmed the CPC's general strategy of building socialism in alliance with the USSR and the other countries of the socialist community. However, as early as 1958 and 1959 the first signs appeared to indicate a revision of the decisions of the 8th Congress of the CPC. Later on, in the 1960s and 1970s, the Chinese leaders began to undertake actions that ran counter to the Soviet-Chinese Treaty and revealed what an unreliable partner China actually was. They stopped participating in international actions to ensure peace and security, and directed their efforts toward wrecking the policy of peaceful coexistence, heightening inter-ational tensions, and hastening "the military showdown with imperialism."...

Finally, the Chinese leaders also violated those provisions of the Treaty which obligated the parties concerned to build their relations in a spirit of friendship and cooperation and in conformity with the principles of equality, mutual interest as well as mutual respect for national sovereignty and territorial integrity, and non-intervention in each other's internal affairs. From 1964 on, various quarters in China, including those at top levels, began to make territorial claims against their neighbor and, later on, urged a united international front against the Soviet Union. The USSR was formally declared to be a state hostile to China. That policy climaxed in border incidents provoked by China in 1969.

Long before the 30-year term of the Soviet-Chinese Treaty of Friendship, Alliance and Mutual Assistance was due to expire, there had been speculation in Peking to the effect that this document had "lost all meaning," had "become a scrap of paper," "outlived its usefulness," etc.

It is necessary to emphasize that even during those years when the Chinese authorities started to play down the significance of the Treaty, the government of the USSR invariably continued to hold a clear and consistent position in respect of that document and just as invariably proceeded from the assumption that the Treaty was as valid as ever and that the commitments both parties had assumed under it remained in force and were therefore honored by the Soviet Union. The Soviet government officially informed the Chinese side of this, notably through diplomatic channels. Nevertheless, the Standing Committee of the National People's Congress of China announced

on April 3, 1979, that it was terminating the Treaty.

The Soviet Government qualified this as an unfriendly act in its Statement of April 4....

After China chose to repudiate the Treaty of Alliance with the USSR, the Soviet side put forward further proposals more than once for restoring confidence and cooperation between the two countries and for laying equal and mutually acceptable foundations under international law for Soviet-Chinese relations. In top-level statements in March and September 1982, the USSR declared itself ready to seek agreement with China on urgent questions of bilateral relations "without any preconditions." In 1983, China was invited to join the Soviet Union in framing a common position and undertaking common action against the resurgence of Japanese militarism.... In August 1983, the Soviet leaders went on record for raising the level of bilateral relations, carrying out confidence-building measures along the common border, and for a dialogue with China on matters relating to the promotion of peace and international security. As Konstantin Chernenko, General Secretary of the CPSU Central Committee and President of the Presidium of the Supreme Soviet of the USSR has stressed, "As we consistently implement the principled line adopted at the 26th Congress of the CPSU we invariably work for improved relations with the PRC and take the appropriate steps in that direction. We always keep the door open to constructive negotiations with China."

Regrettably, the official Chinese approach to relations with the Soviet Union remains ambiguous.... The Chinese media are still quite often trying to make the average Chinese see the Soviet Union as a source of threats to China's security and sovereignty.

The unvarying view of the Soviet Union is that there have never been any objective reasons, nor are there any now, for any estrangement between the peoples of our two countries. The Soviet Union will speak out against any moves in Chinese policy that are unfriendly to it or to other fraternal nations; yet it is to be hoped that sooner or later common sense and a proper appreciation of the Chinese people's objective interests will prevail in Peking. The Soviet Union is in favor of carrying on a dialogue with China and normalizing relations with the People's Republic of China, provided that it is true normalization in the interest of all socialist nations, and not at the expense of our country's friends and allies.

Suggested Readings

Byrnes, Robert F. (ed.): *After Brezhnev: Sources of Soviet Conduct in the 1980s* (Bloomington, IN: Indiana University Press, 1983).

Hough, Jerry: "Andropov's First Year," *Problems of Communism* November–December 1983, pp. 49–64.

Luttwak, Edward: *The Grand Strategy of the Soviet Union* (New York: St. Martin's Press, 1983).

Medvedev, Zhores: *Andropov* (New York: W. W. Norton, 1983).

Meyer, Stephen: "Soviet Theater Nuclear Forces, Part I: Development of Doctrine and Objectives," *Adelphi Papers,* no. 187 (London: International Institute for Strategic Studies, 1984).

Nogee, Joseph L. (ed.): *Soviet Politics: Russia After Brezhnev* (New York: Praeger, 1985).

Potter, William: "Nuclear Proliferation: US-Soviet Cooperation," *Washington Quarterly,* Winter 1985, pp. 141–153.

Shevchenko, Arkady: *Breaking with Moscow* (New York: Ballantine, 1985).

Solovyov, Vladimir, and Elena Klepikova: *Yuri Andropov: A Secret Passage into the Kremlin* (New York: Macmillan, 1983).

Zlotnik, Marc D.: "Chernenko Succeeds," *Problems of Communism,* March–April 1984, pp. 17–31.

CHAPTER SEVEN

Soviet Foreign Policy under Gorbachev— A New Era? (1985–)

The long-awaited transition to the younger generation of Soviet leaders finally took place on 11 March 1985. Shortly after the death of K. U. Chernenko, it was announced that his successor as General Secretary of the CPSU would be Mikhail S. Gorbachev, whose political patron had been Yuri Andropov. It was Andropov who had brought Gorbachev into the upper echelons of the Soviet leadership during the latter part of the Brezhnev administration. Gorbachev's résumé suggested that the attention of the new Soviet leader would be turned inward to the intractable problems of the Soviet economy. The first lawyer (by education) since Lenin to become General Secretary, he also was a trained agricultural expert with practical experience.[1] There was no special reason to believe that Gorbachev would excel at foreign policy and diplomatic matters, inasmuch as he had almost no experience in these spheres. Indeed, first on Gorbachev's agenda was reform of the entire domestic economic system. After only a few months in power, he openly declared to the West that a new and far-reaching detente was the sine qua non for such domestic changes to occur,[2] thereby directly linking his domestic reform agenda to foreign policy.

To put it in Leninist terms, Gorbachev needed a ''breathing space'' of relaxation of tension with the West to resuscitate a flagging economy bloated on excessive defense spending, which had not appreciably improved Soviet national security. Radical reform of the decrepit eco-

---

[1] See Gorbachev's official biography in *Pravda*, 12 March 1985, p. 1. His law degree was from Moscow State University.
[2] See ''An Interview with Gorbachev,'' *Time Magazine*, 9 September 1985, pp. 22–29.

nomic system at home and detente abroad were parts of the formula that Gorbachev devised to "restructure" the Soviet Union, with the goal of making it competitive with the rest of the world. Everywhere Gorbachev traveled during this time—in Europe, Asia, North America, and within the Soviet Union—"new thinking" was promoted as the centerpiece of both Soviet domestic and foreign policy. The stark admission of deep-seated structural problems throughout the Soviet system soon became a common element of the Soviet self-criticism that Gorbachev initiated. This was the first time that the West had heard such words since Stalin's evaluation of the First Five-Year Plan in 1933.

Perestroika (restructuring, rebuilding) and *glasnost* (openness, publicity) both at home and abroad would help to create a second revolution in Soviet society, according to Gorbachev, one which would lead Soviet society into a prosperous era of technological and economic competitiveness, the implications of which for future Soviet military performance were amply apparent. It soon became clear, however, that this entire scheme amounted to a frontal assault on the heavily bureaucratized system of social management that Stalin had created, which stood in the way of technological and economic progress and the advent of the super-computerized information age to the Soviet Union.

While the struggle to reform the economic system continued into 1990 with little palpable success, the first genuine elections since 1918, held on 26 March 1989, augured well for the possibility of expanded political reforms. *Glasnost* allowed for the improvement of diplomatic relations and U.S.-USSR people-to-people contacts, such as during and after the devastating Armenian earthquake of December 1988, but the inertia of the huge Soviet bureaucracy continued to present the foremost obstacle to the massive restructuring Gorbachev consistently promoted.

Unlike previous Soviet leaders and their often formulaic and rhetorical approach to the issue of conflict and discord between the two su-

perpowers, Gorbachev early on began to exhibit substantial interest in improving the cold war atmosphere that had reappeared after the Soviet invasion of Afghanistan in late 1979. It has been suggested that Gorbachev's stress on the commonality of U.S.-Soviet security concerns in an increasingly interdependent world "distinguishes his philosophy from the historic Soviet search for security through advantage."[1] Of course, caution should be observed in extrapolating from select and limited actions by one Soviet leader over the near term to a fundamental Soviet change in world outlook.

And yet, it cannot be denied that the Soviet-U.S. relationship and the full range of Soviet global activities and international relations began to undergo what seemed to be extraordinary changes in the first four years of Gorbachev's leadership. Four U.S.-Soviet summits (Chapter 7, documents 6, 11, and 21) , an historic accord eliminating an entire class (INF) of nuclear weapons and delivery systems (Chapter 7, document 20), a Soviet agreement to withdraw from Afghanistan (Chapter 7, documents 22 and 24), and a Soviet change of attitude toward the UN (Chapter 7, documents 16 and 25), including a promise of payment in arrears of its share of UN operating costs, all represented substantive evidence of real change in Soviet policies. Indeed, Mr. Gorbachev seemed in his first four years to be, as Prime Minister Margaret Thatcher of Britain assessed, a man with whom the West could "do business."

Do the changes that Mr. Gorbachev proposes for the Soviet system mean that an irreversible shift has taken place in the emphasis and direction of Soviet foreign policy and in the Soviet worldview? The opening reading by Seweryn Bialer and the documents in this chapter offer evidence in answer to this question that can be in-

---

[1]Comments attributed to Prof. Michael Mandelbaum during a Congressional roundtable. See "Gorbachev's Era," *Congressional Roundtable on US-Soviet Relations* (Washington, DC: Peace through Law Education Fund, 1987), 10.

terpreted in different ways. Professor Bialer sees fundamental changes in Soviet foreign policy taking place. He analyzes what is behind the "new thinking" that Gorbachev has adopted as a popular slogan and finds that, indeed, there are new and hopeful signs of both tactical flexibility and strategic changes.

Many of the documents in this section can be viewed as historical milestones. The candor with which Soviet spokesmen have addressed issues and engaged in types of self-criticism which, prior to the Gorbachev era, were taboo, marks the documents as particularly significant, especially in comparison with earlier periods of Soviet foreign policy. While there is certainly much more that the USSR must accomplish in terms of societal openness regarding its own past, some of these documents exhibit the first steps in this direction. There is, however, room for much more change in Soviet domestic and foreign policy before an unequivocal "yes" can be given to the question of irreversible change in the Soviet system. True, Marxist-Leninist language and class analysis of Soviet policy seem to have begun to change, but some aspects of the documents included here indicate that old ways die hard, even under an apparent pragmatist such as Gorbachev.

The barometer of openness has registered little change yet in the military dimension of Soviet foreign policy. By the early part of 1989, the key economic gauge of military allocations had not yet shown the kinds of reductions to indicate that a significant trickle down effect of Gorbachev's approach was occurring. And yet, Gorbachev's landmark UN speech of December 1988 (Chapter 7, document 25) held out the prospect of progress in the resolution of many issues, including Strategic Arms Reduction Talks (START), settlement of regional issues (Cambodia, Angola), and the general improvement of bilateral U.S.-Soviet relations. In this speech, a small but significant unilateral step was taken by the Soviet leader to reduce the level of Soviet forces in Europe. However, it remains to be seen whether real change in Soviet policy is so extensive such that there will be no possibility of a repeal of reform by a post-Gorbachev leadership or of its suffocation by the weight of bureaucratic forces beyond Gorbachev's control. Only with time will the questions of continuity versus change in Soviet foreign policy come into clearer perspective.

"New Thinking" and Soviet Foreign Policy

Seweryn Bialer

THE ORIGINS OF "NEW THINKING"

From the Western point of view, the nature of Mikhail Gorbachev's leadership, the internal situation of the Soviet Union and the directions of its development are critically important because of their potential impact on Soviet international behaviour. On the Soviet side, the new leadership understands better than any of its predecessors since Stalin that domestic strength decisively influences foreign-policy success. Khrushchev was a gambler who frequently bluffed and tried to achieve foreign-policy success on the cheap. Brezhnev was cautious and conservative, and although he presided over his country's attainment of strategic parity with the United States, he let the domestic power of the country slip to a point where it became insufficient to support the Soviet Union as an ascending global power. Gorbachev is clearly convinced that domestic strength and internal resources are key factors in Soviet foreign policy. In this respect Gorbachev's domestic programme is at the same time his most basic foreign-policy statement.

While engaged in a radical process of comprehensive reforms at home that has introduced into the international language the Russian term *perestroika* (restructuring), the Soviet leadership is at the same time engaged in a major revision of its conduct of foreign affairs. The equivalent of domestic *perestroika* in the revision of its international policies has become known within the Soviet Union and abroad as the "New Think-

ing." The real "newness" of Soviet thinking in this respect is rather questionable. Most of the ideas that it subsumes were developed in the West in the late 1960s or 1970s, though of course their partial adoption by the USSR is new. What is most impressive in the "New Thinking," is not so much its newness, but the very fact that the Soviet leadership really is engaged in serious thinking about international affairs. In the 1970s and early 1980s, Soviet foreign policy was governed by inertia and unquestioned traditional dogmas. This state of affairs, and the predictability of Soviet international behaviour, has been sharply reversed by Gorbachev.

What are the sources of this "New thinking"? Very often in Western writing these sources are identified in a simplified and trivialized fashion. Most often they are reduced to the proposition that, because of very serious domestic economic difficulties, the USSR is forced to reduce its international commitments, and therefore can no longer afford the strategic arms race. In reality, the most important causes of the "New Thinking" are much deeper and more varied. It is important to identify the range and depth of these sources correctly. Only then can the seriousness and potential longevity of the Soviet "New Thinking" be assessed realistically and accurately.

On the domestic side, the main source of Soviet "New Thinking" is a systemic crisis that is political, social, economic, ideological and cultural in nature. Gorbachev inherited a system in an advanced state of political breakdown where the flow of authority from the center downwards and the flow of information from the peripheries to the centre were seriously disrupted. Almost all strata of the population were becoming increasingly alienated from the regime. The professional and middle classes, whose support was necessary for running society, were ignored by the Party leadership and denied access to power, professional autonomy or appropriate economic rewards. The Soviet social organism was sick, beset by all sorts of problems (e.g., rampant al-

"'New Thinking' and Soviet Foreign Policy," *Survival*, July–August 1988, pp. 291–309. Copyright The International Institute for Strategic Studies. Reprinted by permission.

coholism, all-embracing corruption, increased mortality rates, the breakdown of medical service, and a steep decline of the work ethic). The Stalinist model of the economy was still intact, and the Soviet leadership's attempt to switch the strategy of growth from extensive to intensive methods was entirely unsuccessful, and in fact impossible without structural changes. Soviet ideology became fully routinized, eliminating a common denominator of relations between the ruler and the ruled even within the Communist Party itself.

Culturally, the Soviet Union became a wasteland where high culture survived in the forbidden zone of *samizdat* literature, and the mass culture, of both native and Western origin, was alive in the tangential gray area that was neither sanctioned nor effectively rejected by the authorities. The deepening, multi-dimensional crisis of the Soviet system called for the ruling elite to reorder their priorities and reorientate their efforts towards domestic concerns. Under these conditions, the basic function of Soviet foreign and security policies was to provide favourable conditions for domestic revitalization, whenever possible retaining the international gains of the past.

The domestic crisis of the Soviet system coincided with the development of the Third Industrial Revolution abroad—the rapid, explosive technological growth in capitalist countries in America, Europe and Asia. For the first time in Soviet history, the economic and technological gap between the Soviet Union and major and minor capitalist countries was opening at an alarming and accelerating rate instead of gradually closing. This called into question the basic Soviet belief that time works for them, that history is on their side. Only shortly after the USSR attained strategic parity with the United States, doubt was cast on the Soviet long-range ability to compete even militarily with its adversaries and the magnitude of the opportunity costs of such a competition increased immensely. The visible and rapidly growing technological gap se-

verely wounded the national pride of the Soviet political elite, creating a psychological shock of immense intensity. It also brought home the truth that the USSR was in need of a fundamental and comprehensive change; not to catch up but simply to keep up with capitalist industrial democracies. The external dimension of the Soviet systemic crisis gave a sense of urgency to Soviet reform plans and reinforced the conviction of the necessity to concentrate on domestic tasks.

Finally, Soviet foreign policy itself had reached a point of impasse. On the strategic military side, the resurgence of the United States in the late 1970s and early 1980s, showed clearly that the Soviet dream of strategic superiority was unattainable. The implementation of the INF dual-track decision demonstrated the cohesion and resolve of the Western Alliance. The *Solidarity* crisis in Poland in 1980–81 was a watershed in Soviet evaluation and understanding of the dangerous situation in its East European empire. The invasion of Afghanistan created a situation not unlike the American predicament in Vietnam, a decade earlier. Moreover, the return on Soviet investment in civil wars and regional conflicts in Africa could hardly be counted a success. Soviet adventures in the Third World demonstrated the limits of translating military power into political power and influence in the international arena. The policy of the USSR's Vietnamese ally to dominate Indochina by the invasion of Kampuchea bogged down in the face of local resistance and Chinese resolve to prevent its success. By the mid-1980s, there were probably more so-called National Liberation Struggles directed against Soviet-supported states than there were earlier against American clients.

Soviet influence in the Middle East had reached its lowest point in the post-Stalin era. The influence of the Soviet-supported PLO declined considerably as a result of the civil war in Lebanon. Syria became the USSR's only ally in the Middle East; unruly, defiant and beyond control. At times the Syrian ally was outright dangerous because of its potential to involve the Soviet Union in confrontations with the United States. Syrian clashes with Israel also demonstrated the inferiority of Soviet weapons. The USSR's other semi-ally, Libya, was more of an embarrassment than a help to Soviet international stature. The overthrow of the Shah of Iran, with whom the Soviet Union had enjoyed good relations and stable borders, and the explosion onto the international scene of the elemental force of Islamic fundamentalism created new dangers for the Soviet Union. In short, the Soviet security and foreign-policy strategy of the 1970s and early 1980s failed while the aging Soviet leadership continued to pursue its old course, unwilling and unable to make necessary fundamental readjustments in the international arena.

By the late 1970s and particularly by the early 1980s, Soviet foreign policy in almost all its dimensions had reached a dead-end and required major strategic modifications, because of its impact on the domestic situation and its international repercussions. Yet the mounting pressure of such a change would have most likely remained unheeded were it not for the Soviet leadership succession, which contained some unusual characteristics and led to some unlikely consequences.

The succession encompassed three changes in the position of General Secretary. Consequently, personal loyalties sometimes established by decades of association were weakened or broken. Possession of a political network ceased to be necessary to contend for the top position. This permitted Gorbachev, a newcomer and relative outsider in the top leadership, whose support for reform was known before his victory, to win the top prize without a political machine. Moreover, the succession involved a major turnover within the top leadership and the elite in all spheres of Soviet life, and coincided with a generational change. Gorbachev inherited a leadership group that, with the exception of China's was probably the oldest in the world. The succession has replaced the political gen-

eration that grew up in Stalinist Russia with a leadership that is more apt to support change and to recognize the need for domestic reforms and foreign-policy changes.

Finally, the historical accident that succeeded in bringing Gorbachev to power is of major importance. It promoted to the Moscow leadership an individual who was both innovative and pragmatic, despite his archtypical Party *apparatchik* background, and placed him in the top position of General Secretary. Gorbachev's personal role in promoting and leading major domestic and foreign-policy reforms during his as yet short tenure in office is considerable. His vision of far-reaching changes has been more radical and comprehensive than any of the other members of his Party leadership generation.

To appreciate the serious nature of Gorbachev's "New Thinking," it is absolutely necessary to comprehend the depth of the intertwined root causes of Soviet domestic and foreign-policy reforms. Far from being a breathing spell designed to facilitate improvements in Soviet economic performance, "New Thinking" represents an innovation as radical as *perestroika* and *glasnost* (openness). Moreover, "New Thinking" as a process of profound reassessment of the Soviet approach to international relations has only started. It holds the promise of further evolution and long-term change in Soviet international behaviour.

TACTICAL, STRATEGIC AND PROGRAMMATIC CHANGE IN SOVIET POLICY

The "New Thinking" in Soviet foreign affairs can be analysed according to two criteria: the depth of actual or potential change in comparison to the past; and the extent of assimilation in the process of Soviet foreign policy-making. The first criterion would distinguish between tactical, strategic and programmatic modification. Tactical changes are short-term alterations of forms, while strategic changes are intermediate-range adjustments in direction. Programmatic changes are long-range redefinitions of goals and aspirations. The second criterion would differentiate between novel ideas that entered the process of Soviet foreign policy decision-making, and actual policy changes.

Tactical Changes

The changes in Soviet foreign policy at the tactical level are primarily reflected in the new and impressive flexibility of Soviet diplomacy and approaches to negotiations. An example of this diplomatic flexibility is the effort to improve relations with all capitalist states or, to take another example, to try to resume direct relations with the state of Israel. Yet in most cases this effort is not associated with significant changes in basic attitudes regarding the resolution of outstanding issues with those countries. A typical example here is provided by Soviet policy toward Japan. Verbal modifications of Soviet policy, such as Gorbachev's statement that the USSR recognizes that the issue of the northern territories (the four Japanese islands annexed by the USSR after World War II) is of major importance to Japan, are not followed by the slightest sign of Soviet willingness to enter into negotiations. Another example of tactical flexibility is provided by Soviet willingness to reach a compromise on the delineation of the Sino-Soviet border on the Amur River, and the withdrawal of two Soviet divisions deployed in Mongolia on the Chinese border. This withdrawal was simply a tactical gesture that in no way responded to the Chinese demand for changes in the mode of deployment or for significant reduction in the number of Soviet forces stationed on Chinese borders (about one third of the entire Soviet conventional force).

Another example of Soviet tactical flexibility, this time in negotiations, is provided by the Soviet-American agreement on the abolition of intermediate-range nuclear forces (INF). New flexibility was demonstrated first of all in the USSR being prepared to separate the INF negotiations from strategic arms negotiations, a separation strongly resisted in the past. An even more impressive example of tactical flexibility in arms-control negotiations was Soviet willingness to avoid a confrontation on the Strategic Defense Initiative (SDI) issue that would derail the INF agreement. Before Gorbachev came to power, and even in the first 18 months of his rule, the Soviet leadership was obsessed with President Reagan's SDI programme. This obsession started visibly to decline in 1987, although Soviet concern over SDI is still significant and remains prominent in strategic arms-reduction negotiations. Yet, to help to achieve an INF agreement, the USSR agreed in the final step of the negotiations to a formulation of the SDI issue so ambiguous that each side was free to interpret it as a victory for their own position. The Soviet leadership embraced this tactic to reach the INF accord and leave the SDI issue for the future, when a new president and an already reluctant Congress may themselves move away from "Star Wars."

Strategic Changes

At the strategic level, the modification of Soviet foreign-policy thinking is best exemplified by the evolution of military doctrine towards the principles of "Active Defence." This doctrine, implicitly, and from time to time even explicitly, recognizes for the first time the legitimacy of NATO's apprehension about the size, structure and particularly the mode of deployment of Soviet conventional forces in Europe. The USSR accepts NATO's evaluation of the offensive nature of the Soviet force-mix and deployments in Europe.

The doctrine of "Active Defence," if implemented in the European theatre, will require at least three major modifications to Soviet conventional forces—in their size, structure and mode of deployment. The exact balance, or rather imbalance, of NATO and Warsaw Pact forces in Europe is a matter of debate both in the NATO countries and in the Soviet Union. There is, however, a consensus in the West that the Soviet forces are preponderant by a significant margin. The new Soviet doctrine would require either a unilateral cut in the size of its deployed forces, or a bilateral but asymmetrical cut in the forces of the two military blocs.

The structure of deployed Soviet forces is heavily weighted in favour of elite and "heavy" divisions. Their force mix is geared clearly to large offensive operations. The new Soviet doctrine, if serious, would require the thinning of those force components that are most oriented towards offensive operations—heavy tanks, battlefield air support, heavy helicopter gunships. The mode of deployment of Soviet forces in Europe follows the standard strategy adopted by the USSR from its World War II experience—deployment of assault troops close to the front line, heavy concentration of armour and artillery along the main "corridors" of the eventual attack to assure major superiority of numbers and breakthrough capacity, and significant armour and air cavalry reserves close to the front line to follow breakthroughs and exploit in depth the success of the first wave of troops. The new Soviet doctrine, if implemented, would require at least the thinning of the front-line troops and their dispersal away from the corridors of the main offensive directions.

The military doctrine of "Active Defence" is a serious and authentic strategic modification in Soviet military thinking imposed on the military by the political leadership. It may lead to some Soviet unilateral steps in the directions discussed above. In any case, it should facilitate the immensely difficult negotiations on conventional forces on which the US and the USSR will embark seriously in the near future.

Programmatic Changes

On the programmatic level, one element stands out as being particularly important—the fundamentally modified definition and approach to national security. The traditional Soviet concept of "national security" has been at the heart of Soviet domestic and international policies almost from the beginning of the Soviet state. Stalin's forced industrialization, the creation by force of the East European Soviet empire, the concept of "capitalist encirclement," the belief in the inevitability of wars between the Soviet Union and the West, Khrushchev's international offensive in the Third World, Brezhnev's military build-up beyond any definition of sufficiency—all were expressions of an understanding of "national security" that was uniquely Soviet. Each major country seeks to eliminate or reduce potential sources of threat to its survival and interests and subscribes to what can be called in strategic terminology a "damage-limiting" philosophy. Yet the Soviet leadership seemed to carry it further than most countries, as if satisfied only with "absolute security." But the search for "absolute security" is self-defeating, because it requires measures and military policies that other states find inimical to their own vital interests. Consequently, other states adopt countermeasures that in the end diminish the security of the USSR itself. If the Soviet Union can feel secure only when other countries feel insecure, its understanding of its own national security neither promotes global stability nor a fundamental decline of international tensions.

The main sources of the traditional Soviet concept of "national security" were the lengthy Soviet experience of international isolation and clashes with other powers, and the Leninist doctrine of Imperialism that defined the 20th century as an era of "wars and revolution," where revolutions grow out of wars. Khrushchev's ideological innovation at the 20th Party Congress in 1956, that wars are no longer inevitable, did almost nothing to change the totalistic Soviet concept of "national security." Most disturbing was that the achievement in the early 1970s of strategic parity with the US, the breakthrough in the balance of military power that the USSR had sought from the beginning of the Cold War, evidently did not have sufficient psychological impact to push Soviet leaders away from the traditional concept of "national security." Nor did it change Soviet military doctrine or reduce significantly the military build-up. Gorbachev's new understanding and redefinition of Soviet national security in the nuclear age, under conditions of Soviet-American strategic parity, are the first authoritative revisions of the traditional concept. Several elements of this revision are central.

The first is the idea of "nuclear sufficiency," which proclaims that nuclear build-up beyond Mutual Assured Destruction is meaningless, and that a much lower level of nuclear weapons achieved by radical mutual reductions will lessen the existing psychological tensions, diminish the danger of an accidental nuclear strike and increase the security of both super-powers and the world.

The second element is the concept of "common security" (or "mutual security"), that expresses in Soviet *thinking* a major departure from the *practice* of traditional Soviet defence policies. The idea behind the concept of "common security" is as simple as it is revolutionary. It proclaims that US reactions to perceptions of military insecurity endanger Soviet military security and consequently do not serve Soviet interests. Soviet reactions to perceptions of military insecurity have the same negative implications for US interests. Therefore, each side must seriously consider the probable impact of its defence policy on the other side—any build-up of military power will likely initiate an arms-race cycle that in the end will not increase the security of either side.

It is sometimes said that the simple truths are the most difficult to catch, particularly by political leaders whose thinking is highly ideologized. Gorbachev's conceptual departure from the traditional Soviet understanding of "national security," and the adoption of the notion of "common security" may therefore seem very obvious and undramatic. In fact it represents more discontinuity in the Soviet way of thinking, a revolutionary departure from the principles on which Soviet defence policies have been based. If the conceptual modification is implemented in practical Soviet defence policies its importance will be immense.

Gorbachev's redefinition of "national security" also concerns the inclusions into this concept of factors that are not directly military. The most obvious broadening of the notion of "national security" by Gorbachev concerns Soviet economic power. The domestic morale and order, the vitality of the country, and the state of its alliances all find a place in the understanding of "national security" that Gorbachev is trying to impose on the military and to explain to the political elite. He is postulating a paradoxical proposition that, particularly in the light of Soviet traditions, is very innovative: a Soviet Union that participates in a strict arms-control regime, that cuts its nuclear forces significantly, that devotes equal or even more attention to its civilian economy, that is flexible and ready for even difficult compromises in its foreign policy, will be more secure than it is now, or than it would be by deploying thousands of new weapons. This idea was expressed most succinctly by Soviet Foreign Minister Eduard Shevardnadze in a speech to the Soviet Diplomatic Academy in June 1987:

> The main thing is that the country not incur additional expenses in connection with the need to maintain its defence capacity and protect its legitimate foreign-policy interests. This means that we must seek ways to limit and reduce military rivalry, eliminate confrontational features in relations with other states, and suppress conflict and crisis situations.

It seems that this fact of the reconceptualization of "national security" by the new Soviet leader is an almost necessary precondition to dynamism and success in his domestic programme. Gorbachev must convince the political elite and persuade or force the military to accept his truth.

Without it, the reordering of national priorities and his programme of "renewal" will probably end in his political defeat.

CHANGING ASSUMPTIONS IN SOVIET THINKING

Gorbachev's "New Thinking" has significantly influenced the process of shaping Soviet foreign policy. In many cases this influence is reflected in the ideas that percolate throughout the Soviet foreign-policy community, including at the leadership level. In some cases this influence has already been expressed by changes in policies.

It is often asserted that changes that have taken place in Soviet foreign policy under Gorbachev are limited to words only. But one should not so easily discount the importance of words, particularly in such a centralized and ideological state as the Soviet Union, and especially if the "words" are pronounced by an authoritative leader and may be of a programmatic nature. It is also entirely normal in the USSR that policy changes start with words.

Some of the ideas that circulate in the Soviet foreign-policy establishment and find their way into print reflect new underlying assumptions about "world capitalism" that differ from the well-established "self-evident truths" of the past. Soviet leaders and their aides are at last unable and unwilling to negate the overwhelming evidence that modern capitalism is very different from the images that were conveyed to generation after generation of Soviet leaders, Party members, and the population of the USSR. Five assumptions underlying the newly-shaped attitudes toward modern capitalism are of special importance and interest.

First, the "new" world capitalism is not in a state of general crisis, but is a dynamic force that pushes forward technological development on an unprecedented scale. The stimulant of competition, far from being a destructive and wasteful influence, promotes economic growth and productivity. Second, the new capitalism disposes

of major reserves of internal sociopolitical stability. It was able to eliminate or diminish significantly the social ills that beset its early history. The old idea of the pauperization of the working classes under capitalism in absolute terms has been abandoned, and the idea of the "relative impoverishment" is now being questioned. Third, for many third-world countries the capitalist path of development brought explosive growth, technological progress and improvements in the standard of living. Fourth, the conviction that world capitalism is doomed by history to disintegrate under the weight of its own contradictions is now being questioned. Many in the USSR now believe that the political and economic contradictions among "the Imperialists" are containable and can to a large extent be regulated by bilateral agreements or supranational bodies. And, fifth, the Soviet leadership now believes that the United States and NATO are not posed to strike eastwards, that they do not present an imminent danger to the Soviet Union, and that "bourgeois democracy" constitutes a barrier against war preparations in the West.

A new Soviet insight into the process of international relations that has evolved from the re-evaluation of old perceptions concerns the seemingly simple but very important understanding of the role of action-reaction in relations between states. Soviet leaders have started to address the self-defeating anomaly in their thinking, that was infuriating to states that had to deal with them; namely, the role of the process of action-reaction in the evolution of Soviet-American relations. Each country's international behaviour is shaped above everything else by two factors: domestic and historical determinants, and the actions of other states. In the past, however, when trying to explain American actions or those of other adversaries, the USSR put all the weight on the first determinant, and, by and large, ignored the second as an explanatory factor. This approach was by no means restricted only to the USSR, but in its case this distortion of reality was of ridiculous proportions. At no time did it recognize that its own conduct could explain much in the behaviour of other countries. There are indications that this astigmatism on the part of Soviet foreign policy-makers is giving way to a more realistic interpretation. The recognition by Gorbachev of the notion of "mutual" or "common security" is probably the most important example of this more realistic assessment of the role of action-reaction in the Soviet-American relations. Yet this is only a beginning. In most cases, American foreign and security policies still seem to the USSR to have a momentum of their own, a momentum that is not greatly influenced by Soviet behaviour and is decisive in shaping the US course. Until Soviet (and American) policy-makers recognize the role of their own decisions in shaping the decisions of the other side, Soviet-American foreign- and security-policy behaviour will preclude lasting agreements.

Another key issue in Soviet relations with the United States and other capitalist countries that has been refurbished and reassessed by the "New Thinking" is the concept of "peaceful co-existence" between countries with different socio-political systems. The USSR claims that this fundamental concept was originated by Lenin. This is true, but its meaning for Lenin was quite different from the present one. For Lenin (and Stalin), "peaceful co-existence" meant simply that in the struggle with the capitalist countries the Soviet revolutionary and expansionist pressure could not continue without a break and that, when the conditions did not favour revolutionary and expansionist goals, the USSR should retrench and wait for better times. For Lenin and Stalin, "peaceful co-existence" signified simply an enforced pause in their attack on international capitalism, a *peredyshka* (breathing space) that would end when conditions were ripe for another round of revolutionary expansion, a round that would probably include military conflicts.

"Peaceful co-existence" acquired a different meaning under Khrushchev, the first Soviet leader to begin to understand the international realities of the nuclear age. He proclaimed that wars between capitalist and Communist countries were no longer inevitable. For both Khrushchev and Brezhnev, "peaceful co-existence" meant that Soviet expansion would be achieved without war. Gorbachev's "New Thinking" changes the concept of "peaceful co-existence" still further. It proclaims not only that these concepts denote much more than a transitional "breathing space," but that the idea of Soviet-orchestrated world-wide victory of socialism even without a war, is being abandoned. An adviser to the Soviet leadership wrote in July 1987 in *Pravda* that: "Interstate relations...cannot be the sphere in which the outcome of the confrontation between world socialism and world capitalism is settled." In relations between Soviet foreign policy and Communist ideology "fire breaks" should be established that separate the one from the other. "We have," said Gorbachev in his book *Perestroika,* "taken the steps necessary to rid our [foreign] policy of ideological prejudice."

For domestic purposes, the Soviet leadership is seeking doctrinal justification for this unorthodox way of thinking that will make it legitimate to the believers. For example, a high-ranking Party intellectual showed a Western academic a quote from Lenin's collected works to justify Soviet moderation in support of the revolutionary process abroad. In the work, the Soviet "founding father" states "that situations may arise when the interest of humanity at large takes precedence over the class interest of the proletariat." If such proclamations in fact become true in Soviet international practice, and the USSR abandons its position as "the helper of history," Gorbachev's "New Thinking" will represent a fundamental change that goes to the roots of the Soviet-American conflict.

Another element of the "New Thinking" promoted by Gorbachev concerns the question of "interdependence," which in the discussion of international relations in the West has become almost trite, but in fact constitutes a new theme in Soviet analysis and policy deliberations. One central phenomenon of the Third Industrial Revolution is the exponential growth in global interdependence, first in the economic sphere, but also in science and culture. There is growing evidence to suggest that this process is beginning to be recognized by the new Soviet leaders, and that they are aware of the insufficiency of Marxist and Leninist concepts to explain it.

The idea of a "global economy" is especially troublesome for the Soviet leadership to grasp, and even more difficult to understand in its consequences for individual industrial countries. The Soviet Union, except for the initial phase of its industrialization, developed in a state of virtual autarky. Although Stalin's successors rejected economic self-isolation, the Soviet economy, despite its immense size, plays only a marginal role in the global arena. For example, the structure of Soviet exports is typical of an underdeveloped country (i.e., dominance of raw materials). In addition, Soviet economic circulation in the global arena, as expressed by the share of imports and exports of goods, credit *and* capital in the Gross National Product, is so much lower than that of any other industrial country as to be globally insignificant, and to large extent marginal, for the Soviet Union itself.

Globalization of national economies introduced common thresholds and standards of modernity. To keep up with these standards, let alone to provide in particular areas the cutting edge of modern technology, requires self-generated national thrust and effort that demands adjustments in organization and social and cultural patterns. To be successful, however, this self-generating technological progress requires an opening of the economy to the global circulation of theoretical and applied science, managerial methods and skills, and capital. Gorbachev's policies and economic reforms move in the right direction insofar as they intend to open up more of the Soviet economy and science to global influences. These steps, still

mostly on paper however, are pitifully inadequate and hardly serve as a broad-gauged plan for the future.

The Soviet "New Thinking" about economic, scientific and cultural "interdependence," if serious, will have significant consequences for Soviet international relations. Economic and scientific needs will have to play a much stronger role in Soviet foreign-policy formation than the traditionally understood "security" requirements. Scientific and cultural sectors of Soviet society will have to become open to global interchange, which will drastically curb its current pattern of secrecy. In order for the global standards of modernity to influence Soviet development, Soviet enterprises will have to enter into international competition not primarily for the sake of earning hard currency, but to expand the islands of modernity within the Soviet economy and use them as levers for broader domestic modernization. Whether in the long run the political prerequisites of Soviet power will permit such transformations is an open question.

The Soviet understanding of "interdependence" goes beyond strictly economic, scientific and cultural questions. Most importantly, the growing understanding of the contemporary meaning of "interdependence" is conducive to a new way of thinking about international phenomena that stresses shared interests and ceases to view international relations as a "zero-sum" game. This type of thinking, alien to the traditional Soviet world-view, will require a long period of gestation to influence significantly the new leadership's basic approach to international relations. Certainly, for such a way of thinking to achieve a "critical mass" in the Soviet elite, it will also have to find a counterpart in "non-antagonistic" thinking in the West....

CONCLUSIONS

The vicissitudes of Soviet-American relations in the post–World War II era reflected a lack of synchronization between the two super-powers and the two alliance systems. Moreover, efforts towards improving relations inevitably dealt with the consequences of the Cold War and not the root causes. Currently, for the first time Soviet and American thinking seems to be in phase and is starting to deal with the main sources of the Cold War. The leadership of each super-power is by now convinced that it cannot achieve strategic superiority over the other. While in the 1970s and early 1980s national security concerns were given in both countries priority over economic matters, in the late 1980s and probably in the 1990s the primacy of economic concerns will be established. In both countries there is a movement away from interventionism and from the spirit of ideological crusade. Both countries and their allies are starting to re-evaluate old international commitments in the light of new political, military and economic realities. The new detente therefore holds the promise of being deeper and much longer lasting than the old.

DOCUMENT 1

Pravda Interview with Gorbachev

8 April 1985

Editor's commentary: In a Pravda interview less than one month after assuming his new position as General Secretary of the CPSU, Mr. Gorbachev spoke perhaps more candidly than any previous Soviet leader about the necessity to improve U.S.-Soviet relations, stressing the centrality of these relations for stability in world politics. Along these lines, he expressed Soviet fears over SDI and held out an olive branch to the United States regarding

Pravda, 8 April 1985, as translated in *Reprints from the Soviet Press*, vol. 40, no. 8, 30 April 1985.

INF and START, promising real progress in arms control at the Geneva talks by announcing a temporary moratorium on further INF deployments in Europe. What is perhaps most significant about these wide-ranging comments is that they were offered in such an authoritative manner so soon after his rise to the top leadership position.

Question: Our newspaper is getting many letters, both from Soviet people and from abroad, on international affairs. How would you describe the present international situation?

Answer: I can well understand the increased interest that people have in international affairs....

And this is not mere chance. The world today is full of complex problems—political, economic and social. There is the reality of two opposite social systems, socialism and capitalism, existing side by side. Also, dozens of new states with their own histories, traditions and with their own interests are active in the international arena....

In order to develop international relations in the world today, one cannot help but take this into account. One must not ignore the interests of other states or, more importantly, try to deny them, their right to choose their road of development without outside interference. In the broad context this is precisely (the meaning of) the policy of peaceful coexistence, under which each of the systems has to prove, by force of example and not by force of arms, which of them is better.

Another conclusion that is just as urgent is the necessity of ending the arms race. The development of the international situation has reached a point at which the question arises: Where do we go from here?...

There is an acute need for international co-operation in developing dialogue, in searching for realistic solutions that would ease tensions in the world and help block the road of the arms race....

Question: Much in the world is being associated with the state of Soviet-American relations. In your opinion, have any possibilities of these relations changing for the better appeared?

Answer: Relations between the USSR and the USA are an exceptionally important factor in international politics. But we can hardly look at the world only through the prism of these relations. We understand the importance of other countries in international affairs and take this into consideration when evaluating the general world situation.

Are there currently any changes for the better in Soviet-American relations? There is no simple answer to this question. Some things give reason for hope: but there is still a lot that causes alarm.

New Soviet-American talks on nuclear and space arms have begun in Geneva. This is a positive fact.

Jointly with the United States, we defined the subject and aims of the talks and, to put it briefly, defined them as follows: not to start an arms race in space; to stop it on Earth; and to start radical reductions of nuclear arms, their total liquidation being the ultimate aim.

Now it is necessary to fulfill this agreement. The Geneva talks are important. I am saying this first of all because the direction of the further development of Soviet-American relations and world development as a whole is now being decided. The choice is as follows: either an arms race in all directions and a growing threat of war or the strengthening of universal security and a more durable peace for all.

True, there are some shifts in other areas of Soviet-American relations, but only very minimal ones. On the whole, relations remain tense.

In Washington those in power are banking on strength, and aren't even concealing this. Moreover, they are counting on building up superior strength that would subordinate the rest of the world to the USA. For them, diplomacy and talks are virtually subordinate to missiles and bombers. For it is a fact that the new strategic arms

programs being pushed though congress are sponsored, among others, by the very same men who on behalf of the United States are conducting the talks in Geneva....

Since people intuitively sense the danger in the "Star Wars" plans, their authors hope to convince them that the plans supposedly amount to nothing more than harmless research, which, moreover, supposedly holds the promise of technological benefits. By using such bait Washington proposes to turn its allies, too, into accomplices in this dangerous project.

It is even claimed that by creating space arms it is supposedly possible to reach the point of liquidating nuclear arms. A fraudulent method. Just as the appearance of nuclear arms did not eliminate conventional types of weapons and only generated an accelerated race in the manufacture of both nuclear and conventional arms, so the creation of space weapons will have only one result—the arms race will become even more intensive and will encompass new spheres.

I have singled out the elements which especially complicate Soviet-American relations, sometimes bringing them to the brink of acute tension. But it appears that there are also those in the United States who regard such a state of affairs as normal and view confrontation as almost a natural state.

We do not agree. Confrontation is not an innate flaw in our relations. It is rather an anomaly. Its continuation is not inevitable at all. We regard the improvement of Soviet-American relations not only as extremely necessary, but also as possible. But of course, one cannot do much without reciprocity....

Question: From what you have said, Mikhail Sergeyevich, it follows that it is necessary to work on a broad front. Still, what do you regard as the main lever for achieving a breakthrough?

Answer: Intensive mutual efforts. And, indeed, efforts on a broad front. Mutual understanding on the need to facilitate the settlement of conflict situations in the world would have a beneficial influence on both our bilateral relations and international relations in general. Much can be done to our mutual benefit in developing the bilateral ties between the USSR and the United States.

But still, what you have called the main lever lies in the sphere of security. What could be a concrete beginning here?

If one has taken one's seat at the negotiating table to work on arms reduction, then one should at least refrain from further increasing armaments. That is why we propose that the USSR and the USA introduce for the entire duration of the talks a moratorium on the development (including research, testing and deployment) of strike space arms, plus a freeze on strategic offensive arms.

At the same time, the deployment of American intermediate-range missiles in Europe should be terminated and, correspondingly, the buildup of our retaliatory measures.

The American leaders are telling us they are for radical reductions of armaments. If that is so, it would be logical to first put a brake on the arms race and then immediately get to work on arms reduction.

We are for an honest dialogue. We are prepared to demonstrate our goodwill once again. Starting today—and I want to emphasize this—the Soviet Union is introducing a moratorium on the deployment of its intermediate-range missiles and suspending the implementation of other retaliatory measures in Europe. The duration of the moratorium is until November of this year. The decision we will make after that date will depend on whether the United States follows our example: Will it or will it not stop the deployment of its intermediate-range missiles in Europe?

Summing up, let me say the following. The possibilities do exist for improving Soviet-American relations and improving the general international situation. These possibilities should not be missed. They should be directed onto the plane of specific policies and practical decisions.

Gorbachev Address to Warsaw Treaty Anniversary Meeting

26 April 1985

Editor's commentary: This speech was delivered shortly after Mr. Gorbachev's appointment as General Secretary of the CPSU. Although he pays tribute to the notion of "socialist internationalism" as the principle underlying the unity of the Warsaw Pact nations, he does not dwell on East bloc affairs in this address. Instead, he uses the occasion of the Warsaw Pact's renewal to promote his ideas on East-West relations and disarmament, the success of which would have positive effects on his domestic reform program. These themes dominated the foreign policy agenda of the Gorbachev administration in its first four years.

Dear comrades and friends:

First, permit me on behalf of the Soviet delegation and of all the other participants in this meeting to express our appreciation to the leaders of the Polish United Workers' Party and the Polish state for the hospitality extended to us here. We also convey fraternal greetings to the residents of the heroic and beautiful city of Warsaw and to all the working people of People's Poland, and especially our good wishes for their success in building socialism.

We are all keenly aware that an act of historic importance has today taken place here in Warsaw, the city that has given its name to our alliance. The Treaty of Friendship, Cooperation and Mutual Assistance signed 30 years ago has been renewed. It was renewed, as Comrade Jaruzelski said earlier, with the conviction that

TASS, 26 April 1985, as translated in *Reprints from the Soviet Press*, vol. 40, no. 9, 15 May 1985, pp. 5–9, *excerpts.*

our alliance is vitally necessary to all its members, and vitally needed to strengthen peace and the security of peoples.

As Vladimir Ilyich Lenin always stressed, "Revolution must be able to defend itself." And in the Warsaw Treaty the peoples of our countries have a staunch weapon for defending their revolutionary gains. What has the Warsaw Treaty given us all? It has given us the possibility to pursue peaceful creative work. It has firmly ensured the reliability of our borders. A stout barrier has been put in the way of the latter-day subverters of socialism, those who lay claim to world dominance.

History has never witnessed another alliance such as ours, wherein relations are based on the full equality and comradely mutual assistance of an alliance of peoples, an alliance which is, in the true sense of the word, an alliance of peoples, an alliance which does not threaten anyone but is wholly devoted to the defense of peace. We build relations with the countries of the other social system on the principle of peaceful coexistence—the sole sensible basis there can possibly be, especially in the nuclear age.

It is via the Warsaw Treaty that the major initiatives of our countries, aimed at consolidating peace in Europe and ensuring detente, are introduced. Today's meeting has reaffirmed our shared readiness to continue our collective search for ways of eliminating the threat of war and expanding international cooperation. We stand for making the confrontation of the two military-political alliances less acute, which would meet the interest of all peoples everywhere.

It is not the Soviet Union and the other socialist states that have initiated the split in Europe and the whole postwar world. That was the work of the architects of NATO, while our alliance was formed only six years later. Since then, we have more than once expressed a readiness to dissolve the Warsaw Treaty Pact if NATO agrees to respond in kind. On this principled position we continue to stand firm. But,

regrettably, the other side doesn't show any such intention. On the contrary, it is putting forward new aggressive doctrines, and exerting crash efforts to build up both nuclear and conventional arms before our very eyes. And this now makes us think of further enhancing the Warsaw Treaty Organization.

Mankind has to make a choice: either it must succeed in rectifying the unfavorable course of events, or the risk of an outbreak of nuclear war will continue to escalate. And this risk is multiplied by the USA's military plans for space. No matter what the authors of these plans say and how they justify themselves, the essence of these plans is clear: to acquire the capability to deal the first nuclear blow and to do so with impunity. Since the United States and NATO flatly refuse to follow the example of the USSR and pledge not to be the first to use nuclear weapons, their intentions assume an especially dangerous nature.

The development of weapons for "Star Wars" is just beginning. But it is already causing the present-day world to develop a fever and is leading to destabilizing of the entire system of international relations, to even sharper political and military confrontation. This should not be lost sight of by either the initiators of the provocative undertaking I have just mentioned or by those who are being invited to share in it.

We take a fundamentally different approach: not to make space into a new source of a war threat, not to create space attack weapons, and to scrap all existing antisatellite systems.

Simultaneously, we propose that we come to terms on a radical reduction of nuclear systems and then move forward to complete elimination of nuclear weapons once and for all.

So simple and natural a move as a freeze on the nuclear potentials of both sides immediately suggests itself. But an objection has been raised: to agree to such a course means to secure the Soviets' military superiority. But, in the first place, no such superiority exists—this is something we have repeatedly proved, citing facts and figures, and Washington has failed to disprove any of them. And besides, who said that we want merely to stop at a freeze? On the contrary, we insist that drastic reduction in nuclear arms follow it.

We have already suggested that by way of an opening move both sides reduce strategic offensive arms by one quarter. But we would have no objections whatever to making deeper cuts. All this is possible provided no arms race begins in space—if space remains peaceful.

The Soviet Union and the Warsaw Treaty countries seek no superiority either on Earth or in space. We are not striving to compete at who will succeed in building a higher nuclear fence. But we shall prevent the military-strategic parity being upset. This is the common position of the Warsaw Treaty Organization, and we stand firm on it. If preparations for ''Star Wars'' continue, we will have no other choice but to take appropriate measures in response to them, including, of course, a buildup and improvement of offensive nuclear arms.

The just-ended first round of Soviet-US negotiations on nuclear and space arms has demonstrated that there will be no clear sailing in this area. It is plain that the negotiations can only be a success if the principle of equality and equal security is strictly observed, and that the agreement on the objective of the negotiations and the interrelated resolution of the questions discussed is adhered to.

The Soviet Union, as has already been announced, has unilaterally halted the deployment of intermediate-range missiles and the implementation of other response measures in Europe. The moratorium went into effect April 7. The world public and many sober-minded American and West European politicians have evaluated this move of ours at its true worth. We most certainly hope that Washington and the capitals of the other NATO countries will turn out to be more serious and thoughtful in assessing our initiative and, in their turn, will show restraint on the issue of siting US missiles in Western Europe. For mutuality on that issue could assist in directing the Geneva negotiations onto the plane of practical decisions and play its role in the settlement of far more complex problems.

The Warsaw Treaty has been in effect for almost a third of a century now, and all through that period of time it has served as an initiator of constructive ideas directed toward detente and arms limitation, and toward developing European cooperation. Its growing weight in international politics has had a positive effect on the general climate throughout the world. This, of course, is a result of collective efforts, the contribution of each of the fraternal countries.

Comrades, on the eve of the fortieth anniversary of the great victory over fascism, we once again recall the solemn oath that the victors swore over the graves and ruins of World War II: ''War must not recur!'' We remember this, we remember what the lessons of war teach us. And one of the most important of these lessons is the example of the cooperation among the powers of the anti-Hitler coalition. Today we call upon all the states of Europe and of other continents to rise above their differences and become partners in fighting the new danger that threatens all humanity—the danger of nuclear extinction.

As we extend the Warsaw Treaty, we once again express the same firm conviction: Wars can and must be prevented through joint efforts. Such is the will of the peoples of our countries. This is what the policy of our Parties and Governments, and all the activities of the defensive alliance of socialist states, are directed at.

Here's to the further cooperation of our Parties and states, to their ever stronger unity and cohesion based on the principles of Marxism-Leninism and socialist internationalism! May the fraternal alliance of socialist countries—

the Warsaw Treaty Pact—grow stronger and stronger!

Statement Announcing Soviet Moratorium on Nuclear Weapons Tests

Mikhail Gorbachev

30 July 1985

Editor's commentary: General Secretary Gorbachev began to display his considerable talent for international diplomacy early on in his administration. This proclamation of a unilateral Soviet moratorium on nuclear testing was made on the eve of the tenth anniversary of the signing of the Final Act of the Conference of Security and Cooperation in Europe at Helsinki in 1975. Appealing to world public opinion, the Soviet leader claimed the moral high ground when the United States rejected the Soviet offer, claiming that the Soviet testing program had outdistanced that of the United States.

The continuing race in nuclear armaments harbors a staggering threat to the future of all of the world civilization. It leads to higher tensions in the international arena and to intensification of the war menace, while also diverting enormous intellectual and material resources from constructive purposes.

Since the very beginning of the nuclear age the Soviet Union has consistently and vigorously fought for ending the accumulation of nuclear

---

Pravda, 30 July 1985, as translated in *Reprints from the Soviet Press* vol. 41, no. 3–4, 15–31 August 1985, pp. 5–7.

arsenals, for curbing military rivalry, for strengthening trust and peaceful cooperation between and among states.... The Soviet Union is not seeking military superiority—it favors maintaining the balance of military forces at its lowest possible level.

It is our conviction that ending all tests of nuclear weapons would become a major contribution to consolidating strategic stability and peace on Earth. It is no secret that new, ever more perilous kinds and types of weapons of mass annihilation are being developed and perfected in the course of such tests.

In the interest of creating favorable conditions for an international treaty on a complete and universal ban on nuclear weapons tests, the USSR has repeatedly proposed that nuclear states agree on a moratorium on all nuclear blasts, starting with an agreed-upon date. Regrettably, it has not yet been possible to take this important step.

Striving to facilitate the termination of the dangerous competition in building up nuclear arsenals, and wishing to set a good example, the Soviet Union has decided to discontinue unilaterally any and all nuclear explosions starting with August 6 this year. We call on the Government of the United States to also put an end, starting with this same date which is observed worldwide as the anniversary of the Hiroshima tragedy, to its planned nuclear explosions. Our (Soviet) moratorium is proclaimed until January 1, 1986. It will remain in effect, however, as long as the United States, on its part, refrains from conducting nuclear explosions.

Unquestionably, a mutual moratorium by the Soviet Union and the United States on any and all nuclear blasts would set a good example for other states possessing nuclear weapons.

The Soviet Union expects the United States to respond positively to this initiative and so to stop its nuclear explosions.

This would meet the aspirations and hopes of all nations.

Address at the Tenth Anniversary of the Helsinki Conference

Edvard Shevardnadze

30 July 1985

Editor's commentary: Combined with Gorbachev's announcement of a Soviet moratorium on nuclear testing on the same day, this statement on the anniversary of the Helsinki Final Act was, first and foremost, part of a vigorous "peace offensive" aimed at Western Europe against NATO INF deployments and Star Wars. The new Soviet foreign minister (handpicked by Gorbachev) also affirmed that detente and "the Leninist course of…peaceful coexistence" would remain Soviet policy toward Western Europe.

I think no one today will dispute that the signing of the Final Act of the Conference on Security and Cooperation in Europe ranks as one of the major events of the postwar period in international affairs. That document, which is of truly historic significance, was ratified right here in the capital of Finland on August 1, 1975, and bears the signatures of 35 leaders of European states, the USA and Canada. . . .

All the leaders at that time went part of the way toward a concerted accord. In consequence, the Final Act became a code of constructive mutual obligations. It orients states toward living in peace, cooperating fruitfully, and refraining from imposing on others views and social systems alien to them.

Wherein lies the vital force of the Final Act? Primarily in that it rests on the foundation of peaceful coexistence of states with different socioeconomic and political systems.

The objective need for peaceful coexistence was keenly foreseen by Lenin, the founder of our Soviet state. It was corroborated in practice by the entire content of 20th century history. There simply is no sensible alternative to peaceful coexistence today, in the nuclear age. Expressing the will of the Soviet people, Mikhail Gorbachev, General Secretary of the CPSU Central Committee, has stressed: "We will firmly follow the Leninist course of peace and peaceful coexistence.". . .

The Soviet Union has strongly advocated the prohibition of nuclear weapons ever since their appearance. Throughout these years our country has consistently and energetically struggled against the stockpiling of nuclear arms, seeking to put an end to rivalry in the development of more advanced systems of such weapons. . . .

Seeking to contribute toward ending dangerous rivalry in the buildup of nuclear arms arsenals, the Soviet Union then took another bold step—it decided to terminate unilaterally all nuclear explosions as of August 6 this year. . . .

Deployment of US first-strike nuclear missiles began some time ago and continues in Western Europe contrary to the interests of Europe's peoples. Every component of the US strategic offensive nuclear potential is being intensively built up. NATO is going ahead with a long-term program to develop ultramodern conventional weapons, which approximate nuclear weapons in their effects, and has adopted an aggressive doctrine of their employment. The development of advanced types of chemical weapons, including binary weapons, which are planned for deployment specifically on the European continent as well as elsewhere, is in full swing in the USA. . . .

The US Administration is seeking to carry through by all the means at its disposal its "Star Wars" plans, and hopes to involve its allies in that dangerous venture. Implementation of these plans is fraught with grave adverse consequences for security in Europe and all over the world.

Pravda, 30 July 1985, as translated in *Reprints from the Soviet Press* vol. 41, nos. 3–4, 15–31 August 1985, pp. 7–17, *excerpts.*

The peoples are expecting a good deal from the Soviet-US talks on nuclear and space weapons. The failure so far to make real progress at those talks cannot help disappointing them.

We are motivated at the Geneva talks by the firm desire to reach accords. This desire is manifest in well-substantiated constructive proposals both in Geneva and elsewhere....

I would like to stress once again that the Soviet Union favors accords on a fair and equitable basis, which would help all the sides to advance toward the desired objective of the total elimination of the nuclear war menace and the consolidation of the foundations of universal peace.

One more thing should be made clear. If anyone hopes to conduct talks with the Soviet Union "from a position of strength," let him abandon these illusions. In the face of the acceleration of military preparations by the NATO bloc, the Soviet Union and its allies will be able to take care of their security, to safeguard their legitimate rights and interest. Any attempts to upset the existing military balance, to gain unilateral advantages, will continue to meet effective counteraction on our part.

It is our firm belief, however, that confrontation, whether in the military, political or economic spheres, is not the road that Europe should be taking....

Cooperation between states in trade, in the economic, industrial, scientific and technical spheres and in environmental protection is far from attaining its full capacity. The socialist countries favor the expansion of ties in these spheres, using time-tested forms. We would also open up new channels, as is evidenced by our proposal for establishing direct business relations between the Council for Mutual Economic Assistance (CMEA) and the European Economic Community (EEC)....

The Soviet Union is a convinced supporter of international cooperation in resolving humanitarian issues and in developing all-around, effective relations in the sphere of culture and education. Obviously, such contacts and exchanges should contribute to the spiritual enrichment of the individual, to improving mutual understanding and friendly ties between peoples. The same applies to the promotion of respect for human rights on the principled basis of the Helsinki Accords.

All these issues directly concern the sphere of ideology, in which the socialist states and the world of capitalism stand on opposite positions. It is therefore necessary to learn to distinguish carefully between ideological differences and interstate relations.

This is precisely what the Soviet Union is doing. But our country has never allowed, nor will it now allow, anyone to interfere in its domestic affairs. Slander of any kind against our system, against socialist democracy, will meet with a fitting rebuff in the future as well....

The vital interests of the European peoples demand that Europe follow the path charted ten years ago at Helsinki. Europe can and should play an active role in averting the war menace that is looming so large over mankind and in redirecting international relations back toward detente and peaceful cooperation.

DOCUMENT 5

A Dangerous United States Move (ASAT)

17 September 1985

Editor's commentary: Antisatellite weapons, an important component of the United States' Strategic Defense Initiative (SDI, Star Wars), remained a target of intensive Soviet polemics even after Mr. Gorbachev gained the top post in the Kremlin. As this Pravda editorial clearly indicates,

Pravda, 17 September 1985, as translated in *Reprints from the Soviet Press*, vol. 41, no. 7, 15 October 1985.

the new Soviet leaders worry about the strategic implications that testing of components of SDI has for Soviet security. Concerns over a new escalation of the arms race can also be seen as closely tied to the weakness of the Soviet economy and Mr. Gorbachev's plans for perestroika, or restructuring, which could imply substantial shifts from defense spending. Despite such concerns, this article makes clear Soviet intentions to maintain strategic parity with the United States, whatever the cost.

...On September 13 the USA test-fired a spacecraft, the antisatellite missile system ASAT, at a live target. This was the third test of the system. The first two, which did not involve the hitting of a target, took place in 1984.

It should be noted that the last test was conducted at a time when the USSR's unilateral moratorium on the deployment of all types of antisatellite weapons was already in force. Announcing that moratorium, the USSR said it would remain in force so long as other countries, including the USA, did likewise. The USSR assumed such an obligation because it believed a moratorium could provide a good basis for radical measures to prevent militarization of space and create conditions conducive to halting the arms race in all fields. The decision to impose a moratorium testified to the USSR's goodwill and determination to strengthen peace and international security. When our country took that step, it hoped that the USA would follow its example.

But Washington ignored the opportunity to work with the USSR toward preventing militarization of space, lessening international tension and curbing the arms race. The White House ignored the stern warning contained in the TASS statement of September 5 regarding the consequences of the USA's continued testing of an antisatellite weapon and chose to continue a policy of destabilizing the situation, escalating confrontation and seeking military superiority.

The test of the antisatellite system, held by the US military, is a step in a dangerous direction. It paves the way to setting up a new class of armaments—strike space weapons, the emergence of which would inevitably undermine stability and open new channels for an unbridled race in nuclear arms, primarily strategic ones. This would reduce security around the world.

The Washington Administration claims that the tests of US antisatellite means have been necessitated by the fact that the USA must "catch up" with the USSR in the development of antisatellite defenses. Such claims are pure fabrications. The USA started developing antisatellite weapons as early as the 1950s.... The Soviet Union...began to test its antisatellite means much later. Furthermore, these tests were stopped in 1983 in connection with the unilateral moratorium declared by the USSR, and have not been held since.

Development of American antisatellite weapons as a kind of strike space means is directly linked with the implementation of the "Star Wars" program, itself a component of the general US military-strategic system aimed at gaining military superiority over the USSR. The USA tried to translate this system into reality from the time of the emergence of nuclear weapons, but the nuclear arms race it launched failed to give it any advantages. None of its attempt to gain superiority over the USSR has produced the desired effect. Each time the USSR has brought all these efforts to naught....

Isn't it clear that implementation of the "strategic defense initiative" (SDI) by Washington would inevitably lead to torpedoing the Soviet-American accords in the sphere of strategic arms limitation, primarily the ABM Treaty of 1972? No arguments or pseudo-arguments can help the US Administration disprove this fact. The aims of the ABM Treaty and the SDI are diametrically opposed. While the Treaty is directed against deployment of a large-scale ABM system and prohibits even the development of a basis for such systems, the main objective of SDI is to set up a universal multilayer antimissile system. Thus each move toward implementation of SDI leads to undermining the ABM Treaty and hence the entire process of strategic arms limitation and reduction.

The creation and deployment of attack weapons by one side will require the other side to restore the strategic equilibrium, inevitably leading to an increased amount and qualitative improvement of strategic nuclear arms and making their limitation and reduction impossible. Therefore it is irresponsible for the US Administration to try to assure the public that strategic nuclear arms cuts are achievable without a ban on space attack weapons, and that the question of SDI must be excluded from consideration at the Geneva talks on nuclear and space armaments. As M. S. Gorbachev has declared, "If there is no prohibition of space militarization, if there is no averting an arms race in outer space, there will be nothing at all."...

The Soviet Union has more than once urged the US Administration to consider the inevitable negative consequence of testing antisatellite weapons for the prospects of the Geneva talks. As pointed out in a recent TASS statement, once the USA carries out antisatellite weapons tests involving a target in space, the Soviet Union could consider itself free of the unilateral obligation not to put antisatellite weapons in orbit. This means that the USA's claims to attain military superiority over the USSR would again be destined not to materialize....

DOCUMENT 6

Joint Soviet-American Statement from the Geneva Summit

22 November 1985

Editor's commentary: The Geneva summit (19–21 November 1985) was the first encounter between the leaders of the two superpowers since Jimmy

Pravda, 22 November 1985, as translated in *Reprints from the Soviet Press*, vol. 41, nos. 11–12, 15–31 December 1985.

Carter met with Leonid Brezhnev in 1978 to sign the SALT II accords in Vienna, and the first of four face-to-face meetings between Ronald Reagan and Mikhail Gorbachev. Geneva can be considered a watershed, insofar as it ushered in a new era of detente between the superpowers. It was labeled a useful "get-acquainted" meeting by both sides, even though no agreements were finalized. It was at Geneva that the basic formula for START—50 percent reductions of strategic weapons—began to play a prominent role in the actual process of superpower arms negotiations.

I. The two sides, having discussed key security issues and conscious of the special responsibility of the USSR and the USA for maintaining peace, are stating that a nuclear war cannot be won and must never be fought. Recognizing that any conflict between the USSR and the USA could have catastrophic consequences, they emphasize the importance of preventing any war between them, whether nuclear or conventional. Neither of them will seek to achieve military superiority.

They agreed to accelerate the work at these negotiations, with a view to accomplishing the tasks set down in the joint Soviet-US statement of January 8, 1985, namely: to prevent an arms race in space and to terminate it on earth, and to limit and reduce nuclear arms and to enhance strategic stability.

Noting the proposals recently introduced by both the Soviet Union and the United States, they called for early progress, particularly in areas where there is common ground, including the principle of 50 percent reductions in the nuclear arms of the two sides, appropriately applied, as well as the idea of an interim agreement on medium-range missiles in Europe. During the elaboration of these agreements, effective measures for verification of compliance with obligations assumed will be agreed upon.

The two sides agreed to study the question, at the level of experts, of centers to reduce nuclear risk, taking into account the issues and developments in the Geneva negotiations. They noted with satisfaction such recent steps in this direction as the modernization of the US-Soviet hotline.

Mikhail Gorbachev and Ronald Reagan reaffirmed the commitment of the USSR and the USA to the Treaty on the Nonproliferation of Nuclear Weapons....

The two sides plan to continue to promote the strengthening of the International Atomic Energy Agency....

In the context of discussing security problems, the two sides reaffirmed that they are in favor of a general and complete prohibition of chemical weapons and the destruction of existing stockpiles of such weapons....

The two sides emphasize the importance they attach to the Vienna negotiations on the mutual reduction of armed forces and armaments in Central Europe and expressed their willingness to work for positive results there.

Attaching great importance to the Stockholm Conference on Confidence- and Security-Building Measures and Disarmament in Europe and noting the progress made there, the two sides stated their intention to facilitate, together with the other participating states, an early and successful completion of the work of the Conference....

II. Mikhail Gorbachev and Ronald Reagan agreed on the need to put on a regular basis, and also to intensify, dialogue at various levels. Along with meeting between the leaders of the two countries, this envisages regular meetings between the USSR Minister of Foreign Affairs and the US Secretary of State, as well as between the heads of other ministries and agencies....

Recognizing the usefulness of the already held exchanges of views on regional issues, including those at expert level, they agreed to continue such exchanges on a regular basis.

The two sides intend to expand the programs of bilateral cultural, educational and scientific-technical exchanges, and also to develop trade and economic ties....

They believe that there should be greater understanding between our peoples, and to this end they will encourage more travel and more extensive person-to-person contacts....

The two leaders noted with satisfaction that, in cooperation with the Government of Japan, the Soviet Union and the United States have agreed to a set of measures to promote safety on air routes in the North Pacific and have worked out steps to implement them.

They acknowledged that delegations from the USSR and the USA have begun negotiations aimed at the resumption of air services between the two countries. Both leaders expressed their desire to reach a mutually beneficial agreement on that score at an early date. In this regard, an agreement was reached on the simultaneous opening of consulates-general in New York and Kiev respectively.

Both sides agreed to contribute to the preservation of the environment....

The two leaders emphasized the potential importance of the work aimed at utilizing controlled thermonuclear fusion for peaceful purposes and, in this connection, advocated the broadest practicable development of international cooperation in obtaining this source of energy, which is essentially inexhaustible, for the benefit of all mankind.

. DOCUMENT 7

Plan for the Elimination of Nuclear Weapons

M. S. Gorbachev

15 January 1986

Editor's commentary: Several weeks prior to the convening of the Twenty-seventh CPSU Congress, TASS released a long statement by Mr. Gorbachev regarding the elimination of nuclear weapons by

Pravda, 16 January 1986, pp. 1–2, as translated in *Foreign Broadcast Information Service*, Soviet Union (Washington, DC: *n.p.*, 16 January 1986, pp. AA1–AA8, *excerpts*.

the year 2000. The statement also included some suggestions (not included here) for eliminating chemical weapons and lowering troop levels in Europe. While these proposals were dismissed in some quarters as propaganda designed to forestall the development of SDI, subsequent negotiations have borne out at least some of Gorbachev's optimism. Clearly, the likelihood of achieving all these goals in practical terms is slim. As many have pointed out, nuclear weapons cannot be "un-invented." Others have noted that even the elimination and/or reduction of forces in Europe could in effect leave the Soviet Union with a clear edge in some conventional categories. Still others have claimed this to be a bold visionary plan which should be taken seriously. In any event, it must be noted that Gorbachev's acceptance of strict verification here opened the way for the INF Treaty and rekindled the START talks. Moreover, notwithstanding the unwillingness in this speech to link regional issues with arms talks, the Soviet side later showed signs of accepting the interrelationship of these problems.

... How in practical terms does the Soviet Union see the procedure for reducing nuclear arms—both delivery vehicles and charges [warheads]—down to their complete elimination? In summary form our proposals boil down to the following.

First Stage. Over a period of 5–8 years the Soviet Union and the United States will halve the nuclear arms which can reach each other's territory. No more than 6,000 charges [warheads] will be retained on the delivery vehicles of this kind which they are left with.

It goes without saying that such a reduction is possible only given the mutual renunciation by the Soviet Union and the United States of the development, testing and deployment of space strike weapons. As the Soviet Union has warned repeatedly, the development of space strike weapons will cancel hopes for a reduction of nuclear arms on earth.

The first stage will see the reaching and implementation of a decision on the complete liquidation of Soviet and US medium-range missiles in the European zone—both ballistic and

cruise missiles—as a first stage on the path to freeing the European continent of nuclear weapons.

Here the United States must adopt a pledge not to supply its strategic and medium-range missiles to other countries; Britain and France must adopt a pledge not to build up their own corresponding nuclear arms.

Right from the start it is necessary for the Soviet Union and United States to agree to ending any nuclear explosions and call on other states to join in this moratorium as swiftly as possible.

And if the first stage of nuclear disarmament applies to the Soviet Union and the United States, it is because it is precisely they that must set an example for the other nuclear powers. We stated this with the utmost frankness to US President R. Reagan during the Geneva meeting.

Second Stage. During this stage, which must begin no later than 1990 and last 5–7 years, the other nuclear powers will begin to join in nuclear disarmament. They would first adopt a pledge to freeze all of their nuclear arms and not to have them in the territories of other countries.

During this period the Soviet Union and the United States will continue the reductions on which they agreed during the first stage, will implement further measures to eliminate their own medium-range nuclear weapons, and will freeze their tactical nuclear means.

After the Soviet Union and the United States complete the 50-percent reduction in their relevant arms during the second stage, yet another radical step will be taken: All of the nuclear powers will eliminate tactical nuclear weapons, that is means with a range (radius of operation) of up to 1,000 KM.

At this stage the Soviet-US accord on a ban on space strike arms would have to become multilateral, with compulsory participation by the leading industrial powers.

All nuclear powers would end nuclear-weapons tests.

A ban would be established on the creation of nonnuclear weapons based on new physical principles, and on approaching nuclear or other means of mass destruction in terms of their casualty producing capabilities.

The Third Stage will begin no later than 1995, during which the elimination of all remaining nuclear arms will be completed. By the end of 1999 no nuclear weapons will be left on Earth. A universal accord on ensuring that these weapons are never revived again will be elaborated.

It is envisioned that special procedures for the destruction of nuclear weapons and for the dismantling, conversion, or destruction of delivery vehicles will be elaborated. In the process, the quantity of weapons subject to elimination at each stage, the places where they will be destroyed, and so forth will be agreed on.

Verification of the armaments subject to destruction and limitation would be implemented via both national technical means and on-site inspection. The Soviet Union is prepared to reach agreement on any other additional verification measures.

The adoption of the program of nuclear disarmament that we are proposing would certainly have a beneficial influence on the talks being held in bilateral and multilateral forums. It would determine clearly defined routes and landmarks, would establish specific timetables for reaching and implementing accords, and would make talks purposeful and single-minded. The dangerous tendency whereby the pace of the arms race outstrips the fruitfulness of talks would be stopped.

Thus, we propose entering the third millennium without nuclear weapons on the basis of mutually acceptable and strictly verified accords. If the US administration—as it has repeatedly stated—is committed to the goal of completely eliminating nuclear weapons everywhere, it is being given a practical opportunity to actually do just that. Instead of spending the next 10–15 years creating new weapons in space, which are extremely dangerous for mankind and are allegedly intended to make nuclear arms unnecessary, is it not more sensible to tackle the destruction of these arms themselves—and ultimately reduce

them to zero? The Soviet Union, I repeat, proposes precisely this course.

The Soviet Union appeals to all peoples and states—primarily, of course, the nuclear states—to support the program for eliminating nuclear weapons by the year 2000. It is quite obvious to any unprejudiced person that nobody will lose out as a result of the implementation of such a program, but everybody will benefit. It is a problem of importance to all mankind; it can and must be resolved jointly. And the faster the program is translated into the language of practical action, the more secure life on our planet will be....

DOCUMENT 8

Report of the Central Committee to the Twenty-seventh Congress of the CPSU

M. S. Gorbachev

26 February 1986

Editor's commentary: The following excerpts from Mikhail Gorbachev's report to the Twenty-seventh Congress of the CPSU reflected a change in tone in Soviet foreign policy and held out as well to the West the prospect of substantive change in content. According to Gorbachev, what is needed are innovative policies and a break with the past. Although he uses much of the familiar doctrinal language of his forerunners ("crisis of capitalism," "correlation of forces"), Mr. Gorbachev sees the need for a comprehensive detente. In the face of the possibility of nuclear war, collaboration with the United States to avoid this catastrophe is seen

Pravda, 26 February 1986, pp. 2–10, as translated in *Foreign Broadcast Information Service*, Soviet Union, Supplement (Washington, DC: *n.p.*, 28 March 1986, *excerpts*.

as imperative. The major theme of the international part of the speech was the "contradictions" of the modern epoch. In this context, the stress on growing interdependence as the basic global condition is noteworthy. Although national liberation movements were lauded, the speech was also significant for claiming that militarily "encouraging revolutions from the outside" in the third world is "futile." What is clear throughout the section on foreign affairs is the centrality that Mr. Gorbachev ascribes to U.S.-Soviet relations under conditions of interdependence in solving the wide array of world problems, from the strategic nuclear dilemma to environmental questions.

The modern world is complicated, diverse and dynamic, and shot through with contending tendencies and contradictions. It is a world of the most intricate alternatives, anxieties and hopes. Never before has our home on earth been exposed to such great political and physical stresses. Never before has man exacted so much tribute from nature, and never has he been so vulnerable to the forces he himself has created....

The first and most important group of contradictions in terms of humanity's future is connected with **the relations between countries of the two systems, the two formations.** These contradictions have a long history. Since the Great October Revolution in Russia and the split of the world on the social-class principle, fundamental distinctions have come to light in the assessment of current affairs and in the views concerning the world socialist perspective.

Capitalism regarded the birth of socialism as an "effort" of history which should be "rectified." It was to be rectified at any cost, by any means, irrespective of law and morality: by armed intervention, economic blockade, subversive activity, sanctions and punishments, or refusal of any and all cooperation. But nothing could interfere with the consolidation of the new system and its historical right to live....

The policy of total contention, of military confrontation, has no future. Flight into the past is no response to the challenges of the future. It is rather an act of despair which however, does not make this posture any less dangerous. Washington's deeds will show when and to what extent it will understand this. We, for our part, are ready to do everything we can in order to radically improve the international situation. To achieve this, socialism need not renounce any of its principles or ideals. It has always stood for, and continues to stand for, the peaceful coexistence of states belonging to different social systems. (*Prolonged applause.*)

As distinct from imperialism, which is trying to halt the course of history by force, to regain what it had in the past, socialism has never, of its own free will, related its future to any military solution of international problems. This was borne out at the very first major discussion that took place in our country after the victory of the Great October Revolution. During that discussion, as we may recall, the views of the "Left Communists" and the Trotskyites, who championed the theory of "revolutionary war" which, they claimed, would carry socialism to other countries, were firmly rejected. This position, as Lenin emphasized in 1918, "would be completely at variance with Marxism, for Marxism has always been opposed to 'encouraging' revolution, which developed with the growing acuteness of the class antagonisms that engender revolutions." Today, too, we are firmly convinced that encouraging revolutions from outside, and doubly so by military means, is futile and inadmissible....

In the years to come, the main struggle will evidently center on the actual content of the policy that can safeguard peace. It will be a complicated and many-sided struggle, because we are dealing with a society whose leading circles refuse to assess the realities of the world and its perspective in sober terms, or to draw serious conclusions from their own experience and that of others. All this is an indication of the wear and tear suffered by its internal systems of immunity, of its social senility, which reduces the probability of far-reaching changes in the policy of the dominant forces and augments its degree of recklessness.

That is why it is not easy at all, in the current circumstances, to predict the future of the relations between the socialist and the capitalist countries, the USSR and the United States. The decisive factors here will be the correlation of forces on the world scene, the growth and activity of the peace potential, and its capability of effectively repulsing the threat of nuclear war. Much will depend, too, on the degree of realism that Western ruling circles will show in assessing the situation. But it is unfortunate when not only the eyes but also the souls of politicians are blind. With nuclear war being totally unacceptable, peaceful coexistence rather than confrontation of the systems should be the rule in interstate relations.

The second group of contradictions consists of the **intrinsic contradictions of the capitalist world itself.** The past period has amply confirmed that **the general crisis of capitalism** is growing deeper. The capitalism of today, whose exploitative nature has not changed, is in many ways different from what it was in the early and even in the middle 20th century....The traditional forms of conservatism are giving place to authoritarian tendencies.

Special mention should be made of anti-communism and anti-Sovietism, a most dangerous aspect of the crisis of capitalism. This concerns not only foreign policy. In the modern-day system of imperialism it is also a most important area of domestic policy, a means of putting pressure on all the advanced and progressive elements that live and fight in the capitalist countries in the non-socialist part of the world.

True, the present stage of the general crisis does not lead to any absolute stagnation of capitalism and does not rule out the possible growth of its economy and the mastery of new scientific and technical trends. It "allows for" sustaining

concrete economic, military, political and other positions, and in some cases even for possible social revanchism, the regaining of what had been lost before. But lacking positive aims and guidelines that would express the interest of the working masses, capitalism now has to cope with the unprecedented interweaving and mutual strengthening of all groups of its contradictions. Never before in all the centuries of its development has it known so many social, and other, impasses....

The relations between the three main centres of present-day imperialism—the United States, Western Europe and Japan—abound in visible and concealed contradictions. The economic, financial, and technological superiority which the United States enjoyed over its closest competitors until the end of the sixties has been put to a serious test. Western Europe and Japan managed to outdo their American patron in some things, and are also challenging the United States in such a traditional sphere of US hegemony as that of the latest technology....

The clash of centrifugal and centripetal tendencies will, no doubt, continue as a result of changes in the correlation of forces within the imperialist system. Still, the existing complex of economic, political-military and other common interests of the three centers of power can hardly be expected to break up in the prevailing conditions of the present-day world. But with the framework of this complex, Washington should not expect unquestioning obedience to US dictation on the part of its allies and competitors, and especially so to the detriment of their own interests....

A new, complex and mobile set of contradictions has taken shape between imperialism and the developing countries and peoples. The liberation of former colonies and semi-colonies was a strong political and ideological blow to the capitalist system. It has ceased to exist in the shape that it had assumed in the 19th century and in which it extended into the first half of the 20th. A slow, arduous, but unstoppable process of socioeconomic transformation is under way in the life of nations comprising the majority of mankind. This process, which has brought about no few fundamental changes, has also encountered considerable difficulties....

Analysis of yet another group of contradictions—those on a global scale, affecting the very foundations of the existence of civilization, leads to serious conclusions. This refers first of all to pollution of the environment, the air and oceans, and to the exhaustion of natural resources....

The global problems, affecting all humanity, cannot be resolved by the efforts of one state or a group of states. This calls for cooperation on a worldwide scale, for close and constructive joint action by the majority of countries. This cooperation must be based on completely equal rights and respect for the sovereignty of each. It must be based on conscientious compliance with accepted commitments and with the standards of international law. Such is the categorical call of the times in which we live....

The course of history, of social progress, requires ever more insistently that there should be **constructive and creative interaction between states and peoples on the scale of the entire world.** Not only does it so require, but it also creates the requisite political, social and material premises for it.

Such interaction is essential in order to prevent nuclear catastrophe, in order that civilization could survive. It is essential in order that other worldwide problems that are growing more acute should also be resolved jointly in the interests of all concerned. The realistic dialectics of present-day development consist in a combination of competition and confrontation between the two systems and in a growing tendency towards interdependence of the countries of the world community. This is precisely the way, through the struggle of opposites, through arduous effort, groping in the dark to some extent, as it were, that the contradictory but **interdependent and in many ways integral world** is taking shape.

DOCUMENT 9

TASS On U.S. Aid to Contras

30 June 1986

Editor's commentary: The funding of the Nicaraguan guerrilla "freedom fighters" by the U.S. government in 1986 provided ammunition for TASS to attack the Reagan administration's sincerity in ending the Central American conflict. This editorial is a representative example of the official Soviet view of the matter.

The US House of Representatives has endorsed the White House's request for 100 million dollars to finance the US mercenary Somocista counterrevolutionary bands which terrorize the civilian population and undermine Nicaragua's economy. That action constitutes a most flagrant breach of international law, of the UN charter and of the norms of civilized conduct of states. The UN International Court has declared unlawful the US interference in the affairs of Nicaragua and the use of mercenaries by the USA.

A new and extremely dangerous step has been taken to sharpen tension in Central America and to escalate the undeclared war which the United States has been conducting against the peoples of the region for several years. Washington cynically uses those bands which are in the pay of the United States and are US-controlled to prevent normalization of relations between Central American countries, to provoke and stir up conflicts between them....

The actions of the Reagan Administration expose it as a rabid opponent of a political settlement in Central America. The administration

Pravda, 30 June 1986, as reproduced in *Reprints from the Soviet Press*, vol. 48, nos. 3–4, 31 August 1986, pp. 75–77, *excerpts*.

seeks to prevent by any means a development of events precisely in such a direction. It is no coincidence that Washington is banking on the "contras" precisely at a time when hopes for success in the Contadora process have appeared and when a mutually acceptable solution to the problems has begun to come into view. In many respects this has proved possible because the Government of Nicaragua has put forward a number of new constructive proposals opening the way to untangle the unresolved matters pertaining to a political settlement.

And the United States is impudently defying not only the Contadora Group, which enjoys broad international support. The USA is defying all Latin America, which looks to resolve conflict situations in that part of the world through negotiations, on its own, without interference from the outside.

This is a US challenge to the entire international community. This is an attack on the very foundations of international law and order and on the peoples' sacred rights to sovereignty, independence and freedom, and on their right to choose their way of life and to decide their future themselves.

Washington is expanding the material basis to unleash a large-scale armed conflict in Central America, which may involve many countries. Such a development is fraught with ruinous consequences, and not only for Latin America. It will inevitably affect the general world situation and will not fail to impact upon Soviet-US relations....

The USSR proceeds from the assumption that the crisis situation in Central America can be resolved only along lines of a peaceful, political settlement, on a just basis of the generally recognized norms of international law.

The Soviet Union resolutely condemns the new and extremely dangerous US step aimed to escalate aggressive actions in Central America, and demands that an end be put to it. The Soviet people's solidarity and firm support have been and will be on the side of the just cause of the people of Nicaragua who are fighting for their independence and freedom, for peace in Central America and for the dignity of all sovereign countries.

DOCUMENT 10

Gorbachev's "Pacific Power" Speech in Vladivostok

29 July 1986

Editor's commentary: In this major speech, Gorbachev emphasized the Soviet Union's status as a Pacific power and announced the intention of the Soviet Union to develop its regional interests in a comprehensive way. Characteristic of Gorbachev's "new thinking," the General Secretary held out an olive branch to the United States, Japan, and China, the big Pacific powers, and invited them to a conference, similar to Helsinki, to resolve outstanding disputes and set a new agenda for Pacific region development.

...The main problem confronting humankind today—that of survival—is equally acute and urgent for Europe, Africa, America and Asia. Yet in each part of the world it looks different. Therefore, here in Vladivostok it is natural to look at international policy issues from an Asian-Pacific viewpoint.

Such an approach is justified for many reasons. Because in the first place, east of the Urals, in Asia—in Siberia and the Far East—lies the greater part of our country's territory. It is here that many national targets advanced by the Party

Pravda, 29 July 1986, as translated in *Reprints from the Soviet Press,* vol. 43, no. 5, 15 September 1986, pp. 5–38, *excerpts.*

Congress will be resolved. Hence the situation in the Far East as a whole, in Asia and the ocean expanses washing it, where we are permanent inhabitants and seafarers of long standing, is of national, state interest to us.

Many major states of the world, including the USSR, the United States, India, China, Japan, Vietnam, Mexico and Indonesia, are situated on the enormous expanses of this territory spreading over almost half of the earth. Here lie states which are considered to be medium-sized but are big by European standards—Canada, the Philippines, Australia and New Zealand, and along with them there are dozens of comparatively small and tiny countries. Some of them have a history of millennia or many centuries, others have formed in modern times, and still others have formed quite recently.

Asia, which awakened to a new life in the 20th century, has enriched world progress with its diversified and unique experience of the fight for freedom and independence. This is not only history. This is a living legacy making up an important foundation to the current political realities in this part of the world....

Socialism is an inalienable factor in the large-scale and complex changes in this region. It gained firm positions in Asia as a result of the Great October Revolution and the victory over fascism and Japanese militarism, as a result of the great Chinese revolution, after the new socialist system was consolidated in Mongolia, and on Korean land where the people displayed outstanding steadfastness in the struggle for the socialist future of their country, and then in Vietnam and Laos. But here in Asia it has been confronted with the most brutal and cynical counteraction. Vietnam is the most graphic example. Its heroic experience and the lessons of its victory over imperialism have high-lighted once again the irresistible strength of the ideas of freedom and socialism.

This region, Asia, saw the formation of the concept of nonalignment, a movement which now includes more than a hundred nations. It is seeking to come up with its own response to the challenge of the time, is actively working to overcome the world's division into military blocs and is looking for ways to diminish the nuclear threat. In rejecting and condemning exploitation, the policy of aggression, and neocolonialism, the non-aligned movement is urging humanity's unity, cooperation in combating hunger and the glaring poverty of hundreds of millions of people.

The great India, with its moral authority and traditional wisdom, with its specific political experience and huge economic potentialities, is the recognized leader of this movement. We have a high opinion of its contribution to asserting the standards of equitable coexistence and justice in the international community. Friendly relations between the USSR and India have become a stabilizing factor on a worldwide scale.

Japan has become a power of front-rank importance. The country which became the first victim of US nuclear weapons has covered a great path in a brief period, and made striking accomplishments in industry, trade, education, science and technology. These successes are due not only to the self-control, discipline and energy of the Japanese people, but the "three non-nuclear principles" which officially underlie its international policy, although lately—and this must be emphasized—the...peaceful provisions of Japan's constitution, are being circumvented ever more openly.

But we also see many other things in Asia and Oceania. Colonialism's insults to peoples' dignity and a legacy of poverty, illiteracy and backwardness, along with profound prejudices, preserved conditions for mistrust and hostility between peoples, including those who live within one state. Imperialism speculates on the difficulties and prejudices, and that brings about local conflicts, ethnic and religious strife, and political instability....

The Soviet Union is also an Asian and Pacific country. It is aware of the complex problems of this vast region. It is directly contiguous to them. This is what evokes a balanced and overall view of that giant part of the world with its mass of diverse nations and peoples. Our approach to it is based on recognizing and understanding the existing realities.

At the same time our interest is not a claim to privileges and special position, not an egoistic attempt to strengthen our security at someone else's expense, not a search for benefit to the detriment of others. Our interest is in pooling efforts and in cooperation, with full respect for each people's right to live as they choose and resolve their problems on their own in conditions of peace.

We are in favor of building together new, fair relations in Asia and the Pacific.

Recently, I have had many meetings with leaders of European nations, with various political figures of European countries. Involuntarily, I compare the situation in Asia with that in Europe.

The Pacific region has not as yet been militarized to the same extent as Europe. But the potentialities of its militarization are truly immense, and the consequences are extremely dangerous. A glance at the map will convince one of that. Major nuclear powers are situated here. Powerful land armies and mighty navies and air forces have been established. The scientific, technological and industrial potential of many countries—from the Western to the Eastern fringes of the ocean—makes it possible to intensify any arms race. The situation is being exacerbated by the preservation of conflict situations. Let us not forget: it was in Asia that American imperialism waged the two biggest wars since 1945—in Korea and in Indochina. One can scarcely find a few years in the past four decades when flames of war have not blazed in one or another part of the Asian and Pacific region....

One has to state that the militarization and escalation of the threat of war in this part of the world are picking up dangerous speed. The Pacific Ocean is turning into an arena of military political confrontation. This is what gives rise to growing concern among the peoples living here. This is also alarming for us from all viewpoints, including considerations of security in the Asian part of our country.

The Asian and Pacific direction in the Soviet Union's foreign policy is an integral part of the CPSU's international activity, worked out by the April plenary meeting and the 27th Party Congress. But a platform is not a chart that can be applied to any situation; it is rather a set of principles and a method relying on experience.

Proceeding from that, how will it be possible to perceive the process of shaping international security and peaceful cooperation in this vast region?

First of all, in keeping with the principled policy set out at the 27th Congress, the Soviet Union will seek to lend dynamism to its bilateral relations with all countries situated here without exception....

A noticeable improvement has occurred in [Sino-Soviet] relations in recent years. I would like to reaffirm: the Soviet Union is prepared—any time, and at any level—to discuss with China questions of additional measures for creating an atmosphere of goodneighborliness. We hope the border dividing us (I would prefer to say joining us) will become a line of peace and friendship in the near future.

The Soviet people's attitude to the objectives advanced by the Communist Party of China to modernize the country and build a socialist society worthy of a great people is that of understanding and respect.

As far as it is possible to judge, we and China have similar priorities—those of accelerating social and economic development. Why not support each other? Why not cooperate in implementing our plans wherever this will clearly benefit both sides? The better the relations, the more we shall be able to exchange our experience....

On relations with Japan. There are emerging signs of a turn for the better here as well. It would be good if the turn did take place. The objective position of our two countries in the world demands profound cooperation on a sound realistic basis, in a calm atmosphere free from the problems of the past. A beginning was made this year: Foreign Ministers exchanged visits. And exchange of top-level visits is on the agenda....

In the Pacific region, the Soviet Union also shares a border with the United States. It is our next-door neighbor in the literal meaning of the word, with only seven kilometers dividing us—the exact distance between the Soviet island of Big Diomede and the American island of Little Diomede.

We realize clearly that the United States is a great Pacific power, primarily because a considerable part of the US population lives on the shores of that ocean. And the Western part of the US, gravitating towards that area, is playing a growing part in the country's life, and features dynamism. Besides, the United States undoubtedly has important economic and political interests in the region.

Clearly, without the US, without its participation, it is impossible to resolve the issue of security and cooperation for the Pacific Ocean in a way that would satisfy all. Regrettably, Washington has yet to show interest in this and is not even contemplating a serious talk on the Pacific subject. If this topic is broached, the conversation is led off down the well-trodden path of a "Soviet threat" with saber-rattling to match the myth....

By way of an objective, even if a rather remote one, we would propose a conference along the lines of the Helsinki conference, to be attended by all the countries gravitating toward the ocean. If and when an agreement is reached on its convocation, it will be possible to come to terms on a site. One option is Hiroshima. Why should not that city, the first victim of nuclear evil, become the "Helsinki" for Asia and the Pacific Ocean?

Summing up, I would like to emphasize that we stand for integrating the Asian Pacific region into the general process of establishing a comprehensive system of international security as proposed at the 27th Congress of the CPSU....

Mobilizing the potential for common sense existing in the world, for partnership in reason is now more important than ever to arrest the slide to catastrophe. Our resolve to do our utmost for this remains unchanged. Peoples of all countries and states can be sure of this.

Such is, in brief, the state of our affairs now. Such is the general outline of the international situation in which the role of the Asian-Pacific part of the world will be steadily growing. We must draw practical conclusions from all this so as to act with still greater energy, rebuilding our life for the better.

<hr>

DOCUMENT 11

Gorbachev Statement on Reykjavik Summit

14 October 1986

Editor's commentary: Realistically, the agenda of the Reykjavik Summit between Ronald Reagan and Mikhail Gorbachev, their second meeting, was too ambitious to yield practical results. In Gorbachev's evaluation, the American side had come unprepared to discuss seriously the far-reaching proposals of disarmament which he brought with him, including a 50 percent reduction proposal on strategic systems within five years, to be followed by the complete elimination of these weapons by 1996. The Americans were unwilling to make any concessions on SDI or the "broad" interpretation of the ABM Treaty. Although Reykjavik provided a useful sounding board for future directions in arms

Moscow Television, 14 October 1986, as transcribed and translated in *Foreign Broadcast Information Service*, Soviet Union (Washington, DC: *n.p.*, 15 October 1986, pp. DD1–DD11, *excerpts*.

control, it was suggested at the time that both sides were merely utilizing the meeting for ulterior purposes: Reagan to try to help in retaining Republican control of the Senate in midterm elections, and Gorbachev to take the moral high ground in European (and world) public opinion as the great innovator in pursuing peace.

Dear comrades, you know that the day before yesterday, on Sunday, my meeting in Iceland with Ronald Reagan, the President of the United States of America, ended. A press conference took place on television on the results of the meeting. The text of the speech and my replies to journalists have been published. Having returned to the homeland, I consider it my duty to tell how things went and how we evaluate what has taken place in Reykjavik....

A whole package of major measures was put on the table which, if adopted, would initiate a new epoch in the life of mankind—a nuclear-free epoch. Herein is the essence of a fundamental turning point in the world situation, the possibility of which was evident and real. What was involved was not limitation of nuclear weapons, as was the case in the SALT I and SALT II treaties and other treaties, but the elimination of nuclear arms in a relatively short period.

The proposal dealt with strategic offensive weapons. I stated our readiness to cut these by 50 percent during the first 5 years. This involved halving strategic arms on land, at sea, and in the air. To make an agreement easier, we made a great concession: We removed our former demand to the Americans to include American medium-range missiles able to reach our territory, and the American forward-based arms, in the strategic equation.

We were also ready to take into account the concern of the United States about our heavy missiles. We viewed the proposal about strategic weapons in the context of their complete elimination as proposed by us on 15 January this year.

Our second proposal dealt with medium-range missiles. I suggested to the President the com- plete elimination of Soviet and American mis- siles of this class in Europe. And here, too, we made a great concession: We stated that, in con- trast to our former position, the nuclear missiles weapons of Great Britain and France need not be counted in.

We took as our starting point the need to clear the way to detente in Europe, to free the Euro- pean peoples from the fear of a nuclear disaster, and then to progress to the elimination of all nu- clear arms. You will agree that this is also a bold step on our part.

Knowing in advance the objections there might be, we stated that we were willing to freeze nuclear weapons with a range of less than 1,000 km, and to start immediately on talks about their further fate. As for medium-range missiles in the Asian part of our country, a question which has always been present in the global option of Pres- ident Reagan, we proposed starting talks on that question immediately.

As you can see, here, too, our proposals were of a major and serious nature, providing the op- portunity for fundamentally resolving this prob- lem, too.

The third issue, which I put before the Pres- ident in the very first conversation, and which was an integral part of our package of proposals— that is the existing treaty on antimissile defense and its ban on nuclear testing. Our approach is this: Once we enter a completely new situation, when a considerable reduction of nuclear weap- ons and their elimination over a visibly short period are starting, it is necessary to safeguard oneself against all surprises. We are talking about weapons that up to now constitute the core of the defense of our country: therefore, everything that could undermine equality in the course of disarmament has to be excluded; any possibility of developing weapons of a new type securing military superiority must be excluded....

It became clear, comrades, that the Ameri- cans came to Reykjavik completely empty- handed. The impression was created that they had come there only to gather the fruit into their basket with empty hands. The situation was dramatic. The US President was not prepared to decide the question of principle in a major way, to come part way to meet us, so as to really give an impulse to talks that would produce results and give rise to hope. This is what I called for in my letter to the President in which I put forward the idea of holding the urgent and immediate meeting so as to give a powerful impulse at the level of the top leaders of the two countries, an impulse to the talks on disarmament, nuclear disarmament.

Convinced that our proposals had been carefully thought out, taking into account the interest of our partner, we decided not to give up on our efforts to achieve a breakthrough at the meeting....

I said to the President: Both you and we have an acknowledged triad of strategic offensive weapons: these are land-based missiles, strategic submarines, and strategic bombers. So let us reduce each part of this triad by 50 percent. This does away with the need for all sorts of levels, sub-levels and all sorts of calculations. After lengthy debates, we managed to reach mutual understanding on this issue.

Then a discussion developed on the problem of medium-range missiles. The Americans stubbornly defended the so-called interim option, which envisaged retaining a part of their missiles remaining in Europe, including Pershing II missiles, and, of course, retaining our corresponding missiles, the SS-20, likewise. We came out categorically against this. I have already explained why. Europe deserves to be rid of nuclear weapons, to cease being a nuclear hostage. The President for his part, had difficulty fighting against his own zero option, which he had been pushing for such a long time. Nevertheless, we sensed the Americans' intention to frustrate any agreement, under the guise of special concern for their allies in Asia. A lot was said about that by the American side and was unfounded. There is simply no point in repeating all this today.

And things started going well only when we made yet another step to meet them, on this issue as well. We agreed to the formula: zero missiles in Europe, and 100 warheads each on medium-range missiles in the East of our country, and correspondingly for the Americans on the territory of the United States respectively.

The main thing is that we managed to come to agreement on ridding the European Continent of nuclear missiles. Agreement was thus reached, too, on the issue of medium-range missiles. An important breakthrough was made in this aspect of nuclear disarmament, too.

The American Administration did not succeed in evading our persistent striving to get positive results. But the questions of ABM and a ban on nuclear explosions still remained....

An impasse had arisen. We proposed major, really large-scale things that were clearly compromises. We made concessions. However, I did not see even the slightest desire on the American side to reply to us in the same way or to make any movement to meet us. We began to think of how to end this meeting, these discussions.

Nevertheless, we continued our endeavors to get our partners to follow a constructive path.

The conversation planned as the final one had exceeded the permitted time period. In this situation, instead of going away, we to Moscow and they to Washington, we agreed once again to have a break, let the sides think everything over, and to meet again after dinner. Returning to the mayor's house after the break, we made another attempt to end the meeting with success. We presented the following text as a basis for reaching a positive result. Here is that text. I quote:

The USSR and the United States would pledge, for a period of 10 years, to refrain from using their given right to abandon the indefinite ABM Treaty, and for the duration of this period strictly adhere to all of its provisions. The testing of all space elements of an antimissile defense in space is forbidden, except research and testing carried out in laboratories. During the first 5 years of this 10-year period, up to 1991 inclusive, the strategic offensive weapons of the sides will be reduced by 50 percent. During the following 5 years of this period the remaining 50 percent of the strategic offensive weapons of the sides will be reduced. Thus, by the end of 1996 the strategic offensive weapons of the USSR and of the United States will be totally eliminated.

Commenting on this text, I made an important addition, referring to a document handed to the President at the close of our first conversation. Its essence lay in saying that at the end of 10 years, when there would be no nuclear weapons, we propose the elaboration at special talks of a mutually acceptable decision on how to proceed further.... But the longer this went on, the clearer it became that the Americans were not going to agree to limiting research, development and testing in the SDI program to the laboratory. They are dying to have weapons in space.

I stated firmly that we will never agree to helping with our own hands to wreck the ABM Treaty. For us this is a matter of principle, of our national security. And so, finding ourselves literally one, or two, or three steps from making decisions that could be historic for the whole nuclear space age, we could not take this step, or these steps. There was no turning point in world history, although—and once again I say this with conviction—it was possible.

But our conscience is clear. There is nothing to reproach us with. We did everything we could. Our partners did not have sufficient breadth of approach, understanding of the unique nature of the moment, and in the final analysis courage, responsibility and political determination, which are so necessary in solving such most important, urgent world problems.... Briefly summing up these highly concentrated days...The recent meeting was a major event. A reappraisal took place. A qualitatively new situation has come about. Nobody can now act in the same way as he acted before. The new meeting was a useful one. It prepared a possible step forward, toward a real shift to the better, if the United States will finally adopt realistic positions and renounce illusions in its appraisals. The meeting persuades us of the correctness of the course we have chosen, of the need for and the constructive nature of the new political thinking in the nuclear age....

DOCUMENT 12

Delhi Declaration on the Principles of a Nuclear-Free and Nonviolent World

27 November 1986

Editor's commentary: Mikhail Gorbachev's trip to India late in 1986, soon after his second meeting with President Reagan at Reykjavik, resulted in the signing of a document composed of ten principles directed toward a "nuclear free and nonviolent world." The tone of the document reinforced public opinion about the new and innovative approach to foreign affairs of the Soviet Union under Gorbachev. The leitmotif of the entire speech was a sober recognition of the basic condition of complex global interdependence, irrespective of ideological mold or social system.

...Conscious of our common responsibility for the destinies of our two nations and of mankind, we hereby set forth the following principles for building a nuclear-weapon free and nonviolent world.

1. Peaceful coexistence must become the universal norm of international relations:

Pravda, 28 November 1986, p. 1, as translated in *Foreign Broadcast Information Service*, Soviet Union (Washington, DC: *n.p.*, 3 December 1986, pp. D14–D16, *excerpts*.

In the nuclear age it is necessary that international relations are restructured so that confrontation is replaced by cooperation, and conflict situations resolved through peaceful political means, not through military means.

2. Human life must be recognized as the supreme value:

It is only man's creative genius that makes progress and development of civilization possible in a peaceful environment.

3. Nonviolence should be the basis of community life...:

Philosophies and policies based upon violence and intimidation, inequality and oppression, and discrimination on the basis of race, religion or color, are immoral and impermissible. They spread intolerance, destroy man's noble aspirations, and negate all human values.

4. Mutual understanding and trust must replace fear and suspicion:

Mistrust, fear and suspicion between nations and peoples distort perceptions of the real world. They engender tensions and, in the final analysis, harm the entire international community.

5. The right of every state to political and economic independence must be recognized and respected:

A new world order must be built to ensure economic justice and equal political security for all nations. An end to the arms race is an essential prerequisite for the establishment of such an order.

6. Resources being spent on armaments must be channeled towards social and economic development:

Only disarmament can release the enormous additional resources needed for combating economic backwardness and poverty.

7. Conditions must be guaranteed for the individual's harmonious development:

All nations must work together to solve urgent humanitarian problems and cooperate....A world without nuclear weapons and violence would open up vast opportunities for this.

8. Mankind's material and intellectual potential must be used to solve global problems:

Solutions must be found to global problems such as shortage of food, the growth of populations, illiteracy and environmental degradation through the efficient and appropriate uses of the resources of the earth....

9. The "balance of terror" must give way to comprehensive international security:

The world is one and its security is indivisible. East and west, north and south regardless of social systems, ideologies, religion or race must join together in a common commitment to disarmament and development.

International security can be guaranteed through the adoption of integrated measures in the field of nuclear disarmament using all available and agreed measures of verification and confidence building; just political settlement of regional conflicts through peaceful negotiations; and cooperation in the political, economic and humanitarian spheres.

10. A nuclear-weapon free and non-violent world requires specific and immediate action for disarmament....

Pending the elimination of nuclear weapons, the Soviet Union and India propose that an international convention banning the use or threat of use of nuclear weapons should be concluded immediately. This would constitute a major concrete step towards complete nuclear disarmament.

Building a nuclear-weapons free and non-violent world requires revolutionary transformation of outlook and the education of people and nations for peace, mutual respect and tolerance. The propaganda of war, hatred, and violence should be forbidden and the stereotyped perception of other nations and peoples as enemies should be discarded.

Wisdom lies in preventing the accumulation and aggravation of global problems which, if not solved today require even greater sacrifices tomorrow.

The danger that threatens mankind is grave. But mankind has the power to prevent a catastrophe, and to pave the way to a nuclear free civilization.... The time for decisive and urgent action is now.

[signed] M. Gorbachev, General Secretary of the
   CC CPSU
   R. Gandhi, Prime Minister of the Republic of India

[dated] New Delhi, 27 November 1986

DOCUMENT 13

Soviet Government Statement on U.S. Abandonment of SALT II

6 December 1986

Editor's commentary: The Reagan administration had planned for some time to allow the SALT II treaty to lapse as its expiration date approached. "Breaking out" of the limits of the treaty in this case meant the fitting of another B-52 with cruise missiles, which technically put the U.S. in violation. Although the US Senate had never ratified the SALT II treaty, the Reagan Administration had remained within its limits for nearly six years. Subsequent events suggested that this action was a clear signal to the Kremlin concerning the necessity to make headway on INF and START, rather than an attempt to scrap arms limitations entirely. The U.S. did begin retiring old systems after 31 December before deploying new ones covered by the treaty; and within a year, the INF treaty was reality.

The other day, the United States additionally put into service a 131st heavy bomber equipped to carry long-range cruise missiles, without dismantling an equivalent nuclear-weapon delivery vehicle in compensation. In taking this action, it overstepped the aggregate limit fixed in the SALT-2 Treaty of 1320 units on the number of MIRVed strategic ballistic missile launchers and cruise missile-armed heavy bombers. The US does not conceal that this amounts to its total abandonment of the SALT-2 Treaty which, as the US Administration put it, was left behind. Therefore, practical actions followed President Reagan's statement last May of intent to break out of the 1972 Interim Agreement and the 1979 SALT-2 Treaty, a statement that drew anxiety and condemnation around the world.

A treaty which has sealed military parity between the USSR and the United States and limited the nuclear arms race for a number of years in its central area—the field of strategic offensive arms—has now been trampled underfoot. The value and usefulness of this agreement consisted in its provisions on the sides' commitments to observe restrictions in both quantity and quality of their strategic nuclear systems. The SALT-2 Treaty provided for substantially narrowing possibilities to modernize such systems. In addition, it set corresponding limits on the main groups of strategic systems. Compliance with all these provisions, based on the sides' recognition of the principle of equality and equal security, guaranteed strategic stability and served as the point of departure in the search for ways to reduce and eliminate nuclear weapons.

The decision to augment the US arsenal of strategic systems and to violate the SALT-2 Treaty has been dictated by nothing other than Washington's desire to upset the military balance between the USSR and the United States and assure itself military superiority. These actions could seriously affect international security....

The United States has now dealt the final blow to the SALT-2 Treaty, but it has been undercutting it for more than a year. In the very first days after taking office, the Reagan Administration rejected ratification of that Treaty. At the

---

  Pravda, 6 December 1986, p. 1, as translated in *Reprints from the Soviet Press*, vol. 44, no. 1, 15 Janaury 1987, pp. 24–28, *excerpts.*

same time it launched activities that were in clear violation of the SALT-2 Treaty. Ignoring special restrictions set by the Protocol to the Treaty, for example, the United States has started mass deployments of long-range cruise missiles. Washington has also circumvented the Treaty by stationing its medium-range missiles in Western Europe as a supplement to the US strategic potential.

Work has forged ahead, at full tilt, in the meantime, on an unprecedented program to modernize and build up strategic offensive arms in all areas, with new MX and Midgetman intercontinental ballistic missiles. B-1B and Stealth strategic bombers and nuclear-powered submarines carrying Trident-1 and Trident-2 missiles [are] being developed and built....

Washington is making a big mistake. Exceeding the limits set by the SALT-2 Treaty will not strengthen US security. The six years the present Administration has been in office confirm: In the field of arms limitation the Administration, without constructing anything, has destroyed and is destroying a great deal.

As the Soviet Government warned in its Statement of May 31, 1986, the US decision gives the Soviet Union every ground to regard itself free from its commitments under the 1972 Interim Agreement and the SALT-2 Treaty.

At the same time, the Soviet side believes there is still an opportunity to stop the dangerous course of events being provoked by the irresponsible actions of the present US Administration.

In the US and outside it, it may be presumed, there is still enough political wisdom and even a sense of self-preservation to not allow the entire structure of accords limiting strategic arms—built over 15 years—to be wrecked.

Taking into account the immense universal importance of the issue and the need to preserve the key constraint on the strategic arms race, the USSR will refrain for the time being from abandoning the limitations under the SALT-1 and SALT-2 Treaties....

Soviet Government Statement on the Unilateral Nuclear Testing Moratorium

19 December 1986

Editor's commentary: The moratorium announced by M. S. Gorbachev on 30 July 1985 had evoked no interest on the part of the United States, which claimed that the American testing program was behind that of the Soviets. This announcement, coming 18 months later, seemed to accept the U.S. unresponsiveness to a comprehensive test ban with equanimity. The statement was also meant to absolve the Soviet Union of responsibility for the situation and prepare world public opinion for the resumption of Soviet testing, which began, as promised, after the first U.S. test of 1987.

Almost eighteen months have passed since the Soviet Union, guided by a desire to help end the dangerous competition in building up nuclear arsenals and wishing to set a good example for the other nuclear powers, took a decision to impose a unilateral ban on all nuclear explosions and called on the United States to follow suit....

It is a very regrettable fact that the present US Administration has not given a positive reply to the Soviet call to join its peace initiative....

It is only natural that those who are bent on developing more and more sophisticated nuclear weapons and carrying out Star Wars plans to spread the arms race into new spheres, have no need for a moratorium. Unwilling to give up its plans to achieve military superiority through space, the US Administration has rejected all So-

Pravda, 19 December 1986, as translated in *Reprints from the Soviet Press*, vol. 44, no. 1, 15 January 1987, pp. 29–32, excerpts.

viet proposals to begin meaningful negotiations and ban nuclear testing for good.

There is still no evidence that the United States is going to follow the Soviet example and stop conducting nuclear explosions. Moreover, the United States continues to carry out its nuclear testing program at the same fast pace. While the Soviet moratorium has been in force and while there has been silence at Soviet testing grounds the United States has conducted 20 announced and four unannounced nuclear weapons tests.

Since the United States stubbornly continues to carry out its nuclear testing program with the aim of developing and building new nuclear arms, the Soviet Union cannot exercise unilateral restraint forever. A situation has taken shape, which, if it continues, may seriously impair the security of the USSR and its allies.

After a thorough consideration of this question in all its aspects, the Soviet leadership deems it necessary to declare the following.

First The Soviet Union once again proposes beginning full-scale negotiations without delay to ban all nuclear tests. It is prepared to hold such negotiations in any constituent form and at any forum, but necessarily with the participation of the United States. These negotiations should also resolve the issue of control so that compliance with such an agreement is effectively verified. In the course of the nuclear test ban talks the Soviet Union would be prepared to negotiate a gradual solution of the question, meaning ratification of the Soviet-American treaties of 1974 and 1976, and putting interim limits on the number and yield of nuclear explosions.

Second The Soviet Union is prepared to continue to abide by its moratorium. However, it will resume nuclear tests after the first US nuclear explosion in the coming year.

Third If the United States halts nuclear tests, the USSR will halt, on a mutual basis, the imple-

mentation of its nuclear testing program any day and any month.

The Soviet Union's decision to end its moratorium after the first US nuclear explosion in the coming year is a forced measure prompted exclusively by security interests. The USSR remains a confirmed advocate of a comprehensive nuclear test ban, considering it a measure of paramount importance in the effort to achieve the main goal of curbing the nuclear arms race and then eliminating nuclear weapons entirely. The Soviet Union will continue seriously to work towards the attainment of this goal. It is convinced that its position on the matter will be properly understood and have the support of all peace-loving forces on our planet.

DOCUMENT 15

Soviet Government Statement on the Persian Gulf Situation

4 July 1987

Editor's commentary: Following the logic of Mr. Gorbachev's "new thinking" in Soviet policy, the Soviet Union in 1987 began to shift its attitude towards a multilateral resolution of the Persian Gulf war, in its eighth year, and displayed interest in stabilizing the region. In more practical terms, the Soviets had even begun to lease oil tankers to Kuwait. Refraining from polemics, the government statement below gave notice of Soviet intent to become a force in the settlement of Persian Gulf problems. The critical remarks directed toward the United States are striking in their proclamation of traditional national interests and balance-of-power diplomacy, rather than stale Marxist-Leninist formulas.

Pravda, 4 July 1987, as translated in *Reprints from the Soviet Press*, vol. 45, no. 4, 30 August 1987, pp. 45–46.

Recently tension in the Persian Gulf has been dangerously growing. A drastically increased number of warships, including those of states located thousands of kilometers away from this important area, are plying international waters traditionally used for trade and other peaceful passage. The continuation of the long, senseless war between Iran and Iraq objectively facilitates the aggravation of the situation. As a result, events there are approaching a danger level beyond which exists the risk of the regional conflict developing into an international crisis.

It is absolutely clear that these processes, if not stopped in time and placed under proper control, might pose a serious threat to international peace and security even contrary to the will and intent of the states drawn into them. This turn of events gives rise to the legitimate alarm of the international community. Likewise, this cannot but provoke the concern of the Soviet Union which is located in the direct proximity of the expanding seat of conflict.

In these conditions there is a pressing need to adopt urgent and effective measures that will promote a radical defusing of tension in the Persian Gulf and an early end of the Iran-Iraq war. Real steps toward attainment of the said aims are needed. Pseudomeasures, supposedly motivated by concern for the safety of shipping or "ensuring stabilization" in the Persian Gulf but in reality prompted by selfish designs, are absolutely impermissible. Such actions are now being undertaken by the United States which wants to exploit the present alarming situation in the Persian Gulf area to achieve its long-harbored plans of establishing military-political hegemony in this strategically important area of the world, an area that Washington is trying to represent as a sphere of American "vital interests." Such is the real explanation of the U.S. policy of building up its military presence, although it tries to cover this up with stereotype contentions about the existence of a "Soviet threat."...

Proceeding from the need for radical measures to improve the situation in the region, the Soviet government suggests that all warships of states not situated in the region be withdrawn soon from the Gulf and that Iran and Iraq, in turn, should abstain from actions that would threaten international shipping. Such measures, taken in the context of an all-embracing settlement of the Iran-Iraq conflict, would help pacify the situation and eliminate the threat of the spread of an explosive seat of military tension.

The Soviet Union reaffirms its principled stand in favor of ending the Iran-Iraq war and resolving outstanding issues between Iran and Iraq at the negotiating table rather than on the battlefield.

In this connection we attach special importance to political efforts within the framework of the United Nations to find a peaceful solution to the Iran-Iraq conflict.

In agreement with other members of the UN Security Council, we are in favor of effective measures in this direction, specifically an immediate cease-fire and cessation of all hostilities, and a withdrawal of all troops to the internationally recognized borders without delay.

The UN secretary-general can play a substantial role in achieving a fair settlement acceptable to both sides.

The Soviet Union supports the peace-making mission of the UN secretary-general and calls on all other countries to render every kind of assistance to its successful outcome.

The acuteness of the situation in the Persian Gulf area and the need to quickly bring about an end to the Iran-Iraq conflict require that all countries pursue a policy of genuinely constructive deeds, a policy prompted by the overriding interest in preserving peace and effectively strengthening international security, rather than practicing "gunboat diplomacy."

The Soviet Union is ready to cooperate with all those who really share these aims.

The Reality and Guarantees of a Secure World

Mikhail S. Gorbachev

17 September 1987

Editor's commentary: A milestone in Soviet foreign policy, this article signals a key change in Soviet policy toward international organizations, and especially the UN. Accompanied as it was by a promise of payment in arrears of the Soviet share of UN operations, this statement appeared to be more than mere rhetoric. In its sweeping scope and idealism, Mr. Gorbachev's vision of the possibilities that international organizations hold for providing greater stability in an unstable world could be compared in its breadth and scope to Woodrow Wilson's Fourteen Points for the peace settlement after the First World War. It is interesting to note as well that this announcement preceded by three months a UN-sponsored negotiated settlement of the war in Afghanistan.

The 42nd session of the UN General assembly opened a few days ago. It is this fact that suggested the idea of this article. Objective processes are making our complex and diverse world increasingly interrelated and interdependent. It increasingly needs a mechanism which is capable of discussing its common problems in a responsible fashion and at a representative level and being a place for the mutual search for a balance of differing, contradictory, yet real, interests of the contemporary community of states and nations. The United Nations organization is called upon to be such a mechanism by its un-

Pravda, 17 September 1987, pp. 1–2, as translated in *Foreign Broadcast Information Service*, Soviet Union (Washington, DC: *n.p.*, 17 September 1987, pp. 23–28, *excerpts*.

derlying idea and origin. We are confident that it is capable of fulfilling that role....

I....The security plan proposed by us provides, above all, for continuity and concord with the existing institutions for the maintenance of peace. The system could function on the basis of the UN Charter and within the framework of the United Nations. In our view, its ability to function will be ensured by the strict observance of the charter's demands, additional unilateral obligations of states as well as confidence measures and international cooperation in all spheres—politico-military, economic, ecological, humanitarian and others.

I do not venture to foretell how the system of all-embracing security would appear in its final form. It is only clear that it could become a reality only if all means of mass annihilation were destroyed. We propose that all this be pondered by an independent commission of experts and specialists which would submit its conclusions to the United Nations organization....

The system proposed by us precisely presupposes a definiteness of measures which would enable the United Nations organization, the main universal security body, to ensure its maintenance at a level of reliability.

II. The division of the world's countries into those possessing nuclear weapons and those not possessing them has split also the very concept of security. But for human life security is indivisible. In this sense it is not only a political, military, juridical but also a moral category. Contentions that there has been no war for already half a century do not withstand any test on the touchstone of ethics....There are dozens of regional wars flaring in the world....

Unconditional observance of the UN Charter and the rights of peoples sovereignly to choose the roads and forms of their development, revolutionary or evolutionary, is an imperative condition of universal security. This applies also to the right to social status quo. This, too, is exclusively an internal matter. Any attempts, direct or indirect, to influence the development of "not one of our own" countries, to interfere in this development should be ruled out. Just as impermissible are attempts to destabilize existing governments from outside....

It appears to us that with the aim of strengthening trust and mutual understanding it could be possible to set up under the aegis of the UN organization a mechanism for extensive international verification of compliance with agreements to lessen international tension, limit armaments and for monitoring the military situation in conflict areas. The mechanism would function using various forms and methods of monitoring to collect information and promptly submit it to the United Nations. This would make it possible to have an objective picture of the events taking place, to timely detect preparations for hostilities, impede a sneak attack, take measures to avert an armed conflict, prevent it from expanding and becoming worse.

We are arriving at the conclusion that wide use should be made of the institute of UN military observers and UN peace-keeping forces in disengaging the troops of warring sides, observing ceasefire and armistice agreements....

The Security Council permanent members could become guarantors of regional security. They could, on their part, assume the obligation not to use force or the threat of force, to renounce demonstrative military presence. This is so because such a practice is one of the factors of fanning regional conflicts.

A drastic intensification and expansion of the cooperation of states in uprooting international terrorism is extremely important. It would be expedient to concentrate this cooperation within the framework of the United Nations organization. In our opinion, it would be useful to create under its aegis a tribunal and investigate acts of international terrorism.

More coordination in the struggle against apartheid as a destabilizing factor of international magnitude would also be justified.

As we see it, all the above-stated measures should be organically built into an all-embracing system of peace and security.

III....the problem of economic security. A world in which a whole continent can find itself on the brink of death from starvation and in which huge masses of people are suffering from almost permanent malnutrition is not a safe world. Neither is a world safe in which a multitude of countries and peoples are stifling in a noose of debt....

Ecological security. It is dangerous in the direct meaning of the word when currents of poison flow along river channels, when poisonous rains pour down from the sky, when the atmosphere polluted with industrial and transport waste chokes cities and whole regions, when the development of atomic engineering is justified by unacceptable risks.

Many have suddenly begun to perceive all that not as something abstract, but as quite a real part of their own experience. The confidence that "this won't affect us," characteristic of the past outlook, has disappeared. They say that one thorn of experience is worth more than a whole wood of instructions. For us, Chernobyl became such a thorn....

Realizing the need for opening a common front of economic and ecological security and starting its formation mean defusing a delayed-action bomb planted deep inside mankind's existence by history, by people themselves.

IV. Human rights....

First of all, it is necessary that national legislation and administrative rules in the humanitarian sphere everywhere be brought in accordance with international obligations and standards.

Simultaneously it would be possible to turn to coordinating a broad selection of practical steps, for instance, to working out a world information program under UN auspices to familiarize peoples with one another's life, the life as it is, not as someone would like to present it. That is precisely why such a project should envisage ridding the flow of information of the "enemy image" stereotypes, of bias, prejudices and absurd concoctions, of the distortion and unscrupulous violations of the truth.

There is much promise in the task of coordinating unified international legal criteria for resolving in the humanitarian spirit issues of family reunification, marriages, contacts between people and organizations, visa regulations and so on. What has been achieved on this account within the framework of the all-European process should be accepted as a starting point....

V. The suggested system of comprehensive security will be effective to the extent in which the United Nations, its Security Council, and other international institutions and mechanisms will effectively function. It will be required to enhance resolutely the authority and role of the United Nations and the IAEA. The need for establishing a world space organization is clearly felt. It could work in the future in close contact with the United Nations as an autonomous part of its system. UN specialized agencies should also become regulators of international processes. The Geneva Conference on Disarmament should become a forum that would internationalize the efforts on transition to a nuclear-free, nonviolent world.

One should not forget the capacities of the international court either. The general assembly and the Security Council could approach it more often for consultative conclusions on international law disputes. Its mandatory jurisdiction should be recognized by all on mutually agreed upon conditions. The permanent members of the Security Council taking into account special responsibility, are to make the first step in that direction.

We are convinced that a comprehensive system of security is at the same time a system of universal law and order ensuring the primacy of international law in politics.

The UN Charter gives extensive powers to the Security Council. Joint efforts are required to ensure that it could use them effectively. For this purpose, there would be sense in holding meetings of the Security Council at foreign ministers' level when opening a regular session of the General Assembly to review the international situation and jointly look for effective ways for its improvement....

We are convinced that cooperation between the United Nations and regional organizations could be considerably expanded. Its aim is the search for a political settlement of crisis situations.

In our view, it is important to hold special sessions of the General Assembly on the more urgent political problems and individual disarmament issues more often if the efficiency of the latter's work is to be improved.

We emphatically stress the need for making the status of important political documents passed at the United Nations by consensus more binding morally and politically. Let me recall that they include, among others, the final document of the first special session of the UN General Assembly devoted to disarmament, the charter of economic rights and obligations of states, and others.

In our opinion, we should have set up long ago a world consultative council under UN auspices uniting the world's intellectual elite. Prominent scientists, political and public figures, representatives of international public organizations, cultural workers, people in literature and the arts, including laureates of the Nobel prize and other international prizes of world-wide significance, and eminent representatives of the churches could seriously enrich the spiritual and ethical potential of contemporary world politics.

To ensure that the United Nations and its specialized agencies operate at full capacity one should come to realize that it is impermissible to use financial levers for bringing pressure to bear on it. The Soviet Union will continue to cooperate actively in overcoming budget difficulties arising at the United Nations.

Finally, about the UN secretary general. The international community elects an authoritative figure enjoying everybody's trust to that high post. Since the secretary general is functioning as a representative of every member-country of the organization all states should give him the maximum of support and help him in fulfilling his responsible mission....

Why are we so persistent in raising the question of a comprehensive system of international peace and security?

Simply because it is impossible to put up with the situation in which the world has found itself on the threshold of the third millennium—in the face of a threat of annihilation, in a state of constant tension, in an atmosphere of suspicion and strife, spending huge funds and quantities of work and talent of millions of people, only to increase mutual mistrust and fears.

One can speak as much as he pleases about the need for terminating the arms race, uprooting militarism, or about cooperation. Nothing will change unless we start acting.

The political and moral core of the problem is the trust of the states and peoples in one another, respect for international agreements and institutions. We are prepared to switch from confidence measures in individual spheres to a large-scale policy of trust which would gradually shape a system of comprehensive security. But such a policy should be based on the unity of political statements and real positions.

The idea of a comprehensive system of security is the first plan for a possible new organization of life in our common planetary home. In other words, it is a pass into the future where security of all is a token of the security for everyone. We hope that the current session of the UN General Assembly will jointly develop and concretize this idea.

DOCUMENT 17

USSR-China: For Further Development of Cooperation

25 September 1987

Editor's commentary: The author of this article appearing in the Soviet government newspaper, Izvestiia, *the director of the Institute of the Far East in the USSR Academy of Sciences, reviewed the positive development of Sino-Soviet relations since the early 1980s, and especially in consequence of Gorbachev's "new thinking" in foreign policy. The author outlined the prospects for the future in glowing terms. According to this view, the new Soviet policy toward China is directed toward a "total liquidation" of all past inequities and transgressions in Sino-Soviet relations. While a return to the heyday of the Sino-Soviet alliance seemed unlikely, implications of an invigorated Soviet Chinese policy appeared portentous. Indeed, Sino-Soviet relations were formally normalized less than 2 years later, on 16 May 1989, during Gorbachev's historic visit to the PRC, where the Soviet leader met with Deng Xiao Peng at the summit in Beijing.*

The past several years have been marked by a substantial improvement in USSR-PRC relations. Bilateral cooperation, filled with new content, is becoming ever wider in scope. The level of statesmen's mutual contacts has risen.

Visit exchanges by deputy heads of the two countries' governments have been regular since December 1984. The Soviet and Chinese ministers of foreign affairs had a number of meetings during UN General Assemblies. Political consultations on bilateral and key international issues are now systematic; border talks have been resumed; and the Soviet-Chinese commission for economic and scientific-technical cooperation keeps on meeting.

A significant event in normalizing Soviet-Chinese inter-state relations was the resumption, after a break of more than 20 years, of links between legislative bodies. By now these contact have already assumed a permanent character....

In 1987 a new consular treaty took effect. Consulates general of the USSR and the PRC have been opened in Shanghai and Leningrad as a result. A two-year (1986–87) plan of cultural co-

Izvestiia, 25 September 1987, as translated in *Reprints from the Soviet Press,* vol. 45, no. 8, 30 October 1987, pp. 24–31, *excerpts.*

operation is being successfully realized, and ties have been established between trade unions, women's and youth organizations and friendship societies.

Mutual trade has grown rapidly. Between 1981 and 1986 it rose tenfold in value terms, reaching 1,822 million rubles.

The facts of wider, developing Soviet-Chinese cooperation cannot but evoke deep satisfaction in our country. It is obvious that improved relations between the two largest socialist states are vital for the destinies of world peace and the cause of socialism. History has placed special responsibility on the Soviet and Chinese peoples, especially for the preservation of peace in Asia.

Developing Soviet-Chinese relations as both countries have embarked on large-scale economic reforms to streamline and unfold the advantages of the socialist system, presupposes a broad exchange of the experience of construction in all fields, and is a powerful stimulating factor of rapid realization of the aims and tasks of perestroika and modernization so as to drastically improve the well-being of the Soviet and Chinese peoples. In the coming 21st century the issue of historical peaceful competition between the two socio-political systems will largely depend on the successes of perestroika in the Soviet Union and reforms in the PRC and other socialist lands.

The concept of new political thinking has been the chief methodological guideline in our country's approach to China, just as to other world problems since the April 1985 Plenum of the CPSU Central Committee. It helps clear swiftly and consistently our relations of negative accumulations of the past, and give them a genuinely equitable, mutually beneficial character with regard for each other's current and long-term national interest. In practical terms it has helped give proper dynamism and flexibility to the USSR foreign policy line in promoting links with our great socialist neighbor. The philosophy of new political thinking calls for listening to and understanding other countries and peoples, placing at the center of relations the common interests and aims, the identical or similar aspects of home and foreign policy, and viewing them in the broad context of world relations and interests.

Set out by Mikhail Gorbachev in Vladivostok, the idea of a comprehensive approach to safeguarding peace and security in the Asia-Pacific region has the most direct bearing on Soviet-Chinese relations. Ultimately the part of the Vladivostok proposals concerning the PRC envisages not only a total liquidation of the negative accumulations from an earlier period in Soviet-Chinese relations, but also, based on the experience and lessons of the past, helps set in full motion the huge potential of cooperation and neighborliness.

Such objective factors as the same socio-economic system, geographical proximity, the same priorities in strategic tasks, aimed at more rapid socio-economic development and the self-refinement of socialism, and the historically established mutually complementary nature of the Soviet and Chinese economies offer a clear and significant perspective in this direction.

The chief task at this stage of Soviet-Chinese relations is to assure continuity and dynamism of this process and to create the most favorable conditions for its qualitative development....

The Soviet Union is fully conscious of the role of the PRC as a great power, conducting a self-determined and independent foreign policy directed toward strengthening peace all over the world. Our country has invariably supported China's efforts to defende and uphold its national sovereignty, including its rightful stand in respect to Taiwan as an inalienable part of the PRC.

While welcoming the enhancement of China's constructive effort in international affairs, the Soviet Union sees it as a key factor of international and regional security. There can be no fair and stable solution of international problems, either on an Asian or global scale, without China—a great socialist power, which assisted at the origin of the five principles of peaceful coexistence and has a ramified system of international 1⋯ s and interest....

The Soviet Union does not idealize the picture of Soviet-Chinese relations. Often, they are motley enough. We do not disregard the differing approaches and discrepancies demonstrated by the two nations. However, we do not see them as something fatally unavoidable. We are for a tireless search for ways to resolve existing contradictions. The Soviet leadership has more than once stated it is ready, at any time and on any level, to discuss in the most serious manner with China additional measures for good-neighborliness.

The two countries have made only the first major steps on the road of cooperation and good neighborliness on which they have resolutely embarked. This is the beginning of a long way. As Mikhail Gorbachev put it, ''As for the future, Soviet-Chinese cooperation has tremendous reserves. They are great because this cooperation is in the interests of both countries and because socialism and peace, which the two nations treasure most of all, are inseparable.''

DOCUMENT 18

Great October: The Revolution Continues

M. S. Gorbachev

2 November 1987

Editor's commentary: In these excerpts from Mikhail Gorbachev's keynote address at the celebrations surrounding the seventieth anniversary of the Great October Socialist Revolution, the emphasis is on respecting what Khrushchev labeled "different roads to socialism." While Mr. Gorbachev does accept this principle, it is interesting to note his stress on the principles of "socialist internationalism" and the responsibilities that parties have to the communist movement in the context of the WTO and CMEA, which implies that limits continue to exist to independent action on the part of socialist states in these organizations.

Comrades, in these festive days we are paying due tribute to the merits of the international Communist movement. The October Revolution, which has retained to this day its international stimulus, is the source of its viability. The international Communist movement is growing and developing on the soil of individual countries but there is something in common in the very image of the communist, whatever nation he may belong to and in whatever country he may work. This is his dedication to the idea of a better communist society and his loyalty to the working people, above all to the working class, the struggle for their vital interests, for peace and democracy. (*Applause.*)

I believe that on this our anniversary the Third Communist International also deserves to be mentioned. We have yet to restore the full truth about it and to write its authentic and complete history. For all the shortcomings and miscalculations in its work, and however bitter it may be to recall certain pages of its history, the Comintern is part of the great past of our movement. Born of October, it not only became a school of internationalism and revolutionary brotherhood, it made internationalism a practical weapon in the struggle for the interests of working people, of the social progress of the nations and peoples. From its ranks arose the cohorts of the true knights of the 20th century: people of duty and honor, of lofty flight and inflexible courage, who felt the grief of the millions of the oppressed throughout the world, heard their call and summoned them to the struggle. (*Applause.*)...

Later, and now, with the same irreconcilability and bravery, the communists are in the first ranks against all reaction and all obscurantism.

Moscow Television Service, 2 November 1987, as transcribed in *Foreign Broadcast Information Service*, Soviet Union (Washington, DC: *n.p.*, 3 November 1987, pp. 54–61, *excerpts*.

They are people of legendary heroism and self-sacrifice. They are not just individuals, but hundreds of thousands of people, organized and united by a single will, iron discipline, and incorruptible ideological commitment. The days of the Comintern, of the Informburo, and even of binding international conferences have passed; but the international Communist movement exists. All parties are fully and irreversibly independent. We said that as long ago as the 20th congress. True, it took time to free ourselves from the old habits. Now, however, this is an immutable reality. In that sense the 27th CPSU Congress was also a final and irrevocable milestone. I believe we have shown this by our actions, in our relations with the fraternal parties and in the course of restructuring. (*Applause.*)

The international Communist movement is at the crossroads, and like world progress itself, its driving force. The Communist Parties are seeking their new place in the profound changes at the turn of the centuries. Meanwhile, their international movement is renewing itself, gaining cohesion by respect . . . renewed norms of trust, equality of rights and sincere solidarity.

The movement is open to dialogue, to cooperation, to interaction and alliance with all other revolutionary, democratic and progressive forces. The CPSU has no doubt about the future of the communist movement, the carrier of the alternative to capitalism, the movement of the bravest and most consistent fighters for peace, and for the independence and progress of their countries, for friendship among all peoples of the earth. (*Applause.*)

Comrades: The most important milestone in post-October world history is the emergence of the world socialist system. For four decades now, socialism has been the common destiny of many peoples and a highly important factor of modern civilization. Our party and the Soviet people value greatly their opportunity to interact with our friends, who for several decades now have borne, as we do, responsibility at state level for socialism and for its advance.

All the socialist states have amassed much interesting and useful experience in solving the so-cial, economic and ideological tasks of building a new life. The socialist system and the quest and experience which it has tested in practice are of universal human significance. . . . From the heights of what has been covered, much is clearer. Life has amended our conceptions of the logical patterns and speeds of the transition to socialism and understanding of socialism's role on a world scale. We are far from thinking that all the progressive changes taking place in the world are due only to socialism, but the way in which the most important problems for mankind are presented and in which the search for their solution is proceeding affirms an indissoluble link between world progress and socialism as an international force. (*Applause.*) This link is especially visible in the struggle to avert a nuclear catastrophe and in the presence of a correlation of world forces that permits various peoples to defend their socialist and political choice with greater success.

The experience accumulated permits relations among the socialist countries to be better constructed on generally recognized principles. These are unconditional and total equality, the responsibility of the ruling party for affairs in its state, and for patriotic service to its people; concern for the general cause of socialism, respect for one another, a serious attitude toward what has been achieved and tried out by friends; voluntary and varied cooperation, and the strict observation by all of the principles of peaceful coexistence. The practice of socialist internationalism rests upon these.

The world of socialism rises before us now in all its national and social variation. This is good and useful. We have become convinced that unity does not mean being identical or uniform. We have also become convinced that socialism does not, and cannot have, a model, against which all are compared. The criterion for its development at every stage and in every country is the totality and quality of the real successes which have reconstructed society in the interests of the working people. (*Applause.*)

We also know what damage can be done by

a weakening of the internationalist principle in mutual relations of socialist states, by deviation form the principles of mutual benefit and mutual aid, and by a lack of attention to the general interests of socialism in action on the world arena. It is with satisfaction that we state that recently our relations with all socialist states have acquired dynamism and are improving. Of course, cooperation within the framework of the Warsaw Pact and CEMA has become more fruitful and more businesslike, which, incidentally, in no way of principle separates their participants from the other socialist countries.

The 27th Congress gave a precise definition of the stance of the CPSU in politics and in all other areas of our cooperation with each socialist country. What is decisive is what ensures a combination of mutual interest and those of socialism as a whole. The strengthening of friendship and the all-round development of cooperation with the socialist countries is the main priority of the international policy of the Soviet Union. Welcoming today the delegations from the socialist countries, in their person we welcome the peoples of the socialist countries. (*Applause.*)

a gathering of Communists and leftists from all over the world. The speech displayed a new dimension of openness as he criticized "the arrogance of omniscience" in Soviet dealings with other Communist parties in the past and reemphasized the necessity to avoid the stagnation of the Brezhnev years by striking out in new economic and political directions. As such, the address sounded more like a traditional social-democratic campaign speech than a keynote address by a Soviet Communist, something the Western communists in attendance were no doubt pleased to hear.

...The potential of socialism has not yet developed to the full, by far. In essence, a most profound social revolution is going on, with its origins in the October Revolution. But the duration, novelty, and unevenness of it, the combination and coexistence of progressive moves and recessions, the interchange and interconnection of revolutionary and evolutionary process, make any logical schemes composed according to old text books unviable....

The fact is that real socialism, as far as its technological development is concerned, is still lagging behind capitalism, and is also impeded in the passage to a new level of understanding these processes. The prerequisites for overcoming this lagging behind are taking shape during the course of the revolutionary restructuring of socialist society, of its transition to a qualitatively new condition....

Now it is no longer possible to view world development merely from the viewpoint of the struggle between two opposing social systems. The dialectic of this development represents unity, confrontation, competition, and interaction of a multitude of factors. It is precisely in this interaction between various societies that

---

DOCUMENT 19

Address to the Fraternal Parties on the Seventieth Anniversary of the Great October Socialist Revolution

M. S. Gorbachev

4 November 1987

Editor's commentary: As part of the celebratory activities of the Great October Revolution's Seventieth anniversary, Gorbachev addressed

Moscow Television Service, 4 November 1987, as transcribed in *Foreign Broadcase Information Service*, Soviet Union (Washington, DC: *n.p.*, 4 November 1987, pp. 22–24, excerpts.

each one of them is put to the test. Naturally, this is not tantamount to some sort of unification between them, some convergence.

We will not forgo, not by one iota, the real values of socialism. On the contrary, we will enrich and develop them, ridding ourselves of all that which distorted the humanistic essence of our system. We are certainly not striving for our class enemy to fall in love with us, we do not need that at all. What we are counting on is that life will compel him to take realities into account and to become aware that we are all in the same boat and that we must behave in such a way that it does not capsize....

Representing the CPSU here, I would like to add a few words to what I said about it the day before yesterday in my report. Like much else in today's world, the communist movement needs renewal and qualitative changes. Now it is particularly important that it is not only a national but, in its very nature, an international force. Such a force is particularly needed by contemporary mankind. As far as the CPSU is concerned, it does not imagine its internal plans and deeds outside of the international context, and not, of course, outside of the correlation with the significance which they have or may have for our brothers in ideals and for progressive forces in general.

We ourselves felt strongly how, in the period of stagnation, the international impetus of socialism had lessened, so that restructuring in the USSR became vital from this point of view as well. We are fully aware of the significance of our work at the new stage, not only in the world economic and political context, but also in the context of moral support for the forces of socialism, democracy, and progress. But mere parallel activities in our countries are insufficient. Cooperation is also necessary, but in contemporary forms of course. A more perfect standard, if one may put it like this, of mutual relations between progressive forces is required, such a standard which might make it

possible to accumulate the whole diversity of experience, and help to understand the world surrounding us in all of its multitude of colors and contradictions.

The arrogance of a belief in one's omniscience is akin to fear of one's inability to master new problems; it bears witness to the tenacious habit of rejecting out of hand others' points of view. Here you get neither dialogue nor productive discussion, but the main thing is that the cause suffers. Just as it was impossible in the beginning of the century to dogmatically extrapolate all of the tenets put forward by Marx and Engels for the age of imperialism, so still more it is impossible to carry out such an operation in assessing modern times with the aid of postulates which arose in the fifties, sixties, or even the thirties.

The theoretical legacy which our predecessors created in the name of man's social liberation must be read again in such a way as would make it possible to have a precise analysis of the new realities and to arrive at the optimally correct political conclusions. Many questions have to be answered in the search for a programmatic alternative to a society of antagonisms, and of confrontational tension on the world arena.

Our party and its theorists and scientists began to tackle these questions seriously, ridding themselves of the concepts and schemes born of another time and of different opportunities for creativity. We invite not only the fraternal parties, communists, but also socialists and social democrats and representatives of other trends in political thought and action, all who hold dear the accomplishments of man's spirit and who wish to preserve and make use of them for the coming generations, to cooperation and search jointly.

This is vitally important for understanding the new situation, when the renewal of civilization merges with the task of mankind's survival....

Treaty Between the Union of Soviet Socialist Republics and the United States of America on the Elimination of Their Intermediate-Range and Shorter-Range Missiles

8 December 1987

Editor's commentary: The INF Treaty was the first arms control treaty in history to eliminate an entire class of weapons. After about a decade, NATO's "two-track" proposal had finally been successful. The treaty follows in abridged form.

The Union of Soviet Socialist Republics and the United States of America...have agreed as follows:

Article I

In accordance with the provisions of this Treaty ...each Party shall eliminate its intermediate-range and shorter-range missiles, not have such systems thereafter, and carry out the other obligations set forth in this Treaty.

Article II

For the purposes of this Treaty:

1. The term "ballistic missile" means a missile that has a ballistic trajectory over most of its flight path. The term "ground-launched ballistic missile (GLBM)" means a ground-launched ballistic missile that is a weapon-delivery vehicle.

2. The term "cruise missile" means an unmanned, self-propelled vehicle that sustains flight through the use of aerodynamic lift over most of its flight path. The term "ground launched cruise missile (GLCM)" means a ground-launched cruise missile that is a weapon-delivery vehicle....

Department of State Bulletin, vol. 88, no. 2131, February 1988, pp. 24–30, *abridged.*

5. The term "intermediate-range missile" means a GLBM or a GLCM having a range capability in excess of 1,000 kilometers but not in excess of 5,500 kilometers.

6. The term "shorter-range missile" means a GLBM or a GLCM having a range capability equal to or in excess of 500 kilometers but not in excess of 1,000 kilometers.

7. The term "deployment area" means a designated area within which intermediate-range missiles and launchers of such missiles may operate and within which one or more missile operating bases are located:...

Article III

1. For the purposes of this Treaty, existing types of intermediate-range missiles are:

(a) for the Union of Soviet Socialist Republics, missiles of the types designated by the Union of Soviet Socialist Republics as the RSD-10, the R-12 and the R-14, which are known to the United States of America as the SS-20, the SS-4 and the SS-5, respectively; and

(b) for the United States of America, missiles of the types designated by the United States of America as the Pershing 2 and the BGM-109G, which are known to the Union of Soviet Socialist Republics by the same designations.

2. For the purposes of this Treaty, existing types of shorter-range missiles are:

(a) for the Union of Soviet Socialist Republics, missiles of the types designated by the Union of Soviet Socialist Republics as the OTR-22 and the OTR-23, which are known to the United States of America as the SS-12 and the SS-23, respectively; and

(b) for the United States of America, missiles of the type designated by the United States of America as the Pershing 1A, which is known to the Union of Soviet Socialist Republics by the same designation.

Article IV

Each party shall eliminate all its intermediate-range missiles and launchers of such missiles, and all support structures and support equipment of the categories listed in the Memorandum of Understanding associated with such missiles and launchers, so that no later than three years after entry into force of this Treaty and thereafter no such missiles, launchers, support structures or support equipment shall be possessed by either Party.

2. To implement paragraph one of this Article, upon entry into force of this Treaty, both Parties shall begin and continue throughout the duration of each phase, the reduction of all types of their deployed and non-deployed intermediate-range missiles and deployed and non-deployed launchers of such missiles and support structures and support equipment associated with such missiles and launchers in accordance with the provisions of this Treaty. These reductions shall be implemented in two phases so that:

(a) by the end of the first phase, that is, no later than 29 months after entry into force of this Treaty:

(1) the number of deployed launchers of intermediate-range missiles for each Party shall not exceed the number of launchers that are capable of carrying or containing at one time, missiles considered by the Parties to carry 171 warheads;

(2) the number of deployed intermediate-range missiles for each Party shall not exceed the number of such missiles considered by the Parties to carry 180 warheads;

(3) the aggregate number of deployed and non-deployed launchers of intermediate range missiles for each Party shall not exceed the number of launchers that are capable of carrying or containing at one time missiles considered by the Parties to carry 200 warheads;

(4) the aggregate number of deployed and non-deployed intermediate-range missiles for each Party shall not exceed the number of such missiles considered by the Parties to carry 200 warheads; and

(5) the ratio of the aggregate number of deployed and non-deployed intermediate-range GLBMs of the existing types for each Party to the aggregate number of deployed and non-deployed intermediate-range missiles of existing types possessed by that Party shall not exceed the ratio of such intermediate-range GLBMs to such intermediate-range missiles for that Party as of November 1, 1987, as set forth in the Memorandum of Understanding; and

(b) by the end of the second phase, that is, no later than three years after entry into force of this Treaty, all intermediate-range missiles of each Party, launchers of such missiles and all support structures and support equipment of the categories listed in the Memorandum of Understanding associated with such missiles and launchers, shall be eliminated.

Article V

1. Each Party shall eliminate all its shorter-range missiles and launchers of such missiles, and all support equipment of the categories listed in the Memorandum of Understanding associated with such missiles and launchers, so that no later than 18 months after entry into force of this Treaty and thereafter no such missiles, launchers or support equipment shall be possessed by either Party.

2. No later than 90 days after entry into force of this Treaty, each Party shall complete the removal of all its deployed shorter-range missiles and deployed and non-deployed launchers of such missiles to elimination facilities and shall retain them at those locations until they are eliminated in accordance with the procedures set forth in the Protocol on Elimination. No later than 12 months after entry into force of this Treaty, each Party shall complete the removal of all its non-deployed shorter-range missiles to elimination facilities and shall retain them at those locations until they are eliminated in accordance with the procedures set forth in the Protocol on Elimination.

3. Shorter-range missiles and launchers of such missiles shall not be located at the same elimination facility. Such facilities shall be separated by no less than 1,000 kilometers.

Article VI

1. Upon entry into force of this Treaty and thereafter, neither Party shall:

(a) produce or flight-test any intermediate-range missiles or produce any stages of such missiles or any launchers of such missiles; or

(b) produce, flight-test or launch any shorter-range missiles or produce any stages of such missiles or any launchers of such missiles.

2. Notwithstanding paragraph 1 of this article, each Party shall have the right to produce a type of GLBM, not limited by this Treaty which uses a stage which is outwardly similar to, but not interchangeable with, a stage of an existing type of intermediate-range GLBM having more than one stage, providing that Party does not produce any other stage which is outwardly similar to, but not interchangeable with, any other stage of an existing type of intermediate-range GLBM.

Article VII

For the purposes of this Treaty:

1. If a ballistic missile or a cruise missile has been flight-tested or deployed for weapon delivery, all missiles of that type shall be considered to be weapon-delivery vehicles.

2. If a GLBM or GLCM is an intermediate-range missile, all GLBMs or GLCMs of that type shall be considered to be intermediate-range missiles. If a GLBM or GLCM is a shorter-range missiles, all GLBMs or GLCMs of that type shall be considered to be shorter-range missiles.

3. If a GLBM is of a type developed and tested solely to intercept and counter objects not located on the surface of the earth, it shall not be considered to be a missile to which the limitations of this Treaty apply.

4. The range capability of a GLBM not listed in Article III of this Treaty shall be considered to be the maximum range to which it has been tested. The range capability of a GLCM not listed in Article III of this Treaty shall be considered to be the maximum distance which can be covered by the missile in its standard design mode flying until fuel exhaustion....GLBMs or GLCMs that have a range capability equal to or in excess of 500 kilometers but not in excess of 1,000 kilometers shall be considered to be shorter-range missiles. GLBMs or GLCMs that have a range capability in excess of 1,000 kilometers but not in excess of 5,500 kilometers shall be considered to be intermediate-range missiles.

5. The maximum number of warheads an existing type of intermediate-range missile or shorter-range missile carries shall be considered to be the number listed for missiles of that type in the Memorandum of Understanding.

6. Each GLBM or GLCM shall be considered to carry the maximum number of warhead, listed for a GLBM or GLCM of that type in the Memorandum of Understanding.

7. If a launcher has been tested for launching a GLBM or a GLCM, all launchers of that type shall be considered to have been tested for launching GLBMs or GLCMs.

8. If a launcher has contained or launched a particular type of GLBM or GLCM, all launchers of that type shall be considered to be launchers of that type of GLBM or GLCM.

9. The number of missiles each launcher of an existing type of intermediate-range missile or shorter-range missile shall be considered to be capable of carrying or containing at one time is the number listed for launchers of missiles of that type in the Memorandum of Understanding.

10. Except in the case of elimination in accordance with the procedures set forth in the Protocol on Elimination, the following shall apply:

(a) for GLBMs which are stored or moved in separate stages, the longest stage of an intermediate-range or shorter-range GLBM shall be counted as a complete missile;

(b) for GLBMs which are not stored or moved in separate stages, a canister of the type used in the launch of an intermediate-range GLBM, unless a Party proves to the satisfaction of the other Party that it does not contain such a missile, or an assembled intermediate-range or shorter-range GLBM, shall be counted as a complete missile; and

(c) for GLCMs, the airframe of an intermediate-range or shorter-range GLCM shall be counted as a complete missile.

11. A ballistic missile which is not a missile to be used in a ground-based mode shall not be considered to be a GLBM if it is test-launched at a test site from a fixed land-based launcher which is used solely for test purposes and which is distinguishable from GLBM launchers. A cruise missile which is not a missile to be used in a ground-based mode shall not be considered to be a GLCM if it is test-launched at a test site from a fixed land-based launcher which is used solely for test purposes and which is distinguishable from GLCM launchers.

12. Each Party shall have the right to produce and use for booster systems, which might otherwise be considered to be intermediate-range or shorter-range missiles, only existing types of booster stages for such booster systems. Launches of such booster systems shall not be considered to be flight-testing of intermediate-range or shorter-range missiles provided that:

(a) stages used in such booster systems are different from stages used in those missiles listed as existing types of intermediate-range or shorter-range missiles in Article III of this Treaty;

(b) such booster systems are used only for research and development purposes to test objects other than the booster systems themselves;

(c) the aggregate number of launchers for such booster systems shall not exceed 35 for each Party at any one time; and

(d) the launchers for such booster systems are fixed, placed above ground and located only at research and development launch sites which are specified in the Memorandum of Understanding.

Research and development launch sites shall not be subject to inspection pursuant to Article XI of this Treaty.

Article VIII

1. All intermediate-range missiles and launchers of such missiles shall be located in deployment areas, at missile support facilities or shall be in transit. Intermediate-range missiles or launchers of such missiles shall not be located elsewhere.

2. Stages of intermediate-range missiles shall be located in deployment areas, at missile support facilities or moving between deployment areas, between missile support facilities or between missile support facilities and deployment areas.

3. Until their removal to elimination facilities as required by paragraph 2 of Article V of this Treaty, all shorter-range missiles and launchers of such missile support facilities or shall be in transit. Shorter-range missiles or launchers of such missiles shall not be located elsewhere.

4. Transit of a missile or launcher subject to the provisions of this Treaty shall be completed within 25 days.

5. All deployment areas, missile operating bases and missile support facilities are specified in the memorandum of Understanding or in subsequent updates of data pursuant to paragraphs 3, 5(a) or 5(b) of Article IX of this Treaty. Neither Party shall increase the number of, or change the location or boundaries of, deployment areas, missile operating bases or missile support facilities, except for elimination facilities, from those set forth in the Memorandum of Understanding. A missile support facility shall not be considered to be part of a deployment area even though it may be located within the geographic boundaries of a deployment area.

6. Beginning 30 days after entry into force of this Treaty, neither Party shall locate intermediate-range or shorter-range missiles, including stages of such missiles, or launchers of such missiles at missile production facilities, launcher production facilities or test ranges listed in the Memorandum of Understanding.

7. Neither Party shall locate any intermediate-range or shorter-range missiles at training facilities.

8. A non-deployed intermediate-range or shorter-range missile shall not be carried on or contained within a launcher of such a type of missile, except as required for maintenance con-

ducted at repair facilities or for elimination by means of launching conducted at elimination facilities.

9. Training missiles and training launchers for intermediate-range or shorter-range missiles shall be subject to the same locational restrictions as are set forth for intermediate-range and shorter-range missiles and launchers of such missiles in paragraphs 1 and 3 of this Article.

Article IX

1. The Memorandum of Understanding contains categories of data relevant to obligations undertaken with regard to this Treaty and lists all…missiles, launchers…and support structures and support equipment…possessed by the Parties as of November 1, 1987.…

2. The Parties shall update that data and provide the notifications required by this Treaty through the Nuclear Risk Reduction Centers.…

3. No later than 30 days after entry into force of this Treaty, each Party shall provide the other Party with updated data, as of the date of entry into force of this Treaty, for all categories of data contained in the Memorandum of Understanding.

4. No later than 30 days after the end of each six-month interval following the entry into force of this Treaty, each Party shall provide updated data.…

5. Upon entry into force of this Treaty and thereafter, each Party shall provide the following notifications to the other Party:

(a) notification, no less than 30 days in advance, of the scheduled date of the elimination of a specific deployment area, missile operating base or missile support facility;

(b) notification, no less than 30 days in advance, of changes in the number or location of elimination facilities, including the location and scheduled date of each change;

(c) notification, except with respect to launches of intermediate-range missiles for the purpose of their elimination, no less than 30 days in advance, of the scheduled date of the initiation of the elimination of intermediate range and

shorter-range missiles, and stages of such missiles, and launchers of such missiles and support structures and support equipment associated with such missiles and launchers.…

(d) notification, no less than 10 days in advance, of the scheduled date of the launch, or the scheduled date of the initiation of a series of launches, of intermediate-range missiles for the purpose of their elimination.…

(e) notification, no later than 48 hours after they occur, of changes in the number of intermediate-range and shorter-range missiles, launchers of such missiles and support structures and support equipment associated with such missiles and launchers resulting from elimination as described in the Protocol on Elimination.…

(f) notification of transit of intermediate-range or shorter-range missiles or launchers of such missiles, or the movement of training missiles or training launchers for such intermediate-range and shorter-range missiles, no later than 48 hours after it has been completed.…

6. Upon entry into force of this Treaty and thereafter, each Party shall notify the other Party, no less than 10 days in advance, of the scheduled date and location of the launch of a research and development booster system as described in paragraph 12 of Article VII of this Treaty.

Article X

1. Each Party shall eliminate its intermediate-range and shorter-range missiles and launchers of such missiles and support structures and support equipment associated with such missiles and launchers in accordance with the procedures set forth in the Protocol on Elimination.

2. Verification by on-site inspection of the elimination of items of missile systems specified in the Protocol on Elimination shall be carried out in accordance with Article XI of this Treaty, the Protocol on Elimination and the Protocol on Inspection.

3. When a Party removes its intermediate-range missiles, launchers of such missiles, and support equipment associated with such missiles

and launchers from deployment areas to elimination facilities for the purpose of their elimination, it shall do so in complete deployed organizational units. For the Union of Soviet Socialist Republics, these units shall be RSD-10 regiments composed of two or three battalions. For the United States of America these units shall be Pershing II batteries and BGM-109G flights.

4. Elimination of intermediate-range and shorter-range missiles and launchers of such missiles and support equipment associated with such missiles and launchers shall be carried out at the facilities that are specified in the Memorandum of Understanding or notified in accordance with paragraph 5(b) of Article IX of this Treaty, unless eliminated in accordance with Sections IV or V of the Protocol on Elimination. Support structures, associated with the missiles and launchers subject to this Treaty, that are subject to elimination shall be eliminated in site.

5. Each Party shall have the right, during the first six months after entry into force of this Treaty, to eliminate by means of launching no more than 100 of its intermediate-range missiles.

6. Intermediate-range and shorter-range missiles, which have been tested prior to entry into force of this Treaty, but never deployed, and which are not existing types of intermediate-range or shorter range missiles listed in Article III of this Treaty, and launchers of such missiles, shall be eliminated within six months after entry into force of this Treaty in accordance with the procedures set forth in the Protocol on Elimination. Such missiles are;

(a) for the Union of the Soviet Socialist Republics, missiles of the type designated by the Union of Soviet Socialist Republics as the RK-55, which is known to the United States of America as the SSC-X-4; and

(b) for the United States of America, missiles of the type designated by the United States of America as the Pershing IB, which is known to the Union of Soviet Socialist Republics by the same designation.

7. Intermediate-range and shorter-range missiles and launchers of such missiles and sup-

port structures and support equipment associated with such missiles and launchers shall be considered to be eliminated after completion of the procedures set forth in the Protocol on Elimination and upon the notification provided for in paragraph 5(c) of Article IX of this Treaty.

8. Each Party shall eliminate its deployment areas, missile operating bases and missile support facilities. A Party shall notify the other Party pursuant to paragraph 5(a) of Article IX of this Treaty once the conditions …are fulfilled….

Such deployment areas, missile operating bases and missile support facilities shall be considered to be eliminated either when they have been inspected pursuant to paragraph 4 of Article XI of this Treaty or when 60 days have elapsed since the date of the scheduled elimination which was notified pursuant to paragraph 5(a) of Article IX of this Treaty. A deployment area, missile operating base or missile support facility listed in the Memorandum of Understanding that met the above conditions prior to entry into force of this Treaty, and is not included in the initial data exchange pursuant to paragraph 3 of Article IX of this Treaty, shall be considered to be eliminated.

9. If a Party intends to convert a missile operating base listed in the Memorandum of Understanding for use as a base associated with GLBM or GLCM systems not subject to this Treaty, then that Party shall notify the other Party, no less than 30 days in advance of the scheduled date of the initiation of the conversion, of the scheduled date and the purpose for which the base will be converted.

Article XI

1. For the purpose of ensuring verification of compliance with the provisions of this Treaty, each Party shall have the right to conduct on-site inspections. The Parties shall implement on-site inspections in accordance with this Article, the Protocol on Inspection and the Protocol on Elimination.

2. Each Party shall have the right to conduct inspections provided for by this Article both

within the territory of the other Party and within the territories of basing countries.

3. Beginning 30 days after entry into force of this treaty, each party shall have the right to conduct inspections at all missile operating bases and missile support facilities specified in the Memorandum of Understanding other than missile production facilities, and at all elimination facilities included in the initial data update required by paragraph 3 of Article IX of this Treaty....

4. Each Party shall have the right to conduct inspections to verify the elimination, notified pursuant to paragraph 5(a) of Article IX of this Treaty, of missile operating bases and missile support facilities, which are thus no longer subject to inspections pursuant to paragraph 5(A) of this Article. Such an inspection shall be carried out within 60 days after the scheduled date of the elimination of that facility....

5. Each Party shall have the right to conduct inspections pursuant to this paragraph for 13 years after entry into force of this Treaty. Each Party shall have the right to conduct 20 such inspections per calendar year during the first three years after entry into force of this Treaty, 15 such inspections per calendar year during the subsequent five years, and ten such inspections per calendar year during the last five years. Neither Party shall use more than half of its total number of these inspections per calendar year within the territory of any one basing country. Each Party shall have the right to conduct:

(a) inspections, beginning 90 days after entry into force of this Treaty, of missile operating bases and missile support facilities other than elimination facilities and missile production facilities, to ascertain, according to the categories of data specified in the Memorandum of Understanding, the numbers of missiles, launchers, support structures and support equipment located at each missile operating base or missile support facility at the time of the inspection; and

(b) inspections of former missile operating bases and former missile support facilities eliminated pursuant to paragraph 8 of Article X of

this Treaty other than former missile production facilities.

6. Beginning 30 days after entry into force of this Treaty, each Party shall have the right, for 13 years after entry into force of this Treaty, to inspect by means of continuous monitoring:

(a) the portals of any facility of the other Party at which the final assembly of a GLBM using stages, any of which is outwardly similar to a stage of a solid-propellant GLBM listed in Article III of this Treaty, is accomplished; or

(b) if a party has no such facility, the portals of an agreed former missile production facility at which existing types of intermediate-range or shorter-range GLBMs were produced. The Party whose facility is to be inspected pursuant to this paragraph shall ensure that the other Party is able to establish a permanent continuous monitoring system at that facility within six months after entry into force of this Treaty or within six months of initiation of the process of final assembly described in subparagraph (a). If after the end of the second year after entry into force of this Treaty, neither Party conducts the process of final assembly described in subparagraph (a) for a period of 12 consecutive months, then neither Party shall have the right to inspect by means of continuous monitoring any missile production facility of the other Party unless the process of final assembly as described in subparagraph (a) is initiated again. Upon entry into force of this Treaty, the facilities to be inspected by continuous monitoring shall be: in accordance with subparagraph (a) for the Union of the Soviet Socialist Republics, the Votkinsk Machine Building Plant, Udmurt Autonomous Soviet Socialist Republic, Russian Soviet Federative Socialist Republic; in accordance with subparagraph (b), for the United States of America, Hercules Plant Number 1, at Magna, Utah.

7. Each Party shall conduct inspections of the process of elimination, including elimination of intermediate-range missiles by means of launching, of intermediate-range and shorter-range missiles and launchers of such missiles and support equipment associated with such

missiles and launchers carried out at elimination facilities....

8. Each Party shall have the right to conduct inspections to confirm the completion of the process of elimination of intermediate-range and shorter-range missiles and launchers of such missiles and support equipment associated with such missiles and launchers....

Article XII

1. For the purpose of ensuring verification of compliance with the provisions of this Treaty, each Party shall use national technical means of verification at its disposal in a manner consistent with generally recognized principles of international law.

2. Neither Party shall:

(a) interfere with national technical means of verification of the other Party operating in accordance with paragraph 1 of this Article; or

(b) use concealment measures which impede verification of compliance with the provisions of this Treaty by national technical means of verification carried out in accordance with paragraph 1 of this Article. This obligation does not apply to cover or concealment practices, within a deployment area, associated with normal training maintenance and operations, including the use of environmental shelters to protect missiles and launchers.

3. To enhance observation by national technical means of verification, each Party shall have the right until a Treaty between the Parties reducing and limiting strategic offensive arms enters into force, but in any event for no more than three years after entry into force of this Treaty, to request the implementation of cooperative measures at deployment bases for road-mobile GLBMs with a range capability in excess of 5,500 kilometers, which are not former missile operating bases eliminated pursuant to paragraph 8 of Article X of this Treaty. The Party making such a request shall inform the other Party of the deployment base at which cooperative measures shall be implemented. The Party whose

base is to be observed shall carry out the following cooperative measures:

(a) not later than six hours after such a request, the Party shall have opened the roofs of all fixed structures for launchers located at the base, removed completely all missiles on launchers from such fixed structures for launchers and displayed such missiles on launchers in the open without using concealment measures; and

(b) the Party shall leave the roofs open and the missiles on launchers in place until 12 hours have elapsed from the time of the receipt of a request for such an observation.

Each Party shall have the right to make six such requests per calendar year. Only one deployment base shall be subject to these cooperative measures at any one time.

Article XIII

1. To promote the objectives and implementation of the provisions of this Treaty, the Parties hereby establish the Special Verification Commission....

2. The Parties shall use the nuclear risk reduction centers which provide for continuous communication....

Article XIV

The Parties shall comply with this Treaty and shall not assume any international obligations or undertakings which would conflict with its provisions.

Article XV

1. This Treaty shall be of unlimited duration.

2. Each Party shall, in exercising its national sovereignty, have the right to withdraw from this Treaty if it decides that extraordinary events related to the subject matter of this Treaty have jeopardized its supreme interests. It shall give notice of its decision to withdraw to the other Party six months prior to withdrawal form this Treaty. Such notice shall include a statement of the extraordinary events the notifying Party regards as having jeopardized its supreme interests.

Article XVI

Each Party may propose amendments to this Treaty. Agreed amendments shall enter into force in accordance with the procedures set forth in Article XVII governing the entry into force of this Treaty.

Article XVII

1. This Treaty, including the Memorandum of Understanding and Protocols, which form an integral part thereof, shall be subject to ratification in accordance with the constitutional procedures of each Party. This Treaty shall enter into force on the date of the exchange of instruments of ratification.

2. This Treaty shall be registered pursuant to Article 102 of the Charter of the United Nations.

Done at Washington on December 8, 1987, in two copies, each in the Russian and English languages, both texts being equally authentic.

FOR THE UNION OF SOVIET SOCIALIST REPUBLICS: M. Gorbachev, General Secretary of the Central Committee of the CPSU

FOR THE UNITED STATES OF AMERICA: R. Reagan, President of the United States of America

---

DOCUMENT 21

Joint Soviet-U.S. Summit Statement

10 December 1987

Editor's commentary: The Washington summit was the third, but not the last, meeting between Ronald Reagan and Mikhail Gorbachev. It was, however, the most productive of all the Reagan-Gorbachev summits, the most concrete result being the conclusion of the INF Treaty. A broad array of topics was also discussed and slated for future agendas in the new detente relationship between the United States and the USSR.

Mikhail S. Gorbachev, General Secretary of the Central Committee of the Communist Party of the Soviet Union, and Ronald W. Reagan, President of the United States of America, met in Washington on December 7–10, 1987....

I. The two leaders signed the Treaty between the Union of Soviet Socialist Republics and the United States of America on the elimination of their Intermediate-Range and Shorter-Range missiles. This treaty is historic both for its objective—the complete elimination of an entire class of Soviet and U.S. nuclear arms—and for the innovative character and scope of its verification provisions. This mutual accomplishment makes a vital contribution to greater stability.

The General Secretary and the President discussed the negotiations on reduction in strategic offensive arms. They noted the considerable progress which has been made toward conclusion of a treaty implementing the principle of 50 percent reductions. They agreed to instruct their negotiators in Geneva to work toward the completion of the treaty on the reduction and limitation of strategic offensive arms and all integral documents at the earliest possible date, preferably in time for signature of the treaty during the next meeting of leaders of state in the first half of 1988....

Taking into account the preparation of the treaty on strategic offensive arms, the leaders of the two countries also instructed their delegations in Geneva to work out an agreement that would commit the sides to observe the ABM treaty, as signed in 1972, while conducting their research, development, and testing as required, which are permitted by the ABM treaty, and not to withdraw from the ABM treaty, for a specified period of time....

Department of State Bulletin, vol. 88, no. 2131, February 1988, pp. 13–16, *excerpts.*

The General Secretary and the President reviewed a broad range of other issues concerning arms limitation and reduction. The sides emphasized the importance of productive negotiations on security matters and advancing in the main areas of arms limitation and reduction through equitable, verifiable agreements that enhance security and stability....

The leaders also welcomed the prompt agreement by the sides to exchange expert visits to each other's nuclear testing sites in January 1988 and to design and subsequently to conduct joint verification experiments at each other's test site....

The General Secretary and the President reaffirmed the continued commitment of the Soviet Union and the United States to the non-proliferation of nuclear weapons and in particular to strengthening the Treaty on Non-Proliferation of Nuclear Weapons....

The General Secretary and the President expressed support for international cooperation in nuclear safety and for efforts to promote the peaceful uses of nuclear energy....

The leaders welcomed the signing on September 15, 1987, in Washington of the agreement to establish nuclear risk reduction centers in their capitals....

The leaders expressed their commitment to negotiation of a verifiable, comprehensive and effective international convention on the prohibition and destruction of chemical weapons....

The General Secretary and the President discussed the importance of the task of reducing the level of military confrontation in Europe in the area of armed forces and conventional armaments....

They expressed their determination, together with the other 33 participants in the Conference on Security and Cooperation in Europe, to bring the Vienna CSCE follow-up conference to a successful conclusion, based on balanced progress in all principal areas of the Helsinki Final Act and Madrid concluding document.

II. The leaders held a thorough and candid discussion of human rights and humanitarian questions and their place in the Soviet-US dialogue.

III. The General Secretary and the President engaged in a wide-ranging, frank and business-like discussion of regional questions, including Afghanistan, the Iran-Iraq war, the Middle East, Kampuchea, Southern Africa, Central American and other issues. They acknowledged serious differences but agreed on the importance of their regular exchange of views. The two leaders noted the increasing importance of settling regional conflicts to reduce international tensions and to improve East-West relations. They agreed that the goal of the dialogue between the Soviet Union and the United States on these issues should be to help the parties to regional conflicts find peaceful solutions that advance their independence, freedom and security. Both leaders emphasized the importance of enhancing the capacity of the United Nations and other international institutions to contribute to the resolution of regional conflicts.

IV. The General Secretary and the President reviewed in detail the state of Soviet-U.S. bilateral relations. They recognized the utility of further expanding and strengthening bilateral contacts, exchanges and cooperation.

Having reviewed the state of the ongoing Soviet-U.S. negotiations on a number of specific bilateral issues, the two leaders called for intensified efforts by their representatives, aimed at reaching mutually advantageous agreements on: maritime shipping, fishing, marine search and rescue, radio navigational systems, the USSR-U.S. maritime boundary in Chukchee Sea, and Arctic and Pacific Oceans and cooperation in the field of transportation and other areas....

The two sides took note of progress in implementing the Soviet-U.S. general exchanges agreement in the area of education, science, culture and sports signed at their November 1985 Geneva meeting....

With reference to their November 1985 agreement in Geneva to cooperate in the preservation of the environment, the two leaders approved a bilateral initiative to pursue fount studies in global climate and environmental change....

The General Secretary and the President agreed to develop bilateral cooperation in combating international narcotics trafficking....

The two leaders exchanged views on means of encouraging expanded contacts and cooperation on issues relating to the Arctic....

The two leaders welcomed the conclusion of negotiations to institutionalise the COSPAS/SARSAT space-based global search and rescue system....

The two sides stated their strong support for the expansion of mutually beneficial trade and economic relations....

Both sides agreed on the importance of adequate, secure facilities for their respective diplomatic and consular establishments, and emphasized the need to approach problems relating to the functioning of Embassies and Consulates General constructively and on the basis of reciprocity.

V. The General Secretary and the President agreed that official contacts at all levels should be further expanded and intensified, with the view of achieving practical and concrete results in all areas of US-Soviet relations.

General Secretary of the CPSU CC M. Gorbachev reaffirmed the invitation he extended during the Geneva summit for President R. Reagan to visit the Soviet Union. The President accepted it with pleasure. The visit will take place in the first half of 1988.

Statement on Afghanistan

M. S. Gorbachev

8 February 1988

Editor's commentary: As the Geneva negotiations over the issue of Afghanistan were coming to a conclusion, Gorbachev addressed the Soviet people *and the world regarding the intentions of the Soviet Union not only abide by the accords themselves, but to work for the resolution of other regional conflicts—"bleeding wounds," in his words—and continue to work for disarmament and peaceful relations. Note Mr. Gorbachev's reference to decades of previous Soviet-Afghan relations as "an example of peaceful coexistence" (of states with different socialist systems). Such language implied that perhaps Afghanistan's future social system would not necessarily be cut from the same cloth as that of the Soviet Union.*

The military conflict in Afghanistan has been going on for a long time now. It is one of the most bitter and painful regional conflicts. Judging by everything, certain prerequisites have now emerged for its political settlement. In this context the Soviet leadership considers it necessary to set forth its view and to make its position totally clear....

By now documents covering all aspects of a settlement have been almost fully worked out at the Geneva negotiations....

So what remains to be done? To establish a time frame for the withdrawal of Soviet troops from Afghanistan that would be acceptable to all. Precisely that—a time frame, since the fundamental political decision to withdraw Soviet troops from Afghanistan was adopted by us, in agreement with the Afghan leadership, some time ago, and announced at that same time....

The question of the withdrawal of our troops from Afghanistan was raised at the 27th Congress of the Communist Party of the Soviet Union.

That was a reflection of our current political thinking, of our new, modern view of the world. We wanted thereby to reaffirm our commitment to the traditions of good-neighborliness, good will and mutual respect which trace back to Vladimir Lenin and the first Soviet-Afghan treaty in 1921. Progressive forces of Afghan society have un-

TASS, 8 February 1988, as transcribed in *Foreign Broadcast Information Service,* Soviet Union (Washington, DC: n.p., 8 February 1988, pp. 34–36, *excerpts.*

derstood and accepted our sincere desire for peace and tranquility between our two neighboring countries, which for several decades were showing an example of peaceful coexistence and mutually beneficial equitable cooperation.

Any armed conflict, including an internal one, can poison the atmosphere in an entire region and create a situation of anxiety and alarm for a country's neighbors, to say nothing of the suffering and losses among its own people. That is why we are against any armed conflicts. We know that the Afghan leadership, too, takes the same attitude.

It is well known that all of that has caused the Afghan leadership, headed by President Najibullah, to undertake a profound rethinking of political course, which has crystallized in the patriotic and realist policy of national reconciliation....

Success of the policy of national reconciliation has already made it possible to begin withdrawing Soviet troops from portions of the Afghan territory. At present there are no Soviet troops in 13 Afghan provinces—because armed clashes have ceased there....

The Afghans themselves will decide the final status of their country among other nations. Most often it is being said that the future peaceful Afghanistan will be an independent, non-aligned and neutral state. Well, we would only be happy to have such a neighbor on our southern borders....

And now about our boys, our soldiers in Afghanistan. They have been doing their duty honestly, performing acts of self-denial and heroism.

Our people profoundly respect those who were called to serve in Afghanistan. The state provides for them, as a matter of priority, good educational opportunities and a chance to get interesting, worthy work.

The memory of those who have died a hero's death in Afghanistan is sacred to us. It is the duty of party and Soviet authorities to make sure that their families and relatives are taken care of with concern, attention and kindness.

And, finally, when the Afghan knot is untied, it will have the most profound impact on other regional conflicts too.

Whereas the arms race, which we are work-

ing so hard—and with some success—to stop, is mankind's mad race to the abyss, regional conflicts are bleeding wounds which can result in gangrenous growth on the body of mankind.

The earth is literally spotted with such wounds. Each of them means pain not only for the nations directly involved but for all—whether in Afghanistan, in the Middle East, in connection with the Iran-Iraq war, in southern Africa, in Kampuchea, or in Central America.

Who gains from these conflicts? No one except the arms merchants and various reactionary expansionist circles who are used to exploiting and turning a profit on people's misfortunes and tragedies.

Implementing political settlement in Afghanistan will be an important rupture in the chain of regional conflicts.

Just as the agreement to eliminate intermediate- and shorter-range missiles is to be followed by a series of further major steps towards disarmament, with negotiations on them already underway or being planned, likewise behind the political settlement in Afghanistan already looms a question: which conflict will be settled next? And it is certain that more is to follow.

States and nations have sufficient reserves of responsibility, political will and determination to put an end to all regional conflicts within a few years. This is worth working for. The Soviet Union will spare no effort in this most important cause.

DOCUMENT 23

Soviet-Yugoslav Declaration

19 March 1988

Editor's commentary: The result of Mikhail Gorbachev's official visit to Yugoslavia, 15 to 19

Pravda, 19 March 1988, pp. 1–2, as translated in *Foreign Broadcast Information Service,* Soviet Union (Washington, DC: *n.p.,* 21 March 1988, pp. 34–38, *excerpts.*

March 1988, was the following joint declaration. The document was somewhat anticlimactic, inasmuch as more Soviet self-criticism in line with Mr. Gorbachev's policy of glasnost *had been expected. However, the document does reaffirm several times "separate roads to socialism" and noninterference in internal affairs. It also expresses official Soviet interest in exploring the Yugoslav economic "self-management" model's relevance for the restructuring process in the Soviet Union and other communist societies.*

I.

1. The USSR and the SFRY emphasize the historical role and abiding value of the universal principles contained in the Belgrade (1955) and Moscow (1956) Declarations; namely: Mutual respect for independence, sovereignty, and territorial integrity, equality, and impermissibility of interference in internal affairs under any pretext whatsoever. Their consistent implementation played a key role in the normalization of interstate relations and the unfolding of all-around and stable cooperation. The sides will continue to adhere to these principles.

The USSR and the SFRY build and improve their relations on the basis of unconditional respect for the specific features of the ways and forms of their socialist development and for the differences in international positions.

2. The relations of friendship between the peoples of the two countries have long-standing traditions. They were particularly strengthened during the joint struggle against fascism in World War II. Soviet-Yugoslav relations also underwent grave ordeals. The accretions and burden of the past were eliminated thanks to rigorous adherence to mutually approved principles....

3. The successful and all-around development of stable and mutually advantageous economic cooperation is of paramount importance for relations in their totality. Relying on the considerable achievements in this sphere...the USSR and the SFRY will continue to strive for broader introduction of modern forms of cooperation and...will make joint efforts to improve the structure of commodity turnover and ensure stable and balanced commodity exchange and economic ties as a whole as the material base of cooperation....

II.

1. The CPSU and the LCY assess highly the level of mutual relations achieved and consider them an important factor in stable, all-around Soviet-Yugoslav cooperation and the strengthening of friendship between the two countries' peoples.

They reaffirm their readiness to continue to develop and enrich the content of their relations, acting on the basis of the principles of independence, equality and noninterference, the responsibility of each party to the working class and people of its country, and mutual respect for different ways of building socialism and for their international situation. On this basis they will improve voluntary and mutually advantageous cooperation and constructive and comradely dialogue....

Proceeding on the basis of the conviction that no one has a monopoly of the truth, the sides declare their lack of any claim to impose their own ideas about socialist development upon anyone else whomsoever. The success of each of their paths to socialism is tested by sociopolitical practice and confirmed by concrete results.

The CPSU and LCY will seek to enrich cooperation and will devote constant attention to political dialogue with a view to the in-depth exchange of opinions and experience on topical questions of socialist building in the two countries and socialism as a world process, and also on global problems of peace and social progress, equitable international cooperation, and the strengthening of trust among peoples....

The sides consider the improvement of socialist self-management in relation to each countries' peculiarities to be a question of paramount importance. It ensures true people's power and freedom of the individual and is a reliable guarantee against administrative and bureaucratic distortions of socialism and against dogmatism and voluntarism.

The experience accumulated by Yugoslavia in the development of the political system of socialist self-management and the course of consistent implementation of the principles of people's socialist self-management in the Soviet Union offer new opportunities for the mutual enrichment of knowledge about its present-day forms and means of functioning.

2. The CPSU and the LCY reaffirm the universal significance of democratic principles in relations among Communist, workers' socialist, social democratic, revolutionary democratic, and other progressive parties and movements, based on their inalienable right to autonomously make decisions on the choice of paths of socialist development....

3. Socialism is at a turning point, on the threshold of the more complete uncovering of material and spiritual potential and the deepening of humanist foundations. The processes of reforms and radical transformations in the socialist countries confirm socialism's vitality and its readiness to respond to the challenges of the times....

DOCUMENT 24

United Nations Sponsored Accords on Afghanistan

14 April 1988

Editor's commentary: The following excerpts are from key sections of the United Nations–sponsored Afghanistan accords, allowing for the removal of Soviet forces within 9 months from the date signed, the resolution of the refugee problem which resulted from the Soviet occupation of the country, and the mutual assent of Afghanistan, Pakistan, the United States, and the Soviet Union to respect the agreement. Note that although the accords

Department of State Bulletin, vol. 88, no. 2135, June 1988, pp. 56–60, *excerpts*.

also provided for the nonalignment of Afghanistan and noninterference in its internal affairs, none of the mujahadeen (Afghan guerrillas) participated in the talks or agreed to abide by this arrangement. Although the agreement was initially jeopardized by accusations from all sides that it was being abrogated, Soviet forces completed their withdrawal as scheduled on 15 February 1989.

THE PRINCIPLES OF MUTUAL RELATIONS BETWEEN AFGHANISTAN AND PAKISTAN IN PARTICULAR ON NONINTERFERENCE AND NONINTERVENTION

Article I
Relations between the High Contracting Parties shall be conducted in strict compliance with the principle of noninterference and nonintervention by states in the affairs of other states.

Article II
For the purpose of implementing the principle of noninterference and nonintervention each...undertakes to comply with the following obligations:

1. To respect the sovereignty, political independence, territorial integrity, national unity, security and non-alignment of the other..., as well as the national identity and cultural heritage of its people;

2. To respect the sovereign and inalienable right of the other...freely to determine its own political, economic, cultural and social systems, to develop its international relations and to exercise permanent sovereignty over its natural resources, in accordance with the will of its people...;

3. To refrain from the threat or use of force in any form whatsoever so as not to violate the boundaries of each other, to disrupt the political social or economic order of the other..., to overthrow or change the political system of the other..., or to cause tension between [them];

4. To insure that its territory is not used in any manner which would violate the sovereignty, political independence, territorial integrity and national unity or disrupt the political, economic and social stability of the other...;

5. To refrain from armed intervention, subversion, military occupation or any other form of intervention and interference, overt or covert...;

6. To refrain from any action or attempt in whatever form or under whatever pretext to destabilize or to undermine the stability of the other...;

7. To refrain from the promotion, encouragement or support, direct or indirect, of rebellious or secessionist activities against the other...;

8. To prevent within its territory the training, equipping, financing and recruitment of mercenaries from whatever origin for the purpose of hostile activities...;

9. To refrain from making any agreements or arrangements with other states designed to intervene or interfere in the internal and external affairs of the other...;

10. To abstain from any defamatory campaign, vilification or hostile propaganda for the purpose of intervening or interfering in the internal affairs of the other...;

11. To prevent any assistance to or use of or tolerance of terrorist groups, saboteurs or subversive agents...;

12. To prevent within its territory the presence, harboring, in camps and bases or otherwise, organizing, training, financing, equipping and arming of individuals and political, ethnic and any other groups for the purpose of creating subversion, disorder or unrest in the territory of the other...;

13. Not to resort to or to allow any other action that could be considered as interference or intervention.

Article III
The present agreement shall enter into force on 15 May 1988....

DECLARATION ON INTERNATIONAL GUARANTEES

The Governments of the Union of Soviet Socialist Republics and of the United States of America,

Expressing support that the Republic of Afghanistan and the Islamic Republic of Pakistan have concluded a negotiated political settlement designed to normalize relations and promote good neighborliness between the two countries as well as to strengthen international peace and security in the region;

Wishing in turn to contribute to the achievement of the objectives that the Republic of Afghanistan and the Islamic Republic of Pakistan have set themselves, and with a view to insuring respect for their sovereignty, independence, territorial integrity and nonalignment;

Undertake to invariably refrain from any form of interference and intervention in the internal affairs of the Republic of Afghanistan and the Islamic Republic of Pakistan and to respect the commitments contained in the...Principles of Mutual Relations in Particular on Noninterference and Nonintervention [see above];

Urge all states to act likewise.

The present declaration shall enter into force on 15 May 1988.

ON VOLUNTARY RETURN OF REFUGEES

Article I
All Afghan refugees temporarily present in the territory of the Islamic Republic of Pakistan shall be given the opportunity to return voluntarily to their homeland in accordance with the arrangements and conditions set out in the present agreement [conditions follow]....

AGREEMENT ON THE INTERRELATIONSHIPS FOR THE SETTLEMENT OF THE SITUATION RELATING TO AFGHANISTAN

1. The diplomatic process initiated by the Secretary General of the United Nations with the support of all governments concerned and aimed at achieving, through negotiations, a political settlement of the situation relating to Afghanistan has been successfully brought to an end....

5. The Bilateral Agreement on the Principles of Mutual Relations, in Particular on Noninterference and Nonintervention; the Declaration on International Guarantees; the Bilateral Agree-

ment on the Voluntary Return of Refugees, and the present Agreement on the Interrelationships for the Settlement of the Situation Relating to Afghanistan will enter into force on 15 May 1988. In accordance with the time frame agreed upon between the Union of Soviet Socialist Republics and the Republic of Afghanistan there will be a phased withdrawal of the foreign troops which will start on the date of entry into force mentioned above. One half of the troops will be withdrawn by 15 August 1988 and the withdrawal of all troops will be completed within nine months.

6. The interrelationships in Paragraph 5 above have been agreed upon in order to achieve effectively the purpose of the political settlement, namely, that as from 15 May 1988, there will be no interference and intervention in any form in the affairs of the parties; the international guarantees will be in operation; the voluntary return of the refugees to their homeland will start and be completed within the time frame specified in the agreement on the voluntary return of the refugees; and the phased withdrawal of the foreign troops will start and be completed within the time frame envisaged in Paragraph 5. It is therefore essential that all the obligations deriving from the instruments concluded as component parts of the settlement be strictly fulfilled and that all the steps required to insure full compliance with all the provisions of the instruments be completed in good faith.

7. To consider alleged violations and to work out prompt and mutually satisfactory solutions to questions that may arise in the implementation of the instruments comprising the settlement, representatives of the Republic of Afghanistan and the Islamic Republic of Pakistan shall meet whenever required.

A Representative of the Secretary General of the United Nations shall lend his good offices to the parties and in that context he will assist in the organization of the meetings and participate in them....

In order to enable him to fulfill his tasks, the representative shall be assisted by such person-

nel under his authority as required. On his own initiative, or at the request of any of the parties, the personnel shall investigate any possible violations of any of the provisions of the instrument and prepare a report thereon. For that purpose, the representative and his personnel shall receive all the necessary cooperation form the parties, including all freedom of movement within their respective territories required for effective investigation....

DOCUMENT 25

Gorbachev's Address to the United Nations

7 December 1988

Editor's commentary: Gorbachev's address to the UN was widely hailed as a significant political event. The Soviet press emphasized that this was the first-ever address to the UN by a Soviet head of state (Mr. Gorbachev had gained the Soviet presidency in 1988). In the speech, the Soviet leader announced the unilateral reduction of Soviet ground forces and tanks in Europe and promised reductions in Asia as well.

Esteemed Mr. Chairman, esteemed Mr. Secretary General, esteemed delegates. We have arrived here to express our respect for the United Nations organization, which is ever increasingly displaying its ability to be a unique international center in the service of peace and security. We have arrived here to express our respect for the dignity of this organization, capable of accumu-

Pravda, 7 December 1988, as translated in *Foreign Broadcast Information Service*, Soviet Union (Washington, DC.: n.p., 8 December 1988, pp. 11–19, *excerpts.*

lating the collective reason and will of mankind. Events are increasingly confirming the world's need for such an organization. It its turn, the organization needs the active participation of all its members in supporting its initiatives and actions, and in enriching its activity by their potential and original contribution. Somewhat over a year ago, in the article "The Reality and Guarantees of a Safe World," I set out a number of thoughts concerning the problems within the scope of the United Nations organization. The time that has passed has given new food for thought. A turning point has come, indeed, in the development of world events....

Very profound social changes for the better are taking place. Hundreds of millions of people, be they in the East or in the South, in the West or in the North, new nations and states, new social movements and ideologies have moved to the front of the historical stage. In large-scale, not infrequently stormy people's movements, the surge toward independence, democracy, and social justice is expressed in all its many aspects and contradictoriness. The idea of the democratization of the entire world order has turned into a mighty sociopolitical force.

At the same time the scientific-and-technical revolution has turned many problems—economic, food, energy, ecological, informational and demographic—which not so long ago we dealt with as national or regional ones—into global problems. Thanks to the latest means of communications, mass information, and transportation, the world has, as it were, become more visible and perceptible for everyone. International contact has been simplified in an unprecedented way. Today it is hardly possible to preserve some sort of "closed" societies. This requires a decisive revision of views on all problems of international cooperation as a major element of universal security.

The world economy is becoming a single organism, outside of which not a single state can develop normally, whatever social system it belongs to or whatever economic level it has

reached. This puts the drafting of a fundamentally new mechanism for the functioning of the world economy, for a new structure for the international division of labor, on the agenda. At the same time the growth of the world economy exposes the contradictions and limits of industrialization of the traditional type. Its further spread "in breadth and depth" threatens an ecological catastrophe. However, there are still many countries where industry is not sufficiently developed, while others have not yet left the pre-industrial stage. Whether the process of their economic growth will follow the old technological patterns, or whether they will be able to join in the search for clean production, from the ecological point of view, is a major problem.

Another problem is that the gap between developed countries and the majority of developing ones is failing to narrow, and is becoming an ever greater threat on a global scale. This makes it necessary to begin searching for a fundamentally new type of industrial progress, the type which would correspond to the interests of all peoples and states. In a word, new realities are changing the entire world situation. The differences and oppositions inherited from the past are being alleviated or removed. But new ones are appearing. Some former disagreements and arguments are losing their significance. Their place is being taken by conflicts of another sort....

The history of the past centuries and millennia has been a history of almost ubiquitous wars, and sometimes desperate battles, leading to mutual destruction. They occurred in the clash of social and political interests and national hostility, be it from ideological or religious incompatibility. All that was the case, and even now many still claim that this past—which has not been overcome—is an immutable pattern. However, parallel with the process of wars, hostility, and alienation of peoples and countries, another process, just as objectively conditioned, was in motion and gaining force: The process of the emergence of a mutually connected and integral world.

Further world progress is now possible only through the search for a consensus of all mankind, in movement toward a new world order. We have arrived at a frontier at which uncontrolled spontaneity leads to a dead end. The world community must learn to shape and direct processes in such a way as to preserve civilization, to make it safe for all and more pleasant for normal life. It is a question of cooperation that could be more accurately called "cocreations" and "codevelopment." The formula of development "at another's expense" is becoming outdated. In light of present realities, genuine progress by infringing upon the rights and liberties of man and peoples, or at the expense of nature, is impossible....

The compelling necessity of the principle of **freedom of choice** is also clear to us. The failure to recognize this...is fraught with very dire consequences, consequences for world peace. Denying that right to the peoples, no matter what the pretext, no matter what words are used to conceal it, means infringing upon even the unstable balance that it has been possible to achieve....

The de-ideologization of interstate relations has become a demand of the new stage. We are not giving up our convictions, philosophy, or traditions. Neither are we calling on anyone else to give up theirs. Yet we are not going to shut ourselves up within the range of our values. That would lead to spiritual impoverishment, for it would mean renouncing so powerful a source of development as sharing all the original things created independently by each nation. In the course of such sharing, each should prove the advantages of his own system, his own way of life and values, but not through words or propaganda alone, but through real deeds as well. That is, indeed, an honest struggle of ideology, but it must not be carried over into mutual relations between states. Otherwise we simply will not be able to solve a single world problem; arrange broad, mutually advantageous and equitable cooperation between peoples; manage rationally the achievements of the scientific and technical revolution; transform world economic relations; protect the environment; overcome underdevelopment; or put an end to hunger, disease, illiteracy, and other mass ills. Finally, in that case, we will not manage to eliminate the nuclear threat and militarism.

Such are our reflections on the natural order of things in the world on the threshold of the 21st century. We are, of course, far from claiming to have the infallible truth, but having subjected the previous realities—realities that have arisen again—to strict analysis, we have come to the conclusion that it is by precisely such approaches that we must search jointly for a way to achieve the **supremacy of the common human idea** over the countless multiplicity of centrifugal forces, to preserve the vitality of a civilization that is possibly the only one in the universe.

Is there not here a certain romanticism, an exaggeration of the potential and maturity of public awareness in the world? We hear such doubts and questions both at home and from some of our Western partners. I am convinced that we are not losing touch with reality. Forces already have formed in the world which one way or another are inducing the **start of a period of peace**...

Perhaps the term "restructuring" is not very suitable in this case. But I am, indeed, advocating **new international relations.** I am convinced that the times and the realities of the modern world demand that a stake is placed on the **internationalization** of dialogue and negotiating process. This is the **main generalizing conclusion** that we have reached from our study of world processes, which lately have been gathering strength, and from our participation in world politics....

Now about the most important topic, without which no problem of the coming century can be resolved: **disarmament.**

International development and contacts have been deformed by the arms race and militarization of thinking:

On 15 January 1986 the Soviet Union put forward, as is known, a program for building a nuclear-free world. Its embodiment in real negotiating positions has already provided material results. Tomorrow is the first anniversary of the signing of the treaty scrapping intermediate and shorter-range missiles. With still greater satisfaction, I say that the implementation of that treaty—the destruction of the missiles—is proceeding normally, in an atmosphere of trust and efficiency. It would seem that a breach has been made in the impenetrable wall of suspicion and hostility. Before our eyes we are seeing a new historic reality arising, **a turnaround from the principle of over-abundance of weaponry to the principle of reasonable sufficiency for defense.** We are present to see the first glimmers of the formation of a new model of ensuring security, not with the help of increasing weapons—as was almost always the case—but on the contrary through reducing them on the basis of compromise. The Soviet leadership has decided once again to demonstrate its readiness to strengthen this healthy process, not only in words, but in **deeds.**

Today I can inform you of the following: The Soviet Union has made a decision on reducing its armed forces. In the next 2 years, their numerical strength will be reduced by 500,000 persons, and the volume of conventional arms will also be cut considerably. These reductions will be made on a **unilateral basis**, unconnected with the negotiations on the mandate for the Vienna meeting. By agreement with our allies in the Warsaw Pact, we have made the decision to withdraw six tank divisions from the GDR, Czechoslovakia, and Hungary, and to disband them by 1991. Assault landing formations and units, and a number of others, including assault river-crossing forces, with their armaments and combat equipment, will also be withdrawn from the

groups of Soviet forces situated in those countries. The Soviet forces situated in those countries will be cut by 50,000 persons, and their arms by 5,000 tanks. All remaining Soviet divisions on the territory of our allies will be reorganized. They will be given a different structure from today's, which will become unambiguously defensive, after the removal of a large number of their tanks.

At the same time, we will also cut the numbers of the personnel of our forces and the quantity of arms in the European part of the USSR. Altogether, in that part of our country and on the territory of our European allies, the Soviet Armed Forces will be reduced by 10,000 tanks, 8,500 artillery systems, and 800 combat aircraft.

Over these 2 years we will substantially reduce the grouping of armed forces in the Asian part of the country, too. By agreement with the government of the Mongolian People's Republic, a considerable part of the Soviet troops temporarily present there will return home. In adopting these decisions of fundamental importance, the Soviet leadership is voicing the will of a people engaged in an in-depth renewal of its entire socialist society. We will maintain our country's defense capability on a level of reasonable and reliable sufficiency, so that no one should find themselves tempted to infringe upon the security of the USSR and its allies.

By this act, just as by all our actions aimed at the demilitarization of international relations, we would also like to draw the attention of the world community to another topical problem, the problem of changing over **from an economy of armament to an economy of disarmament.** Is the conversion of military production realistic? I have already had occasion to speak about this. We believe that it is, indeed, realistic. For its part, the Soviet Union is ready to do the following. Within the framework of the economic reform we are ready to draw up and submit our internal plan for conversion, to prepare in the course of 1989, as an experiment, the plans for the conversion of two or three defense enterprises, to publish our experience of job relocation of specialists from the military industry, and also of using its equipment, buildings, and works in civilian industry. It is desirable that all states, primarily the major military powers, submit their national plans on this issue to the United Nations....

We are not inclined to oversimplify the situation in the world. Yes, the tendency toward disarmament has received a strong impetus, and this process is gaining its own momentum, but it has not become irreversible. Yes, the striving to give up confrontation in favor of dialogue and cooperation has made itself strongly felt, but it has by no means secured its position forever in the practice of international relations. Yes, the movement towards a nuclear-free and nonviolent world is capable of fundamentally transforming the political and spiritual face of the planet, but only the very first steps have been taken. Moreover, in certain influential circles, they have been greeted with mistrust, and they are meeting resistance.

The inheritance and the inertia of the past are continuing to operate. Profound contradictions and the roots of many conflicts have not disappeared. The fundamental fact remains that the formation of the peaceful period will take place in conditions of the existence and rivalry of various socioeconomic and political systems. However, the meaning of our international efforts, and one of the key tenets of the new thinking, is precisely to impart to this rivalry a quality of sensible competition in conditions of respect for freedom of choice and a balance of interests. In this case it will even become more useful and productive from the viewpoint of general world development; otherwise, if the main component remains the arms race, as it has been till now, rivalry will be fatal. Indeed, an ever greater number of people throughout the world, from the man in the street to leaders, are beginning to understand this....

DOCUMENT 26

Joint Sino-Soviet Communiqué

18 May 1989

Editor's commentary: Gorbachev's historic visit to China formally ended 30 years of Sino-Soviet estrangement and normalized party and state relations between the two communist giants. Gorbachev met with Chinese leader Deng Xiao Peng on the morning after his arrival; however, ceremonies planned in the Soviet leader's honor were cancelled due to unprecedented massive student demonstrations in Beijing's Tiananmen Square. These dramatic developments shifted international attention away from the historic visit. The summit's communiqué is notable for the absence of ideological verbiage; its emphasis is wholly pragmatic and reaffirms Soviet willingness to resolve long-standing issues separating the two sides, including Soviet support of the Vietnamese occupation of Kampuchea (Cambodia), the presence of Soviet forces in Mongolia, and Sino-Soviet border problems. Prospects for improved trade between the two sides are also highlighted.

1. At the invitation of the President of the People's Republic of China...M. S. Gorbachev made an official visit to the PRC from 15–18 May 1989....

2. The leaders of the USSR and the PRC consider that the exchange of opinions on Soviet-Chinese relations was useful. Both sides expressed the common opinion that the Soviet-Chinese summit marks the normalization of interstate relations between the Soviet Union and China. This meets the fundamental interests and aspirations of the peoples of the two countries and promotes the maintenance of peace and stability throughout the world. The normalization

---

Pravda, 19 May 1989, p. 1, *excerpts*. Editor's translation.

of Soviet-Chinese relations is not directed against third countries and does not infringe upon the interests of third countries.

3. Both sides declare that the USSR and the PRC will develop mutual relations on the basis of universal principles of interstate contacts: mutual respect for sovereignty and territorial integrity, nonaggression, noninterference in the internal affairs of each other, equality and mutual advantage, and peaceful coexistence.

4. The Soviet and Chinese sides are prepared to solve all contentious issues between the two countries by way of peaceful negotiations and will not resort to force or threat of the use of force against each other in any form whatsoever, including through the use of the territory, territorial waters, and air space of third countries adjacent to the other side.

The USSR and the PRC hold that strict compliance with these conditions will promote the strengthening of mutual trust and the establishment of friendly good-neighborly relations between the two countries.

5. The leaders of the USSR and the PRC reaffirm the declaration of 6 February 1989 concerning the Kampuchean problem.... The Soviet and Chinese sides express interest in, and deem it essential, that after the complete withdrawal of Vietnamese troops a civil war should not break out in Kampuchea. They proceed from the premise that Kampuchea will be an independent, peaceful, neutral, and nonaligned country. With this goal, the sides favor national reconciliation in Kampuchea with the participation of the four Kampuchean sides.

The Soviet side abides by the position that Kampuchea's internal problems, including the preparation and holding of general elections under international control, should be solved by the Kampucheans themselves. It welcomes the intensification of the inter-Khmer dialogue and expresses readiness to support any agreements on various aspects of settlement worked out by the Kampuchean parties.

The Chinese side advocates, in the transitional period following the complete withdrawal of Vietnamese troops and prior to the completion of the general elections, the creation in Kampuchea of an interim four-party coalition government with Prince Sihanouk at its head.

Both sides will respect the results of the general elections conducted by the Kampuchean people under international control.

They hold that, as Vietnamese troops are being withdrawn from Kampuchea, all states concerned should realize a gradual cut of military aid to all Kampuchean parties, leading up to its eventual complete cessation.

The USSR and the PRC advocate the earliest possible convocation of an international conference on the Kampuchean problem.

The Soviet and Chinese sides confirm that they will continue to exert every effort to assist a fair and rational settlement of the Kampuchean problem by political means. They agreed to continue the discussion of the questions of the Kampuchean settlement, among them those on which there still exist differences between them.

6. Both sides agreed to take measures to reduce armed forces in the area of the Soviet-Chinese border to a minimal level in line with normal good-neighborly relations between the two countries, and also to apply efforts toward the goal of building up trust and preserving calm in the border areas.

The Chinese side welcomes the announcement by the Soviet side about the withdrawal of 75 percent of its troops stationed in the Mongolian People's Republic, and expresses the hope that the remaining Soviet troops will be fully withdrawn from Mongolia within relatively short terms.

7. Both sides advocate solving the remaining long-standing border issues between the Soviet Union and China fairly and rationally on the basis of treaties on the present Soviet-Chinese border, according to the generally recognized norms of international law, and in the spirit of equitable consultations, mutual understanding, and mutual compliance.

In keeping with the aforementioned principles, the leaders of the USSR and the PRC agreed to intensify the consideration of the parts of the Soviet-Chinese border, on which agreement has as yet not been reached, with the aim of working out mutually acceptable solutions simultaneously on the eastern and western parts of the border. They entrusted the two countries' foreign ministers with holding, in case of necessity, a special discussion on border issues.

8. The Soviet Union and China will, on the basis of principles of equality and mutual benefit, develop relations in economic, trade, scientific, technological, cultural, and other fields actively and in a planned manner, and they will assist in the deepening of mutual understanding and contacts between the people of the two countries.

9. The sides consider it useful that the two countries exchange information and experience in the field of building socialism, restructuring, and reform, as well as opinions on issues of mutual interest concerning bilateral relations and the international situation. Disagreements on these or other issues should not hinder the development of relations between the two states.

10. The Soviet and Chinese sides agreed that the Communist Party of the Soviet Union and the Communist Party of China will pursue contacts and exchanges in keeping with principles of independence, full equality, mutual respect, and noninterference in each other's internal affairs.

11. The Chinese side reaffirms that Taiwan is an integral part of the territory of the PRC.... The Soviet side supports this position of the government of the PRC.

12. The Soviet side declares that in its foreign policy it proceeds from an idea of the world as the supreme value, consistently strives for real disarmament, including nuclear disarmament, holds that the security of some states cannot be insured at the expense of others, advocates the priority of universally shared values and the peaceful competition of different socioeconomic systems in conditions of freedom of choice and a balance of interests.

The Chinese side reaffirms that the PRC follows an independent, peaceful foreign policy, and firmly abides by the principled position of not forming alliances with any country whatsoever.

13. Both sides declare that neither the Soviet Union nor China lays claims to hegemony in any form whatsoever in the Asian-Pacific region or in other parts of the world. International relations should be free from actions and attempts by any state to impose its will on others and to strive for hegemony in any form and anywhere whatsoever.

14. Both sides consider that peace and development have become the two most important issues of the times. They welcome the started relaxation in the international situation, which remained tense for a long time, and assess positively steps by various nations of the world in arms reduction and easing military confrontation, as well as progress achieved in the settlement of regional conflicts. The Soviet Union and China expressed readiness to continue on each side to apply efforts in these fields.

The Soviet and Chinese sides call for increasing the authority of the United Nations and for it to play a more active role in world affairs, disarmament, the resolution of issues of a global character, and the settlement of regional conflicts. All states of the world—big and small, strong and weak—have the right to take part in international life on an equal basis....

Suggested Readings

Bialer, Seweryn, and Joan Afferica: "Gorbachev's World," *Foreign Affairs* 64/3 (America and the World 1985) pp. 605–644.

Bradsher, Henry: *Afghanistan and the Soviet Union* Durham: Duke University Press, 1987).

Brown, Archie. "Gorbachev: New Man in the Kremlin," *Problems of Communism,* May–June 1985, pp. 1–24.

Carnesale, Albert, and Richard Haas: *Superpower Arms Control: Setting the Record Straight* (Cambridge, MA: Ballinger, 1987).

Colton, Timothy: *The Dilemma of Reform in the Soviet Union,* rev. ed. (New York: Council on Foreign Relations, 1986).

Dallin, Alexander, and Condoleeza Rice (eds.): *The Gorbachev Era* (Stanford, CA: Stanford University Press, 1986).

Golan, Galia. "Gorbachev's Middle East Strategy," *Foreign Affairs,* Fall 1987, pp. 41–57.

Gorbachev, Mikhail S.: *Perestroika: New Thinking for Our Country and the World* (New York: Harper & Row, 1987).

Gustafson, Thane, and Dawn Mann: "Gorbachev's First Year: Building Power and Authority," *Problems of Communism,* 35, May–June 1986, pp. 1–19.

Horelick, Arnold (ed.): *US-Soviet Relations: The Next Phase* (Ithaca, NY: Cornell University Press, 1986).

Hough, Jerry: "Gorbachev's Strategy," *Foreign Affairs,* 64, Fall 1985, pp. 35–55.

Medvedev, Zhores A.: *Gorbachev* (New York: W. W. Norton, 1986).

Meyer, Stephen: "Soviet Strategic Programs and the US SDI," *Survival,* November–December 1985, pp. 279–283.

Mikheyev, Dimitri: *The Soviet Perspective on the Strategic Defense Initiative* (New York: Pergamon-Brassey's, 1987).

Nelson, Daniel N., and Roger B. Anderson (eds.): *Soviet-American Relations—Understanding Differences, Avoiding Conflicts* (Wilmington, DE: Scholary Resources Books, 1988).

Ploss, Sidney: "A New Soviet Era?" *Foreign Policy,* 62, Spring 1986, pp. 50–54.

Pravda, Alex: *Soviet Foreign Policy: Priorities Under Gorbachev* (London: Routledge, 1988).

Shulman, Marshall (ed.): *East-West Tensions in the Third World* (New York: W. W. Norton, 1986).

Valkenier, Elizabeth Kridl: "New Soviet Thinking About the Third World: A Hands-Off Approach to Radical Change," *World Policy Journal,* Fall 1987, vol. 4, no. 4, pp. 651–674.